THE STUDENT'S DICTIONARY

OF

ANGLO-SAXON

SWEET

THE

STUDENT'S DICTIONARY

OF

ANGLO-SAXON

BY

HENRY SWEET, M.A., Ph.D., LL.D.

CORRESPONDING MEMBER OF THE MUNICH ACADEMY OF SCIENCES

28473

OXFORD
AT THE CLARENDON PRESS

Oxford University Press, Walton Street, Oxford OX2 6DP

OXFORD LONDON GLASGOW
NEW YORK TORONTO MELBOURNE WELLINGTON
IBADAN NAIROBI DAR ES SALAAM LUSAKA CAPE TOWN
KUALA LUMPUR SINGAPORE JAKARTA HONG KONG TOKYO
DELHI BOMBAY CALCUTTA MADRAS KARACHI

ISBN 0 19 863107 3

First edition 1896
Tenth impression 1978

Printed in Great Britain
at the University Press, Oxford
by Vivian Ridler
Printer to the University

PREFACE

—◆—

THIS dictionary was undertaken at the request of the Delegates of the Clarendon Press, who, feeling the want of an abridgement of the large Anglo-Saxon dictionary (BT) still in progress, applied to me. From a variety of reasons I felt myself obliged to undertake the work. As the book was wanted as soon as possible, with a view to forestalling unauthorized abridgements, I could only undertake to do my best within a limited space and a limited period. Every dictionary is necessarily a compromise. If done ideally well and on an adequate scale, it is never finished—and an unfinished dictionary is worse than useless—or, if finished, is never uniform as regards materials and treatment. A dictionary which is good from a practical point of view—that is, which is finished within a reasonable time, and is kept within reasonable limits of space—must necessarily fall far short of ideal requirements. In short, we may almost venture on the paradox that a good dictionary is necessarily a bad one.

Sources.—When I first began this work all the existing Anglo-Saxon dictionaries were completely antiquated. The old Bosworth is an uncritical compilation, which falls far short of the scientific requirements even of the period of its first publication. Ettmüller's *Lexicon Anglosaxonicum* is far superior as regards accuracy and fullness, but its unhappy arrangement of the words under hypothetical roots makes it practically useless to the beginner. Leo's *Angelsächsisches Glossar* combines the faults of both its predecessors with a recklessness in inventing new forms and meanings which is without a parallel even in Anglo-

Saxon lexicography. I had hardly begun to work steadily at this dictionary when a *Concise Anglo-Saxon Dictionary* was brought out by Dr. Clark Hall (CH), an American scholar. CH is a work of great industry, and contains a good deal of new and valuable matter; but it is terribly uncritical, and embodies an enormous number of spurious words and meanings.

I have already said that this dictionary was undertaken as an abridgement of BT. But BT consists really of two fragments of dictionaries. The first part (A–FIR), for which Bosworth alone is responsible, is far inferior to the succeeding portions of the work, which have been edited by Prof. Toller: these show a great and progressive improvement in fullness, accuracy and method. I have, of course, throughout checked and supplemented BT by the other dictionaries and glossaries —including my own glossaries to the *Anglo-Saxon Reader* and *Oldest English Texts* —and by a MS. dictionary of my own, begun many years ago, when I had scarcely emerged from boyhood. CH has also been of considerable service, as he gives references for many of the rarer words. But the labour of testing these, and separating the grains of wheat from the mass of chaff, has been great, and has materially retarded my progress. I have also found time to gather a good deal of fresh material from the texts themselves.

Difficulties.—The great difficulty of Anglo-Saxon lexicography is that we have to rely for our material solely on a limited number of carelessly written and often badly edited manuscripts—there is no long series of native critics, grammarians and lexicographers to help us. The greatest difficulties are with the glossaries of detached words. In many of these English (that is, Anglo-Saxon) explanations of the Latin words are only occasionally interspersed among Latin renderings; and it is often a difficult task to determine whether a word is English or a miswritten word in Latin or some other language. One editor even prints *resuanas* as an English gloss to *ineptias*, not seeing that it stands simply for *res vanas*! And even when we are certain that a word is English we cannot be sure that it has not been displaced, so that it really has nothing to do with the Latin word it follows. Hence the imaginary word *blere*, 'onyx,' which still encumbers all the dictionaries except the present one. The connexion between the English gloss and its original is often very vague, as when *napta* (=*naphtha*) is glossed *tynder*, 'tinder,' on account of its inflammability! Again, the Latin words are often misspelt beyond recognition, and even when correctly spelt often cannot be found in any Latin dictionary, either classical or mediaeval. To deal fully and

successfully with these glossaries would require a combination of qualities that has never yet been achieved, together with several lifetimes. The investigator of Old-English as a whole—to whom these glossaries are only subordinate sources of information—is therefore often obliged to work by guesswork, until some one else guesses better, and to be thankful for an occasional ray of light.

We have similar difficulties with the place-names in the Charters. Even in connected texts there are often great difficulties : such poems as Beowulf and the Exodus teem with obscurities, many of which will probably never be cleared up.

Doubtful matter.—Although I have tried, as a general rule, to keep doubtful matter out of the dictionary, I have been careful to leave a margin, especially in dealing with a well-known text such as Beowulf. But I have often put the reader on his guard by adding (?), or by referring (by *Cp.*) to some other word of which the doubtful word may be a variant, or by indicating the source of an obscure word ; thus R. tells him that the word or meaning occurs only in the Rhyming Poem, which is the most obscure of all the poems. The doubtfulness of a word is greatly increased when it occurs only once ; accordingly in such cases I often add the warning *once.* Doubtful endings are printed in thin letters ; thus **gambe** *f.* means that the word occurs only in the inflected form *gamban*, which may point either to a feminine *gambe* or a masculine *gamba*. So also **pyf**fan means that the word occurs only in forms which leave it in doubt whether the infinitive is *pyffan* or *pȳfan.*

Late words.—All Anglo-Saxon dictionaries contain words which are not Old-English, but belong to Transition-English (1100–1200), or even to Middle-English. Thus all dictionaries except the present one give a form *abbot* for *abbod* with a reference to the year 675 of the Chronicle, which certainly seems early enough. But unfortunately the whole of that entry is an interpolation in Transition- or Early Middle-English, so that the form *abbot* has no claim whatever to be regarded as Old-English. Another source of these forms are collections of texts such as Kluge's *Lesebuch* and Assmann's *Homilien*, which contain late Transition texts mixed up with Old-English ones, so that late forms get into the glossaries to these books, whence they are copied by uncritical compilers. But I have thought it right to keep many of the words which occur in the later portions of the Chronicle, partly on the chance of their being really older than their first occurrence, partly because of the continuity and great importance of the Chronicle.

Words that first occur towards the end of the eleventh century are marked $vL.=$ 'very late.'

Unnatural words.—As the Old-English literature consists largely of translations, we may expect to find in it a certain number of words which are contrary to the genius of the language, some of them being positive monstrosities, the result of over-literal rendering of Latin words. I often warn the reader against them by adding (!). These unnatural words are not confined to interlinear translations. The translator of Bede's History is a great offender, and I have had constantly to add the warning Bd. Among the poetical texts the Psalms are especially remarkable for the number of unmeaning compounds they contain, evidently manufactured for the sake of the alliteration; this text also contains many other unnatural words and word-meanings; hence the frequent addition of Ps.

Brevity.—In a concise dictionary so much must be omitted that it is necessary to follow strict principles of selection, so as to omit what is least essential and to give most space to what is most important. Otherwise we might easily fall into the error of giving more space to a demonstration of the spuriousness or unnaturalness of a word than to a statement of the meanings and constructions of some really important word. The test of a dictionary is not the number of words it contains, but the fullness of treatment of the commonest words.

Brevity and conciseness have not only the negative advantage of saving space, but also the positive one of facilitating reference by enabling the eye to take in at a glance what would otherwise be scattered over a wide space. It will be seen that the three-column arrangement of the present dictionary, together with the use of systematic contractions and typographical devices, has made it possible to carry compactness and brevity further than has yet been done, and without any loss of clearness. Thus, instead of the lengthy *w. dat. of pers. and gen. of thing*, I write simply *wdg*. Much, too, may be done by omitting what is superfluous. Thus, by adding its class-number to each strong verb, I dispense with the addition of *str. vb.* Again, as nearly all verbs are recognizable by their ending *-an*, the absence of the class-numbers serves all the purposes of adding *wk. vb.*, the classes of the weak verbs being easily discriminated by the presence or absence of a mutated vowel in the root. The ignoring of *ge-* in the alphabetic arrangement (p. xii) has also been a great saving of space: under the old arrangement the reader was often obliged to look up a verb twice, perhaps only to find that the *ge*-forms

were confined to the preterite participle ; as if a student of German were expected to look up *nahm* under *nehmen* and *genommen* under *genehmen* !

Meanings.—The first business of a dictionary such as the present one is to give the meanings of the words in plain Modern English, discriminating clearly the different meanings of each word, but doing this briefly and without the attempt to give all the English words that may be used to translate the Old-English word. Etymological translation should be avoided ; thus *geþofta* does *not* mean 'one who sits on the same rowing-bench.' Less mischievous, but equally silly, is the practice of translating an Old-English word by some obsolete or dialectal word, which is assumed—sometimes falsely—to be connected with the Old-English one. Thus, when we have once translated *bearn* by 'child' there is no more reason for adding 'bairn' than there is for adding 'kid' or any other synonym. It is curious that this kind of thing is done only in the Germanic languages : no one thinks of translating *un veau, c'est le petit d'une vache* by 'a veal, it is the little of a cow,' or of telling us that 'a veal is less grand than a beef.' One practical advantage of avoiding this kind of translation is that when the reader finds in a dictionary such as the present one *lǣce* explained as meaning 'leech' as well as 'physician,' he feels quite certain that the former word is not a mere repetition of the meaning of the latter. But in some cases where there is no example of the primitive meaning of a word, and yet there is reason to believe that it actually existed in Old-English, I give it in ( ) ; thus under *wacan* I give (awake).

The distinct meanings are separated by (;), groups of meanings being further marked off by | and ‖, the latter being especially used to separate the transitive and intransitive meanings of verbs.

The ambiguity of many English words makes it difficult to define meanings with certainty without full quotations. The best method is to add part of the context in ( ): thus I explain *ādragan* by 'draw (sword),' *seomian* by 'hang heavy (*of* clouds),' where the italic *of* stands for 'said of.'

Quotations are next in importance to definitions, though an extensive use of them is quite incompatible with the nature of a concise dictionary. But idioms ought to be given whenever they offer difficulty. Sometimes, too, a quotation is shorter than a detailed explanation. Whenever space has allowed it, I have also given quotations even when they are not absolutely necessary.

References I omit entirely, as being inconsistent with the plan of this dictionary. But I indicate the sources of words in many cases; and † = 'poetical' is practically a reference to Grein's *Glossar*, where full references may be found.

Constructions are given with considerable fullness.

Irregular forms which can be better studied in an ordinary grammar are dealt with very briefly. Thus I characterize *bēc* as 'pl. of *bōc*' without going into further details, while under the rarer *āc* I give fuller details.

Cognate words are given only in Old-English itself. It would, indeed, have argued a strange want of the sense of proportion if I had sacrificed my quotations in order to tell the reader that *mann* is cognate with Danish *mand*, or to refer him from the perfectly transparent compound *līc-hama* to the misleading German *leichnam*. But I give the sources of borrowed words—or, at least, indicate the language from which they are taken—as this information is definitely limited, and throws direct light on the meaning of the word.

Spellings.—In this dictionary the head-words are given in their Early West-Saxon spellings, with, of course, such restrictions and exceptions as are suggested by practical considerations. Feminine nouns in *-ung, -ing* are given under the former spelling, unless they occur only in the latter. The ending *-nis, -nes* is always written *-nes*; *-o* interchanging with *-u*, as in *bearo, menigo*, is always written *-o*, to distinguish it from the *-u* of *sunu, caru*. The silent *e* in *c(e)aru, sc(e)ort* is always omitted in the head-words. It is evident that it would have been idle to attempt to do justice to such minute variations in a work like the present one. So also I ignore the diphthong *io*, always writing it *eo*, in spite of its etymological value in certain texts.

As the regular variations of spelling are given in the List (p. xiv) in alphabetical order, they are not repeated under each word. To save space I have made some use of etymological diacritics. Thus the West-Saxon *ǣ* which corresponds to Anglian and Kentish *ē* is written *ǣ* (as in *dǣd*). So also *ie, iė, iẹ* all represent the same Early West-Saxon sound, but each corresponds to a different vowel in the other dialects, namely *i, e, ẹ* respectively, as in *bierhto, sciėld, ciẹle* = Anglian and Kentish *birhto, sceld, cẹle*. Variations of spelling which require to be specially noted are given—as in my *History of English Sounds*—in an abridged form; thus *wita, io* implies *wiota*, the diphthong being given to show that the *i* of *wita* is

short. So also *bēn, oe* implies *boen* ; *feorm, a* implies *farm*, the diphthongs *ea, eo, ia, io, ie, oe* being treated as simple vowels. Where necessary, the place of the vowel is indicated thus : *a-* (first syllable), *-a* (last syllable), *-a-* (middle syllable). Forms that do not occur are marked *. Hence *brīesan*, ȳ* means that the word occurs only in the spelling *brysan*, but that this is probably only a late spelling, and that if the word occurred in an Early West-Saxon text it would probably be written with *ie*. As the reader cannot possibly know beforehand whether the spelling he believes or knows to be the normal one actually occurs or not, it is surely better to put the word in the place where he expects to find it than to give way to a too great distrust of hypothetical forms.

Cross-references are given sparingly, and only when really useful to those for whom the dictionary is intended. The reader who wants a cross-reference from *bundon* to *bindan* — and perhaps expects to have it repeated with *forbindan* and all the other derivatives—had better devote a few hours to my *Anglo-Saxon Primer*. There is no system of cross-references which will enable people ignorant of the elements of Old-English to read charters and other original texts in Old-English ; and cross-references for forms which occur only in interlinear glosses are of no use to beginners, for no beginner would think of reading such texts with a dictionary— or, indeed, of reading them at all. No one who has an elementary knowledge of West-Saxon will have the slightest difficulty in recognizing such a word as *woruld* by its context, even in the disguise of *wiarald*. If he has, he need only turn to the list of various spellings, where he will find *ia=eo*, and in the dictionary itself he will find *weoruld* with a reference to *woruld*.

In conclusion, I venture to say that, whatever may be the faults and defects of this work, I believe it to be the most trustworthy Anglo-Saxon dictionary that has yet appeared.

OXFORD,
October 1, 1896.

ARRANGEMENT AND CONTRACTIONS

—•◦•—

THE order is alphabetic, *æ* following *ad*, and *þ* (which also stands for *ð*) following *t*. But *ge-* is disregarded (*gebed* under *b*), and is generally omitted before verbs, except where accompanied by distinctions of meanings, as in *gegān*.

Compounds and derivatives generally come immediately after the simple word, whose repetition is denoted by ~, as in **bī-spell,** ~**bōc** = *bīspellbōc*. If only part of the word is repeated, that part is marked off by an upright stroke, as in **bann|an,** ~**end** = *bannend*. So also in the first quotation given under **mǣn|an,** the ~**e** stands for *mǣne*; but if nothing is added to the ~ when used in this way, it necessarily implies repetition of the complete head-word, whether the head-word contains a | or not: thus in all the quotations given under **gemǣn|e** the ~ stands for *gemǣne*.

* denotes hypothetical or non-existent forms (p. xi).

† signifies that the word or idiom or meaning occurs only in poetry, (†) that it is mainly poetical, but occurs also in prose. When all the compounds of a word marked † occur only in poetry, the † is omitted after them; otherwise the † is repeated after them when necessary, or the exceptions are marked *Pr.*='prose.' † after an isolated vowel means that the shortness or length of the vowel is proved by the metre; thus *i*† under *wiga* means that the metre shows that the *i* is short, while *ō*† under *þrowian* means that although the *o* does not seem to be accented—in which case *ó* would have been added—the metre shows it to be long—at least in some dialects.

(?) denotes doubtful words, forms, or meanings (p. vii).

(!) denotes words formed in slavish imitation of Latin (p. viii).

The ( ) in (*m.*) means that the gender of the noun is doubtful, but probably masculine ; (*f.*) means that it is probably feminine, and so on. When the second of two final repeated consonants is put in ( ), it implies that the uninflected word ends in a single consonant, which is doubled before an inflectional vowel; thus **fæsten(n)** means nominative *fæsten*, dative *fæstenne*, &c.

For the meaning of the thin *e* in **gambe,** &c., see p. vii.

For the diacritics in *ê, iĕ, iẹ*, see p. x.

In words divided by a hyphen, the stress is generally on the first syllable, if no stress-mark is used ; if the stress is on any other than the first syllable, it is marked by · before the letter with which the stress begins, as in *be·cuman*, which has the same stress as *become*, while in such a word

as *bī-spell* the stress is on the first syllable. In such compounds as *ongēan-cyme* the first element is assumed to have the stress in the same place as in *on'gēan*, that is, on the second syllable.

The parts of speech are not generally marked in the case of adjectives, numerals, pronouns, and weak verbs, strong verbs being indicated by the number of their class. Anomalous verbs are marked *vb.*, especially the preterite-present verbs, such as *cann*, which are given under this form, not under their infinitives.

A. Anglian.
a. accusative, accusative singular.
abs. absolute.
abst. abstract.
act. active.
aj. adjective.
an. analogy.
av. adverb.

Bd. Bede's History.

cj. conjunction.
coll. collective.
comp. composition.
correl. correlative.
cp. compare.
cpv. comparative.
Ct. Charter.

d. dative.
def. definite.
dem. demonstrative.
dir. direct.

e, E. early.
esp. especially.

f. feminine (noun).
fem. feminine.
fig. figurative(ly).
Fr. French.

g. genitive.
gen. generally.
ger. gerund.
Gk. Greek.
Gl. glossary.

i. instrumental.
impers. impersonal.
impv. imperative.
indc. indicative—*w. indc.* with the conj. *þæt* followed by vb. in indc.
indecl. indeclinable.
indef. indefinite.
indir. indirect.
inf. infinitive.
infl. influence.
intens. intensitive.
interj. interjection.
interr. interrogative.
intr. intransitive.

K. Kentish.

l, L. late.
lit. literally.
LL. Laws.
Lt. Latin.

M. Mercian.
m. masculine (noun).
masc. masculine.
met. metaphorical(ly).

N. Northumbrian.
n. neuter (noun).
neut. neuter.
no. noun.
nom. nominative.
nW. non-West-Saxon.

occ. occasional(ly).
of said of (p. ix).

pass. passive.
pers. person(al).

pl. plural, nominative and accusative plural, noun in plural.
pleon. pleonastic(ally).
poss. possessive.
Pr. Prose.
pro. pronoun.
prp. preposition.
prs. present.
prt. preterite.
Ps. Psalms (metrical).
ptc. participle, preterite participle.

R. Rhyming Poem.
rel. relative.
rfl. reflexive in form, that is, taking a rfl. pronoun.

sbj. subjunctive — *w. sbj.* with the conj. *þæt* followed by vb. in sbj.
Scand. Scandinavian (Scand. words are given in their Icelandic forms).
sg. singular.
spl. superlative.
st. strong.

tr. transitive.

v. very.
vb. verb (generally implying anomalous vb.).

W. West-Saxon.
w. with—*waa.* with double accusative, *wdg.* with dative of person and genitive of thing, and so on.
wk. weak.

Note that these contractions are often combined : *mf.* noun which is both *m.* and *f.*, *eW.* early West-Saxon, *ld.* dative in the later language, *vL.* very late (p. viii).

VARIATIONS OF SPELLING

[The spellings which follow the = are those under which the word must be sought in the dictionary, if it cannot be found under the original spelling. Unaccented vowels are disregarded.]

a = æ, ea.
æ = a, æg, e, ea.
æi, æig = æg.
æo = ea.
b = f.
c = g, h.
ce = c.
ch = c, h.
ci = c.
cs = sc, x.
ct = ht.
d = þ.
dd = þd.
ds = ts.
ð = þ.
e = æ, ea, eg, eo, ie, y.
ea = æ, a, eo, gea, i.
ei = e, eg.
eo = e, ea, geo, i, ie, oe (= e).
eu = eo, eow.
ew = eow.

f = w.
fn = mn.
g = h, w, x.
ge = g.
gg = cg.
gi = g.
gu = geo.
h = c, g.
hs = sc, x.
i = eo, g, ie, ig, ige, y.
ia = eo.
ig = i.
io = eo.
iu = eo, geo.
iw = eow.
k = c.
m = mn, n.
nc = c(e)n, ng.
ng = g(e)n.
o = a, og.
oe = e, æ.

ps = sp.
pt = ft.
qu = cw.
sc = s.
sce = sc.
sci = sc.
sþ = st.
t = þ.
th = þ.
u = f, ug, v, w.
uu = ū, w.
v = f.
weo = wo, wu.
wi = wu.
wo = weo.
wu = w, weo, wo, **wy**.
wy = weo, wi.
x = cs, hs, sc.
y = e, i, ie, yg.

INFLECTIONS

(EARLY WEST-SAXON.)

NOUNS: REGULAR.

Strong: Masculine.

			Neuter.
Singular	Nominative [1]	stān	scip, hūs
	Dative	stāne	scipe
	Genitive	stānes	scipes
Plural	Nom.	stānas	scipu, hūs
	Dat.	stānum	scipum
	Gen.	stāna	scipa

Strong Feminine.

		1 a.	1 b.
Sg.	Nom.	giefu, synn	dǣd
	Acc.	giefe, synne	dǣd
	Dat.	giefe	dǣde
	Gen.	giefe	dǣde

Strong Feminine.		1 a.	1 b.
Pl.	Nom.	giefa	dǣda
	Dat.	giefum	dǣdum
	Gen.	giefena, synna	dǣda

Weak :		Masc.	Neut.	Fem.
Sg.	Nom.	nama	ēage	sunne
	Acc.	naman	ēage	sunnan
	Dat.	naman	ēagan	sunnan
	Gen.	naman	ēagan	sunnan
Pl.	Nom.	naman	ēagan	sunnan
	Dat.	namum	ēagum	sunnum
	Gen.	namena	ēagena	sunnena

[1] When the Accusative (Acc.) is not given separately, it is the same as the Nom.

IRREGULAR.

	U-Nouns : Masc.	Fem.
Sg. Nom.	sunu	duru, hand
Dat.	suna	dura, handa
Gen.	suna	dura
Pl. Nom.	suna	dura
Dat.	sunum	durum
Gen.	suna	dura

	Mutation-Plurals : Masc.	Fem.
Sg. Nom.	fōt	bōc
Dat.	fēt	bēc
Gen.	fōtes	bōce, bēc
Pl. Nom.	fēt	bēc
Dat.	fōtum	bōcum
Gen.	fōta	bōca

	R-Nouns : Masc.	Fem
Sg. Nom.	brōþor	sweostor
Dat.	brēþer	sweostor
Gen.	brōþor	sweostor
Pl. Nom.	brōþor, brōþru	sweostor
Dat.	brōþrum	sweostrum
Gen.	brōþra	sweostra

Masc. ND-Nouns.

Sg. Nom.	frēond, būend	
Dat.	frīend, būend	
Gen.	frēondes	
Pl. Nom.	frīend, būend	
Dat.	frēondum	
Gen.	frēonda, būendra	

Masc. E-Plurals.

Pl. Nom.	Ęngle	
Dat.	Ęnglum	
Gen.	Ęngla	

Indeclinable Fem. : *bieldo, bieldu*

ADJECTIVES.

Strong.

	Masc.	Neut.	Fem.
Sg. Nom.	sum, gōd	sum	sumu, gōd
Acc.	sumne	sum	sume
Dat.	sumum	sumum	sumre
Gen.	sumes	sumes	sumre
Instr [1]	sume	sume	(sumre)
Pl. Nom.	sume	sumu, gōd	sume
Dat.		sumum	
Gen.		sumra	

[1] Instrumental.

Weak.

	Masc.	Neut.	Fem.
Sg. Nom.	gōda	gōde	gōde
Acc.	gōdan	gōde	gōdan
Dat.		gōdan	
Gen.		gōdan	
Pl. Nom.		gōdan	
Dat.		gōdum	
Gen.		gōdena, gōdra	

NUMERALS.

	Masc.	Neut.	Fem.
Pl. Nom.	twēgen	twā	twā
Dat.		twēm	
Gen.		twēg(r)a	

So also *bēgen* ' both.'

Pl. Nom.	þrīe	þrēo	þrēo
Dat.		þrim	
Gen.		þrēora	

PRONOUNS.

Sg. Nom.	ic	þū	hē	hit	hēo
Acc.	mē	þē	hine	hit	hīe
Dat.	mē	þē	him	him	hire
Gen.	min	þīn	his	his	hire
Pl. Nom.	wē	gē		hīe	
Acc.	ūs	ēow		hīe	
Dat.	ūs	ēow		him	
Gen.	ūre	ēower		hira, heora	

	Masc. and Fem.	Neut.
Sg. Nom.	hwā	hwæt
Acc.	hwone	hwæt
Dat.	hwēm	
Gen.	hwæs	

	Masc.	Neut.	Fem.	Masc.	Neut.	Fem.
Sg. Nom.	se	þæt	sēo	þes	þis	þēos
Acc.	þone	þæt	þā	þisne	þis	þās
Dat.	þǣm	þǣm	þǣre	þissum	þissum	þisse
Gen.	þæs	þæs	þēre	þisses	þisses	þisse
Instr.	þȳ	þȳ	(þǣre.	þȳs	þȳs	(þisse)
Pl. Nom.	þā			þās		
Dat.	þǣm			þissum		
Gen.	þāra			þissa		

VERBS.

		Strong.	'Hear.'	Weak.'Wean.'	'Love.'
Indic.			'Hear.'	'Wean.'	'Love.'
Pres. Sg.	1	*binde*	*hīere*	*węnige*	*lufige*
	2	*bintst*	*hīerst*	*węnest*	*lufast*
	3	*bint*	*hīerþ*	*węneþ*	*lufaþ*
Pl.		*bindaþ*	*hīeraþ*	*węniaþ*	*lufiaþ*
Pret. Sg.	1	*band*	*hīerde*	*węnede*	*lufode*
	2	*bunde*	*hīerdest*	*węnedest*	*lufodest*
	3	*band*	*hīerde*	*węnede*	*lufode*
Pl.		*bundon*	*hīerdon*	*węnedon*	*lufodon*
Subj.					
Pres. Sg.		*binde*	*hīere*	*węnige*	*lufige*
Pl.		*binden*	*hīeren*	*węnigen*	*lufigen*
Pret. Sg.		*bunde*	*hīerde*	*węnede*	*lufode*
Pl.		*bunden*	*hīerden*	*węneden*	*lufoden*
Infinitive		*bindan*	*hīeran*	*węnian*	*lufian*
Gerund		(*tō*) *bindenne*	*hīerenne*	*węnienne*	*lufienne*
Partic.					
Pres.		*bindende*	*hīerende*	*węniende*	*lufiende*
Pret.		(*ge bunden*	*hīered*	*węned*	*lufod*

GROUPS OF STRONG VERBS.

I. Fall-group.

(a) eo-preterites.

INFINITIVE.	THIRD PRES.	PRET. SG.	PRET. PL.	PTC. PRET.
feallan	*fielþ*	*fēoll*	*fēollon*	*feallen*

(b) e-preterites.

hātan	*hǣtt*	*hēt*	*hēton*	*hāten*

II. Shake-group.

scacan	*scæcþ*	*scōc*	*scōcon*	*scacen*

III. Bind-group.

bindan	*bint*	*band*	*bundon*	*bunden*

IV. Bear-group.

beran	*bierþ*	*bær*	*bǣron*	*boren*

V. Give-group.

INFINITIVE.	THIRD PRES.	PRET. SG.	PRET. PL.	PTC. PRET.
sprecan	*spricþ*	*sprǣc*	*sprǣcon*	*sprecen*
giefan	*giefþ*	*geaf*	*gēafon*	*giefen*

VI. Shine-group.

scīnan	*scīnþ*	*scān*	*scinon*	*scinen*

VII. Choose-group.

cēosan	*cīest*	*cēas*	*curon*	*coren*
lūcan	*lȳcþ*	*lēac*	*lucon*	*locen*

PRETERITE-PRESENT VERBS.

		Indic.	Subj.
Pres. Sg.	1	*wāt*	*wite*
	2	*wāst*	*wite*
	3	*wāt*	*wite*
Pl.		*witon*	*witen*

Pret. *wiste*. Imper. *wite, witaþ*. Infin. *witan.*
Ptc. Pres. *witende*, Pret. *witen.*

ANOMALOUS VERBS.

Ind. Pres. Sg.	1	*wile, nyle*	*eom, bēo*	*dō*	*gā*
	2	*wilt, nylt*	*eart, bist*	*dēst*	*gǣst*
	3	*wile*	*is, biþ*	*dēþ*	*gǣþ*
Pl.		*willaþ, nyllaþ*	*sind(on), bēoþ*	*dōþ*	*gāþ*
Pret. Sg.	1	*wolde, nolde*	*wæs*	*dyde*	*ēode*
	2	*woldest*	*wǣre*	*dydest*	*ēodest*
	3	*wolde*	*wæs*	*dyde*	*ēode*
Pl.		*woldon*	*wǣron*	*dydon*	*ēodon*
Subj. Pres. Sg.		*wile*	*sīe, bēo*	*dō*	*gā*
Pl.		*willen*	*sīen, bēon*	*dōn*	*gān*
Pret. Sg.		*wolde*	*wǣre*	*dyde*	*ēode*
Pl.		*wolden*	*wǣren*	*dyden*	*ēoden*
Imper. Sg.		*wile*	*wes, bēo*	*dō*	*gā*
Pl.		*willaþ*	*wesaþ, bēoþ*	*dōþ*	*gāþ*
Infin.		*willan*	*wesan, bēon*	*dōn*	*gān*
Partic. Pres.		*willende*	*wesende*	*dōnde*	*gangende*
Pret.		—	—	*gedōn*	*gegān*

ANGLO-SAXON DICTIONARY.

ā *av.*, ō *N.*, *W.* always, ever; at all. ne . . ā never; not at all, not. ā on ēcnesse, ā būton ende for ever and ever ‖ *of space*, continuously : ā oþ *wa.* all the way to . . [āwa].

~brēmende ever-celebrating.

~libbende everlasting.

~wunigende continual.

a-, ā- *occ.* = ǣ-, on-.

aæþan = āīeþan.

ab = ōwębb woof.

ā·bacan 2 bake.

ā·bǣdan force out, extract (oil by pressure); force away, ward off (death); obtain by force, exact.

ābǣligan = ābięlgan.

ā·bǣran disclose, reveal.

abǣre = ǣbǣre.

abǣrnan *tr.* burn = on-.

abal = afol.

ā·bannan 1 summon, command—~ūt call out (the militia); proclaim.

ā·barian, ābor-, disclose, make public [bær].

abbod *m.* abbot [*Lt.* abbatem].

~dōm *m.*, ~hād *m.*, ~rīce *n.* dignity *or* rule of an abbot, abbacy.

~isse *f.* abbess.

ā·bēatan 1 beat to pieces; beat; beat down, make to fall.

ābēcēdē (*n.*) alphabet.

ā·bedecian*, ābeþ- get by begging *or* asking.

ā·belgan 3 *w. d. or a.* anger, irritate, offend, injure — ābolgen

wesan *or* weorþan ‖ *wd.* be angry *or* offended (with).

ā·bēodan 7 *wda.* announce, state | offer *w. sbj.* | command; summon—ūt ~ call out (militia). | appoint (festival)| —hǣlo ~ *wd.* wish good luck, greet, take leave of.

ā·bēowan = ābīewan.

ā·ber|an 4 carry with effort; endure, suffer; *rfl.* restrain oneself, (not) know what to do; take upon oneself, put up with | take away, remove |ūp~ raise, lift up | reveal, make known.

~endlic endurable.

ā·berED, *once* -rd, cunning.

ā·berstan 3 *intr.* force one's way out; burst out, appear, *often w.* ūt; escape *w.* fram.

abepecian = abed-.

ā·bīd|an 6 remain; remain alive, be spared; remain behind | wait, wait patiently; *wg.* wait for, await, expect; experience.

~ung *f.* waiting.

ā·biddan 5 *wa.*, *w. sbj. and* æt (him) request, pray for | obtain (by prayer or request).

ā·bīeg|an bend *tr.*; subdue; convert.

~endlic flexible.

ā·bięlgan*, y, abæligan make angry, offend [belgan].

ā·biernan 3 burn *intr.*

ā·bīewan*, ȳ, ēo rub, polish; purify; adorn.

ā·bifian, eo tremble.

ā·bītan 6 bite (to death); devour, eat; *wg.* taste, partake of.

ā·biterian become bitter.

ā·blāc|ian, ~od bēon become pale *or* pallid.

ā·blǣc|an make pale, whiten.

~nes *f.* paleness, gloom = ǣ-.

~ung *f.* paleness, pallor.

ā·blǣst with strong blast (*of* flame).

ā·blāwan 1 *tr.* blow (trumpet); breathe: God him on-āblēow gāst.

ā·blendan blind; delude, deceive.

ā·blERED *ptc.* bare, uncovered (neck) [blēre].

ā·blīcan 6 shine (forth), appear, be bright—ic bēo āblicen dealbabor.

ā·blinn|an 3 *intr.* cease; desist (from) *w.g.*, fram.

~e(n)dnes *f.* cessation, interruption.

ā·blissian make glad, please.

ā·blycg|an grow pale ‖ strike with consternation, amaze, *esp. in ptc.* ~ed.

ā·blys|ian blush, be ashamed.

~ung *f.* blushing, shame.

ā·bolgennes *f.* irritation [ābelgan].

āborian = ābarian disclose.

ā·borgian be security for *wa.*; borrow *w.* æt.

ā·brac|ian— ~od engraved in relief.

ā·brǣdan dilate, stretch out.

ā·braslian *intr.* (re)sound.

ā·brecan 4 break through *or* down

(wall); take (fortress); break (command) ‖ *intr.* force one's way (into), break away (from).

ā·bredwian destroy, kill.

ā·brēgan terrify.

ā·bregdan, -ēdan 3 *tr.* move quickly, snatch, draw (sword), up~ raise; ~ of, fram remove, take away ‖ *intr.* start up, awake.

ābrēmende, *under* ā.

ā·brēot|an 7, *also wk., prt.* -ēat, -ēot, -ēotte destroy.

~nes *f.* extermination.

ā·brēoþan 7, *prt. pl.* -uþon deteriorate; prove untrustworthy, fail; hit ābrēaþ, hē ābrēaþ æt þǣre þearfe; perish, come to an end. *ptc.* -open degenerate, worthless ‖ *tr., prt.* -ēodde, destroy *M.*

abrerdan = onbryrdan.

ā·brīetan*, ȳ, *A.* ēo destroy. *Cp.* ābrēotan.

ā·broþen *ptc. of* ābrēoþan.

~nes *f.* degeneracy, cowardice.

a·bufan *av.* above *vL.* [= onbufan].

ā·būgan 7 *intr.* bend, be bent; bow down; incline | turn (to *or* from, withdraw | *wd.* submit (to), do homage.

abūtan = onbūtan.

ā·bycgan buy; requite; redeem | perform (oath).

ā·byffan mutter.

ābylg-, *see* æbylg-.

ā·bysg|ian, i occupy, trouble, engross (the mind): ~od on, mid ‖ *intr.* ~ on engage in, undertake.

~ung *f.* occupation.

ac, á, *A.* ah I. *cj.* but; and. II. *av. interr. A.* numquid—ah-ne nonne.

āc *f., d., nom. pl.* ǣc, *g.* āce, *ld.* āc oak; † ship of oak ‖ *m. the Runic letter* a.

~bēam *m.* oak-tree.

~cynn *n.* kind of oak.

~drenc *m.* drink made from acorns (?).

~lēaf *n.* oak-leaf.

~melo *n.* acorn-meal.

~mistel *m.* oak mistletoe.

~rind *f.* oak-bark.

~trēow *n.* oak-tree.

ac-lǣc = āg-lāc.

acan 2 ache.

ā·cǣgl|ian — ~od serrated (back).

ā·calan 2 become cold.

accent *m.* accent [*Lt.* accentus].

ā·cealdian become cold.

ā·cēlan *tr.* cool; quiet.

ācelma, *see* æc-.

ācen = ǣcen.

ā·cenn|an bear (child): hē wæs ~ed of hire; produce (result).

~ed born, (his) own (child).

~edlic native Gl.

~ednes, *E.* ācennes *f.* birth.

ā·ceoc|ian, -coc- *tr.* choke (to death) ‖ *intr.* burn itself out (*of* fire).

~ung *f.* 'choking up,' ruminating.

ā·ceorfan 3 cut (off head, down tree).

ā·cēosan 7 choose, pick out— ācoren Gode chosen in the sight of (by) God.

ā·ciegan call forth, summon.

ā·cierr|an *tr.* turn; turn aside ‖ *intr.* turn, go; return.

~ednes *f.* turning away, apostasy, revolt.

āclian terrify [ācol].

ā·clǣnsian purify *w.* fram.

ā·clēofan 7 *tr.* split.

ā·clingan 3—*ptc.* āclungen contracted.

ā·clipian, eo call forth, summon.

ā·cofrian *intr.* recover (from illness).

ācol, ā†, ~mōd terrified, excited.

ge~mōdian terrify, dispirit.

ā·cōlian become cool *or* cold.

acolitus *m.* light-bearer (in church) [*lLt.* acolythus].

ā·coren *ptc. of* ācēosan, chosen.

~lic eligible, estimable.

ā·costnian try, test.

ā·cræftan devise (plan).

ā·crammian cram.

ā·crēop|ian creep, crawl—wyrmum ~ed swarming with worms.

ā·crimman 3 cram, stuff.

ācsian = āscian.

ā·cum|an 4 come; descend (from ancestor): eal mancyn þe him of-ācōm ‖ *tr.* endure, withstand (temptation).

~endlic endurable.

~endlicnes *f.* possibility Gl.

ā·cumba *m.*, -e *f.*, ǣ-, ācuma oakum, tow; ashes of the same | clippings, prunings [cemban].

ā·cunnian test, try, find out; experience: ~ on mē selfum.

acustan accuse *lM.*

ā·cwacian tremble.

ā·cweccan shake *tr. and intr.*

ā·cwelan 4 die, perish.

ā·cwellan kill, destroy.

ā·cwencan extinguish (fire, light).

ācweorna, *L.* ācwern *m.* squirrel.

ā·cweorran 3—ācworren surfeited, crapulatus. *Cp.* metecweorra.

ā·cweþan 5 say: ~ hine fram reject.

ā·cwician, āc(w)ucian revive *tr. and intr.*, come to life again (*of* the dead).

ā·cwielman kill.

ā·cwīnan 6 dwindle, become extinct (*of* fire).

ā·cwincan 3 be extinguished (*of* fire, light); be eclipsed (*of* moon); vanish.

ā·cȳþan make known, show, reveal; proclaim, announce; prove, confirm.

ād *m.* heap; funeral pile | fire, flame.

~faru† *f.* funeral procession.

~fȳr† *n.*, ~līeg† *m.* pile-fire.

~lama† *m.* one crippled by fire, demon.

ā·dǣlan separate, part.

ā·dēadian become dead *or* torpid, decay.

ā·dēaf|ian become deaf.

~ung *f.* becoming deaf.

adel|a *m.* putrid mud, filth.

~iht muddy, filthy.

~sēap *m.* cesspool, sewer.

ā·delfan 3 dig (pit, grave).

ā·dēman decree: ~ hine fram *d.* deprive of ‖ try, afflict.

ā·deorc|ian, ~od wesan become dim *or* tarnished; be eclipsed (*of* moon).

ades|a *m.*, ~e *f.*, ads- adze.

ā·dīedan put to death, destroy— *ptc.* ādīedd dead.

ā·diefan deafen, surpass in sound [dēaf].

ā·dihtan compose, write.

ā·dihtian arrange, decree.

ā·dīl(e)gian, *L.* ȳ destroy, do away with, annihilate, ‖ erase.

ā·dimm|ian, ~od wesan become dim; lose clearness of sight (*of* eyes).

ādl, *A.* āld *f.* disease.
~ig diseased, ill.
~þracu† *f.* virulence of disease.
~wērig† weary with illness.
ādl|ian be sick, be ill, become infirm *or* weak. *ptc.* geādlod sick (person).
~ung *f.* illness.
ā·dōn *vb.* take away, send away ‖ destroy ‖ put : þanon ~ remove, ~ of expel, deliver.
adrǣdan = ondrǣdan.
ā·drǣfan drive away, expel.
ā·dragan 2 draw (sword).
adreminte *f.* feverfew.
ā·drencan drown, immerse.
ā·drēog|an 7 perform, practise ; pass (life, the night) | endure, suffer | tolerate, put up with.
~endlic endurable.
ā·drēopan 7 drip, drop.
ā·drēosan 7 fall ‖ be diminished, fail.
ā·drīegan endure [drēogan].
ā·drīfan 6 drive away *or* out, drive, pursue — ~ spor follow track ; ~ ford mid pīlum stake ford with piles. *ptc.* ādrifen engraved, embossed.
ā·drincan 3 be drowned ; be quenched by water (*of* fire).
ā·drūgian, -ūwian dry up *intr.*
ā·drȳgan cause to dry up (well, sea) ; wipe dry.
ā·dumbian become silent, dumb.
adun- = ofdūn-.
adustrigan = andūstrigan.
ā·dwǣscan extinguish (fire, light) ; destroy (enemies).
ā·dwellan, -elian, *prt.* -ealde lead into error, seduce (from God).
ā·dwīnan 6 dwindle, waste away, disappear.
ā·dysg|ian, ~od wesan become foolish.
ǣ, ǣw *f., g. etc.* ǣ(we) divine law ; scripture, book of the Bible ; religion ; rite, religious ceremony | human law—būton ǣ outlaw ; custom | marriage | wife | life† *once. In lW. there is a tendency to restrict the form ǣw to the meaning 'marriage.'*
~bebod *n.* commandment.
~bōc *f.* book of the law.
~boda *m.* preacher.

ǣ|brǣce law-breaking ; adulterous.
~breca, -y- *m.* adulterer.
~brucol sacrilegious.
~bryce *m.* adultery.
~crǣft *m.* skill in law.
~crǣftig skilled in law.
~fæst pious | married.
~fæstlīce *av.* piously.
~fæsten *n.* legal *or* public fast.
~fæstnes *f.* piety ; religious creed, religion.
~fremmende pious.
~fyllende pious.
~glēaw learned in the law.
~lǣdend *m.* lawgiver (!).
~lǣrend *m.* teacher of the law.
~lagol law-giving.
~lic of the law, lawful.
~līce *av.* lawfully.
~riht *n.* code of law.
~sellend *m.* lawgiver.
~swice *m.* violation of God's law ; adultery (?).
~we-weard *m.* priest.
~wita *m.* lawyer, councillor.
~wrītere *m.* law-giver.
ǣ·eargian become cowardly.
ǣ-bǣre, ā-, -ere notorious, openly known [āberan].
ǣ·ebbian ebb away, recede from.
ǣ-blāce pale.
~nes, ā- *f.* pallor.
ǣbs, ǣps [*confusion w.* ǣps = ǣspe aspen] (*f.*) fir-tree [*Lt.* abies].
ǣ-byl(i)g|an, ā-, -il- make angry *or* indignant ; offend.
~nes *f.* anger.
~þ(u), ǣbylþ, ābyl(i)gþ *f.* anger ; offence, injury : Crīstes ~ offence against C., þæt him tō ~e gedōn wæs that which had offended him.
ǣc *see* āc oak.
ǣc-lǣca *see* ag-.
ǣ-cambe *f.* oakum. *Cp.* ācumba, camb.
ǣ-celm|a, āc-, *M.* ecilma chilblain [ācalan].
~eht with chilblains.
ǣcen, ā- of oak [āc].
ǣcer *m.* (cultivated) field | acre.
~ceorl *m.* farmer.
~hege *m.* field-hedge.
~mann *m.* farmer.
~sǣd *n.* seed for an acre (?).
~splott *m.* small field (?).

ǣcer|spranca *see* ǣcern.
~tēoþung *f.* tithe of the produce of the soil.
~tȳning *f.* fencing.
ǣcern, -irn, ǣcren *n.* acorn.
~spranca*, ǣcer- *m.* ilex, oak sapling (?) Gl.
ǣ-cnōsl|e degenerate, not noble Gl.
ge~iende degenerating Gl.
ǣcumba = ācumba.
ǣ-cyrf clippings, what is cut off [āceorfan].
ǣd(d)re *f., pl.* ǣdran, ǣdra, *A.* hēþir, ēþre vein—ǣdrum hrīnan, ǣdran hrepian feel the pulse ; nerve, sinew ; *in pl.* kidneys | spring (of water).
~seax, ǣdderseax *n.* lancet.
~weg *m.* artery, vein.
ǣdre *av.* at once, forthwith | (know) fully, clearly†.
ǣfen(n), *lN.* ēfern *m.* evening.
~gebed *n.* evening prayer *or* service.
~drēam *m.* even-song.
~giefl *n.* twilight.
~glōm(a) *m.* twilight.
~gram† fierce in the evening.
~lāc† *n.* evening sacrifice.
~lǣcan become evening.
~leoht† *n.* evening light.
~lēoþ† *n.* evening song.
~lic of the evening.
~lof *n.* lauds.
~mete *m.* supper.
~rǣding *f.* evening reading.
~gereord *n.*, -u *pl.* supper.
~gereordian sup.
~repsung *f.* nightfall.
~rest† *f.* evening rest.
~sang *m.* evening song.
~scima *m.* evening light.
~scop† *m.* evening bard.
~sprǣc† *f.* speech of the evening before.
~steorra *m.* evening star.
~tīd *f.*, ~tīma *m.* evening time.
~þegnung, ~þēn- *f.* (divine) evening service ; supper.
~þēowdōm *m.* (divine) evening service.
ge·ǣf(e)nian become evening.
ǣfnung *f.* evening.
ǣfesn, *L.* ~e *f.* special pasturage (of swine) ; charge for pasturage | luxury, wantonness (?).

[3]

æf(e)st, æ†, *mfn.* envy, malice; zeal, rivalry [ēst].
~**full** envious.
~**ian** be envious.
~**ig** envious, jealous.
æf-gielp, -ælþ (*f.*) superstition Gl.
æf-grynde *n.* abyss.
ǣ-fielle*, **æfelle** peeled [fell].
ǣ-fiermþa*,*yf.* sweepings, rubbish.
æf-lāst† *m.* swerving (?) *once.*
æfnan, **ę**, perform, do, make (ready), carry out (commands) | cause, excite (anger) | endure, suffer.
ǣfre *av.* always : ne . . ~ never | at any time ‖ *L. indf.* ever : eall þæt ~ betst wæs whatever was best ; ~ ǣlc each.
æftan *av.*, ~**weard** *aj.* from behind, behind.
æftemest *spl.* hindmost, last *in time and order.*
æfter, y- I. *prp. w. d.* (*a.*) behind, after *place, order, time* | *extension in space and time* along, through, during | *pursuit, aim, object of vb.* (dig a. gold, ask a.) | *according to* | in consequence of ‖ ~ þǣm, ~ þon afterwards. ~ þǣm þe *cj.* after. II. *av.* after(wards). III. ~**ra**, *L.* **æft(e)ra** *cpv. aj.* following, next, second.
~**boren** posthumous.
~**cweþan** 5 speak afterwards; repeat (what is said *or* dictated).
~**cwepend†** *mpl.* posterity.
~**ealo** *n.* small beer.
~**folgere** *m.* successor.
~**folgian, ~fyl(i)gan** succeed; pursue.
~**fylgend** *m.* successor.
~**fylgung** *f.* pursuit.
~**gang** *m.* succession.
~**genga** *m.* successor; posthumous child.
~**gengel** *m.* successor.
~**gengnes** *f.* succession, extremity.
~**gield** *n.* additional payment.
~**hǣþe** *f.* after-heat.
~**hyr(i)gan** imitate.
~**ield(o)** *f.* old age† ; future period.
~**lēan** *n.* reward ; retribution.
~**lic** second Gl.
~**rāp, ~rǣpe** *m.* crupper.
~**ryne** *m.* encountering (!).
~**sang** *m.* matins.
~**singend** *m.* succentor.

æfter͡sōna *av. IN.* again ; afterwards.
~**sprǣc** *f.* after-claim.
~**sprecan** 5 claim.
~**spyrian** follow ; inquire.
~**weard** following. .
~**weardnes** *f.* posterity.
æf-þanc(a) *m.* grudge, displeasure ; insult.
æf-weard absent.
~**nes** *f.* absence.
æf-wierdelsa, ǣwy- *m.* injury,loss.
æf-wierdla *m.* injury, loss ; fine for injury *or* loss.
ǣg, ǣ† *n., pl.* ~**ru**, egg.
~**er-felma** *m.* film of an egg.
~**er-geolu** *n.* yolk of egg.
~**līm** *m.* white of egg.
~**(ge)mang** *n.* egg-mixture.
~**sciell** *f.* egg-shell.
~**wyrt** *f.* dandelion.
æg-flota = īeg-.
æg-læca &c., *see* **ag-**.
ǣgen = āgen.
ǣg-hwā *no.* each one, every one ; any one ‖ *n.* -hwæt everything ; something *or* other, anything. -hwæs *av.* in every way, entirely.
ǣg-hwǣr, -ār, ǣgwern *av.* everywhere, in every direction ; anywhere | in every respect, in every way.
ǣg-(hwǣ)þer *no., aj.* each (of two *or* more), both : heora ǣg(hwæ)þer; on ǣgþere healfe on both sides. ǣgþer . . and, ǣgþer . . ge . . (ge) *cj.* both . . and . . (and).
ǣg-hwanon(e) *av.* from all sides ; on all sides, everywhere.
ǣg-hwelc, i, y *no., aj.* each (one), every (one) ; who-, what-soever. ~ ānra *no. wg.* each. ~es *av.* in every way.
ǣg-hwider *av.* in every direction ; everywhere.
ǣ-gift *n.* repayment.
ǣ-gilde, y without compensation, unatoned for (*of* man killed).
ǣgnan *pl.* chaff.
ǣgþer = ǣghwǣþer.
ǣgwern = ǣghwǣr.
ǣ-gylt *m.* trespass, offence.
ǣ-gype worthless, nugatory.
æhher = ēar ear of corn.
ǣ-hīw *n.*, ~**nes** *f.* want of colour, paleness.

ǣ-hīwe pallid.
ǣ-hlīep *m.* violence, breach of peace LL. *Cp.* æthlīep.
æht† hostility, strife.
æhte *f.* pursuit, persecution.
æht = eaht.
ǣht *f. gen. pl.* power, possession ; property.
~**boren** born in serfdom.
~**eland** *n.* territory.
~**emann** *m.* serf, farmer.
~**eswān** *m.* unfree herdsman.
~**spēdig** wealthy.
~**gesteald** *n.* possession.
~**gestrēon** *n.* possessions, riches.
~**geweald** *n.* power, possession.
~**wela** *m.* wealth.
~**welig** wealthy.
geǣhtan†, *prt.* -ehte *once* subdue.
geǣhtle† *f.* esteem (?) [eahtian].
ǣl *m.* eel.
~**fisc** *m.* eel.
~**hyde** eel-receptacle (?).
~**nett** *n.* eel-net.
~**epūta** *m.* eel-pout, burbot.
ǣl = āwel awl.
ǣl- 'all-' *interchanges with* eall-.
ǣl- = ęl-.
ǣl͡an, ǣ†, burn, burn up ; kindle, light (lamp).
~**ing** *f.* burning ; ardour.
ǣ-lǣte I. *f.* divorced woman. II. *n.* desert place [ālǣtan].
ǣl-beorht†, eall- all-bright, very bright.
ǣlc *no., aj.* each, every, all ; any, *esp. after* būton : on ānum bāte būton ǣlcum gereþrum. ~ . . ōþer the one . . the other.
ǣl-ceald† very cold.
ǣl-cræftig† all-powerful.
ǣlc(w)uht *n.* everything [ǣlc wiht].
ǣled†, g. ǣldes, *m.* fire, firebrand.
~**lēoma** *m.* gleam of fire, firebrand.
ǣ-leng|e tedious, tiresome [lang].
~**nes** *f.* tediousness.
ælf *m., pl.* ięlfe fairy, elf, incubus.
~**ādl** *f.* nightmare.
~**cynn** *n.* race of elves.
~**scīene†** elf-sheen, beautiful as a fairy.
~**siden(n)** *f.* nightmare.
~**sogoþa** *m.* hiccup.
~**þone** [o=a *or* ō?] *f.* nightshade (plant).
ǣl-fǣle†, cal-felo dire (poison).

æl-faru† *f.* host.
ælfen = ielfen fairy.
æl-frem(e)de, el- foreign; free (from).
æl-fylce† *n.* foreign (hostile) army; foreign land.
æl-grēne†, eall- all-green.
ællyfta = endlyfta.
ælmes|se, *L.* -ysse *f.* alms [*Lt.* eleemosyna].
~bæþ *n.* gratuitous bath.
~dǽd *f.* almsdeed.
~gedāl *n.* distribution of alms.
~feoh *n.* alms.
~full charitable.
~georn charitable.
~giefa *m.* giver of alms.
~giefu *f.* almsgiving.
~hlāf *m.* dole of bread.
~land *n.* land granted in frank-almoigne.
~leoht *n.* candle *or* light given to church by layman.
~lic, *once* -estlic charitable.
~lice *av.* charitably.
~mann *m.* beggar.
~pening *m.* alms-penny.
~riht *n.* right of receiving alms.
~selena, ~sylena *fpl.* almsgiving.
~weorc *n.* almsgiving.
æl-midde *f.* exact middle.
æl-mierca*, y† *m.* Ethiopian.
æl·mihtig, æll-, eal(l)-, al(l)-, -e(a)htig, -ahtig, -æhtig almighty (*only of* God).
~nes *f.* omnipotence.
ælpig = ān-liepig.
ælren of alder [alor].
æl-tǽwe, -tēowe, -towe, perfect; in sound health; excellent, good; true; famous.
æ-mel|le insipid.
~nes *f.* tedium, weariness, sloth.
æ-men(ne) depopulated, desert [mann].
ǽmerge, ǽmyrie *f.* embers, ashes.
ǽmet|te, ~e *f.* ant.
~hyll *m.* ant-hill.
ǽmet|te, ǽm(e)te, *vE.* ēmōte *f.*, ǽmta *m.* leisure, want of occupa-tion [mōt, gemōt].
~hwil *f.* leisure (time).
~tig, ǽm(e)tig at leisure, free from (occupation) *w. g. or* fram; de-prived of, without; empty.
ǽmettigian, ǽm(e)t(ig)ian, -gan be at leisure *abs., rfl. w. g. or* fram

and tō keep oneself free: hū hīe hīe ge~ scoldon ōþerra weorca; ǽmtigaþ ēow tō rǽdinge!
ǽ-mōd out of heart, dismayed.
ǽmte = ǽmette.
ǽ-mynde*, -i- *n.* forgetfulness.
æn- = ān-.
ǽne, āne *av.* once *in time*; *repeti-tion* one time, once (in multiplica-tion): ~ seofon bēoþ seofon || ~sīþa once.
ænet = ān-.
ænetre = enitre, ān-wintre.
ǽnig, -iht *no.,* *aj.* any(one)— ~e þinga *av.* somehow, anyhow.
æniht = āwiht.
ǽn|lic single, only (son); unique, incomparable, excellent; beauti-ful; of high rank.
~lice *av.* splendidly.
ǽnne, *see* ān.
ǽ-note useless.
æppel, a-, *pl.* -p(p)la(s), *m.* apple, fruit; ball; eye-ball.
~bǽre apple-bearing.
~bearo *m.* orchard.
~cyrnel *n.* pip; pomegranate (!).
~fæt *n.* apple-vessel Gl.
~fealo reddish yellow.
~hūs *n.* apple-storehouse.
~lēaf *n.* violet.
~scala *fpl.* core of apple.
~scrēada *fpl.* apple-parings.
~trēow *n.* apple-tree.
~tūn *m.* orchard.
~þorn *m.* crab-apple.
~wīn *n.* cider.
æppledē† ball-shaped, embossed.
æps = æsp.
æps = æbs fir-tree.
ǽr = ār brass.
ǽr *aj.* only in *cpv. and spl.* ǽrra, ǽrest, *which see, and in* (on) ǽrne-morgen (*see under* ǽr-morgen).
ǽr *av.* formerly; previously, before; already—ǽr oþþe æfter sooner or later; ǽr and sīþ always; ne ǽr ne siþþan never; swā wē ǽr (above) cwǽdon; on ǽr before-hand, previously; *to make prt. into pluperfect*: ǽr brohte had brought. || ǽr, *lN.* ār soon: tō ǽr too soon; swā ǽr swā as soon as *w. indc.*; sǽles bīdeþ hwonne ǽr hēo .. cȳþan mōte how soon, when.

ǽr|or *av. cpv.* formerly; previously, beforehand.
~est, ǽst, *lN.* ārest *av. spl.* first (in time *or* order), for the first time, at first.
ǽr *cj.* before *w. sbj., occ. w. indc.*: cwǽdon þæt Crīst nǽre ǽr hē ācenned wæs of Mārian; *correl.* ǽr, ǽrest (*avs.*) . . ǽr (*cj.*): hine hæfde ǽr Offa āflīemed .. ǽr hē cyning wǽre; þū meaht ǽlcne unþēaw on þǽm menn ǽrest be sumum tācnum ongi-etan .. ǽr hē hit mid wordum cȳþe.
ǽr *prp. wd.* before (in time). ~ þǽm (*or* þām), þon (*or* þan) *av.* before that (time), formerly; *cj. w. sbj.* before. ~ þǽm þe &c. *cj. w. sbj.* before.
~adl† *f.* early disease.
~ǽt *m.* feasting early.
~boren† first-born.
~cwide† *m.* prophecy.
~dǽd *f.* former deed.
~dæg *m.* early part of day; *pl.* former days, ancient times.
~dēaþ† *m.* early death.
~gedōn done before.
~fæder† *m.* forefather.
~gōd† good of old (?).
~ieldo *f.* former age.
~lice *av.* early.
~(ne)morgen, -me-, -ma- early morning [*cp.* ǽr *aj.*].
~(ne)morgenlic matutinal.
~genemned, ~gesǽd above-men-tioned.
~sceaft† *f.* piece of antiquity.
~gestrēon† *n.* ancient treasure.
~wacol early awake.
~wela† *m.* ancient wealth.
~geweorc† *n.* ancient work (sword).
~gewinn† *n.* former war *or* trouble.
~woruld† *f.* primeval world.
~gewyrht† *n.* former deserts.
ǽra *m.* scraper, strigil [ār].
ǽrce, a-, e- *m.* archiepiscopal pallium [*Lt.* archi-].
~biscop *m.* archbishop.
~biscop-dōm *m.* -rīce *n.* arch-bishopric.
~biscop-stōl *m.* archiepiscopal see.
~diacon, archi- *m.* archdeacon.
~hād *m.* episcopal dignity.
~rīce *n.*, ~stōl *m.* archbishopric.

ǣren of brass [ār].

ǣrend|e *n.* errand, message, tidings.

~bōc *f.* written message, letter.

~fæst bound on errand.

~gāst *m.* angel.

~(d)raca, -wraca, -wre(o)ca *m.* messenger, ambassador, (angel, apostle).

~scip *n.* ship, boat Gl.

~secg *m.* messenger.

~spræc *f.* message.

~wreca, *see* ~raca.

~gewrit *n.* letter.

ǣrend|ian, *gen.* ge~, carry message, go on errand : ~ him þæt undertake that commission for him ; negotiate, enter into treaty for : ~ his hlāforde wīfes ; intercede, use one's influence with: ~ tō Gode ymb . . ; ~ him þæt hē forgēafe . .

~ung *f.* errand ; commission, mandate.

ǣrendra *m.* messenger ; representative, proxy.

ǣrig-, *see* earh arrow.

ǣring *f.* dawn [ǣr].

ǣrist, -est *f., m.* resurrection ; origin ; pedigree [ārīsan].

ǣrn *n.* house [*an older form* ræn- *appears in composition : see* mete- *and next word*].

~þegn*, *vE.* rendegn *m.* house-officer.

ǣrn|an ride (fast), gallop ; ride race [*causative of* iernan].

~eweg *m.* road fit to ride on ; race-course.

~ing *f.* riding, racing.

geǣrnan *intr.* gallop, ride ‖ *tr.* reach by riding, gallop up to.

ǣror *see* ǣrra.

ǣrra *aj. cpv.* former, earlier, old (times, wars). ǣror *av.* before, formerly ‖ *spl.* ǣrest first (in time) : æt ~an in the first place (in enumerating).

ǣs *n.* carrion, food.

æsc *m.* ash-tree ; spear† ; boat, Scandinavian war-ship ; *the Runic letter* æ.

~berend†, ~bora† *m.* spear-bearer, warrior.

~berende spear-bearing.

~here† *m.* ship-band, (Danish) army.

~holt† *n.* spear.

~mann *m.* (Danish) pirate.

~plega† *m.* spear-play, battle.

æsc|rind *f.* ash-bark.

~rōf† warlike, illustrious.

~stede† *m.* battle-place.

~tīr‖ *m.* glory in war.

~þracu†*f.* spear-violence, battle.

~þrote, -u *f.* vervain (?).

~wiga† *m.* warrior.

~wlanc† warlike.

~wyrt *f.* vervain (?).

æsc = æx axe.

æsc|e = asce ashes.

~fealu ashy-coloured.

~grǣg ashy gray.

æsc|e *f.* inquiry, questioning ; search, investigation [āscian].

~an demand (legally).

ā̆-scēare, ā̆-, -ǣre unshorn, with untrimmed hair [scieran].

ā̆-sceda *fpl.* (?) refuse (?) Gl. [āscādan].

æscen I. *f.,* (*m.*) wooden vessel, bucket, cup. II. *aj.* of ash.

ā̆-smogu *npl.* slough, cast-off skin (of snake) [āsmūgan].

æsp|e, *L.* æps *f.* aspen, white poplar.

~en of aspen.

~rind *f.* bark of aspen.

ā̆-sprynge, *L.* -inge source (of running water) ; starting-point, origin ; spring (of water), fountain [āspringan].

ǣst = ǣrest.

æstel *m.* book-mark [*lLt.* (h)astula].

ā̆-swic (*n.*) scandalum, stumbling-block, offence ; sedition ; deceit, seduction ; crime.

ā̆-swic|ian scandalizare, become an offence ; offend ; betray ; become an apostate.

~end *m.* offender ; hypocrite ; traitor.

~ung *f.* offence, stumbling-block ; deceit ; sedition.

ā̆-swica *m.* offender ; deceiver ; hypocrite ; traitor, deserter.

ā̆-swicce rebellious.

ā̆-swind inert [āswindan].

æt, *rare A.* ot, *prp. wd.* at *of time* —þā æt nēxtan thereupon, then ‖ *of place—pleon.* : in þǣre stōwe þe is genemned æt Searobyrȝ, is called Salisbury ‖ *motion* to ‖ source, origin : geleornian æt ‖ *deprivation,* from : āniman æt ‖ *specification* : onfēng hine æt fulwihte ‖ *equivalence, price* : āgefe þēr-æt . . ‖ *instrument* :

wearþ ācweald æt his witena handum.

æt *m.* food ; eating [etan].

~giefa† *m.* feeder.

~wela† *m.* abundance of food.

ā̆-etan 5 eat up, devour.

æt·beran 4 carry, carry off ; bring, show.

æt·berstan 3 break away, escape, *w. d. or* þanon.

æt·bregd|an, -ēdan 3 take away, deprive *wda.* : hē ætbrǣd hine (*rfl.*) lustum.

~endlic ablative (case).

æt·clifian adhere.

æt·clīpan *once* adhere.

æt·dēman refuse.

æt·dōn *vb.* take away, deprive *wda.*

æt·ealdod too old (for) *wg.*

æt·eglan molest.

æt·fæstan *wda.* inflict ; impart, endow with ; *wad.* join (in marriage), commit, entrust.

æt·feallan 1 fall out (of chariot) ; fall away, deteriorate ; be deducted (from sum paid).

æt·fele (*m.*) adhesion.

æt·feng *m.* taking possession of, reclaiming (cattle).

æt·feohtan‖ 3 : ~ folmum grope.

æt·fēolan, *prt.*-fealh 3 *wd.* adhere ; apply oneself to, continue in.

æt·ferian carry away *wda.*

æt·flēon 7 escape.

æt·flōwan 1 be abundant (!).

æt·foran I. *prp. wd.* before, in the presence of. II. *av.* beforehand (time).

æt·gǣd(e)re *av.* together ; at the same time [gadrian].

æt·gǣre, -ǣre *n.,* -gār *m.* javelin.

æt·giefan 5 give *wda.*

æt·grǣpe† seizing, aggressive.

æt·habban *vb.* retain, withhold.

æt·hebban 2 take away, withhold —*rfl.* separate oneself from, exalt oneself above *w.* fram.

æt·hindan *prp. wd., av.* behind, after.

æt·hlēapan 1 *wd.* run away, escape.

æt·hliep *m.* assault.

æt·hrīnan 6 touch *w. g., a.*

æt·hrine *m.* touch.

æt·hwā *no.* every one, each.

æt·hweg(u), -a *av.* somewhat, a little ; how.

æt·hweorfan 3 (re)turn, go.

æt-hwōn *av.* almost.

æt·iec|an, *M.* ot- add to, increase.

~nes *f.* increase.

æt·iernan 3 run away.

æt·iew|an; -ēowan *occ. W.*; -ēo-
wian *lW. often*; -ēawan *A.*;
otēawan *eM.*; at- *tr.* show,
display, reveal; *rfl.* appear ‖ *intr.*
appear.

~(ed)nes *f.* appearance; manifestation, revelation.

~ung *f.* showing, manifestation,
Epiphany.

æt·lǽdan lead away, take away.

ætlic eatable Gl. ǽ- *or* e- (?).

æt·licgan 5 lie useless.

æt-limpan 3 *wd.* disappear, escape
(from); become an apostate (from
God).

æt·lūtian lie hid; *wd.* hide from.

ætnes edibility (?) Gl. *Cp.* ætlic.

æt·niman 4 take away, deprive *wda.*

æt·reccan *wda.* declare forfeited.

geæt(t)red, -od poisoned, poisonous.

ǽt(t)ren, ǽt(t)ern poisonous,
poisoned.

~mōd† venomous in mind.

ǽttr|an, ~ian poison.

ǽtrig poisonous.

æt-rihte, y, e I. *aj.* near (in place
and time). II. *av.* nearly, almost.

æt·sacan 2 *w. g., a.* deny.

æt·samne *av.* together.

æt·scūfan 7 push away.

æt·sittan 5 stay, wait.

æt·slidan 6 slip, glide.

æt·sporn|an, u 3 stumble, knock
against *tr., intr., rfl. w.* æt | rebel.

~ung *f.* stumbling, misfortune.

æt·springan 3 spring out, flow out.

æt·sprung(en)nes *f.* failing [æt-
springan].

æt·stand|an 2 stand (still); be
present; cease—*ptc.* ~en stopped
(*of* urine, veins).

æt·standende standing by.

æt·steall† *m.* place (?); help (?).

æt·stillan *tr.* still, calm.

æt·swerian 2 deny with oath.

æt·swigan become silent; keep
silence about, not speak of *w.* be.

æt·swimman 3 swim away, escape
by swimming.

æt·swingan 3 *wda.* deprive.

ǽttren = ǽtren.

æt·þringan 3 force out, deprive *wda.*

æt·weaxan 1 *intr.* increase.

æt·wegan 5 take away, carry off.

æt·wenian *wda.* wean from (evil).

æt-wesende at hand.

æt·windan 3 *wd.* escape; fly away.

æt·wist *f.* presence; (?) sustinence,
food [*through confusion with*
edwist].

æt·wītan 6 *wda.* reproach with.

æt·wrencan *wda.* deprive by
fraud.

ǽþian *intr.* breathe ‖ *tr.* breathe,
blow, inspire.

geǽþed sworn (witness) [āþ].

geǽþelian ennoble, make renowned.

æþel|e noble (by birth or char-
acter); vigorous (plants); good
(in character); valuable, of high
price; pleasant (*of* odours).

~boren of noble birth; freeborn.

~borennes *f.* nobility of birth.

~cund of noble origin.

~cundnes *f.* nobility of origin.

~cyning *m.* king (Christ).

~duguþ *f.* retinue.

~ferþing-wyrt, -fyrding- *f.* a
plant.

~nes *f.* nobility.

~stenc *m.* sweet odour.

~tungol *n.* noble star.

geæþele *wd.* inborn, natural (to),
suitable.

æþeling king's son, heir apparent;
nobleman; †hero, man.

æþel(l)ic noble, excellent.

æþellīce *av.* nobly, excellently.

æþelu *f.* origin, lineage *gen. pl.*;
nobility, excellence; produce,
growth (of the earth).

æþm *m.* breathing, breath; vapour;
blast (of fire).

~ian give out vapour.

ǽ-þrīet*, -ȳ troublesome, tedious
[āþrēotan].

~nes *f.* tedium.

ǽ-þrot *n.* disgust, weariness
[āþrēotan].

~sum*, ā- irksome.

ǽw = ǽ law.

ǽwan contemn, scorn.

ǽ-wǽde without clothes.

ǽwda, ~mann *m.* witness.

ǽw(e) lawful (wife); (brother) of
the same marriage [ǽ].

ǽwen related by marriage, (brother)
of the same marriage [ǽ].

ǽ-wēne hopeless, uncertain, doubtful.

ǽ-wielm *m.* source (of river),
spring, fountain : origin [āweal-
lan].

ǽwierdelsa = ǽf-.

ǽwis-firina, ē(a) *lM.* notorious
sinner, publicanus. *Cp.* ǽwisc-.

ǽwisc, ~e I. *n.* disgrace, offence,
scandalum. II. *aj.* disgraced,
abashed; indecent.

~berende shameful.

~firenend*, a- *m.* public sinner Gl.

~lic shameful.

~mōd abashed.

~nes *f.* disgrace, sense of shame;
shamelessness—(?) on ~se in pro-
patulo, publicly; reverence.

ǽwn|ian marry [ǽ].

~ung *f.* wedlock.

ǽwum-boren legitimate (child)
[ǽ].

ǽwung—on ~e openly Gl. *Cp.*
ēawunga.

ǽ-wyrp throwing-away, rejection;
what is rejected [āweorpan].

æx, æcus, acus, æces, æsc, eax *f.*
axe.

ā·fǽgan draw, depict [fāg].

ā·fǽgrian make beautiful; embroider. *confusion w.* āfǽgan (?).

ā·fǽman foam out, breathe out.

ā·fǽran terrify.

ā·fǽstan fast, perform (fast).

ā-fǽst-lā *interj.*

ā·fǽst(e)nian make firm, confirm;
fix (eyes on); build; write; affix,
add (in writing).

ā·fand|ian test, try; experience.

~igendlic, ~odlic capable of being
tested, probabilis.

~ung *f.* trial.

ā·faran 2 go out, depart.

ā·feallan 1 fall down; fall (in
battle); fall off, decline, decay.

ā·fēdan nourish, feed; maintain,
support; rear, bring up; bring
forth, produce.

ā·feohtan 3 attack, assail; pluck out.

ā·feorm|ian clean(se), remove
(pimples), purge (stomach);
purify (spiritually).

~ung *f.* clean(s)ing, purging.

afeorran = āfierran.

ā·feorsian, -ie, y remove, expel;
depart.

ā·ferian carry away, remove.

ā·ferscian become fresh (*of* water).
ā·fiellan fell (tree); kill; subvert, abolish.
ā·fierran, eo remove, deprive *w. d. or* fram.
ā·figen fried *once* Gl.
afindan = onfindan.
ā·flēan 2 strip off (piece of skin).
ā·flēon 7 flee; escape.
ā·flēogan 7 fly—biþ āflogen tō is addicted to.
ā·flīegan put to flight; expel (fever, devils).
ā·flīeman put to flight; expel; banish.
ā·flōwan 1 flow.
afogian = āwōgian.
afol†, *once* abal *n.* strength, might.
afon = onfōn.
āfor, ā, harsh (to taste); †fierce, vehement.
afora = eafora.
ā·forhtian be afraid.
ā·frēfr(i)an comfort, console.
ā·fremd|an, *A.* -emþan alienate.
~ung *f.* alienation.
ā·frēoþan 7 froth.
ā·fūlian become foul *or* impure, decay.
ā·fȳlan foul; defile.
ā·fyllan *w. a. and g. or i.* fill; satisfy (desires); complete.
ā·fȳran deprive *wai.*; castrate.
ā·fyrhtan—*ptc.* āfyrht afraid.
ā·fȳsan make to hasten, drive on *or* away; incite, impel (mind).
āg-lāc, æg-, -æc I.† *n.* misery, torment. II. *aj.* sagacious (?).
~cræft *m.* evil art.
~hād *m.* misery.
~wif *n.* wretched, monstrous woman.
āg-læca†, āh-, æg- *m.* wretch, monster; warrior, hero.
ā·gān *vb.* come forth, appear; pass (*of* time); happen; grow.
ā·gǣl|an hinder, frustrate; neglect —*ptc.* ~ed neglectful, remiss | engross, occupy: eall þæt folc wearþ mid him ānum āgǣled (in trying to capture him).
ā·gǣlwan astonish, alarm.
ā·galan 2 *tr.* sound; sing.
ā·gāl|ian—*ptc.* ~od remiss, neglectful.
ā·gānian yawn.

āgen, *occ. eW.* ǣ- I. own. II. *n.* (own) property; own country [āh].
~nama *m.* proper name (in grammar).
~nes *f.* possession, property.
~slaga *m.* suicide.
~spræc *f.* idiom.
agen = ongēan.
āgend *m.* possessor; the Lord [āh].
~frēa, āgenf-, -frēo, -frīg(e)a, -frīg, *d. &c.* -frēan, -frēo, *m., f.* owner, master, mistress.
~līce *av.* as one's own, imperiously; accurately, properly.
ā·geolwian become yellow.
ā·gēomerian mourn, grieve.
ā·gēotan 7 pour out, shed (blood); melt, found (metal images); destroy; deprive *wg.* ‖ *intr.* flow out.
ā·giefan 5 *wda.* give, render, give up; restore, repay.
ā·gieldan 3 pay, requite, render (account, retribution), repay, offer (sacrifice); make possible, allow —þā mē sǣl āgeald, when I had an opportunity.
ā·gielpan 3 exult in *wd.*
ā·gīemelēasian neglect.
ā·giet|an 5, *also wk. ptc.* ~ed, destroy.
ā·gieta *m.* waster, prodigal.
agift = ǣgift.
ā·gimmed gemmed, set with jewels.
aginnan = onginnan.
agita = āgīeta.
ā·gleddian moisten.
ā·glīdan 6 glide, slip, stumble.
āgn|ian possess; claim (possession); take possession, appropriate, adopt; hand over.
~iend *m.* possessor.
~iendlic, ge- possessive (in grammar).
~ung *f.* possession; claim.
āgnettan appropriate [āgen].
ā·gnīdan 6 rub (off)—*ptc.* āgniden threadbare.
ā·gniden(n) *f.* rubbing *once* Gl.
ā·gotennes *f.* shedding (of blood) [āgēotan].
ā·graf|an 2 engrave, inscribe, sculpture.
~enlic sculptured, graven.
ā·grāpian grasp.

ā·grīsan, ȳ shudder, fear: ~for helle.
ā·grōwan 1: *ptc.* ~en mid overgrown, covered with.
ā·gryndan descend [grund].
agrysan = āgrīsan.
agu *f.* magpie.
ā·gyltan be guilty, incur guilt, trespass *w.* wiþ.
ah = ac.
āh *vb., prt.* āhte, *inf.* āgan possess, have, get possession of; ought: nāh hē þæt tō dōnne.
ā·habban restrain; *rfl.* abstain *w.* fram.
ā·haccian pick out.
ā·hafen, æ *ptc. of* āhebban.
~nes *f.* elevation, rising (of the sea); pride.
ā·hātian become hot.
ā·heardian become hard, firm; become hardy, inured; be insisted upon, be maintained.
ā·hēawan 1 cut, excavate, cut down (tree), cut wood into planks.
ā·hebban 2 lift up, raise; extol, praise; exalt (thoughts), *rfl.* be presumptuous; *ptc.* āhafen leavened, raised (*of* bread).
ahebbian = āebbian.
ā·hefigian make heavy, weigh down; make sad.
ā·helpan 3 *wg.* help.
ā·heolorian weigh, consider.
ā·hēoran *or* ā·heordan† *once* rescue (?).
ā·herian (fully) praise.
ā·hieldan*, e, y, i bend, incline; lay down, rest ‖ turn away, avert [heald. *Cp.* onhieldan].
ā·hieltan*, y make lame, trip up; supplantare.
ā·hīenan humble.
ā·hierd|an *tr.* harden; encourage, strengthen.
~ing *f.* hardening.
ā·hladan 2 draw (water); deliver.
ā·hlǣnan *rfl.* exalt oneself.
ā·hlǣnsian become lean; make lean, macerare.
ā·hlēapan 1 leap up.
ā·hlēfan*, oe pull out *LN.*
ā·hliehhan 1 laugh; exult; laugh at, ridicule *wg.*
ā·hlocian pull out, dig out.
ā·hlōwan 1 resound.
ā·hlūttrian make clear, purify.

[8]

ā·hlȳttran = ā·hiūttrian.
ahnian = āgnian.
ā·hnēopan† 7 *prt.* -ēap*, -ēop pluck.
ā·hnescian become soft, weak; become effeminate ‖ *tr.* weaken.
ā·hnīgan 6 *intr.* bow, fall.
ā·hogian think out, devise.
ā·holian hollow; engrave, emboss | pull out.
ā·hōn 1 b *tr.* hang; kill by hanging; crucify.
ā·hopian hope.
ā·hredd|an save: hē hī æt hungre āhredde | rescue, recapture.
~ing *f.* deliverance, salvation.
ā·hrēof|ian become leprous—*ptc.* ~od leprous.
ā·hrēosan 7 fall; rush.
ahreran = onhrēran stir.
ahrinan = onhrīnan.
ā·hrisian, y shake; shake off.
ahsian = āscian.
āht = āwiht anything.
~līce *av.* worthily, bravely.
āhte *prt.* of āh.
ā·hwā *no.* any one.
ā·hwǣn|an vex, tease, grieve—*ptc.* ~ed afflicted, sad.
ā·hwǣr, -ār, āwer, ōwer(n) *av.* anywhere; in any way; ever.
ahwærgen = āhwergen.
ā·hwæt *no.* anything.
ā·hwæþer, ā(w)þer, āþor I. *no.* either (of two); anything (?). II. *av.* āwþer, oþþe . . oþþe either . . or. *Cp.* ōþar.
ā·hwanon, *IN.* ōwana *av.* from anywhere; on any side.
ā·hweorfan 3 *intr. and tr.* turn away, remove, avert.
ā·hwergen, -æ- *av.* anywhere.
ā·hwettan excite, incite; provide; repudiate, renounce.
ā·hwider *av.* in any direction, from any source.
ā·hwielfan cover (with vault), overwhelm. ūp~ pull up, loosen [hwealf].
ā·hwierfan *tr.* turn away.
ā·hwonne, -ænne *av.* at any time.
ā·hycgan think out, devise.
ā·hȳdan hide; *rfl. w.* wiþ.
ā·hȳrian hire.
ā·hȳpan plunder, destroy.

ā·idlian be free *w.* fram | make useless, annul, frustrate (plans); profane; get rid of (disease).
ā·iernan 3 run, flow; pass, expire (*of* time).
ā·iepan† lay waste, destroy.
āl- fire [ǣled, ǣlan].
~fæt *n.* cooking vessel.
~geweorc *n.* fire-making, tinder Gl.
āl = awel awl.
ā·lādian excuse, justify.
ā·læccan catch.
ā·lǣdan lead away, take away; lead: eft~ bring back; bring forth, cause to grow.
ā·lǣnan lend.
ā·lǣran teach.
ā·lǣt|an 1 b send forth, shed (tears); let, permit; let go, give up; let alone, leave: þā þæt fȳr hīe ālēt; remit, pardon; deliver.
~nes *f.* loss.
alan 2 †nourish, produce; appear (!) *IN.*
ā·lāþian become distasteful.
albe *f.* alb [*Lt.* alba].
aldot = *ealdoþ.
ā·lecg|an lay down, put down; place, put | desist from, remit (tribute), give up: ~ende word deponent verb | conquer, put down, refute; diminish, withhold | inflict.
~endlic deponent (verb).
ā·lēf|an, -ian, -wan injure, maim, weaken—*ptc.* ~ed ill [lēf].
aleon = onlēon lend.
ā·lēodan 7 grow.
ā·lēogan 7 tell lies *w.d. of person*; deny *wda.*; belie, not keep (vow).
ā·lesan 5 pick out, gather.
alet = ǣled fire.
alewan = ālēfan.
alewe = aluwe.
ā·libban, āleof-, ālif- live, pass (life); survive (injury).
ā·licgan 5 *w.d. of pers.* fail, cease, perish.
ā·lief|an *wda., w.d. and sbj.* allow; give up, surrender (fortress).
~ed lawful, allowable.
~edlic allowable.
~edlīce *av.* allowably.
~ednes *f.* permission.
ā·lies|an loosen, take off (helmet); release; ransom, redeem.
~(ed)nes *f.* redemption.

ā·lies|end *m.* releaser; Redeemer.
~endlic bond-loosening, liberating (rune *or* charm).
~ing *f.* redemption.
ā·lieþran*, ē *tr.* lather, rub with soap [lēaþor].
ā·lihtan lighten, alleviate, relieve, help; take away *or* off; alight.
ā·limpan 3 happen.
ā·linnan, -linian pull out; deliver, set free.
ā·lipian, eo dismember; loosen, separate (soul from body).
ā·liþrian loosen, remove.
ā·loccian entice out.
alor, -er, alr *m.* alder.
~drenc *m.* alder drink.
~holt *m.* alder wood.
~rind *f.* alder bark.
alter, altare *m.* altar [*Lt.* altare].
ā·lūcan 7 pull up, pull away, separate.
ā·lūtan 7 *intr.* bend, bow—*ptc.* āloten bowed down, humble.
aluwe, al(e)we *f.* aloes (a spice) [*Lt.* aloe].
am *IN.* = eom am.
ām, uma† reed (of loom).
ā·mǣllad [æ = ie?] *M.* made empty *or* useless. *Cp.* ǣmelle.
ā·mǣran make famous, proclaim.
ā·mǣstan fatten (pig).
aman = onman *vb.*
ā·manian demand, exact.
amang, *see* gemang.
ā·mānsum|ian excommunicate.
~ung *f.* excommunication.
ā·marod confused, confounded.
ā·masod confused, confounded.
ā·māwan 1 mow down.
amb = ām.
amber *mf.* jar, pitcher, bucket; a measure (dry and liquid) [*Lt.* amphora].
ambiht, -eht, (o)e- I. *n.* office, service; commission, command, message. II. *m.* officer, attendant, servant, messenger.
~hiera† *m.* obedient servant.
~hūs *n.* office.
~ian*, e- serve *IN.*
~mann *m.* official, attendant.
~mecg†, æ *m.* servant.
~scealc† *m.* official, servant.
~secg† *m.* official, messenger.
~smiþ *m.* official smith, carpenter, &c.

ambiht|sumnes*, ę-f. service LN.
~þegn† m. attendant, servant.
ambyre favourable (wind) [and-, byre].
ā·mearcian mark out, define (limits of); delineate, draw; destine, appoint.
amel m. vessel for holy water [lLt. amula].
ā·meldian betray, reveal.
ā·meltan 3 intr. melt—ptc. āmolten melted (metal).
ā·męrian, y purify (esp. melted metals); test, examine.
ā·met|an 5 measure; assign, bestow; plan, form, make.
~endlīce av. compendiously (!) Gl.
ā·mētan paint; adorn.
ā·mętsian provide with food, provision.
amidlod = unmīdlod.
ā·mięltan*, y tr. melt.
ā·mierran hinder, wag. hinder one in (from) ..; disable, injure, corrupt, destroy.
ā·molsnian decay, become weak (of eyes).
amore, vE. emer, omer a bird Gl.
ampella m. bottle [Lt. ampulla].
ampre f. dock (plant), sorrel.
ā·mundian protect.
ā·myrgan cheer.
ā·myrþran murder.
an, an- = on, on-.
ān I. a.m. ānne, ǣnne, no., aj. one (always strong: þæt ān) w. g. or of. ān and ān, ān æfter ānum one by one, one after the other. ān .. ōþer the first .. the second | same : on ānum gēare forþ·fērdon | only, alone : būton him ānum | a certain (one), a | any : būton synne ānre || þæt ān av. only : nā þæt ān (þæt w. indc.) .. ac not only .. but. for ān av. only. on ān av. continually; always, continuously; immediately; together; (tell him) once for all. ānes hwæt a portion, only a part (of the whole); gewearþ him ānes they made an agreement. ānum av. alone, solely; tō ānum gecierdon joined together. ānra gehwelc each. II. av. only.
~bīeme made of one trunk.

ān|boren only (child).
~būend† m. anchorite.
~cęnned only (child).
~cummum av. one by one LN.
~cyning† m. unique king.
~dǣge lasting one day.
~daga m. appointed day, term.
~dagian appoint day or term w. d. and of; adjourn.
~ēage(de) one-eyed.
~ęcge one-edged.
~feald(lic) simple, single; singular (number); unique, superior; honest, modest.
~fealdlīce av. simply.
~fealdnes f. concord; simplicity.
~fēte one-footed.
~floga† m. solitary flyer.
~forlǣtan 1 b relinquish, forsake, lose.
~forlǣtnes f. desertion.
~genga† m. solitary; also aj.
~gięld(e) n. single (fixed (!), cp. āndaga) compensation — ~gielde av. with such a compensation; fixed price.
~haga m. recluse.
~hende one-handed.
~hoga m. = ~haga.
~horn(a) m. unicorn.
~hygdig, ~hȳdig steadfast, stubborn, self-willed.
~hyrne one-horned; m. unicorn.
~hyrned(e) one-horned.
~īege one-eyed.
~lǣcan unite.
~lǣtan 1 b relinquish.
~legere with one husband.
~liepe, ~lape, ~liepig, ǣlpig isolated, single; unattached, without ties, private.
~liepnes f. loneliness.
~lic only, solitary, unique [cp. ǣnlic].
~mēde n. unanimity.
~mōd unanimous; resolute, brave, fierce; obstinate.
~mōdlīce av. unanimously; resolutely.
~mōdnes f. unanimity; constancy.
~nes f. oneness, unity; agreement; solitude.
~pæþ m. one-by-one path, narrow path.
~rǣd(e) unanimous; resolute, of firm character.
~rǣdlic unanimous; resolute.

ān|rǣdlīce av. unanimously; resolutely.
~rǣdnes f. unanimity, agreement; constancy.
~seld n. hermitage.
~setl n. hermitage.
~setla m. hermit.
~spilde unique (medicine).
~sprǣce speaking together.
~standende standing alone.
~stapa m. lonely wanderer.
~stelede with one stalk.
~stīg f. = ~pæþ.
~strǣc pertinacious.
~streces av. continuously [stręc·can].
~sum whole.
~sumnes f. virginity.
~sunu m. only, unique son.
~swēge harmonious.
~tīd† f. fixed time (?).
~getrum† n. unique, noble host.
~wędd n. security, pledge.
~wīg n. single combat.
~wiglīce av. in single combat.
~wille I. obstinate. II. av. obstinately.
~willīce av. obstinately.
~wil(l)nes f. obstinacy.
~wintre, ǣnetre, enetere of one year, one year old.
~wīte n. simple fine.
~wuniende solitary.
~wunung f. solitary abode.
geāned united Bd.
anung once f. zeal LN.
āna wk. mf. solitary, alone; only : God – wāt.
ana-wyrm [ā- ?] m. intestinal worm.
ānad-, -æd- n. desert.
anan-bēam m. spindle-tree.
an-bid, i† (n.) expectation, suspense; interval.
~stōw f. place of waiting.
an(d)-bīd|ian, ge- w. g., a. expect, wait for || intr. ge- wait.
~ung f. expectation.
an-bringelle f. instigation.
anbroce† once f. timber, wood.
an-brucol rugged.
anclēow f. ankle.
ancor, -er, ancra m. anchor [Lt. ancora].
~bęnd, ~rāp, ~stręng m. cable.
~mann m. anchor-man, proreta.
~setl n. prow.

ancra, ancer, -or *m.* hermit [*Lt.* anachoreta].
ancer|lic, ancor- of a hermit.
~līf *n.* hermit's life.
~setl *n.* hermitage.
~stōw *f.* hermitage.
and, *cA.* ęnd *cj.* and.   gelīce and *w. sbj.* as if.
and- *occ.* = on- (an-), rarely = ā-.
and|a envy, malice; anger, grudge, vexation; indignation, zeal; injury, hostility.
~ian envy; be zealous.
~ig envious, jealous.
and-bita tasting *or* feast (?) *once* Gl.
an(d)-byrd|an strive, *w.* ongēan, on resist.
~nes *f.* resistance.
and-cwiss *f.* answer.
and-ēages*, -æges† *once av.* face to face.
andefn, anddyfen *f.* proportion, amount [gedafenian].
andetla *m.* confession.
andett|an, andhet(t)an confess, give praise *wda.* [and, hātan].
~a, ~end, ~ere *m.* confessor, praiser.
~ing, ~nes *f.* confession.
and-feax bald.
and-fęnga *m.* taker up, defender, susceptor [fōn].
and-feng|e acceptable, fit.
~nes *f.* receiving; receptacle.
~estōw *f.* receptacle.
and-fęngend *m.* defender.
and-giet *n.* intellect; comprehension; sense (the five senses); meaning, purport.
~full intelligent, knowing.
~fullic intelligible.
~fullīce *av.* intelligibly, clearly.
~lēas foolish.
~lēast, ię *f.* folly.
~lic intelligible.
~līce *av.* intelligibly.
~ol intelligent.
~tācen† *n.* intelligible sign, symbol.
and-giéte*, -gete† manifest.
and-hēafod *n.* unploughed headland of a field, *gen. pl.*
andlang, *A.* ollung I. *aj.* continuous, whole (day). II. ~, ~es *prp. wg.* along(side).
and-lēan† *n.* retribution.
and-leofen, -lifen, y *f.* sustenance, food; wages [libban].

and-(ge)lōman, -uman, -aman *mpl.* utensils.
and-mitta = an-mitta.
an-drysn|e, andd- awe-inspiring; terrible, horrible.
~o† *fpl.* awe, reverence; etiquette.
~lic, ondrys(t)lic terrible.
and-sac|a *m.* denier, renouncer, apostate; enemy.
~ian deny.
and-sæc *n.* denial; refusal; resistance.
an(d)-sǽte hateful, repugnant, repulsive, hostile.
and-slieht†, y, *written* hand- *but alliterating with vowels, m.* stroke.
and-spyrnes *f.* stumbling-block, scandalum [onspornan].
and-swar|ian, -orian, -erian, -eorian, answer *wda.*
~u, ans-, *lN.* ondsuer- *f.* answer.
andūstr|igan protest, deny *lA.*
~ung *f.* protest, denial.
and-wǽt moist.
and-weard opposite; present (in place and time).
~lic present.
~līce *av.* present: hine ~ gesāwon.
~nes *f.* presence (in place and time).
and-weorc *n.* substance, thing; material; cause.
and-wig *n.* resistance.
and-wīs knowing, skilful in *wg.*
~nes *f.* experience.
and-wist *f.* station (?); support (?).
and-wlita, -iota; -eata *A.*; -ata *m.* face, countenance; surface (of earth); form, shape.
and-wlit|e, onwlite *m.* face, forehead.
~full proud Gl.
and-wrāþ† hostile *wd.*
and-wyrd|an answer *wd.*
~e *n.* answer.
~ing *f.* conspiratio.
āne = ǽne once.
ā-nęmnan declare, proclaim.
ānett, ǽ- *fn.* (*or m.*?) solitude.
an-filte (*n.*) anvil.
an-forht alarmed.
ang-*, o-.
~nora, nere *m.* corner of the eye (?).
anga *m.* prickle, sting, goad.
ānga sole, only [ān].

ang|e *av.* anxiously—him was ~ on his mōde he was anxious.
~brēost *n.* asthma.
~mōd anxious, sad.
~mōdnes *f.* distress of mind.
~nægl *m.* corn (on foot).
~nes *f.* anxiety, distress.
~set(a) *m.* pustule, carbuncle.
~sum, ~sumlic troublesome.
~sumian trouble.
~sumlīce *av.* painfully.
~sumnes *f.* trouble, perplexity, pain.
Angel *n.* Anglen (in Schleswig).
~cyning *m.* king of the English.
~cynn *n.* English race.
~þēod *f.* English people.
angel *m.* fish-hook.
~twicca, -æcca *m.*, ~twicce *f.* (?) earthworm.
an-ginn *n.* beginning; rising (of sun); enterprise; design; action.
Angle *pl.* = Ęngle English.
an-grisenlīce*, y *av.* terribly.
an-grisla, o- *m.* terror, horror.
angris(t)lic, o- terrible, horrible.
an-gryrlic*, o- *once* terrible. *a blending of* angrislic *and* gryre.
ā-nīedan force — ~ fram separate forcibly, ~ ūt drive out, expel.
ā-nīehst† *av.* last (in order of mention).
ā-niman 4 take away, deprive *w.* æt.
āninga, ānunga, ǽninga *av.* at once; absolutely, entirely, certainly.
ā-niþ(e)rian thrust down; condemn.
an-lēc, -æc, -ic *m.* 'looking-on,' regard, respect [lōcian].
anlic, angelīc, *eW.* o, *wd.* similar; equal.
~nes *eW.* a, o, *f.* likeness, similitude; form, stature: on næddran ~se; illustration, parable; portrait; statue, idol.
anlīc|e, o- *av.* similarly: ~ost swelce *w. sbj.* as if.
geanlīcian *wda.* compare; make like.
an-mēdla, o- *m.* pride, pomp, glory; presumption; courage [mōd].
gean-mēttan encourage [mōd].
an(d)-mitta, onm- *m.* balance, scales (for weighing).

ann *vb.*, *prt.* ūþe, *inf.* unnan, *wdg.* grant; not grudge, wish (a person to have something); wish *w. d.* *and sbj.* — unnendre handa voluntarily.

anoþa *m.* fear.

an-sīen; -ēon *A.*; o- *f.* face, countenance; aspect, appearance, form; view, contemplation; spectacle.

an-sīen*, onsȳn† *f.* lack, want.

an-spilde salutary.

an-stiellan*, y put in stall *or* stable [steall].

an-sund, o- whole, entire, sound, uninjured.

~nes *f.* soundness, wholeness.

Ante-crīst *m.* Antichrist [*Lt.*].

antefn, antifen *mf.* anthem [*Lt.* antiphona].

~ere *m.* book of anthems.

an-timber *n.* material; reason, pretext.

antre *f.* radish.

an-þrācian, andþ-, onþ-, apfear *wg.*, *w.* þæt *and* sceolde.

an-þrēce dreadful, repulsive.

anung *after* ān.

an-weald, and-, o- *m(n)*. authority, rule, prestige; jurisdiction, territory.

~a, onwalda *m.* ruler, sovereign; the Lord. = ān-?

an-weald, ān- *aj.* powerful, soleruling (?).

~ig [ān-?] powerful.

an-wealg, onwealh unimpaired, uninjured, safe.

~līce *av.* wholly.

~nes *f.* wholeness, soundness, chastity.

anwīg-gearo† *once* [= and-] ready for war.

an-wille*, on-† *once* desired.

an-wlōh† *once* adorned (?).

apa *m.* ape.

ā·pǣcan seduce (retainer from his allegiance).

ā·parian take in the act (hine þæræt).

ā·pins|ian estimate; consider, ponder [*Lt.* pensare].

~ung *f.* weighing Gl.

ā·plantian plant.

ā·platod plated (?) Gl.

apostata *m.* apostate [*Lt.*].

apostol, *lN.* postol *m.* apostle [*Lt.*].

apostol|hād *m.* apostolate.

~(l)ic apostolic.

appel = æppel.

Aprelis *m.* April [*Lt.*].

ā·priccan prick, make (dot).

aprotane *f.* wormwood [*Lt.* abrotonum].

apulder, apuldre *fm.* apple-tree [æppel].

~rind *f.* bark of apple-tree.

~tūn *m.* orchard.

apytan = āþȳtan.

ār† *m.* messenger (angel, apostle), herald; servant, soldier [ǣrende].

ār *f.* honour, dignity; reverence, respect; property, revenue, estate, benefice; prosperity; benefit, help; kindness; mercy.

~cræftig pious *or* distinguished (?).

~dǣde merciful, charitable.

~dagas *mpl.* feast-days.

~fæst distinguished; virtuous; pious, dutiful; merciful, kind, gracious.

~fæstlīce *av.* piously; kindly.

~fæstnes *f.* piety; virtue; kindness.

~full venerable; merciful, kind.

~fullīce *av.* kindly, mercifully.

~giefa† *m.* beneficent one.

~hwæt† eager for glory.

~lēas impious, wicked; merciless, cruel.

~lēaslīce *av.* wickedly, impiously; cruelly.

~lēasnes *f.* wickedness, impiety.

~lēast *f.* wickedness, wicked deed; cruelty.

~līc honourable, distinguished; honest; befitting; pleasant; merciful, kind.

~līce *av.* honourably; kindly, mercifully.

~scamu *f.* shame, modesty.

~stafas† *mpl.* kindness, help.

~þegn *m.* servant.

~wierþe, -eorþ, -urþ, -yrþ venerable, distinguished.

~weorþfull honourable.

~weorþian, u, y honour, reverence, worship.

~weorþlic, u, y venerable.

~weorþlīce, u, y *av.* honourably; kindly.

~weorþnes, u, y *f.* honour, dignity.

~weorþung, u *f.* honour.

~wesa *once* respected.

ār *f.* oar.

ār|blæd *n.* blade of oar.

~gebland† *n.* sea.

~loc *n.* rowlock.

~wela† *m.* sea.

~wiþþe *f.* oar-withe, rowlock.

~ȳþ† *f.* wave.

ār, ǣr *n.* brass, copper. grēne ~ orichalcum.

~fæt *n.* brass vessel.

~gēotere *m.* brass-founder.

~glæd*, ǣr-† brass-bright.

~sāpe *f.* verdigris.

~gescōd, ǣr-† brass-shod.

~smiþ *m.* brass-smith.

~gesweorf *n.* brass filings.

ār = ǣr early.

ār|ian *wa.* honour, treat with respect; endow | *wd.* care for (the poor), be kind; be merciful, spare (life), pardon.

~igend *m.* benefactor.

~ing, ~ung *f.* honour; pardon.

ā·rǣcan get at, attain; hand, give.

ā·rǣd† (?) wise (?); resolute, inexorable (?)

ā·rǣd|an 1, *but gen. wk.* decree, settle, arrange, appoint, prepare; prophesy; solve (riddle); expound, explain; utter; read (to oneself *or* aloud).

~nes, ared- *f.* agreement, condition.

a·rǣfn|an, -ian carry out, accomplish; endure (patiently); suffer; ponder, consider.

~(i)endlic endurable.

ā·rǣfsan, arǣpsan, e intercept.

ā·rǣman elevate — *rfl.* elevate, improve oneself || rise.

ā·rǣr|an lift up, raise; raise (to life); set up (cross), build; establish, create, disseminate; ūp~ bring up, educate.

~nes *f.* raising, exaltation (in power).

ā·rǣsan rush.

ā·rāfian unravel, unwind (ball of thread).

ā·rās|ian, -acsian explore; detect, take in the act of; reprove, correct (faults). *ptc.* ~od trained, skilled.

arblast *vL. m.* crossbow [*Old Fr.* arbaleste].

arc = earc.

ardlic = ārodlic.

ā·rēafian† separate (?).

ā·reccan stretch out, raise up— āreahtum ēagum with astonished eyes | explain, expound ; translate ; relate, tell, speak.

ā·rēcelēasian be negligent.

ā·redian prepare, provide ; carry out, perform ; contrive, manage | find (right time for); find, find the way : ūt ~ find the way out, oferdruncen mann ne mæg tō his hūse ~, þone weg ~, þā ceastre ~ reach | find out, understand.

arednes = ārǣdnes.

ā·rēodian intr. redden, blush.

ā·rētan cheer.

Ārianisc Arian [Lt.].

ā·rīdan 6 ride (out).

ā·riepan*, y strip off.

ariht = on riht rightly.

ā·rīman count ; enumerate, relate.

ā·rīsan 6 stand up, get up (from bed), rise ; be forthcoming (of money) ; arise, happen (of temptation) ; originate.

armelu wild rue [Lt. harmala].

arn prt. of iernan.

arod (m.) arum.

ārod energetic | brisk ; quick.

~lic quick.

~līce, ārd- av. vigorously ; quickly.

~nes f. boldness.

~scipe m. boldness, energy.

aron are, see wesan.

arunnen = āurnen ptc. of āiernan.

arwe, arewe f. arrow.

ā·ryddan, -dran, -tran strip, plunder.

ā·sǣlan bind.

ā·sānian become languid, weak (of love) [sǣne].

ā·sāwan 1 sow.

āsc|ian, ācs-, āx-, āhs- try for, demand ; question, ask waa., w. æfter, w. hwȳ &c., w. sbj. ; call to account wag. ; experience (calamity).

~iendlic interrogative (in grammar).

~ung f. interrogation.

geāsc|ian learn by inquiry, be told, hear of w. a. and æt, w. indc., ~ode þis þus gedōn | discover.

~ung f. inquiry.

ā·scacan 2 shake off w. a. and of ; shake, brandish ǁ intr. flee, desert.

ā·scafan 2 shave.

ā·scalian peel off (bark).

ā·scam|ian be ashamed.

~elic shameful.

asce, axe, æ- f., pl. -an ash, ashes.

~geswǣp n. cinders.

ā·scēadan, -scādan 1 b w. a. and g. or fram or of, separate, exclude ; distinguish ; purify.

ā·sceltan once separate, dissolve (?).

ā·scēotan 7 shoot (arrow); lance (swelling) ǁ intr. dart out, fall.

ā·scielian*, i shell, peel [scalu].

ā·scieppan 2 appoint, give, esp. ~ him naman.

ā·scier|ian*, i, y w. a. and g. or fram separate ; deprive, purify ; destine, appoint.

~igendlic disjunctive (in grammar).

ā·scierpan sharpen (eyesight).

ā·scīmian shine.

ā·scīnan 6 shine (forth); be evident, clear.

ā·scīran*, ȳ make clear, transparent.

ā·scortian run short, fail ; seem short or elapse (of time).

ā·scrēadian prune, lop.

ā·screncan trip up, make to fall.

ā·screpan 5 scrape.

ā·scrincan 3 shrink up.

ā·scrūtnian investigate.

ā·scūfan, -scēofan 7 push (away), expel.

ascunian = on-.

ā·scylfan once destroy Gl.

ā·scyndan take away, deprive.

ā·sēarian dry up intr.

ā·sēcan seek out, select ; penetrate, pervade ; ~ hine līfes aim at his life.

ā·secg|an say fully, express, tell, say.

~endlic utterable.

ā·sēdan*, oe satiate [sǣd].

ā·segnian*, āsēngan† once show.

ā·sellan give up ; expel.

ā·sencan tr. sink.

ā·sēon once 5 see. L. for gesēon.

ā·sēon 7 strain (through sieve).

ā·seolcan 3 become languid. ptc. āsolcen slothful, remiss.

ā·seonod ' unsinewed,' relaxed Gl. [seono].

ā·sēoþan 7 boil ; smelt (metals), purify by smelting—āsoden gold pure gold ; try (by affliction), chasten.

ā·sett|an place, put—hī ~on hī (rfl.) ofer (av.) crossed (the Channel) ; build ; plant ; appoint ; ~ sīþ make a journey.

~nes (?) f. law = gesetnes.

ā·sēþan affirm, confirm (statement) [sōþ].

ā·sīcan sigh.

ā·siftan sift.

ā·sīgan 6 sink down, fall down ; be neglected.

ā·sincan 3 sink down, fall to pieces.

ā·singan 3 sing, deliver (speech).

ā·sittan 5 settle intr. ; run aground (of ship) | expect, be apprehensive of w. sbj. ǁ tr. ūt ~ starve out (garrison).

ā·sīwan, ēo sew.

ā·slac|ian become slack, become weak ; decline, diminish.

~igendlic remissive (adverb).

ā·slæccan once loosen Gl. [slæc].

aslǣpan = onslǣpan.

ā·slāwan blunt, make dull [slāw].

ā·slāwian become dull, slothful.

ā·slēan 2 strike, cut—of ~ cut off (head); beat out (metal); geteld ~ put up tent.

ā·slīdan 6 slip (of foot) ; fall.

ā·slītan 6 tear off ; tear to pieces ; destroy.

ā·slūpan 7 slip away ; disappear (of sorrow).

ā·smēa(ga)n scrutinize, investigate ; conceive, realize ; consider, reflect on ; treat of (in writing) ; settle (plan).

āsmēagung f. investigation.

ā·smiþian forge, make (metal objects).

ā·smorian suffocate, kill by suffocating, choke (growth of plants).

ā·smūgan 7 investigate, consider.

ā·snǣsan, ā transfix, spit, rfl. stake oneself.

ā·snīþan 6 cut off, cut (corn).

ā·solian become dirty.

ā·solcennes f. torpor, sloth [āseolcan].

ā·spanan 2 allure, entice ; introduce in an underhand way ; induce.

ā·spēdan make prosperous.

ā·spelian be deputy for, represent *wa*.

ā·spendan spend *wa*.— ~ þear-fum give to the poor ; squander [*Lt.* expendere].

aspide *f.* viper, serpent [*Lt.* aspidem].

ā·spinnan 3 spin.

ā·spiwan, ȳ 6 vomit up.

ā·sprecan 4 speak fully, speak.

ā·sprengan send flying, fling out.

ā·sprindlian rip up.

ā·spring|an, -incan 3 spring up, rise ; flow ; spread (*of* fame, heresy, &c.) ; originate, be descended (from) ; come into being, appear, rise ; fail, decline, cease.

~ung *f.* failing, being wanting.

ā·sprungennes *f.* failing, decline, exhaustion, eclipse.

ā·sprūtan 7 sprout out.

ā·spryttan cause to grow, produce (*of* the earth).

ā·spylian wash oneself. *Cp.* swillan.

ā·spyr|ian follow tracks of, trace (lost cattle) ; investigate ; discover.

~igend *m.* investigator.

ass|a *m.* donkey.

~miere *f.* donkey mare.

asse, assen *f.* she-donkey.

āst kiln.

ā·stǣnan adorn with gems.

ā·stand|an 2 stand up, rise *often w.* ūp ; stand firm, persist, endure.

~(en)nes *f.* existence, entity, substance ; perseverance.

ā·stellan set, put ; establish, create ; institute, set on foot, set (example) ; undertake, begin, undergo.

ā·stemnian found, build.

ā·stempan stamp (metal).

ā·steorfan 3 die. *ptc.* āstorfen (flesh) of animal having died a natural death. | *n.* flesh of such an animal.

asterion pellitory [*Lt.*].

ā·stiep|an*, *A.* ēo (ēa) bereave—*ptc.* ~ed having lost parents or child ; *wag.* deprive.

~nes *f.* privation.

ā·stierfan*, y kill [steorfan].

ā·stierred*, y starred [steorra].

ā·stīfian become stiff.

ā·stīgan 6 ascend *w. a. and* on— ~ on scip go on board ; descend ; go, pass—niþer ~ descend.

ā·stīgend *m.* rider.

ā·stig(en)nes *f.* ascent.

ā·stiht|an decree.

~ing *f.* doctrine.

ā·stingan 3 pierce out, put out (eyes), *also w.* ūt || ~ on *a.* lay claim to, usurp (estate).

ā·stīþian become strong, grow up ; dry up *intr.*

astorfen *n., see* āsteorfan.

ā·streccan *tr.* stretch out, extend —fēoll āstreaht fell flat, at full length ; *rfl.* prostrate oneself || *intr.* be erect, haughty.

ā·stregdan scatter ; sprinkle.

ā·streng|an—*ptc.* ~d malleable Gl.

ā·strienan, ēo beget.

ā·strowennes *f.* being extended, length Gl. *Cp.* strewian.

ā·stundian be responsible for, take upon oneself.

ā·stȳfician, ī extirpate.

ā·styltan be astonished.

ā·styntan make dull, stupid ; confute [stunt].

ā·styr|ian *tr.* agitate, raise (doubt) ; move— ~ fram remove. *ptc.* ~ed agitated (in mind) ; irritated, angry.

~iend *m.* stirrer, ventilater (!) Gl.

~iendlic movable.

~ung *f.* motion.

ā·sūcan, -ūgan 7 suck out, suck, drain.

āsundrian = āsyndran.

ā·sūrian become sour.

ā·swǣman wander about,*w.* fram depart | suffer, grieve.

ā·swǣrn|ian, ā be confounded, ashamed.

~ung *f.* bashfulness, shame.

ā·swǣtan burst out in perspiration.

ā·swāmian† cease (?).

ā·swāpan 1, *ptc.* -āpen, -ōpen sweep (away).

ā·swārcian abash, confound.

aswarnian = āswǣrnian.

ā·sweartian become black *or* dim.

ā·swebban, *ptc.* -efed make to cease, lull (storm), destroy, annul ; kill.

ā·swefecian root up, eradicare.

ā·swellan 3 *intr.* swell.

ā·sweltan 3 die.

ā·swengan shake off, cast off.

ā·sweorcan 3 become depressed (*of* the mind).

ā·sweorfan 3 file off, polish.

ā·swerian 2 swear.

ā·swican 6 *wd.* desert, betray ; offend, scandalizare.

ā·swician offend, scandalizare.

ā·swīfan 6 wander about, lose the way.

ā·swindan 3 languish away, become enervated — *ptc.* āswunden sluggish ; disappear, perish.

ā·swōg|an 1 suffocate, choke—*ptc.* ~en overrun (with weeds).

ā·sworettan sigh ; grieve *intr.*

ā·swundennes *f.* sluggishness [āswindan].

ā·sȳcan*, ī wean.

ā·syndran, -ian, -sundrian separate.

at- *occ.* = æt-.

ā·tǣsan wound ; wear out, injure ; *once* soothe (?).

āt|e *f.*, ǣ-, *gen. pl.* ātan oats.

~lēag *m.* oat-field (?) Ct.

ategār = ætgār.

atelic = atollic.

ā·tellan reckon up, count ; enumerate, tell ; explain.

ā·temian tame.

ā·tend|an set on fire ; trouble, perplex (?).

~end *m.* incendiary.

~ing *f.* incitement.

ā·tēon 7 draw out *or* away ; draw, drag, pull, take — ~ of extract, take out ; protract, continue ; treat (well *or* ill), behave to ; dispose of, do (as one likes) with || *intr.* go, make expedition.

ā·tēor|ian become tired, languish ; fail, cease ; perish.

~igendlic perishable, fleeting (world).

~odnes *f.* cessation.

~ung *f.* failing ; weariness.

ā·teran 4 tear away, remove.

ātes-hwōn *once av.* at all [āwiht].

ā·tiefran depict, draw.

ā·timbr(i)an build.

atol, ~(l)ic, atelic I. terrible, dire, horrid, loathsome. II. *n.* what is terrible, terror.

ge~ian*, ge~hīwian disfigure.

~iende disfiguring.

ge~od*, -atel- monstrous.

āt(t)or, ǣ- *n.* poison, venom.

~bǣre, ~berende poisonous, venomous.

ātor|coppe f. spider.
~cræft m. art of poisoning.
~cynn n. (kind of) poison.
~drinca m. poisonous draught.
~lāþe f. cock's-spur grass.
~lic poisonous.
~scapa† m. venomous enemy, dragon.
~spere n. poisoned spear.
~tān† once m. poison-twig = ~tēar* m. drop of poison (?).
ā·trahtnian treat, discuss.
ā·tredan 4 ūt ~ wd. extort from. Or = ātrẹddan?
ā·trẹddan investigate, explore.
ā·trẹndlian roll tr.
atrum (n.) ink [Lt. atramentum].
ā·tȳdran bring forth (progeny, growth), produce.
ā·tyht|an incite, entice; stretch, extend, turn, direct — ēarum ~um with attentive ears.
ā·tȳnan — ūt ~ exclude. Also = ontȳnan.
āþ m. oath.
~bryce m. perjury.
~fultum m. confirmers of an oath.
~gehāt n. promise on oath, oath.
~loga m. perjurer.
~stæf m. oath.
~swaru f., -a m. oath.
~swẹrung, ~swaring f. swearing an oath.
~swyrd, eo f. oath.
~wẹdd (?) n. promise on oath Gl.
~wierþe worthy of credit.
aþamans adamant [Lt. adamantem].
āþẹcgan† destroy, kill (?).
ā·þẹgen ptc. distended Gl.
ā·þẹn|ian, -þẹnnan stretch out (hand), stretch (bow) — ptc. ~ed distended; rfl. prostrate oneself; concentrate (mind) w. on.
~e(d)nes f. extension.
ā·þencan devise, invent; intend.
ā·þĕostr|ian, īe become dim, obscure; be eclipsed—ptc. ~od dim (of the eyes), eclipsed.
ā·þerscan* 3 'thresh out'—ptc. āþroxen robbed.
āþexe f. lizard.
ā·þīedan, ēo separate.
ā·þierran wipe.
ā·þīetan sound or blow (horn) [þēotan].

ā·þindan 3 swell—ptc. āþunden swollen.
aþol-ware† once pl. citizens. for ēþel-?
ā·þolian hold out, endure.
aþracian = onþrācian.
ā·þrǣstan wrest out, deprive.
ā·þrāw|an 1, ptc. -āwen, ō twist (out); flow: is mīn swāt ~en.
ā·þrēatian be irksome ‖ dissuade from : him his yfel ~.
ā·þrēotan 7 impers.—hine āþrīett wg., w. sbj. be weary, find irksome |personal hē wæs āþroten þæs.
ā·þrīetan tr. weary, bore.
ā·þringan 3 tr. force out ; ptc. ūt-āþrungen embossed ‖ intr. force one's way out, rush out.
ā·þrintan* 3 intr. swell—ptc. ā-þrunten swollen.
ā·þrotennes f. wearisomeness. [āþrēotan].
aþrowen, see āþrāwan.
aþroxen, see āþerscan.
ā·þrūt|an* 7 swell—ptc. ~en swollen.
ā·þrȳ(a)n—ptc. āþrȳd robbed.
ā·þrys(e)man, -ian stifle, suffocate.
āþum m. son-in-law; brother-in-law.
~swerian† once mpl. father- and son-in-law.
ā·þundennes f. being swollen, swelling [āþindan].
ā·þwǣnan soften.
ā·þwēan 2 ptc. -wagen, æ, e wash, cleanse.
ā·þweran 4 churn (butter).
ā·þwītan 6 disappoint, frustrari.
ā·þȳn press—ūt ~ extract (oil); imprint.
ā·þȳtan expel Gl.—ūt ~*, apytan pull out, put out (eyes).
ā·þȳwan push away, expel. = *ā-þīen.
āwa, see ā.
ā·wacan 2 intr. awake; come into existence, arise, be born.
ā·wacian intr. awake.
ā·wācian become weak; become languid, relax efforts; wd. fall away (from God).
ā·wǣcan weaken.

ā·wæcnian, -ac(e)nian, -nan come to life; come into being, appear; be result of, arise from, be descended from.
ā·wǣgan make nugatory, annul, rel ut (testimony); deceive.
ā·wǣlan roll, roll away; afflict.
ā·wannian become pale.
ā·wascan 1 wash.
ā·weahtnes, -weht- f. exciting [āwẹccan].
ā·weallan 1 gush forth, issue; have source, emanate.
ā·weardian defend.
ā·weaxan 1 grow; grow up; come into being, arise.
awebb = ōwẹbb woof.
ā·wẹccan, āwrẹ- wake tr.; bring to life; beget, suscitare; incite, excite; cause.
ā·wẹcgan move away, move; ~ fram, of dissuade.
ā·wēdan go mad [wōd].
ā·wefan 5 weave.
aweg = on weg away.
ā·wegan 5 carry away; carry off, carry; weigh, weigh out.
āwel, owul, āl, ǣl mf. awl, hook, fork.
ā·wẹmman, -æmmian pollute; curtail, shorten.
ā·wẹnian, -ẹnnan disaccustom, wean (child).
ā·wẹnd|an tr. turn away, turn; turn upside down, ransack (house) | pervert; alter, change; ~ tō transform into, turn into; ~ of . . on translate ‖ intr. turn; go; ~ fram secede, desert.
~e(n)dlic changeable.
~e(n)dlicnes f. mutability.
~ednes f. change.
~ing f. subversion.
ā·wēodian extirpate.
ā·weorpan, u, y 3 throw; throw out, throw away, throw down; expel, degrade (from dignity, office); reject, divorce—āworpen wīf.
ā·weorþan 3 perish, become worthless—ptc. āworden worthless (person).
ā·wẹrian defend, protect — w. a. and g. or d. defend . . against; restrain, hinder.
ā·wẹrian wear, wear out (clothes).
awesc = ǣwisc.

B

ā·wēst|an lay waste, ravage, destroy.
~(ed)nes f. desolation.
~end m. devastator.
ā·wīdlian pollute, profane.
ā·wielgan*, prt. -wiligdon roll.
a·wiellan (cause to gush forth) —†wynnum ~ed joyful; boil tr.
ā·wieltan roll tr.
ā·wierd|an injure; corrupt, deprave; destroy—ptc. āwærd worthless, contemptible [weorþan].
~nes f. injury, destruction.
ā·wierg|an, L. -yrgian curse — ptc. ~ed (ac)cursed, execrable [wearg].
~e(n)dlic wicked.
~(ed)nes f. malediction.
ā·wiftan—ūt~ exhale Gl.
ā-wiht, āwuht, ā(u)ht, ōwiht, IN. āeniht I. no. anything, something. tō āhte at all. āhtes serviceable: þā scipu þe āhtes wēron. II. āht aj. of worth, good: hwæþer hē ~ sȳ oþþe nāht. III. av. at all, by any means.

ā·wildian become wild, fierce.
āwiligan = *āwielgan.
ā·windan 3 intr. wind, plait; turn off, slip; become relaxed or weak.
ā·windwian winnow away, disperse (enemies).
ā·winnan 3 strive; overcome; gain, acquire.
ā·wisnian dry up intr.
ā·wistlian hiss, pipe (of weak voice).
ā·wlacian be lukewarm met.
ā·wlǣtan make loathsome, deform, spoil.
ā·wlancian become proud, exultare.
ā·woff|ian be insolent; be mad— ptc. ~od insane.
ā·wōgian woo.
awoh = on wōg.
ā·wordennes f. worthlessness, degeneration [āweorþan].
ā·worpen|lic worthy of rejection or condemnation [āweorpan].
~nes f. rejection; exposure (of children by parents).

ā·wrǣstan wrest from, extort.
ā·wrecan 5 drive away, drive | strike, pierce | avenge; punish | recite, relate.
āwreccan = āweccan awake.
ā·wreþian prop, support; sustain, help.
ā·wrīdian grow, be descended.
awrigennes = onwrigennes.
ā·wringan 3 squeeze out.
ā·wrītan 6 write; depict, draw, carve; compose, write, describe.
ā·wrīþan 6 twist; bind, bandage (wound).
awriþan = on·wrīþan unbind.
awþer = āhwæþer.
ā·wunian remain (in place); continue (in time).
ā·wundrian wda. make to seem wonderful.
ā·wyrcan do.
āwyrdla = ǣ- injury.
ā·wyrgan strangle, kill.
ā·wyrtwalian root up; extirpate.
ā·ȳtan drive out, expel.

B.

bā, see bēgen.
bacan 2 bake.
gebacu*, -bæcu npl. back parts.
bād f. pledge, thing distrained; impost | expectation [bīdan].
~ian take a pledge abs.
bæc n. back. clǣne ~ habban be free from deceit. on ~, ofer ~, under ~ av. back(wards), behind.
~bord n. left side of ship, port.
~ling—on b. av. back, behind.
~slitol slandering.
~þearm m. rectum; pl. ~as bowels.
bæc (?) brook. See bece.
bæc-, see bacan.
~ere m. baker.
~ern, ~hūs n. bake-house.
gebæc n. baking, what is baked.
bæcering (m.) gridiron.

bæcestre, -istre, y fm. baker (male or female).
bæd prt. of biddan.
bǣd|an compel; urge on, incite; solicit, require wag.; afflict, oppress.
~end m. impeller.
bǣddel m. hermaphrodite.
bǣde-weg, beadowig n. cup.
bǣdling m. sodomite, effeminate one.
bǣdzere = bǣzere.
bæfta m. back [bæftan].
bæftan, beæ- prp. wd., av. behind: hī ætsǣton ~ remained at home (instead of serving in the militia); time after(wards): hēr~.
~sittende slothful.
bǣl n. funeral pile; fire, blaze.

bǣl|blǣse†, ~blys(e)† f. blaze of fire.
~egsa† m. terror of fire.
~fȳr† n. funeral fire.
~stede† m. place of a funeral pile.
~þracu† f. strength of fire.
~wielm† m. intensity of fire.
~wudu† m. wood of a funeral pile.
bælc† once covering (?).
bælc† (m.) pride.
bælcan† vociferate.
bælignes = *belignes.
bǣm d. of bēgen.
bær bare, naked.
~(e)fōt bare-footed.
~līce n. evidently.
~synnig, bearswinig notoriously sinful IN.
bǣr f. bier; litter [beran].

[16]

bǽr-mann *m.* bearer; porter.
bǽr-disc *m.* tray = ber- (?).
bærn = bern barn.
bærn|an *tr.* burn ; light (fire, lamp) [biernan].
~elāc *n.* burnt offering.
~ing *f.* burning *tr.*
~(n)es *f.* burning.
bærnet(t), -yt *n.* burning *tr.*; arson.
bærs, bears *m.* perch (a fish).
bærst *prt. of* berstan.
bærstlian = brastlian.
gebǽr|u *npl.* behaviour, manner, customs; gesture; cries [beran].
~an behave.
~nes *f.* behaviour.
bærwe = bearwe wheelbarrow.
bæst (*m.*) bast (inner bark of the lime).
~en of bast.
bæstere = bæzere.
bǽt|an furnish with bit, bridle; coerce, restrain | hunt, bait, worry [bītan].
~ing *f.* cable (of ship).
gebǽt|u *npl.,* ~el *n.* bit, bridle, trappings of horse.
~an furnish with bit, bridle, curb.
bæþ *n.* bath.
~fæt *n.* bath.
~hūs *n.* bath-house.
~stede *m.,* ~stōw *f.* bath-place.
~weg† *m.* sea.
bæ(d)zere, bæp(c)ere, bæstere *m.* baptist [*Lt.* baptista, *through Celtic*].
bala-niþ = bealo-.
balc *m.* (?) ridge between two furrows.
balca *m.* heap.
bals-minte *f.* spear-mint.
balsam *n.* balsam, balm. ~es tēar juice of balsam [*Lt.*].
bām *d. of* bēgen.
bān *n.* bone (ivory. whalebone); leg *only in composition.*
~beorge *f.,* -an *pl.,* ~gebeorg *n.* (*pl.* ?) greaves.
~gebrec *n.,* ~bryce *m.* bone-fracture.
~cofa† *m.* body.
~fæt *n.* body.
~fāg† adorned with bone? (hall).
~hring† *m.* vertebra.
~hūs† *n.* body.
~lēas boneless.

bān|loca† *m.* body.
~rift greaves.
~sele† *m.* body.
~wærc *m.* pain in the bones.
~wyrt *f.* violet (?)
ban-helm† *m.* helmet.
ban|a *m.* slayer, murderer.
~gār† *m.* deadly spear.
~snaca *m.* venomous snake.
gebann *n.* summons, proclamation, command ; the indiction (cycle of fifteen years).
~gēar *n.* year of indiction.
bann|a 1 a, b summon— ~ūt call out (militia); proclaim, command.
~end *m.* summoner Gl.
bannuc *m.* cake of bread, scone.
~camb *m.* wool-comb Gl.
bār *m.* wild boar.
~spere *n.,* ~sprēot *m.* boar-spear, hunting-spear.
barian make bare, uncover; depopulate [bær].
barda *m.* beaked ship.
barþ (*m.*) light ship.
basing *m.* cloak, mantle.
bāsn|ian expect, await [bīdan].
~ung *f.* expectation.
baso, ea, *pl.* baswe, purple, crimson. se baswa stān topaz.
~hǽwen purple.
~rēadian*, beso- make reddish-purple, colour purple.
bastard *m.* bastard *L.* [*Fr.*].
baswian stain purple *or* red (with blood) [baso].
bāt *m.* boat.
~swegen *m.* boatman *L.* [*Scand.*].
~weard† *m.* boat-guarder.
bat|ian *intr.* be in good condition *or* health, grow fat : wæs ge~ad healed (*of* wound).
batt club, stick.
batwa, *see* bēgen.
baþian bathe, *tr., intr., rfl.*; provide (poor men) with baths [bæþ].
be, bi; bī(g)*through confusion w.the adverb* bī. I. *prp. wd., place and motion* by (*nearness*), along, in | *time*—be him lifgendum during his lifetime || *defining*, by: ge-hæfted be þām healse | *manner, cause, instrument*: be hrēow-sunge dǽdbētende, be his hǽse, be hlāfe libban | *according to* : ǣghwilc gilt be his gebyrdum | *forming adverbs*: be

fullan fully | concerning: be manna crǣftum (*title of poem, &c.*) | *to express object of vb.* about : cwepan be, āwrītan bōc be, āxian hine be, him bebēad be þē. II. be norþan, be sū-þan, &c. *prp. wd.* north of, &c. III. be-þǣm-þe *av.* in proportion to, as much as.
bēac(e)n *n.* sign, token, beacon ; standard, banner.
~fȳr *n.* beacon-fire, light-house.
~stān *m.* beacon-fire rock, farus.
gebēacn *n.* sign.
beacnian = bīecn(i)an.
beado†, *g.* bead(u)we, *f.* battle, war.
~cāf prompt in battle, warlike.
~crǣft *m.* skill in war.
~crǣftig skilful in war.
~cwealm *m.* violent death.
~folm *f.* war-hand.
~grīma *m.* helmet.
~grimm fierce in war.
~hrægl *n.* coat of mail.
~lāc *n.* battle.
~lēoma *m.* sword.
~mǣgen *n.* battle-strength.
~mēce *m.* battle-sword.
~rǣs *m.* onset.
~rinc *m.* warrior.
~rōf warlike.
~rūn *f.* theme of quarrel.
~scearp sharp in battle (*of* sword).
~scrūd *n.* coat of mail.
~searo *n.* armour.
~sierce *f.* coat of mail.
~þrēat *m.* army.
~wǣpen *n.* war-weapon.
~wang *m.* field of battle.
~weorc *n.* war-work.
~wig = bǽdeweg.
beæftan = bæftan.
be-ǣwnian join in marriage.
beaftan lament *lN.*
bēag *m.* ring (of gold), bracelet, torque, crown [būgan].
~giefa† *m.* giver of rings, patron.
~giefu† *f.* ring-giving, liberality.
~hord† *n.* treasure.
~hroden† adorned with rings, &c. [hrēodan].
~sǽl† *n.,* ~sele† *m.* hall in which gold is distributed.
~þegu† *f.* receiving of rings.
~wriþa† *m.* bracelet, &c.
bēagian crown.

bealcan; be(a)lcettan, i, y belch forth, utter.

bealcett (*n.*) belching.

beald, *vE.* balþ self-confident, bold.

~e, ~līce, *lN.* ballīce *av.* boldly.

~ian be bold.

~wyrde bold of speech.

bealdor† *m.* prince, king.

beallucas *m.* testicles.

bealo† *g.* beal(o)wes I. *n.* evil, calamity, injury, wickedness. II. *aj.* evil, dire, pernicious, wicked.

~bend (*m.*) severe bond, chain.

~benn *f.* severe wound.

~blanden pernicious.

~clamm *m.* dire bond.

~cræft *m.* evil art, magic.

~cwealm *m.* violent death.

~dǣd *f.* crime.

~full evil, wicked.

~fūs prone to evil.

~hycgende, ~hygdig, -hȳdig meditating evil, hostile.

~inwit *n.* malice.

~lēas innocent.

~nīþ *m.* pernicious malice, vice, wickedness.

~rāp *m.* dire rope, bond.

~searo *n.* dire machination.

~sīþ *m.* fatal journey, misfortune.

~sorg *f.* dire sorrow.

~spell *n.* dire tidings.

~þanc *m.* evil thought.

bēam *m.* tree; the Cross; pillar (of fire); beam; †ship.

~sceadu *f.* shadow of a tree.

~telg† *m.* 'wood-dye,' (carbon) ink.

bēan *f.* bean.

~belg, -codd *m.* bean-pod.

~cynn *n.* species of bean.

~scalu *f.* bean-pod.

bēanen of beans.

bearce*, *A.* æ *f.* barking [beorcan].

beard *m.* beard, *occ. pl. in sg. meaning.*

~lēas beardless.

bearg *m.* pig.

bearhtm, eo, y, e; *A.* æ; breaht(u)m *m.* glance (of the eye)— ēagena~ the evil eye [beorht].

~e *av.* instantly [*i. of* bearhtm].

~hwæt swift as a glance of the eye.

~hwīl *f.* moment, instant—āne ~e suddenly.

bearhtm = breahtm noise.

bearm *m.* bosom, lap; middle, inside; †possession.

~clāþ, ~hrægl *n.* apron.

bearm-teag, *see* beo-.

bearn *n.* child.

~gebyrda *fpl.* child-bearing.

~ēacen, ~ēaca (?), ~ēacniend pregnant.

~lēas childless.

~līest, ~lēast *f.* childlessness.

~lufe *f.* adoption.

~myrþre *f.* infanticide.

~gestrēon *n.* begetting children.

~tēam *m.* begetting children.

bearn *prt. of* beiernan.

bearo, *g.* bear(o)wes, *m.* grove, wood.

~næss† *m.* woody tract, grove.

bears = bærs.

bearwe, æ, e, -uwe, -ewe *f.* basket, wheelbarrow.

be·āscian *tr.* question; request *waa. (or wag. ?).*

gebēat *n.* beating.

bēat|an 1 beat; clash together; tramp, tread on.

~ere *m.* pugilist Gl.

bēaw (*m.*) gadfly.

be·baþian *tr.* bathe, wash.

be·bēod|an 7 *wda.* offer; commit, entrust; command, ask; announce.

~end *m.* master, praeceptor.

~endlic imperative (mood).

be·beorgan 3 *w. d. and a.* or *inst. rfl.* ward off from oneself, avoid.

be·beran 4 *wad.* supply, provide with.

be·bindan 3 bind.

be·bod *n.* command, mandate, (moral) precept.

~dæg *m.* appointed day.

be·brǣdan *tr. w.* mid spread, cover.

be·brecan 4 *wad.* deprive of by breaking; *wa.* consume.

be·bregdan *lN.* pretend, simulate.

be·brūcan 7 practise (virtue).

be·būgan 7 encompass, surround; avoid, escape ‖ *intr.* extend *w.* geond.

be·bycgan sell: on gold ~ sell for gold.

be·byrig|an, -rgan bury.

~(ed)nes *f.* burying, burial.

bēc *pl. of* bōc.

bēcan, ge- *wda.* assign by charter [bōc].

be·cæfed*, e adorned.

becca *m.* pickaxe, mattock.

bece *m.* brook.

bēc|e, oe *f.* beech-tree [bōc].

~en of beech.

be·cēapian sell : ~ wiþ fēo.

becefed = becæfed.

be·ceorfan 3 cut off: hine hēafde ~.

be·ceorian *tr.* complain of, lament.

be·cēowan 7 gnaw (through).

be·cīepan sell [becēapian].

be·cierran *tr.* turn, make to revolve; give the slip to, avoid; betray.

be·clǣman glue together.

be·clemman† fetter, enclose.

be·clingan 3 enclose, bind.

be·clipian, eo summon, sue at law.

be·clyppan embrace, encompass.

be·clȳs|an enclose, shut up, close [clūse].

~ing *f.* cell; period, syllogism.

be·cnāwan 1 know.

be·cnyttan tie up.

be·crēopan 7 creep — wæs becropen lay hid, was kept concealed.

be·cuman 4 come; meet with, fall among; happen— ~him tō ēadignesse make him happy.

be·cweþan 5 say; reproach; bequeath *wda.*

be·cwiddian deposit Gl.

be·cyme (!) *m.* event Bd.

bed = gebed *occ. in composition :* ~dagas, ~hūs, ~rǣden.

~rīp, bider- compulsory reaping [*cp.* bēnrīp].

gebed *n.* prayer; religious ordinance *or* ceremony.

~dagas *mpl.* prayer-days.

~giht *f.* evening Gl.

~hūs *n.* oratory, chapel, temple.

~mann *m.* worshipper, priest.

~rǣden *f.* prayer.

~stōw *f.* place of prayer, oratory.

gebedian pray, worship.

be·dǣlan deprive *wag., wai.*

bedd *n.* bed; (garden) bed, plot.

~bolster *n.* bolster.

~būr *m.* bedchamber.

~clēofa, -clȳfa; ~cofa *m.* bedroom.

~clāþ *m.* bed-covering, *pl.* bedclothes.

~felt blanket, sheet.

bedd|gemāna *m.* cohabitation.
~rēaf *n.* bed-clothes.
~reda, i, y *m.* one bed-ridden; *also aj.*
~rest *f.* bed.
~gerid *n.* (ants') nest (?).
~þegn *m.* chamberlain.
~tīd *f.* bed-time.
~wāgrift bed-curtain.
bedd|ian make a bed : ~ him for him.
~ing *f.* bedding, bed-clothes; bed.
gebed|da *f.* consort, wife.
~cleofa*, ȳ *m.* lair, den.
~scipe *m.* cohabitation, marriage.
bedecian beg [gebed(ian)].
be·delf|an 3 dig round; bury.
~ing *f.* digging round.
beden *ptc. of* biddan.
be·dician fortify with mound.
be·dīegl(i)an, -dēaglian hide, conceal, keep secret.
be·dīepan*, ē, ȳ dip. *Cp.* bedyppan.
be·diernan conceal *wda.*
be·dōn shut, close (door).
bedol suppliant.
be·drēosan† 7—bedroren wearþ *or* wæs was deprived of *wi.*; came into the power of.
be·drīfan 6 drive; assail, beat, cover : stēame bedrifen.
be·drincan 3 drink in, absorb.
be·drōg† *Old-Saxon prt.* beguiled [=*OE.* *bedrēag*].
bedu *f.* request [biddan].
be·dūfan 7 be submerged—*ptc.* bedofen drowned.
be·dydrian deceive; conceal (from) *w. a. and* wiþ *a.*
be·dyppan dip [*cp.* bedīepan].
be·ebb|ian : ~od wæs was left aground by the tide going out (*of* ship).
be·fæstan fasten, fix; establish; make safe; apply, utilize; entrust, commit *wda.*
be·fæþman embrace, encircle
be·faran 2 *tr.* traverse; attack; ūtan ~ surround (army), blockade || *intr.* proceed, go.
be·fealdan 1 fold; fold round, cover; surround.
befealh *prt. of* befēolan.
be·feall|an 1 fall; ~ on *a., d.* incur (death, guilt), fall into (habit) | *ptc.* ~en *wi.* deprived (of).

be·fēgan *tr.* join *w.* on *a.*
be·feohtan 3 *wai.* deprive of by fighting : fēore befohten dead.
be·fēolan 3, *prt.* -fealh, *ptc.* -fōlen *tr.* put away (under the earth); *wda.* impose, grant, consign : him wæs Hālig Gāst befōlen, hē hine rōde befealh crucified him || *intr. wd.* apply oneself (to prayer, learning), importune (a person); *w.* on *d.* fall into (a certain state) : ~ on slǣpe.
be·fēran traverse, encompass.
be·fician deceive.
be·fiell|an knock down, fell, throw down | *ptc.* ~ed deprived *wi.*†
be·flēan 2 flay, take off skin : take off bark — beflagen flǣsc viscera.
be·flēon 7 flee from, escape *tr., and intr. w.* fram.
be·flēogan 7 fly.
be·flōwan 1 flow over, flood.
be·fōn 1 b grasp, seize; take possession of; take (in the act), detect (in a crime); entrap | surround, encompass, encircie; contain, hold (a quantity).
befōlen *ptc. of* befēolan.
be·foran I. *prp. w. d. and more rarely a.* in the presence of | in the name of : ic þē bebēode ~ Gode | before *order, time.* II. *av.* before, in front; above (in book) : þæs cynn is ~ āwriten; beforehand, ready; openly, publicly.
be·forhtian dread.
be·fōtian depriving of feet.
be·frēo(ga)n free.
be·frign|an, -frīnan 3 question; ask for, request '*wag*
~ung *f.* inquiry, investigation.
be·fullan *av.* completely [be, full].
be·fȳlan defile.
be·fylgan follow, pursue.
be·fyllan fill.
bēg* *pl.* ~er berry.
~bēam*, beig- *m.* bramble.
bēga *g. of* bēgen.
be·gān, -gangan *vb.* go over, traverse; occupy, possess (country), surround — ūtan ~ besiege; cultivate (land), take care of; honour, worship; perform, practise, do.
~nes *f.* calends (!) Gl.

be·galan 2 sing incantations over, bewitch.
be·gang, bī-geng *m.* circuit; tract, space | observance, practice, business; service, worship.
beganga = bīgenga.
be·geat *n. gen. pl.* gains, property.
bēgen, ē†, oe, *fem. and neut.* bā, bātwā, bū(tu) both.
begenga = bīgenga.
be·gēomerian lament.
be·geondan *av., prp. w. d., a.* beyond.
be·gēotan 7 pour over, cover (with fluid) : mid blōde begoten; pour.
bēger *pl. of* *bēg berry.
be·giellan† 3 scream around *or* sing about (?).
be·giem|an *wg.* take care of, attend to.
~en *f.* attention, looking out for.
~ung *f.* taking care.
be·gietan 5 get, obtain, attain, conquer, acquire (wealth); find; happen to, come upon (*of* danger, evil, &c.); beget *or* conceive (child).
be·gīnan 6 gape at *once.*
be·ginnan 3 begin.
be·gleddian stain (with blood).
be·glīdan 6 depart from *wd.*
be·gnagan 2 gnaw.
be·gnornian lament. *Cp.* be-grornian.
bēgra *g. of* bēgen.
be·grafan 2 bury.
be·grētan† *once wk.* lament.
be·grinian, y ensnare.
be·grindan 3 polish; †deprive *wai.*
begroren† *once ptc.* — sūsle ~ overwhelmed (?).
be·grornian lament. *Cp.* be-gnornian.
be·gyldan gild.
be·gyrdan gird; clothe; surround.
be·habban surround; comprehend; detain.
be·hǣs (*f.*) vow *vL. Blending of* hǣs *and* behāt.
be·hǣttian scalp (as punishment).
be·hamelian *tr.* strip naked (?).
be·hammen (*of* shoe).
be·hāt *n.* promise; vow.
be·hātan 1 *wda.* promise; vow; threaten with.

be·hāwian look carefully, take care.
be·hēafd|ian behead.
~ung *f.* beheading.
be·hēafodlic capital (punishment) Gl. [be, hēafod].
be·heald|an 1 hold, keep; guard; possess, have; *rfl.* act, behave | look at, observe; consider, reflect on; pay regard to, observe, keep (laws) — *rfl. w. sbj.* be careful; practise, perform | signify, mean; be of importance, avail.
~en cautious; assiduous (in) *wi.*
~nes *f.* regard.
be·hēawan 1 hew, cut into shape (timber); bruise, beat; *wai.* cut off (head), deprive of: ~ hine hēafde, fēore.
be·hēf|e, oe, ~(e)lic suitable; necessary [behōfian].
~nes *f.* utility.
be·helan 4 cover over, conceal.
be·helian cover over, conceal.
be·helmian cover over, shroud (with darkness), conceal.
be·hēofian lament, mourn for.
be·heonan, -hinon *av., prp. wd.* on this side of (river, sea). gīet ~ citerius Gl.
be·hīepan surround (with heaps).
be·hindan *av., prp. w. d., a.* behind.
behinon = beheonan.
be·hlænan surround anything by leaning other things against it: ~ fæt holte, surround.
be·hlēap|an 1 leap; his mōd biþ ~en on . . his mind is fixed on.
be·hlemman *tr.* dash together, close (jaws).
be·hlīdan 6 cover up, close *tr., intr.*
be·hliehhan 2 deride.
be·hliepan*, ȳ deprive, strip.
be·hligan, (hē) behliþ, defame: ~ hīe wammum.
be·hōn 1 b behang, hang round with, *esp. in ptc.* behangen *w. i. or* mid.
be·hōf|ian need, require *wg.*
~lic necessary.
be·hog|ian take care of.
~odlīce *av.* carefully.
~odnes *f.* exercising, practising Gl.
be·horsian — hīe wurdon ~ode were deprived of their horses.

be·hrēosan 7 fall | *ptc.* behroren *wi.* covered; deprived of.
be·hrēows|ian repent; atone.
~ung *f.* repentance.
be·hrīman cover with hoar-frost.
be·hringan encircle, surround.
be·hrōpan 1 importune.
be·hrūmian besmirch.
be·hrūmig besmirched, sooty.
bēhte *prt. of* bēcan.
bēhþ†*f.* sign.
be·hweorf (!) *m.* exchange.
be·hweorfan 3 *tr.* turn; spread out | arrange, put in order (house), tend, prepare (corpse for burial) | change; exchange for *wai.*
be·hwielfan vault over, cover.
be·hwierfan *tr.* turn, turn round; ūtan ~ encompass; exercise, train | change, convert; exchange for *w. a. and* on *d.,* mid.
be·hycgan bear in mind, consider; trust *w.* on.
be·hȳdan hide, conceal.
be·hȳdignes (!) *f.* desert.
be·hygdig, -hȳdig vigilant, careful, solicitous.
~līce, -hȳdelīce *av.* carefully.
~nes *f.* solicitude, anxiety.
be·hyhtan *w.* on set hopes (on), trust in.
be·hyldan skin, flay.
be·hȳr|an hire out.
~ing *f.* hiring out, letting.
be·hȳpelīce *av.* sumptuously Gl.
be·ierfeweardian disinherit.
be·iernan 3 run (into), be involved (in sin); occur (to the mind): þā bearn him on mōde þæt hē cōme he thought he would come | biþ beurnen mid blōde covered.
beinnan = binnan.
be·lācan 1 b sport round, surround (of waves).
be·lād|ian exculpate, clear *wag.*
~igend *m.* excuser, defender.
~igendlic excusable.
~ung *f.* excuse : þǣr is sum ~ on þǣre segene there is some excuse for your saying so.
be·lǣdan lead, impel *gen. in bad sense* : on synna ~.
be·lǣfan *tr.* spare, leave undestroyed || *intr.* remain, be left.
be·lǣþan make hateful, pervert.
be·lǣw|an betray.
~ing *f.* betrayal, treason.

be·lāf *f.* remainder.
belagen *ptc. of* belēan.
be·landian deprive of land.
belced - sweora† puff - necked [bælc].
belcettan = bealcettan.
gebeldan, *prt.* gibēlde *IN.* cover *or* bind (book).
be·lēan 2 blame, forbid, dissuade from *wda.*
be·lecgan *wai.* cover, envelop, *met.* overwhelm (with contempt); treat (ill), afflict — *wg.* hē wæs swelces dōmes belēd þæt . . he had such a reputation; charge (with crime) *w. a. and* mid.
be·lendan deprive of land *vL.* [belandian].
belene, beolone *f.* henbane.
be·lēogan 2 deceive.
be·lēoran *A.* pass by *intr.*
be·lēosan† 7 be deprived of *wi.* — *ptc.* beloren deprived of *wi.*
gebelg *n.* anger; arrogance.
bel(i)g = byl(i)g.
~nes*, bælig- *f.* offence, injury *IN.*
belgan 3 *intr. and rfl.* be angry *w.* wiþ *a.,* for, tō—*ptc.* gebolgen angry, fierce.
gebelgan 3 offend *wd.*
be·libban — *ptc.* belifd lifeless.
be·licgan 5 surround.
be·līēf|an *L.* believe — ~ed believing *w.* on *a. Cp.* gelīēfan.
be·līfan 6 remain, be left.
be·līfian kill.
be·limp *n.* occurrence.
be·limpan 3 belong to, concern, appertain *w.* tō; happen, befall *wd.*
be·lis(t)nian castrate.
be·līpan† 6 — *only in ptc.* beliden deprived *w.g. or i.*; lifeless.
bellan 3 bellow, grunt.
bell|e *f.* bell.
~flies *n.* bell-wether's fleece.
~hring (*m.*) bell-ringing.
~hūs *n.* bell-tower.
~tācen *n.* showing time by bell ringing.
belt (*m.*) belt [*Lt.* balteus].
be·lūcan 7 lock up, confine; close (house); enclose (with wall); bind (with fetters); impede, choke; *wad.* protect against.
be·lūtian lie hid.
be·lyrtan deceive, cheat *IN.*

be·lytigian deceive, entrap.
be·mǣnan lament.
be·metan 5 estimate — *rfl.* hīe hīe selfe tō nohte ne bemǣton thought themselves of no account, hīe hīe ne bemǣton nānes anwealdes they did not consider they had any power.
be·mīþan 6 conceal (from) *wda.*
be·murc(n)ian murmur, grumble.
be·murnan 3 bewail ; care for, take heed of.
be·mūtian exchange (for) *w.* on *a.* [*Lt.* mutare].
be·myldan bury [molde].
bēn, oe, *f.* prayer, petition, request.
~dagas *mpl.* rogation-days.
~feorm *f.,* ~ierþ *f.,* ~rīp food, ploughing, harvest-work required from a tenant.
~tīd *f.* prayer-time, rogation-days.
~tigþe, -īþ(ig)e successful in prayer, successful ; gracious.
gebēn *f.* prayer.
bēna *m.* petitioner — ~wesan request.
be·nacodian*, -nacian lay bare. *The shortening into* -nacian *is to avoid the clumsy prt.* -nacodode*.
be·nǣman deprive *w. a. and g. or i.* [niman].
benc *f.* bench.
~sittend(e)† *m.* guest.
~swēg† *m.* revelry.
~þel† *n.* bench-floor.
bencian make benches.
bend *mfn.* band, ribbon, chaplet, crown ; bond, chain [bindan].
bendan bind ; stretch, bend (bow).
be·neah *vb., pl.* -nugon, *prt.* -nohte, *wg.* enjoy, have benefit of ; require.
be·nemnan declare, certify.
be·nēotan 7 *wai.* deprive.
be·neoþan, -niþan, y *av., prp. wd.* beneath, below.
be·niman 4 *wag., wai.* deprive.
beniþan = beneoþan.
benn† *f.* wound [bana].
~geat *n.* opening of a wound.
~ian wound.
benohte *prt. of* beneah.
be·notian use up, consume (provisions).
bēnsian supplicate [bēn].
benugon *prt. pl. of* beneah.
benyþan = beneoþan.

bēo *f., g.* ~n bee.
~(n)brēad *n.* beebread, honeycomb.
~nbroþ *n.* drink made of honey.
~ceorl, ~cere *m.* bee-keeper.
~gang *m.* swarm of bees.
~mōdor *f.* queen-bee.
~þēof *m.* stealer of bees.
~wyrt *f.* bee-wort, sweet flag.
bēo-hata† once *m.* warrior, chief.
bēon, *see* wesan.
bēod *m.* table ; bowl.
~ærn, bēod(d)ern *n.* dining-room, refectory.
~bolla *m.* bowl.
~clāþ *m.* table-cloth.
~fæt *n.* table-vessel, cup Gl.
~fers *n.* grace sung at mealtimes.
~giest *m.* guest at meals.
~hrægl *n.* table-cloth.
~lāfa *fpl.* table-leavings.
~land *n.* land for supplying the food of a monastery, glebe-land.
~genēat *m.* meal-companion.
~gereord(u) *n(pl).* feast.
~scēat *m.* napkin.
~wist *f.* meal, food.
bēod|an, ge- 7 *wda.* offer *w. sbj.* : him gefeoht ~ challenge to fight ; inflict : him wītu ~ ; behave to, treat (well or ill) : uton ~ ōþrum þæt wē willen þæt man ūs ~e ! | announce, proclaim ; bode ; threaten | command, decree, enjoin — ~ ūt *wd.* call out (militia), banish.
bēod(d)ian do joiner's work [bēod].
beofor *m.* beaver.
bēogol, ge~, y forgiving [būgan].
beolone = belene.
bēom = bēo am.
bēor†, *rarely Pr., n.* beer [bēow].
~byden *f.* beer-barrel.
~hierde† *m.* butler.
~scealc† *m.* feaster.
~sele† *m.* hall of festivity.
~setl* *n.* †bench at banquet.
~þegu† *f.* beer-drinking.
gebēor *m.* boon-companion, guest.
~scipe, b- *m.* convivial meeting, feast.
beorc *f.* birch-tree ; *the Runic letter* b [bierce].
gebeorc (*n.*) barking.
beorcan 3 bark ; bark at *wa.*
beorg *m.* hill, mountain ; heap of stones, mound.

beorg|ælfen *f.* oread.
~hliþ *n.* hill-slope.
~iht*, beorhtt- mountainous.
~seþel *n.* mountain dwelling.
~stede *m.* mound.
gebeorg† once *n.* mountain.
gebeorg, -rh *n.* defence, refuge, safety, precaution.
~lic safe, advisable.
~nes *f.* refuge.
~stōw *f.* place of refuge.
beorg|an, ge- 3 *wd.* preserve, save ; abstain from injuring, spare ; *w. a. and d. or* wiþ guard, save — *rfl.* avoid : hīe him yfel ~aþ, ~aþ ēow wiþ yfel ! | avoid, beware of *w.* wiþ.
beorht, y I. *aj.* bright ; clear-sighted ; clear (sounding), loud ; magnificent, glorious, noble. II. *n.* brightness, light ; sight ; twinkling — ēagan ~ moment.
~e *av.* brightly ; (see) clearly.
~hwīl *f.* moment.
~ian be bright ; (sound) clear *or* loud.
ge~nian*, -brehtnian *IN.* become bright.
~lic bright ; clear - sounding* ; glorious.
~līce *av.* brightly ; distinctly.
~nes *f.* brightness, splendour.
~rodor† *m.* heaven, æther.
~word clear of speech.
beorhtt- = beorgiht*.
beorm|a *m.* yeast.
~tēag*, bea- *f.* yeast-box.
beorn† *m.* brave man, warrior, man of rank, rich man, prince, king.
~cyning *m.* king of warriors.
~þrēat *m.* band of warriors.
~wiga *m.* warrior.
beornan = biernan.
Beornice *mpl.* Bernicians.
beorþor, byr- *n.* childbirth ; fetus [beran].
~cwealm *m.* dead birth, abortion.
~þignen*, byrþ-þīnenu *f.* midwife.
gebeorþor*, y *n.* birth.
bēost (*m.*) biestings, first milk of cow after calving.
bēot *n.* promise ; vow ; boast ; threat ; danger [=*bi-hāt].
~ian promise ; vow ; boast.
~lic boastful, arrogant ; threatening.
~līce *av.* threateningly.

bēot|ung f. threatening.
~word† n. boast; threat.
gebēot n. vow; boast; threatening
— tō ~es assiduously (!).
bēow n. barley.
beowan = bīewan polish.
be·pǣc|an deceive.
~end m. deceiver.
~estre f. deceiver, harlot.
~ung f. deceiving, alluring Gl.
beprenan, see beprīwan.
beprepan, see beprīwan.
be·prīwan, -prēwan*, -prenan
[n for u], -prepan wink (eye).
Cp. prēowt-hwīl.
beran 4 carry, wear (hat), bring,
carry off; produce, bring forth,
bear | endure, tolerate; suffer ‖
~ ūp open (a case).
berian make bare, clear (benches)
[bær].
bera m. bear.
be·rǣdan deprive w. a. and g. or i.
or æt; deliberate on, prepare;
get the better of.
be·rǣsan rush.
berbene f. verbena [Lt.].
bere m. barley.
~corn n. barley-corn.
~flōr f. barn-floor.
~gafol n. rent paid in barley.
~grǣs n. green barley.
~hlāf m. barley loaf.
~sǣd n. barley seed.
~tūn, bertūn m. threshing-floor,
barn.
~wīc f. hamlet.
be·rēafian wag. despoil, deprive.
be·rēcan make to smoke.
be·reccan relate; justify, excuse
gen. rfl.
gebered crushed; afflicted, oppressed.
be·regnian*, -rēni-† cause
(strife).
beren = biren bear's.
beren of barley.
beren = bern barn.
berenian = beregnian*.
be·rēofan† 7 deprive wi.
be·rēotan 7 bewail.
berern = bern barn.
be·rīdan 6 surround on horseback,
besiege; overtake, take possession of, seize.
be·rīefan deprive wag.
be·rīepan wag. despoil, plunder of.

berig|e, berge f. berry.
~drenc m. drink made of mulberries.
be·rihte*, biryhte prp. wd. close
by, by.
be·rindan take off bark.
be·rinnan 3 wet.
bern, beren, LN. berern n. barn
[bere-ærn].
~hūs n. barn.
be·rōwan 1 row round.
geberst n. intr. breaking, bursting.
berstan prt. bærst 3 intr. burst,
break; dash, break (of waves);
resound | escape; fail — gif him
āþ burste.
bertun = bere-tūn.
ber-winde f. navel-wort.
be·sǣtian lie in wait for, beset.
be·sārg|ian be sorry for; lament;
condole with.
~ung f. sorrowing.
be·sāwan 1 sow.
be·sceadan† cast in the shade,
overshadow.
be·scēadan 1 b separate; discriminate; sprinkle tr.
be·scēaw|ian look at, survey;
consider, pay regard to; watch.
~odnes f. vision, sight.
~ung f. contemplation.
be·scencan give to drink wai.
be·scēotan 7 intr. dart, rush ‖ tr.
send, instil (thoughts).
be·scerwan = bescierian.
be·scīelan*, ȳ look at w. on.
be·sciēran 4 shear, shave — ~hine
tō prēoste like a priest.
be·scier|ian, once -scerwan de-
prive wag., wai., fram, of.
~ednes f. deprivation.
be·scīnan 6 shine upon.
be·scītan 6 cover with filth, be-
daub.
be·screpan 5 scrape.
be·scūfan 7 thrust, throw, precipitate.
be·secgan say: him on ~ accuse
him; announce; plead cause, rfl.
defend oneself (in court of law).
be·sellan surround wai.
besema = besma.
be·sencan tr. sink, plunge.
be·sengan singe; burn.
be·sēon intr., rfl. look up, look
about, see; w. on a., tō look at,
pay regard to ‖ tr. go to see, visit.
be·settan set (hope on); appoint;

set about, adorn wai.; beset:
searopancum beseted; keep,
guard; institute, set going.
be·sīdian regulate, determine.
be·sierwan ensnare, take by surprise, overcome; deprive by
treachery wai.
be·silfran silver.
be·sincan 3 sink intr.
be·singan 3 sing incantations over,
bewitch; sing of, bewail.
be·sittan 5 besiege, beset, block-
ade, gen. w. ūtan; possess.
be·sīw(i)an, ēo sew.
be·slǣpan 1 b sleep.
be·slēan 2 wai. cut off (head); deprive of.
be·slīepan tr. slip, put, clothe.
be·slītan 6 deprive of by tearing
away wai.
bes(e)ma m. broom; rod (for
beating).
bēsm|an — ptc. ge~ed curved Gl.
[bōsm].
~ing f. curve Gl.
be·smierwan besmear.
be·smitan 6 defile.
be·smitennes f. defilement, impurity [besmītan].
be·smittian defile.
be·smiþian work (metals), forge.
be·smocian tr. smoke, envelop
with incense.
be·snǣdan wai. deprive by cutting,
prune.
be·snīwian snow on, cover with
snow.
be·snyppan†, prt. -yþede deprive
wai.
beso = baso.
be·solcen torpid, inert.
be·sorg subject of solicitude, dear
to wd.
be·sorgian be sorry for; care for,
be solicitous about; scruple, fear.
be·spanan 2, 1 entice, persuade.
be·spearrian*, a shut, bar.
be·sprecan 5 tr. speak about,
complain of, charge.
be·sprengan sprinkle.
be·spyrian follow tracks of, trace.
be·stæppan 2 go, proceed.
be·stand|an 2 stand round, sur-
round; afflict — mid ādle ~en.
be·stealcian go stealthily.
be·stecan 5 close, bar (door).
be·stefn|an — ~d fringed Gl.

be·stelan 4 intr., rfl. move stealthily, steal ‖ tr. him sum þing on ~ accuse of, charge with.
be·stīeman wet [stēam].
be·stingan 3 thrust, push — ~ fȳr on a. set fire to.
bestredan = *bestregdan.
be·stregdan*, -ēdan bestrew, cover (with earth).
be·strēowian bestrew, cover.
be·strīdan 6 mount (horse).
be·strīepan strip of, plunder wag. — ~ hīe æt landum.
be·strūdan 7 despoil, deprive wai.
be·styrian heap up Bd.
be·styrman assail, agitate (mind).
be·sūt|ian — ~od dirty.
be·swǣlan scorch, burn.
be·swāpan 1 cover, envelop wai. or mid; shelter against (wiþ), protect; ~ him on mōd persuade.
be·swemman make to swim [swimman].
be·sweþian bind up, bandage.
be·swic, bi- deceit, treachery; snare.
~a*, bi- m. deceiver.
~fealle f. trap.
~ol deceitful.
be·swīc|an 6 deceive; lead astray; seduce (woman); offend, scandalizare; get the better of, conquer, disable.
~end m. deceiver, seducer.
~ung f. deception.
be·swician tr. escape from, evade; wd. be free from (disease).
be·swincan 3 tr. labour at, make with labour; till (land).
be·swingan 3 beat, flog.
be·sylian, -sw- soil, stain.
bet av. better, see gōd.
~lic† excellent, magnificent.
bēt|an, oe improve; ~ fȳr make or light fire; reform, make amends for, atone [bōt].
~end† once m. builder (?).
~nes f. reparation, atonement.
be·tǣcan wad. hand over; hand down (tradition); entrust, commit, give in charge of; appoint; without d. send; pursue, hunt.
bēte, oe f. beet-root [Lt. beta].
be·teldan 3 wai. or mid cover, surround; overwhelm (with grief) [geteld].

be·tellan rfl. clear oneself (of charge) w. æt.
be·tēon 6, 7 prt. -tāh, -tēah, ptc. -tigen, -togen accuse; bequeath.
be·tēon 7 cover; enclose, contain.
beter|a cpv. of gōd good.
~ian, betrian make better; trim (lamp) ‖ become better.
~ung, bet(t)rung f. improvement.
be·tierwan tar.
be·tihtlian accuse.
be·tillan decoy.
be·timbran build.
be·togen(n)es f. accusation [be·tēon].
betonice f. betony (a plant) [Lt.].
be·tredan 4 tread on.
be·treppan, æ entrap, surprise (enemies' forces).
be·trymman, -trymian besiege.
betst, betest spl. of gōd good.
~boren eldest.
betuh, betweoh = betweox.
be·twēonan, -twēonum; bi-twihn vE.; -twin-, -twyn-, betwēon prp. w. d., or a. (gen. of motion) between, among — met. of social relations; difference: hwæt biþ ~ mannes and nȳtenes and gyte, gif .. Often follows case, esp. when a pronoun: cwǣdon him ~. Tmesis: be sǣm twēonum.
be·tweox, ~n, -twoxn, -twix, -tweoh, -t(w)uh, -twih, -y-, -hs prp. w. d.; rarely a., which gen. implies motion, between (of space, distinction, &c.), among. time between (two dates); during — ~ þissum meanwhile. Often follows case, sometimes w. word between: hī him healdaþ betwuh sibbe.
~ǣlegednes, -ǣworpennes f. interjection.
~gangan vb. go between (!).
~licgan 5 lie between (!).
~sendan send between (!).
~gesett interposed.
betwīnan = betwēonan.
be·tȳn|an enclose (with wall); shut (door), close (opening) — ūte ~ þæt folc shut out; finish [tūn].
~ing f. conclusion.
beþ|ian tr. bathe, foment [bæþ].
~ing f. hot bath; fomentation.

be·tyrnan rfl. prostrate oneself (!).
be·þearf vb., pl. -þurfon, prt. -þorfte, wg. require, need.
be·þeccan cover, conceal wai. or mid.
be·þencan consider, bear in mind —rfl. reflect; form plan, think of; w. tō entrust, abs. trust, confide.
be·þennan, -þenian cover.
be·þēodan join, associate.
be·þrāwan 1 afflict.
be·þridian, y circumvent, overcome.
be·þringan 3 wai. press on; surround.
be·þryccan tr. press on.
be·þuncan† once = beþencan.
be·þwēan 2 wash, wet.
be·þwēor|ian*, ȳ — ptc. ~ad depraved Gl.
be·þȳn prt. -ȳd(d)e thrust, push.
beufan = bufan.
beutan = būtan.
be·wacian watch.
be·wadan† once 2 deprive (?).
be·wǣfan wrap round, dress.
be·wǣgan deceive, frustrate.
be·wǣgnan (!)† once offer wda.
be·wǣlan wai. afflict.
be·wǣpnian deprive of weapons.
be·wǣrlan pass by LN.
be·warian tr. watch over, guard; ward off, avoid; rfl. avoid, beware of w. wiþ a.
be·war(e)nian intr. w. wiþ beware of, guard against ‖ tr. ward off (from oneself) w. rfl. d.: him ~ hellewītu.
bewarnian = bewarenian.
be·wāt vb., pl. -witon, prt. -wiste watch over; superintend, have charge of.
be·wāw|an† 1 — ptc. ~en blown upon (by winds) wi.
be·weallan 1 tr. boil away.
be·wealwian wallow.
be·weardian guard, watch, protect.
be·weax|an 1 —ptc. ~en overgrown wi.
be·wedd|ian betroth, marry.
~endlic relating to marriage.
~ung f. betrothal.
be·wefan 5 cover.
be·wegan† 5 cover wai. or mid ‖ kill.
be·wēlan join.

be·węndan *tr.* turn ; *intr.*, *rfl.* turn (round).

be·węnnan, -węnian entertain (hospitably).

be·weorpan 3 throw ; surround *wai.*

be·wēp|an 1 bewail, mourn for.

~endlic lamentable.

be·węr|ian defend ; prohibit.

~e(d)nes *f.* prohibition.

~igend *m.* protector.

~ung *f.* defence.

be·windan 3 twist round, bind, swaddle, wrap *wai.* or mid ; encircle, surround — *met.* hēafe ~ bewail ; brandish ; turn over (in mind).

be·witian, eo watch, observe ; watch over ; perform (journey).

be·wlātian gaze at, contemplate.

be·wlītan 6 look.

bewōpen *ptc.* of bewēpan.

be·wrec|an 5 drive, send ; *ptc.* ~en beaten *or* afflicted all round, surrounded *wai.*

be·wręncan deceive.

be·wrēon 6, 7 cover *wai.* or mid ; conceal ; protect *w.* fram.

be·wrītan† 6 write about (?).

be·wrīpan 6 bind round, encompass.

be·wuna *adj. indecl.* in the custom of, wont.

be·wyrcan make| cover, surround, adorn *wai.* or mid, on ; wall in, imprison.

bezera = bæzere.

bicce *f.* female dog, bitch.

bi-cwide *m.* proverb.

bīd (*n.*) halt—† on ~ wrecan bring to bay, make to halt.

~fæst† stationary.

~steall† *m.* halt— ~ giefan halt, stand at bay.

bīd|an 6 *intr.* remain, continue ; *wg.* await, wait for, wait long enough for, live till, *w. indc.* wait till || *tr.* endure, experience.

~ing *f.* abiding, abode.

bidd|an 5 entreat, request, demand, challenge (to duel) *wag* , *w. a.* or *g.* of thing and æt, *w. rfl. d.*: ānwīges bæd ; him fultumes bæd ; ~aþ ēow þingunge æt him ! | pray : bæd Dryhten for his þēowan hǣlo ; bitt his sāwle onlihtinge ; þus ~ende :

.. but this meaning is generally expressed by gebiddan | late or doubtful command : bæd hine faran.

biddere *m.* petitioner.

gebidd|an 5 pray, worship *often w. rfl. pro. in d.*, *lW.* in *a.* : for þǣm stǣnendum gebæd ; hē sceal him fore ~ ; ~ aþ þǣre sāwle ! for the soul *vE.* ; hē nolde him (*lW.* hyne) ~ tō Gode ; rarely *w.* thing expressed : ~ ūre wǣstma genyhtsumnesse.

bide-rip = bed-.

bīecn|an, bīcnian, bē(a)cnian *w. d.* or tō make signs, nod, beckon ; point out (place), indicate (time) ; show (with words), hint ; signify, be a symbol of ; summon [bēacn].

ge·~iend *m.* forefinger.

~iendlic allegorical ; indicative (mood).

~iendlīce *av.* allegorically.

~ung, ~ing *f.* beckoning ; symbol, figure.

bīecnol indicating Gl.

bīeg|an *tr.* (*rfl.*) bend, bow ; turn ; force ; convert (heathen) ; humiliate ; overcome || *intr.* bend (of point of spear) [būgan].

ge·~ednes *f.* inflection (in grammar).

(ge)~endlic flexible.

~nes *f.* flexibility.

~ung *f.* bending, curvature.

bīegels *m.* arch, vault.

gebield boldness [beald].

gebielde*, i bold.

bieldan encourage, animate.

bieldo *f.* boldness.

bīem|e *f.* trumpet [bēam].

~ere, ~esangere *m.* trumpeter.

~ian sound trumpet.

bierc|e, eo, byre *f.* birch [beorc].

~holt *n.* birch wood.

biercen of birch.

gebierded *ptc.* bearded [beard].

bierhtan, eo, bryhtan *intr.* shine [beorht].

gebierhtan *tr.* make bright ; heighten (beauty) ; make clear *or* distinct ; make famous, celebrate || *intr.* be bright, shine—also *rfl.*

bierhto *f.* brightness.

gebierm|an ferment ; leaven—*ptc.* ~ed *n.* leavened bread ; *ptc.* ~ed puffed up, proud *wi.* [beorma].

biernan 3, *A.* eo, *prt.* born, a *intr.* burn, be burnt down : sēo burg barn ; sēo eorþe wæs tō axan geburnen.

bīesting (*m.*) thick milk, first milk of cow after calving [bēost].

bīetel *m.* mallet [bēatan].

bīewan*, ȳ, ēo polish.

bifian, eo tremble.

bi-fylce *n.* neighbouring people *or* region.

big = bī by.

bī-geng|a, be- *m.* cultivator (of land) ; inhabitant ; benefactor [begān].

~ere *m.* one who plies (a trade) ; attendant.

~estre *f.* attendant.

~nes *f.* cultivation, study.

bigspell = bīspell.

bī-gyrdel girdle ; purse ; treasury.

bile *m.* bird's bill, beak.

gebilod having a beak.

bī-leofa *m.* sustenance, food ; wages.

bī-leofen, -lifen *f.* sustenance, food.

bile-wit, bil(i)-, bilwet-, ~witt- gentle, kind ; innocent, simple [bile, hwīt].

~līce *av.* innocently.

~nes *f.* innocence.

bill† *n.* sword.

~hęte *m.* hostility, warfare.

~geslieht *n.* sword-clash, battle.

~swæþ *n.* sword-track, field of battle.

bī-nama *m.* pronoun.

gebind† *n.* what is bound together —waþema ~ frozen waves† ; costiveness.

bind|an 3 bind, fetter—*ptc.* bunden (sweord) with hilt adorned with gold chains† ; make prisoner, imprison ; *met. esp. in pass.* be bound (by duty, obligation), be under constraint.

~ere *m.* binder.

binde *f.* head-band, fillet.

binn *f.* manger.

binnan, beinnan *av.*, *prp. w. d.* within, in (of place, time) ; into ; of quantity within, less than.

biren(e) *f.* she-bear [bera].

biren, beren of a bear [bera].

bī-sæc *f.* †once visit (?).

bī-sæc (*n.*) litigation.

biscep, -op *m.* bishop; high-priest, heathen chief-priest [*Lt.* episcopus].

~dóm *m.* bishopric; excommunication.

~ealdor *m.* high-priest.

~gegierelan *pl.* episcopal robes.

~hád *m.* bishopric, episcopate.

~hám *m.* bishop's estate.

~héafodlín *n.* bishop's head-ornament.

~híered *m.* clergy Gl.

~líc episcopal.

~ríce *n.* bishopric.

~rocc *m.* bishop's rochet.

~scír *f.* diocese; episcopate.

~setl, ~seld, ~seþel *n.* episcopal see.

~sinoþ, eo *m.* synod of bishops.

~stól *m.* episcopal see, bishopric.

~sunu *m.* godson at confirmation.

~þegnung, -þénung *f.* bishop's office.

~wíte *n.* bishop's fee for visiting, procuration fee.

~wyrt *f.* marsh-mallow.

biscep|ian, -opian confirm.

~ung, biscpung *f.* confirmation.

bisn, bisen, *L.* **y** *f.* example, pattern — **ástellan, settan ~e, ást., st.** (hit) tó ~e set (as) example (to be imitated or avoided); similar case, parallel; original (of copy); similitude, parable.

ge~ere *m.* imitator.

~ian *wd.* set *or* give an example (to); take example by, imitate : ~ on hiera unþéawum.

(ge)~ung *f.* example; similar case, parallel.

bisen-, y blind.

bises, í [*or* **-iss-**]† *m.* day added in leap-year [*Lt.* bissextus].

bisgo, bys(i)go *f.* occupation, labour; trouble, care, affliction.

bisg|ian, bys(i)gian occupy *tr. and rfl.*, engross (mind); trouble, worry, afflict.

~ung *f.* occupation.

bisig, *L.* **y** busy, occupied.

bismer, by-, -or *nm.* insult, mockery—on ~ by way of insult; joke; blasphemy; calumny; ignominy, disgrace—tó ~e gerénian, getáwian humiliate.

~full abominable, disgraceful.

~glíw*, éo *n.* shameful lust.

~léas irreproachable.

bismer|léoþ *n.* scurrilous song, nenia (!).

~líc disgraceful, ignominious.

~líce *av.* disgracefully; contemptuously.

~spréc *f.* blasphemy.

~word *n.* insult.

bismer|an, bismran, by-, -ian insult, mock, deride; blaspheme, revile; disgrace, injure, ill-treat.

~iend *m.* mocker.

~nes *f.* mockery; blasphemy.

~ung *f.* mockery; blasphemy; infamy, being object of contempt.

ge~ung *f.* illusion Gl.

bí-spell *n.* parable, proverb, example; story.

~bóc *f.* book of proverbs.

bissexte leap-year [*Lt.* bissextus].

bist (thou) art.

bita *m.* morsel, bit [bítan].

bít|an 6 bite—biton heora téþ him tógéanes gnashed their teeth at him; cut, wound.

~a *m.* wild beast.

bit|e *m.* bite; cutting, (sword) cut; cancer.

~mælum *av.* piecemeal.

bitel *m.* beetle.

biter, tt bitter; painful, severe (grief, &c.); fierce [bítan].

~e, bitre *av.* severely, very.

~líce *av.* severely : ~ wépan.

~nes *f.* bitterness.

~wyrde severe in speech, bitter.

~wyrt-drenc *m.* bitter drink.

biterian be bitter; make bitter.

bitol bridle [bítan].

bítol*, bitela biting Gl.

gebitt *n.*—tóþa ~ gnashing of teeth [bítan].

biþ is.

biwáune, *see* bewáwan.

bí-wist *f.* sustenance, provisions.

bí-word *n.* proverb, saying; adverb.

bizant *m.* bezant, a gold coin [*Lt.* Byzanteum].

blác bright, white; pale.

~ern, æ *n.* lantern.

~hléor† white- *or* pale-cheeked, fair (woman).

~ian become pale.

~ung *f.* pallor.

blǽ-hǽwen, blǽwen, blǽhwen light blue.

blæc *n.* ink.

blæc black — ~ berige blackberry; swarthy, dark-complexioned.

~feaxede black-haired.

~gimm *m.* jet.

~pytt *m.* naphtha-pit.

~te(o)ru *n.* naphtha.

~þrúst *m.* leprosy.

blǽc *n.* leprosy.

blǽcan make pale, bleach [blác].

blǽcern = blácern lantern.

blǽco *f.* pallor [blác].

blǽd *n.* leaf; blade (of oar).

blǽd I. *m.* blowing, blast; breath; inspiration; life ‖ prosperity, glory; plenty, riches. **II.** *f.* shoot, flower, fruit; harvest, crops. *See* bléd [bláwan].

~ágend(e)† *m.* prosperous, glorious.

~belig, y *m.* bellows.

~dæg† *m.* day of prosperity.

~fæst†, ge- glorious.

~fæstnes*, bleof- *f.* delight.

ge~fæstnes *f.* sustenance, provisions.

~giefa† *m.* giver of prosperity.

~horn *m.* trumpet.

~wela† *m.* riches, plenty.

blǽdnessa *fpl.* blossoms.

blǽddre = blǽdre.

blǽd(d)re *f.* blister; bladder [bláwan].

blǽge *f.* gudgeon.

blǽs *m.* blowing, blast. *Cp.* blǽst.

~belg *m.* bellows.

blǽs|e, -ase *f.* torch, fire. *Cp.* blyse.

~ere *m.* incendiary.

blǽst *m.* blowing, blast, wind; flame, glare [bláwan].

~belg, blǽst- *m.* bellows.

blǽstan blow.

blǽtan bleat.

blǽwen = blǽ-hǽwen.

blagettan weep.

blanca (†) *m.* steed, horse.

bland *once* = gebland.

gebland† *n.* what is mixed together, commotion.

bland|an† 1 b mix : *ptc.* ge~en mixed, disturbed; infected, corrupted, injured *w. i.* (*g. once*).

~en-feax† having mixed-coloured *or* grey hair, old.

blase = blǽse.

blast = blǽst.

blát† *once* sound, cry (?).

blát† pale, livid. *Cp.* bléat.

blāt|e *av.* : ~e forbærnan *tr.* burn with livid flame (?).

~ian* be pale.

~ende pale.

blāw|an I *intr.* blow (*of* wind); blow (with mouth), breathe; snort (*of* horse); be blown, sound : **~ende bīeman** ‖ *tr.* blow (trumpet); inflate (bladder).

~ere *m.* one who blows (furnace).

~ung *f.* blowing (trumpet).

blēat† bringing misery, *once.* *Cp.* blāt.

~e† *av.* miserably *once.*

blēaþ timid, sluggish.

blęce *m.* blight [blæc].

blęcþa *m.* blight [blæc].

blēd *f.* shoot, branch ; fruit, flower [blōwan].

~hwæt† *once* quick-growing (?).

blēd|an bleed—se ~enda fīc a disease [blōd].

bledsian = bletsian.

bledu *f.* dish, bowl, cup.

blegen, blegne *f.* boil, ulcer; blister.

blegne = blegen.

blęncan deceive, cheat.

blęndan blind ; deceive [blind].

blēo, bleoh [*by an. of* feoh, fēos], *g.* **blēos**, *dpl.* blēo(wu)m *n.* colour; appearance, form.

~bord† *n.* chess-board.

~brygd-† *pl.* various colours, changing colours.

~cræft *m.* embroidery.

~fāg parti-coloured.

~rēad purple.

~stǣning *f.* mosaic work.

geblēo, -bleoh *n.* colour [blēo].

geblēod variegated [blēo].

bleoh = blēo.

blēowum, *see* blēo.

blēre; blērig (?) bald.

blēri-pittel, blēria pyttel (*m.*) mouse-hawk.

blets|ian, blœdsian bless, consecrate [blōd ?.

~ing-bōɔ *f.* book of formulae for blessing.

~ing-sealm *m.* the Benedicite.

~ung *f.* blessing.

blician shine, appear [blīcan].

blīcan 6 shine, glitter ; appear, be laid bare (*of* bone).

blice *m.* laying bare, exposure (of bone through wound) [blīcan].

blicettan glitter, vibrate.

---

blicettung *f.* coruscation.

blind blind ; unintelligent ; dark (prison) — ~ slite wound whose opening is not visible. sēo ~e nętele blind (non-stinging) nettle.

ge-fellian blindfold.

~līce *av.* blindly ; thoughtlessly.

~nes *f.* blindness.

~þearm *m.* caecum. Or blind þearm (?).

blinn cessation—būton ~e.

blinnan 3 *intr.* cease ; be vacant (*of* bishopric) ; desist from, forfeit *w. g. or* fram [= belinnan].

blisgere = blysiere.

bliss, blīþs *f.* joy, merriment, happiness ; friendship, grace, benevolence [blīþe].

~ian, blīþsian rejoice *w. g. or* ofer, on. **~ian, blitsian** [*infl. of* bletsian] gladden ; make prosperous, endow.

~igendlic exulting.

(ge)blissung *f.* rejoicing, joy.

blīþ|e joyful, merry ; kind, gentle ; calm, peaceful ; pleasant.

~e, ~elīce *av.* gladly, kindly.

~heort cheerful ; friendly.

~(e)mōd cheerful ; friendly.

~nes *f.* joy, happiness.

blīþs = bliss.

blīwum, *see* blēo.

blōd *n.* blood — ~es flōwnes flux of blood ; vein. ~ (for)lǣtan bleed.

~drynce *m.* bloodshed.

~egesa† *m.* sanguinary horror.

~fāg† bloodstained.

~forlǣtan I b bleed Bd.

~gēotende sanguinary.

~gita *m.* shedder of blood [*Cp.* āgieta. Or formed from ~gyte (?)].

~gyte *m.* bleeding ; bloodshed.

~hrǣcung *f.* spitting blood.

~(h)rēow sanguinary.

~iernende having issue of blood Bd.

~lǣs(wu), *g.* ~lǣs(w)e blood-letting, bleeding.

~lǣtere *m.* blood-letter.

~lēas bloodless.

~gemęnged bloodstained.

~orc *m.* sacrificial vessel.

~rēad blood-red.

~rēow = ~hrēow.

~ryne *m.* flux of blood, issue.

~seax *n.* lancet.

---

blōd|spīwung, blōtspīung *f.* spitting blood.

~wīte *n.* fine for bloodshed Gl.

~wyrt *f.* bloody dock.

blōdig bleeding ; bloodstained.

~tōþ† with bloodstained teeth.

blōdgian be bloodthirsty Gl. ; cover with blood.

blōma *m.* moss of metal.

blōstm|a, blōsma, blōstm *m.* blossom, flower.

~bǣre, ~berende flowery.

~frēols *m.* floral festival Gl.

~ian blossom.

(ge)blōt *n.* heathen sacrifice of human beings—tō blōte gedōn kill as a sacrifice.

blōt|an I sacrifice *wda., w.d. and* mid.

~ere sacrificer Gl.

~mōnaþ *m.* November.

~ung *f.* sacrificing.

blōw|an I bloom, flower — *ptc.* ge~en blooming.

~endlic blooming.

blycgan terrify.

blys|a, i *m.*, ~(ig)e *f.* torch, fire. *Cp.*

~iere, blisgere *m.* incendiary.

blyscan blush.

bōn = bōgan boast.

bōc, *pl.* bēc, oe, *f.* book ; document, charter [bēce].

~æcer *m.* field granted by charter.

~blæc*, e *n.* ink.

~cięst *f.* book-chest.

~cræft *n.* literature.

~cræftig learned.

~fell *n.* vellum.

~hord *m.*, ~hūs *n.* library.

~lǣden *n.* literary Latin.

~land *l.* land held by charter.

~lār *f.* learning, doctrine.

~lic of books, literary, biblical.

~rǣdere *m.* reader.

~rǣding *f.* reading books.

~rēad *n.* vermilion.

~riht *n.* right of granting by charter.

~gestrēon *n.* library.

~tǣcing *f.* teaching by book ; Scripture.

~talu *f.* Scripture.

bōcian grant by charter *wda.* ; furnish with books.

bōcere author ; Scribe.

bēc *f.* beech.

bōc|holt *n.* beech-copse.
~scield *m.* shield of beech-wood.
~stæf *m.* letter, character; Runic letter.
~trēow *n.* beech.
~wudu *m.* beech-forest.
(ge)bod *n.* command, precept.
(ge)~scipe *m.* message, command.
bodlāc decree *vL.*
bod|ian *wda.* announce, proclaim, preach; foretell, prophecy.
~ere *m.* teacher *lN.*
~igend *m.* preacher.
~igendlic to be proclaimed.
~ung *f.* preaching.
~ung-dæg *m.* Annunciation-day.
boda *m.* messenger, herald, angel, apostle; prophet.
bodan = botm.
bode *prt. of* bōgan.
bodig *n.* trunk, body; stature.
bōg *m.* shoulder, arm; bough, branch (of tree); progeny.
~incel *n.* small bough.
~scield *m.* shoulder-shield.
bōg|an, bōn, bōgian, *prt.* bōde boast, *also rfl.*
~ung, bōung *f.* boasting, arrogance.
bōgian *L. intr.* dwell, take up one's abode *w. rfl. d.* ‖ *tr.* inhabit [būan].
bog|a *m.* bow (to shoot with); bend, fold [būgan].
~efōdder *m.* quiver.
~enętt, ~anętt *n.* basket for catching fish.
bogetung *f.* curve Gl. [boga].
bŏl, oo eel.
bolca *m.* gangway (of ship).
bold *n.* dwelling, house, palace [botl].
~āgend† *m.* house-owner.
~getæl *n.* regular dwelling-place; district, region.
~getimber† *n.* house.
~wela† *m.* wealth, (splendid) dwelling-place.
bolgen-mōd† angry [belgan].
bolla *m.* bowl.
bolster *n.* bolster, pillow.
bolstrian support with pillows.
bolt *m.* bolt, arrow.
bōn *f.* ornament of a ship.
~ian polish, burnish.
bōnda, u *m.* householder; free man, plebeian; husband. [*Scand.* bōndi].

bōndeland *n.* leased land (?) *vL.*
bor gimlet.
~ian bore, perforate.
borlīce *av.* accurately, exactly, very.
borcian bark [beorcan].
bord *n.* board, plank; table;†shield; framework, side of ship — on ~e in a ship, on board.
~hæbbende warrior.
~haga *m.* testudo, phalanx.
~hrēopa, ē *m.* phalanx; shield.
~gelāc *n.* weapon.
~rand *m.* shield.
~rima *m.* rim.
~stæp *n.* shore.
~þaca *m.* testudo.
~weall *m.* phalanx; shield; shore, landing-place.
~wudu *m.* shield.
borda *m.* fringe.
geboren born, own (kinsman, brother) [beran].
borettan brandish [beran].
borg *m.* pledge, security, bail; person who gives security, surety; debtor.
~bryce *m.* breach of surety *or* bail.
~fæst bound by pledge, dependent on.
~fæstan *wda.* bind by pledge — ~ þām cyninge.
~gielda *m.* debtor; money-lender, usurer, creditor.
~hand *f.* pledger, surety.
~lēas without security, for which no pledge has been given.
~geliefde*, e pledge, security Gl. *Or = two words* (?).
~wędd *n.* pledge.
borg|ian borrow *w.* æt; lend.
~iend *m.* money-lender, usurer.
bōsig, -ih cow-stall *lN.*
bōsm, bōsum *m.* bosom, breast; womb.
~ig curved Gl.
bōt *f.* mending; remedy; cure; compensation, satisfaction, atonement, repentance.
~ettan keep in repair.
~lēas what cannot be compensated.
~wierpe what can be compensated.
botl, ge- *n.* dwelling, house, building.
~gestrēon *n.* household property.
~weard *m.* steward.
~wela *m.* village.

botm, bodan *m.* bottom; ship's keel.
bōþ, *see* bōgan.
boþen rosemary; thyme; darnel.
box (*m.*) box-tree; box [*Lt.* buxus].
~trēow *n.* box-tree.
brac-hwil = bearhtm-hwil moment.
braccas *once mpl.* breeches.
brād- roasting.
~hlāf *m.* toast.
~panne *f.* frying-pan.
brād, *cpv.* brādra, æ broad, wide, spacious — ~ hand open hand, palm ‖ copious.
~e *av.* far and wide.
~æx *f.* broad axe.
~brim† *n.* ocean.
~lāst-æx *f.* broad axe.
~eleac *m.* broad leek.
~nes *f.* surface; extent; liberality — ~ heortan.
~þistel *m.* sea-holly.
brādian be broad; extend *w.* fram . . oþ ‖ *tr.* spread.
bræc rheum [brecan].
~copu *f.* epilepsy.
~sēoc, ge- lunatic, epileptic.
gebræc, ~eo phlegm, cough.
brād† *once* flesh (?).
bræd = brægd trick.
bræd-īsen *n.* chisel.
brād|an *tr.* broaden, extend (territory); increase, extend (fame); expand (wings), stretch out (hands) ‖ *intr. and rfl.* extend; grow (*of* trees) [brād].
~els *m.* covering, carpet.
~ing *f.* spreading (fame).
brād|an roast; fry.
~epanne, ~ing-panne *f.* frying-pan.
brāde roast meat.
brādo *f.* breadth; extent.
brægd, e, brād *m.* trick, deceit [*cp.* gebregd].
~boga *m.* treacherous bow.
~en crafty.
~wīs crafty.
(ge)brægden, e cunning.
ge-līce *av.* cunningly.
brǣdra, ā *cpv. of* brād.
brægen, bra- *n.* brain.
~loca† *m.* head.
~panne*, brægp- *f.* skull.
~sēoc brain-sick.
brǣm(b)el = brēmel.

bræs *n.* brass.

~en of brass ; †bold, mighty.

bræþ *m.* odour ; exhalation, vapour.

bræw, brēaw, brēag, *A.* brēg *m.* eyelid.

bran-.

~wyrt *f.* bilberry bush.

brand *m.* fire-brand ; fire ; sword, *esp.*†.

~hāt ardent (love, hate).

~hord† *m.* R.

~īsen *n.* fire-dog, grate.

~ōm rust produced by burning, hammer scales.

~rād *f.*, ~rida, e *m.* fire-dog, grate.

~stefn† = brant-.

brant† lofty, high (ship) ; deep (water).

~stefn*, brondstæfn† steep-prowed (ship).

brasian, æ do brass-work [bræs].

gebras(t)l *n.* crackling (of flames).

brastl|ian crackle, rattle (*of* thunder, falling tree, fire).

~ung, barstlung *f.* crackling, crashing sound.

bratt cloak *IN.* [*Celtic*].

brēad *n.*, *pl.* ~ru morsel, crumb ; bread.

gebre(a)dad† regenerated.

brēag = bræw.

breahtm, e, *A.* æ ; bearhtm, eo, y noise, clamour [brecan].

~ian*, brehtnian, bearhtmian resound.

breahtm, breorht atom [bearhtm].

breahtm = bearhtm glance.

breard = brerd.

brēaþ *once* brittle.

brēaw = bræw eyelid.

breawern = brēow- brew-house.

brēc breeches, *pl.* of brōc.

~hrægl *n.* breeches.

gebrec *n.* noise, clamour.

~drenc *m.* emetic. *Or* = gebrǣc-(?).

brec|an 4 *tr.* break, burst, burst through, penetrate, break down, take by storm (town, fortress) | violate (oath, peace), break (command), curtail, injure, annul | urge, *in* hine firwet brǣc he felt curiosity *or* desire || *rfl.* retch —ongann hine ~ tō spīwenne || *intr.* burst forth (*of* stream), be violent (*of* wind) ; make one's way with effort, burst.

brecung *f.* breaking (bread)

brecþa† *m.* grief.

bred board ; surface ; tablet (of stone).

~en = briden of boards.

bre(o)dwian† prostrate.

brēfan epitomize, set down in writing [*Lt.* brevis].

brēg|an terrify, induce by intimidation *w. sbj.* [brōga].

~nes *f.* terror.

brega = brego.

bregd = brægd trick.

gebregd *n.* change (of weather) || skill, cunning [bregdan ; *cp.* brægd].

~stafas† *mpl.* learning.

bregdan, brēdan, *prt.* brægd, brǣd, *pl.* brugdon, brūdon, *ptc.* brogden, brōden *tr.* *often w. i.* *of thing in E., always a. in lW.* move quickly (hands in swimming, oars), brandish, drag, pull, draw (sword), put : ~ sweord(e), sweord of scēaþe, rāp on his sweoran ; throw (in wrestling) ; draw (breath) | weave | change (colour), transform (*of* wizard) : ~ blēom, hē brǣd his hīw (form) | deceive || *rfl.* pretend : hē gebrǣd hine sēocne || *intr.* be transformed *w. to.*

(ge)bregden = brægden cunning.

brego† *m.* chief, prince, king.

~rīce *n.* kingdom.

~rōf mighty.

~stōl *m.* throne ; principality, kingdom.

~weard *m.* chief, king.

brehtm = breahtm.

bremb|el, ~er = brēmel.

brēm|e [œ ?], ē† celebrated, illustrious, famous, noble.

~e *av.* gloriously.

~an celebrate, commemorate.

~endlic celebrated.

brēmel, brēmbel, brēmber, æ *m.* bramble.

~æppel *m.*, ~berige *n.* blackberry.

~brēr *m.* bramble.

~lēaf *n.* bramble-leaf.

~rind *f.* bramble-rind.

~þyrne *f.* bramble.

brem|man, *brēmian resound, roar.

~ung *f.* roaring.

brengan = bringan.

brenting† *m.* ship [brant].

breord = brerd.

brēosa *m.* gadfly.

brēost *n.* *often pl.*, *m.* breast, chest ; mind, heart.

~bān *n.* breast-bone.

~byden, e *f.* breast, chest.

~beorg *f.*, ~geborg *n.* bulwark.

~byden *f.* chest, thorax Gl.

~caru† *f.* anxiety.

~cofa† *m.* mind, heart.

~hord† *m.* mind, heart.

~gehygd†, ~gehȳd *fn.* thought, mind.

~līn *n.* breast-cloth.

~loca† *m.* mind.

~nett† *n.* corslet.

~rocc *m.* chest-clothing.

~sefa† *m.* mind, heart.

~toga† *m.* chief.

~geþanc† *m.* thought, mind.

~gewǣde† *n.* corslet.

~wærc *m.* pain in the chest.

~weall *m.* bulwark.

~weorþung† *f.* ornament on breast.

~wielm† *m.* teat ; agitation of mind.

brēotan† 7 break, destroy, kill.

Breoten = Breten.

breoton† *once* spacious.

brēow|an 7 brew.

~ern*, ēa *n.* brew-house.

~lāc, brȳw- *n.* brewing.

brēr, ǣ *m.* briar.

brerd, eo, ea *m.* brim, border ; bank ; surface.

~full brimful.

Breten, eo, y, i, tt, -on *f.* Britain.

~land *n.* Britain ; Wales. *See also under* Brettas.

~wealda, Bretw- chief king of Britain.

Brett|as, y, i, Britas *mpl.* Britons.

~land *n.* Britain.

~wealas, ~walas *mpl.* Britons.

~wīelisc*, Brytwylsc British.

brēþer *d.* of brōþor.

bridd, *lN.* *pl.* birdas, *m.* young bird ; chicken.

brīdel *m.* bridle.

~þwang *m.* bridle-thong.

brīdels *m.* bridle.

~hring *m.* bridle-ring.

briden, e (wall) of boards [bred].

brīdlian bridle, restrain.

bries|an*, ȳ bruise ; season (food).
ge~ednes f. crushing.
brig = brīw.
brigd (n.) once change [gebregd, bregdan].
-briht, see beorht.
brihtan = bierhtan.
brim†, y [confusion w. brymme] n. sea, ocean, water (of sea) gen. pl.
~ceald sea-cold.
~clif n. sea-cliff.
~faroþ n. sea-shore.
~flōd m. sea ; deluge.
~fugol m. sea-bird.
~gięst m. sailor.
~hengest m. ship.
~hlæst m. fishes.
~lād f. sea-way.
~līpend(e) m. mariner.
~mann m. sailor, pirate.
~nesen (?) safe sea-passage.
~rād f. sea.
~stæp n. sea-shore.
~strēam m. sea's current, sea ; broad river.
~þisa m. ship.
~więlm m. sea-surge, waves.
~wīsa m. sea-captain.
~wudu m. ship.
~wylf f. sea-wolf, she-wolf of the lake.
bring once m. offering, sacrifice.
bring|an, ę wk., †3 ptc. broht, †brungen bring ; bring forth, produce (fruits).
~nes f. oblation.
bring|e* f. chest (?).
~ādl f. epilepsy (?).
Briten = Breten.
Brittas = Brettas.
Brittisc, y, Brytisc British [Brettas].
brīw, briig m. pottage, porridge.
brīwan prepare (food).
broc n. affliction ; labour ; disease [brecan].
~ian afflict ; injure, maim ; oppress.
~lic full of hardship.
~ung f. affliction ; illness.
gebroc n. fragment ; affliction, trouble.
brōc m. brook.
~minte f. brookmint.
brōc f. trousers | pl. brēc, ǣ breech, hind quarters ; trousers.
brocc m. badger.
~en (coat) of badger's skin.

brōd f. brood, also of bees ; fetus.
~ig broody (hen).
broddian be luxuriant = brordian* (?).
brōden ptc. of bregdan.
brōdettan = brogdettan.
brōg|a m. terror, prodigy, danger.
~þrēa†, brōh- m. dire calamity.
brogden, brōden ptc. of bregdan.
~mǣl† once n. inlaid sword. Or = brōden mǣl (?).
brogdett|an, brōdettan brandish ‖ intr. tremble.
~ung f. trembling ; figment Gl.
brogn-, ge~ branch, twig LV.
brord m. point ; first blade of grass, young plant.
brōm m. broom (the plant).
~fæsten n. thicket of broom (?) Gl.
brosn|ian crumble, decay ; perish, pass away.
~iendlic, ge~odlic corruptible.
(ge)~ung f. corruption, ruin.
gebrot n. fragment [brēotan].
broþ n. broth [brēowan].
brōþor, d. brēþer, pl. ~, ge~, brōþru m. brother lit. and fig. ; monk.
~bana† m. fratricide (person).
~cwealm† m. fratricide (action).
~dohtor f. niece.
~gięld† n. vengeance for brothers (?).
~lēas brotherless.
~lic fraternal.
~licnes f. brotherliness.
~rǣden(n) f. brotherhood.
~sibb f. relationship between brothers ; brotherly love.
~slaga m. fratricide (person).
~slęge m. fratricide (action).
~sunu m. nephew.
~þīnen = beorþor-þignen.
~wīf n. sister-in-law.
~wyrt f. pennyroyal.
gebrōþor, -brōþru mpl. brothers.
~scipe m. brotherhood.
brū f., pl. ~(w)a, gpl. ~na eyebrow ; eyelid, eyelash.
brūcan 7 wg., rarely i. or a. make use of, enjoy — brocen worn (coat) ; eat ; spend (life) ; possess, keep.
brūn brown.
~baso purple.
~ęcg† brown-edged (sword).
~eþa m. erysipelas.
~fāg brown-coloured.

brūn|wann dark brown.
~wyrt f. water-betony.
brycian wd. benefit [bryce].
bryc|e I. m. breaking ; fragment. II. aj. brittle, worthless [brecan].
~mǣlum*, bre- av. piecemeal.
gebryce once breaking.
bryce m. making use of, use, enjoyment [brūcan].
brȳce, ȳ† useful [brūcan].
brycg f. bridge.
~bōt f. bridge-repair.
~ian make a bridge, also abs. (of ice) ; make plank path.
~weard m. bridge-defender.
~geweorc n. bridge-construction.
brycsian wd. benefit [bryce].
brȳd f. bride ; †wife ; †woman.
~bedd n. nuptial bed.
~bletsung f. blessing the bride.
~boda m. bridesman.
~būr, ~cofa m. bridal chamber.
~ealo(þ) n. marriage feast.
~giefu f. dowry ; pl. wedding.
~gift f. betrothal.
~guma m. bridegroom.
~lāc npl. marriage ; married life.
~lēoþ n. epithalamium.
~(e)lic bridal.
~loca m. bridal chamber.
~lōp n. wedding L. [Scand.].
~lufe† f. love of a bride.
~niht f. wedding-night.
~rēaf n. wedding-dress.
~rest f. nuptial bed.
~sang m. marriage song.
~þing npl. nuptials.
bryd = brygd.
brȳd|ian — ptc. ge~od married (woman) [brȳd].
brygd, brȳd drawing (weapon) [bregdan].
-bryht, see beorht.
bryhtan = bierhtan.
brymme m. border, shore (of sea) ; sea. Cp. brim.
bryne m. burning, flame(s), fire ; inflammation (of body) [biernan].
~ādl f. fever.
~brōga† m. fire-terror.
~gięld† n. burnt-offering.
~hāt† burning hot.
~lēoma† m. flame.
~tēar† m. hot tear.
~więlm† m. conflagration.
brȳne (m.) brine.
brynig fiery [bryne].

bryrd|an stimulate [brord].
~nes *f.* stimulus.
Bryten = Breten.
bryten-†. *Cp.* breoton.
~cyning *m.* great king.
~grund *m.* spacious earth.
~rīce *n.* spacious kingdom.
~wangas *mpl.* the world.
brytn|ian deal out, distribute, arrange [brēotan].
~ere *m.* steward.
~ung *f.* distribution.
brȳtofta *pl.* wedding [brȳd, þoft].
(ge)brytsen *f.* fragment.
gebryttan, *ptc.* -bryted break to pieces; destroy [brēotan].
brytt|a† *m.* distributor (of wealth), perpetrator (of crime), Lord (of heaven, glory, &c.).
~ian tear to pieces, divide; distribute; possess, enjoy; share, exercise: mægen ~ wiþ metode (*of* Satan).
Bryttas = Brettas.
Bryttisc = Brittisc.
bryþen brewing — ān ~ mealtes; drink, beverage [broþ].
bū *pl.* bȳ *n.* dwelling.
bū|an, būn, būgan, bū(g)ian, būwian, bōgian *prt.* būde, *ptc.* gebū(e)n, gebūd *int.* dwell ‖ *tr.* inhabit, occupy (house); cultivate (land).
~end *m.* inhabitant.
būc *m.* pitcher; stomach.
bucc *m.* buck, male deer; beaver (of helmet).
bucca *m.* he-goat.
bufan, be·ufan *av., prp. w. d.,* or *a.* (*expressing motion*) above, higher than; above, away from : be Lygan, xx mīla ~ Lundenbyrig; *superiority,* above. þǣr ~ &c. above *mention in book* [ufan].
~cweden, ~nęmd above-mentioned.
būgan 7 *intr.* bow down, stoop; bend, swerve (sideways *or* up and down) | turn, go; flee *w.* fram | turn (the mind) : ~ tō hǣþenscipe become a heathen, ~ tō woruldþingum, ~ fram yfele avoid ; go over to, submit *w.* tō, *rarely w. d. only — ptc.* gebogen converted (to Christianity).
būgan = būan dwell.
būian = būan.

bul, ~a ornament [*Lt.* bulla].
~berende wearing an ornament Gl.
bul|a *m.* bull (?) — ~an wylle Ct.
bulentse *f.* a plant.
bulluc *m.* bull-calf.
bulot cuckoo-flower.
bunda = bōnda.
bunden *ptc. of* bindan bind.
~heord† (?).
~stęfna† with bound prow.
ge~nes *f.* obligation.
būne *f.* cup.
būr *m.* chamber; cottage, villa.
~cniht *m.* chamberlain.
~cot *n.* bedroom.
~rēaf *n.* tapestry.
~geteld† *n.* pavilion.
~þegn, ~þēn *m.* chamberlain.
gebūr *m.* peasant, farmer.
~gerihtu *npl.* peasants' rights *or* dues.
~scipe *m.* neighbourhood.
burg, bur(u)h, *pl.* byrig, burga *f.* fortified place; (fortified) town, city.
~āgend † *m.* city-possessor.
~bōt *f.* repairing fortress.
~bryce *m.* burglary; fine for burglary.
~ealdor *m.* mayor.
~fæsten† *n.* fortress.
~geard *m.* castle-yard.
~geat *n.* city-gate.
~geat-setl *n.* law-court held at city-gate.
~hlip† *n.* city-slope [*confusion w.* beorg-hlip ?].
~lagu *f.* civil law.
~land† *n.* native city.
~lēode *mpl.* citizens.
~loca† *m.* city.
~mann, byrig- *m.* citizen.
~gemōt *n.* meeting of townsmen.
~ręced† *n.* city-dwelling.
~rǣden(n) *f.* citizenship.
~gerēfa *m.* chief magistrate of a town.
~rūn(e) *f.* sorceress.
~sæl† *n.* house.
~sǣta *m.* citizen.
~scipe *m.* municipality.
~scīr *f.* corporation, city.
~sęle† *m.* house.
~sittend(e)† *m.* citizen.
~sittende city-dwelling — ~ mann.

burg|sprǣc *f.* urbane speech.
~steall† *m.* city.
~stęde† *m.* city.
~tūn *m.* city.
~þelu *f.* castle-floor.
~þegn = būrþegn (?).
~geþincþ (?) town-council LL.
~ware, -an *pl.,* -u *f. coll.* citizens; -u city.
~waru-mann *m.* citizen.
~wealda *m.* alderman.
~weall *m.* city-wall.
~weard†, byrig- *m.* city-defender, citizen.
~weg *m.* street.
~wela† *m.* city-wealth.
~werod *n.* crowd of citizens.
~wīgend *m.* warrior.
~wita *m.* town-councillor.
burn|e *f.,* burn(n)a, brunna *m.* stream, brook.
~sęle† *m.* bath-house.
bute = būton.
buter|e *f.* butter [*Lt.* butyrum].
~flēoge, buttor-, *f.* butterfly.
~stoppa *m.* butter-vessel.
~geþwēor *n.* butter.
būton, būtan | būte (*cj.*) *W. I. av.* outside. II. *prp. w. d., and rarely a.* (*to express motion*) outside ; without ; free from : ~ hæftnīede ; against, without : ~ þæs cyninges lēafe, ~ lēodrihte ; except — ~ þām þe *cj.* besides that *w. ind.* III. *cj. w. sbj.* unless ; *w. ind.* except that ; but ; *without vb.* except.
butruc, bute-, butu- *m.* leather bottle.
butse-carl *m.* sailor *L.*
buttuc *m.* end ; piece of land : on þā ~as Ct.
butu, *see* bēgen.
by, *see* bū.
bycgan buy *w.* æt ; get done, see after.
bydel *m.* messenger, herald, forerunner ; beadle, police-officer [bēodan].
byden *f.* vessel, tub, barrel ; a measure, bushel.
~botm *m.* bottom of a vessel.
~fæt *n.* bushel.
byffan mutter.
byge *m.* traffic [bycgan].
byge *m.* curve ; corner ; cone (of helmet) [būgan].
gebygel obedient = gebēogol.

byht *m.* bend [būgan].
byht *n.* dwelling [būan].
bylda† *m.* builder [bold].
bȳle, bȳl *m.* boil, carbuncle.
byled-brēost† puff-breasted.
byl(i g, *A.* bęlg, æ *m.* leather bag *or* bottle; bellows [belgan].
bylgan bellow.
byndel(l)e, i *f.* binding (a man) [bindan].
bȳne inhabited, cultivated [būan].
gebyr|ian *impers. wd.* happen: him ~ede þæt hē wæs . . ; be fitting, proper ‖ *personal* happen: him ~ied ~ede — him ~ede þæt feorh earfoþlīce he recovered with difficulty; befit: stōr ~eþ tō Godes þegnunge; be assigned to (the devil) [beran].
~edlic suitable.
~edlīce *av.* conveniently.
byrd *f.* birth, *pl. in sg. meaning* [beran].
~scipe *m.* child-bearing.
gebyrd, ~o *f. often pl. w. sg. meaning* birth; parentage: good birth, high rank; condition, nature — on ~ † according to fate *or* in order (?).
~boda *m.* announcer of (Christ's) birth.
~dæg *m.*, ~tīd *f.* birthday.
~wiglere, ~witega *m.* astrologer.
gebyrd burdened *IN.*
byrd|an fringe, embroider [borda].
~icge *f.* embroideress.

byrde of high birth *or* rank [beran].
gebyrde innate, natural *wd.*
~līce *av.* (besiege) vigorously *or* methodically. *Cp.* gebyrd.
byre†, *pl.* ~, -as *m.* son; youth.
byre *m.* mound.
(ge)byre *m.* opportunity; time, period.
gebyrelic suitable, agreeing.
bȳre *n.* (cattle)stall; shed, hut [būr].
byrel|e, byrle *m.* cupbearer, butler [beran].
~ian give to drink, serve with liquor *wda.*
byres *f.* borer, chisel [bor].
byrg *d. of* burg.
gebyrg — bēon on ~e *wd.* help, protect [beorgan].
gebyrg*, i *n. IN.* taste.
byrga, byriga *m.* one who gives bail, surety [borg].
byr(i)g|an bury [beorgan].
ge~ednes *f.* burial.
~end *m.* burier.
~ere *m.* corpse-bearer.
~nes *f.* burying.
~sang *m.* dirge.
byr(i)g|an taste; eat.
~nes *f.* taste.
byrgels *m.* burial-place; tomb.
~lēoþ *n.*, ~sang *m.* dirge.
byrgen(n) *f.* sepulchre, tomb.
~lēoþ *n.* epitaph.
~sang *m.* dirge.

byrgen-stōw *f.* burial-place.
-byrht-, *see* beorht, bierhtan.
byrig *d. of* burg.
byrla *m.* body, barrel (of horse).
byrn|e *f.* corslet.
~ham† *m.* corslet.
~wiga†, ~wīg(g)end† *m.* warrior.
ge~od corsleted.
byrst *m.* loss, injury [berstan].
~full calamitous *vL.*
~ig broken.
byrst, *vE.* bryst (?) *f.* bristle.
byrstan roar *IN.*
byrþ* birth [beran].
~þignenu*, -þin- *f.* midwife.
byrþen(n), byrden *f.* burden, load; impost, charge [beran].
~mǣlum *av.* by loads.
~strang strong for burdens (*of* donkey).
byrþere, byrþre I. *m.* bearer (of corpse); support; horse, &c. (for riding or driving). II. *f.* she who bears (a child), mother.
byrþestre *f.* carrier.
bytl|an, -ian build; fortify [botl].
~a *m.* builder.
(ge)~ung *f.* act of building; edifice.
gebytle *n.* edifice, house.
bytm|e, byþme, byþne bottom; keel (of ship) [botm].
~ing *f.* bottom, ground floor (of ark).
bytt *f.* leather bottle, wine-skin; cask.
~fylling *f.* filling casks.
byxen of box-wood [box].

C.

cæfer-tūn = cafor-.
cæfester (*n.*) halter [*Lt.* capistrum].
cǣg, ~e *f.* key.
~bora *m.* key-bearer.
~hierde *m.* key-keeper.
~loca *m.* keeping under lock and key.
cǣlic = calic.
cæppe *f.* hood; cap [*Lt.* cappa].

cæren = ceren.
cærfille = cerfille.
cærse = cerse cress.
cāf prompt; active; bold.
~e, ~līce *av.* promptly; boldly.
~lic bold.
~scipe *m.* activity; courage.
cafor-tūn, ea, cæfer- *m.* courtyard, vestibule; hall, mansion.

cafstrian bridle, curb [cæfester].
cāl = cawel cabbage.
calan 2 be cold *intr.*: hine cælþ, him cælþ.
calc sandal; horse-shoe* [*Lt.* calceus].
~rand† shoed (horse) (?).
calca-trippe = colte-træppe.

[31]

cālend, ā† *m.* calend; month; †allotted time, span of life [*Lt.* calendae].

calic, cęl(i)c *m.* cup, chalice [*Lt.* calicem].

calo, *g.* **calwes** bald.

calwa *m.* mange [calo].

calwer = cealer.

cāma *m.* muzzle, collar [*Lt.* camus].

camb I. *m.* comb; (cocks)comb, crest (of helmet). **II.** *f.* honeycomb.

~iht crested.

camel *m.* camel [*Lt.* camelus].

cammoc *m.* (?) a plant.

camp *m.* battle, war, contest [*Lt.* campus].

~dōm *m.*, ~hād *m.*, ~rǣden(n)† *f.* contest, war.

~ealdor *m.* general.

~gefēra *m.* fellow-soldier.

~gimm *m.* precious gem.

~stęde † *m.* battle-field.

~wǣpen† *n.* weapon.

~werod *n.* army.

~wīg† *n.* battle.

~wisa *m.* champion.

~wudu† *m.* shield.

gecamp (*n.*) warfare.

camp|ian fight.

~ung *f.* fighting.

gecampian gain by fighting.

gecanc (*n.*) derision.

canceler *m.* chancellor *vL.* [*lLt.* cancellarius].

cancer, -or *m.*; ~ādl *f.* cancer [*Lt.* cancer].

cancett|an, -etan cackle (in laughing), deride.

~ung *f.* loud laughter.

candel, *g.* ~le *f.*, *n.* candle [*Lt.* candela].

~bora *m.* acolythus.

~leoht candle-light.

~mæsse *f.* Candlemas.

~snietels*, ~ȳ *m.* snuffers.

~stæf *m.*, ~sticca *m.*, ~trēow *n.* candlestick.

~twist (*m.*) pair of snuffers Gl.

~weoce *f.* wick.

~wyrt *f.* mullein.

cann *f.* cognizance, asseveration; clearance (from accusation).

cann, ge- *vb.*, *pl.* cunnon, *prt.* cūþe know; experience; know how to, be able.

canne *f.* can.

canonic *m.* canon (person) [*Lt.*].

~lic canonical.

Cant-war|e, Cęnt- *pl.* people of Kent.

~aburg *f.* Canterbury.

~amǣgþ *f.* people of Kent.

cantel *m.* or *n.* buttress, support.

cantel-cāp *m.L.*, **canter-cæppe** *f.* cope (vestment).

canter|e *m.* singer [*Lt.* canto].

~stafas *mpl.* (?) Ct.

cantic *m.* canticle, sacred song [*Lt.* canticum].

capian *once* turn, face *intr.*

capellān *m.* chaplain *vL.* [*Fr.*].

capitol *m.* chapter (cathedral *or* monastic); chapter (of book) [*Lt.* capitulum].

~hūs *n.* chapter-house.

~mæsse *f.* first mass.

capūn (*m.*) capon, fowl [*Fr.*].

carcern, cea-, -ærn; *lA.* carcrænn; carcern-ern *n.* prison [*Lt.* carcer, ærn].

~weard *m.* jailor.

c(e)arian care, reck *w.* ymb; sorrow, be anxious [caru].

caric- dry fig [*Lt.* carica].

carl, ea *m.* man — ~es wǣn Charles's Wain, constellation of the Great Bear [*Scand.*].

~fugol *m.* male bird.

~mann *m.* male, man.

carr *m.* stone, rock *lN.* [*Celtic*].

carte *f.* paper, piece of paper; deed, document [*Lt.* charta].

car|u, ea *f.* anxiety, grief, trouble, care.

~full anxious; solicitous, careful.

~fullīce *av.* carefully, diligently.

~fulnes *f.* anxiety; solicitude.

~gāst† *m.* sad spirit, demon.

~gealdor† *n.* song of sorrow.

~ig† anxious, sad; painful (bonds).

~lēas free from anxiety, cheerful.

~lēasnes, ~lēast *f.* freedom from care.

~(e)līce *av.* wretchedly.

~seld† *n.* place of sorrow.

~sīþ† *m.* sad journey, fate.

~sorg† *f.* anxious sorrow.

~więlm† *m.* flood of care.

case-bill ? *n.* club Gl.

cāser|e *m.* emperor [*Lt.* Caesar].

~dōm *m.* emperor's rule.

~ing *m.* a coin.

cāser|lic imperial.

~n *f.* empress.

casol (*m.*) short cloak.

cassoc *m.* sedge, coarse grass.

~lēaf *n.* sedge-leaf.

castel *n.* village [*Lt.* castellum].

castel *L.* *m.* castle [*Fr.*].

~mann *m.* castle-man.

~weall *m.* castle-, city-wall.

~weorc *n.* castle-building.

castenere (*m.*) cabinet, chest.

catt *m.*, **catte** *f.* cat.

cawel, caul, cāl *m.* cabbage [*Lt.* caulis].

~lēaf *n.* cabbage-leaf.

~sǣd *n.* cabbage-seed.

~stela *m.* cabbage-stalk.

~wyrm *m.* caterpillar.

caw(e)l, ceawl, eo, cowel *m.* basket.

cēac *m.* pitcher, jug, basin.

~bora *m.* yoke for carrying buckets, &c.

cēac|e *f.* jaw.

~bān *n.* jaw-bone.

ceaf *n.* chaff.

~finc *m.* chaffinch.

ceafl*, cæfl (*m.*) halter.

cēafl *m.* jaw.

ceafor *m.* cockchafer, beetle.

ceahhett|an, -etan laugh loudly.

~ung *f.* laughter; jest(ing).

cealc *m.* chalk, lime; plaster [*Lt.* calx].

~pytt, ~sēap *m.* chalk-pit.

~stān *m.* chalk.

ceald I. cold. **II.** *n.* cold.

~heort† cruel.

~ian become cold; become torpid.

cealer, cealre, ceoldre *f.*, **calwer** *m.* curds.

~brīw, calwer-clīm *m.* pottage of curds.

cealf, A. ę, ǣ *n.*, *pl.* ~as, ~ru, *A.* calfur, calferu calf.

~ian calve.

ceallian† shout.

cēap *m.* price — dēop ~ high price; bargain, commercial transaction — ~ drīfan make bargain; marketing, market; cattle.

~cniht, cīepe- *m.* slave.

~dæg *m.* market-day.

~ēadig rich in cattle.

~gięld *n.* price.

~hūs*, cǣpe- *n.* storehouse.

cēap|mann, cīep(e)- *m.* merchant, pedlar.

~scamol, cīep- *m.* custom-house, toll-booth.

~scip *n.* trading-ship.

~setl, cīep- *n.* toll-booth.

~stōw, cīepe- *f.* market-place, commercial centre.

~strǣt, cīep- *f.* trade-street.

~þing, cīepe- *n.* merchandise.

cēapian buy; bargain; buy and sell, trade; acquire *wda.*

cēapung,-ing *f.* marketing, buying and selling, trading.

~gemōt *n.* meeting for trade, market.

cearc|ian creak; gnash (teeth).

~etung *f.* creaking.

cearm = cierm cry.

cēas *f.* quarrel, strife; reproof.

cēast *f.* quarrel, strife, sedition, seditio.

~full quarrelsome, turbulent.

ceaster *f.* city [*Lt.* castra].

~æsc *m.* black hellebore.

~būend† *m.* citizen.

~hlid† *n.* city-gate.

~hof† *n.* house.

~ware, -an, ~gewaran, *pl.*, ~waru *f.* citizens.

~wīc *f.* village.

~wyrt *f.* black hellebore.

ceawl = cawel basket.

cēcel, oe, i *m.* little cake; morsel.

cedelc *f.* mercury (a plant).

ceder *n.*, ~bēam *m.*, ~trēow *n.* cedar [*Lt.* cedrus].

cedrisc of cedar [ceder].

cēl|an, oe cool *tr.* [cōl].

~ing *f.* coolness; cool place.

(ge)~nes *f.* coolness.

celdre = cealer.

cele *m.* keel.

celeþonie, cyleþenie *f.* celandine [*Lt.* chelidonium].

cell (monastic) cell *vL.* [*Lt.*].

cel(l)endre *f.*, cel(l)ender *n.* coriander [*Lt.* coriandrum].

celmert-mann *lN. m.* hired servant.

cellod†, celod† round (?) *or* embossed (?) (*of* shield).

cemban, *prt.* cemde comb [camb].

cemes *f.* shirt [*Lt.* camisia].

cemp|a *m.* soldier, warrior [camp].

~estre *f.* female novice Gl.

cēn† *m.* torch; *the Runic letter* c.

cēn|e, oe bold.

~līce *av.* boldly.

~þu *f.* boldness.

cenep *m.* moustache.

cenn|an, y bear (child), produce; declare, attest, give information; *wda.* assign, ascribe, give (name) || *rfl.* clear oneself (of accusation), disavow.

~ende parent.

~endlic genital.

~estre, cy- *f.* mother.

cenning *f.* begetting; birth.

~stān *m.* testing-stone.

~stōw *f.* birth-place.

~tīd *f.* time of birth.

Cent *f.* Kent [*Lt.* Cantia].

~ingas *mpl.* men of Kent.

~isc Kentish.

~land, ~rīce *n.* Kent.

~ware = Cant-ware.

centaurie *f.* centaury (a plant) [*Lt.* centaureum].

cēo *f.* jackdaw.

cēod *m.*, ~e *f.* (?) pouch, vessel.

cēol *m.* ship.

~pelu† *f.* ship.

ceoldre = cealer curds.

ceole *f.* throat.

ceolfor- = cilfor-.

ceolor *m.* throat.

ceor|ian murmur, grumble.

~ung *f.* grumbling.

ceorc|ian* complain.

~ing *f.* complaining.

ceorf|an 3 cut. cut down (tree), excavate (sepulchre in rock)—*ptc.* corfen cut off; engrave; tear.

~æx *f.* axe.

~ing-īsen *n.* branding-iron (!).

ceorl *m.* free man of the lowest class; free man; common man, plebeian; husband; †man, hero.

~boren of low birth.

~folc *n.* common people, vulgar.

~ian marry (*of* woman).

~isc = cierlisc.

~(l)ic common, popular (not learned).

~(l)īce *av.* vulgarly.

~strang strong as a man (*of* woman).

ceorran 3 creak *once.*

cēosan *prt. pl.* curon, *ptc.* coren 7 choose *w. a.*, *rarely g.*; select — Gode gecoren chosen (man) in the sight of God; accept; decide.

ceosol, cisel, y (*m.*) gravel; cesol gizzard Gl.

~stān *m.* pebble.

ceosol cottage.

cēowan 7 chew; gnaw; eat, consume.

ceowl = cawel.

cēpan *wa.* observe, notice | *wg.* attend to, not neglect, keep (appointment) | *wdg.* take (to flight), betake oneself (to shelter); devise, meditate: hē nolde him nānes flēames cēpan, hē mē hearmes cēpþ | strive: hē cēpte symle hū hē cwēmde Gode [gecōp].

ceren, oe, æ, y (*n.*) sweet wine [*Lt.* carenum].

ceren = cyren churn.

cerfille, cæ-, cy-, -elle *f.* chervil [*Lt.* cerefolium].

cerlic (*m.*) charlock (a plant).

cerse, æ, cresse *f.*, cressa *m.* cress.

cesol = ceosol.

cete = cyte cottage.

cewl = cawel.

chor *m.* dance; choir [*Lt.* chorus].

~glēo *n.* dance.

cīan *pl.* gills.

cicel = cēcel little cake.

gecīd *n.* strife.

cīd|an quarrel; complain; blame *w. d. or* wiþ *a.*

~ung, ~ing *f.* rebuke.

ciefes, ~e *f.* concubine, prostitute.

~boren illegitimate.

~dōm, ~hād *m.* concubinage, fornication.

~gemāna *m.* fornication.

cieg|an call *tr. and intr.*, call out, call to, invoke; summon; call by name.

ge-(ed)nes *f.* calling; name.

~endlic vocative (case).

~ere *m.* caller, crier out.

cielian *L.* be cold [ciele].

cield(o) *f.* cold [ceald].

ciele *m.* cold [calan].

~gicel *m.* icicle.

~wearte *f.* goose-skin.

~wyrt *f.* sorrel.

geciełf (cow) with calf [cealf].

cīep(e)- *see* cēap-.

cīep|an buy, sell, trade in [cēap].

~a, ~end *m.* merchant, trader.

~ing *f.* trade, marketing; market, market-place.

gecīepe for sale.

[33]

cīepe f. onion [Lt. caepa].
~lēac m. leek.
cierlisc, ceo- rustic, common (man) [ceorl].
~nes f. clownishness.
cierm, ea, eo m. shout, clamour, cry.
~an shout, cry out tr. and intr.
cierr m. time, occasion — æt sumum ~e; (first, second, &c.) time; affair, business.
cierr|an tr. turn, bring into a certain state, convert (to Christianity); reduce to subjection — him tō ge~; transform, turn ‖ intr. turn; go, return — hine ~, ge~ return to.
ge~ednes f. entrance, admission; conversion (to Christianity).
~ung f. conversion.
cīes fastidious (about food) [cēosan].
~nes f. fastidiousness.
cīes|e, ǣ m. cheese [Lt. caseus].
~(e)fæt n. cheese-vat.
~hwǣg n. whey.
~lybb n. rennet.
~gerunn n. rennet.
~wuce f. cheese-week.
ciést f. chest; coffin [Lt. cista].
~ian put in coffin.
ciétel m. kettle.
~hrūm (n.) soot of kettle.
cild n., pl. cild(ru) child — wearþ mid (þām) ~e became pregnant.
~a hierde schoolmaster, pædagogus. ~a mæssedæg Innocents'-day. ~trog cradle.
~clāþ n. swaddling-cloth.
~cradol m. cradle.
~faru f. carrying children.
~fōstre f. nurse.
~geogoþ f. period of childhood.
~geong infantine.
~hād m. childhood.
~hama m. womb; afterbirth.
~ieldo f. childhood.
~isc childish.
~lic infantine.
cileþonie = celeþonie.
cilfor-lamb, eo n. ewe-lamb.
cilic m. hair-cloth [Lt. cilicium].
cimb|an*.
~ing f. joint.
~īren n. edge-iron (?).
cimbal(a) m. cymbal [Lt. cymbalum].
cīnan 6 gape, crack.
cinc-.

cinc|daþen ornamented in some way: hyre ~an cyrtel Ct.
cincung f. loud laughter.
cine (m.) folded sheet (of parchment) Gl. Cp. geclofa. [cīnan].
cin|e, ~u wk. f. chink, fissure.
~iht, io cracked.
cinn f. chin.
~bān n. jaw.
~beorg f. visor.
~tōþ m. grinder.
cinnan† once R.
cinu = cine chink.
ciper-sealf f. henna-ointment [Lt. cypros].
cipp m. log, trunk; ploughshare; weaver's beam.
circul, -ol m. circle [Lt.].
~ādl f. shingles (a disease).
~cræft m. knowledge of the zodiac.
ciric|e, circe, cyr- f. church.
~ǣw f. ecclesiastical marriage.
~bell f. church-bell.
~bōc f. church-book.
~bōt f. church-repair.
~bryce m. breaking into a church.
~dor m. church-door.
~friþ m. (right of) sanctuary.
~fultum m. church-help.
~gang m. going to church.
~georn diligent in attending church.
~griþ n. (right of) sanctuary.
~hād m. order of the church.
~hālgung f. consecration of a church.
~hata m. persecution of churches.
~lic ecclesiastical.
~mǣrsung f. dedication of a church.
~gemāna m. congregation.
~mangung f. simony.
~mitta m. church-measure.
~nied, ēo f. need or use of the church.
~nytt f. church-service.
~pæþ m. church-path.
~ragu f. church-moss.
~rān*, e church-robbery.
~geryht n. church-due.
~sang m. church-hymn.
~sangere m. church-singer.
~sceatt m. church-tax or rate.
~sōcn f. (right of) sanctuary; going to church.
~steall, ~stede m. site of a church.
~stīg f. church-path.
~tīd f. church-time.
~tūn m. churchyard.
~þegn, ~þen m. minister.

ciric|þegnung, -þēn- f. church-service.
~þingere m. priest.
~wǣcce f. vigil.
~wǣd f. church-vestment.
~wāg f. church-wall.
~waru f. congregation.
~weard m. churchwarden, sacristan.
cir(e)s|bēam, ciser-, m., ~trēow n. cherry-tree [Lt. cerasus].
cirps, y, crisp curly (hair); curly-haired.
~ian curl.
ciser- = cirs-.
cistel*, y (f.) chestnut-tree [cp. cisten].
cisten (f.), cist(en)-bēam m. chestnut [Lt. castanea].
citel|ian tickle.
~ung f. tickling.
cit(e)re f. harp [Lt. cithara].
cīþ m. germ (of plant), spire, young shoot, sprout; mote (in eye); seed.
~fæst well rooted, growing.
clā = clawu claw.
clacian, ea hurry, hasten intr.
clac|u* f. strife.
~lēas, clæc- undisputed, free.
clador*, ea, clader-sticca m. rattle.
clæc = clac-.
clǣfre, ā, clǣfer-wyrt f. clover.
clǣg (m.) clay.
~ig*, clǣig aj. clayey.
clǣm|an smear, plaster, caulk [clām].
~ing*, mm f. smearing.
clǣn|e I. clear, open (field); pure, clean, wg. free from, devoid of; innocent, free from guilt; chaste. II. clǣne, ā av. entirely.
~georn desiring to be pure-hearted.
~heort pure-hearted.
~lic pure (love).
~līce av. purely.
~nes f. purity.
clǣns|ian, clā-, clǣsnian, ā, clǣnsnian clean(se), clear (land of weeds), purge (stomach); purify (heart), chasten (with affliction); wg. clear (of accusation).
~ere m. purifier.
(ge)~ung f. purifying; expiation; chastity.
clǣnsnian = clǣnsian.

[34]

clæppett|an, -etan throb (of sinew).

~ung f. throbbing, pulse.

clæsnian = clǣnsian.

clafre = clǣfre clover.

clām m. mud, paste.

clamm m. grasp ; bond, chain.

clāne = clǣne av.

clāsnian = clǣnsian.

clāte f. burdock, burr.

clatr|ian clatter.

~ung f. clattering.

clāþ m. cloth ; pl. clothes.

clāþian LN. clothe.

clauster n. enclosure ; cloister ; fortress. Cp. clūstor [Lt. claustrum].

clāw|an claw.

~ung f. gripes, colic.

clāwu, clā, A. clēa, clēo f. claw ; hoof ; iron claw, pl. pincers.

clēa = clawu.

cleac f. stepping-stone Ct. [Celtic].

clemman*, imper. clæm once contract (hand) (?).

cleofian = clifian.

cleōf|an 7 split, cleave tr.

~ung f. cleaving, sectio.

cleofa, y m. chamber, cell ; den (of wild beasts).

cleopian = clipian.

cleric, cleroc, cli- m. secular clergyman [Lt. clericus].

~hād m. the clerical office.

clewepa m. itch [clāwan].

clibbor adhesive [clifian].

geclibs = geclips*.

clidren(n) f. clatter.

clif n. cliff ; crag, rock.

~hliep m. leap from cliff (?) Gl.

~ig steep.

~iht(ig) steep.

~stān m. rock.

clif-wyrt*, y f. foxglove.

clifian, eo, y adhere.

clife f. burdock.

clifer m. claw.

~fēte claw-footed (bird), with talons.

clifiht adhesive.

clifr|ian scratch [clifer].

~ung f. scratching.

gecliht ptc. of clyccan compress.

climman, L. climban 3 ; †clymmian once climb.

clingan 3 shrink, contract intr. ; wither.

clip|ian, y, eo call (out) intr. wd. || tr. summon, call ; w.a. nom. call, name.

~iendlic vocal (sound), vowel ; vocative (case).

~ol vowel.

~ung f. clamour ; articulation (of sounds) ; vL. claim.

clipol, clipor m. clapper (of bell).

geclips*, -ibs, -ysp n. clamour [clipian].

cliroc = cleric.

clite f. colt's-foot.

clīpa, y m. poultice, plaster (for wound).

clīwen, y, eo, clywe n. ball of thread, clew ; anything in the shape of a ball.

cloccian cluck (of hen).

clod-.

~hamer m. fieldfare once.

geclofa m. half of a folded sheet ; duplicate of a document [clēofan].

clofe f. buckle.

clof|e, u f. clove, bulb or tuber of plant — gārlēaces ~ [clēofan].

~eht bulbed.

~þung, -e f. crow-foot.

~wyrt f. buttercup.

clott- lump Gl.

clūd n. rock.

~ig rocky.

cluf- = clof-.

clugge f. bell.

clūmian mumble, speak indistinctly.

clūse f. confinement, prison ; bond, chain ; (mountain) pass [Lt. clausum].

clūstor n. lock ; barrier ; confinement, prison [Lt. claustrum].

~cleofa m., ~loc n. prison.

clūt m. piece of cloth, patch ; metal plate.

~ian patch.

clyccan bring together, clench — gecliht clenched (hand).

clyfa = cleofa.

geclyfte cloven Gl [cleofan].

clympre f. lump of metal, metal.

clyne (m.) lump of metal.

clynnan, clynian (re)sound intr.

clypp (m.) embracing.

clyp|pan embrace ; affect, seize (heart) ; cherish, love.

~nes f embrace.

geclyps = geclips*.

clȳs|an* enclose [clūse].

~ung, ~ing f. enclosing ; chamber ; conclusion (of sentence).

clyster, geclystre n. cluster, bunch (of berries).

cnǣpling m. youth [cnapa].

cnǣpp m. top ; mountain-top | brooch.

gecnǣwe conscious of, acknowledging (sin) wg. ; known, manifest [cnāwan].

cnafa = cnapa.

cnapa, cnafa m. boy ; youth ; servant.

gecnāw|an 1 (cnāwan very rare ; never in W.) know : hine gecnēow þæt hē wæs Godes sunu ; understand (language) ; recognize (opposite of ignore).

~nes f. acknowledgement.

cnearr† m. small war-ship.

cnēat|ian dispute.

~ung f. dispute, investigation.

cnedan 5 knead.

cnēodan = cnōdan.

gecneord, cneord intent on, zealous, diligent.

~lǣcan be diligent.

~lic diligent.

~lice av. diligently.

~nes f. diligence, study.

cnēoris(s), -isn f. generation, family, race, tribe.

~bōc f. Genesis.

cnēo(w), A. cnēo n. knee ; degree of relationship, generation.

~gebed n. prayer on one's knees.

~bīeging f. kneeling.

~eht knotty (plant).

~holen n. butcher's broom.

~mǣg m. kinsman.

~rift m knee-hose (?).

~rīm m. progeny, descendants.

~sibb f. race, family.

~wærc m. pain in knees.

~wrist, ~wyrst f. knee-joint.

cnēow ian, cnēowan kneel.

~ung f. kneeling.

cnēowlian kneel.

cnīdan once 6 beat LM. [cp. gnīdan].

cnīf m. knife.

cniht, eo, A. e m. boy ; attendant, servant, retainer.

~gebeorþor n. (male) child-bearing.

~cild n. boy.

~geogoþ f. youth.

cniht|geong young.

~hād *m.* youth ; (male) virginity.

~lēas without attendants.

~lic boyish.

~wesende† young, in boyhood.

~wīse *f.* manner of a boy.

cnocian, u knock (at door) ; pound (in mortar).

cnōdan, ō†, ēo *wda.* attribute (qualities to a person).

cnoll *m.* hill-top, hill.

gecnos *n.* collision [cnyssan].

cnōsl *n.* progeny, kindred, family, native country.

cnossian dash, strike *intr. w.* be.

cnot|ta *m.* knot.

~mǣlum *av.* concisely Gl.

cnucian = cnocian.

cnū(w)ian pound (in mortar).

gecnycc- bond *lN.*

cnyll *m.* sound of bell.

~an, *lN.* cnyllsan sound bell.

cnyss|an *tr.* beat against, dash against, toss (storm . . ship)| defeat, crush (in battle), overcome (*of* temptation) ; hard press, trouble, afflict [cnossian].

~ung *f.* stroke, impulse (of air).

cnytt|an tie [cnotta].

~els *m.* string, sinew.

cōc *m.* cook [*Lt.* coquus].

cocc *m.* cock.

coccel *m.* corn-cockle, darnel, tares.

cōcer-panne *f.* frying-pan.

cōcn|ian*, cōca- cook [cōc].

~ung, cōcu- *f.* thing cooked.

cocor *m.* quiver ; sword (!), spear (!).

cōcor- [cōc].

~mete *m.* cooked food.

~panne *f.* frying-pan.

cod-æppel *m.* quince [*Lt.* cydonia, æppel].

codd *m.* bag ; cod, shell, husk, skin (of grape).

cof|a, o†, *m.* chamber.

~godas *mpl.* house-gods, penates.

~incel *n.* little chamber, hand-mill (!).

cohhetan† shout (?), cough (?).

col *n.* live coal, (piece of) charcoal.

~māse *f.* titmouse (a bird).

~pytt *m.* coal-pit.

~þrǣd *m.* blackened thread, plumb-line.

cōl cool ; appeased, calm (*of* anxiety, grief).

~cwield *f.* ague (?) Gl.

cōlnes *f.* coolness.

cōlian *intr.* cool, become cold ; cool (*of* love).

coliandre *f.* coriander [*Lt.* coriandrum].

collen-fer(h)þ† bold.

~an*, -ferhtan make empty, exhaust Gl.

collon-crog *m.* water-lily.

colt *m.* colt.

~grǣg colt's-foot.

~etræppe, coltræppe, calcatrippe *f.* Christ's thorn.

columne, -umbe *f.* column [*Lt.* columna].

cōm *prt. of* cuman.

consolde *f.* comfrey [*Lt.* consolida].

consul *m.* consul [*Lt.* consul].

coorte *f.* cohort [*Lt.* cohors].

cōp (*m.*) an outer garment.

gecōp fit, suitable.

~līce *av.* fitly, well.

cōpenere *m.* lover.

copor *n.* copper [*Lt.* cuprum].

copp *m.* summit.

~ede having the top cut off, polled (tree).

cops = cosp.

cor- [cēosan].

~snǣd *f.* 'trial-morsel,' piece of consecrated bread whose swallowing was a test of innocence.

gecor *n.* decision [cēosan].

cordewānere *m.* shoemaker Ct. [*Fr.*].

coren-bēag *f.* crown [*Lt.* corona].

coren, ge- chosen [cēosan].

ge~lic elegant.

ge~līce *av.* elegantly.

(ge)~nes *f.* choice ; goodness.

ge~scipe *m.* election ; excellence.

corflian mince, cut small [ceorfan].

corn *n.* corn ; grain (of mustard), pip, berry ; corn (on foot).

~æppel *m.* pomegranate.

~æsceda *fpl.* corn-sweepings, chaff.

~bǣre, ~berende corn-bearing.

~hrycce *f.* corn-rick.

~hūs *n.* granary.

~gesǣlig rich in corn.

~gesc(e)ot *n.* contribution of corn.

~tēopung *f.* tithe of corn.

~trēow *n.* cornel-tree.

~trog *m.* corn-bin.

~wurma *m.* weevil.

cornoc = cranoc (cronoc).

corōnian crown [*Lt.* corona].

corþer, -or *n.* troop, assemblage, retinue ; pomp.

cosp, cops *m.* fetter.

~ian fetter.

coss *m.* kiss.

~ian kiss.

cost *m.* (?) costmary (a plant).

cost — þæs ~es þe on condition that [*Scand.* kostr].

gecost†, cost tried, proved, chosen, excellent [cēosan].

cost|ian, costnian *w.g. or a.* try, test ; tempt, afflict.

~ere, ~i(g)end *m.* tempter.

~ung, ~ing *f.* temptation, trial, tribulation.

ge~nes *f.* trial, temptation.

cot *n.* cottage, house ; chamber ; den (of thieves).

~līf *n.* hamlet.

~setla *m.* cottager, tenant.

~stōw *f.* hamlet.

cottuc, cotuc *m.* mallow.

coþu *f.* disease, pestilence. sēo micle ~ elephantiasis, leprosy.

crā (*n.*) croaking (of frogs and crows) Gl.

crabba *m.* crab.

cracian resound.

cræcett|an croak.

~ung, cræcetung *f.* croaking.

cradol, -el *m.* cradle.

~cild *n.* infant.

cræft *m.* skill, ability ; cunning, device ; knowledge, science ; art, trade, profession | good quality, excellence, virtue | strength, power ; cause.

~glēaw† wise.

~lēas unskilled.

~lic artificial ; skilfully made, skilled (labour).

~līce *av.* skilfully.

~weorc *n.* clever work.

cræftan exercise a craft.

cræftig skilful, skilled—*wg.* skilled in ; cunning | excellent, virtuous | strong, powerful.

~līce *av.* skilfully.

cræft(i)ga, cræft(i)ca, cræfta *m.* artificer, workman.

cræt *n.*, *gpl.* ~(en)a chariot.

~ehors *n.* horse for driving.

~wǣn *m.* chariot.

~wīsa *m.* charioteer.

craf|ian, æ demand (one's rights) ; summon (before court of law).

~ung, f. claim, demand.

cram-pul = cran-pōl.

crammian cram, stuff.

crampiht crumpled, wrinkled.

cran m. crane.

~pōl*, crampul m. crane-pool Ct.

cranc-.

~stæf m. weaving-implement.

cranic m. chronicle, record [Lt. chronicus].

cranoc, cornoc m. crane [cran].

crās (f.) food, dainty.

crāwan 1 crow.

crāw|e f. crow.

~lēac, ~an- m. crow-garlic.

Crē(a)cas, Crēce mpl. Greeks.

crēas-.

~nes f. pride, elation Gl.

Crēcisc, ēa Greek [Crēacas].

crēda m. creed [Lt. credo].

cręncestre f. weaver [cranc].

crēop|an 7 creep, crawl.

~el, y m. cripple.

~ere m. cripple.

~ung f. creeping.

cribb f. crib, stall.

crīepan*, y, i contract, clench (hand).

crīepel m. burrow [crēopan].

crimman 3 cram, insert ‖ crumble.

crīn vb. flow Gl.

crincan = cringan.

cringan, crincan 3 fall in battle, perish.

crism|a m. chrism, holy oil used for anointing after baptism ; chrisom, white vesture put on a child after baptism ; wearing a chrisom [Lt. chrisma].

~hālgung f. consecration by chrism.

~līesing f. taking off chrisom.

crismal m. or n. chrisom. Cp. crisma.

crisp = cirps.

Crīst m. Christ — ~es bōc f. the Gospels. ~es mǣl, tācn the cross [Lt.].

~līc Christian.

~mæsse L. f. Christmas.

cristall|a m. crystal ; flea-bane (a plant) [Lt. crystall|us, ~ium].

~isc of crystal.

crīstel-, cyrstel- [Crīst].

~mǣl n. cross.

crīsten Christian.

crīsten|dōm m. Christianity.

~nes*, crīstnes f. Christianity.

crīst(e)n|ian christianize ; christen ; anoint with holy oil.

~ung f. christening.

croc|c mf., crocca m. earthenware vessel, pot.

~sceard potsherd.

~wyrhta m. potter.

gecrod n. throng, crowd [crūdan].

croft m. small field.

crōg, oo m. pot, vessel.

~cynn n. kind of pot.

croh (m.) saffron [Lt. crocus].

crōp*, cnop n. bleating, croup (?) Gl.

cropp m. sprout, bunch (of flowers or berries), ear (of corn) ; crop (of bird) ; kidney.

~iht bunchy.

~lēac m. garlic.

crūce f. pitcher.

crūdan 7 intr. press, make one's way w. on a.

cruft crypt, vault [Lt. crypta].

cruma m. crumb.

crumb, crump crooked.

crundel mn. cavity, chalk-pit (?), pond (?) Ct. [Celtic ?].

crūs(e)ne f. robe of skins, fur coat.

crycc f. crutch ; staff, crozier.

cryccen of clay [crocc].

crymb|an* bend tr. [crumb].

~ing f. bending.

crympan curl [crump].

crypel = crēopel cripple.

cryppan bend, crook (finger).

cū, g. cū(e), cȳ, d. cȳ, pl. cȳ(e), gpl. cū(n)a, dpl. cū(u)m f. cow.

~butere f. cow's-milk butter.

~cealf n. calf.

~ēage n. cow's eye.

~hierde m. cowherd.

~horn m. cow's horn.

~meol(u)c f. cow's milk.

~migoþa m. cow's urine.

~sealf f. suet.

~slyppe, ~sloppe f. cowslip.

~tægel m. cow's tail.

cucler, -e, cucul-, cucel- m. spoon, spoonful [Lt. cochlear].

~mǣl n. spoonful (measure).

cucu = cwic alive.

cucurbite f. gourd [Lt. cucurbita].

cudele f. cuttle-fish.

cudu, cwidu, cweodu, cwudu, g. cwidwes, -u(w)es, -owes n. what is chewed, cud ; mastic (a gum).

cuffie f. hood.

cūg(e)le, cūhle, cūle f. (monk's) hood, cowl [lLt. cuculla].

culfre, culfer f. pigeon, dove.

culmille f. small centaury. Cp. curmelle.

culp|e (f.) fault [Lt. culpa].

~ian humble oneself, cringe.

culter (m.) dagger ; coulter (of plough) [Lt. culter].

cum-mǣse f. once a bird Gl.

cum|an 4 prt. cwōm, cōm, ptc. ~en, cy- come — w. inf. cōm gān came (walking), cōm grētan came to greet ; ~ ūp land ; hwǣr cōm middangeardes gestrēon what has become of . . ? ; go ‖ happen, come upon one — ~ forþ come off, be carried out ; result : hit cōm to þām þæt indc. ‖ come to oneself, recover intr.

cum|a m. stranger ; guest — ~ena būr guest-chamber, spare-room. ~ena hūs, inn, wīcung hostel, inn.

~feorm f. entertainment of strangers.

~līþe hospitable.

~līþian show hospitality.

~līþnes f. hospitality.

cumb m. valley [Celtic].

cumb m. a liquid measure.

cumbol†, cumbor n. banner, sign.

~gebrec n. crash of banners, battle.

~haga m. phalanx.

~hete m. war.

~gehnāst n. crash of banners, battle.

~wiga m. warrior.

cumbor = cumbol banner.

cumendre f. woman living in monastery, priest's housekeeper [lLt. commater].

cuml, cumul, cumbl n. swelling (of wound).

cumpæder m. godfather [Lt. compater].

cuneglæsse f. hound's-tongue (a plant) [Lt. cynoglossos].

cūnelle f. thyme.

cunn|ian w g. or a. explore, search ; try, test, tempt ; experience.

~ere m. tempter.

~ung f. trial, testing.

cuopel boat, ship *IN*.

cuppe *f.* cup.

curmelle, -ealle, -ille *f.* centaury (a plant). *Cp.* culmille.

curon *prt. pl.* of cēosan.

curs curse *L.*

~ian curse *vL.*

~ung *f.* cursing.

cursumbor *IN*. incense.

cūsc chaste, modest, virtuous.

cūscote *f.* wood-pigeon, ring-dove.

cuter (*m.*) resin.

cūþ known; certain; manifest; clear; well known, famous; familiar, intimate.

~a *m.* acquaintance, friend, relative.

~e *av.* clearly.

~ian be known.

~lǣcan be friendly, make alliance.

~(e)lic known, certain.

~līce *av.* certainly, clearly; familiarly, kindly.

~nama *m.* surname.

~nes *f.* knowledge.

cwac|ian quake, tremble, chatter (*of* teeth).

~ung *f.* quaking.

cwalu *f.* killing, violent death, destruction [cwelan].

cwānian lament *tr. and abs.*

cwatern the number four (in dice) [*Lt.* quaternus].

cwēad *n.* dung, excrement.

cwealm, cwelm, y *m.* killing, murder; death; mortality; pestilence, plague; pain, torment [cwelan].

ge~bǣran, -cwelm- torture.

~bǣre deadly; bloodthirsty.

~bǣrnes *f.* destruction, persecution; mortality.

~bealo† *n.* deadly evil.

~cuma† *m.* deadly guest.

~drēor† *n.* blood of slaughter.

ge~full*, -cwylm- pernicious.

~nes *f.* torment, pain.

~stede *m.* death-place, arena.

~stōw *f.* place of execution.

~þrēa *f.* deadly affliction.

cweartern *n.* prison.

~lic of a prison.

cwecc|an, *prt.* cwe(a)hte *tr.* shake (head), brandish (weapon) [cwacian].

~ung *f.* shaking.

cwece-sand *m.* quicksand Gl.

gecwed *n.* declaration [cweþan].

~fæsten *f.* appointed fast.

gecwed|rǣden *f.* agreement, conspiracy.

~stōw *f.* appointed place, place of meeting.

cweddian = cwiddian.

cweden *ptc.* of cweþan.

cwedol eloquent Gl. [cweþan].

cwelan 4 die.

cwell|an, *prt.* cwealde kill [cwelan].

~end, ~ere, cwelre *m.* killer, persecutor, executioner.

cwēm|an, oe *wd.* please; comply.

~ing *f.* pleasing, satisfaction.

ge~(ed)lic pleasant.

~nes, ge~ednes *f.* satisfaction, pleasing.

gecwēm|e, cwēme agreeable, acceptable, convenient.

~līce *av.* agreeably, acceptably.

cwēn, oe *f.* queen; wife.

cwen|e *f.* woman, female serf; prostitute.

cwenlic†, *or* ē, *once* feminine *or* queenly (?).

cweodu = cudu.

cweorn, ~e, cwyrn, *d.* ~a *f.* (hand) mill.

~bill *n.* chisel.

~stān *m.* millstone.

~tēþ *mpl.* grinders, molars.

cweþan 5 say, speak *w. a. of thing* (word), †wi. (wordum), tō *of person*; *w.* direct narration, *w.* subj. († *omission of* þæt), *more rarely w. indc.*; †*impers.*: be þǣm ilcan se sealmscop cwæþ: . . cwæþ tō him þæt hē wǣre . . cweþaþ hē sīe . . þæt godspell cwiþ þæt R. beweþọ . . | mention: þā þing þe wē ǣr bufon cwǣdon. swā hit on bōcum cwiþ. cweþaþ þæt hit sīæ . . | call, name it | ~ on hine assign to him | ~ ongēan *a.* raise objections to || name, call, account, consider: on þǣre stōwe þe is gecweden Crecganford. þā sind gecwedene þā heardestan menn. baþu þe wǣron hālwende gecwedene || proclaim, summon (meeting) || determine, resolve: cwæþ on his heortan þæt hē wolde . . cwǣdon betweox him þæt hī woldon . . II. cwist þū, cweþe gē *interr. av., translating Lt.* numquid.

gecweþan 5 speak, utter: hē word ne mihte ~ | proclaim, summon, order: gecwæþ ānwīg wiþ hine = challenged him to . . gecwæþ tō gefeohte *abs.*, ~ hine ūtlah | agree, resolve *w. sbj., esp.* wolde: gecwǣdon þæt him lēofre wǣre þæt . ., gecwǣdon þæt hīe wolden . .

cwic, cwuc, cwicu, cucu (*also neut. and def.*: cucu nēat, sēo cucu) living, alive.

~ǣht *f.* live stock, cattle.

~bēam *m.* aspen.

~bēam-rind *f.* aspen-bark.

~fȳr *n.* sulphur.

~hrērende moving alive, living.

~līce *av.* in a living manner, vigorously.

~lifigende† living, alive.

~seolfor *n.* mercury.

~sūsl *n., f.* hell-torment.

~sūslen of hell.

~trēow *n.* aspen, white poplar.

cwic|ian, c(w)ucian *intr.* come to life, revive || *tr.* bring to life.

ge~ung *f.* coming to life again.

cwice *f.* couch-grass.

cwidd|ian, cwy- speak *wa., w.* be.

~ung *f.* saying, report.

cwide *m.* what is said, expression, statement; proverb, saying; proposal; judgement, verdict; decree, enactment; discourse, essay, sermon; will, testament [cweþan].

~bōc, cwid- *f.* book of proverbs.

~giedd† *n.* song.

~lēas speechless; intestate.

cwidele, y *f.* inflamed swelling, boil.

cwidu = cudu.

cwield *fmn.* destruction; death; pestilence [cwelan].

~bǣre destructive, deadly; pestilential.

~bǣrlīce *av.* pestiferously.

~eflōd *m.* deluge.

~eht diseased (body).

~full destructive.

~rōf† destructive, savage (*of* wolves).

~seten *f.* beginning of night.

~tīd *f.* evening.

cwield - rede *, cwyldhreþe, cwealdæræde *f.* bat (animal).

cwielmian*, y *intr.* suffer (torment).

cwielman kill, torment, oppress [cwealm].

cwięlm|ing *f.* affliction, cross.
~nes, ea *f.* torment.
cwiesan*, y *tr.* bruise, dash against, squeeze.
cwiferlíce *av.* zealously.
cwinod wasted (with love).
cwíp|an lament *tr. and intr.*
~nes *f.* lamentation.
~ung *f.* complaint.
cwiþa, cwiþ *m.* womb.
cwōm *prt. of* cuman.
cwuc = cwic.
cwudu = cudu.
cȳcen, i *n.* chicken.
cȳ(e), *see* cū.
cycene *f.* kitchen [*Lt.* coquina].
cycgel (*m.*) dart.
cȳdde = cȳpde.
cȳf, ~e *f.* tub, vessel.
cyl(e)n *f.* kiln, oven.
cyleþenie = celeþonie.
cylle *m.*, cyll(e) *f.* leather bottle, flagon, vessel [*Lt.* culeus].
cyl|u, ~ew speckled Gl.
cym- = cum-.
cym|e *m., pl.* cyme, ~as coming, advent.
cȳm|e †, ȳ†, ~lic† beautiful, splendid.
~líce *av.* beautifully.
cymed *n.* wall-germander (a plant).
cymen *m.* cummin [*Lt.* cuminum].
cynce *f.* artichoke.
gecynd, cynd *fn.* kind, species; nature, quality, manner; gender; origin, generation; offspring; genitals.
~bōc *f.* Genesis.
~lim *n.* womb; *in pl.* genitals.
gecynd|e, cynde, (ge)cyndlic innate, natural, suitable.
~elíce *av.* naturally.
~nes *f.* nation.
cyne- royal; *in L. sometimes made into* cyning-.
~beald*, cyningb-† nobly brave, noble.
~bearn† *n.* royal child.
~boren of royal birth.
~bōt *f.* king's compensation.
~botl *n.* palace.
~cynn *n.* royal line, royal family.

cyne|dōm, cyning- *m.* royal power, kingdom, empire.
~gięld *n.* king's compensation.
~gięrd, e(a) *f.* sceptre.
~gięrela, cyningg- *m.* royal robe.
~gōd† excellent, noble.
~gold† *n.* crown.
~hād *m.* royal dignity.
~hām *m.* royal manor.
~helm *m.* crown, diadem.
~helmian crown.
~hlāford *m.* sovereign, liege lord.
~lic royal | suitable = cynnlic.
~líce *av.* royally.
~lícnes *f.* kingliness, kingly bearing.
~ríce *n.* royal authority, kingdom.
~riht *n.* royal prerogative.
~rōf† noble, illustrious.
~scipe *m.* royalty.
~setl *n.* throne; capital.
~stōl *m.* throne; capital.
~strǣt *f.* high road.
~þrymm† *m.* royal host; majesty.
~wǣden*, -pen of royal purple.
~gewǣdu *npl.* royal robes.
~wierþe very worthy *or* excellent.
~wíse *f.* kingdom, state.
~wiþþe *f.* diadem.
~word† *n.* fitting word. *Cp.* ~líc.
cyng = cyning.
cyning, -ig, cyneg-, cyng, i *m.* king. ~es feorm *f.* obligation to entertain the king. ~es tūn *m.* royal residence. ~es wyrt marjoram.
cyning- *L.* = cyne-.
~feorm = ~es feorm.
~gereord *n.* royal banquet.
cyninge *once f.* queen.
cyn|n I. *n.* kind, species, variety; race, progeny; sex, (grammatical) gender. II. *aj.* proper, suitable.
~lic, cynelic proper, suitable; reasonable, right.
~líce *av.* suitably.
~ręc(c)enes *f.* genealogy.
cynnan = cęnnan.
cynren, -yn *n.* kind, species; family, kin, generation; progeny [cynn, ryne].
cynsian *once* be eager *or* agitated (*of the mind*).
cypera *m.* spawning salmon.

cyp(e)ren of copper [copor].
cypresse *f.* cypress [*Lt.*].
cypsan = cyspan.
cyre *m.* choice, free-will [cěosan].
~āþ *m.* select oath.
~líf *n.* choice of (way of) life.
cyren *f.* churn.
cyrnan churn.
cyrf (*m.*) cutting [ceorfan].
cyrfel (*m.*) peg.
cyrfette, -ætte *f.*, -æt gourd [*Lt.* cucurbita].
cyrfille = cerfille.
cyrnel *mn.* kernel, seed, pip; pimple, hard swelling [corn].
cyrs- = cires- cherry.
cyrstel- = cristel-.
cyrtel *m.* coat, cloak.
cyrten beautiful, elegant; smart, intelligent [*Lt.* cohors].
~lǣcan make elegant.
(ge)~líce *av.* elegantly, neatly, perfectly, well.
~nes *f.* elegance.
cyspan, cypsan fetter [cosp].
cyssan kiss [coss].
cyst *f.* choice; what is choicest of its kind, the best, ideal *wg.*; goodness, excellence; virtue; munificence [cěosan].
~ig liberal, bountiful; morally good.
~ignes *f.* bounty; goodness.
~lēas reprobate.
~líc munificent.
~(e)líce *av.* bountifully.
cystan spend *vL.*
cyt-wer *m.* weir for catching fish.
cȳta *m.* kite, bittern.
cyte, e *f.* cottage, chamber, cell [cot].
cȳþ|an *prt.* cȳpde, *L.* cȳdde *wda.* make known, announce, proclaim, reveal; testify (with oath); prove; perform (miracle) [cūþ].
~ere *m.* witness; martyr.
(ge)~nes *f.* testimony; (Old and New) Testament.
gecȳþig knowing *lN.*
cȳþling *m.* relation *lN.*
gecȳþþ *f.* native country.
cȳþþ(o) *f.* knowledge; acquaintance; relationship; friendship; native country.

D.

dá *f.* doe.

dǽd *f.* action; deed, exploit; event.

~bana *m.* perpetrator of homicide, murderer.

~bēta *m.* penitent.

~bētan make amends, give satisfaction, be penitent.

~bētnis, ō *f.* penitence.

~bōt *f.* making amends, penance, repentance.

~cēne† bold in deeds.

~fram† strenuous.

~fruma† *m.* performer of exploits, hero; worker, toiler; perpetrator (of crime).

~hata† *m.* active hater, persecutor.

~hwæt† prompt in deeds.

~lēan† *n.* recompense.

~lic active (verb).

~rōf† valiant.

~scua† *m. for* dēaþ- (?).

~weorc† *n.* great deed, work.

dǽde = dyde.

gedǽftan, dǽftan make smooth; put in order, arrange.

gedǽft|e gentle, meek [gedafen].

~(e)līce *av.* seasonably, fitly.

dæg *m., gpl.* dag(en)a day — ~es, on ~e by day. (tō) ānes ~es in a single day. þȳ ~e, þȳ ~es, on þām ~e on that day. ǽlce ~e every day. tō ~ to-day | life, life-fime — on his ~e. ofer minne ~, æfter mīnum ~e. his ~ *av.* during his life. | *the Runic letter* d. | ~es ēage *n.* daisy.

~candel(1)† *f.* sun.

~fæsten *n.* a day's fast.

~feorm *f.* a day's provisions.

~hlūttre† *av.* with the clearness of day.

~hwām *av.* daily.

~hwāmlic, -o- daily.

~hwāmlīce *av.* daily.

~hwīl† *f.* period of a day; *pl.* period of life.

~lang† lasting one day.

~langes *av.* during one day.

dæg|lic daily.

~mǽl *n.* time-piece, dial.

~mǽl-scēawere *m.* horoscope (!).

~mete *m.* daily food.

dæg-red *n.* dawn.

~lic of the dawn.

~sang *m* matins.

~wōma† *m.* dawn.

dæg|rīm† *n.* number of days.

~rima *m.* dawn.

~sang *m.* daily service.

~sciéld† *m.* screen by day.

~steorra *m.* day-star.

~tīd *f.* day-time — ~tīdum by day; time.

~tīma *m.* day-time, day.

~wæcce *f.* day-watch.

~weard *m.* day-watchman.

~(e)weorc† *n.* day's work; day-time.

~weorþung *f.* commemoration.

~wine a day's pay.

~wist *f.* a day's food.

~wōma† *m.* dawn.

dǽge *f.* bread-maker [dāg].

dægþerlic daily: on þisum ~an dæge on this very day [dæg].

dægþern I. *f.* a day's space. **II.** daily.

dæl *n.* valley; gulf, abyss. *Cp.* dell.

dǽl *m.* part, quarter (of globe); fraction; portion, share; part of speech, word | quantity — gōd ~, micel ~ much. ~ wintra many years. be ǽnigum ~e at all. sume ~e, be sumum ~e to some extent, partly. cȳþan be ~e make one-sided statement [gedāl].

~lēas portionless, deficient.

~mǽlum *av.* piecemeal.

~nimend *m.* participator *wg.*; participle (in grammar).

~nimendnes *f.* participation.

~nimung *f.* share-taking, share.

~numol* share-taking, participating.

~numolnes *f.* participation.

dǽlan divide, share — †hilde ~,

fight; tear, rend (?); give away, spend; *wda.* distribute; get as one's share, get, gain.

gedǽledlīce *av.* separately.

dǽl|end *m.* divider, distributor.

~ere *m.* distributor, steward; giver.

dærst|e *f., lN.* dǽrst, ea leaven; *pl.* dregs, lees.

~ig, drǽstig dreggy.

ge-an leaven.

gedafen I. suitable, fitting; **II.** *n.* due, right, what is fitting.

gedafn|ian, dafnian, -dafen-, æ *wd., gen. impers.* be fitting *or* becoming.

~igendlic suitable, proper.

~igendlīce *av.* suitably.

~lic, -daflic fitting, proper, right.

~līce *av.* fitly, rightly.

~licnes *f.* fitness, propriety; opportunity.

dāg (*m.*) dough; mass of metal.

dag|ian dawn, become day; be day [dæg].

~ung *f.* dawn, daybreak.

gedāl *n.* separation, division, distribution — līces ~ death [dǽl].

~land, -dǣl- *n.* common land.

dalc, o *m.* brooch, bracelet.

dalmatice *f.* dalmatic (vestment) [*Lt.*].

darian once lurk, be hidden.

daroþ†, ea, -eþ *m.* javelin.

~hæbbende javelin-bearing.

~lācende javelin-brandishing.

~sceaft *m.* javelin-shaft.

daru *f.* hurt (physical); damage; harm, injury [derian].

datārum *m. indecl.* date — on þām ~ idus Aprilis [*Lt.*].

dēacon = diacon.

dēad dead | congealed (blood); sluggish (stream) | torpid, dull (life).

~bǽre, dēaþ-,~bǽrlic, ~berende deadly.

~bǽrnes *f.* mortality.

~boren dead-born.

dēad|hrægl *n*. shroud.

~lic, dēaþlic subject to death, mortal (man); deadly, sanguinary (victory).

~lice *av.* deadly.

~licnes *f.* being subject to death, mortality; mortal frailty.

~spryng *m.* ulcer, carbuncle.

~wielle barren.

dēaf deaf; ~ corn empty ear of corn.

dēafo *f.* deafness.

dēag *f.* dye; colour (of cloth).

~ian dye.

~ung *f.* dyeing; colour (of cloth).

~wyrmede = dēaw- gouty.

dēaggede = *dēaw-wyrmede gouty.

dēagol = dīegle.

dēah, *pl.* dugon, *prt.* dohte *vb.* avail, be of use, be good: ne dohte hit there was no goodness (in the country); *wdg.* be equivalent to, able to procure | be vigorous: hrīþer dugunde | be (a) worthy (man), be virtuous, be liberal.

deall† proud (of), exulting (in), resplendent (with) *wi.*

dearep = daroþ.

dearf bold *IN.*

dearnunga, dy-, -inga *av.* secretly, privately, clandestinely.

dearr *vb.*, *sbj.* dyrre, u, *pl.* durron, *prt.* dorste dare, venture.

dearste = dærste.

dēaþ *m.*, *once f.* death.

~bære = dēad-.

~bēacnigende boding death.

~bēam† *m.* tree of death.

~bedd† *n.* grave.

~berende† deadly, fatal.

~cwalu† *f.* deadly pain; deadly destruction, fatal infliction.

~cwealm† *m.* slaughter.

~cwielman kill.

~dæg† *m.* day of death.

~gedāl† *n.* separation of body and soul in death.

~denu† *f.* valley of death.

~drepe† *m.* death-stroke.

~fǣge† fated to die.

~godas *mpl.* manes.

~lic = dēadlic.

~līeg† *m.* deadly flame.

~mægen† *n.* death-bringing troop.

~rǣs† *m.* sudden death.

dēaþ|rēaf *n.* spoils Gl.

~reced† *n.* sepulchre.

~rēow† deadly cruel, savage.

~scua, scufa *m.* shadow of death; deadly phantom.

~scyld *f.* capital crime, deadly sin.

~scyldig guilty of a capital crime.

~sele† *m.* hall of death.

~slege† *m.* death-blow, deadly stroke.

~spere† *n.* deadly spear.

~stede† *m.* death-place.

~þegnunga, -þēn- *fpl.* funeral service, funeral.

~wǣge† *n.* deadly cup.

~wang† *m.* plain of death.

~wērig† dead.

~wīc† *n.* death-dwelling.

~wyrda *fpl.* fates Gl.

gedēaþian kill *IN.*

dēaw *mn.* dew.

~drēos*, iaþ fall of dew.

~ig, dewy.

~ig-feþer†, -a dewy-winged.

dēaw-wyrm *m.* ring-worm.

~ede*, dēagw-, dēaggede gouty.

dēcan, é smear, plaster.

declīn|ian* decline (in grammar) [*Lt.*].

~igendlic declinable.

~ung *f.* declension.

gedēf|e, oe I. fitting, seemly; gentle, meek. II. *av.* fittingly [gedafen].

~(e)lic, dēflic fitting.

~līce *av.* fitly, becomingly.

~nes *f.* gentleness.

dēgolfull [ē = ēa *or* īe]† *once* mysterious.

dehter *d.* of dohtor.

gedelf *n.* digging; trench.

delf|an 3 dig, burrow.

~ere *m.* digger.

~ing *f.* digging.

~īsen *n.* spade.

delfīn *m.* dolphin [*Lt.* delphinus].

dell (*n.*) valley (?) Ct. *Perhaps weak (unaccented) form of* dæl. *Cp.* pull *weak form of* pōl.

delu *f.* nipple (of breast).

dēm|an, oe judge, decree, assign *gen. w. d. of person*: ēow biþ ge~ed, ~ unryht; *wda.* ~ him selfum wīte | condemn *w. a.* and tō: ~ hine tō dēaþe | consider, estimate; glorify, praise.

~end†, ~ere *m.* judge.

dēma, oe *m.* judge [dōm].

demm *m.* damage, injury, loss, misfortune.

gedēn = gedōn.

Den|e *pl.*, *g.* ~igea, ~a Danes, Scandinavians. ~a lagu Danish law; district under Danish law, East-Anglia, &c. ~a-mearc, ~em- *f.* Denmark.

~isc Danish.

den|n *n.* den.

~bǣre swine-pasture.

den|u *f.* valley.

~eland *n.* valley Gl.

dēofol, -el *n.* devil, demon [*Lt.* diabolus].

~cræft *m.* art of the devil; witchcraft.

~cund like the devil, diabolical.

~dǣd† *f.* diabolical deed.

~gield *n.* idol; idolatry.

~gielda *m.* idolater.

~gield-hūs *n.* heathen temple.

~lic, dēoflic devilish, of the devil.

~scin *n.* diabolical phantom.

~sēoc possessed with a devil.

~sēocnes *f.* demoniacal possession.

~wītga† *m.* wizard.

dēogol = dīegle.

dēop I. deep; profound (learning, mystery), awful, terrible, excessive, great (crime), high (price). II. *n.* deep place, depth, abyss.

~e *av.* deep (wounded), deeply (consider), thoroughly, seriously.

~hycgende†, ~hygdig†, -hȳd- deeply meditating, thoughtful.

~lic profound, thorough.

~līce *av.* profoundly.

~nes *f.* deepness; deep place, depth, abyss, gulf; mystery.

~pancol thoughtful.

dēor *n.* (wild) animal; deer, reindeer.

~cynn *n.* species of animal.

~en of a wild animal.

~fald *m.* deer-park.

~fellen made of hides.

~friþ *m.* preservation of deer.

~hege *m.* deer-fence, park-fence.

~nett *n.* hunting-net.

~tūn *m.* park.

dēor† brave, bold; severe, full of hardship; fierce.

~lic brave (deed).

~mōd brave.

dēoran = dīeran.

[41]

deorc, y dark; obscure; gloomy, sad; terrible; evil, wicked; unintelligent, ignorant (mind).
~e av. darkly, sadly.
~egrǽg dark grey.
~full dark.
~līce av. gloomily.
~nes f. darkness.
~ung f. twilight.
dēor|e = dīere beloved.
~boren of noble birth.
~līce av. preciously.
~ling = dierling.
dēor-wierþ|e, -weorþ, -wurþ, dīer- valuable, precious.
~līce av. dearly : ~ healdan.
~nes f. precious thing, treasure.
gedeorf, deorf n. labour, effort; hardship.
~lēas fruitless (?) Gl.
~nes f. tribulation.
~sum vL. grievous.
(ge)deorfan 3 labour | perish.
depp(ett)an = dy-.
der|ian wd. injure, hurt, annoy [daru].
~igendlic hurtful, noxious.
~ung f. injuring.
Dēre pl. inhabitants of Deira.
derodin, dy- (m.) scarlet dye [Lt. teredinem].
dēp, see dōn.
diacon, ea, eo m. deacon [Lt. diaconus].
~hād m. deaconship.
~rocc m. dalmatic.
~þegnung, -þēn- f. ministration of a deacon, deaconship.
dīc, î m. wall of earth, embankment, rampart, stone wall | mf. ditch, moat.
~sceard n. gap in stone wall.
dīc|ian dig, make embankment.
~ere m. digger.
~ung f. digging a ditch.
dīedan put to death [dēad].
dīef|an*, y dip [dūfan].
~ing f. immersion.
gedīegan carry out with safety, survive (danger, illness), abs. fēore ~ [dēah].
dīegel|līce, -elīce, -ol-, ēa, ēo av. secretly.
~nes f. secrecy; secret, mystery; privacy.
dīegl|e, dīhle, dēagol, dēogol, dȳgel, dȳgol, î, A. dēgol I.

secret, hidden; mysterious, profound; doubtful, unknown. II. n. secret, mystery; secret place, grave. on ~e, on ~um in secret. III. av. secretly, stealthily.
dīegl(i)an hide.
dīepan*, ē, ȳ tr. dip, baptize; (deepen), increase (oath) [dēop].
dīepe, dīep(o) f. depth; the deep, sea; deep place (in river); abyss, gulf [dēop].
dīeran, ēo esteem, praise, extol.
dīer|e, dēore I. beloved; precious, costly; respected, glorious, noble. II. av. at great cost. See dēore.
~ling, ēo m. favourite.
dīerfan*, y injure [deorfan].
dīernan conceal; keep secret; rfl. conceal one's identity.
dīern|e hidden, secret — ~ ge-ligre adultery; deceitful, wicked [dearnunga].
~hǽmend m. fornicator.
~licgan fornicate.
~geliger f., ~geligerscipe m. adultery.
~gewrit n. apocryphal book.
dīersian*, y glorify, praise [dīere].
diht n. direction, command; arranging, ordering; administration, office, action, conduct; purpose, intention.
~fæstendæg m. appointed fast.
diht|an, diht(n)ian compose, write || wd. direct, command; arrange [Lt. dictare].
~ere, dihtnere m. informant, expositor.
~ung f. ordering.
gediht n. composition, literary work.
dile, y m. dill.
dīl(e)gian, ȳ erase (writing); destroy, blot out.
dilignes f. destruction.
dim|m dark; unknown, obscure (disease); wicked (deed).
~hīw n. of dark colour.
~hof n. hiding-place.
~hūs n. prison.
~lic dark; secret.
~nes f. darkness; mist; dimness (of eye-sight).
~scua m. darkness (of mind).
dīner-, dign- m. a coin, piece of money [Lt. denarius].
ding = dyng, d. of dung.

dinge†, dinne (n.) (?).
dirige f. dirge, 'vigilia' Gl. [Lt. dirige!].
disc m. dish, plate, bowl [Lt. discus].
~berend, ~þegn, -þēn m. dish-bearer, waiter, seneschal.
discipul m. disciple, pupil [Lt. discipulus].
~hād m. pupilage.
disme (?) f. tansy (a plant).
distæf (m.) distaff.
dōn; dōan, ic dōm A.; (hē) dēþ, oe; prt. dyde, e, ǽt; ptc. gedōn, gedēn, oe vb. do, perform, act : ~yfel; ~swā; ~ælmessan; gif hē elles dēþ; siþþan þis ge~ wæs when this had happened; hwæt dō ic? what shall I do? or what will become of me? | wda. do good or evil to .. | w. rfl. d.: dyde ic mē tō gamene ganetes hlēoþor I made the gull's song a solace to me | ne dēþ hē nān þing tō gōde will do no good (to himself or others) | ~ tō nāhte annul. hwæt dō we ymbe hine? do with him | make (statues) || half auxiliary : se mōna dēþ ǽgþer, ge wyxþ ge wanaþ | to take place of verb: Crīst wēox swāswā ōþre cild dōþ. þā getīmode him swāswā dēþ fisce || cause : ~ hine tō cyninge. dyde hine lǽssan þonne hē wæs made him out to be .. tō witanne. dyde hine forlǽtan .. dēþ þæt fȳr cymþ. || put, give, &c., also met.: þā handa dōþ þone bīgleofan þām mūþe. gen. w. av. or prp.: fur-þor ~, ~ tō hīerran hāde promote. ~tō ānum unite. ~six dagas oþ þām getele subtract | w. advs.: ~on, of put on, off (clothes). ~ þanon take away. ~ūp put ashore: þā dyde hē on his byrnan.
gedōn vb. do, act, make; cause; put, &c.: hē gedyde þæt nān cyning ǽr gedōn ne dorste. hē hīe tō hīersumnesse gedyde reduced to subjection. hē gedyde dumbum menn sprǽce. hē gedyde Crēcas on his geweald conquered | w.avs.: ~forþ manifest. ~ūp exhume || encamp,

halt *w.* æt, on ; cast anchor (in-nan Sæferne-mūþan).

docce *f.* dock (a plant).   sēo fealwe ~ . sēo rēade ~ . sēo scearpe ~ sorrel. ~ sēo þe swimman wile water-lily.

dōere *m.* doer, agent.

gedof *n.* fury, madness.

dof|ian rage.

(ge)~**ung** *f.* frenzy, madness.

dogian (?) once† endure.

dogga*, cg *m.* dog.

dōgor(†), *d.*, *i.* ~, dog(o)re *n.* day — uferan ~e at some future time [dæg].

~**rīm**, ~gerīm *n.* number of days, term of life.

dohte, *prt. of* dēah.

dohtig *L.* (man) of worth ; doughty, vigorous ; good (man), respectable [*from* dyhtig *by infl. of* dohte].

dohtor, *d.* dohtor, dehter, oe *f.* daughter.

dohx = dosc dark.

dol I. foolish, presumptuous ; dull-witted, stupid.   **II.** *n.* folly, conceit.

~**gielp** *n.* foolish pride, brag.

~**lic** foolish ; rash.

~**lice** *av.* foolishly ; rashly.

~**scapa**† *m.* rash depredator.

~**scipe** *m.* folly.

~**spræc** *f.* foolish speech, loquacity.

~**willen**† **I.** rash. **II.** *n.* rashness.

~**wīte**† *n.* Or two words (?).

dolc = dalc.

dolg *n.* wound, scar.

~**benn**† *f.* wound.

~**bōt** *f.* compensation for wound.

~**drenc** *m.* wound-potion.

~**ian** wound.

~**rūne** *f.* pellitory.

~**sealf** *f.* wound-salve, poultice, wound.

~**slege**† *m.* wound, stroke.

~**swaþu** *f.* scar.

~**wund**† wounded.

dōm *m.* (free) will, option, choice : bēad him hira ägenne ~ fēos ; opinion ; judgement, judicial sentence, decree, law, court of law, meeting | authority, power, dominion ; magnificence ; reputation, glory | interpretation (of dream) || ~es dæg *m.* day of judgement, doomsday.

~**bōc** *f.* law-book, code.

dōm|dæg *m.* doomsday, last day.

~**ēadig** glorious.

~**ern** *n.* judgement-hall, law-court.

~**fæst**† just ; glorious.

~**fæstnes** *f.* justice.

~**georn**† ambitious, noble, righteous.

~**hūs** *n.* tribunal, law-court.

~**hwæt**† ambitious.

~**isc** of the day of judgement.

~**lēas**† inglorious ; powerless.

~**lic** judicial, canonical ; glorious.

~**lice**† *av.* judicially ; gloriously.

~**setl** *n.* judgement-seat, tribunal.

~**settend** *m.* lawyer, judge.

~**stōw** *f.* tribunal.

~**weorþung** *f.* glory, honour.

dōm|ian glorify.

~**ere** (?) *m.* judge = dēmere.

domne lord [*Lt.* dominus].

dop|ened *f.*, ~**fugol** *m.* waterfowl.

doppettan dive, plunge (*of waterbirds*).

dor *n.* door, gate ; pass [duru].

dora *m.* humble-bee.

dorste *prt. of* dearr.

dosc*, dohx dark-coloured.

dott *m.* speck, head (of boil).

dox = dosc dark.

draca *m.* dragon.   ~an blōd dragon's blood (a juice) [*Lt.* draco].

dracent(s)e, -conze *f.* dragon-wort [*Lt.* dracontea].

-**drædan** 1 b *prt.* -drēd, *A.* -drēord, *in* on~ dread.

dræf = drāf.

dræf|an, oe drive — ūt~ expel [drīfan].

~**end** *m.* hunter.

gedræg = gedrēog.

dræg|e *f.* drag-net [dragan].

~**nett** *n.* drag-net.

dræstig = dærstig.

drāf, æ *f.* drove ; herd ; crowd, band [drīfan].

dragan 2 drag, draw || *intr.* go.

drān, æ *f.* drone.

gedrēag† *n.* crowd, troop, tumult, lamentation.

dreahnian, dreh- strain ; strain out (a gnat).

drēam *m.* joy, bliss ; mirth, revelry ; musical sound, melody ; musical instrument.

~**cræft** *m.* music.

drēam|ere *m.* musician.

~**hæbbende**†, ~**healdende**† joyful, blessed.

~**lēas**† joyless.

~**lic** pleasant ; musical.

~**nes** *f.* singing.

~**swinsung** *f.* harmony.

drecc|an trouble, annoy ; vex ; afflict, torment.

~**ing** *f.* tribulation.

(ge)~**ednes**, -dreced- *f.* affliction.

drēf|an, oe make turbid, stir up (water), ruffle | trouble (in mind), afflict [drōf].

~**ere***, drēfre *m.* disturber.

ge~**edlic** thick (darkness).

(ge)~**ednes**, gedrēfnes *f.* tribulation, disturbance, grief, scandal.

~**ing** *f.* disturbance.

drefel- rheumy, snivelling (person) (?) Ct.

drefliende once suffering from rheum Gl.

drehnian = dreahnian.

drenc *m.* what is drunk, drink — wīnes ~ wine ; (medical) drink, draught | drowning [drincan].

~**cuppe** *f.* drinking-cup.

~**fæt** *n.* cup.

~(e)**flōd**† *m.* deluge.

~**horn** *m.* drinking-horn.

~**hūs** *n.* drinking-house.

drencan give to drink ; ply (with liquor), intoxicate | submerge, drown.

dreng *m.* (Scandinavian) warrior *L.* [*Scand.*].

gedrēog I. *n.* what is useful or suitable, keeping (shoes) in good condition — tō ~e gān privy. **II.** *aj.* sober.

~**læcan** put in order (temple), attend to, manage (farm).

~**lice** *av.* suitably, carefully ; drēohlīce *L.* humbly.

drēogan 7 do (with effort), perform, carry out (will of God), wage (war), commit (crime), lead (a certain life), enjoy ; suffer, endure || *intr.* be employed, be busy, strive.

drēop|an 7 *intr.* drop, drip.

~**ian**, *A.* ēa *intr.* drop, drip.

~**ung** *f.* dropping.

drēor† (*m.*) blood [drēosan].

~**fāg** blood-stained.

~**lic** *see* ~iglic.

drēor-sele *m.* dreary hall.

drēor|ian*.

~ung *f.* falling.

-drēord *A. prt. of* -drǽdan dread.

drēorig† blood-stained, gory | sad, sorrowful.

~ferþ† sad.

~hlēor† sad of countenance.

~lic, drēor(i)lic sanguinary, cruel ; sad, mournful.

~līce *av.* sadly.

~mōd† sad.

~nes *f.* sadness.

drēorgian fall, crumble away.

drēos|an, *ptc.* droren 7 fall ; come to ruin, perish—*prs. ptc.* ~ende perishable.

gedrep *n.* stroke (of darts).

drep|an 5 strike, hit (with weapon) —*ptc.* ~en struck down (by disease) ; kill.

drepe, y *m.* (death) stroke, blow.

gedrīehþ *f.* sobriety, moderation [gedrēog].

drīem|an rejoice ; play on a musical instrument, make melody — *ptc.* ge~ed harmonious.

~ing *f.* susurrus.

(ge)drīeme melodious, cheerful [drēam].

drīepan let drop, pour a drop ; moisten [drēopan].

drif *f.*, ge~ fever *lA.*

gedrif *n.* what is driven, regions (of air and water) ; stubble.

drīfan 6 drive ; expel ; pursue — ~ spor follow track ; do, practise, transact — ~ cēap make bargain ; ~ sprǽce carry on a lawsuit || *intr.* move with violence, dash.

gedrinc, y *n.* carousal.

drinc- = drync-.

drinc|an 3 drink — *ptc.* druncen intoxicated, flushed.

~ere *m.* drinker, drunkard.

gedrincan 3 drink up ; engulf.

drinca *m.* drink, something to drink.

drit (*n.*) dirt.

drīt|an cacare.

~ing *f.* digestion Gl.

drōf, ge~ turbid, muddy.

~lic sad, irksome.

drōfe *av.* grievously, severely.

gedrofenlic full of trouble.

droge *f. once* excrement.

---

droht (*m.*) manner of life [drēogan].

droht|ian ; ~nian *L.*, *intr.* pass life, live, dwell, continue ; behave.

~aþ, ~noþ *m.* way of life ; circumstances, condition ; dwelling, sojourn ; society, intercourse.

~(n)ung *f.* (way of) life, conduct ; circumstances, condition.

drop|ian drop *intr.*

~ung *f.* dropping.

drop|a *m.* drop ; a disease.

~fāg spotted.

~mǽlum *av.* drop by drop.

droppett|an, -etan, -ian *intr.* drop, drip.

~ung *f.* dropping.

droren *ptc. of* drēosan.

drōs, ~na *m.*, ~ne *f.* dregs ; dirt ; ear-wax.

drūg|ian, drūw- *intr.* become dry, dry up [drȳge].

~aþ, ~oþ *m.* dryness ; drought ; dry ground (!).

~ung *f.* drought ; dry place (!).

drunc-mennen† *n.* drunken female serf.

druncen I. intoxicated.   II. *n.* drunkenness [drincan].

~georn drunken.

~hād *m.* drunkenness *L.*

~(n)es *f.*, ~scipe *m.* intoxication.

~willen drunken.

druncn|ian become intoxicated ; be drowned.

~ing *f.* becoming intoxicated.

drūt† *f.* beloved one [*German*].

drūsian become languid, sluggish (through old age).

drūwian = drūgian.

drȳ *m.* magician ; sorcery [*Celtic*].

~cræft *m.* sorcery.

~cræftig skilled in magic.

~ecge *f.* sorceress.

~lic magic.

~mann *m.* sorcerer.

gedrycned *once* afflicted.

drȳgan *tr.* dry ; wipe, wipe off.

drȳg|e I. dry.   II. *n.* dry land : on ~um [drūgian].

~nes *f.* dryness.

~scōd dry-footed.

dryht† *f.* troop (of retainers), multitude, army ; *pl.* men, mankind.

~bearn *n.* princely child.

~cwēn *f.* queen.

~dōm *m.* judgement Pr.

---

dryht|ealdor *m.* bridesman Gl.

~folc *n.* multitude ; nation.

~guma *m.* retainer ; warrior ; man.

~lēoþ *n.* noble song, hymn.

~lic lordly, noble ; of the Lord.

~līce *av.* in a lordly, divine, noble manner.

~māþm *m.* noble treasure.

~nē *m.* dead body of a warrior.

~scipe *m.* sovereignty, power ; nobility, courage, virtue.

~sele *m.* princely hall.

~sibb *f.* peace, alliance.

~gesīþ *m.* retainer, warrior.

~gestrēon *n.* noble treasure.

~wer *m.* man.

~weorþ divine.

~wuniende living among the people.

gedryht† *f.* troop, body of retainers.

~a *m.* fellow-soldier Gl.

dryhten *m.* lord, prince ; the Lord (God *or* Christ).

dryhten- *L. for* dryht-.

~bēag *m.* money paid to the king for killing a freeman.

~bealo† *n.* great evil, extreme misery.

~dōm *m.* glory, majesty.

~hold loyal.

~lic of the Lord.

~līce *av.* according to the Lord.

~weard *m.* king.

drync, drinc *m.* drinking ; drink, potion [drincan].

~(e)fæt *n.* cup.

~elēan *n.* tributary drink (!) LL.

~wērig overcome with drink.

drync|an *once* give to drink *tr.*

ge~nes *f.* immersion, baptism.

drype = drepe.

dryre *m.* falling, fall ; cessation, loss [drēosan].

dryslic terrible.

drysmian† become gloomy.

drysn|an extinguish *lN.* [drosn].

~ian vanish.

dubbian *L.* dub, knight.

dūce *f.* duck.

dūfan 7 *intr.* dive ; sink, be drowned.

dūfe-doppa *m.* pelican (!).

dugon *pl. of* dēah.

duguþ, -oþ *f.* those of mature age *coll.* (*opposed to* geoguþ the

[44]

young) ; body of retainers, retainers *coll.*, nobility *coll.*, flower
(of a nation) | army, host ; multi-
tude, nation, people ; *pl.* men,
mankind | power, rule, majesty,
glory | excellence, virtue ; good
thing, benefit, happiness ; deco-
rum, etiquette [dēah].
duguþ|ealdor *m.* president.
~giēfu *f.* gift, donation.
~līce *av.* with authority.
dulmun *m.* warship [*Lt.* dro-
munda, dromo].
dumb dumb, silent.
dūn *f.*, *locative* -dȳne (?) Ct., hill,
mountain ; down. *See* ofdūne.
~ælf, ~elfen *f.* mountain fairy.
~land *n.* hilly country.
~lendisc hilly.
~līc belonging to mountains.
~sǣte *pl.* (Welsh) mountaineers.
~scræf *n.* mountain cave.
dūne = ofdūne down.
dung* *f.*, *d.* dyng*, i† *once* prison.
dung *f.* dung, manure.
dunn dun, dark brown.
~falo tawny.
~grǣg dusky.
~ian *tr.* obscure (light of stars).
dureras *mpl.* folding doors.
durron *pl* of dearr.
dur|u, *g.* ~a *f.* door.
~(u)stod, ~stodl *n.* door-post.
~uþegn *m.* door-keeper.
~uþignen, ~eþīnen *f.* door-keeper.
~uweard, ~e- *m.* door-keeper.
dūst *n.* dust.
~drenc *m.* drink made of pounded
seeds.
~scēawung *f.* contemplation of
dust.
dūp-.
~hamor, dȳp- *m.* papyrus.
dwǣs, ge- I. dull, stupid, foolish.
II. *m.* impostor (?).

dwǣs|ian become stupid.
~līce *av.* foolishly.
~nes *f.* stupidity.
dwǣscan extinguish (fire, crime,
enmity).
dwal- = dwol-.
dwealde *prt. of* dwellan.
dwelian *tr.* lead astray ; lead into
error, wrong-doing ; deceive ; pre-
vent, thwart, afflict || *intr.* lose
the right direction, go astray ;
wander (*of* the planets).
dwellan, *prt.* dwealde lead astray,
deceive — *ptc.* gedweald man
heretic.
dweorg *m.* dwarf.
~edwos(t)le *f.* pennyroyal (a
plant).
gedwield, dwild *n.* error, heresy
[dwellan].
~æfterfolgung *f.* heresy.
~līc deceptive.
gedwimor *n.* spectre ; illusion,
delusion.
~līc illusive.
~līce *av.* illusively, without
reality.
dwīnan 6 become smaller, dwindle ;
waste away.
gedwol heretical.
dwol|ian stray ; err.
~ung *f.* insanity.
gedwol|a, dwola, dwa- *m.* error,
heresy | deceiver, heretic.
~biscop *m.* heretical bishop.
~cræft *m.* illusion, conjuring.
~god *m.* idol, false god.
~līc heretical.
~līce *av.* heretically.
~mann *m.* heretic.
~mist *m* mist of error.
~sprǣc *f.* heretical talk.
~sum erroneous.
~þing *n.* imposture, idol.
gedwolen perverse, wrong.

dwolma *m.* chaos.
dyde *prt. of* dōn.
dyd(e)r|ian delude.
~ung *f.* illusion, phantasmagoria ;
delusion, deceit.
dydrin *once* yolk (of egg).
dyge, duge *sbj. of* dēah.
dyhtig strong. *Cp.* dohtig [dēah].
dylst|a *m.* matter, pus.
~iht festering, mucous.
dyn|e *m.*, ge~ noise, loud sound.
~ian resound — gif ēaran ~ien if
there is a singing in the ears.
-dȳne, see dūn.
dyng|an* manure [dung].
~ung*, dingiung *f.* manuring.
dynge*, i, e fallow land [dung].
dȳnige *once, f.* a plant [dūn].
dynt *m.* stroke, blow ; bruise.
dyple double [*Lt.* duplex].
dypp|an, e dip ; baptize.
~ettan*, *vE.* e dip ; baptize.
gedyre *n.* door-post [duru].
dyrodin = derodin.
dyrre, see dearr.
gedyrst† *once* tribulation (?).
(ge)dyrstig bold, daring, reckless
[dearr].
~ian dare, presume.
~līce, -dyrstel- boldly.
~nes *f.* boldness.
dyrstlǣcan dare, presume.
dysi(g) I. foolish, irrational. II. *n.*
folly.
~dōm *m.* folly, ignorance.
~līc*, dys(e)līc foolish.
~līce*, dys- *av* foolishly.
~nes *f.* folly, blasphemy.
dys(i)g|ian, dysian be foolish, act
foolishly, blaspheme.
~ung *f.* foolishness.
dȳstig dusty [dūst].
dyttan shut (ears), stop (mouth).
dȳp-hamor = dūp-.

E.

ē, *see* ēa.

ēa, *g.* ēa(s), īe, ē *f.* river ; stream.
~cerse *f.* water-cress.
~docce *f.* water-dock.
~fisc *m.* river-fish.
~lād *f.* watery way, ocean.
~land *n.* island = īeg-land.
~lifer *f.* (a plant).
~lipend† *m.* sailor.
~ōfer *n.* river-bank.
~risc *f.* bulrush.
~rīp *m.* stream.
~spring *m.* spring = ǣspring.
~stæp *n.* shore, bank.
~strēam *m.* stream, water.
~wyrt *f.* burdock.
ēac *prp. wd.* in addition to, besides,
  and — ~þon *av.* also.
ēac *av.* also. and . . ~, ge . . ~ and
  . . also. ~ swelce (swelce . . ~),
  ~swā, ~swā same also. ~ hwæþre
  (hwæþre ~) nevertheless.
ēacian increase *intr.*
ēac|a *m.* increase, addition—tō ~an
  prp wd. besides ; interest (on
  money lent), usury.
ēacen (*ptc.*) increased, enlarged ;
  endowed ; strengthened, strong,
  mighty, vast, great ; pregnant.
~cræftig† mighty, great.
ēacn|ian increase *intr.* conceive,
  be pregnant ; ｜ e in child-birth.
(ge)~ung *f.* conception.
ēad† *n.* prosperity, happiness, (eternal bliss, wealth.
~fruma *m.* author of prosperity.
~giefa *m* giver of prosperity.
~giefu *f.* gift of prosperity.
~hrēþig happy, blessed, triumphant.
~lufe *f.* love.
~mōd = ēaþ-mōd humble.
~nes = ēadignes.
~wela *m.* riches ; prosperity, joy.
ēaden† (*ptc.*) granted.
ēadig prosperous, rich, happy,
  blessed, perfect.
~lic prosperous, happy ; abundant
  (harvest).

ēadig|līce *av.* happily.
~nes, ēadnes *f.* prosperity, happiness.
ēad(i)gian, -igan count fortunate ;
  bless.
eafora†, a- *m.* son, child, de-
  scendant.
eafoþ† *n.* strength, might.
ēag|e *n.* eye ; eye (of needle).
~æppel *m.* ball of the eye.
~gebyrd† *f.* nature of the eye.
~duru *f.* window.
~flēah *m.* disease of the eye,
  albugo.
~hring *m.* socket of eye.
~hyrne*, heahhyrne *m.* corner of
  the eye.
~sealf *f.* eye-salve.
~sēoung *f.* cataract.
~sīen|e visible, conspicuous — ~es
  with one's own eyes, visibly.
~þyrel *n.* window.
~wræc *m.* pain in the eyes.
~wund *f.* wound in the eye.
~wyrt *f.* eye-bright (a plant).
eago-spind = heago- cheek.
ēagor, ē (*n.*) flood, tide ; †sea.
~here† *m.* flood.
~strēam† *m.* sea.
eaht, *A.* æht *f.* council, deliberation, consulting — æht besittan†
  hold council ｜ estimation, esti-
  mated value.
eaht|ian watch over ; hold council,
  deliberate, consider — ræd(es) ~
  consult together ; discuss, mention ｜ estimate (at right value) ;
  esteem ; criticize ; praise.
ge-endlic estimable.
~ere *m.* estimator, valuer.
(ge)~ung *f.* deliberation ; estimation, valuation, esteem.
eahta eight.
~feald eightfold.
~hyrnede eight-cornered.
~tīene eighteen.
~tēoþa eighteenth.
~tig=hundeahtatig eighty.

eahta-wintre eight years old.
eahtoþa eighth.
geeahtle*, æt† *f.* esteem.
eal- *under* eall.
eal- *occ.* = æl-.
ēa-lā, ēaw- oh ! alas !
eald, *cpv.* ieldra, *spl.* ield(e)st
  old — ~ fæder grandfather ｜ *spl.*
  chief, eminent.
~gecynd *n.* original nature.
~cȳþþ(u) *f.* old country, home.
~dagas *mpl.* days of old.
~dōm *m.* (old) age, antiquity.
~(e)fæder *m.* grandfather ; ancestor.
~fēond *m.* old enemy, Satan.
~hād *m.* old age.
~hettende† *mpl.* old foes.
~hlāford *m.* hereditary lord.
~lic senile ; venerable.
~emōder *f.* grandmother.
~genēat† *m.* old companion.
~nes *f.* (old) age.
~genīþla† *m.* old enemy, Satan.
~(ge)ryht *n.* ancient right.
~seaxe *mpl.* Old Saxons.
~gesegen† *f.* old tradition.
~gesiþ† *m.* old companion.
~spell *n.* old story ; history.
~sprǣc *f.* old tradition, history.
~gestrēon† *n.* old treasure.
~geweorc† *n.* ancient work (*of the*
  earth).
~wērig† accursed of old.
~gewinn† *n.* ancient war.
~gewinna† *m.* old adversary.
~wita *m.* sage.
~wrītere *m.* historian.
~gewyrht† *n.* old desert, former
  guilt.
eald|ian grow old.
~ung *f.* (old) age.
ealdor *m.* chief, prince — hīredes ~
  head of a family, paterfamilias ;
  parent, ancestor.
~apostol *m.* chief apostle.
~biscop *m.* chief bishop ; high
  priest.
~botl *m.* king's residence.

[46]

ealdor|burg† *f.* capital, metropolis.

~dēma† *m.* chief judge, prince.

~dōm *m.* right of primogeniture, eldership; authority, dignity, rule.

~dōm-scipe *m.* office of duke.

~duguþ† *f.* chief nobility.

~frēa† *m.* chief lord.

~lic princely, chief, magnificent.

~lice *av.* excellently.

~licnes *f.* authority.

~mann *m.* duke, magistrate, chief.

~nes = **~licnes**.

~sācerd *m.* chief priest.

~scipe *m.* authority.

~stōl† *m.* seat of authority.

~þegn† *n.* chief officer.

~wīsa† *m.* chief.

ealdor† *n.* life, vitals ; eternity—(ǣfre) on ealdre ever, *w.* ne never. tō ealdre, ā(wa) tō ealdre, ǣfre tō ealdre for ever.

~bana *m.* life-destroyer.

~bealo *n.* injury to life, terrible evil.

~caru *f.* life-care, great sorrow.

~dagas *mpl.* life-days.

~gedāl *n.* separation from life, death.

~geard *m.* body.

~lang lifelong *or* eternal.

~lēas lifeless.

~legu *f.* fate ; death.

~neru *f.* preservation of life, salvation.

~gesceaft *f.* condition of life.

~gewinna *m.* mortal adversary.

ealdoþ*, vE.* aldot, aldaht trough, vessel Gl.

ealfara *once m.* camel.

ealgian defend.

ealh† *m.* temple.

~stede *m.* temple.

eall I. all. ealne weg, ealneg *av.* always. II. *av.* entirely. III. *n.* everything, all. ofer ~ everywhere : mid ~e entirely. ~es of all *w. spv.* (~es swīþost) ; entirely, quite, much : ~es tō gelōme. ~ra of all *w. spv.* : ~ra mǣst.

~beorht† all-bright.

~biernende burning all over.

~cræftig all-powerful.

~fela very much.

~felo†, æl-fæle dire (poison).

~geador *av.* all together.

eall|gearo† quite ready.

~gōd perfectly good.

~grēne† all-green.

~gylden† all of gold.

~hālig† all-holy.

~hwīt all-white.

~īren all of iron.

~īsig all-icy, very cold.

~gelēaflic believed by all, catholic.

eallencten *m.* season of Lent.

eallic catholic.

eall|mægen† *n.* all one's power, utmost effort.

~mǣst *av.* nearly all, almost.

~mihtig = æl- almighty.

~nacod quite naked.

~nīwe quite new.

~offrung *f.* holocaust.

~rūh quite rough *or* hairy.

~sealf *f.* a plant.

~seolcen quite of silk.

~tela† *av.* quite well.

~wealda†, **~wealdend** *m.* omnipotent one.

~wealdende omnipotent.

~wihta† *fpl.* all creatures.

~wundor† *n.* very wonderful thing (?).

ealling = ealneg.

eal(l)neg, ealnig, ealne weg, ealnuweg, -ning *av.* always [ealne weg].

eal(l)-swā, eall . . swā quite so, in the same way, likewise ; as.

eallunga, -inga *av.* entirely.

ealo *n.* ale.

~benc† *f.* ale-bench.

~fæt *n.* ale-vat.

~gafol *n.* ale-tax.

~gāl† excited with ale.

~hūs *n.* ale-house.

~mealt *n.* ale-malt.

~scop *m.* minstrel.

~wǣge† *n.* ale-cup.

~geweorc *n.* making ale, brewing.

~wosa† *m.* drunkard.

ealoþ *n.* ale [ealu].

eam = eom am.

ēam *m.* (maternal) uncle.

geēan yeaning (sheep).

ēanian bring forth (lamb).

ēar, *lN.* æhher *n.* ear (of corn).

ēar (*m.*)† sea.

~gebland *n.* surge.

~grund *m.* depths of the sea.

ēar (*m.*)† earth ; *the Runic letter* ea.

earc *f.* ; arc *m. L.* (Noah's) ark ; chest, box, coffin [*Lt.* arca].

eard *m.* native country, home. dwelling-place, native soil (of plants) ; place ; earth.

~begenga *m.* inhabitant.

~begengnes *f.* dwelling, habitation.

~cȳþþ o) *f.* old acquaintance.

~fæst settled, dwelling.

~geard† *m.* dwelling-place ; world.

~giefu† *f.* gift from one's native country.

~hæbbend† *m.* dweller.

~land†, **~rīce†** *n.* native country.

~lufe† *f.* (?).

~stapa† *m.* wanderer.

~stede† *m.* dwelling-place.

~weall *m.* cliff.

~wīc† *n.* dwelling-place.

~wrecca *m.* exile.

~wunung *f.* dwelling in one's native country.

eard|ian dwell ‖ *tr.* settle, occupy (country).

~igend *m.* dweller.

~igendlic habitable.

eardung, -ing *f.* dwelling ; tabernacle.

~burg *f.* city of tabernacles.

~hūs *n.* dwelling.

~stōw *f.* dwelling-place.

ēar|e *n.* ear.

~clǣnsend *m.* 'ear-cleaner,' little finger.

~copu *f.* ear-disease.

~efinger *m.* 'ear-finger,' little finger.

~hring *m.* earring.

~læppa *m.* lobe of the ear.

~(e)lippric *lN. n.* lobe of the ear.

~plætt *m.* box on the ear.

~plættan box one's ear.

~prēon *m.* earring.

~scripel, y *m.* little finger.

~sealf *f.* ear-salve.

~spinl *f.* earring.

~gesp(r)eca *m.* whisperer.

~wærc *m.* ear-ache.

~wicga *m.* earwig.

ēarede having ears (*of* vessel).

ēarendel, ēo- *m.* ray of light, dawn.

earfan *pl.* tares.

earfoþ, earfeþe I. full of hardship, grievous, troublesome, diffi-

[47]

C

cult. II. *n.* hardship, suffering, trouble, difficulty.

earfoþ|cierre difficult of conversion (to Christianity).

~**cynn** *n.* perverse generation.

~**dǣde** difficult.

~**dǣg**† *m.* day of tribulation.

~**e** *av.* with difficulty.

~**fēre** difficult to pass.

~**fynde** hard to find.

~**hāwe** difficult to be seen.

~**hịelde***, -**y** perverse.

~**hwīl**† *f.* hard time.

~**lǣre** difficult to be taught.

~**lǣte** difficult to be discharged (*of* urine).

~**lic** full of hardship, difficult.

~**līce** *av.* with difficulty, hardly; painfully, sorely.

~**licnes** *f.* difficulty (of urine).

~**mẹcg**†, -**æ** *m.* unhappy man.

~**nes** *f.* hardship, trouble; bodily trouble *or* disturbance (of women); misfortune; difficulty.

~**rẹcce** difficult to be told.

~**rīme** difficult to be counted; difficult to be enumerated, innumerable.

~**sǣlig**† unblessed, unfortunate.

~**sīþ**† *m.* toilsome journey; misfortune.

~**tǣcne** difficult to be shown.

~**þrāg**† *f.* time of trouble.

earfoþian trouble.

earg inert; cowardly; bad, depraved.

~**e** *av.* badly.

~**ian** be slothful *or* remiss; lose heart, be cowardly.

~**lic** slothful; bad.

~**līce** *av.* timidly; basely, treacherously.

~**scipe** *m.* sloth, cowardice.

earh†, **earg**-, **ærig**- *f.* arrow *not* W.

~**faru** *f.* flight of arrows.

earm *m.* arm; arm (of the sea).

~**bēag** *m.* bracelet.

~**gegịerela** *m.* bracelet.

~**hrēad**† *f.* arm-ornament.

~**scanca** *m.* arm-bone.

~**sliefe** *f.* sleeve.

~**strang**, ~**swīþ** strong in the arm.

earm wretched, miserable, despicable, poor.

~**cearig**† careworn.

~**e** *av.* wretchedly, badly.

earm|heort merciful; humble.

~**ian** commiserate *wd., vL.*; him ~**ode** þæt he was sorry because of it.

~**ing** = **ịerming** wretch.

~**lic** wretched, miserable.

~**līce** *av.* miserably, cruelly.

~**sceapen**† wretched, miserable.

earmelle *f.* sleeve.

earn *m.* eagle.

~**cynn** *n.* eagle-kind.

~**gēat**, ~**gēap** *m.* vulture.

earn|ian *w.g., rarely a.* deserve, merit, earn.

(ge)~**ung**, ~**ing** *f.* merit.

earning-land *n.* land earned *or* made freehold.

earon are *not* W.

earp dusky, dark.

ears *m.* podex.

~**endu** *npl.* buttocks.

~**ling** — on ~ *av.* back(wards).

~**līra***, -**e** *m.* buttocks.

~**ode** tergosus.

~**þỹrel** *n.* anus.

eart (thou) art.

earþ = **ịerþ**.

earþ = **eart**.

earwunga, **a**- *lN.* *av.* gratis; without cause.

ēast I. *av.* east, eastwards, in the east. **II.** *aj., only in cpv.* ~(**er**)**ra** eastern, *spl.* ~(**e**)**mest** in the extreme east.

~**cẹntingas** *mpl.* people of East Kent.

~**dǣl** *m.* eastern quarter, the East.

~**ẹnde** *m.* eastern extremity, east quarter.

~**ẹngle** *pl.* East-Anglians, East-Anglia.

~**francan** *pl.* East-Franks.

~**healf** *f.* east side.

~**land** *n.* the East.

~**lang** *av.* along the east side, east : se wudu is ~ .. mīla lang.

~**gemǣre** *n.* east boundary.

~**norþ** *av.* north-east.

~**norþ-wind** *m.* north-east wind.

~**rīce** *n.* eastern kingdom, the East.

~**rodor** *m.* east part of sky.

~**ryhte** *av.* due east.

~**sǣ** *f.* east sea.

~**seaxe** *mpl.* East-Saxons, Essex.

~**sūþ** *av.* south-east.

~**sūþlang** *av.* from east to south.

~(**e**)**weard** east(ward).

ēast-weg *m.* eastern way, the East.

ēastan, ~**e** *av.* from the east; in the east. **be** ~ *prp. wd.* east of. **wiþ** ~ *av.* on the east side.

~**norþan** *av.* from the north-east.

~**sūþan** *av.* from the south-east.

~**sūþan-wind** *m.* south-east wind.

~**wind** *m.* east wind.

ēaste *f.* the East.

Ēaster|ǣfen(**n**) *m.* Easter-eve [Ēastron].

~**dǣg** *m.* Easter Sunday — ōþer ~ Easter Monday; day of the Passover.

~**fæsten** *n.* Easter-fast.

~**feorm** *f.* Easter-feast.

~**lic** paschal.

~**mōnaþ** *m.* April.

~**niht** *f.* Easter-eve.

~**tīd** *f.* Easter-time.

~**þegnung**, ~**þēn**- *f.* Easter-service, paschal feast, passover.

~**wuce** *f.* Easter-week

ēasterne eastern (wind, people).

Ēastr|e *f., nearly always pl.* ~**on** (~**an**) *rarely* ~**o**, ~**a**, *indecl. except occ. d.* ~**um**, *g.* ~**ena** Easter; passover.

~**ian** — oþ fīftēne niht bēon ge~ ode until fifteen days of Easter have elapsed.

Ēastron, *see* **Ēastre**.

ēaþ = **īeþ** more easily.

ēaþ = **ēaþe** easily.

ēaþ-mēd|an, **ēad**-, *gen.* ge- humble, humiliate | *rfl.* condescend; submit | *wd.* worship, *also rfl.* [**ēaþ-mōd**].

~**e** humble, gentle.

~**o**, -**mẹtto** *npl.* humility; kindness — ~**um** humbly; kindly.

ēaþ-mōd, **ēad**- humble; kind.

~**ian**, ge- humble || *intr.* deign Bd.

~**ig**, ~**lic** humble; kind.

~**līce** *av.* humbly.

~**nes** *f.* humility.

ēaþe *aj.* = **īeþe** easy.

ēaþe, **īeþe** *av., cpv.* **īeþ**, **ēaþ**, *spl.* **ēaþost**, **īeþest**, **īeþost** *av.* easily; willingly.

~**lic** easy; scanty, insignificant, contemptible.

~**līce** *av.* easily.

ēawesclīce *av.* openly, clearly.

ēawis-firina = **ǣwis**-.

ēawlā = **ēalā**.

ēawunga, -winga av. openly, publicly [īewan].
eax f. axle-tree; axis.
~faru*, æx- f. Gl.
eaxl f. shoulder.
~cláp m. shoulder-cloth, scapular.
~(e)gespann† n. place where beams of cross intersect.
~gesteallat† m. comrade.
ębb|a m. ebb, low tide.
~ian ebb, go out (of tide).
~ung f. ebbing.
Ebr|ēas mpl. Jews.
~(ē)isc Hebrew, Jewish.
ęce m. ache, pain [acan].
ēc|e I. eternal.   II. av. eternally.
~elic eternal.
~elīce av. eternally.
~nes f. eternity — ā on ~se for ever.
ęced, æ- nm. vinegar [Lt. acetum].
~fæt n. vinegar-vessel.
~wīn n. wine mixed with vinegar (?).
ęcg f. edge; †weapon, sword.
~bana† m. slayer, murderer.
~heard† hard of edge.
~hęte† m. hostility.
~lāst† f. edge (of sword).
~plega† m., ~pracu† f. battle.
~wælt† n. slaughter.
ęcg|an, prt. ęgede harrow.
~ung f. harrowing.
ed-byrdan regenerate.
ed-cēlnes, -oe- f. becoming cool again.
ed-cęnn|an regenerate.
~ing f. regeneration.
geed-cīegan recall.
ed-cięrr m. return; return (of disease).
~ian, -cucian intr. revive.
ed-frēolsian re-grant by charter.
ed-geong† growing young again.
ed-gięld n. repayment.
edgięld|an* 3 repay.
~end m. remunerator.
ed-gift f. restitution.
ed-grōwung f. re-growing.
ed-hiertan refresh, encourage.
ed-hīwian refashion.
ed-hwyrft m. change, reverse of fortune.
edisc n. enclosure, park; pasture.
~hęnn f. quail.
~weard m. park-keeper.

ed-lǣc|an* do again, repeat.
~ung f. repetition.
ed-lǣstan repeat.
ed-lēan n. reward, retribution.
ge~end m. requiter.
~ian reward, requite.
(ge)~ung f. recompense, requital.
ed-lesend|lic reciprocal, relative.
~līce av. relatively.
ed-lesung f. relating Gl.
ed-mǣle n. festival Gl.
ed-nīw|e, -nēowe, īo I. renewed, new — ~an av. anew.   II. av. anew.
~ian renew; restore; reform.
~igend m. renewer, repairer.
~ung f. renewal; mending, reparation.
~unga, -inga av. anew.
ed-recan, eodorcan ruminate [cp. edroc, ~ian].
ed-roc rumination.
~ian ruminate.
ed-sceaft f. new creation, regeneration.
ed-stapel|ian (re)establish.
~ig restored, made strong again.
(ge)~igend m. restorer.
(ge)~ung f. restoration.
ed-þingung f. reconciliation.
ed-węnden† f. change, reverse of fortune; destruction, end (of the world).
ed-wielle m. whirlpool, eddy.
ed-wielm† m. whirlpool (of fire).
ed-wierp|an* recover (from illness).
~ing f. recovery (from illness).
ed-winde once f. whirlpool.
ed-wist f. substance. Cp. ætwist.
~ian feed, support.
~lic substantive (verb).
ed-wīt n. reproach, contumely, disgrace.
~full, ~fullic disgraceful.
~fullīce av. disgracefully.
~līf†† n. life of disgrace.
~scipe† m. disgrace — þurh ~ ignominiously.
~spræc† f. scorn.
~spreca† m. reviler.
~stæf† m. reproach, contumely.
edwītan = ætwītan reproach.
efe-lang = efen-.
efe(n)-lāste† f. everlasting (a plant).
efen, efn; emn, in composition em(ne)-. The f-forms are not

strict W. I. level; even (temper), unchanged. II. av. equally.
efen|æþele equally noble.
~ametan 5 compare.
~behēfe equally necessary or useful.
~beorht equally bright.
~biscop m. co-bishop.
~blissian rejoicing equally wd.
~ceasterwaran pl. fellow-citizens.
~cęmpa m. fellow-soldier.
~cristen m. fellow-Christian.
~cuman 4 assemble; agree.
~gedǣlan share equally.
~dīere equally dear, equally beloved.
~ēadig equally blessed.
~eald of the same age, contemporary.
~eardigende dwelling together w. mid.
~ēce co-eternal wd.
~edwistlic of the same substance, consubstantial wd.
~ęsne m. fellow-servant.
~etan 5 eat as much as wd.
~fela equally many, as many.
~gefēon 5 rejoice together.
~gōd equally good.
~hēah equally high.
~hēap m. fellow-soldier (!).
~hęrenes f. praising together.
~herian praise together.
~hlēoþor n. unison.
~hlyte*, -ete equal in rank.
~hlytta m. partaker, sharer.
~ierfeweard m. co-heir.
~ieþe equally easy.
~lǣcan imitate wd.
~lǣcend, ~lǣcere m. imitator.
(ge)~lǣcestre f. imitator.
ge)~lǣcung f. imitation.
~lang, efelang of equal length.
~lange*, emn- prp. wd. along.
~lēof equally pleasant w. d. of person.
~lic, ge- equal wd.; of the same age or period.
~gelic equal.
~(ge)līca m. equal.
·līce av. equally, alike.
ge~līcian make equal.
~licnes f. equality.
~ling m. equal.
~gemǣcca m. equal, fellow.
~mǣre of equal fame or importance.

[49]

efen|mæssepreost *m.* fellow-priest.

~micel of equal size *or* greatness.

~mid middle.

~mihtig equally mighty.

~mōdlīce *av.* with equanimity.

~gemyndig equally mindful.

~nēah equally near.

~niht, emniht *f.* equinox.

~nes, efnes *f.* equality ; equity.

~rēþe equally ferocious.

~rīce of equal power.

~sācerd *m.* fellow-priest.

~sār *n.* equal sorrow.

~sārig equally grieved *wd.*

~sārgian commiserate.

~sārgung *f.* sympathy.

~scearp equally sharp.

~scolere *m.* school-fellow.

~scyldig equally guilty.

~spēdiglic, -delic consubstantial.

~stālian prepare Gl.

~swīþ equally strong.

~swiþe *av.* equally.

~tōwistlic consubstantial.

~twā — on emtwā *av.* in two.

~þēow\a) *m.*, ~þēowen *f.* fellow-servant.

~þrōwian sympathize.

~þrōwung *f.* sympathy.

~wæge *f.* counterpoise.

~wierþe, ~weorþ equivalent.

~wyrcend *m.* co-operator.

~wyrhta *m.* colleague.

efenehp *f.* plain [efen-hiehþ].

efes *f.* eaves ; border (of forest). *Cp.* yfes.

efes|ian, efs- shear, cut (hair).

~ung *f.* shearing, tonsure.

efet|e *f.*, *once* ~a newt.

geefn(i)an compare *LN.*

efne (*f.*) alum.

efne, *strict W.* emne I. *av.* equally — ~ gefeohtan (*of* drawn battle); with fairness, justly ; exactly, just — ~ swā just as. II. *interj.* behold ! ecce. *often intens. or pleon.* truly, indeed — ~ nū (even) now ; behold ! ecce. ~ þā just then ; behold !

efstan, oe-, *intr.*hasten ; endeavour *w.* hū *and sbj.* [ofost].

eft *av.* a second time, again ; afterwards ; *order of statement, argument, &c.* again, rursum : eft Hē hīe þrēade þurh þone wītgan : back : wendan ~ hāmweard.

eft|cyme† *m.* return.

~edwītan 6 reprove (!).

~hweorfende recurring.

~lēan *n.* recompense.

~liesing *f.* redemption.

~sittan sit again (!).

~sīþ† *m.* return *intr.*

~sīþgende retreating.

~sōna *av.* again.

~spellung *f.* recapitulation (!).

~wyrd† *f.* future fate.

eftgan repeat ; restore, strengthen (voice).

ēg-clif = īeg-.

ege *m.* fear — habban ~ tō fear.

~full terrible.

~lēas fearless.

~lēaslīce *av.* fearlessly.

~lēasnes *f.* fearlessness.

~wielm† *m.* wave of terror.

egede, *prt. of* ecgan harrow.

egenu *f.* chaff.

eges|a, egsa fear ; what is terrible [ege].

~full, ~fullic terrible.

~fullīce *av.* terribly.

~fulnes *f.* terribleness.

~grīma *m.* spectre.

~lic terrible.

~līce *av.* terribly ; excessively.

eges|ian, egs- terrify.

~ung *f.* terrifying, threatening.

egeþ|e, egþe *f.* harrow [ecgan].

~ere *m.* harrower.

~getigu *npl.* some implement of harrowing.

geeggian incite *LN.* [*Scand.*]

egl (*f.*) mote (in eye).

egl|an, -ian *wd.* molest, trouble (*esp. of* diseases).

~e troublesome ; horrible, repulsive ; sad.

egle, egile *f.* dormouse.

ēgor = ēagor.

Egypt|e, -ipte *mpl.* Egyptians.

~isc Egyptian.

eh- = eoh-.

eht|an, ē ?, oe *w. g. or a.* pursue, persecute [oht].

~end, ~ere *m.* persecutor.

~ing, ~nes *f.* persecution.

geehte, *or* *geæhtan subdue.

ei, *see* ēa.

eig = īeg.

eiseg *once*† = egesig (?) terrible.

el (*m.*) *the letter* l.

~leoht elision of *l* Gl.

el-boga = eln-.

elc|ian, ieldcian *intr.* delay *w. sbj.* || *tr.* delay, retard [eald].

~end *m.* procrastinator.

~ung *f.* delay.

elcor, ellicor, *once* ellcra *av.* elsewhere ; otherwise, else — noht ~ nothing besides [ele-].

elcra *cpv.* se ~ the latter (*as opposed to* the former) [elcor].

eldcung = elcung.

ele, oe *m.* oil [*Lt.* oleum].

~bacen baked in oil.

ele-bēam *m.* olive-tree.

~en of the olive-tree.

~stybb *m.* olive-stump Ct.

ele|ber(i)ge *f.* olive.

~bytt *f.* oil-vessel.

~fæt *n.* oil-vessel.

~horn *m.* oil-flask.

~lēast *f.* lack of oil.

~sealf *f.* oil-salve.

~seohhe *f.* oil-strainer.

~tredde *f.* oil-press.

~trēow *n.* olive-tree.

~trēowen of olive-trees.

~twig *n.* olive-twig.

elehtre, *vE.* elot(h)r lupin (a plant) [*Lt.* electrum].

elfen = ielfen.

el-hygd *f.* distraction (of mind).

el(e)-land† *n.* foreign country.

elle *aj. pl.* remaining *lM.*

ellefne = endlufon.

ellen *nm.* courage, zeal — on ~ boldly.

~campian contend zealously.

~cræft† *m.* might.

~dǣd† *f.* deed of courage.

~gāst†, ǣ *m.* bold demon.

~heard† brave.

~lǣca† *m.* champion.

~lēas wanting in courage.

~lic brave.

~līce† *av.* daringly.

~mǣrþo† *f.* fame of courage.

~rōf† brave.

~sēoc† dying.

~sprǣc† *f.* speech, voice.

~þriste† courageous.

~weorc† *n.* deed of courage.

ellen-wōd† furious.

~ian be zealous, emulate.

~nes *f.* zeal.

ellen, -ern (*n.*) I. elder-tree. II. of elder.

~rind *f.* elder-bark.

ellen|stybb *m.* alder-stump.
~wyrt *f.* dwarf elder.
ẹl(e)-lẹnd e, ~isc foreign [ẹlland].
ellern = ellen alder.
ẹlles *av.* otherwise; if it were
  otherwise, else — ~hwæt, ~wiht,
  ~ āwiht anything else [ẹle-].
~hwǣr, ~hwergen *av.* elsewhere.
~hwider *av.* elsewhither.
ẹllor† *av.* elsewhither, elsewhere
  (motion) — ~ landes in another
  country.
~fūs ready to depart (from life).
~gāst, ǣ *m.* alien sprite.
~sīþ *m.* departure, death.
elm *m.* elm [*Lt.* ulmus].
~rind *f.* elm-bark.
elmestlic = ælmeslic.
ẹln *f.* ell.
~gemet *n.* ell-measure.
~boga, ẹl(e)-, ẹlm- *m.* elbow.
ẹln|ian *tr.* encourage; *rfl.* take
  heart, be revived ‖ *intr.* be zealous, emulate [ẹllen].
~ung *f.* encouragement; zeal, emulation.
elpend, -ent, y-, ylp *m.* elephant
  [*Lt.* elephantus].
~bān, elpen-, ylpen-, ylpes- *n.*
  ivory.
~bǣnen, elpen-, ylpesbānen of
  ivory.
~tōþ *m.* elephant's tusk.
elra† (?).
ẹl(1)-reord, ~ig barbarous, foreign.
~ignes *f.* barbarism Gl.
ẹltst = iẹldest, *see* eald.
ẹl-þēod, ẹll- *f.* foreign nation, *pl.*
  foreigners; exile (?) = ẹlþīede.
  pl. = æl-þēoda* all people (?).
ge~an make strange, disturb Gl.
ẹl-þēodig, ælpīedig I. foreign, in
  exile; *met.* estranged. II. *n.* exile.
~līce *av.* abroad.
~nes *f.* living abroad, exile.
~ian, ~an, ẹlþēodgian live abroad,
  be a pilgrim *or* exile.
ẹl-þēod(g)ung *f.* residence abroad,
  exile.
ẹl-þēodisc foreign.
ẹl-þīede, -ēo- *n.* (?) exile [ẹlþēod].
ẹl-wiht*, æ- *f.* strange monster.
em (*m.*) *the letter* m.
~leoht *n.* elision of *m* Gl.
em- = efen-.
em(b)- = ymb-.
embiht, oe = ambiht.

ẹmbren (*n.*) bucket [amber].
emdenes = ẹndemes.
emel = ymel caterpillar.
emer = amore a bird.
emn(e) = efen, efne.
emnet- *n.* plain [efen].
emnettan level *fig.*, destroy; make
  equal; compare.
emrene = ymbryne.
emswāfela = efen-swā-fela just
  as many.
ẹnd = and and.
ẹnd|ian end *tr. and intr.*; die.
(ge)~ung *f.* ending, end; death.
geẹndadung *IN.* = geẹndung.
ẹnde *m.* end | limit, border; quarter,
  direction : be ǣghwilcum ~;
  district, region | part, portion,
  quantity | species, kind | death |
  result, end : oþ man wiste tō
  hwām se ~ gehwurfe how things
  would turn out | þæt hē gesāwe
  þone ~.
~byrd *f.* arrangement, order.
~byrdan put in order, arrange.
~byrdes *av.* in an orderly manner,
  properly.
~byrdlic ordinal (number).
~byrdlīce *av.* in order, successively.
~byrdnes *f.* order.
~dæg† *m.* last day (end, death).
~dēaþ† *m.* death.
~dōgor† *m.* last day, death.
~lāf† *f.* last remnant.
~lēan† *n.* final retribution.
~lēas, ~lēaslic endless.
~lēaslīce *av.* endlessly.
~lēasnes *f.* eternity.
~līf† *n.* death.
~mann *m.* man of the present day.
~nīehst last — æt ~an finally.
~rīm† *n.* number.
~sǣta† *m.* borderer, coast-guard.
~sp(r)ǣc *f.* epilogue.
~stæf† *m.* end; destruction.
ẹnd-wærc *m.* pain in anus.
ẹndemes, ẹmdenes, ẹmdemes,
  -est *av.* completely; equally,
  uniformly, unanimously, together
  — ealle ~ all (together), likewise.
endlufon, -le(o)f-, -lyf-, enl-,
  ændlefen, ellefne eleven.
endlyfta eleventh.
ẹned *f.* duck.
ẹnge narrow; causing anxiety,
  painful, severe [ange].
~an — *ptc.* ge~ed anxious.

ẹngu *f.* narrowness; confinement.
ẹngel *m.* angel [*Lt.* angelus].
~cund angelic.
~cynn *n.* race of angels; order,
  rank of angels.
~lic angelic.
Ẹngl|e, Angle *mpl.* the English
  [Angel]. ~a-land *n.* England.
Ẹnglisc I. English. II. *n.* English
  (language).
~gereord *n.* English language.
enitre, enetere, enwintre one
  year old [ān-wintre].
enlefan = endlufon eleven.
ẹnt *m.* giant.
~cynn *n.* race of giants.
~isc of giants.
enwintre = enitre.
ēode *prt. of* gān go.
e(o)dor *m.* enclosure, fence, hedge;
  court, dwelling; region, zone;
  †prince, king.
~breþ, ~bryce *m.* fence-breaking,
  trespass.
~gang *m.* refuge.
~wīr† *m.* enclosing wire.
eofole *f.* a plant [*Lt.* ebulum].
eofor *m.* (wild) boar; †figure of
  boar on helmet.
~cumbol† *n.* boar-shaped ensign,
  standard.
~fearn *n.* polypody (a fern).
~līc† *n.* image of a boar.
~sprēot† *m.* boar-spear.
~swīn *n.* boar pig, male pig.
~þring (*n.*) the constellation Orion.
~prote *f.* carline thistle.
eofot, *vE.* ebhat *n.* debt; crime
  [*from* *ef-hāt].
eoful-sæc† *n.* blasphemy.
eofulsian blaspheme [*from* ef-
  hālsian ?].
eoh, *g.* ēos, *mn.* (war) horse†; *the*
  Runic letter eo.
~heolope *f.* elecampane (a plant).
ēoh† = īw yew; *the Runic letter* ēo.
eolet† *once* (*n.*) sea-journey.
eolh *m., g.* ēoles elk; *name of a*
  Runic letter.
~sand *m.* amber.
~secg, *vE.* ilug- *m.* sedge.
eolone, elene *f.* elecampane (a
  plant).
eom am.
eorc(n)an-stān, ea, eorclan-,
  lM. ercna(n)-, *m.* a precious
  stone.

ēored, -od *nf.* troop (of cavalry), legion [eoh, rād].
~cyst†, ie *f.* troop.
~geatwe† *fpl.* military trappings.
~hēap *m.* troop, host.
~mann *m.* horseman.
~mecg†, æ *m.* horseman.
~gerid *n.* troop of cavalry.
~prēat† *m.* troop.
~werod *n.* troop.
ēorendel = ēa-.
eorl *m.* nobleman, ealdormann, earl, chief; † (brave) man.
~gebyrd† *f.* noble birth, nobility.
~cund noble.
~dōm *m.* earldom.
~isc noble.
~(l)ic manly.
~(l)ice *av.* strongly, excessively.
~mægen† *n.* troop of warriors.
~ryht *n.* right *or* privilege of an earl.
~scipe† *m.* manliness
~gestrēon† *n.* treasure.
~gewǣde† *n.* armour.
~werod† *n.* troop of warriors.
eormen-†, yrmen-
~cynn *n.* mankind.
~grund *m.* the earth.
~lāf *f.* great legacy.
~strynd *f.* generation, race.
~pēod *f.* great people.
eornan = iernan.
eornes *f.* provocation [ierre].
eornost, -est I. [*or* ~e ?] earnest, serious. II. *f.* zeal, earnestness on ~(e), þurh ~e in earnest.
~e *av.* earnestly, in earnest; fiercely.
~lice *av.* strictly; in truth, indeed, therefore, but, and.
eorp = earp swarthy.
eorre = ierre angry.
eorþ *f.* earth, ground, world.
~æppel *m.* cucumber.
~ærn† *n.* tomb, grave.
~ber(i)ge *f.* strawberry.
~bifung, eo *f.* earthquake.
~bīgenga *m.* inhabitant of earth.
~bīgengnes *f.* agriculture.
~būend†, ~būgigend *m.* inhabitant of earth.
~burg *f.* earth-fortification.
~(ge)byrst *n.* landslip.
~ceafor *m.* beetle.
~cenned earth-born.
~cræft *m.* geometry (!).
~crypel, pp *m.* paralytic person.
~cund earthly.

eorþ|cyning† *m.* earthly king; king of the land.
~cynn† *n.* terrestrial species.
~draca† *m.* earth-dragon.
~dyne *m.* earthquake.
ern = ~ærn.
~fæst fixed in the earth.
~fæt† *n.* the body.
~gealla *m.* lesser centaury (a plant).
~grǣf *n.* ditch, pit.
~grāp† *f.* earth's grasp.
~hnutu *f.* earth-nut.
~hrērnes *f.* earthquake.
~hūs *n.* earth-house, subterranean chamber.
~īfig *n.* ground ivy.
~lic earthly.
~lice *av.* in an earthly manner.
~ling = ierþling.
~mægen† *n.* earthly *or* temporal power.
~maþa*, -ta *m.* earth-worm.
~gemet *n.* geometry (!).
~mistel *m.* basil (a plant).
~nafola, -naf(e)la *m.* asparagus.
~reced† *n.* cave.
~rest *f.* bed on the ground Gl.
~rice *n.* country; the earth.
~rima *m.* a plant.
~gesceaft† *f.* earthly creature.
~scræf† *n.* cave; sepulchre.
~sele† *m.* cave.
~slihtes *av.* level with the ground (*of* grazed grass).
~stede† *m.* earth.
~styrennes, ~styrung *f.* earthquake.
~tierwe *f.* bitumen.
~tilia *m.* farmer.
~tilþ *f.* agriculture.
~tūd(d)or† *n.* earth-progeny, mankind.
~wæstm *m.* fruit of the earth.
~waru *f.*; -e, -an *pl.* mankind.
~weall *m.* earth-wall, mound.
~weard† *m.* country *for* ~geard (?).
~weg† *m.* earth.
~wela *m.* fertility; wealth.
~weorc† *n.* earthly work.
~werod *n.* inhabitants of earth.
Ēotas *mpl.* Jutes.
eoten† *m.* giant.
~isc of giants.
~weard† (?).
Eotenas *pl.* Jutes.
Eotol-, Etel- Italy [*Lt.* Italia].

Eotol-ware *pl.* Italians.
ēow, ēaw, ēw *m.* sheep; ~u, ~e *f.* ewe.
~estre *m.* sheep-fold.
~(o)cig of a ewe.
~(o)d *f.* flock; sheep-fold.
~(o)de, ~ede *n.* flock, herd.
~ohumele *f.* female hop-plant.
ēow = īw yew.
ēow = gīw griffin.
ēow you.
ēow(i)an = iewan show.
ēowā, ēow! *interj.* alas!
ēowend (*m.*) membrum virile.
ēower your.
~lendisc of your country Gl.
ēowunga = ēawunga.
epistol *m.* letter [*Lt.* epistola].
er|ian plough.
~iung *f.* ploughing.
~ing-land *n.* arable land.
erce- = ærce-.
ern = ærn house.
ersc stubble-field.
~henn *f.* quail.
ēse *pl. of* ōs heathen god.
esne *m.* labourer, servant; retainer; man.
~cund of a labourer Gl.
~lice, esnl- *m.* manfully, strenuously.
~wyrhta *m.* hireling, labourer.
esol, eosel *m.* ass.
~cweorn *f.* mill turned by an ass, mill-stone.
eosele she-ass.
ess (*m.*) *name of letter* s [*Lt.*]
ēst, oe *fm.* favour, grace, bounty; will: ofer mīne ~ against my will | *pl.* ~as delicacies || ~um *av.* kindly, willingly, bounteously.
~ēadig*, eft-† living in luxury, prosperous.
~(e)full kind, devoted, helpful; devout, pious | fond of luxury.
~fullice *av.* kindly, devotedly.
~fulnes *f.* devotion, zeal; luxury, lechery.
~georn fond of luxury.
~ig gracious, bountiful *wg.*
~ignes *f.* kindness.
~mete *m.* dainty — *pl.* -mettas luxury.
ēstan live luxuriously.
ēst|e gracious, bountiful *wdg.*
~(e)lice *av.* graciously; gladly, willingly; delicately, luxuriously.

et|an, *prt.* ǣt 5 eat ; consume.
~end, ~ere *m.* eater, glutton.
~ing *f.* eating.
ęte-land *n.* pasture land [ęttan].
eten-lǣs *f.* pasture.
etol gluttonous.
~nes *f.* gluttony.
ęttan *tr.* pasture (land) [etan].
ēþ|ian, oe *intr.* breathe ; rush,
rise (*of* flame) ‖ *tr.* blow on ;
smell (odour).
~(g)ung *f.* breathing ; hard breathing.
ēþel, oe *mn.* country, native land

—†hwæles ~ the sea ; *the Runic
letter* ǣ = *later* ē.
ēþel|boda† *m.* apostle of a country,
native preacher.
~cyning† *m* king of the land.
~drēam† *m.* home joy.
~eard† *m.* native dwelling.
~fæsten† *n.* fortress.
~land† *n.* (native) land.
~lēas† homeless.
~mearc† *f.* territory.
~rīce† *n.* native kingdom, country.
~riht† *n.* rights of a native, hereditary privilege.

ēþel|seld†, ~setl† *n.* settlement.
~stæf *m.* support of country *or*
family, heir.
~staþol† *m.* settlement.
~stōl *m.* settlement, habitation ;
metropolis, capital.
~stōw† *f.* dwelling-place.
~turf† *f.* country.
~þrymm† *m.* glory of one's country.
~weard† *m.* king ; man.
~wynn† *f.* joy of country.
ēþr- = ǣþr-.
eþþa = oþþe or.
exen, oe *pl. of* oxa ox.

F.

fā, *see* fāh hostile.
~lǣcan be at feud with.
gefā *m., pl.* ~n enemy.
fācian try to get, aspire to
[fǣcan].
fāc(e)n *n.* deceit, fraud, treachery ;
injury, malice, crime.
~gecwiss conspiracy.
~dǣd *f.* sin.
~full deceitful.
~lēas guileless.
~lic deceitful.
~līce, ǣ *av.* deceitfully, treacherously.
~searo† *n.* treachery.
~stafas† *mpl.* treachery.
~geswipere† *n.* treachery.
~tācen† *n.* deceitful token.
fācne = fǣcne.
fad|ian set in order, arrange, direct,
dispose.
~ung *f.* order, arrangement, dispensation.
fǣn*, *vE.* fǣhan; *prt.* fǣde paint Gl.
fæc *nm.* space ; period of time,
interval.
~full spacious.
fǣc|an deal : gif hwā tō ōþrum
mid yrfe ~e ⌊fācian].
fæcele *f.* torch. *Cp.* þæcele.
fǣcne, fācne I. deceitful, fraudu-
lent, treacherous ; wicked. II. *av.*

deceitfully ; maliciously, wickedly ;
†exceedingly.
gefǣd orderly, proper, well-regu-
lated (in character) [fadian].
~lic suitable, proper.
~līce properly.
fǣder, *d.* ~ ; *g.* ~, ~es, fǣdres, *A.*
f(e)adur ; *pl.* ~as, fædras *m.*
father ; *in pl.* parents, ancestors ⌊
eald ~ grandfather ; ancestor [*cp.*
eald-fæder]. þridda ~ great-
grandfather.
~æþelo† *pl.* patrimony ; genealogy.
~ēþel *n.* birth-place, native land.
~feoh *n.* father's money, marriage
portion of widowed daughter re-
turned to the father.
~geardas† *mpl.* birth-place, home.
~lēas fatherless.
~lic of a father, paternal ; ancestral.
~līce *av.* in a paternal manner.
~rīce *n.* hereditary kingdom.
~slaga *m.* parricide.
~gestrēon *n.* patrimony.
~swica *m.* traitor to one's father.
fǣdera *m.* (paternal) uncle [fæder].
gefæder|a *m.* godfather.
~e *f.* godmother.
fæd(e)ren paternal.
~brōþor *m.* full brother.
~cnōsl *n.* father's kin *or* family.
~cynn *n.* father's family, pedigree.

fæderen|healf *f.* father's side (*in*
genealogy).
~mǣg, fædering- *m.* paternal relative.
~mǣgþ *f.* paternal kindred.
gefæderen, gefædred born of the
same father as *wd.*
fædrunga *m., f.* parental relative,
mother.
fǣge on the point of death, doomed
to death, fated ; dead ; damned,
accursed ; afraid, cowardly.
fægen, ge~ glad, rejoicing *wg.*
⌊gefēon].
fægen|ian, fægn-, fahn- rejoice,
exult, be pleased with *wg.* ;
~, on ~ fawn (*of* dog).
(ge)~ung *f.* rejoicing.
fæger, ǣ†, æ† beautiful, fair ;
pleasant, sweet (sound, odour) ;
fair (words).
~e, fægre *av.* beautifully ; pleasantly ; kindly ; gently ; fittingly,
well.
(ge)~nes *f.* beauty.
~wyrde smooth-speaking, concili-
ating.
fægrian *intr.* become beautiful ‖
tr. adorn.
fǣhþ(o), fǣgþ-*f.* feud, enmity [fāh].
~bōt *f.* feud-compensation.
fǣlǣcan = fā-.

[53]

fǣle†, ǣ† I. faithful, kind, pleasant. II. *av.* faithfully, pleasantly.

fælging = fielging.

fǣlsian† purify [fǣle].

fǣman foam [fām].

fǣmig = fāmig.

fǣmn|e *f.* virgin ; †woman.

~(an)hād *m.* virginity — ~es mann virgin.

~(en)lic, fǣmhādlic virginal.

fǣr *n.* going ; journey, passage — mannes ~; thoroughfare, road ; removal *intr.*; military expedition | (course of) life ‖ movable possessions | ship [faran].

~eht, ~riht (!) *n.* fare, passage-money (in ship) [fǣr, ǣht].

~sceatt *m.* fare, passage-money.

fǣr- = for-.

fǣr *m.* (sudden) danger, calamity, attack.

~befangen† encompassed with danger.

~blǣd *m.* sudden *or* terrible blast.

~bryne† *m.* terrible heat.

~ciele† *m.* terrible cold.

~clamm *m.* sudden *or* terrible grasp.

~cwealm *m.* pestilence.

~dēaþ *m.* sudden death.

~drype† = ~drepe *m.* sudden stroke *or* ~dryre sudden fall.

~fiell *m.* sudden fall—on ~ headlong.

~gripe† *m.* sudden grasp.

~gryre† *m.* danger, terror.

~haga† *m.* environment of danger.

~inga, -unga, -unge *av.* quickly, soon ; suddenly.

~lic, fǣredlic sudden.

~lice *av.* suddenly.

~niþ† *m.* hostility.

~sc(e)apa† *m.* enemy.

~scyte† *m.* dangerous shooting *or* shot.

~searo† *n.* artifice, stratagem.

~sēaþ *m.* terrible pit, abyss Gl.

~slide† *m.* sudden slip.

~spell† *n.* terrible news.

~stice *m.* sudden stitch (pain).

~stylt amazement *LN.* = forstylt ?

~wundor† *n.* prodigy.

gefǣr *n.* going, course, march (of army).

fǣr|an alarm, terrify.

~ing*, ē *f.* simulatio Gl.

fǣrben|a, *vE.* ~u [*for* ~o] *m.* sailor.

fǣreld, -elt *n.* journey, expedition,

---

company ; motion, locomotion ; passover.

fǣreld-frēols *m.* feast of the passover.

fǣs *n.* fringe.

fǣsl† (*n.*) progeny, offspring.

fæst firm, fixed, stiff (soil) — ~ innoþ constipated ; fortified (by nature *or* art) ; heavy (sleep) ; steadfast, firm (mind, faith) ; religious, Christian (book).

~e *av.* firmly ; (sleep) heavily ; vigorously, (forbid) strictly.

~gangol†, fæsten- persevering, firm (mind).

~hafol tenacious ; miserly.

~hafolnes *f.* parsimony.

~heald firmly fixed.

~hygdig†, -hȳdig firm in mind, constant.

~lic fixed, steadfast, vigorous (warfare).

~līce *av.* firmly, steadfastly, vigorously.

~mōd firm in mind, constant.

~nes *f.* firmness, massiveness ; fortification, firmament, sky ; kindness, *for* ǣfæstnes (?).

~rǣd steadfast, firm (mind).

~līce *av.* steadfastly.

~nes *f.* fortitude.

~steall† firm.

fæstan make firm ; entrust ‖ fast — fæsten ge~ keep a fast ; abstain from (food) *wi.*

fæsting *f.* taking care of child.

~mann *m.* king's purveyor (?).

fæsten(n) *n.* fortress, castle, cloister ; firmament, sky ‖ fast.

~behæfednes *f.* parsimony Gl., *for* fæst- (?).

~bryce *m.* breach of fasting.

~dæg *m.* fast-day.

~dīc *m.* moat.

~gangol = fæst-.

~geat *n.* gate of fortress.

~tīd *f.* fast-time, fast.

~geweorc *n.* liability for repair of fortifications.

~wuce *f.* week of fasting.

fæstn|ian fasten, fix, *met.* fix (hopes on God) ; conclude (peace), ratify (agreement) ; betroth.

~ung *f.* fixing ; ratification ; pledge, engagement ; security.

fæt *n.* vessel, casket, cup, pot.

~fyllere, ~fylre *m.* cup-bearer.

---

fǣtan put ; ~ inn take in, swallow.

fǣted, ǣ†, fǣtt ornamented with gold — golde ~ sweord.

~hlēor† with ornamented cheeks (*of* horse).

~sinc† *n.* treasure.

fǣtels *m.* tub, vessel ; pouch, bag.

~ian put into a receptacle *or* vessel.

fǣtt fat, fatted (calf).

~ian grow fat ‖ *tr.* fatten.

~nes *f.* fatness.

fǣtt = fǣted.

fæþm *m.* outstretched arms ; embrace | bosom, lap, womb ; envelopment, interior, midst | grasp ; control, power ; protection | expanse | cubit, fathom.

~lic embracing, enclosing.

~rīm† *n.* (cubit-)measure.

fæþm(i)an surround, envelop ; clasp, seize.

fāg (*m.*) plaice, flounder.

fāg variegated, pied (horse) ; discoloured, stained, blood-stained ; adorned.

~ian *intr.* vary in colour ‖ *tr.* embroider.

~nes *f.* scab, ulcer, eruption.

~ung *f.* variety.

~wyrm *m.* basilisk.

fāgett|an, -etan *intr.* change colour ; mid wordum ~ speak evasively.

~ung *f. intr.* changing colour (*of* sky in storms).

fāh, fāg, *pl.* fā hostile ; proscribed, outlawed ; guilty *wi.*

fǣt†, *dpl.* fǣt(t)um metal plate, gold ornament.

faldian make sheep-fold, hurdle off sheep [falod].

fal(o)d *m.* sheep-fold. ox-stall.

~gang *m.* going to sheep-fold.

fals I. false (weight), counterfeit (coin). II. *n.* fraud, dishonesty ; counterfeit coin [*Fr. or Lt.*].

fām *n.* foam.

~blāwende discharging foam.

fāmgian foam [fāmig].

fāmig, ǣ foamy.

~borda† with foamy sides.

~bōsma† foamy-bosomed.

~heals† foamy-necked.

fana *m.* banner.

fandian *w. g. or a.* investigate, explore ; try, test, tempt.

fandung *f.* investigation, testing, proof, temptation.

fan|e, ~u *f.* banner ‖ iris (a plant).

fang *once* booty *L.* [fōn ; *or Scand.*].

fann *f.* winnowing-fan [*Lt.* vannus].

~ian fan.

fant, o *m.* (baptismal) font [*Lt.* fontem].

~bæþ *n.* baptism.

~fæt *n.* font.

~hālgung *f.* consecration of font.

~wæter *n.* font-water.

far|an 2 go, march, travel (by land or sea)—*in pass. sense* cōm of ~endum wege. on~ *wd., w.* on *a.* assail, take (city) | lead life, behave, act : mid hīwunge ~ be hypocritical | fare, be : wel~ prosper, ~ būtan bearnum be childless.

~ennes*, fæ- *f.* passage, *lM.*

gefaran 2 go &c.; accomplish (journey *or* distance) | fare &c.; *tr.* suffer (shipwreck); behave, act | die — gefaren deceased | attack (hīe mid fierde) | take possession of, occupy (country) gain (victory).

fāra *gpl. of* fāh.

gefara *m.* fellow-traveller, companion. *Cp.* gefēra.

Farisēisc Pharisean — ~ mann Pharisee [*Lt.*].

faroþ† (*n.*) shore.

~hengest *m.* ship.

~lācende, ~rīdende sailing, seafaring.

~strǣt *f.* ocean.

faru *f.* going, transit, journey ; march, expedition | course of life, life, proceedings ; adventures ‖ troop, retinue, companions | movable property, baggage.

fatian = fętian.

faþ|e, ~u *f.* paternal aunt.

faul (*m.*) evil spirit (?).

fēa, ~we, ~wa, *d.* feā(wu'm, *g.* fēara I. few. II. *av.* (not) even a little.

~lōg† *wg.* destitute.

~(w)nes *f.* fewness, scarcity.

~sceaft(ig)† destitute *wg.*; poor, miserable.

gefēa, -ia, fēa *m.* joy [gefēon].

~lic pleasant.

gefēald† *n.* (?).

fēald|an 1 fold.

~estōl, fyldstōl *m.* camp-stool.

feale-for = felo-.

fealg, fealh, æ, e *f.* felly (of wheel) ‖ harrow.

~ian harrow.

~ing *f.* harrowing.

fealh *prt. of* fēolan.

feall = fiell.

gefeall, *lN.* æ [= īe] *n.* falling; ruin.

feall|an 1 fall, *met.* fall (into vice), fall down ; prostrate oneself : him tō fōtum ~ | rush — on ~ assail ; flow (*of* river) | come to an end, decay (*of* kingdom), fall (in battle).

~endlic perishable, transient.

gefeallan 1 fall — *met.* his mōd gefēoll on hyre lufe | perish ‖ *tr.* him dęmm ~ make a slaughter of them.

fealle *f.* trap.

fealo, *pl.* fealwe I. dull-coloured, yellow, yellowish-red, brown, bay (horse). II. *n.* fallow ground.

~hilte† yellow-hilted.

fealwian grow yellow; change colour ; ripen, wither.

fēar = fearh.

fearh, fēar *m.* pig, boar.

gefearh (sow) with young.

fearn *n.* fern.

~bedd *n.* fern-bed.

fearr *m.*, ~hrȳþer *n.* bull.

fēaw, *see* fēa few.

feax *n.* hair of the head, head of hair.

~clāþ *n.* cap.

~ēacan *pl.* forelocks.

~ode with hair — ~ steorra comet. ge~ode, ge~en, ge~e having a head of hair.

~fang *m.* seizing by the hair.

~feallung *f.* loss of hair, mange.

~hār grey-haired.

~nǣdl *f.* curling-iron.

~nes*, fæxnis *f.* head of hair (!) Gl.

~nętt *n.* hair-net.

~prēon *m.* hair-pin.

~sceacga *m.* bunch of hair.

~sceacgede shaggy.

~sceāra *fpl.* hair-cutting scissors.

febbres, *see* fefer.

fęccan = fętian.

fēd|an, oe feed, suckle, bring forth (fruit, children), rear, bring up [fōda].

~(ed)nes *f.* nourishment.

fēd|els, ~esl *m.* feeding, keep ; fattened animal Gl.

~ing *f.* feeding.

~nes *f.* nourishment Bd.

fefer, -or, *once* febbres, *m.* fever.

~ādl *f.* fever.

~fuge *f.* feverfew (a plant) [*Lt.* febrifugia].

~sēoc feverish.

gefēg *n.* joining, joint.

fēg|an, oe join, unite, fix [gefōg].

ge~(ed)nes *f.* joining.

(ge)fēging, -ung *f.* joining ; conjunction (in grammar).

fēl|an, oe feel *wg.*

~elēas without sensation.

(ge)~nes *f.* feeling, sensation.

fel-cyrf foreskin (!).

fel-tūn *n.* privy.

fela, *vE.* felo- many, much : ~ manna, *L.* ~ męnn ; *also* no.

~fǣcne† very treacherous.

~feald manifold, various.

~frēcne† very fierce.

~gēomor† very sad.

~geong† = ~gęnge* having travelled much.

~hrōr† very brave.

~īdel-sprǣce very loquacious.

~lēof† very dear.

~mihtig†, ea very mighty.

~mōdig† very brave.

~sprǣce loquacious.

~sp(r)ecol loquacious.

~sp(r)ecolnes *f.* loquacity.

~synnig† very guilty.

~wlanc† very proud.

~wyrde loquacious.

~wyrdnes *f.* loquacity.

feld, *d.* ~a, ~e *m.* field, plain, field of battle.

~bēo *f.* locust (!).

~biscopwyrt *f.* a plant.

~cirice *f.* country church.

~ęlfen *f.* field-fairy.

~gangende field-traversing.

~hrīper *n.* field-ox.

~hūs *n.* tent.

~land *n.* flat country, lower land.

~lic rural.

~mǣdere *f.* rosemary.

~minte *f.* wild mint.

~more, -u *f.* parsnip.

~oxa *m.* ox kept in field.

~rūde *f.* wild rue.

~swamm fungus.

feld|wēsten(n), oe *f.* desert plain.

~wōp *m.* plantain.

~wyrt *f.* gentian.

felg = fealg.

fell *n.* skin (of man or animal), hide, fur.

~en of skins.

felo-for, *vE.* feolufer, -fe(a)rþ; feal(e)for fieldfare (a bird).

fēlon *A. prt. pl. of* fēolan.

felt (*m.*) felt (?).

~wurma *m.* wild marjoram (a plant).

~wyrt *f.* wild mullein (a plant).

fenester *n. or m.* window [*Lt.* fenestra].

fęng *m.* grasp; booty [fōn].

~nett *n.* net.

~tōþ *m.* canine tooth.

gefęng *IN. n.* taking, capture.

fēng, *prt. of* fōn.

fęngel† *m.* prince, king.

fēnix, e† *m.* phœnix; date palm [*Lt.* phoenix].

fęnn *nm.* mud, dirt; fen.

~cerse *f.* water-cress.

~fearn *n.* osmunda regalis (a fern).

~friþu† *f.* refuge in fen.

~hliþ† *n.* fen-retreat.

~hop† *n.* fen-retreat.

~ig muddy.

~gelād† *n.* fen-tract.

~land *n.* fen-country.

~lic of fens.

~minte *f.* water-mint.

~þæc *n.* fen-covering.

~ȳce*, fenȳce† *f.* frog.

fēo *d. of* feoh.

fēo-laga *m.* partner, associate [*Scand.* fēlaʒi].

fēon, fēogan hate.

fēo(u)ng, fēowung *f.* hatred, hostility.

gefēon, *prt.* -eah, -ǣgon, *ptc.* -ǣgen ₅ rejoice *w. g. or i.*

fēogan = fēon.

feoh, *d.* fēo, *gpl.* fēona *n.* cattle — money — licgende ~ gold and silver, money; property, wealth | *the Runic letter* f.

~behāt *L.* promise of money.

~bōt *f.* pecuniary compensation.

~fang *m.* taking bribes.

~giéfu *f.* bounty.

~gīfre† avaricious.

~gift *f.* gift of money.

feoh|gītsere *m.* miser.

~gītsung, fēog- *f.* avarice.

~gehāt *n.* promise of money.

~hord *m.* treasury.

~hūs *n.* treasury.

~lǣnung *n.* money-lending.

~lēas without money; †not to be bought off (*of* homicide).

~lēasnes *f.* want of money.

~sceattas† *mpl.* wages.

~spēda *fpl.* riches.

~spilling *f.* waste of money.

~gesteald† *n.* possession of riches.

~strang opulent.

~gestrēon† *n.* acquiring money; riches, treasures.

feoht *n.*, ~e *f.* fighting, battle.

~gegięrelan *pl.* implements of war Gl.

~ehorn*, fy- *m.* fighting-horn.

~lāc *n.* fighting.

~ling*, y- *m.* warrior.

~wīte*, y- *n.* fine for fighting.

gefeoht *n.* fight, battle; war.

~dæg† *m.* day of battle.

feoht|an ₃ fight, *w.* wiþ, *w.* on *a.* attack — on ~ attack.

~ere *m.* fighter.

gefeohtan ₃ fight; *wa.* fight (duel) || *tr.* gain by fighting, gain (victory).

fēol, fīl *f.* file.

~heard† hard as a file (?)—*for* fela-heard (?).

~ian file.

fēolan, *prt.* fealh, fēal, *pl.* fulgon, fūlon, fēlon; *ptc.* folgen, fōlen ₃ enter (into a state): inne ~ get in, penetrate; cn flēame ~ take to flight; *wd.* adhere; apply oneself to, persevere in || *tr.* experience (treachery).

fēond, *pl.* fīend, ēo, ~as *m.* enemy; fiend, devil [fēon].

~ǣt† *m.* eating what is sacrificed to idols.

~giéld† *n.* idolatry; idol.

~grāp† *f.* hostile grasp.

~lic hostile.

~līce *av.* hostilely.

~rǣden(n) *f.* enmity.

~rǣs† *m.* hostile attack.

~sc(e)aþa† *m.* enemy, robber, villain.

~scipe *m.* hostility, enmity.

~sēoc possessed by a devil.

~ulf *m.* villain Gl. [ulf = -wulf].

fēond-wīc *n.* hostile camp.

feor, *see* feorr.

~būend† *m.* one dwelling far off, foreigner.

~cumen, ~cund = feorran-.

~cȳþþ† *f.* distant country.

~land *n.* distant land.

~nes *f.* distance.

~weg *m.* distant part.

feor-stuþu *f.* support, prop Gl.

feorh, feorg, *g.* fēores, *nm.* life — be fēore on pain of death; soul —†tō (wīdan) fēore, ā(wa) tō fēore, ǣfre tō fēore, ealne wīdan ~ for ever | living being, person.

~ādl *f.* mortal disease.

~bana† *m.* homicide, murderer.

~bealo† *n.* deadly evil.

~benn† *f.* mortal wound.

~gebeorg† *n.* refuge.

~berend† *m.* living being.

~bold† *n.* body.

~cwalu† *f.* death, slaughter.

~cwealm† *n.* death.

~cynn† *n.* living species *or* kind.

~dæg† *m.* day of life.

~gedāl† *n.* death.

~dolg† *n.* deadly wound.

~ēacen† living.

~fǣgen glad of being allowed to live.

~geong young, *or two words* (?).

~giéfa *m.* giver of life.

~giéfu† *f.* gift of life.

~gōma† *m.* jaw.

~hama*, fea- *m.* womb *or* caul (?) Gl.

~hierde† *m.* preserver, protector.

~hord† *m.* soul.

~hūs† *n.* body.

~lāst† *m.* track, step.

~lēan *n.* gift of life (?).

~legu† *f.* life.

~lif† *n.* life.

~loca† *m.* breast.

~lyre *m.* loss of life.

~nęre† *m.* refuge; sustenance; salvation (of soul).

~gener *n.* being allowed to live, life.

~genipla† *m.* mortal enemy.

~rǣd† *n.* soul's benefit, salvation.

~scyldig having forfeited one's life, guilty of a capital offence.

~sēoc† sick to death.

~swęng† *m.* deadly blow.

feorh|þearf† f. extreme need.
~wund† f. mortal wound.
feorlen = fierlen.
feorm, _IN._ a, æ f. feeding; provisions, food; feast | entertaining, taking in (strangers), harbouring (criminals)] goods, property, stores; rent in kind; use, benefit.
~fultum m. contribution of provisions.
~ehām m. farm vL.
feorm|ian supply with food, feed, support; entertain (as guest) | cherish; profit, benefit | clean, polish | consume.
~end m. entertainer; (sword) polisher.
~endlēas† without a polisher.
~ere m. purveyor.
~ung f. entertaining, harbouring; polishing, cleaning.
feorr av., aj. (rarely inflected) far w.i. or fram, distant, at a distance — ~ and wīde in every direction; far back in time | moreover, besides, = fierr cpv. (!) || cpv. fierra aj. more distant, further (Spain). av. fierr further || spl. fierrest aj., av. most distant w.i., furthest.
feorr|ian intr. keep at a distance; depart.
~ung f. departure, being removed.
feorran, feorrane, y- av. from afar, at a distance — ~ and nēan from all quarters.
~cumen, feorc- come from afar.
~cund, feorc- having come from a distance, foreign.
feorran, feorsian = fie-.
feort|an* 3.
~ing f. pedatio.
fēorþ|a, fēowerþa fourth [fēower].
~ling, ~ung m. fourth part; farthing.
fēower four.
~feald fourfold — be ~um av. fourfold.
~fealdlīce av. quadruply.
~fēte, ~fōtede four-footed.
~gīeld n. fourfold payment or compensation.
~scīete four-cornered, square.
~tēoþa, ~teog(o)þa fourteenth.
~tiene fourteen.
fēowertig forty.
~feald fortyfold.

fēowertig|lic of forty.
~oþa fortieth.
fer = for.
fer|ian carry, convey, lead, bring || intr. take to, deal in w. i. or on; go, depart [faran].
~bedd n. portable bed.
~iend m. bringer, leader.
~(e)sceatt m. passage-money, fare.
fēr|an, oe go, march, sail, travel— wa. of distance; set out, depart | ~forþ go forth, go on; die | behave, act.
~end m. messenger; sailor.
~ing f. going, travelling.
~nes f. going, passing.
gefēr|an go; fare; behave, act || tr. accomplish (journey, distance) | reach, attain (place), gain (victory) — āxode hwæt hī ~don what had become of them | suffer (misfortune).
gefēr|a, fēra, oe m. companion, friend; wife; associate (in an undertaking); equal; retainer, attendant [faran].
~lǣcan associate, unite.
~lic associated.
~līce av. sociably, together.
~rǣden(n) f. companionship: body of people, retinue; association, congregation; compact.
~scipe, f- m. companionship; body of people, retinue, band; association, guild.
~scipian _IN._ unite tr.
ferc|ian, ferec- tr. bring (a person); support (life), feed — met. cram (with lies) || intr. go, proceed.
~ung f. sustenance, food.
fēre serviceable (ship), fit for military service.
gefēre I. accessible. II. n. body of people; community; party, side.
ferht honest.
~lic honest, just.
fer(h)þ† mn. mind, spirit, understanding; life—wīdan ~ for ever.
~bana m. murderer.
~cearig anxious in mind.
~cleofa, ~cofa m. breast.
~gedāl*, friþ-† n. death.
~frec bold in spirit.
~friþende life-protecting, life-sustaining.
~glēaw sagacious, wise.
~grimm fierce.

ferhþ|loca m. breast, heart; body.
~lufe f. heartfelt love.
~genīþla m. deadly foe.
~sefa m. mind.
~wērig soul-weary, sad.
~gewitt n. understanding.
fers n. sentence; verse [Lt. versus].
~ian make verses Gl.
fersc fresh (water).
fēster-, fēstr- = fōstor-, fōstr-.
fēt, see fōt.
fetan 5 fall.
fetian, once a, feccan, fettan, prt. fette fetch; summon; seek; take, seize; gain; marry.
fetel (m.) belt.
~hilt n. belted hilt.
feter, fetor f. fetter.
~wrāsen† f. fetter.
fettian once contend.
fēþ|an.
~ung f. walking, motion.
fēþa, oe m. troop, band of infantry.
fēþe n. walking, movement, power of motion.
~cempa† m. active warrior, footsoldier.
~gang† m. foot-journey.
~georn† eager to go.
~giest† m. traveller.
~here m. infantry.
~hwearf† m. troop on foot.
~lāst† m. step.
~lēas† without feet; crippled.
~mann m. foot-soldier.
~mund† f. fore-feet (of badger).
~spēdig† quick walking.
~wīg† n. battle on foot.
feþer f. feather; pen; pl. feþra wings.
~bǣre winged.
~bedd n. feather-bed.
~berende feathered.
~cræft m. embroidery.
~gearwe ⊦ fpl. feathering (of arrow).
~hama† m. plumage; feather-coat, flying apparatus, wings.
~geweorc n. embroidery in feathers.
feþer-scēat = fiþer-.
gefīc n. deceit, treachery.
fīc m. fig; ~, se blēdenda ~ piles, hemorrhoids.
~ādl f. piles.
~æppel m. fig.
~bēam m. fig-tree.
~lēaf n. fig-leaf.
~trēow n. fig-tree.

[57]

fīc|wyrm m. intestinal worm.
~wyrt f. fig-wort.
ficol cunning, tricky [gefic].
fielg|an* harrow [fealg].
~ing*, ~æ, ~y f. harrowing, harrow.
fięll, ea m. fall (falling, cause of fall) | ruin, destruction; death, slaughter | case (in grammar) [feallan].
~wērig*, fylw-† killed, dead.
fięll|an, A. æ make to fall, fell, pull down (house); destroy, kill; humble; LN. offend, scandalizare; †ge~ wag. deprive (of kinsmen) by killing.
~nes f LN. offence, scandalum.
ge~nes f. LN. fall; transmigration (!).
fięlle|sēoc epileptic.
~sēocnes f., ~wærc m. epilepsy.
fīend, see fēond.
gefīend pl. enemies — wæron ~ were at enmity.
fięrd f. militia, army; military expedition, campaign; camp (!) for ~wīc [faran].
~cræft m. art of war, warfare.
~ęsne m. soldier.
~færeld n. (liability to) military service.
~faru f. military service.
~geatwa† fpl. arms.
~ham† m. corslet.
~hrægl † n. armour, corslet.
~hwæt† warlike.
~lāf f. remnant of an army.
-lēas without an army, undefended.
~lēoþ† n. war-song.
~lic military.
~gemaca m. companion in arms.
~mann m. soldier.
~rinc† m. soldier, warrior.
~sceorp† n. armour.
~scip n. war-ship.
~searo† n. armour.
~sōcn f. military service.
~gestealla† m. companion in arms, fellow-soldier.
~stemn m. detachment of militia.
~tiber n. military sacrifice (?) Gl.
~getrum n. band of soldiers, cohort.
~truma m. cohort, army.
~wæn m. military wagon Ct.
~weard f. military watch.
~werod n. army.

fięrd|wīc n. camp.
~wierpe† distinguished in war.
~wīsa† m. general.
~wise f. military manner.
~wīte n. fine for neglect of military duties.
fięrd,ian, fyrdrian serve in army; march; be at war with.
~ing, -ung f. expedition; army; camp.
fiergen-, i, y mountain.
~bēam† m. mountain-tree.
~bucca m., ~gāt f. chamois.
~hēafod† n. mountain-headland.
~holt† n. mountain-wood.
~strēam† m. mountain-stream.
fierlen*, e(o), y I. distant, remote — on ~e, on ~um far away. II. n. distance.
fiermþ, frymþ f. entertainment, harbouring (criminals) || cleansing, washing [feorm].
fierr(a), fierrest, see feorr.
fiersian*, y, eo intr. go beyond || tr. remove; rfl. depart.
fiersn† once f. heel.
fīf five.
~ecgede with five edges or corners.
~feald fivefold.
~fēte(d) five-footed.
~flēre five-storied.
~læppede having five lobes.
~lēaf n. cinquefoil.
~wintre five years old.
fīf-mægen = fīfel-.
fīfealde, fiff- f. butterfly.
fīfel† (n.) monster, giant.
~cynn n. race of monsters.
~dor n. the river Eider (between Holstein and Slesvig).
~mægen*, fīfm- n. magic power.
~strēam, ~wæg m. ocean.
fifele f. buckle [Lt. fibula].
fīfta fifth.
fīf-tēopa fifteenth.
fīf-tiene fifteen.
fīftig fifty.
~feald fiftyfold.
~opa, -eog- fiftieth.
fihte (n.) rag LN.
fīl = fēol file.
~ian rub (!) Gl.
fild milking, quantity milked at one time.
~cumb n. milk-pail.
filde level (land) [feld].
gefilde n. plain.

filiþ|e n. hay.
~lēag m. meadow Ct.
filmen, y n. film, thin skin; prepuce.
fīn heap of wood, wood-store.
fīna m. woodpecker.
finc m. finch.
find|an (3) prt. funde, fand find, meet: funde hine licgan; ~ cweartern beclȳsed; find out (hwelc hē sīe); ~ æt obtain — met. ic ne mæg æt mē selfum ~ þæt ic hine æfre gesēo I cannot bring myself to . ., I cannot bear to . . | think of (plan), devise, invent: se cyning funde þæt him man sæt wiþ made arrangements for opposing their landing, fundon þæt hīe sendon æfter him agreed on the plan of sending. .
~end m. finder.
finger m. finger.
~æppel m. date.
~doccan pl. finger-muscles.
~līc of a finger.
finn m. fin.
~iht*, finiht finny.
finol, finugl m., finu(g)le f. fennel [Lt. foeniculum].
~sæd n. fennel-seed.
finta† m. tail; consequence, result.
fīras† mpl. men, mankind.
firen, fy- f. crime, sin; violence; torment, suffering. firnum av. wickedly, excessively.
~bealo† n. sinful evil.
~cræft† m. wickedness.
~dæd† f. crime.
~earfoþ† n. terrible suffering.
~fremmende† sinful.
~full†, ~georn†, ~lic† sinful.
~lice† av. violently, rashly.
~ligerian commit fornication.
~lust m. sinful lust, luxury.
~lustfull luxurious, wanton.
~synnig† sinful.
~pearf† f. dire need or distress.
~weorc† n. crime.
~wyrcend(e)†, ~wyrhta† m. evil-doer.
fir(e)nian sin, commit adultery; revile.
firenicg|a* m., ~e* f., fyrenhycga, fyrnhicge adulterer, adulteress, &c.
firmdig = frymdig.

[58]

firmettan ask, request *w. a. and sbj.*

firn, y I. ancient. II. *av.* long ago. *cpv.* (gīet) ~or.

~dagas† *mpl.* days of old.

~geflit† *n.* former quarrel.

~geflita† *m.* old enemy.

~gēar† *npl.* former years, lapse of time.

~gēara† *av.* of old.

~giédd† *n.* ancient tradition, prophecy.

~lic former, ancient.

~mann† *m.* man of old.

~gemynd† *n.* old tradition.

~scapa† *m.* old enemy.

~gesceap† *n.* old decree.

~segen† *f.* ancient tradition.

~gesetu† *npl.* ancient seats or abode.

~strēamas† *mpl.* ancient streams, ocean. *Cp.* fiergen-.

~gestrēon† *n.* ancient treasure.

~synn† *f.* ancient sin.

~(ge)weorc† *n.* ancient work.

~gewinn† *n.* ancient war.

~wita† *m.* sage, councillor.

~gewrit† *n.* ancient writing, scripture.

~gewyrht† *n.* former deserts, fate.

gefirn *av.* long ago, far back (in time); for a long time, *spl.* ~ost furthest back (in time) — ~ worulde long ago.

~dagas *mpl.* days of old.

~gewiten long past (time).

first *f.* roof, ceiling.

first, ie, y *m.* space of time; respite; time (to finish something).

~hrōf *m.* ceiling, *or two words* (?).

~mearc *f.* space of time, appointed time, interval.

~gemearc *n.* space of time.

firwit, -et, fy-, fe(o)- *n.* curiosity. hine ~ bræc, hine ~ frægn þæs he was curious.

~full inquisitive.

~georn inquisitive, curious.

~geornnes *f.* curiosity.

~nes *f.* curiosity.

firwit, -tt curious, inquisitive.

fisc, *pl.* ~as, fixas *m.* fish.

~brȳne (*m.*) brine.

~cynn *n.* fish kind, species of fish.

~dēag *f.* purple.

~flōd(u)† *m.* sea.

~hūs *n.* fishing-house.

fisc|mere *m.* fish-pond.

~nett *n.* fishing-net; net of fishes.

~pōl *m.* fish-pool; pool in river.

~prūt *m.* small fish *IN.*

~wer *m.* fish-weir (for catching fish).

~wielle I. abounding in fish. II. *m.* fish-pond Gl.

fisc|ian, fix- fish.

~ere *m.* fisher; kingfisher.

~(n)oþ, fisc(n)aþ *m.* fishing.

fīsting *f.* fesiculatio, *following* pedatio *in Gl.*

fitt *f.* song, poem.

~an sing, tell in verse.

fitt† *once* fight.

fitung *f.* fighting LL.

fiþel|e *f.* fiddle.

~ere *m.*, ~estre *f.* fiddler.

fiþer-, e(o), *L.* fēower- [fēower].

~dǣled quadripartite.

~fēte, ~fōte four-footed.

~flēdende flowing in four streams (river) Gl.

~hīwe quadriform.

~ling *m.* quarter.

~rīca *m.* tetrarch.

~scēatas*, fe-† *mpl.* four quarters (?).

~scietan quarter Gl.

~sciete quadrangular.

~tīeme four-teamed (chariot).

fiþer|e *n.* wing [feþer].

~bǣre, ~berende winged.

ge~hamod feathered.

ge~ian feather, wing.

~lēas without wings.

~slieht *m.* flapping wings.

flā = flān.

flacor† flying (*of* arrows).

flǣsc, flǣc *n.* flesh, body, living creature.

~ǣt *m.* meat.

~bana *m.* murderer.

~gebyrd *f.* incarnation.

~cieping *f.* meat-market.

~cofa *m.* body, flesh.

~(c)wellere *m.* executioner

~en of flesh.

~ennes *f.* incarnation.

~hama† *m.* body.

ge~hamod incarnate.

~hord† *n.* body.

~hūs *n.* meat-house.

~lic carnal.

~licnes *f.* incarnation.

~mangere *m.* butcher.

~maþu *f.* maggot.

flǣsc|mete *m.*, *pl.* ~mettas meat.

ge~nes *f.* incarnation.

ge~od incarnate.

~strǣt *f.* meat-market.

~tāwere *m.* executioner.

~tōþ *m.* one of the teeth Gl.

~wyrm *m.* maggot.

flǣþe-camb = fleþe-.

flagg plaster.

flāh† I. treacherous, hostile. II. *n.* treachery.

flān *fm.*, flā *f.*, *pl.* ~a, ~ arrow, dart.

~boga† *m.* bow.

~hred† R.

~iht of an arrow.

~þracu† *f.* attack *or* force of arrows.

~geweorc† *n.* arrows.

flasce, flaxe *f.* flask, bottle [*Lt.* vasculum].

flax-fōte = flox- web-footed.

flēa, flēah (*f.*) flea.

~wyrt *f.* fleabane (a plant).

flēan 2 *ptc.* flagen flay, strip off (piece of skin).

flēah *n.* albugo, white spot in the eye.

flēam *m.* flight — wearþ *or* fealh on ~e took to flight [flēon].

~lāst *m.* apostasy Gl.

fleard *n.* folly, superstition.

~ian grow luxuriantly; play the fool; act wrongly.

gefleard *n.* folly, madness, error.

fleaþe = fleope.

fleax *n.* flax.

~æcer *m.* flax-field.

~līne *f.* flax-winder, reel.

~gescot *n.* contribution of flax.

flecta = fleohta.

flēd|an* flow [flōd].

~ing *f.* flowing.

~e full (river).

flēon *prt.* flēah, *pl.* flugon, *ptc.* flogen 7 flee; put to flight; fly. *Cp.* flēogan.

flēog|an 7 *intr.* fly; move quickly; flee. *Cp.* flēon.

~endlic flying.

gefleogan 7 *intr.* fly || *tr.* fly over.

flēog|e *f.* fly.

~cynn, flēoh- *n.* fly-kind.

~nett *n.* fly-net, mosquito-curtain.

~rift *n.* fly-curtain.

fleoht|an* 3 plait, weave. *See* flohten-fōte.

fleohta*, *vE.* flecta *m.* hurdle.

flēos = flīes.

flēot *m.* mouth of river, estuary; bay | sea, water | raft, ship, vessel. ~**wyrt** *f.* seaweed.

flēotan 7 float, sail; swim.

fleoþe, ea *f.* water-lily.

flēring *f.* flooring, story [flōr].

fleswian *once* whisper.

flętt *n.* floor; dwelling, house, hall. ~**þæþ**† *m.* floor. ~**ręst**† *f.* bed. ~**sittend**† *m.* hall-sitter, courtier. ~**gesteald**† *n.* household goods. ~**werod**† *n.* hall-troop, retainers.

fleþe-camb, æ *m.* weaver's comb.

flēwsa *m.* flux, discharge (in medicine) [flōwan].

flex = fleax.

flicce *n.* flitch (of bacon).

flicerian flutter, hover.

geflīen*, **ȳ, ī, -an** expel (disease) [flēon].

flīem|an put to flight, banish [flēam].

flīem|a *m.* fugitive, outlaw — ~**an** *or* ~**ena fiermþ** *or* **feorm** harbouring an outlaw [flēam]. **ge-~e** fugitive *LN*.

flīes, ēo *n.* fleece.

flīete *f.* cream, curds ‖ punt [flēotan].

fligel (*m.*) flail.

flint *m.* flint; rock. ~**grǣg**† grey as flint.

flit strife; scandalum (!) [flītan]. ~**cræft** *m.* disputation, logic. ~**cræftig** belonging to logic, dialectical. ~**full** contentious. ~**georn** quarrelsome, litigious. ~**mǣlum** *av.* contentiously.

geflit *n.* strife, dissension, contest; dispute, discussion. **tō ~es** emulously.

~**full**, ~**fullic**, ~**georn** contentious. ~**fulnes** *f.* litigiousness. ~**lice**, ~**mǣlum** *av.* emulously.

flit|an 6 contend, struggle (in lawsuit, argument), oppose, quarrel. ~**end**, ~**ere** *m.* wrangler.

flōc (*m.*) a fish.

flōcan† clap, applaud.

flocc *m.* body of men, troop, company. ~**mǣlum** *av.* troopwise, in detachments, flockwise, in flocks. ~**rǣd** *f.* troop of cavalry. ~**slite** *m.* sedition.

flōd *mn.* flowing, stream; flow of tide, tide | river, sea, *pl.* water; deluge, flood [flōwan]. ~**blāc**† flood-pale. ~**egesa**† *m.* terror of flood. ~**en**, ~**lic** of a river. ~**weard**† *f.* sea-wall. ~**weg**† *m.* ocean path, sea. ~**wielm**† *m.* raging flood. ~**wudu**† *m.* ship. ~**ȳþ**† *f.* wave of the sea.

flōde *f.* channel; gutter.

flogettan, gg fluctuate Gl. [flēogan].

flogeþa *m.* liquid Gl.

flōh fragment, piece (of stone).

flohten-fōte web-footed [fleohtan].

flōr, d. ~a, ~e *fm.* floor; ground — scipes ~, gangway. ~**stān** *m.* pavement-stone.

flōrisc flowery [*Lt.*].

flot *n.* sea [flēotan]. ~**here**† *m.* (hostile) fleet. ~**lic** naval. ~**mann** *m.* sailor, pirate, Dane. ~**scip** *n.* ship. ~**smero** *n.* dripping, fat. ~**weg**† *m.* sea.

flotian float *L*.

flota *m.* sailor, pirate†; ship; fleet.

geflota† *m.* floater, swimmer.

floter|ian float, be flooded — mid ~**iendum ēagum** weeping; fly; flutter, be disquieted (*of* heart) [flēotan].

flōw|an 1 flow; be abundant. ~**(ed)nes** *f.* flowing, flux (of blood); overflow, torrent.

flox-fōte, fla- web-footed. *Cp.* flohten.

flugol, flygol [*infl. of* flyge] flying, fleeing; fleeting [flēogan, flēon].

flycgan*, **e** put to flight, disperse [flēon].

flyge *m.* flying, flight (of birds, arrows). ~**rēow**† fierce in flight. ~**wil**† *m.* flying wile.

flygol = flugol.

flyht *m.* flying, flight (of birds, weapons) [flēogan]. ~**hwæt**† brisk in flight.

flyhte-clāþ, vE. flycti- *m.* patch [fleohtan].

flyne *f.* batter.

flytme *f.* lancet [*Lt.* **phlebotomum**].

fnæd, ge- *n.* fringe, hem (of dress). **fnæs** *n.* fringe.

fnæsettan snort.

fnǣst *m.* breath, breathing; blast (of fire). ~**ian** breathe hard.

fnēos|an sneeze. ~**ung** *f.* sneezing.

gefnesan (5) *once* sneeze. *Cp.* fnēosan.

fnora *m.* sneeze [fnēosan].

fōn 1 b (hē) fēhþ, *prt.* fēng, *ptc.* fangen grasp, seize — *abs.* : **him tōgēanes fēng** clutched at him; **tōgædre fēngon** engaged in battle; **him on fultum fēng** came to their help | make prisoner, capture *gen.* **ge-** : **gefēngon hine, micle herehȳþ** | take, receive *A*. **wi.** (fēng wīfe), *W. w.* **tō**, on *a.* : ~ **tō wīfe**, ~ **tō hæþeniscum þēawum**, ~ **on fæsten** take to fasting; ~ **tō rīce** come to the throne, ~ **tō þǣm lande** succeed to the estate; ~ **tō þǣm norþdǣle** begin to describe the North (of Europe); **uton fōn on þæt godspell þǣr wē hit forlēton** return to the discussion of . . ; ~ **tō wurþienne** begin to worship.

foca *m.* cake of bread.

fōda *m.* food.

fōdor, fōdder *n.* food; fodder, food for cattle | case, sheath. ~**brytta** *m.* fodderer, herdsman. ~**hec** fodder-rack. ~**noþ** *m.* sustenance. ~**pegu**† *f.* taking food, food. ~**wela**† *m.* abundance of food.

fōdrere *m.* forager (of army).

gefōg *n.* joining, joint. ~**stān** *m.* key-stone.

fol = full.

gefol with foal.

fola *m.* foal, colt.

folc *n.* people, crowd — ~**es mann** layman; army; nation. ~**āgende**† ruling. ~**bealo**† *n.* severe evil *or* affliction. ~**bearn**† *n.* man. ~**beorn**† *m.* man. ~**cū**† *f.* cow of the people (!). ~**cūþ** celebrated, well known; public (road) (!). ~**cwēn**† *f.* queen.

folc|cyning† *m.* king.
~dryht† *f.* people.
~ęgsa† *m.* terror.
~gefeoht *n.* pitched battle.
~firen† *f.* crime.
~frēa† *m.* lord, king.
~frēo, -frīg folk-free, free as other people.
~isc of the people, popular, common.
~lagu *f.* law of the people.
~land *n.* land of the people.
~lār *f.* homily, sermon.
~lēasung *f.* slander.
~lic of the people, popular, common.
~mægen† *n.* army.
~mǣgþ† *f.* tribe, nation.
~mǣre† celebrated.
~mōt, ~gemōt *n.* popular assembly, folkmoot.
~nīed† *f.* need of the people.
~rǣd† *m.* public benefit.
~rǣden(n)† *f.* decree of the people.
~gerēfa *m.* official.
~ryht, ~geryht *n.* popular right, right of a citizen; common law.
~ryht lawful.
~sǣl† *n.* hall, house.
~scaru† *f.* tribe, nation; † = folc-land, land of the people.
~scaþa† *m.* villain.
~scipe† *m.* people, nation.
~gesęttnes *f.* statute Bd.
~gesiþ† *m.* noble, prince.
~slite *m.* sedition.
~gestealla† *m.* companion in war.
~stęde† *m.* dwelling-place; battle-place.
~stōw *f.* country place (*as opposed to a town*).
~gestrēon† *n.* public treasure.
~swēot† *m.* multitude, army.
~getæl† *n.* number of people.
~talu *f.* genealogy.
~toga† *m.* chief, general.
~getrum† *n.* host.
~truma *m.* people.
~geþrang *n.* crowd.
~welig populous.
~wer† *m.* man.
~wiga† *m.* warrior.
~gewinn† *n.* battle, war.
~wita† *m.* councillor.
~wōh *n.* deception of the people.
fold|e† *f.* earth; mould, soil, ground; country.
~ærn *n.* sepulchre.
~āgend*, folc- *m.* man.

fold|bold *n.* house, palace.
~būend(e) *m.* man.
~grǣf *n.* grave.
~grǣg earth-grey.
~hrērende earth-traversing.
~ręst *f.* rest in the earth, being buried.
~wæstm *m.* fruit of the earth.
~wang *m.* earth.
~weg *m.* path, way; earth.
~wela *m.* earthly wealth *or* prosperity.
fōlen *ptc. of* fēolan.
folg|ian, fyl(i)gan *wd.* succeed (in time); follow, pursue; persecute; obey, observe (law); serve, belong to household of; yield to physical force: gif sēo hringe him ~aþ æt þām forman tyge (pull). *See* fyligan.
~ere *m.* follower, disciple; retainer, freeman belonging to another's household; successor (in office).
folgen *ptc. of* fēolan.
folgaþ *m.* body of followers *or* retainers, province; service, official position (*esp.* at court), office, appointment; condition of life.
folm†, -e *f.* palm of hand; hand.
for, fer, æ, A. fore *prp. w. d., i., a.* before: ~ eaxlum stōd þæs cyninges; weorþode hīe ~ ealle menn above. *These meanings are not W.; they are probably the result of transliterating A.* fore *into* for | *time* before: ~ fēawum dagum a few days ago, nū ~ fēower gēarum | in the sight of, as regards: rīce ~ worulde | *cause*: mōdigode ~ his fægernesse; ~ Godes lufan; swealt ~ þām gylte | *aim*: cōm þider ~ þæs cyninges swicdōme to betray | *benefit*: bæd ~ his cwelleras *or* cwellerum | *equivalence, wa.*: rīxode ~ þone Herōdem in the place of, after; ēage ~ ēage; hæfdon hine ~ ǣnne wītegan | ~ ān only || for-hwȳ, -hwǣm, ā, -hwon, a why.
for-þǣm, ā, -þon, a, A. for(e)-þon therefore; because *w. indc.*
for-þǣm-þe, -þon- because *w. indc.* for-þǣm-þæt in order that *w. sbj.* for-þȳ, ī therefore. for-þȳ-þe, -þon-þȳ . . þe because. for-þȳ-þæt, for-þȳ . . þæt in order that *w. sbj.*

for *av.* too, very, very much.
fōr *f.* movement, motion, course; journey; way of life [faran].
~bedd *n.* litter Gl.
~bōc *f.* itinerary.
~męte *m.* provisions for a journey.
fōr, oo (*m.*) pig Gl.
for-, fer-, æ.
for- *occ.* = fore-.
foran, ~e *av.* in front, before — ~ forrīdan cut off advance (of army); *time* before | foran ongēan *prp. wa.* opposite. foran tō *prp. wd.* before (*time*).
~bodig *n.* chest.
~hēafod, for(e)h- *n.* forehead.
~niht *f.* early part of the night.
for-āþ = fore-.
for·bærn|an *tr.* burn up, burn.
~ednes *f.* being burnt, burn (on body).
for·belgan 3 *rfl.* be angry.
for·bēodan 7 forbid *wda.* (him unryht), *w. sbj., w. ger.*
~endlic dehortative (in grammar).
for·beran 4 endure, suffer, tolerate; restrain || *intr.* forbear, refrain from *w. indc. or sbj.*: forbær þæt hē ne slōg hine.
for·berstan 3 *intr.* break, be broken; come to nothing, fail; let go by default.
for·bieg|an *tr.* bend down, bend; humble.
~els *m.* arch, vault.
for·biernan, eo 3 be consumed by fire, be burnt.
for·bindan 3 tie up (mouth of ox).
for·bītan 6 bite through.
for·blāwan 1 *tr.* blow: wind forblēow hīe ūt on sǣ; blow out— *ptc.* forblāwen suffering from flatulence.
for·blindian *lA. tr.* blind.
for·bod *n.* prohibition.
for·brecan 4 break down; break, destroy — forbrocen decrepit; violate, break (oath, commands).
for·bregdan, -brēdan 3 tear in pieces; cover; transform.
for·brytednes *f.* contrition.
for·bryttan, -brytan break to pieces, crush.
for·būgan 7 *tr.* turn away from, flee from; avoid, refrain from; refuse (office); hold down, prevent from rising.

[61]

for·byrd *f.* abstention, restriction.
~**ian** endure, wait for Gl.
forca *m.* fork [*Lt.* furca].
for·**ceorfan** 3 cut off, out, down, through (tongue, tree, neck).
for·**cēowan** 7 bite off (one's own tongue).
for·**cierr|an** *tr.* turn aside, *rfl.* turn back *intr.*; turn upside down; avoid, escape.
~**ed** perverse.
~**ing** *f.* turning aside.
for·**cinnan**† R.
for·**clǣman** stop up.
for·**clingan** 3 shrink, wither.
for·**clȳsan** *tr.* close, obstruct.
for·**cnīdan** 6 break to pieces, crush.
for·**cuman** 4 overcome, surpass; assail; wear out, destroy.
for·**cūþ** depraved, wicked, bad, foul.
~**e**, ~**līce** *av.* badly.
for·**cweþan** 5 speak ill of; rebuke; reject.
for·**cwolstan** swallow, take (medicine).
for·**cȳþan**† surpass in knowledge, confute.
ford, *d.* -a, -e *m.* ford.
for·**dǣlan** expend (money).
for·**delfan** 3 dig.
for·**dēm|an** condemn.
~**edlic** to be condemned.
~**ednes** *f.* condemnation, proscription.
for·**demman** shut up, stop (ears).
for·**dīcian** block up.
for·**dīl(i)gian** exterminate, destroy.
for·**dimmian** become dark, obscure.
for·**dōn** destroy, ravage, ruin, kill; lead astray, pervert — *ptc.* fordōn corrupt, wicked.
for·**drencan** intoxicate.
for·**drīfan** 6 expel, drive into exile; drive out of course, carry away (*of* current of river).
for·**drincan** 3 — *ptc.* fordruncen intoxicated.
for·**drūgian**, -ūwian *intr.* dry up.
for·**dwīnan** 6 dwindle away, disappear, vanish (from sight); perish.
for·**dwylman***, i confound, obscure (sight) [dwolma].
for·**dyttan** stop up, close.

fore I. *prp. w. d., a., often written* for *in A. and occ. in W.*, before: ~ **ēagum**; mīþan onsīene ~ **him** | *superiority, rank* before, above: for(e) ōþrum (*or* ōþre) bēon | *time* before | *causal*, because, for the sake of | *equivalence*, instead of. II. *av.* beforehand.
for·**eald|ian** grow old, decay — *ptc.* ~**od** superannuated (soldier).
for(e)·**āþ** *m.* preliminary oath.
for·**ēaþe** *av.* very easily.
fore·**bēacen** *n.* portent, prodigy.
fore·**beran** 4 prefer (!).
for(e)·**bīsen** *f.* example.
fore·**bodian** announce, utter (!).
for(e)·**boda** *m.* messenger (of God).
fore·**brēost** *n.* chest, breast.
fore·**burg** *f.* vestibule, entrance; outwork.
fore·**byrd** *f.* authority.
fore·**ceorf|an** 3 cut off front of (!).
~**end** *m.* front tooth.
fore·**costian** profane (!).
for(e)·**cuman** 4 come before, come forward; forestall, prevent.
fore·**cweþan** 5 foretell, predict; mention before *or* above.
fore·**cynren** *n.* progeny (!).
fore·**duru** *f.* porch, vestibule.
fore·**dyre** *n.* vestibule.
fore·**fang***, for-, *E.* for(e)feng *m.* capture *or* recovery of cattle, &c.; reward for such recovery.
~**feoh** *n.* reward for rescuing stolen cattle, &c.
for(e)·**feng** = forefang.
fore·**fērende** going before.
fore·**fōn** 1 anticipate.
fore·**gān**, -gangan precede; take precedence of, excel.
fore·**genga** *mf.* one who goes in front, forerunner; attendant, servant; predecessor (in office); ancestor.
fore·**gengel***, for- *m.* predecessor.
fore·**gīsl** *m.* preliminary hostage.
fore·**glēaw** provident, prudent, wise.
~**līce** *av.* providently, prudently.
fore·**hālig** very holy.
fore·**gehāt** *n.* promise, vow.
for(e)·**hēafod** = foran-.
fore·**iernend** *m.* predecessor.
fore·**lǣrende** teaching.

fore·**mǣr|e**, ~**lic** illustrious, eminent.
~**nes** *f.* eminence, renown.
fore·**manian** forewarn.
fore·**mearcod** before-mentioned.
fore·**mearcung** *f.* chapter *IN.*
fore·**mihtig**, ea very mighty, chief.
~**līce** *av.* very mightily.
fore·**munt** *m.* promontory (!).
fore·**nyme** *m.* taking before.
fore·**rīdel***, for- *m.* fore-rider, mounted messenger.
fore·**rīm** *m.* preface.
for(e)·**rynel** *m.* forerunner, precursor.
fore·**scēaw|ian**, for- foresee, see; appoint, ordain — ~**ode him wununge** provided him with.
~**ere** *m.* appointer.
~**odlīce** *av.* providently, thoughtfully.
~**ung** *f.* foreseeing; prudence; (divine) providence.
fore·**scēotan***, for- 7 anticipate, forestall, prevent.
fore·**scip***, for- *n.* prow of ship.
fore·**scyttels** *m.* bar, bolt.
fore·**secgan** foretell; mention before *or* above.
fore·**sendan** send before
fore·**sēo|n** 5 foresee; provide.
~**nd** *m.* provider.
~**nes** *f.* (divine) providence.
fore·**set|tan**, for- place before *or* in front; shut in, enclose; appoint, intend.
~(**ed**)**nes**, **foregeseten(n)es** *f.* purpose, intention; preposition.
fore·**gesettan** put before.
fore·**singend** *m.* precentor.
fore·**sittan** 5 preside (!).
fore·**smē(ag)an** think *or* consider beforehand.
fore·**snot(t)or**† very prudent *or* wise.
fore·**sp(r)ǣc** *f.* preface, preamble; agreement; (legal) defence, pleading; promise (of godfather at baptism).
fore·**sp(r)eca**, for- *m.* advocate, mediator; sponsor.
fore·**sp(r)ecen**, for- above-mentioned.
for(e)·**stæpp|an**, ę 2 go before, precede; excel; forestall.
~**end** *m.* predecessor.

fore-stæppung *f.* anticipating, preventing.

fore-standan 2 excel (!); preside.

for(e)-steall *m.* assault; fine for assault | forestalling, interference.

fore-stēora *m.* look-out man, pilot.

fore-stigan 6 excel.

fore-stiht|ian preordain.

~ung *f.* preordaining.

for(e)-tācn *n.* foretoken, presage, prodigy.

~ian presage.

fore-tēon *wk.* preordain, settle beforehand.

fore-teohhung *f.* predestination.

fore-tiege (*n.*) porch, vestibule. *Cp.* forþtiege.

fore-tōþ *m.* front tooth.

fore-þanc *m.* forethought, deliberation, consideration, (divine) providence.

~lic provident, thoughtful.

~līce *av.* prudently, thoughtfully.

~ol provident, prudent, wise.

~ol nes *f.* prudence.

for e-þencan consider beforehand.

fore-þing ian plead for, defend (in law-court), intercede.

~ere , ~iend *m.* intercessor.

~rǣden(n), ~ung *f.* intercession.

fore-warnian take warning beforehand Gl.

fore-wāt *vb.* foreknow.

fore-weall *m.* rampart, bulwark.

fore-weard *m.* scout, outpost.

fore-weard *f.* contract, agreement; provision (of agreement).

fore-weard, for-, -word *aj. place* front, front part of, extremity of : ~ hēafod forehead, ~ fōt sole — on ~an gān go on ahead, in advance || *time* early (part of), beginning of: ~ niht beginning of night.

fore-wesan *vb.* be before, take the lead, preside, rule.

fore-wis foreknowing.

fore-witig, -wittig, foreknowing.

fore-witig|ian prophesy

~ung *f.* prophecy.

fore-witol foreknowing.

~nes*, for w- *f.* intelligence.

fore-wítiendlic prescient.

fore-witung *f.* foreknowing.

fore-wost; *m.* chief *IN.*

fore-writen above-written, above-mentioned.

fore-writennes *f.* proscription (!).

fore-wyrcend *m.* servant.

fore-wyrd *f.* predestination.

fore-wyrhta*, for- *m.* agent, representative.

for-faran 2 *tr.* intercept, blockade : forfōron þǣm scipum þone mūþan foran; destroy, kill, ruin || *intr.* perish *vL.*

for-fēran *vL.* perish, be spoilt.

for-ferian *tr.* let (child) die.

for-flēon 7 flee from, escape, avoid.

for-fliegan put to flight.

for-fōn I seize; take by surprise, come upon suddenly; anticipate, forestall — hēo hine forane forfēng prevented him (from prostrating himself); forfeit.

for-fyllan stop up, obstruct.

for-gǣg|an transgress; prevaricate.

~ednes *f.* transgression; prevarication.

~ung *f.* fault, excess.

for-gān *vb.* go *or* pass over; forgo, abstain from; neglect.

for-georne *av.* very earnestly.

for-gief|an 5 *wda.* give; give up; forgive.

~endlic dative (case).

~en(d)lic pardonable, pardoned.

~en(n)es, ~nes *f.* forgiveness.

~ung *f.* giving, donation.

for-gieldan 3 *wda.* repay, requite, recompense, make good — hire be twifealdum forgeald þæs þe . . ; pay, give || *wa.* pay for, buy off (person accused, attack).

for-gielpan 3 — *ptc.* forgolpen made subject of boasting (*of* alms).

for-giem|an neglect; ignore, not heed.

~elēasian neglect.

for-giet|an 5 *w. a. or g.* forget.

~ing *f.* forgetfulness.

for-gietol forgetful.

~nes *f.* oblivion.

for-glendr(i)an devour, swallow up, destroy.

for-gnagan 2 gnaw to pieces, devour.

for-gnidan 6 crush — *ptc.* forgniden contrite; throw down.

forgnidennes *f.* contrition.

for-grindan 3 destroy.

for-grīpan 6 seize, grasp; attack; afflict.

for-grōwan† R.

for-gyltan — *ptc.* forgylt guilty ; *rfl. w.* on (synnum) incur guilt of.

forgyrd = forþgyrd.

for-gyrdan enclose.

for-habb|an keep back, restrain, hinder, prevent; refrain from : ic þē bidde þæt þū þis ne ~e, ac þæt þū cume; be continent — *ptc.* forhæfed continent.

~ende, æ abstinent, continent.

for-hæfed continent [forhabban].

~nes, forhæfd- *f.* continence, temperance.

for-hātan I forswear, renounce — *ptc.* †forhāten reprobate (*of* the Devil).

for-heald|an I misuse, ill-treat, defile (woman); desert — *ptc.* ~en rebel, deserter.

for-heard very hard.

for-heardian become hard.

for-hēawan I cut down, slaughter.

for-helan 4 conceal, keep secret *wd. of pers.*

for-herg|ian, -herigan ravage, plunder, pillage [here].

~end *m.* ravager.

~ung *f.* devastation, pillage.

for-hienan humiliate, crush (in spirit); injure.

for-hierdan *tr.* harden.

for-hog|ian despise, ignore.

~iend *m.* despiser.

~odlic contemptuous.

~odlīce *av.* contemptuously.

~odnes, -hohnes *f.* contempt.

~ung *f.* contempt.

for-hradian be beforehand in doing anything; do anything too soon; anticipate, forestall, frustrate, prevent.

for-(h)raþe *av.* very *or* too soon.

forht, *IN.* froht afraid, timid; formidable, terrible.

~full timorous.

~lic afraid, terrified.

~līce *av.* with fear, anxiously.

~mōd afraid, timid.

~nes *f.* fear, amazement.

forht|ian be afraid; fear.

~iendlic timorous.

~ung *f.* fear.

forhtig *once* afraid, humble.

for-hwega *av.* about (quantity).

for·hweorfan (3) come to an end, be destroyed.

for·hwierf|an remove; change, pervert.

~edlic perverse.

for·hycgan despise; reject; neglect, ignore (command).

for·hȳdan hide.

for·hygdelic despicable, despised.

for·hylman† once neglect (command).

for·ieldan delay, put off.

for·ierman reduce to poverty [earm].

for·lācan 1 b prt. -lē(ol)c lead astray, deceive, betray.

for·lǣdan lead astray; lead into destruction.

for·lǣran lead astray (by bad advice).

for·lǣt|an 1 b leave — bæftan ~ leave behind; abandon; give up; omit, neglect, let go; lose | dismiss; remit, excuse, forgive; grant, give; let ‖ inn ~ let in; ūt ~ let out; ūp ~ direct upwards.

~(en)nes f. abandonment; absence, cessation, end; desolation, destruction, loss; remission (of sins).

for·legenlic mean-looking, ugly.

forlegen(n)es, forlegnes f. fornication [forlicgan].

forleger- = forliger-.

forlegis(s), -es f. prostitute, fornicatress [forlicgan].

~wīf n. prostitute.

for·lēogan 7 tell falsehood, lie — ptc. forlogen perjured; accuse falsely.

for·leornung f. deception.

for·lēosan 7 w. a., †i. lose; destroy — ptc. forloren ruined.

for·licg|an 5 commit fornication rfl. w. wiþ a., tr : hēo hīe forlæg wiþ hine; hē hīe wolde ~ — ptc. forlegen fornicator, adulterer, also = aj.: þā fūle (or fūlan) ~an.

~end m. fornicator.

forliden shipwrecked [forlīþan].

~nes f. shipwreck.

forlig-gang (?) m. fornication Gl.

for·lig(e)r, ~e, -leg- n. fornication.

~bedd n. bed of fornication.

~hūs n. house of ill-fame.

for·ligerlic unchaste.

for·lig(e)r, -līr m. fornicator, adulterer.

for·liger adulterous.

~nes, -leg- f. fornication.

for·ligrian commit fornication.

for·līpan, see forliden.

for·lor destruction, perdition — tō ~e gedōn destroy; loss [forlēosan].

for·loren(n)es f. destruction, perdition [forlēosan].

for·lustlīce av. very cheerfully or willingly.

forma wk. first (in order or rank, or time) [fore].

for·mǣl, -māl (n.) treaty, agreement.

for·manig very or too many.

formelle f. bench [Lt. formella].

for·meltan 3 intr. melt away, be consumed, disappear.

formest = fyrmest foremost.

for·mieltan melt tr. and intr.

for·mog|ian — ptc. ~od decayed.

for·molsnian crumble, decay.

for·myrpr(i)an murder, destroy.

for·nǣm|an — ptc. ~ed worn out, afflicted (with grief).

forne = foran.

for·nēah av. very nearly, almost.

for·nēan av. nearly, almost.

for·nefa m. great-grandson (!).

Fornet (m.) — ~es folm a plant.

for·nēpan rfl. risk one's life.

for·nīedan force.

for·niman 4 plunder; destroy, disfigure — mid fyrhte fornumen overcome with terror; annul.

forod often used as a partic. broken (esp. of arms, legs, and other parts of the body); humbled (of pride); void, useless.

for·oft very or too often.

for·pǣran pervert; destroy, ruin.

for·pyndan† annul, do away with (Eve's sin).

forradian = forhradian.

for·rǣdan betray, injure — hine of līfe ~ betray him to death, cause his death; hine tō dēaþe ~ put him to death.

for·rīdan 6 — foran ~ cut off advance, intercept (of cavalry).

for·rot|ian rot away, putrefy — ptc. ~od purulent (wound).

~odnes f. corruption; pus, matter.

for·sacan 2 wa. refuse; give up, relinquish; deny.

for·sǣtian lay in wait for, surprise (army).

forsāwen occ. ptc. of forsēon.

forsc, pl. ~as, froxas m. frog.

for·scādan, ēa 1 b scatter, disperse.

for·scam|ian impers. wa. be ashamed: hine ~aþ.

~ung f. modesty.

for·scapung f. crime, fault.

for·sceap (n.) crime.

for·scending f. confusion LN.

for·sceorfan 3 devour (of locusts).

for·scieppan 2 tr. transform, change to something worse.

for·screnc|an supplant, oppress, overcome (sins).

~end m. supplanter.

for·scrīfan 6 proscribe; condemn w. a. or d.; †bewitch (by writing runes).

for·scrincan 3 intr. shrink up, wither.

for·scūfan 7 humble (pride).

for·scyld(i)gian convict of crime, rfl. incur guilt, incriminate oneself — ptc. forscyldgod guilty.

for·scyttan forestall, prevent (punishment).

for·sēarian intr. wither, dry up.

for·sēcan afflict.

for·secgan accuse, traduce, slander.

forsegen ptc. of forsēon.

for·sendan send into exile, send to destruction — on wræcsīþ ~ banish.

for·sēon 5 despise; reject, ignore; refrain from.

for·sēones f. care, diligence Bd.

for·sēopan 7 — ptc. forsoden withered.

for·settan obstruct (road, watercourse).

for·sewen, -sāwen, -segen ptc. despised [forsēon].

~lic contemptible, abject.

~līce av. ignominiously.

~nes f. contempt.

for·sittan 5 hem in, obstruct (path); injure; absent oneself from (meeting, militia); put off, delay w. a., i.; neglect.

for·sīpian perish.

for·slāwian be slothful or unwilling.

for·slēan 2 break (bone); kill, slaughter.

for·slegenlic mean, ignominious (death). *Cp.* forlegenlic.

for·slītan 6 devour.

for·smorian smother, stifle, choke.

for·sorgian despond.

for·span|an 2 entice, allure.

~ing *f.* enticement.

for·spēdian make prosperous.

for·spendan squander.

for·spenn|an entice, allure [spanan].

~en(n) *f.* enticement.

~end *m.* procurer.

~endlic seductive, corrupting.

~estre *f.* bawd.

~ing *f.* enticement.

for·spiercan *tr.* dry.

for·spild *m.* destruction.

for·spildan, -spillan destroy, squander, kill.

forspildednes *f.* destruction, perdition, waste.

for·sp(r)ecan 5 *tr.* speak in vain; deny.

forst *m.* frost.

~ig, ~lic frosty, frozen.

for·stalian *rfl.* steal away, run away.

for·standan 2 *wa.* defend — forane~ defend; obstruct, stop (way); understand; *wda.* hinder from; *wd.* help, avail, profit.

for·stelan steal, rob *wda.* — *ptc.* forstolen deprived of, without *wi.*

for·stoppian stop up, close.

for·strang very strong.

for·styntan blunt.

for·sūgan, -can 7 — *ptc.* forsogen hollow, emaciated (stomach).

forsūgian, forsūwian = forswigian.

for·swǣlan burn up, burn, scorch.

for·swāpan 1 sweep away, sweep, dash, hurl.

for·swelgan 3 swallow up, devour; absorb (moisture).

for·sweltan 3 die, perish.

for·sweorcan 3 become dark.

for·sweorfan 3 rub off, grind away.

for·swerian 2 forswear, renounce *wi.*; swear falsely, *rfl.* perjure oneself — *ptc.* forsworen perjured.

for·swigian,-s(w)ūgian,-sūwian

tr. keep silent, not speak of, ignore; pass over in silence, not mention.

for·swiþ very strong.

for·swiþ(i)an overcome, repress.

for·swiþe *av.* very strongly *or* severely, excessively.

for·sworcennes *f.* darkening [forsweorcan].

for·sworennes *f.* perjury [forswerian].

for·syng|ian — *ptc.* ~od sinful, sinner.

for·tendan burn away, cauterize.

for·tēon 7 mislead ‖ cover.

for·timbr(i)an obstruct.

for·togen(n)es *f.* cramp, colic [fortēon].

for·tred|an 5 tread down, trample on.

~ing *f.* treading down.

for·trūw|ian, -ūgian be overconfident — *ptc.* ~od presumptuous.

~odnes *f.* presumption, arrogance.

~ung *f.* presumption.

for·tyhtan entice into wrong, seduce.

for·tyllan lead astray, seduce.

for·tȳnan block, stop (way).

forþ *av.* | *place* forth, out, forwards, on(wards). ~ *mid d.* with; *av.* simultaneously, together with, henceforth, continuously ‖ *time* still, continually, henceforth. ~ *mid* ealle forthwith. (and) swā ~ and so on, then. swā ~ (swā) to the extent that, because.

forþian promote; accomplish.

forþ-bǣre productive, teeming.

forþ-beran 4 bring forward, produce.

forþ-bielding *f.* emboldening.

forþ-boren of high birth.

forþ-bringan bring forward *or* out; bear (fruit), produce, create; accomplish.

forþ-cuman 4 come forward *or* forth; be born; come into being; come to pass; succeed, be a success.

forþ-cyme *m.* coming forth, birth.

forþ-pearl|e *av.* very severely, excessively.

~(l)īce *av.* very much, entirely.

for·þencan despise, *rfl.* distrust

oneself, despair—*ptc.* forþoht in despair, despairing.

forþ-þēon 6, 7 surpass in merit.

forþ-þēon oppress, destroy.

forþ-þēofan steal.

forþ-þēostrian darken.

forþ-fæder *m.* forefather.

forþ-faran 2 die.

forþ-fēr|an die: wearþ ~ed died.

~ednes, ~ing *f.* death.

forþ-folgian, -fylgan follow (!).

forþ-fōr *f.* departure, death.

forþ-forlǣten(n)es *f.* licence.

forþ-fram|ian *intr.* grow; improve.

~ung *f.* prevailing; departure.

forþ-gang *m.* progress, course; success; privy, drain, going to the privy.

forþ-genge progressive, prosperous, effective.

forþ-georn† eager to advance, impetuous.

forþ-gyrd, forg- *m.* fore-girth, martingale.

forþ-heald bent forward, stooping; steep.

forþ-here *m.* van (of army).

forþ-hlīfian be prominent.

forþ-pierrian*, y dry up *intr.*

for·þilman = -þylman choke.

forþ-þindan 3 — *ptc.* forþunden swollen.

forþ-þingian intercede for *wa.*

forþ-lǣd|an bring forth.

~nes *f.* bringing forth, production.

forþ-gelang dependent, depending on.

forþlic forward, advanced *L.*

forþ-mǣre† very illustrious *or* conspicuous (?). *Cp.* foremǣre.

for·þolian be without, want *wi.*

for·þræst|an destroy, afflict.

~ednes *f.* contrition.

forþ-riht*.

~e *av.* at once, instantly.

for·þringan† 3 protect: hīe him ~ protect them from him.

for·þrycc|an press; overwhelm; oppress, afflict; suppress, stop.

~ednes, -yced- *f.* pressure, oppression.

forþ-ryne *m.* course, flow (of river).

for·þrysm(i)an throttle, strangle, choke (growth).

forþ-gesceaft† *f.* created things,

[65]

creation *coll.* ; future state *or* condition, the future.

forþscipe *m.* progress Bd.

forþ-gesīene† visible.

forþ-sīþ *m.* departure; death.

~ian die.

forþ-snottor very wise.

forþ-spell *n.* declaration.

forþ-spōwnes *f.* prosperity.

forþ-tīege (*n.*) porch, vestibule. *Cp.* foretīege.

forþ-þegn *m.* noble.

forþ-weard *m.* pilot.

forþ-weard I. inclined forward, tending; advanced, forward (*of* undertaking *or* work), progressing, growing, ready; future, in future; continual, everlasting. **II.** ~*, forweard†* once *av.* in future, always. ~es *av.* forwards.

forþ-weᵹ *m.* forward way, departure — on ~, in ~ away.

forþ-wīf *n.* matron.

forþ-gewītan 6 go forth; *of time* pass by — *ptc.* forþgewiten past (deeds, tense); die.

forþ-gewiten(n)es *f.* departure.

for-þyldigian, -þyld(e)gian, -þylgian bear patiently, endure.

for-þylman choke; † envelope, encompass, cover, overwhelm.

forþ-yppan display, reveal.

for-ūtan *av., prp. wd.* except *L.*

for-wana = *forwēna.**

for-wand|ian hesitate: hī ~iaþ þæt hī swā ne dōn h. to do so. ~igende hesitating, respectful, scrupulous.

~ung *f.* shame.

forweard† = *forþweard.*

for-weax|an 1 grow too much — *ptc.* ~en overgrown, too big.

for-wĕddian pledge.

for-wegan 5 kill.

for-wel *av.* very well, very much.

for-wēn|an — *ptc.* ~ed insolent.

for-wēna*, -wana once *m.* presumption (?).

for-weornian wither away, fade, decay [forwesan].

for-weoron *ptc. of* *forwesan.

for-weorpan 3 throw; throw away; reject, repulse; squander.

for-weorþan 3 perish; ~ on mōde be grieved.

for-weorþfullic very illustrious.

for-wĕr|ian wear out — *ptc.* ~ed,

~od worn out (clothes), extreme (old age).

for-wĕrednes *f.* extreme old age, decrepitude.

forweren *ptc. of* *forwesan.

for-wes|an* 5 — *ptc.* -weren, -weoron†, -woren decayed, worn out.

~ing *f.* destroying.

for-wiern|an *wdg.* prevent from, restrain, oppose; refuse, deny (favour).

~edlīce *av.* with abstinence.

~ednes *f.* self-restraint, continence.

for-wisnian, eo wither up, decay.

for-witolnes = fore-.

for-wlęncan make proud, puff up.

for-worden|lic perishable [forweorþan].

~(n)es *f.* failure (of crops) *vL.*

forworen *ptc. of* *forwesan.

for-wracned banished.

for-wrecan 5 banish, expel — *ptc.* forwrecen exiled, strange.

for-wrēgan accuse, calumniate.

for-wrītan 6 cut through.

for-wrīþan 6 bandage (wound).

for-wundian wound.

for-wundorlīce *av.* very wonderfully.

for-wyrcan *prt.* -orhte, -yrhte barricade, obstruct (road, bridge), dam up; destroy, ruin; forfeit; *rfl.* incur guilt, perdition | *ptc.* forworht guilty, wrong-doing, convicted, condemned, ruined; ~ mann criminal.

for-wyrd *fn.* destruction, ruin [forweorþan].

~an perish.

~endlic perishable.

forwyrhte, see forwyrcan.

fossere *m.* spade [*Lt.* fossorium].

fōstor, -er, fēster- *n.* feeding, sustenance, food.

~bearn *n.* foster-child.

~brōþor *m.* foster-brother.

~cild *n.* foster-child.

~fæder *m.* foster-father.

~land *n.* 'foster-land,' endowment.

~lēan *n.* payment *or* reward for keep of a child.

~ling *m.* foster-child.

~mann *m.* security.

~mōdor *f.* foster-mother.

~sweostor *f.* foster-sister.

fōsternoþ *m.* sustenance; pasturage.

---

fōstraþ *m.* food, provisions.

fōt *m., pl.* fēt, oe, -as foot; foot (measure).

~ādl *f.* gout.

~bred *n.* stirrup.

~cosp, -cops *m.* fetter.

~coþu *f.* gout.

ge~cypsed fettered [fōt-cosp].

~ece *m.* gout.

~feter *f.* fetter.

~lāst, ǣ *m.* footstep, track; step (distance).

~lic pedestrian.

~mǣl *n.* foot (measure).

~mǣlum *av.* step by step.

~gemearc† *n.* measurement by feet, space of a foot.

~gemet *n.* fetter (!).

~rāp *m.* part of a sail.

~scamol *m.*, ~setl *n.* footstool.

~sīd reaching to the feet (*of* cloak).

~spor *n.* footprint.

~spure (?) *n.* foot-rest, -stool *vL.*

~stān *n.* pedestal.

~swæþ *n.* footprint; foot.

~swyle *m.* swelling of the foot.

~þwēal *n.* washing the feet.

~gewǣde *n.* foot-clothing.

~wǣrc *n.* gout.

~welm, ~wolma *m.* sole of the foot.

fōþor, -er *n.* food, fodder; load (measure); covering, case; basket.

foþorn (*m.*) a surgical instrument, lancet (?).

fox *m.* fox. ~es-clāte *f.* burdock. ~es-clīfe *f.* greater burdock. ~es-fōt *m.* bur reed (a water-plant). ~es-glofe, ~es-clofe *f.* foxglove.

~hyll *m.* fox-hill Ct.

~ung *f.* craftiness.

fracoþ, fracod, *vE.* frǣcuþ **I.** vile, shameful, nasty, abominable; hateful, wicked, bad, useless. **II.** *n.* disgrace, insult; wickedness [*Cp.* forcūþ].

~e *av.* shamefully.

~lic shameful, ignominious, wicked.

~līce *av.* wickedly, with evil intent, disgracefully.

~(lic)nes *f.* vileness, lewdness.

~scipe *m.* vileness, disgraceful conduct.

frǣ- = frēa-.

frǣc = frec.

frǣcuþ = fracoþ.

frǣfele = frefele.

gefrǽge† I. *n.* — mīne ~ as I have heard say. II. *aj.* celebrated, notorious.

gefrǽgen, *see* fricgan.

frǽgn *prt. of* frignan.

gefrǽgnod† *once. For* gefrēc-nod (?).

frǽng = frǽgn *prt. of* frignan.

gefrǽp(pe)gian *lN.* accuse; reverence (!).

frǽt†, ǣ† obstinate, defiant, proud.

~ig, ǽ† proud, perverse.

frǽt *prt. of* fretan.

frǽt-gengia *vE. m.* apostasy (!) Gl.

frǽt-lǽppa *m.* dewlap.

frǽtw|a, -e, ge- *fpl.* ornaments, trappings, armour, treasures [getāwe].

~(i)an, -tew- adorn.

~ednes *f.* ornament.

~ung *f.* ornament.

gefrāgian learn by asking *lN.* [frignan].

fram, freom vigorous, bold, brave.

~līce *av.* vigorously, boldly, promptly.

~nes *f.* vigour.

~scipe *m.* action.

fram I. *prp. w. d., i. motion* (away) from: hī wurdon gegripene ~ mōderlicum brēostum; þā hē him ~ wolde, þā gefēng hē hine | *distance, extent*: fēower mīla ~ þǽm mūþan; ~ sǽ oþ sǽ | *time*: ~ hancrede oþ undren | *origin, source*: swā micel ege stōd dēoflum ~ ēow þæt . . | *agent (with passive)*: wearþ ādrifen of his biscepdome ~ Ecgferþe cyninge | *privative*: frēoh ~ dēaþes sǽrnesse; bugon ~ Godes geléafan; ālíesan ~ . . II. *av.* away: ~ gān depart; ~ ic ne wille I will not run away.

fram|ian avail, benefit.

~igendlic effective (medicine).

fram-byge *m.* apostasy.

fram-cyme *m.* progeny, descendants.

fram-cynn *n.* progeny, offspring; lineage; origin.

fram-faru *f.* excess (!).

fram-fundung *f.* departure.

fram-lād *f.* retreat.

framlic turned away from Gl.

fram-sīþ *m.* departure.

fram-slitnes *f.* desolation *lN.*

framweard about to depart, departing; about to die; enterprising (?).

~es *av.* in a direction away from.

frān *prt. of* frignan.

franca *m.* javelin.

Franc|an *mpl.* Franks.

~land *n.* France.

frās|ian question; tempt.

~ung *f.* questioning; temptation.

gefrāsian find out by inquiry, learn.

frēa† *m.* lord, king, consort; the Lord (God *or* Christ).

~dryhten *m.* lord.

~reccere *m.* prince.

~wine *m.* (beloved) lord.

~wrāsen *f.* splendid chain.

frēa-beorht, frǽ- very bright; glorious.

frēa-bodian proclaim.

frēa-drīeman exult.

frēa-fǽtt*, frǽ- very fat.

frēa-glēaw very prudent.

frēa-hrǽd, frǽ- very quick.

frēa-mǽre, frǽ- very famous.

frēa-micel*, frǽ- very great.

frēa-ofestlīce*, frǽ- *av.* very quickly.

frēa-torht very bright.

frēa-wlitig very beautiful.

frec, æ, *lN.* i *wg.* gluttonous, greedy, bold (in).

~līce *av.* greedily.

~māse *f.* titmouse.

~nes *f.* greediness.

freca† *m.* bold one, warrior.

frec|a*, *vE.* ~eo *m.* glutton.

frēcednes, frēcelnes = frēcen-nes.

frēcelsian endanger.

frēcen *n.* danger [frēcne].

~full, ~(d)lic dangerous.

~līce *av.* dangerously.

~(n)es, frēcnes, frēcednes, frēcelnes *f.* danger; harm.

frēcn|e, oe I. dangerous; terrible; daring, bold; wicked. II. *av.* dangerously; severely; boldly.

~ian — *ptc.* ge~od endangered, †fierce, proud.

frēcnes = frēcennes.

gefrēd|an be sensible of, feel, perceive — *ptc. cpv.* ~ra more perceptible [frōd].

~endlic perceptible.

gefrēd|mǽlum *av.* by degrees (!).

~nes *f.* perception.

frefel, æ (*n.*) cunning.

~e cunning; bold.

~ian be cunning.

~līce, fref(e)līce *av.* cunningly; shamelessly.

~nes *f.* cunning, sagacity.

frēfernes *f.* consolation.

frēfr|an, oe, -ian comfort, console.

~(i)end *m.* comforter, consoler.

~ung *f.* comfort, consolation.

gefregen *ptc. of* fricgan.

freht [e = eo?] divination. *Cp.* frihtere.

frem(e)de, fremþe unfamiliar, strange; estranged (from) *wd.*; foreign; devoid of *wg.*

fremdian alienate, estrange.

fremednes, gefrem(ed)nes *f.* fulfilment.

fremm|an, fremian *tr.* further, advance, raise *fig.*; urge, incite; perform, commit, make, do || *wd.* benefit, do good, profit, avail [fram].

~ing, fremung, ge- *f.* performance; effect.

frem|u, eo *f.* benefit, advantage, prosperity.

~full beneficial.

~fullīce *av.* efficaciously.

~fulnes *f.* utility.

~lic profitable.

~sum beneficial; kind.

~sumlīce *av.* kindly.

~sumnes *f.* benefit; liberality; kindness.

Frencisc French [Francan].

frēo, frēoh, frī(g), *pl.* frīge free; †noble; †joyful.

~bearn *n.* freeborn *or* noble child.

~borg = friþ-.

~brōþor *m.* own brother.

~burg *f.* city.

~dohtor *f.* freeborn daughter.

~dōm *m.* freedom.

~dryhten† *m.* noble lord.

~lāc *n.* oblation.

~lǽta *m.* freedman.

~lic(†) noble; goodly, magnificent; beautiful.

ge~lic *lN.* free.

~līce *av.* freely, without hindrance; nobly.

~mǽg† *m.* (free) kinsman.

[67]

frēo|mann *m.* free man, man.
~nama *m.* surname, cognomen.
~riht *n.* right of free men, privilege.
~sceatt *m.* private property (?).
frēot† *f.* lady, woman.
frēo (*f.*) freedom, immunity Ct.
frēo- = frēa-.
frēon = frēogan.
frēod† *f.* affection, friendship, good-will, peace.
frēo(ga)n, frīgan free ; †love.
gefrigend *m.* liberator.
gefreog-, *see* gefrige.
frēols *m.* freedom, immunity, privilege ; festival, holy day, celebration (of festival) [*from* *frī-hals].
~ǽfen *m.* eve of a festival.
~bōc *f.* charter of freedom.
~bryce *m.* breach of festival.
~dæg *m.* festival day, festival.
~dōm *m.* freedom.
~gēar *n.* jubilee.
~giefa *m.* manumitter.
~lic festive.
~līce *av.* freely ; solemnly.
~mann *m.* freedman.
~stōw *f.* festival-place.
~tīd *f.* festival time, anniversary.
frēols|ian keep as a festival, keep holy, celebrate, keep (Sunday); deliver.
~ung *f.* celebration of festival.
frēond, *d.* friend, ~e ; *pl.* friend, ēo, ~as friend ; relative ; lover [frēon].
~heald friendly.
~healdlic akin.
~lār†*f.* friendly instruction *or* advice.
~laþu† *f.* friendly invitation.
~lēas friendless.
~lēast *f.* want of friends.
~lic friendly.
~līce *av.* kindly.
~lufu† *f.* love, friendship, relationship.
~mynd†*f.* love.
~rǽden(n) *f.* friendship ; love.
~scipe *m.* friendship ; love.
~spēd†*f.* abundance of friends.
~spēdig rich in friends.
frēorig† cold ; dispirited, sad, terrified [frēosan].
~ferþ, ~mōd sad.
frēosan, *ptc.* froren 7 freeze.
frēot *m.* freedom [frēo].
~giefa *m.* manumitter.
~giefu, ~gift *f.* manumission.

frēot-mann *m.* freedman.
freop-, *see* friþ-.
Fresisc = Frīesisc.
fret|an 5 eat up, devour ; destroy ; break [*from* *for·etan].
~ol*, -tt- gluttonous.
frettan eat up, consume, devour [fretan].
fric *LN* = frec greedy.
frīcian, î dance.
fricca, y *m.* herald, crier.
fricgan† 5 *ptc.* -frigen, e, æ, u ask, inquire ; *wag.* question (a person) ; *wg.* seek.
gefricgan† 5 learn by inquiry, hear of.
fricl|an *wg.* seek, desire.
~o *f.* appetite.
frico (*f.*) usury [frec].
gefrīend *mpl.* — ~ bēon be on friendly terms [frēond].
Fries|a, i, e, i† *m.* Frisian.
~cyning† *m.* Frisian king.
~isc Frisian — on ~ in the Frisian manner.
~land *n.* Friesland.
frīg = frēo.
frīgan = frēogan free.
frīga†, î† *fpl.* love.
Frige|ǽfen *m.* Thursday evening.
~dæg, frīgdæg *m.* Friday.
gefrige†, eo *n.* hearsay [gefricgan].
frīgea *m.* lord, master [frēa].
gefrigen *ptc. of* fricgan.
frig(e)nes, ge- *f.* inquiry, question [fricgan].
frign|an, frīnan, frinnan 3, *prt.* frægn, fræng, frān,*ptc.* frugnen, frūnen ask, inquire *wag.*, *w. a.* and æfter, *w. sbj.*
~ung*, frægning *f.* questioning.
gefrignan 3 learn by asking, hear.
frihtere *m.* soothsayer [freht].
frihtr|ian practise divination.
~ung *f.* divination.
Fris|a, ~isc = Fries|a, ~isc.
frist = first.
friþ, fri(o)þu, eo *mn.* peace, truce — ~ habban, niman wiþ *a.* be at peace, make peace ; security, protection ; asylum ; king's peace, public order.
~āþ *m.* peace-oath.
~ubēacen† *n.* sign of peace.
~bēna *m.* petitioner for peace.
~borg *m.* surety for peace.

friþ|brec, æ *f.* (!) breach of peace.
~(u)burg† *f.* peace-city, city of refuge.
~candel†*f.* sun.
~gedāl† ÷ *ferhþ-.
~geard† *m.* enclosure, court.
~georn pacific.
~gield *n.* peace-guild, association for public order.
~gegielda *m.* member of a peace-guild.
~gīsel *m.* peace-hostage.
~hūs *n.* asylum, sanctuary.
~land *n.* peaceful country.
~(u)lēas, friþelēas outlawed.
~lic peaceable.
~māl *n.* article of peace.
~mann *m.* one under protection.
~uscealc† *m.* messenger of peace.
~scipe *m.* peace.
~usibb† *f.* pledge of peace.
~sōcn *f.* asylum, sanctuary.
~uspēd†*f.* protection, prosperity.
~splott *m.* peace-place.
~stōl *m.* sanctuary, refuge, safe quarters.
~stōw *f.* asylum, refuge.
~sum pacific.
ge~sum fortified.
~utācen† *n.* sign of peace.
~uþeawas† *mpl.* peace.
~uwǽr† *f.* peace-agreement.
~uwang† *m.* peaceful plain.
~uwaru† *f.* protection.
~uweard† *m.* protector.
~uwębba† *m.* peace-weaver, peace-messenger.
~uwębbe†*f.* peace-weaver, woman.
~gewrit *n.* article of peace.
friþ|ian, eo *w. d. or a.* protect ; keep peace towards — *also w.* wiþ *a.* ; observe (festival).
~iend *m.* protector.
friþa*, eo† *m.* protector.
frōd†*wg.* old ; old *wg.* (fēores).
~ian be wise.
frōfor *fm.* consolation ; help ; joy.
~bōc *f.* book of consolation.
~gāst *m.* spirit of consolation.
~lic consoling, kind.
~līce *av.* kindly.
~nes *f.* consolation
frōfrian console.
frogga *m.* frog.
froht = forht afraid.
frowe† *f.* lady, woman [*German*].
frox- = forsc frog.

[68]

frugnen, *see* frignan.
frum (?) first.
frum|a *m.* beginning, origin — on ~an at first, wæstma ~an first-fruits ; originator, creator, inventor, doer, maker ; †chief, king.
~bearn† *n.* first-born child.
~bierdling *m.* youth.
~byrd *f.* birth.
~cenned first-born ; primitive, original.
~cierr *m.* first time.
~onēow† *n.* first generation.
~cynn† *n.* genealogy, origin, native country ; race, tribe.
~gār†, ~gāra† *m.* chief, general, patriarch.
~giéfu *f.* prerogative (!).
~giéld *n.* first instalment of a man's *wer* (value).
~gripa *m.* first-born. *Cp.* -rīpan.
~hīwung, ēo *f.* first fashioning *or* forming, creation.
~hrægl† *n.* first garment.
~ieldo *f.* first age.
~lēoht *n.* first light, dawn.
~lic original.
~liehtan dawn.
~mynet-slege *m.* first coinage.
~ræd *m.* primary ordinance.
~ræden(n)† *f.* agreement, period.
~rīpan *pl.* first-fruits.
~sceaft *f.* creation ; origin, place of origin, home ; original state ; created being, creature.
~gesceap *n.* (first) creation.
~sceapen first-created.
~sceatt *m.* first-fruits.
~scieppend *m.* creator, originator.
~scyld† *f.* original sin.
~setnes *f.* authority *LN.*
~setnung *f.* creation *LN.*
~slǣp *m.* first sleep.
~sprǣc *f.* agreement, promise ; introductory remarks.
~stapol† *m.* original condition.
~stemn *m.* prow (of ship).
~stōl original dwelling, paternal mansion.
~talu *f.* first statement (of a witness).
~tīd *f.* beginning.
~tihtle *f.* first accusation *or* charge.
~wæstm *m.* first-fruits.
~weorc† *n.* creation.
~geweorc *n.* first construction.
~wielm *m.* first fervour.

frum|wīfung *f.* first marriage.
~gewrit *n.* deed, document.
~wyrhta *m.* creator.
frūnen *ptc. of* frignan.
frungon, *see* frignan.
frycca = fricca.
frymdig, i inquiring, inquisitive ; desirous — ~ bēon entreat.
frymetling *f.* young cow.
frymþ, ~u *f.* origin, beginning ; created being, creature.
~elic original, primitive.
~ieldo *f.* first age.
frymþ = fiermþ.
frysca *m.* kite, bittern.
fugl|ian fowl, catch birds.
~ere *m.* bird-catcher, fowler.
~oþ, fugelnoþ *m.*, ~ung *f.* fowling.
fugol, -el *m.* bird. fugles bēan vetch. fugles lēac (?). fugles wīse larkspur.
~bana *m.* fowler.
~cynn *n.* bird-kind, species of bird.
~dæg *m.* poultry-day (at dinner).
~doppe *f.* water-bird.
~hǣlsere *m.* augur.
~hwata *m.* augur.
~līm (*m.*) bird-lime.
~nett *n.* fowler's net.
~timber *n.* young bird.
~trēow *n.* perch.
~wielle abounding in birds.
~wiglere, -weohlere *m.* augur.
fūht damp.
fūl I. foul, putrid ; unclean, impure ; vile, wicked ; convicted (of crime), guilty. II. *n.* foulness, impurity, dirt ; guilt, offence.
~bēam *m.* black alder.
~e *av.* foully.
~lic dirty ; repulsive.
~(l)īce *av.* foully, impurely, wickedly.
~nes, fȳ- *f.* foulness ; stench.
~(e)stincende stinking.
~etrēow *n.* black alder.
fūlian decay.
fulgon *prt. pl. of* fēolan.
full *n.* cup.
full I. full *wg.* (*w.* mid *d.*), high (tide) — hand + *wg.*, *a.* hand ~e handful ; complete, perfect. be ~an fully, completely. II. *av.*, *wk. form* fol, fully, completely, very : ~ twā gēar, ~ oft very often, ~ nēah almost.
fullian fulfil, perfect.

full|ian* whiten, full (cloth).
~ere *m.* fuller.
fullian = fulwian baptize.
fulla *m.* assembly (?) *Ct.*
fullǣst, ~est, -āst *f.* help.
~an, -estan *wd.* help.
full·berstan 3 *intr.* break completely.
full·bētan make full amends.
full·boren born complete ; noble-born.
full·brecan 4 violate.
full-bryce *m.* complete violation (of peace).
full·dōn *vb.* satisfy.
full-gedrifen *wg.* driven full, filled (with wild beasts, *of* the earth).
full·endian complete.
full·fealdan 1 explain (!).
full·flēon 7 flee away completely (!).
full·frem|man, -fremian complete, perfect, fulfil, practise. *ptc.* ~ed perfect.
~edlīce *av.* perfectly.
~ednes *f.* perfection, fulfilment.
full·fylgan *wd.* obey, follow.
full·fyllan fulfil.
full·gān, -gangan *vb. wd.* finish, accomplish, perform, follow (desire) ; obey ; imitate ; help.
full·grōwan 1 grow to maturity.
full-healden contented Gl.
full-mægen *n.* great power.
full·mannod fully peopled.
full·trūwian confide.
full·þungen fully grown.
fulluht, fulwiht *n.* baptism.
~bæþ *n.* font, baptism.
~bēna *m.* competitor Gl.
~ere, fulwere *m.* baptist.
~fæder *m.* baptizer.
~hād *m.* baptismal vow.
~nama *m.* Christian name.
~stōw *f.* baptistry.
~tīd *f.* time of baptism.
~þēawas *mpl.* rite of baptism.
~þegnung, -þēn- *f.* baptism.
~wer *m.* baptist.
fulluhtian baptize.
fullunga *av.* fully *LN.*
full·wyrcan complete ; commit (crime).
fūlon *occ. prt. pl. of* fēolan.
fultum, -ēam, -em *m.* help ; army, forces [full, tēam].
~lēas without help, at a loss.
fultumian, fulteman *wd.* help.

fultum|end, ~iend, ge- m. helper.
fulw|ian, fullian baptize; ~fram purify by baptism from (sins).
~ere m. baptist.
fund|ian w. of, tō set out, depart; hasten; go whither one intends, go (to), tend; aspire, desire.
~ung f. departure.
furh, g. fūre, d. fyrh f. furrow.
furh* fir.
~wudu m. fir.
furlang n. furlong [furh, lang].
furþum, furþon av. time first, just: siþþan ~ swealg eorþe Ābēles blōde when . . first; þā hīe þæt geweorc ~ ongunnen hæfdon | even: hē wēneþ furþon þæt hē mann ne sȳ; ~ ænne man; se gītsere wile māre habban, þonne hē ~ orsorh ne brȳcþ his genyhtsumnisse although as it is . .
furþumlic luxurious, effeminate.
furþor, lN. forþor av. further, forwards | quantity further | higher (in rank or consideration), more — ~ dōn promote.
furþra aj. cpv. higher, greater (in rank or consideration); pre-eminent.
fūs ready or eager to set out, hastening; ready, prompt; brave; noble, excellent; about to die, dying [fundian].
~lēoþ n. death-song, dirge.
~lic ready; excellent.
~līce av. readily, gladly.
fyht- = feoht-.
fȳhtan*, i moisten [fūht].
fyl-werig = fiell-.
fȳlnes = fūlnes.
fȳlan defile [fūl].
gefylc|e n. troop, regiment; army [folc].
~a m. companion, friend.
fylc(i)an collect, marshal (army) L. [Scand.].
fyld-stōl = fealde-.
fylg|an, fyli(g)an = folgian follow.
~end m. follower, observer.

fylg|endlic to be imitated.
~estre f. follower.
~ing f. following.
~nes f. observance.
fyll|an w.a. and g., i. or mid fill, fill up (gap), supply (want), cram; satisfy (with food), satiate; wa. fulfil, complete [full].
~(ed)nes, ge- f. satiety; fulfilment; supplement.
~end m. performer.
ge~endlic expletive (in grammar).
~ing f. filling.
ge~ing-tīd f. compline.
fylleþ*.
~flōd m high tide.
fyllo f. fullness, fill; repletion, plenty, feast; impregnation.
fylst f. help [fullæstan].
ge~a m. helper.
~an wd. help.
~end m. helper.
fȳlþ f. filth, impurity [fūl].
fyndele f. invention [findan].
fȳne (m.) mould (fungoid growth).
fynig*, i mouldy.
~ian*, i become mouldy.
fȳr n. fire; a fire.
~bǣre m. fiery.
~bæþ† n. bath of fire, flames.
~bend† m. fire-hardened fastening (of door).
~gebeorg n. fire-screen (?).
~bēta m. fireman.
~gebræc† n. roaring of flames.
~bryne m. conflagration, fire.
~clamm† m. = ~bend.
~crūce f. crucible.
~cynn n. fire (?).
~draca m. fire-dragon.
~en fiery; on fire.
~feaxen with fiery hair.
~gearwunga fpl. materials for a fire.
~gnāst† m. spark of fire.
~hāt† hot as fire.
~heard† hardened by fire.
~hūs n. room with fireplace.
~leoht† n. light of fire.
~lēoma† m. flash of fire.
~loca† m. fiery prison.

fȳr|mǽl† n. mark of fire.
~panne f. firepan.
~race*, ferrece f. fire-iron.
~scofl f. fire-shovel.
~smeortende smarting like a burn.
~spearca m. spark.
~stān m. flint.
~sweart† black with fire.
~tang f. fire-tongs.
~torr m. lighthouse.
~polle f. gridiron.
~wielm† m. flame.
fȳran castrate.
fȳrian tr. supply with fire, keep warm.
fȳrian once cut Gl. [furh].
fȳrclian flash vL. [fȳr].
fyr(e)st I. first (in order); first (in rank). II. av. first [fore].
fyrh, see furh.
fyrht|an, lN. fryhta frighten — ptc. (ge)fyrht afraid || intr. fear lN. [forht].
~nes f. fear.
fyrhto, lN. fryhto f. fear.
fyrmest, fo-, lN. and lA. forþmest spl. of forma I. wg. first (in number); first (in rank). II. av. first (in time); first (in order), most in front; chiefly, most — swā hē ~ mæg to the extent of his power, as far as he can.
fyrs m. furze.
gefyrst (n.) frost [forst].
fyrstig frosty [forst].
fyrþr|an, -ian advance, further, promote; benefit, protect [furþor].
ge~a m. promoter.
~ung f. furthering.
fȳsan, -ian tr. send forth, discharge (arrow); drive away, expel, banish; impel, incite || intr., rfl. hasten [fūs].
fȳst f. fist.
~gebēat n. fighting with fists.
ge~lian beat with the fists.
~slægen struck with the fist.
fyxen, fyxe f. she-fox [fox].
~hȳd f. skin of she-fox.
fyxen of a fox.

G.

gān, gangan, *IN.* geonga;
(hē) gǣþ, *prt.* ēode, †gēng,
†gengde, *ptc.* gegangen *vb.*
walk, go, come, proceed — gan-
gende menn infantry; *also met.*
of origin | happen, turn out | be-
long *met.*: ne gǣþ nā māre tō
metinge būton þæt þū hit
gesēo all that is required for
understanding a picture is . . ||
forþ~ go *or* come out ; continue
of time, action. ūp ~ rise (*of* sun,
stars).

gegān *vb.* go, proceed, *also wa.*:
†~**gryresīþas;** *of time* pass;
happen || *tr.* practice, exercise;
overrun, occupy (country), take
(city).

gabote *f.* small dish Gl.

gād *f.* goad, point.

~īsen *n.* goad.

gād†, ǣ *n.* want, lack *wdg.*

gegada, gada *m.* companion, associate.

gader|scipe, gæ- *m.* matrimony.

~tang continuous, united.

~tangnes *f.* continuation.

~wist *f.* association, intercourse.

ge~wyrhtan *mpl.* assembled work-
men.

gaderung *f.* assembly.

gadr|ian, gæd(e)r- *tr.* gather,
collect, store up.

gegadr|ian *tr.* collect || *intr.* col-
lect together.

~ung *f.* coming together, conflux;
assembly, congregation.

gæd† *once,* (*n.*) fellowship.

gædeling† *m.* companion, kinsman.

gǣl|an hinder, impede; *wag.* hinder
from, prevent from obtaining ||
intr. delay [gāl].

~ing *f.* delay.

gǣlsa *m.* wantonness, pride [gāl].

gærs, græs *n.* grass; young corn;
plant.

~bedd *n.* grave.

---

gærs|cīþ *m.* blade of grass *or* corn.

~grēne grass-green.

~hoppa *m.* grasshopper.

~ierþ *f.* grass-land.

~molde *f.* sward.

~(s)tapa *m.* grasshopper.

~swīn *n.* pastured pig.

~tūn *m.* meadow.

~tūndīc *m.* meadow-dike Ct.

~wang *m.* sward.

gærsum(a) = gersum.

gǣsne, ē, ēa barren ; *wg.* deprived
of, without; wanting, scarce;
dead.

gæst = giest guest.

gǣst = gāst spirit.

gǣstan† afflict, torment.

gǣstlīc† *once* dreary (?).

gǣt *pl.* of gāt goat.

gǣten of goats.

gǣþ (he) goes.

(ge)gaf-sprǣc *f.* foolish talk, scur-
rility.

gafelian rent Ct.

gafeloc *m.* javelin.

gaffetung *f.* scoffing.

gafol, go- *n.* tax, tribute ; rent ;
usury, interest.

~bere *m.* barley given as rent.

~giéld *n.* tribute (?).

~giélda *m.* tributary ; debtor;
tenant.

~giéldere *m.* tributary.

~heord *f.* hive of bees subject to
a tax.

~hwītel *m.* tribute-blanket paid as
the equivalent of rent or tribute.

~ierþ *f.* tribute-land, rented land.

~land *n.* tribute-land, rented land,
land liable to taxation.

~līc fiscal.

~mǣd *f.* tribute-meadow, meadow
whose mowing was part of the
obligation of its renter.

~manung *f.* place of tribute, cus-
toms.

~pening, -ig *m.* tribute-penny,
penny paid as tax or rent.

---

gafol|rǣden(n) *f.* tribute, rent.

~gerēfa *m.* publican.

~swān *m.* tribute-herdsman, swineherd who rents land for feeding
his pigs.

~tȳning *f.* material for fencing as
equivalent of rent.

~wudu *m.* wood as equivalent of
rent.

gafol *f.* fork.

~rand *m.* pair of compasses.

gagat|es, ~stān *m.* agate.

gagel *m.* (?), **gagelle, -olle** *f.* gale,
sweet gale (a plant).

~cropp *m.* top *or* catkins of gale.

gagol, gægl wanton, lascivious.

~bǣre* wanton.

~bǣrnes *f.* wantonness.

gagul-swillan [*or two words*?]
gargle Gl. *Cp.* gēagl.

gāl I. wanton, frivolous; proud;
wicked, bad. **II.** *n.* wantonness,
folly ; pride; wickedness, evil.

~ferhþ† lascivious, lustful.

~frēols *m.* revel *Gl.*

~full lustful, licentious.

~fullīce *av.* lustfully.

~līc lustful, sensual.

~mōd licentious.

~nes, gǣ- *f.* licentiousness ; (boyish)
levity, folly.

~scipe *m.* wantonness, lasciviousness ; pride.

~smǣre given to joking and laughter.

gal|an 2 sing; scream (*of* bird);
intr. sing charms, practise incantation.

~end, ~ere, galdre *m.* enchanter,
incantator.

~ung *f.* incantation.

Gal-w(e)alas *mpl.* Gauls, French-
men; France [*Lt.* **Gallia**].

gambe† *f.* tribute.

gamelian grow old.

gamen *n.* amusement, game, sport,
exhibition of skill, &c., merriment, joy ; jesting, joke.

gamen|lic, gamelic belonging to games, theatrical.
~līce av. deceitfully.
~wǣþ† f. path of joy.
~wudu† m. wood of mirth, harp.
gamen|ian, gamn-, æ play; jest, joke.
~ung f. amusement; jesting.
gamol† old [ge-, mǣl].
~feax grey-haired.
~ferhþ old.
gān|ian yawn [gīnan].
~ung f. yawning.
gan(d)ra m. gander.
gang m. going, progression, gait; path, track, bed (of river); flow, stream; course (of time); drain, privy.
~ærn, -ern n. privy.
~dagas m. Rogation days.
~ehere m. infantry.
~pytt m., **~setl** n., **~stōl** m. privy.
~geteld n. pavilion.
~tūn m. privy.
~weg m. road, cart-road.
~wuce f. Rogation week.
gegang m. event, result.
gangan = gān.
gange - wifre, gangel - wæfre, -weafre f. spider [gān, wefan].
ganot m. gannet, sea-bird — †~es bæþ sea.
ganra = gandra.
gār† m. javelin, spear.
~bēam m. javelin-shaft.
~berend m. warrior.
~cēne brave, warlike.
~clīfe f. agrimony (a plant) Pr.
~cwealm m. slaughter.
~dene pl. (warlike) Danes.
~faru f. warlike expedition.
~hēap m. warlike troop.
~holt n. javelin (-shaft).
~lēac n. garlic Pr.
~mēting*, -mitting f. battle.
~nīþ m. war.
~rǣs m. battle.
~secg, gāsric m. ocean, sea Pr.
~torn m. rage of battle.
~getrum n. band of warriors.
~þracu f. battle.
~þrīste brave.
~wiga, ~wīgend m. warrior.
~gewinn n. battle, violence.
~wudu m. javelin.
gāra m. triangular piece (of land), projection.

gāsric = gār-secg.
gāst, ǣ m. breath; mind, spirit, soul; life; spirit, angel, sprite, demon — se hālga ~ the Holy Ghost.
~bana† m. devil.
~berend† m. living being, man.
~cofa† m. breast, mind.
~cund spiritual.
~cwalu† f. torment, affliction.
~cyning† m. God.
~gedāl† n. death.
~giéfu f. gift of the Spirit.
~hālig† holy.
~gehygd† n. thought.
~lēas dead.
~līc spiritual.
~līce av. spiritually.
~lufe† f. spiritual love.
~gemynd† n. thought.
~geníþla† m. devil.
~gerȳne† n. spiritual mystery.
~sunu† m. spiritual son.
~gewinn† n. trouble of soul, affliction.
gāt, pl. gǣt f. goat. ~ e-trēow cornel - tree. ~ e-þyrne goat's thorn.
~bucca m. he-goat.
~hierde m. goatherd.
ge cj. and. **ge . . ge** both .. and.
gē, gīe ye.
gēa, ia, A. gǣ, gee av. yes: cwæþ ia wiþ consented.
gēac m. cuckoo. ~es sūre wood-sorrel.
geador av. together — on ~ together.
geafl-, see gafol fork.
geaflas mpl. jaws. Cp. cēafl.
geagl mn. jaw.
~swile m. swelling of the jaw.
geaglisc, geg- frolicsome, wanton.
geal-ādl f. jaundice [gealla].
gealdor, æ incantation, charm; magic; divination.
~cræft m. magical art, magic, incantation.
~cræftiga m. magician.
~cwide m. incantation.
~galend, ~galere m. enchanter.
~lēoþ n. incantation.
~word n. magic word, incantation.
gealdricge f. sorceress.
gealg* sad.
~mōd sad.

gealg|a m. gallows, gibbet, cross (for crucifixion).
~trēow, lN. galgatrē n. gallows, cross.
gealla m. gall, bile.
geall|a m. gall, sore on the skin.
~ede galled (horse).
gealloc*, a m. comfrey (a plant).
gēan-, gegn- = ongēan-.
~bōc f. duplicate charter, counterpart.
~cwide m. reply; pl. conversation.
~fær n. return.
~hweorfan 3 return intr.
~hwierft m. turning back intr.
~hworfennes f. return.
~hwurf m. return Gl.
~nes f. meeting Gl.
~pæþ m. hostile path.
~ryne m. meeting.
~slege m. fight.
~þingian reply.
gēan-wyrde or gean-wyrde — hē þæs ~ wæs he confessed it.
gēanol coming to meet, on the road to Gl.
gēap crooked, curved; cunning, deceitful. †steep, lofty, projecting, spacious.
~līc deceitful.
~līce av. deceitfully, cunningly.
~nebb† ? (of corslet).
~scipe m. deceit, cunning.
gēar, gēr n. year; the Runic letter g.
~cyning m. consul Gl.
~dagas† mpl. lifetime; days of yore. Cp. gēara.
~hwāmlīce av. yearly.
~līc yearly, of the year.
~līce av. yearly.
~mǣlum av. year by year.
~market n. yearly market lCt.
~gemearc† n. period of a year.
~gerihte n. yearly due.
~rīm†, ~gerīm† n. number of years.
~getæl n. number of years.
~torht† bright every year, bright in season (of crops, &c.).
~þegnung, ~þēnung f. annual service (of the church).
gear-wutol austere lN.
gēara av. long ago, formerly.
gearcian prepare, supply [gearo].
gearcung f. preparation.
(ge)~dæg m. preparation-day

geard *m.* fence; enclosure, court-yard; dwelling.

geare *av.* = **gearwe**.

gearn *n.* yarn.

~winde *f.* reel.

gearo, *IN.* iare ; *pl.* **gearwe** ready.

~brygd† *f.* quick movement.

~folm† with ready hand.

~gangende† going swiftly.

~lice *av.* completely, well.

~snot(t)or† wise, skilled (in) *wi.*

~þancol† very wise *or* prudent.

~wita *once, m.* understanding, knowledge.

~witol* ready-witted.

~witolnes *f.* sagacity.

~wyrdig† eloquent.

gearor *cpv. of* **gearwe** *av.*

gearw|ian make ready ; make, do ; clothe.

(ge)~**ung** *f.* preparation.

gearw|a*, ~**e**† *fpl.* clothing, ornaments, armour.

gearw|e *f.* yarrow (a plant) — ~**an-lēaf** mallow.

gearwe, **geare** *av.* completely ; well.

geat, *pl.* gatu *n.* gate.

~torr† *m.* gate-tower.

~weard *m.* porter.

gēatan *L.* grant. *Cp.* gēa [*Scand.*].

geatolic† adorned, splendid.

geatw|a, ~**e**† *fpl.* armour, ornaments [getāwe].

gēap† foolishness ; mockery.

gegn* direct — þā gēnran wegas.

gegn- = **gēan-**.

gegnum† *not W. av.* forwards, direct.

gegninga† *not W.*, gea-, gēn-, -unga *av.* straight forwards, direct ; altogether, entirely ; without doubt, certainly.

gehþu = **geohþu**.

gellet basin.

gēmung *f.* marriage *IN.*

~ian marry *IN.*

~lic nuptial *IN.*

gēn- = **gegn-**, **gēan-**.

gēn *not W.* (†), īe, gēna, gēno, *IN.* geona *av.* often preceded by þā, nū | *continuation* still, yet : þēr hē ~ ligeþ — *so also* nū ~(a) þā ~(a) still ; ne wæs mē feorh þā gēn not yet ; geornor þonne hē ~ dyde | *further*: hierde ic secgan ~ be sumum fugle —

so also þā ~ | *still w. cpv.* : ~ mâre, gēna swētre ‖ now, in the immediate future : gif hē his ~ wolde geþafa weorþan þæt . . ; ~ ic þē fēores unnan wille, gif þū . . ‖ *repetition* again : þā ~ sēo fâmne spræc. *Cp.* gīet.

gēng *prt. of* gān.

gengan (†) go *only in prt.* [gān].

gegenga *m.* fellow-traveller ; companion, associate [gān].

genge *n.* troop, gang ; privy.

gegenge *n.* troop, gang.

genge having influence, effective, valid.

gēno = **gēn**.

gēnunga = **gegninga**.

gēo, (g)iū *av.* formerly, of old.

~dǣd† *f.* former deed.

~lēan† *n.* reward for past action.

~mann *m.* man of old.

~mēowle† *f.* (?).

~sceaft† *f.* destiny.

~sceaft-gāst† *m.* doomed sprite.

~wine† *m.* departed friend.

geoc, iuc *n.* yoke ; yoke of oxen ; a measure of land ; *IN.* wife (!).

~boga *m.* yoke.

~ian yoke.

~led, iuclǣte *n.*, iocleta *m.* a measure of land. *Cp.* scīrlett.

~stecca *m.* part of a yoke.

~tīema*, ē *m.* one of a team, animal yoked with another Gl

gēoc(†) *f.* help ; consolation ; safety.

~end *m.* preserver.

~ian preserve, save *w. g. or d.*

gēocor† full of hardship ; sad.

gēocre *av.* severely.

geocs|a = ***giexa** sob.

~ung *f.* sobbing.

geofon†, y, i *n.* ocean, flood.

~flōd *n.* sea.

~hūs *n.* sea-house (the ark).

~ȳþ *f.* wave.

gēog(e)lere *m.* magician.

geogoþ, eo†, iug- *f.* (period of) youth ; young ; young persons, youth ; new-born animals.

~cnōsl† *n.* young progeny.

~feorh† *n.* (period of) youth.

~hād *m.* (state of) youth.

~hādnes *f.* (state of) youth Bd.

~lic youthful.

~lust *m.* lusts of youth.

~myru*f., g. **~myrwe**† *once* youthful joy (?).

geohhol = **gēol**.

geohsa = ***giexa** sob.

gēol, ge(o)hhol, geohel *n.* Yule, Christmas — *also pl.* : ǣr ~um [*Lt.* Julius].

~dæg *m.* Yule-day — se ǣresta ~ Christmas-day.

~mōnaþ *m.* December.

gēola *m.* — se ǣrra ~ December, se æfterra ~ January.

geoloca, geol(e)ca *m.* yolk (of egg) [geolo].

geolo, *pl.* geolwe yellow.

~hwīt pale yellow.

~rand† *m.* yellow shield.

~rēad reddish yellow.

geolstor, *vE.* gelostr *nm.*, gillister *n.*, gillistre *f.* poisonous secretion, pus, matter.

geolstrig secreting poison, purulent.

geoluling*, giu- (*m.*) July (?). *Cp.* gēol.

geolwian become yellow.

gēomor sad, mournful.

~e *av.* sadly.

~frōd† old.

~giedd† *n.* dirge.

~lic sad.

~līce *av.* sadly.

~mōd† sad.

gēomer|ian, gēomr- mourn, complain.

~ung *f.* moaning ; mourning, lamentation.

geon *once* that, yonder.

geond, i I. *prp. wa.* throughout *of* extension and motion ; *of time* during. II. *av.* thither.

geondan *prp.* beyond — fram ~ sæ. *Cp.* begeondan.

geond·blāwan I inspire (?).

geond·brǣdan cover (with cloth, &c.).

geond·drencan intoxicate.

geond·faran *tr.* traverse, pervade.

geond·fēolan 4, *ptc.* -folen fill *wi.*

geond·fēran traverse.

geond·folen, *see* -fēolan.

geond·gān *vb.* traverse.

geond·gēotan 7 pour over, flood, wash.

geond·hierdan harden thoroughly.

geond·hweorfan 3 traverse ; pass through (mind).

geond·iernan 3 run over.

[73]

geond·lācan† 1 traverse.
geond·lęcc|an moisten throughout, water.
~ing f. watering.
geond·liehtan illumine.
geond·męngan† confuse (mind).
geond·sāwan 1 scatter.
geond·scēawian survey.
geond·scīnan 6 shine on, illuminate.
geond·scrīpan 6 traverse.
geond·sęndan† overspread (with army) wi.
geond·sēon 5 survey.
geond·smēa(ga)n investigate, discuss.
geond·spætan syringe.
geond·spręngan sprinkle over.
geond·springan 3 pervade (?) Gl.
geond·sprūtan 7 pervade.
geond·stręgdan, -strēdan sprinkle over.
geond·styrian agitate.
geond·þęncan consider, contemplate.
geond·wadan 2 study, be versed in.
geond·wlītan 6 see through, gaze all over.
geong, iung, cpv. gingra, spl. ging(e)st young.
~lācan be growing up, be young Gl.
~lic, geonlic young.
~licnes f. youth.
~ling m. youth.
geongr|a, i m. youth; disciple, follower; attendant, vassal.
~e*, i f. attendant.
geongor|dōm, ~scipe m. vassalage [Old Saxon].
gēopan† 7 swallow.
geormant-lāf (f.), geormanlēaf n. mallow. Cp. gearwanlēaf.
georn wg. desirous, eager; zealous w. ymb.
~e av. eagerly; earnestly; well, accurately.
~full eager wg.; zealous, diligent.
~fullic zealous.
~fullīce av. zealously, diligently.
~fulnes f. desire, eagerness; zeal.
~lic desirable.
~līce av. diligently, zealously; accurately.

georn(n)es f. zeal.
georstu A. interj. Oh.
geostran = giestran.
gēot|an 7 pour; shed; cast (in metal) ‖ intr. flow— ~ende hęre overwhelming army.
~end m. artery Gl.
~endlic*, ~enlic fluid Gl.
~ere m. (brass)-founder.
geoxa = *giexa sob.
gēr = gēar year.
gęrla (m.) tribute lN.
gersum, æ mn., ~a m. treasure, gift [Scand.].
gesca = *giexa sob.
gesen, iesende, isend, isern entrails Gl.
gestende, see giestan.
gētan = gīetan destroy.
geten-wyrde consenting, agreeing Ct.
giccan itch.
giccig once purulent Gl.
giēcel (m.) icicle, ice. īses ~ icicle.
~a m. ice.
~ig icy.
~stān m. piece of ice, hailstone.
gicþa, ie, io, gihþa, y m. itch; hiccup. Cp. gycenes.
gīdsian = gītsian.
giēdd n. song, poem; speech; narrative, tale; proverb, riddle.
~ian sing; recite, speak; discuss, debate.
~ing f. song; saying, discourse.
giēf|an 5 wda. give, grant; give in marriage.
~a m. giver.
~ung f. granting, consent.
giēfian wd. bestow gifts on, endow; give.
giēfl n. food, piece of food.
giēf|u, gifu f. gift — tō ~e(s) gratis; good thing; (divine) grace; the Runic letter g.
~fæst gifted; capable of wg.
~heall† f. gift-hall, hall in which gifts are distributed.
~ig*, i rich.
~ol bountiful.
~olnes f. liberality.
~sceatt† m. gift.
~stōl† m. throne.
giēld n. payment; tribute, tax | compensation; stead: on þære sunnan ~ instead of the sun | offering (to a god), sacrifice, wor-

ship; heathen god, idol | guild, fraternity.
giēld|dagas m. guild- or festival-days.
~lic of a guild.
~rǣden(n) f. membership of a guild.
~scipe m. association, guild.
~sester m. a measure.
gegiēld n. association, guild.
~a m. member of a guild.
~heall f. guild-hall.
~scipe m. guild.
giēldan 3 wda. pay, pay for; give, render; recompense, requite; punish; make good, make restitution; worship (idols).
giēlda m. member of a guild.
giēlde*, e sterile Gl.
giēllan 3 scream, utter cry, sound intr.
giēlm*, ~a, e, i m. handful, sheaf.
giēlp m. boasting, arrogance; fame, glory.
~cwide† m. boastful speech.
~en boastful.
~georn† eager for glory.
~geornes f. desire of glory.
~hlæden† boastful or illustrious (?).
~lic vainglorious, arrogant; magnificent, splendid.
~līce av. arrogantly.
~plega† m. battle, war.
~sceaþa† m. arrogant enemy.
~sprǣc⊦ f. boastful speech.
~word† n. boastful word, boast.
giēlp|an 3 w.g., rarely i. boast, exult.
~ing f. boasting, glory.
gīem|an wg. take care of; take notice of, reflection.
~end m. keeper, governor.
~ing f. care; gēmung lN. marriage. See gēmung.
gīeme f. care.
gīemelēas careless, heedless; neglected, uncared for; stray (cattle).
~ian neglect.
~lic careless.
~līce av. carelessly.
~nes f. negligence, carelessness.
~t, -līest f. negligence, carelessness; being neglected.
gīemen(n) f. taking care of, care, guardianship; government.
gīen = gēn.
giend = geond.

giendan* *once* drive — *prt.* gynde, e, î.

giengra = geongra.

giẹrd *f.* rod, twig; a measure of land, rood.

~weg*, y *m.* fenced road (?).

~wīte† *n.* rod-punishment, punishment through Moses' rod.

gierede, *prt. of* giẹrwan.

giẹr(e)la, ge- *m.* dress, clothing.

gegiẹrelic of clothes.

giern|an, ~ian, eo *w. g.*, æfter, *rarely a., w. sbj., w. inf.* desire; request, demand [georn].

ge-endlic desirable.

~ing *f.* desire.

giẹrran 3 chatter; creak.

gierstan = giestran.

giẹrwan *prt.* giẹrede prepare, cook (food) : ~ tō mẹte — ~ ūp serve (meal); adorn; clothe, dress [gearu].

giése*, i, y, *lN.* ise *av.* yes [gēa, sīe].

giẹst, æ; ẹ *A.*, also *lW.* [*Scand. form?*] *m.* stranger; guest; †enemy.

~ærn, -ern *n.* guest-chamber, inn.

~hof *n.* guest-house.

~hūs *n.* guest-house, inn.

~ian be guest, lodge.

~ig*, gestig strange, being a stranger *lN.*

~ing*, ẹ *f.* exile.

~līþe hospitable.

~līþnes *f.* hospitality.

~mægen† *n.* troop of guests.

~sẹle† *m.* hall for strangers.

giẹst *m.* yeast.

giéstan* ferment (?) — gestende swelling (madness).

giéstran-, eo, gyrstan-, e(o).

~æfen *m.* — ~e *av.* yesterday evening.

~dæg(e) *av.* yesterday.

~lic*, gysternlic — ~ dæg yesterday.

~niht *av.* yesterday night.

gīet, ~a, ietf *av., often w.* nū, þā *prefixed* still, yet : gȳt mē twēonaþ; hē næs dēad þā ~; hitherto: swā hē nū ~ dyde; further, besides: be þǣm is ~ gecweden..; *w. cpv.* still: swīþor ~.

gīeta = gīet.

gīetan*, ē† destroy.

giéxa*, geocsa, gihsa, *vE.* gesca, iesca *m.* sob. *See* geocsa.

gif, y; e, eo *cj. w. indc., sbj.* : mē þyncþ betre, ~ ēow swā þyncþ, þæt . . ; ~ wē æfre mægen ; whether : þū wāst ~ hit is swā wē secgan hīerdon ; frægn ~ him wǣre niht getǣse whether he had had a pleasant night.

gīfer† *once* (*m.*) glutton (?).

gifeþe† I. granted (by fate). II. *n.* fate, chance.

gifre† *once* useful (?).

gīfer|līce *av.* greedily.

~nes *f.* greediness, voracity.

gīfre greedy, ravenous; rapacious; desirous.

gift *f.* price of wife ; *pl.* ~a, -u marriage, wedding [giéfan].

~būr *n.* wedding-chamber.

~hūs *n.* wedding-house.

~ian give (woman) in marriage *lN.*

~lēoþ *n.* epithalamium.

~(e)lic belonging to a wedding.

gīgant, ī† *m.* giant [*Lt.* gigantem].

~mæcg† *m.* son of a giant.

gihsa = giéxa sob.

gillister, gillistre = geolstor.

gilte *f.* young sow.

gimm *m.* gem, jewel; †sun [*Lt.* gemma].

~bǣre gem-bearing.

~cynn *n.* species of gem, gem.

~ian adorn with gems.

~isc jewelled.

~rẹced† *n.* palace.

~stān *m.* gem, precious stone.

~wyrhta *m.* jeweller.

gimrodor a precious stone.

gin *n.* yawning gulf, abyss.

gin-fæst† ample, liberal (gifts) [ginn].

gīnan 6 yawn.

gin|ian, geonian be wide open, gape [gīnan].

~ung, geo- *f.* gaping, yawning.

gind = geond.

ging = geong.

gingifer, gingiber, gingifere *f.* ginger [*Fr.*].

gingra = geongra.

ginn† spacious.

ginnes *f.* gap, interval.

ginnan = onginnan begin.

gip|ian*, y yawn.

~ung *once f.* gaping, open mouth Gl.

giren = grīn trap.

gegiscan *once* block up Gl.

giscian sob.

gīs(e)l *m.* hostage.

~hād *m.* being a hostage.

gīslian give hostages.

gistran = giestran.

git ye two.

gīts|ian, gīds- *wg.* covet, crave, be greedy, be avaricious.

~ere *m.* covetous man ; miser.

~ung *f.* covetousness, desire, avarice.

gīþ-corn = gȳþ-.

giuguþ = geoguþ.

giung - geong.

gīw, gēow (*m.*) griffin, vulture.

gīw|ian, gīowian *lN.* ask, demand, beg.

~ung *f.* petition.

glad|ian be glad, exult ‖ *tr.* make glad, cheer [glæd].

~ung *f.* cheerfulness, joy.

glæd, æt, ǣt I. †bright, clear; glad, cheerful, merry; kind, courteous. II. *n.* joy† *once.*

~lic bright, splendid ; cheerful, pleasant.

~līce *av.* gladly, cheerfully ; kindly.

~mōd glad, cheerful ; kind, pleasant.

~mōdnes *f.* kindness, liberality.

~nes *f.* joy, cheerfulness.

~scipe *m.* joy.

glædene, a, e *f.* iris, gladiolus.

glǣm† *m.* brightness, splendour, beauty.

glǣr, *pl.* glǣsas (!) *m.* amber.

glǣs *n.* glass.

~fæt *n.* glass vessel.

~hluttor clear as glass, transparent.

glǣsen of glass.

~ēage grey-eyed Gl.

glǣterian glitter.

glappe *f.* buckbean (?).

glēam (*m.*) merriment.

glēaw, ā, *A.* glēu quick-sighted ; sagacious, wise, prudent, clever, skilful, skilled in *w. g.*, on *d.*

~e *av.* wisely ; well.

~ferhþ† wise.

~hycgende† wise.

~hygdig†, -hȳdig sagacious, prudent.

~lic wise, prudent.

~līce *av.* sagaciously, cleverly.

~mōd wise, prudent.

glēaw|nes *f.* sagacity, intelligence, prudence.

~scipe *m.* sagacity, prudence; proof, indication.

glēd, oe *f.* live coal; flame, fire. ge~an make hot, kindle.

~egesa† *m.* terror of fire.

~fæt *n.* chafing-dish.

~scofl *f.* fire-shovel.

~stede † *m.* altar.

gleddian *once* moisten, daub.

gledene = glædene.

glemm blemish, disfigurement.

glendran devour, swallow. geglendrian *LN.* precipitate.

gleng *fm.* ornament; magnificence. ~an adorn; trim (lamp). ge~endlic magnificent. ~full, ~lic adorned, magnificent.

gleoma† R.

glēow = glīw.

glēs|an*, oe gloss, explain [*Lt.* glōssa]. ~ing *f.* glossing.

glīdan 6 glide, slip.

glida, io *m.* kite.

glidder slippery [glīdan]. gliddrian slip.

glīg = glīw.

glis|ian glitter — se ~igenda wibba glowworm.

glisnian glitter.

gliten|ian glitter, shine. ~ung *f.* flash.

glīw, glīg, glēo(w), ī† *n.* music, minstrelsy; mirth, jest, ridicule; pleasure.

~bēam *m.* musical instrument, harp, timbrel (!).

~cræft *m.* music, minstrelsy.

~drēam† *m.* music, mirth.

~georn fond of jesting.

~hlēoþriendlic musical.

~lic mimic.

~mægden, -mæden *n.* female minstrel.

~mann *m.* minstrel, musician; buffoon.

~stafas† *mpl.* joy.

~stōl† *m.* seat of joy.

~word† *n.* song, poem.

glīw|ian, ēo play on musical instrument, sing; play the buffoon, jest, joke; adorn.

~(e)re *m.* buffoon, jester.

~ung *f.* mirth.

glōf, ~e *f.* glove.

glōf|ung *f.* providing with gloves.

~wyrt *f.* lily of the valley; hound's tongue (a plant).

glōm twilight.

~ung *f.* twilight; dim light before dawn.

glōwan I glow (*of* red-hot things).

gnætt *m.* gnat.

gnagan 2 gnaw.

gnāst spark.

gnēaþ, ē niggardly *wg.* (giefa); frugal, austere (life). *Cp.* gnīeþe.

~licnes *f.* frugality.

gnīdan 6 rub; pulverize.

gnīdel (*m.*) pestle.

gnieþ|e scanty [gnēaþ].

~elīce*, ē *av.* sparingly, in small quantities.

~elicnes, gnēa~, ~nes *f.* frugality.

gnorn I. (*m.*) sorrow, affliction. II. sorrowful.

~cearig† sorrowful.

~hof† *n.* prison.

~scyndende† *ptc.* hastening away in sorrow.

~sorg† *f.* sorrow.

~word† *n.* sorrowful word *or* speech.

gnorn|ian *intr.* grieve, be sorrowful; *tr.* lament.

~ung *f.* lamentation; grief.

gnyran *once* creak = gnierran?

gnyrn† sorrow, evil.

~wracu† *f.* enmity.

gō|n* sigh.

~ung *f.* sighing, groaning.

god *m., pl.* ~as, ~u, *gpl.* ~a, ~ena God; heathen god.

~bearn *n.* child of God; godchild.

~borg *m.*?

~bōt *f.* atonement made to the church.

~cund of God, divine, religious, sacred.

~cundlic divine.

~cundlīce *av.* by divine power, divinely.

~cundnes *f.* divinity, Godhead, divine quality; sacred office.

~dohtor *f.* god-daughter.

~drēam† *m.* divine joy.

~fæder *m.* God the Father; godfather.

~ferht, y pious.

~gield *n.* idol.

~gieldlic of idols.

god|gimm *m.* divine gem.

~hād *m.* divine nature.

~ing *m.* son of God *LN.*

~mægen *n.* divinity.

~mōdor *f.* godmother.

~scyld *f.* impiety.

~scyldig impious.

~sibb *m.* sponsor.

~sibbrǣden(n)*f.* sponsorial obligations.

god-spell *n.* gospel.

~bōc *f.* the Gospels.

~bodung *f.* gospel-preaching.

~ere *m.* evangelist.

~ian preach the gospel.

~isc, ~ic evangelical.

~traht *m.* gospel-commentary.

god|(ge)sprǣce *n.* oracle.

~sunu *m.* godson.

~þrymm *m.* divine majesty.

god(e)-webb *n.* precious *or* fine cloth, purple.

~cynn *n.* kind of purple.

~en of purple.

~gierla *m.* cloth of purple.

~wyrhta *m.* weaver of purple.

god-wræc impious, wicked.

~lic impious.

~nes *f.* impiety, wickedness.

gōd I. good, *cpv.* betera, bet(t)ra, *spl.* bet(e)st good *in all the MnE.* meanings | virtuous, suitable, capable | considerable — ~ dæl *wg.* a considerable portion, ~e hwīle *av.* for some time | of high rank —his betera his lord, patron. II. *n.* good: ~ and yfel — swā hwæt swā hē tō ~e gedēþ his good actions; good action, goodness; benefit | property; prosperity.

~æppel, oo = cod-.

~dǣd *f.* good deed; benefit.

~dōnd *m., pl.* -dōnd, ē benefactor.

~lēas unfortunate, wretched.

~lic goodly, noble, magnificent.

~nes *f.* goodness; good thing.

~scipe *m.* goodness.

~spēdig rich.

gōd|ian *intr.* become better, improve — hit ~ode mid him they prospered; be cured, get better (*of* illness) || *tr.* improve, repair (house), reform (morally); enrich, endow.

gofol = gafol.

gold *n.* gold.

gold|æht† *f.* possessions in gold.
~e-āwefen woven with gold.
~(e)beorht† bright with gold.
~blēo(h) *n.* golden colour.
~blōma *m.* gold flower (?) (Christ).
~burg† *f.* town in which gold is distributed.
~fæt† *n.* gold vessel.
~fāg variegated *or* adorned with gold.
~fell *n.* gold plate.
~finc *m.* goldfinch.
~finger *m.* third finger.
~frætwe† *fpl.* gold ornaments.
~fyld covered with gold.
~giéfa† *m.* lord, patron.
~hama† *m.* golden *or* gilt corslet.
~hilted† having a gold *or* gilt hilt.
~hladen† adorned with gold.
gold-hord *nm.* treasure, treasury.
~hūs *n.* privy.
~ian lay up treasure.
gold|hroden† adorned with gold.
~hwæt† (?).
~læfer *f.*, ~lēaf *n.* gold leaf *or* plate.
~mæstling *n.* brass.
~māþm† *m.* treasure.
~sele† *m.* hall where gold is distributed.
~smiþ *m.* goldsmith.
~smiþu *f.* goldsmith's work.
~spēdig† wealthy.
~torht† bright as gold.
~þéof *m.* stealer of gold.
~þræd *m.* gold thread.
~weard† *m.* guardian of gold (a dragon).
~geweorc *n.* gold-work, what is made of gold.
~wine† *m.* liberal patron, lord.
~wlanc† gold-proud, adorned with gold.
~wlenc- gold ornament.
gōma *m.* palate; *pl.* gōman jaws.
gōp, ō† *once* slave, servant (?).
gor (*n.*) dung, dirt.
gorett|an, -etan gaze, stare.
~ung *f.* gazing.
gorst, ~bēam *m.* furze.
gōs *f.*, *pl.* gēs, oe goose.
~fugol *m.* goose.
~hafoc *m.* goshawk.
got-woþe *f.* goatweed (?).
Got|a *m.* Goth.
~land *n.* Gothland.
Gotonisc Gothic Gl

grā-scinnen *vL.* made of grey fur [*Scand.*].
grād *m.*, ~e *f.* step of altar; degree, rank [*Lt.* gradus].
græd, gærd (*m.*) grass.
græde grassy.
grædan (1 b) cry out, call out.
grædig greedy, covetous, eager for *wg.*; rapacious, fierce.
~līce, grædelīce *av.* greedily, eagerly.
~nes *f.* greediness, greed, covetousness.
grædum† *once av.* greedily.
græf *n.* cave; grave [grafan].
~hūs *n.* grave.
græf (*n.*) style (for writing) [*Lt.* graphium].
~ere = grafere.
~seax *n.* graving-tool.
græfa *m.* grove, thicket, bramble, brush-wood (for burning) [grāf].
græft *m.* sculpture, carved object [grafan].
~geweorc *n.* piece of sculpture.
græg grey.
~hæwe grey Gl.
~hama† grey-coated.
~mæl† grey-coloured.
gegræppian seize *LN.*
grætan* weep, *see* grētan.
grāf *m.* grove, copse. *Cp.* græf-.
grafan 2 dig, penetrate; engrave, carve.
~ere, æ *m.* carver, sculptor.
grafett *n.* trench (?) *vlCt.*
gram *w.d.*, wiþ *a.* angry; fierce; hostile; oppressive, unkind.
~bære passionate.
~bærnes *f.* bad temper, anger.
~e *av.* angrily; fiercely; cruelly.
~heort† fierce, hostile.
~hycgende†, ~hygdig†, -hȳdig fierce, hostile.
~lic fierce, cruel, grievous.
~līce *av.* hostilely, fiercely, cruelly.
~mōd fierce, cruel.
~word† *n.* hostile word *or* speech.
gramian rage Gl.
grama *m.* anger.
grammatic|cræft, gramatisc- *m.* grammar [*Lt.*].
~ere *m.* grammarian.
grān|ian groan; lament.
~ung *f.* groaning; lamentation.
grandor.
~lēas† guileless.

gran|u *f.* moustache.
~fisc *m.* a fish.
grāp *f.* grasp [grīpan].
grāp|ian touch, handle, feel ‖ *intr.* grope.
~igendlic tangible.
~ung *f.* sense of touch.
grasian graze *intr.* [græs].
grātan *pl.* *once* groats.
grēada *m.* bosom.
grēat, *cpv.* ~ra, grīetra*, grȳttra, thick, stout, bulky, big; coarse-grained, coarse (salt). ~e wyrt meadow saffron.
~ian become thick *or* big.
~nes *f.* thickness, bigness.
Grēcisc = Crēcisc.
gremian, gremman irritate, provoke; revile (!) [gram].
gremettan = grymettan.
grēn|e, oe green — ~ ār orichalcum Gl.
~hæwen greenish.
~ian become green.
~nes *f.* greenness; *pl.* plants.
grenn|ian grin.
~ung *f.* grinning.
grēofa*, greoua *twice m.* pot Gl.
grēosn *once* gravel, pebble.
grēot *n.* earth, dust, sand.
~hord† *n.* body.
grēotan 7 weep.
grēp(e), oe, y *f.* trench, ditch, drain; burrow.
grēt|an, oe handle, touch: hearpan ~ play the harp; come to, visit; attack; treat (subject); treat (well *or* ill): mid yfle ~; have intercourse with, cohabit; greet, salute, address.
grēting *f.* greeting, salutation; present as acknowledgement of a favour received.
~hūs *n.* audience-chamber.
grētan† [ē = æ] *intr.* weep ‖ *tr.* bewail.
grīeto *f.* bulkiness, great size [grēat].
grillan irritate, tease.
grīm|a† *m.* mask; helmet; ghost, spectre.
~helm *m.* helmet with visor.
grīming *once* spectre Gl.
grimm cruel, fierce; terrible, severe, excessive (cold).
~e *av.* fiercely; cruelly, severely.

grimm|lic fierce, terrible ; san-guinary (battle, victory).

~lice av. fiercely, severely.

~nes f. cruelty, fierceness, severity.

grimman† 3 rage, be proud.

grims|ian rage, be fierce, be excessive.

~ung f. asperity.

grīn, ge-, gīren fn. snare, noose, trap.

~(i)an ensnare.

gegrind† n. grinding together, crash, clash.

grind|an 3 tr. grind ; sharpen by grinding ‖ intr. grind, dash, rub — mid tōþum ~ gnash teeth.

~etōþ m. molar.

grindel† m. bar, bolt, in pl. iron grating (?).

grīng† once slaughter, destruction. Cp. cringan.

~wracu f. punishment.

gringan = cringan.

grīp in 6, always ge- in W. seize, clutch, also met. (of temptation, fear, disease, weapons) ; take possession of, usurp w. on a. ; understand.

~end m. seizer, robber.

~ol capacious Gl.

grīpa m. handful, sheaf [grīpan].

grīpe m. grasp, clutch, hold.

gegripennes f. seizing Gl.

grīpu† f. kettle.

grīst, gyrst I. (n.) grinding ; grist, corn to be ground. II. aj. strident Gl. [grindan].

~bite m. gnashing the teeth.

~bitian, ~bātian grind or gnash the teeth, gnash.

~bitung, ~bātung f. gnashing (of teeth).

gristlung*, y f. once gnashing (of teeth).

grīstra m. baker [grīst].

gristel (m.) gristle.

griþ n. peace, truce ; protection, asylum, guarantee of safety or immunity [Scand.].

~bryce m. breach of peace.

~lagu f. law concerning peace.

~lēas unprotected.

~ian make peace w. wiþ ; protect wa.

grorn† I. sad. II. n. grief.

~e av. sadly.

~hof n. house of woe.

grorn|ian mourn, murmur, complain.

~ung f. complaining LN.

grost once gristle Gl.

grot n. particle [grēot].

~ig gritty, earthy.

grot (n.) once groats, coarse meal Gl. [grēot].

grōw|an 1 grow.

~nes f. growth.

grun|ian grunt.

~ung, nn f. roaring, grunting.

grund m. bottom, floor (of cave) ; ground, earth ; plain, country, land ; depth(s), abyss, interior ; water, sea.

~bedd† n. ground, earth.

~būend† pl. inhabitants of earth, men.

~fūs† hastening to the abyss (of hell).

~hierde† m. guardian of the depths (of a lake).

~lēas bottomless ; boundless (avarice).

~lēaslic boundless.

~lunga, ~linga av. (pull down) from or to the foundations, totally ; to the ground, down.

~scēat† m. tract of the earth, country.

~sele†* m. abysmal dwelling.

~sopa m. a plant.

~stān m. foundation-stone.

~staþolian fix on firm foundation met.

~wang† m. bottom, floor (of cave) ; the earth, world.

~weall m. foundation, also met.

~weallian found.

~weg†, æ m. the earth.

~wela† m. earthly wealth.

~wiergen† f. water-wolf, she-wolf of the deep.

grunde-swelge = gunde-.

grunnettan once grunt Gl. [grunian].

grūt f., d. grȳt coarse meal ; grains (in brewing).

grutt m. gulf, abyss Gl. Cp. grund.

grymet|tan, ~(i)an, gre- roar, grunt ; rage.

~ung f. roaring, grunting.

gryn-smiþ† once m. worker of evil = gnyrn-?

gegrynd n. plot of ground [grund].

gryndan descend [grund].

grynde† once (n.) abyss.

grȳpe = grēpe.

gryre† m. terror, horror (emotions) ; (what causes) terror, horror ; destructiveness.

~brōga m. terror, horror.

~fæst terribly firm.

~fāh terribly hostile or variegated.

~geatwe fpl. terrible armour.

~gīest m. a terrible visitant.

~hwīl f. time of terror.

~lēoþ n. song or cry expressing terror or inspiring terror.

~lic terrible, horrible.

~miht f. terrible power.

~sīþ m. terrible (dangerous) expedition.

gyrrran† once chatter (of teeth). Cp. gnyran.

gryt, see grūt.

grytt|a, ~an pl. grits, coarse meal [grot].

grytte once f. spider Gl.

gū = gēo.

gum|a† m. man, hero.

~cynn n. mankind, men ; race, nation.

~cyst f. liberality, munificence ; virtue, goodness — ~um excellently.

~drēam m. joy among men, life.

~dryhten m. prince, lord.

~fēþa m. troop.

~frēa m. king.

~mann m. man, warrior.

~rīce n. kingdom, country, the earth.

~rinc m. man.

~stōl m. throne.

~þegen m. man.

~þēod f. nation, pl. mankind, men.

gund (m.) pus, matter.

~eswelge, gr-, -swil(i)ge, -swy-f. groundsel.

gung = geong.

guttas mpl. entrails Gl.

gūþ† f. war, battle.

~beorn m. warrior.

~bill n. sword.

~bord n. shield.

~byrne f. corslet.

~caru f. war.

~cræft f. strategy, warfare.

~cwēn f. warlike queen.

~cyning m. warlike king.

~cyst f. bravery or troop (?).

~dēaþ m. death in battle.

~fana m. banner, standard.

gūþ|flā(n) f. battle-arrow.
~floga m. warlike flyer (dragon).
~frēa m. warlike lord or prince.
~frec warlike.
~freca m. warrior.
~fremmend m. warrior.
~fruma m. warrior.
~fugol m. bird of war, eagle.
~gēatas mpl. the warlike Goths.
~geatwe fpl. armour.
~hafoc m. war-hawk, eagle.
~heard warlike, brave.
~helm m. helmet.
~here m. army.
~horn n. trumpet.
~hrēþ (m.) glory in war.
~hwæt warlike, brave.
~gelāca m. warrior.
~lēoþ n. war-song.
~maga, mæcga m. warrior.
~mōd warlike.
~gemōt n. battle.
~myrce pl. Ethiopians.
~plega m. battle.
~ræs m. warlike attack.
~rēaf n. armour.
~(h)rēow fierce in battle
~rinc m. warrior.
~rōf warlike.
~scaþa m. enemy, destroyer.
~scear- slaughter (?).

gūþ|sceorp, ~scrūd, ~searu n. armour.
~sele m. hall of warriors.
~spell n. tidings of war.
~sweord n. sword.
~getāwe = **~geatwe**.
~geþingu npl. battle, contest.
~þracu f. violence.
~þrēat m. martial band.
~gewǣde n. armour.
~weard m. king.
~(ge)weorc n. warlike deed or exploit.
~wērig weary with battle.
~wiga m. warrior.
~wine m. fellow-warrior.
~gewinn n. battle.
~wudu m. spear.
gycenes, i f. itching Gl. Cp. gicþa.
gyden f. goddess [god].
~lic vestal Gl.
gydig insane [god].
gyldan gild [gold].
gylden gold(en).
~bēag m. crown.
~feax golden-haired.
~mūþa golden-mouthed.
gylede prt. of gyllan.
gyllan†, prt. **gylede, y†** shout.
gylt m. guilt, sin; crime, offence; fault.

gylt|ig guilty, liable.
~lic wicked.
gylt|an be guilty.
~end m. offender.
~ing f. sinning.
gyr fir-tree.
~trēow n. fir-tree.
gyr-, see gyrwe-fenn.
gyrdan gird, put girdle on, belt, gird (with sword).
gyrdel m. girdle, belt; purse.
~bred n. pugillar Gl.
~hring m. buckle.
gyrdels m. girdle.
~hring m. buckle.
gyrl|e* f. virgin.
~gyden f. Vesta Gl.
gyrn† n. sorrow, affliction.
~stafas mpl. affliction, tormenting.
~wracu f. revenge.
gyrst = **grīst** grinding.
gyrwe-fenn n. marsh Gl.
gysternlic, see giestran.
gyte m. pouring (out), flood, shedding (of blood, tears) [gēotan].
~sǣl m. joy at the pouring out of wine, pl. revelry.
~strēam m. current.
gȳþ-.
~corn*, ī, L. u n. spurge laurel.
~rife, git- f. cockle.

H.

hā, ? hāne L. rowlock — æt ~ per man [Scand.].
~sǣta L. m. rower in warship [Scand.].
hā hā interj. ha ha!
habban, æ, (hē) hæfþ, hafaþ, prt. **hæfde** w. a., partitive g. have, hold, take, met. possess, hold, have: ~ wiþ þām fȳre; ~ mid him; æt hæbbendre handa with the stolen goods in his possession; wīf ~ have intercourse with; he was thirty; gif hē þæs andgytes hæfþ þæt hē hit

understandan mæg; ~ andan tō bear malice | behave to: yfele ~ ill-treat — ptc. yfele gehæfd tormented, diseased | have an opinion about: þā lǣwedan willaþ ~þone mōnan be þām þe hī hine gesēoþ | necessity, obligation w. ger.: þone calic þe ic tō drincenne hæbbe | to form past tenses w. inflected or (gen.) uninflected ptc.: oþ þæt hīe hine ofslægen(ne) hæfdon.
gehabban hold, keep; rfl. restrain oneself.
haca m. hook.

haccian hack.
hacele f. mantle, cloak.
hacod m. pike (fish).
hād m., g. ~es, rarely ~a rank, order. (holy) office; condition, state, character, nature, form: fǣmnan ~ virginity; to form avs.: þurh hǣstne ~ violently; sex; person, person (in grammar).
~bōt f. compensation for injury to priest.
~breca m. violator of his holy orders.
~bryce m. violation of one's holy orders.

D

hād|griþ *n.* security *or* privilege of those in holy orders.

~es-mann *m.* member of a particular order.

~notu *f.* exercising clerical functions.

hād- chamber (?).

~swǣpa *m.* bridesman.

~swǣpe, ~swāpe *f.* bridesmaid. *Cp.* heorþswǣpe.

hād|ian ordain ; let take the veil.

~od ordained, clerical.

~ung *f.* ordination.

gehāda *m.* fellow-monk.

hādor†, ǣ I. (*n.*) clearness, bright light (of the sky). II. bright ; clear-sounding.

hādre, ǣ *av.* clearly (*of light and sound*).

hæbb- = habb-.

~endlic habilis Gl.

hæc|c, ę *f.* gate, half-grating *or* hatch, grating.

~wer *m.* weir with grate to catch fish.

gehæcca *once* sausage Gl. [haccian].

hæcce *f.* crosier [*Cp.* haca].

hædor = hādor.

hædre† *av.* anxiously.

hæf† *n.* sea.

hæfde *prt. of* habban.

hæfe = hefe leaven.

hæfen, ha- *f.* property, riches [habban].

~lēas poor.

~lēast *f.* poverty.

hæfen *f.* harbour.

hæfer *m.* he-goat.

~blǣte, *vE.* hæfre- *f.* a bird.

hæfern, hrefn, æ *m.* crab.

hæfre-blete = hæfer-blǣte.

hæft *n.* handle [habban].

~mēce† *m.* hilted sword.

hæft† *m.* bond, fetter ; captivity, custody, imprisonment ; captive, prisoner, slave [habban].

~eclamm† *m.* bond ; *pl.* subjection.

~edōm† *m.* captivity.

ge~fæst captive.

~incel *n.* slave.

~ling *m.* prisoner.

~(e)nied *f.* custody, captivity.

~niedling *m.* captive.

~noþ *m.* custody, imprisonment.

hæft|an bind ; confine, imprison, arrest.

ge~(ed)nes *f.* captivity.

hæfting *f.* fastening.

hæftelic captious Gl.

hæften (*f.*) custody *vL.*

hæftn|ian take captive.

~ung *f.* fastening, bond ; captivity, confinement, imprisonment.

hæg- = hagu-.

hæghāl uninjured *LN.*

hæg-weard *m.* hayward, keeper of cattle in a common field.

gehæg- (*n.*) meadow. *Cp.* *gehīege.

hægl = hagol.

hægtesse, hæts(e) *f.* witch. *Cp.* heago-rūn.

hǣl† *once* (*n.*) omen.

hǣl = hǣlo.

hǣl-wyrt *f.* pennyroyal.

hǣl|an heal, cure ; save (soul) [hāl].

hǣlend *m.* Saviour.

~lic salutary.

hǣlnes *f.* salvation, sanctuary.

~griþ *n.* privilege of sanctuary.

hǣlung *f.* healing.

hǣle† *m.* man, hero [hæleþ].

hæleþ† *m.*, *pl.* ~, ~as man, hero.

~helm = heolop-.

hælfter, ea *n.* halter.

hǣlig *once* inconstant, fickle [hāl-stān].

hǣlnes *see* hǣlan.

hǣlo, hǣl *f.* health ; safety ; prosperity ; salvation [hāl].

~bearn† *n.* salvation-child (Christ).

hǣls|ian observe omens. *Cp.* hāl-sian.

~end, ~ere *m.* soothsayer.

~ung *f.* divination.

hǣlþ *f.* healing, cure ; health ; salvation [hāl].

hǣm|an have sexual intercourse, *abs*, *in pl.*, *w.* mid *or* wiþ [hām].

~ere *m.* — unriht ~ fornicator.

-hǣme, e *mpl.* inhabitants Ct. [hām].

hǣmed *n.*, *pl.* ~(r)u sexual intercourse, connexion, marriage.

~ceorl *m.* married man.

~lāc† *n.* sexual intercourse.

~gemāna *m.* matrimony.

~scipe *m.* sexual intercourse.

~þing *n.*, *also pl.* sexual intercourse.

~wīf *n.* married woman.

-hǣmingas *mpl.* inhabitants Ct. [hām].

hǣnan pelt with stones, stone (to death) [hān].

gehǣp, ~lic convenient.

~licnes *f.* convenience.

hæps|e, hæsp *f.* hasp, fastening.

~ian hasp, fasten.

hǣr *n.* hair ; a hair.

~en of hair.

~iht hairy.

~locc *m.* lock of hair.

~sife *n.* hair-sieve.

hǣr-sceard (*n.*) hare-lip.

gehǣre hairy.

hǣre *f.* haircloth, sackcloth.

hǣrfest *m.* autumn.

~handfull *n.* a due belonging to the husbandmen on an estate.

~lic of autumn, autumnal.

~mōnaþ *m.* September.

~tīd *f.*, ~tīma *m.* autumn.

~wǣta *m.* wet weather of autumn.

hǣring *m.* herring.

~tīma *m.* herring-season.

hǣrn, hræn (*f.*) wave ; †sea.

~flota† *m.* ship.

hǣs *f.* command [hātan].

~ere *m.* master, lord *LN.*

hǣsel (*m.*) hazel.

~hnutu *f.* hazel-nut.

~wrid *n.* hazel thicket.

~wyrt *f.* asarabacca (a plant).

hǣslen of hazel.

hǣst† I. violent, severe. II. (*f.*) violence, hostility.

~e, ~līce *av.* violently, fiercely.

hǣtan heat [hāt].

hǣte *f.* heat, inflammation (of body).

hǣteru *npl.* clothes.

hǣto *f.* heat.

hǣts(e) = hægtesse.

hǣtt *m.* hat.

hǣttian scalp (as punishment).

hǣþ *nm.* heath (land) ; heather, heath (the plant).

~berige *f.* bilberry.

~cole *f.* a plant.

~hrycg *m.* heath-ridge.

~iht heathy.

~stapa† *m.* heath-stalker.

hǣþ|a *m.* hot weather.

~ung *f.* heating.

hǣþen heathen, gentile [hǣþ].

~cyning† *m.* heathen king.

~cynn† *n.* heathen race.

~dōm *m.* heathen belief, paganism.

~feoh† *n.* heathen sacrifice.

~gièld *n.* idolatry ; idol.

~gièlda *m.* idolater, heathen.

hǣþen|isc heathenish, heathen.

~mann *m.* Samaritan.

~nes *f.* heathen belief, paganism; *coll.* heathens.

~scipe *m.* heathen belief *or* worship, paganism.

~styrc† *m.* heathen calf (the golden calf).

hǣwen, -e, *vE.* hǣwi, ēa blue.

~ hydele *f.* a plant.

~grēne cerulean Gl.

haf-, *see* habban.

hafela†, heafola *m.* head.

hafen *ptc. of* hebban.

hafenian† grasp.

hafetian, afetigan, hafīt- clap hands, flap (wings).

hafoc *m.* hawk.

~cynn *n.* hawk species.

~ere *m.* hawker.

~fugol *m.* hawk.

~wyrt *f.* a plant.

hafud- = hēafod-.

gehag|ian *impers.* — gif him (*or* hine) tō þām ~ige if he has the money, can afford it.

haga *m.* enclosure; homestead, messuage.

haga *m.* haw, fruit of wild rose.

hago-steald, hæg(e)-, *LN.* hehstald I. *m.* bachelor, one living in the lord's house, youth, warrior. II. *n.* celibacy. III. *aj.* unmarried, young.

~hād *m.* bachelorhood; virginity.

~lic virgin.

~mann *m.* bachelor, young warrior.

~nes *f.* virginity.

hagol, hæg(e)l *m.* hail; *the Runic letter* h.

~faru† *f.* hailstorm.

~ian hail: hit ~ode stānum meteoric stones fell.

~scūr *m.* shower of hail, hailstorm.

~stān *m.* hailstone.

hagu-.

~þorn *m.* hawthorn.

hal-, *see* healh.

hāl- smooth (?). *Cp.* hǣlig.

~stān, aa, *L.* ea *m.* crystal Gl.

hāl whole, uninjured; healthy — wes þū ~, ~ westu, bēo þū ~! hail!

~bǣre wholesome, salutary.

~fæst pious (?).

hāl-wend|e, -y- healing, medicinal; wholesome; salutary,

---

beneficial; conducive to salvation, saving. se ~a the Saviour.

hālwend|lic salutary, conducive to salvation.

~līce *av.* salutarily, in a manner conducive to salvation.

~nes *f.* healthiness.

gehāl whole, uninjured.

hālian heal *intr.*

halc = healh.

hālett|an, hǣ-, -etan hail, greet, salute.

~end *m.* greeter, middle finger (!).

~ung *f.* salutation.

hālgian make holy, hallow (God's name), sanctify, consecrate (church, bishop).

hālgung, ge~ *f.* consecration.

~ramm *m.* ram of consecration.

hālga *m.* saint. ealra hālgena mæssedæg All Saints' day.

hālig holy.

~dæg *m.* Sunday.

hāligdōm *m.* holiness, sanctity; holy things, relics; holy place, sanctuary.

~hūs *n.* sanctuary.

hālig|ern *n.* sanctuary.

~mōnaþ *m.* September.

~nes *f.* holiness, sanctity; holy things, relics; holy place, sanctuary.

~rift, e, y *n.* nun's veil.

~wæter *n.* holy water.

hālor† (*n.*) salvation.

hāls† (*f.*) salvation.

~wurþung *f.* thanksgiving for safety.

hāls|ian exorcise. *Cp.* hǣlsian, healsian.

~ere *m.* soothsayer.

~igend *m.* exorcist; soothsayer.

~ung *f.* exorcism; divination; greeting.

hām *m., d.* ~(e) home; house, dwelling; residence, estate | hām *av.* home(wards). æt ~ at home.

~cūþ familiar.

~cyme *m.* coming home, return.

~færeld *n.* going home.

~fæst resident, settled.

~faru *f.* = ~sōcn.

~henn *f.* hen.

~lēas homeless.

~scīr *f.* ædileship Gl.

~sittende resident, at home.

~sīþ *m.* return home.

---

hām|sōcn *f.* attacking an enemy in his house, house-breaking; fine for the offence.

~steall, ~stede *m.* homestead, residence.

~weard(es) *av.* on the way home, homewards.

~weorþung *f.* ornament of a home.

~werod *n.* household, body of retainers.

~wyrt *f.* house-leek.

gehāmian *rfl. w.* mid make oneself familiar with, master (subject) (?) *LN.*

hama *m.* dress, covering; womb.

hāma *m.* cricket.

hamelian mutilate [hamola].

hāmettan provide with home, house.

hamm *m.* piece of land, dwelling, enclosure.

hamm *f.* inner part of knee, ham.

hamola *m.* one whose head has been mutilated *or* shaved (?): hine on bismer tō ~an bescire LL. [hamelian].

hamol|e *f.* oar-thong, rowlock — æt ǣlcre ~an per man.

hamor *m.* hammer — †hamera lāf sword.

~secg *m.* hammer-sedge.

~wyrt *f.* black hellebore.

hān *f.* stone, rock.

hana *m.* cock *not W.*

han-crēd *m.* cock-crow, part of the night [crāwan].

~tīd *f.* time of cock-crow.

hand *f., d.* ~a hand: brād ~ palm; his sulh on ~a hæfde; hine lædde be þǣre ~a; hēold hine ~ on ~a | side: sette hīe on his swiþran ~: on gehwæþere ~ on both sides (in battle) | person *as agent, receiver, &c.*: tō sēo nīehste ~ tō þǣm lande the nearest heir; gif sēo ~ oþcwolen sīe if the seller is dead | *in phrases expressing agency, control, possession. &c.*: wearþ ācweald æt hira ~um; hine onfēng (*or* nam) æt (*or* tō) biscopes ~a acted as sponsor to him; unnendre ~a ungrudgingly; gemǣnum ~um jointly; him on ~gān surrender; under his ~a authority; on his ~um under his

management; hēoldon þæt land tō his ~a as his vassals; him tō ~a lǣtan deliver up, abandon; þæt feoh becōm him tō ~a; hit hire on ~ āgeaf; sealde him on ~ þæt hē wolde . . promised, engaged; hire on ~ becōm came under her notice; him wel on ~ ēode he prospered; sēo nīed þe ūs nū on ~a stent our urgent need.

hand|æx f. axe.

~**bæft(i)an**, ea lN. lament.

~**bana**† m. slayer.

~**bell** f. hand-bell.

~**bōc** f. hand-book.

~**bred** n. palm of hand, hand.

~**clāþ** n. towel, napkin.

~**cops** m. handcuff, manacle.

~**cræft** m. use of the hands, manual skill, handicraft.

~**cweorn** f. hand-mill.

~**dǣda** m. perpetrator (of homicide).

ge~**fǣstan** betroth.

~**fǣst(n)ung** f. ratification.

~**full** see full.

~**gang** m. laying on of hands; surrender.

~**gift**† f. wedding gift.

~**gripe**† m. grasp.

~**grip** n. peace, protection, security.

~**hamor** m. hammer.

~**hrægl** n. towel, napkin.

~**hrine**† m. touch of hand.

~**hwīl** f. moment.

~**lēan**† n. recompence, requital.

~**līn** n. napkin.

~**locen**† linked or woven by hand.

~**gemaca** m. companion.

~**mægen**† n. strength, might.

~**mitta** = an-mitta.

~**gemōt**† n. battle.

~**nægl** m. finger-nail.

~**plega**† m. fighting, battle.

~**prēost** m. chaplain.

~**rǣs**† m. onslaught, attack.

~**rōf**† strong, renowned for strength.

~**gesceaft**† f. creature.

~**scēo**† m. a proper name.

~**scolu**†, -a- f. retinue.

~**scyldig** liable to losing the hand (as punishment).

~**seax** n. dagger.

~**gesella**† m. comrade.

~**seten** f. signature, signatures coll.

~**slieht**† = and-.

~**smiell***, -æ m. slap lN.

hand|spitel m. spade.

~**sporu** f. talon, claw.

~**gestealla**† m. comrade.

~**stoc** handcuff Gl.

~**swile***, y m. swelling in the hand (?) Gl.

~**geswing**† n. stroke, blow.

~**tam** so tame as to be handled.

~**þegen** m. attendant, manservant.

~**þwēal** n. washing of the hands.

~**geweald**† n. power, possession.

~**weorc** n. manual labour; result of work, work (of a smith).

~**geweorc** n. result of work, work.

~**gewinn** n. manual labour, toil, struggle; warfare.

~**worht** made with hands.

~**wrist***, ~**wyrst** f. wrist.

~**gewrit** n. deed, contract.

~**gewriþen**† twisted or woven by hand.

~**wundor**† n. wonderful piece of work.

~**wyrm** m. hand-worm (supposed to cause disease of the hand).

hand-swā-gelīce av. in the same way.

handl|ian handle, feel; carry on (negotiation); treat of, discuss.

~**ung** f. handling, touching.

handle (?) f. handle [**hand**].

handlinga av. with one's own hands.

hangian intr. hang; depend on, be subordinate to w. on.

gehange† R.

hangelle† once f. hanging thing.

hangen ptc. of **hōn**.

hangra m. hanger, wood on a declivity [**hangian**].

hār grey, hoary; old.

~**(e)hūne** f. horehound.

~**ian** become grey.

~**nes** f. greyness.

~**ung** f. becoming grey.

~**wenge**, ~**wielle** grey-haired.

~**wengnes** f. hoariness.

hara m. hare. **haran hige** hare's-foot (a plant). **haran sp(r)ecel** viper's bugloss (a plant). **haran wyrt, harew-** [a = ā?] a plant.

hare-wyrt, see **hara**.

hās hoarse.

~**ian** become hoarse.

~**nes** f. hoarseness.

~**swēge** sounding hoarsely.

haso, ea pl. **haswe** grey.

haso|fāg grey.

~**pāda**† m. grey-coated one, eagle.

hassoc m. coarse grass.

haswig- grey.

~**feþera**† grey-winged.

hāt I. hot; fervent (love), severe (hunger, disease); inspiring. II. (n.) heat.

~**e** av. hotly, fervidly.

hāt-heort I. angry, fierce, vindictive. II. n. anger.

~**e** f. anger.

ge~**ian** become angry.

~**līce** av. ardently (love); furiously, savagely.

~**nes** f. fervour; anger.

hāt|hiertan rfl. become angry.

~**hyge**† m. anger.

~**wende**† hot.

hāt n. promise lN.

gehāt n. promise; vow.

~**land** n. promised land.

hāt|an 1 b prt. hēt, hēht, pass. prs. and prt. ~**te** | command, bid : **hit dōn hēt**; . . þū dō þæt ic þē (d.) ~e; hēt hine gesund faran; hēton hine þæt hē gewite | name, call, w. a. and nom. or æt d. ; be named, called.

gehātan 1 b command; invite, summon : hīe tō gereordum ~; tō him gehēt; promise : him gehēton; gehēt þæt hē feoh wolde . . | name, call.

hatian hate.

hatigend m. hater.

~**lic** hateful.

hatung f. hating; being hated.

hāt|ian become hot; be eager (of desire).

~**ung** f. becoming hot; inflammation (of wounds).

hatol = hetol.

hātte pass. of **hātan**.

haþo-liþa once m. elbow.

hāw|ian gaze on, survey.

~**ere** m. spectator.

~**ung** f. inspection, observation.

hē he.

hēn vb. = *hīen.

hēa, pl. of **hēah**.

hēa- in comp. = hēah-.

hēaf m. lamentation [hēofan].

~**lic** lamentable, mournful.

sang m. dirge.

hēafian = hēofian.

hēafdeht having a head (of plants).

hēafdian behead.
gehēafdod headed (*of* ring) Gl.
heafela = hafola.
heafo *pl. of* hæf.
heafoc = hafoc.
hēafod *n.* head : æt his hēafdum
at his head. ofer ~ singly, specially. be his hēafde on pain of
death. ~ wiþ hēafde head for
head (of murderer) | top, head (of
plant) ; high ground, upper part
of field ; source (of stream) |
leader, chief ; capital (city) ; originator : ~ tō þām unrǣde, *also
wg.*
~æcer*, hafud- *m.* chief field (?)
Gl.
~ǣdre *f.* cephalic vein.
~bān *n.* skull.
~bēag *m.* crown.
~bend *m.* fetter round head.
~beorg† *f.* helmet.
~beorht† having a bright head.
~biscop *m.* high priest (of the
Jews).
~bolla *m.* skull.
~bolster *n.* pillow.
~botl *n.* chief dwelling, manor.
~burg *f.* chief town, capital.
~cirice *f.* cathedral.
~clāþ *n.* head-dress.
~cwide *m.* important saying ; chapter *lN.*
~ece *m.* headache.
~frætennes *f.* head-ornament.
~gimm† *m.* eye.
~gold *n.* crown.
~gylt *m.* capital crime, deadly sin.
~hǣr *n.* a hair of the head.
~hebba *m.* prime mover, promoter ;
beginning.
~hrægl *n.* head-dress.
~hriefþo *f.* scurf.
~land*, hafud- *n.* top of field,
boundary.
~leahtor *m.* capital crime, deadly
sin.
~lēas headless.
~lic capital *or* deadly (crime).
~ling *m.* equal, companion.
~gemaca, ~gemæcca *m.* equal,
companion.
~mǣg† *m.* near relation.
~māga† *m.* near relation.
~mann *m.* chief, leader.
~mynster *n.* church.
~panne *f.* skull.

hēafod|port *m.* chief town.
~rīce *n.* empire.
~gerīm† *n.* majority.
~sār *n.* pain in the head.
~segn† *n.* helmet.
~sīen† *f.* eye.
~slege *m.* head of pillar (?) Gl.
~smæl (?) Gl.
~stede *m.* chief place.
~stōl *m.* chief place, capital.
~stōw *f.* place for the head.
~swīma *m.* dizziness.
~synn *f.* deadly sin.
~getel *n.* cardinal number.
~þwēal *n.* washing the head.
~gewǣde *n.* veil.
~wærc *m.* pain in the head.
~weard *m.* chief officer.
~weard *f.* guarding the king · chapter *lN.*
~wielm *m.* heat in the head ;
†tears.
~wind *m.* — þā fēower ~as the four
chief winds.
~wīsa† *m.* ruler.
~wōþ† *f.* voice.
~wund *f.* wound in the head.
~wyrhta *m.* chief workman.
hēafre = hēahfore.
hēag-, *see* hēah.
heago- = hago-.
heago-rūn, heahrūn *f.* necromancy, mystery. *Cp.* hægtesse.
heago-spind, *L.* hecga-, -spinn,
vE. -spen, *L.* -swind [*a miswriting through the word having
become obsolete*] *n.* cheek.
hēah I. *a. m.* hēanne, *pl.* hēa(ge),
cpv. hīer(r)a, ~ra, hēar(r)a, *spl.*
hīehst, ēa, *A.* hēst high, deep
(water) ; right (hand) ; sublime,
high (rank), important ; haughty.
II. *av.* high, *cpv.* hēaor.
hēah- *occ. under* hēa-.
hēah- = hīeh-.
~altare *m.* high altar.
~beorg *m.* mountain.
~biscop *m.* archbishop ; high
priest.
~bliss† *f.* exultation.
~boda† *m.* archangel.
~burg *f.* chief town ; †town high
up.
~cāsere† *m.* supreme king.
~cleofa *n.* principal chamber.
~clif *n.* high cliff *or* rock.
~cræft† *m.* high skill.

hēah|cræftiga *m.* architect (!).
~cyning† *m.* great king ; God.
hēa(h)-dēor, -dor *n.* stag, deer.
~hund *m.* stag-hound.
~hunta *m.* stag-hunter.
hēah|diacon *m.* archdeacon.
~ealdor *m.* chief ruler.
~ealdormann *m.* chief patri-
cian (!).
~engel *m.* archangel.
~fæder *m.* patriarch ; God.
~fæst† firm, stable.
~fæsten(n) *n.* chief fortress, city.
~flōd *m.* high tide ; †deep water.
~frēa† *m.* supreme lord.
hēah-frēols *m.* high festival.
~dæg *m.* day of high festival.
~tīd *f.* time of high festival.
hēah|fȳr† *n.* high flame.
~gāst† *m.* lofty spirit.
~gnornung† *f.* lamentation.
~god† *m.* the Highest, God.
~græft *m.* object carved in relief (?)
Gl.
~hād *m.* holy order.
~heort† proud.
~hierde *m.* archimandrite Gl.
~hliþ† *n.* high hill.
~hwēolod having high wheels.
~hylte (*n.*) high wood (?) Ct.
~hyrne = ēag-.
~ieldest (!) most illustrious Gl.
~lǣce, hēal- *m.* physician.
~land† *n.* mountains.
~lāreow *m.* chief teacher.
~leornere *m.* chief learner Gl.
~lufe† *f.* great love.
~mægen† *n.* might ; mighty
troops *coll.*
~mæsse *f.* high mass.
~miht† *f.* might.
hēah-mōd† proud, noble.
~nes *f.* pride.
hēah|munt *m.* mountain.
~nama *m.* illustrious name.
~nes = hēanes.
~reced† *n.* high building.
~gerēfa *m.* high reeve, chief officer.
~rodor† *m.* sky.
~rūn = heago-.
~sācerd *m.* chief priest.
~sǣ† *f.* deep sea.
~sǣl† *f.* great happiness.
~sǣ-þēof *m.* chief pirate (!).
~(ge)samnung *f.* chief synagogue.
~sangere *m.* chief singer.
~gesceaft *f.* exalted creature.

hēah|gesceap† *n.* fate.
~scēawere *m.* pontiff Gl.
~scīremann *m.* procurator Gl.
~seld† *n.* throne.
~sele† *m.* lofty hall.
~setl *n.* seat of honour, dais, throne, tribunal.
~stēap† lofty.
~stede† *m.* high *or* distinguished place.
~stefn† high-prowed.
~strǣt *f.* high-road.
~strengþo†*f.* strength.
~gestrēon† *n.* treasure.
~synn *f.* deadly sin.
~tīd *f.* festival.
~timber† *n.* lofty building.
~getimbrod† high-built.
~getimbru† *npl.* lofty buildings.
~torras *mpl.* the Alps Gl.
~trēow†*f.* solemn compact.
~þearf†*f.* great need.
~þegen *m.* chief officer; apostle; noble.
~þegnung†*f.* high service *or* function.
~þēod *f.* nation.
~þrēa† *m.* panic.
~geþring† *n.* high waves.
~þrymm *m.* ; ~þrymnes† *f.* great glory.
~(ge)þungen of high rank, distinguished, exalted.
~weofod *n.* high altar.
~(ge)weorc *n.* excellent work.
hēahfore, hēafre, hēahfru *f.* heifer.
hēal- *see* healh.
hēal|a *m.* rupture, hydrocele.
~ede ruptured, hydrocelous.
heald (*n.*) protection *L.*
heald, *vE.* halþ bent down; inclined (to evil).
geheald *n.* keeping, custody; protection; guardian; observing (festival) [*cp.* gehield].
~dagas *mpl.* calends Gl.
~sum frugal; chaste.
~sumnes *f.* keeping, observance, keeping (commands); abstinence, continence.
healdan I hold : ~ hine be þǣre handa | possess, keep : rīce ~ reign ; hine gebundenne ~ ; withhold ; lock up (*of* keys), contain ; inhabit | govern ; restrain, *rfl.* restrain oneself — *ptc.*

gehealden frugal, continent | guard, preserve, save : ~ līchaman wiþ leahtras ; support (one's king) | observe, keep (command, promise, festival) ; practise, carry on, do (virtue, war) | behave to, treat ; *rfl.* behave | regard : unweorþlīce ~ despise | ge- satisfy claims of, pay || *intr.* hold out, not surrender ; force one's way ; proceed, go.
heald|end *m.* guardian, ruler.
~nes *f.* observance.
healf *f.* half; side; quarter, part ; party, side (in battle, lawsuit).
healf half — þridde ~ gēar two and a half ; ōþrum ~um lǣs þe þritig wintra 28½.
~clǣmed half-finished (*of* mud-hut).
~clipigende semi-vowel.
~clungen half-withered.
~cwic, -cucu half-dead.
~dēad paralyzed on one side.
~eald half-grown (pig).
~fēþe lame.
~frēo half-free.
~hār half-grey.
~hēafod *n.* (front) part of head Gl.
~hrūh half-shaggy.
~hunding *m.* cynocephalus.
~hwīt whitish.
~mann *m.* half man (!).
~penig-weorþ *n.* halfpennyworth.
~rēad reddish.
~scyldig half-guilty Gl.
~sinewealt semicircular.
~slǣpende half-asleep.
~soden half-cooked.
~tryndel *m.* hemisphere.
~wudu *m.* field-balm.
healfter = hælfter.
healfunga *av.* partially, to some extent, imperfectly.
healh, *L.* hēal ; *pl.* hēalas, halas *m.* corner, hiding-place ; bay, gulf.
~iht*, æ full of corners.
healic (*m.*) a fish Ct.
hēalic high, from a height (*of* fall) ; distinguished, illustrious, pre-eminent ; proud ; excellent ; excessive, great (crime).
~hād *m.*, ~nes *f.* sublimity, excellence.
hēalīce *av.* on high ; in a high

degree, supremely, extremely, greatly.
heall *f.* hall.
~ærn† *n.* hall, palace.
~gamen† *n.* mirth in hall.
~ic palatial.
~rēaf *n.* piece of tapestry.
~reced† *n.* palace.
~sittend† *m.* one who sits in a hall, guest.
~þegen† *m.* hall-officer.
~wāgrift† *n.* piece of tapestry.
~wudu† *m.* woodwork of hall, floor.
healm *n.* haulm, straw, stem (of grass).
~strēaw *n.* stubble.
heals *m.* neck ; prow of ship.
~bēag† *m.* necklace ; torque.
~gebędda† *f.* bedfellow, consort.
~beorg *f.* gorget, hauberk.
~bōc *f.* phylactery.
~fæst stubborn, stiff-necked.
~fang *n.* halsfang, a legal penalty of uncertain nature.
~gund (*m.*) swelling in the neck.
~leþer *f.* reins.
~mǣgeþ†*f.* beloved virgin.
~mene, -myne *m.* necklace.
~ōme *f.* tumour on the neck.
~wriþa *m.* necklace.
~wyrt*, a *f.* daffodil (?).
heals|ian, *lW. and A.* a (= ā !) implore, entreat. *Cp.* hālsian, hǣlsian.
~igendlic deprecable Gl.
~igendlīce *av.* imploringly, with importunity.
healsung, a *f.* entreaty ; augury ; divination.
~gebed*, a *n.* litany.
healsed, halsod (*n.*) head-cloth, napkin.
heals(e)re- pillow.
~feþer† *f.* pillow-feather, down.
healt lame, limping.
~ian limp.
hēamol miserly, frugal Gl.
hēan *vb.* = *hīen exalt.
hēan humiliated, abject ; of low rank, mean ; poor.
~e *av.* ignominiously.
~lic ignominious, disgraceful ; poor ; paltry.
~līce *av.* ignominiously, miserably.
~mōd† dejected, humiliated.

[84]

hēan-spēdig† poor.
hēanes, hēahnes, hēannes *f.*
height ; high place : on ~sum in
excelsis ; sublimity, excellence ;
high rank.
hēanne, *see* hēah.
hēap *mf.* troop, band ; multitude ; social gathering, company ;
association, corporation.
~ian heap — him on ge~.
~mǣlum *av.* in troops *or* flocks.
~ung *f.* heap Bd.
heara = heora of them.
hēara, *see* hēah.
heard hard ; strong (chain) ; stern,
hard, severe ; brave ; stubborn,
hard (heart) ; attended with effort,
hard (labour) ; excessive, strong
(stench).
~cwide† *m.* harsh language, contumely.
~e *av.* fiercely ; excessively.
~ecg hard of edge, sharp.
~fierde difficult to carry.
~hara, ~ra *m.* a fish.
~hēaw chisel Gl.
heard-heort unfeeling, hard-
hearted ; obstinate.
~nes *f.* hard-heartedness ; obstinacy.
heard|hycgende† brave.
~lic severe, excessive.
~līce *av.* vigorously, bravely ; excessively ; harshly.
~licnes *f.* austerity (of hermit's
life).
~mōd self-confident, obstinate,
brave.
~mōdnes *f.* obstinacy.
~nebb having a hard beak.
~nes *f.* hardness.
~rǣd† steadfast, firm.
~sǣlig† unfortunate.
~sǣlnes *f.* calamity.
~sǣlþ *f.* misfortune ; wickedness.
~wendlīce *av.* severely.
heardian harden *intr. and tr.*
hearding† *m.* warrior, hero.
heardra = heard-hara.
hearg *m., pl.* ~as, ~a (heathen)
temple ; idol.
~lic idolatrous.
~trǣf† *n.* (heathen) temple.
~weard† *m.* (heathen) priest.
hearm I. *m.* injury, affliction, evil,
loss ; grief ; insult. II. *aj.* grievous,
cruel, wicked.
~cwalu† *f.* destruction.

hearm|cwedelian calumniate.
~cweþan 5 revile, calumniate.
~cweþend *m.* calumniator.
~cwide† *m.* severe sentence ;
calumny ; blasphemy.
~cwid(d)ian revile, calumniate.
~cwidol speaking ill of others,
calumnious.
~edwīt† *n.* contumely.
~fullic hurtful.
~heortnes *f.* murmuring Gl.
~lēoþ† *n.* song of grief.
~lic injurious.
~loca† *m.* prison ; hell.
~plega† *m.* strife, quarrel.
~scaru† *f.* affliction, punishment.
~scaþa† *m.* terrible enemy.
~slege† *m.* grievous blow.
~sprǣc *f.* calumny.
~stafas† *mpl.* trouble, affliction.
~tān† *m.* twig bringing calamity.
hearmian injure *wd.*
hearma *m.* shrew-mouse (?) Gl.
hearma-scinnen made of ermine-
skins *vL.* [*Scand.*].
hearp|ian play on the harp.
~ere *m.* harper.
~estre *f.* female harper.
~ung *f.* playing on the harp.
hearp|e *f.* harp.
~(e)nægel *m.* plectrum.
~sang *m.* song to the harp, psalm.
~slege *m.* playing the harp ; plectrum.
~streng *m.* harp-string.
~swēg *m.* sound of the harp.
hearra† *m.* lord.
hēarra, *see* hēah.
hearste-panne = hierste-.
heaþo-† war.
~byrne *f.* corslet.
~dēor brave.
~fremmende fighting.
~fȳr *n.* destructive fire.
~geong young in war.
~glemm wound got in battle.
~grimm very fierce.
~helm *m.* helmet.
~lāc *n.* battle.
~lind *f.* shield.
~līþende *m.* war-sailor, sea-warrior.
~mǣre illustrious in war.
~rǣs *m.* onslaught.
~rēaf *n.* armour.
~rinc *m.* warrior.
~rōf brave, famous in war.
~sceard notched in battle.

heaþo|sēoc wounded in battle, dis-
abled.
~sigel *m.* sun.
~stēap towering in battle.
~swāt *m.* blood shed in battle.
~sweng *m.* hostile stroke.
~torht defiant (voice).
~wǣd *f.* armour.
~weorc *n.* fight.
~wērig weary from fighting.
~wielm *m.* intense heat.
heaþorian restrain, confine.
gehēaw *n.* gnashing (of teeth).
hēawan 1 hew, cut ; cut down,
kill ; æftan ~ slander.
hebb|an 2 *prt.* hōf, hefde, *ptc.*
hafen, æ raise, lift up ; raise (cry) ;
ūp ~ raise, exalt ‖ *intr.* ūp ~ rise
in the air, fly.
~endlic exalted *IN.*
hecc = hæcc.
hecga-spind = heago-.
hed-.
~clāþ *m.* chasuble.
hēd|an *wg.* heed, attend to, look
out for ; take possession of, take.
~ærn*, hēddern, y *n.* storehouse.
~endlic captious Gl.
~endlīce *av.* captiously Gl.
heden dress Gl.
hef-, *see* hebban.
hefe *m.* weight ; feeling of oppression (in heart) [hebban].
~full severe.
~lic grievous, severe ; tedious. *Cp.*
hefiglic.
~līce *av.* excessively, severely ; with
difficulty (!).
hefe*, æ *m.* leaven.
hefel- = hefeld-.
~gierd *f.* weaver's shuttle.
~þrǣd *m.* thread for weaving.
hefeld thread for weaving.
~ian begin the web.
hefig heavy ; important ; grievous,
injurious, unpleasant, troublesome ;
hostile ; severe (fighting), hard,
difficult ; excessive [hefe].
~e *av.* severely, painfully.
~lic grievous, severe. *Cp.* hefelic.
~līce *av.* severely, seriously ; with
grief *or* anger.
~mōd troublesome, hostile.
~nes *f.* heaviness, weight ; affliction.
~tīeme, hefet- troublesome, grievous, tedious.
~tīemnes *f.* trouble.

hefigian lie heavy on, burden; oppress, afflict ‖ *intr.* become heavy; become oppressive, troublesome, painful; be aggravated.

heg-, *see* **hege.**

~**stæf** *m.* enclosure Gl.

hēgan† perform, achieve, hold (meeting).

hegian make hedge, fence in; ge~ hedge in, enclose.

hege [**hagu**]. *See* **heg-.**

~**clife** *f.* hedge clivers (a plant).

~**hymele** *f.* hop-plant.

~**rǣw, hægrǣw** *f.* hedgerow.

~**rife** *f.* heyriffe (a plant).

~**sugge** *f.* hedge-sparrow.

hēht *prt. of* **hātan.**

hei-weg *m.* = **hīeg**-hay-road (?) Ct.

geheig- = *****gehīege.

helan 4 cover; hide *w. a. and d. of person or* wiþ *a.*

helian cover; conceal [**helan**].

hēlan*, œ calumniate *IM.* [**hōl**].

hēl|a, oe, ǣ *m.* heel.

~**spure** *f.* heel.

helde *f.* tansy (a plant).

hell *f.* Hades; hell [**helan**].

~**bend†** *mf.* bond of hell.

~**cniht** *m.* demon.

~**cræft†** *m.* hellish art.

~**cund** of hell.

~**cwalu†** *f.* hell-torment.

~**dēofol** *m.* demon Gl.

~**dor†** *n.* gate of hell.

~**firen†** *f.* hellish crime.

~**fūs†** bound for hell.

~**god, helle-** *n.* god of Hades.

~**hēoþo†** hell.

~**ic, hellelic** of hell.

~**rūn** *f.* sorceress.

~**rūna†** *m.* demon.

~**rӯnegu** *f.* sorceress.

~**scaþa†** *m.* fiend.

~**træf†** *n.* heathen temple.

~**trega†** *m.* hell-torment.

~**geþwing†** *n.* restraint of hell, hell-durance.

~**ware, -waran, -wara** *pl.*, -**waru** *f. coll.* inhabitants of hell.

~**werod** *n.* host of hell.

~**wiht** *fn.* devil.

helle|bealo† *n.* woe of hell.

~**brōga** *m.* terror of hell.

~**bryne†** *m.* hell-fire.

~**ceafl†** *m.* jaw of hell.

~**clamm†** *m.* bond of hell.

~**cynn†** *n.* race of hell.

helle|dēofol† *nm.* devil.

~**dor†** *n.* door of hell.

~**duru†** *f.* door of hell.

~**flōr†** *f.* floor of hell.

~**fӯr** *n.* fire of hell.

~**gāst†, ǣ** *m.* demon.

~**geat** *n.* gate of hell.

~**grund†** *m.* abyss of hell.

~**gryre†** *m.* terror of hell.

~**hæft(a)†, -hæftling†** *m.* captive of hell.

~**hinca†** *m.* hell-limper, devil.

~**hund** *m.* dog of hell.

~**hūs†** *n.* hell.

~**mere** *m.* lake of hell, Styx.

~**nīþ†** *m.* hell-torment.

~**rūne** *f.* sorceress.

~**scaþa†** *m.* devil.

~**scealc†** *m.* devil.

~**sēaþ** *m.* hell.

~**þegn†** *m.* devil.

~**wīte** *n.* hell-torment, hell.

~**wīte-brōga** *m.* hell-terror.

helm *m.* helmet; covering; top *or* foliage (of trees); †protector, lord.

~**bære, -berende** leafy Gl.

~**berend†** *m.* warrior.

~**ian** cover.

~**iht** leafy Gl.

helma *m.* rudder.

helor = **heolor.**

help *fm.*, ~**e** *f.* help.

helpan 3 help *w. d. or g.*

helpend *m.* helper.

~**bære, -lic** helpful.

helt = **hilt.**

hemeþ shirt [**ham**].

hemlic = **hymlic.**

hemm *m.* hem, border.

hemming, i (*m.*) shoe of hide.

gehendan† *once* hold [**hand**].

gehend|e I. near; handy, convenient. II. *av.* near; **wel**~ nearly. III. *prp. wd.* near.

~**nes** *f.* nearness, neighbourhood.

henep, œ (*m.*) hemp.

heng-wīte *n.* fine for letting criminal escape.

hēng *prt. of* **hōn.**

henge-clif *n.* steep cliff [**hangian**].

hengen(n) *f.* death *or* punishment by hanging, hanging, torture; gallows; cross; rack; prison, confinement.

~**wītnung** *f.* imprisonment.

hengest, hengst *m.* horse, gelding.

henn *f.* hen. ~**e-belle** *f.*, ~**e-wōl** *m.* henbane.

~**fugol** *m.* hen.

henna *m.* fowl.

hentan pursue *w. g. or* æfter — ~ **his mid flānum** shoot at; seize.

hēo I. she. II. = **hīe** they.

hēo = **hīw** colour.

hēo-dæg *av.* to-day.

hēof (*m.*) lamentation, mourning, grief. *Cp.* **hēaf.**

~**lic** lamentable.

hēof|an 7 (?) *prt.* heōf [*for* heāf?], ~**de** *intr.* lament.

~**endlic** mournful, dismal.

~**endlīce** *av.* dismally.

~**ian, ēa** *intr.* lament, weep; *tr.* bewail.

~**igendlic** mourning.

heofol*, hioful face *IN.*

hēofung *f.* lamentation, mourning, grieving.

~**dæg** *m.* day of mourning.

~**tīd** *f.* time of mourning.

heofon, hef- *m.*, *L.* ~**e** *f.* sky; heaven *often pl. in both meanings.*

~**bēacen†** *n.* sign in the sky.

~**beorht†** heavenly bright.

~**bīeme†** *f.* heavenly trumpet.

~**candel(l)†** *f.* heavenly candle (sun, the fiery pillar).

~**colu†** *npl.* heat of the sun.

~**cund** heavenly.

~**cyning** *m.* king of heaven.

~**dēma†** *m.* celestial judge.

~**drēam†** *m.* joy of heaven.

~**duguþ†** *f.* heavenly host.

~**engel†** *m.* angel.

~**fugol†** *m.* bird.

~**hālig†** of celestial holiness.

~**hām†** *m.* heaven.

~**hēah†** reaching to heaven.

~**heall** *f.* hall of heaven.

~**hlāf†** *m.* bread from heaven, manna.

~**hrōf** *m.* †heaven; ceiling.

~**hūs** *n.* ceiling.

~**hwealf†** *f.* heavenly vault.

~**isc** of *or* from heaven.

~**lēoht†** *n.* light of heaven.

~**lēoma†** *m.* heavenly radiance.

~**lic** of heaven, celestial.

~**līce** *av.* from heaven.

~**mægen†** *n.* heavenly might.

~**rīce** *n.* kingdom of heaven.

~**steorra†** *m.* star.

~**stōl†** *m.* throne in heaven.

heofon|timber† *n.* heavenly structure.
~torht† heavenly bright.
~tungol† *n.* luminary.
~þreat† *m.* heavenly troop.
~þrymm *m.* heavenly glory.
~ware, ~waran *pl.*, **~waru** *f. coll.* dwellers of heaven.
~weard† *m.* guardian of heaven.
~werod *n.* heavenly host.
~wolcen† *n.* cloud.
~wōma† *m.* sound in heaven.
~wuldor† *n.* heavenly glory.
heolfor† (*n.*) blood, gore.
heolfrig† blood-stained.
heolor, helor *f.* scales, balance.
~bledu *f.* scale of balance.
~ian, holrian weigh.
~ung *f.* turning of a scale, momentum Gl.
heoloþ-† covering [helan].
~cynn *n.* inhabitants of hell.
~helm, hæ- *m.* helmet which makes the wearer invisible.
heolstor, *vE.* **helustr** I. (†) *m.* what veils *or* covers ; hiding-place, concealment ; darkness. II.† *aj.* dark [helan].
~cofa† *m.* grave.
~hof† *n.* hell.
~loca† *m.* prison.
~sceado† *f.*, **~scuwa**† *m.* darkness.
heolstrig*, **-icc** dark Gl.
heom *L.* = **him** *pl.*
heonon, i, heonane *av.* hence, away ; (see) from here | from this time. **forþ ~** henceforth.
~forþ *av.* henceforth (time).
~sīþ† *m.* death.
~weard transitory.
heonu, henu, hona *interj.* not W lo ! behold !
hēop|e *f.* hip (berry of dog-rose).
~brēmel *m.* dog-rose ; bramble (?).
heora = **hira** of them.
heorcn|ian, e, (ē ?) listen.
~ung *f.* listening ; power of hearing.
heord *f.* herd, flock | care, custody.
(ge)**~nes, ~rǣden(n), hy-** *f.* custody.
heord = **hīred.**
heordan *pl.* hards of flax.
heorde = **hierde.**
geheordung *f.* guard, watch Gl.
hēore = **hīere.**
heor(o)t *m.* stag.

heorot|ber(i)ge *f.* buckthorn berry.
~brēmbel *m.*, **~brēr** *f.* buckthorn.
~bucc *m.* roebuck.
~clǣfre *f.* hemp agrimony.
~cropp *m.* cluster of hemp agrimony flowers (?).
~sol *n.* stag's wallowing-place Ct.
heorra = **hearra.**
heorr *m.* hinge ; cardinal point.
geheort of good cheer, courageous.
~līce *av.* cheeringly.
heort|e *f.* heart.
~angnes*, **-anc-** *f.* heart-distress Gl.
~coþu *f.* heart-disease.
~ece *m.* pain in the heart.
~gryre *m.* terror of heart.
~hama *m.* pericardium.
~hogu *f.* anxious care.
~lēas dispirited.
~lufe† *f.* heartfelt love.
~sēoc suffering from disease of the heart.
~gesida *pl.* entrails.
~wærc *m.* pain in the heart.
heorten = **hierten.**
heorþ *m.* hearth, fire, furnace ; house, home.
~bacen baked on the hearth.
~cniht *m.* attendant.
~fæst having a house of one's own.
~genēat *m.* retainer.
~pening *m.* house-tax.
~swǣpe *f.* bridesmaid Gl.
~werod† *n.* band of retainers.
heoru† *m.* sword.
~blāc* mortally wounded.
~cumbol *n.* banner.
~dolg *n.* wound.
~drēor *m.* blood.
~drēorig blood-stained ; very sad.
~drync *m.* blood.
~fæþm *m.* deadly gripe.
~gīfre very fierce.
~grǣdig very fierce.
~grimm very fierce.
~hōciht with formidable hooks *or* barbs.
~scearp very sharp.
~sceorp *n.* armour.
~sierce *f.* coat of mail.
~swealwe *f.* hawk.
~sweng *m.* sword-stroke.
~wǣpen *n.* weapon, sword.
~weallende boiling fiercely.
~wearg *m.* bloodthirsty wolf (?).

heoru|word *n.* fierce word.
~wulf *m.* warrior.
hēow = **hīw.**
hēr *av.* here : **~ on lande** in this country — **~ geond** in this neighbourhood | *time* at this date || **~æfter** hereafter. **~ b(e)ufan** before this, (mentioned) above, &c.
~būende† dweller on earth.
~cyme† *m.* advent (of Christ).
her|ian, A. hergan praise.
~enes *f.* praise.
~gere *m.* praiser *lN.*
~igendlic praiseworthy.
~igendlīce *av.* praiseworthily.
~(i)ung, ~ing *f.* praise.
herian = **hergian.**
hercnian = **heorcnian.**
here *m.*, *pl.* **her(g)as** army, predatory troop, band of thieves — **se ~** the Danish army ; devastation ; battle ; multitude, body of people.
~bēacen *n.* banner ; lighthouse.
~bieme† *f.* trumpet.
~blēaþ† cowardly.
~brōga† *m.* terror of war.
~byrne† *f.* corslet.
~cierm† *m.* war-cry.
~cumbol† *n.* military signal.
~cyst† *f.* warlike troop.
~feld† *m.* battlefield.
~feoh *n.* booty.
~fēpa† *m.* martial band.
~flīema† *m.* deserter, fugitive from battle.
~folc† *n.* army.
~fugol† *m.* eagle, bird of prey.
~gang *m.* invasion.
here-geat, hergeat *n.*, *gen. pl. fn.* **~geat(w)a, ~geat(w)e, ~geatu** military equipment ; heriot.
~land *n.* heriot-land.
here|gield *n.* war-tax, Danegeld.
~grīma† *m.* helmet.
~hand *f.* hostile hand *or* power (!).
~hlōþ† *f.* hostile troop.
~hȳþ, -hūþ *f.* plunder, booty.
~lāf *f.* remnant of an army ; spoil, plunder.
~lic martial.
~mæcg† *m.* warrior, man.
~mægen† *n.* army ; multitude.
~mæþel† *n.* national assembly.
~mann *m.* soldier.
~nett† *n.* corslet.
~nīþ† *m.* hostility.

hęre|pād† *f.* coat of mail.
~pæþ, hęrpoþ, -aþ *m.* (main) road.
~rǣs *m.* predatory attack.
~rǣswa† *m.* general, chief.
~rēaf *n.* plunder, booty *coll. and in pl.*
~rinc† *m.* warrior.
~sceaft† *m.* spear.
~sceorp† *n.* armour.
~searo *n.* stratagem.
~sierce† *f.* corslet.
~sīþ† *m.* military expedition.
~spēd† *f.* success in war.
~strǣl† *m.* arrow.
~strǣt *f.* main road, highway.
~swēg† *m.* martial sound.
~tēam *m.* joining a predatory band; devastation, plunder, spoil.
~tiema *m.* general, prince; superior, ruler.
~toga *m.* general; leader of a people, duke.
~þrēat *m.* warlike troop.
~þrymm *m.* phalanx (!).
~wǣd† *f.* armour.
~wǣpen† *n.* weapon.
~wǣsm† (?).
~wǣþa† *m.* warrior.
~weg *m.* main road.
~weorc† *n.* warlike deed.
~wīc *npl.* camp.
~wīsa† *m.* general.
~wōp† *m.* cry of an army.
~wōsa† *m.* warrior.
~wulf† *m.* warrior.
hęre-beorgian take up one's quarters *L.*
hęre-fang*, -fong (*m.*) osprey.
hęre-, *see* hęrian praise.
~lof *n.* fame.
~word *n.* fame, reputation.
hęrg|ian make war, make raid; ravage; carry off captive [hęre].
~oþ *m.* plundering, making war.
~ung *f.* making war, invasion; devastation; plunder; booty; harrowing (of hell).
herþ|an *pl.* testicles.
~belig *m.* scrotum.
hęte *m.* hate, malice, persecution, punishment [hatian].
~grimm† fierce, cruel.
~lic hostile, malignant; violent, excessive.
~līce *av.* fiercely; violently, excessively.

hęte|nīþ† *m.* enmity, malice; wickedness.
~rōf† hostile.
~rūn† *f.* charm causing mischief.
~spræc† *f.* hostile speech.
~swęng† *m.* hostile blow.
~þanc† *m.* hostility.
~þancol† hostile.
hętlen† hostile.
hętol, ha- hostile, fierce.
hęt(t)end† *m.* enemy.
hī = hīe they.
hīce-māse *f.* blue titmouse.
hīd, hīgid *f.* a measure of land, hide [hīwa].
~gięld *n.* hide-tax.
~mǣlum *av.* by hides.
hider *av.* hither: wīsdōm ~ on land sohte in this country — ~ and þider in different directions. *cpv.* ~or nearer.
~cyme *m.* arrival, advent (of Christ).
~geond *av.* thither.
~ryne directed hither Gl.
~weard I. coming here. II. *av.* hither.
hidres *av.* — ~ þidres in different directions.
hīe I. they. II. her *a.*
hīen*, *A.* hēan *vb.*, *ptc.* gehēd, ȳ exalt [hēan].
hīeg *n.* hay; fresh-cut grass; grass [hēawan]. *See* hei-.
~hūs *n.* hay-house.
gehīege*, *lKt.* ei *once* (*n.*) meadow. *Cp.* gehǣg.
hīehþo, hēah- height, above; glory [hēah].
gehīeld *nf.*, *A.* ǣ watching; observance (of festival); protection; guardian; secret place. *Cp.* geheald.
~nes *f.* guarding, observance.
hīeld|an bend, incline, bend down, bow *intr.*, *tr.*, *and rfl.* [heald].
~ing *f.* bending, curvature.
hīelf *m.* handle.
hīelfling*, ę *m.* farthing *lN.* [healf].
hīelto *f.* lameness [healt].
hīen|an fell, strike down; bring to subjection, domineer over; humble, humiliate; treat with contempt, insult; condemn; ill-treat, afflict, injure, destroy [hēan].
~nes *f.* ill-treating, proscription.

hiene = hine.
hīenþ(o) *f.* ignominy, humiliation; harm, injury, mischief; loss [hēan].
hīepe *f.* heap [hēap].
hiepel *m.* heap.
hiera of them.
hiera = hīerra higher.
hīer|an *wa.* hear; hear mentioned, hear of | *wd.* listen to, pay attention to; obey, follow; minister. *Always* ge- *in W. in the above meanings* ‖ *w.* tō, intō, inn on belong, appertain. *Never* ge- *in this meaning.*
~a *m.* subject.
~(e)mann, hȳrig- *m.* subject, subordinate, parishioner.
~ing *f.* hearing.
hīere-borg = hȳre-.
hīernes *f.* obedience, allegiance, subjection; parish.
gehīernes *f.* hearing; obedience.
(ge)hīersum obedient *wd.*
~ian *wd.* obey; *tr.* reduce to subjection.
~nes *f.* obedience; subjection.
hierd|an *tr.* harden; make firm, brace up; *also fig.* [heard].
~ung *f.* strengthening.
hierde, *A.* eo *m.* shepherd; guardian, keeper; pastor [heord].
~belig *m.* shepherd's pouch.
~bōc *f.* pastoral book.
~cnapa *m.* shepherd-boy.
~lēas without a shepherd.
~lic pastoral.
~mann *m.* shepherd.
~wyrt *f.* a plant.
(ge)hierdnes *f.* guard, watch.
hierdrǣden = heord-.
hiere = hire.
hīere†, ēo safe, pleasant, good.
hīer(r)a *cpv. of* hēah.
hierst|an fry.
~e *f.* frying-pan.
~epanne, hearste- *f.* frying-pan.
hiersting *f.* frying.
~hlāf *m.* crust.
~panne *f.* frying-pan.
hiertan cherish; encourage; *rfl.* take heart [heorte].
hierten*, y, eo of a stag [heorot].
hierw|an, -ian despise; deride; blaspheme; condemn; injure.
~end *m.* blasphemer.
~endlic contemptible.

hierw|endlīce *av.* with contempt.

~ing *f.* blasphemy.

~nes *f.* contempt, reproach.

hīewe-stān *m.* hewn stone [hēa-wan].

hīewet(t) *n.* cutting.

hīg = hīe.

hīgian strive for, be intent on.

hīgid = hīd.

hīgna *gpl. of* hīwa.

higora *m.*, higere *f.* magpie *or* woodpecker.

hīgþ *f.* effort Gl. [hīgian].

hil-hāma = hylle- grasshopper.

hild† *f.* war, battle.

~bedd *n.* death-bed.

~egesa *m.* terror of war.

~fram brave.

~(e)freca *m.* warrior.

~fruma *m.* war-chief, general.

~lata *m.* coward.

~stapa *m.* warrior.

~þracu *f.* battle.

hilde|bill *n.* sword.

~bord *n.* shield.

~calla *m.* war-herald (?).

~corpor *n.* warlike troop.

~cyst *f.* valour.

~dēofol *n.* devil, demon.

~dēor brave.

~freca *m.* warrior.

~frōfor *f.* sword.

~geatwe *fpl.* armour.

~giécel *m.* drop of blood.

~giest *m.* enemy.

~grædig eager for battle.

~grāp *f.* hostile grasp.

~hlemm *m.* crash of battle *or* ~hlemma *m.* warrior.

~lēoma *m.* sword.

~lēoþ *n.* war-song.

~mæcg *m.* warrior.

~mēce *m.* sword.

~nædre *f.* arrow.

~pīl *m.* arrow, dart.

~ræs *m.* charge, onslaught.

~rand *m.* shield.

~rinc *m.* warrior.

~sæd wearied with battle.

~sceorp *n.* armour.

~scūr *m.* shower of missiles.

~setl *n.* seat in war (on horse).

~sierce *f.* corslet.

~spell *n.* warlike speech.

~strengo *f.* strength in war.

~swāt *m.* hostile vapour (?).

~swēg *m.* sound of battle.

hilde|torht brilliant in war.

~tūsc *m.* war-tusk.

~þrymm *m.*, ~þrȳþ *f.* valour.

~þrymma*, ~emma *m.* warrior.

~wǣpen *n.* weapon.

~wīsa *m.* chief, general.

~wōma *m.* sound of battle.

~wrǣsen *f.* war-fetter.

~wulf *m.* warrior.

hilman helmet, cover Gl. [helm].

hilt, e *nm.*, ~e *f.* hilt *often pl. w. sg. meaning.*

~ecumbor† *n.* ensign with hilt.

~lēas without a hilt.

gehiltu *npl.* hilt.

hilted having a hilt.

him *d.* him, it, them.

himming = hemming boot.

hīna *gpl. of* hīwa.

hinan = heonon.

hind *f.* hind, female of the hart.

~berige *f.* raspberry.

~brēr *m.* raspberry bush.

~cealf *n.* fawn.

~falod *n.* hind-fold.

~heoloþ(e), -hæleþ(e) *f.* water-agrimony.

hindan *av.* from behind, behind : ~ offaran cut off retreat — æt ~ behind.

~weard *av.* at the further end.

hindema last (in time).

hinder *av.* below, deep down. on ~ down; behind (motion), backwards — on ~ gefadod 'the cart before the horse.'

~gēap cunning, underhand.

~hōc† *m.* stratagem.

~ling I. *m.* contemptible person. II. on ~ backwards.

~scipe *m.* wickedness.

~pēostro† *pl.* nether darkness.

~weard lagging, slow.

hindeweard with wrong end first (*of* spear).

hindrian repress.

hine him *a.*

hin-fūs† ready to depart (die).

hin-gang† *m.* departure, death.

hinon = heonon.

hin-sīþ† *m.* departure, death.

~gryre† *m.* death-terror.

hīon *f.* bone of head (?) *LL.*

hira of them.

hīrd = hīred.

hire her *d., g.*

hīred, *L.* hīrd, heord *m.* household, family, body of retainers, court ; religious community, brotherhood ; association, company [*from* *hīw-rǣd].

~cniht *m.* young retainer, page.

~cūþ domestic, familiar.

~lic domestic, familiar.

~mann *m.* retainer, courtier, officer.

~prēost *m.* chaplain.

~gerēfa *m.* ex-consul (!).

~wifmann *m.* female member of household, female servant.

~wist *f.* familiarity.

his of him, of it.

hit it.

hittan come upon, find.

hīw, ī, *A.* hēow *n.* appearance ; form, shape ; figure of speech ; colour ; beauty.

~beorht† beautiful.

~e beautiful.

~fæst beautiful.

~lēas colourless ; shapeless.

~lic comely.

hīw- family.

~cund domestic, familiar.

hīw-cūþ familiar, intimate *wd.*

~lic domestic.

~līce *av.* familiarly.

~rǣdnes *f.* intimacy.

hīw|gedāl *n.* divorce.

~rǣden(n) *f.* family, household ; brotherhood (of monks).

~scipe, hīg- *m.* family, household ; hide of land.

hīw|ian colour, paint ; shape, fashion, form ; change, transform, transfigure *tr.* : Drihten hine (*rfl.*) tō menn ge~ode ; figure, signify ; simulate, pretend : hē ~aþ hine selfne unforhtne.

~ere *m.* hypocrite.

~ung *f.* form, appearance ; dissimulation, hypocrisy.

hīw|ian marry.

~ung *f.* marriage.

hīwa, hīga *m.*, *gpl.* hī(g)na member of a family, servant ; monk.

hīwen *n.* family, household.

hīwisc *n.* family, household ; hide (of land).

~līce *av.* familiarly.

hlad|an 2 load *wai.—ptc.* ~en *w. i. or g.* ; put as a load, put ; build up (pile) ; draw (water).

hlæd (*n.*) mound, pile.

hlæd|disc *m.* dish.
~hwēol *n.*, ~tryndel *m.* water-wheel.
hlædel (*m.*) ladle.
hlæd d)er *f.* ladder.
~wyrt *f.* Jacob's ladder (a plant).
hlǣfdige, ā *f.* mistress of a household; lady (of rank) — sēo ealde ~ the queen dowager [hlāford].
gehlǣg *n.* scorn, ridicule.
hlǣhan = hliehhan.
hlǣnan cause to lean.
hlǣn|e lean.
~ian *tr.* make lean, mortify (body) || *intr.* become lean.
~nes *f.* leanness.
~sian make lean.
hlǣst *n.* burden; freight — holmes ~ † fish.
~an load, freight; adorn.
~ing *f.* toll on loading a ship.
~scip *n.* trading vessel.
hlǣw, ā *m.* mound, hill; cave.
hlāf *m.* bread; loaf.
~ǣta *m.* servant.
~gebrece†, ~gebroc *n.* piece of bread.
~gang *m.* procession with the host; participation in a meal.
~hwǣte *m.* wheat for making bread.
~lēast *f.* want of bread.
~mæsse, *vL.* hlāmmæsse *f.* Lammas, first of August.
~mæsse-dæg *m.* Lammas-day.
~ofn *m.* baker's oven.
~segnung, -sēn- *f.* blessing of bread.
hlāfdie = hlǣfdige.
hlāford, -ard *m.* lord, patron, master — (uncre) ~as master and mistress [*from* *hlāfweard].
~dōm *m.* domination, authority; patronage.
~hyldo *f.* loyalty.
~lēas without a lord.
~lic noble.
~scipe *m.* domination, supremacy.
~searo *n.* high treason.
~sōcn *f.* seeking service and protection of a lord.
~swica *m.* traitor.
~swice *m.* high treason.
hlāfording *m.* lord, master.
hlagol given to laughter.
~ian, æ sound.

hlām-mæsse = hlāf-.
hlanc lank, lean.
hland (*n.*) urine.
~ādl*, lond- *f.* strangury (?).
hlāw = hlǣw.
hleahtor *m.* laughter, merriment; ridicule.
~bǣre*, leahtor- causing laughter (?) Gl.
~full contemptuous, scornful.
~lic ridiculous.
~smiþ† *m.* laughter-maker.
hlēap|an 1 *vL. prt. pl.* hlupon (leap); dance; run, go — ūt ~ become an outlaw *vL.*
~ere *m.* runner, courier; itinerant monk; dancer.
~estre *f.* dancer.
~ung *f.* dancing.
gehlēapan 1 *tr.* leap over; leap upon, mount (horse).
hlēapettan leap up.
hlēape-wince = lǣpe- lapwing.
hlec leaky (ship).
hlecan (5) — tōsamne ~ cohere.
hled|a, -e *mf.* seat.
hlęmm *m.* noise, sound.
hlęmman† clash, dash (jaws together).
hlęnce† *f.* (link), *pl.* armour.
hlēo = hlēow.
hleomoc, ~e *mf.* brooklime (a plant).
hleonian = hlinian.
hlēonaþ†, ēo† *m.* shelter [hlēow].
hlēonian† *once*, ēo† flourish (?) [hlēow].
hlēor *n.* cheek; face.
~bān *n.* cheek-bone.
~bolster† *n.* pillow.
~dropa† *m.* tear.
~scamu† *f.* blushing.
~slege *m.* box on the ear.
~torht† beautiful.
hlēotan 7 cast lots; obtain by lot, obtain *w. g., i.*
gehlēotan 7 obtain; be allotted *w.* tō, on *d.* — *so also* wæs gehloten was allotted.
hlēoþor† *n.* sound; melody, song; voice, speaking; hearing (sense of).
~cwide *m.* speaking, words, song.
~cyme *m.* coming with sound (of trumpets).
~stede *m.* place of conference.
gehlēoþor harmonious.

hlēoþr|ian make a sound; shout, speak, utter (words) || *intr.* resound.
~ung *f.* utterance, reproof (!).
hlēow†, hlēo *n.* covering; shelter; refuge; protection; protector.
~bord *n.* cover (of book).
~burg *f.* sheltering city.
~dryhten *m.* patron, lord.
~fæst protecting.
~feþer *f.* sheltering wing.
~lēas without shelter, cheerless (dwelling).
~lora *m.* unprotected.
~mǣg *m.* protecting kinsman.
~sceorp *n.* dress.
~stede *m.* sheltered, warm place.
~stōl *m.* asylum, native city.
gehlēow sheltered, warm (place).
hlēowan = hliewan.
hlēowe (?) *once* warm.
hlēowþ = hliewþ.
gehlēþa† *m.* companion, inhabitant [hlōþ].
hlid *n.* cover, lid; aperture [hlīdan].
~fæst with a lid (*of* cup).
~geat *n.* folding-door.
gehlid *n.* cover, roof.
~od covered with a lid.
hliehhan 2 laugh; rejoice; laugh at (what is said), ridicule *wg.*; smile (to show good-will), *wd. of person* smile upon.
hliep *m.* leap, jump [hlēapan].
hliepe *f.* thing to mount (horse) from, horse-block.
hliet- *m.* lot — ~as begān practise divination [hlēotan].
hliew|an, ēo cover, shelter, cherish; warm || ēo become warm [hlēow].
(ge)~ung *f.* sheltering, shelter.
hliewþ, ēo *f.* covering, shelter, warmth.
hlīfian stand high, tower.
hlīgan give a reputation for (wisdom) *wag.*, attribute to.
hlimman 3 resound, clang, roar (*of* sea), make a sound.
hlimme† *f.* torrent.
hlin† a tree.
hlin|bedd† *n.* couch.
~duru† *f.* door.
~reced† *n.* prison.
~scu(w)a† *m.* darkness of a prison.
hlin|ian, eo recline, lie.
~ung *f.* leaning; couch.
hlinc *m.* ridge, slope, hill.

hlinc-ræw *m.* turf balk (?).
hlis|a, hligsa *m.* report, rumour; reputation, fame [hlīgan].
~bære, ~ēadig renowned.
~ēadignes *f.* renown.
~full of good repute, famous.
~fullīce *av.* gloriously.
hliþ *n.* slope, hill-side, hill.
hloccetung *f.* sighing Gl.
hlos|e *f.* sheep-fold (?).
~lēah *m.* Ct.
~wudu *m.* Ct.
hlosn|ian listen for *wg.*; listen in suspense, be astonished.
~ere *m.* listener; pupil.
hlot *n.* lot, allotment — sendan, weorpan ~ cast lots; portion, share [hlēotan].
gehlot *n.* decision (?).
~land *n.* inheritance.
hlōþ *f.* band of brigands *or* pirates; the offence of joining such a band; †troop, multitude | booty, spoil.
~bōt *f.* compensation *or* fine incurred by member of a hlōþ for offence committed by any one of them.
~gecrod† *n.* press of troops.
~slieht *f.* homicide committed by member of a hlōþ.
hlōþ|ian plunder, take booty.
~ere *m.* robber.
gehlōw *n.* lowing, bellowing.
hlōw|an I low; make a loud sound (*of* trumpeter).
~ung *f.* lowing; sound like lowing.
hlūd loud.
~clipol calling loudly.
~e *av.* loudly.
~nes *f.* clamour.
~stefne loud-sounding Gl.
~swēg *m.* loud sound — ~e loudly.
hlupon *occ. prt. pl.* of hlēapan.
hlūt(t)or clear, limpid; fine (weather); pure.
~līce *av.* distinctly, clearly.
~līcnes, ~nes *f.* purity.
hlūt(t)re *av.* brightly; distinctly, clearly.
hlūttrian become clear; make clear, purify.
hlȳd sound [hlūd].
gehlȳd *n.* noise; tumult.
hlȳdan make loud sound *or* noise; shout; resound.
hlȳda *m.* March [hlūd].
hlȳdig garrulous Gl. [hlūd].

gehlyn *n.* noise.
hlynn *m.* loud sound, resonance; clamour.
hlynn *f.* torrent *LN.*
hlynnan, hlynian make a loud sound; resound, roar (*of* sea); shout.
hlynsian make loud sound, resound.
hlysnan listen.
hlyst *mf.* sense of hearing; listening, attention.
~an listen, hear.
~end, ~ere *m.* listener.
~ung *f.* listening.
gehlyst hearing.
~full attentive.
gehlyta *m.* companion [hlot].
hlytta *m.* diviner, augur [hlot].
gehlytto fellowship *LN.*
hlȳttr|an, -ian purify [hlūtor].
~ung *f.* purifying.
hnǣcan = nǣcan kill.
hnǣgan lay low, humble [hnīgan].
hnǣg|an neigh.
~ung *f.* neighing.
hnæpp *m.* cup, bowl.
hnæppan *once* strike (against) *intr.*
gehnǣst, ā *n.* collision, battle [hnītan].
hnāg bowed down, prostrate; contemptible; niggardly [hnīgan].
hnapp|ian, æ doze; sleep.
~ung *f.* dozing, drowsiness.
hnēaw stingy, niggardly *wdg.*
~līce *av.* stingily, sparingly.
~nes *f.* stinginess.
hnecca *m.* nape of neck, back of head.
hneoton = hniton *prt. pl.* of hnītan.
hnescian, hnexian soften *intr.*, *tr.* (?); relax vigour, yield, waver.
hnesc|e soft, tender; luxurious, delicate; lax, feeble.
~lic effeminate.
~līce *av.* laxly, gently, luxuriously.
~nes *f.* softness; soft part of a thing; effeminacy, want of vigour.
hnifol, *m.* hneofule *f.* forehead.
~crumb, ~crump leaning over (?) Gl.
hnīgan 6 *intr.* bend down, bow, sink down.
hnigian *once* bend *intr.*

hnipian droop, bend down *intr.*; be dejected, sad; doze, be drowsy.
hnītan 6 *tr.* butt, gore; *intr.* come into collision, clash together.
hnitol given to butting *or* goring.
hnitu *f.* nit, louse's egg.
hnocc (*m.*) hook (?).
hnoll (*m.*) crown of head.
hnossian beat.
hnot bald-headed; close-cut, pollard (willow).
hnut|u *f.*, *pl.* hnyte.
~bēam *m.* nut-tree.
~cyrnel *n.* kernel of nut.
hnydele = hydele.
hnygel|a, ~e *mf.* shred, clipping.
gehnyscan *once* crush *M. Cp.* hnęsce.
gehnyst† *once* contrite *LK.*
hnyte, see hnutu.
hō = hōh.
hōn I b *prt.* hēng *tr.* hang, hang on gallows, crucify — *ptc.* gehangen hung (with), adorned *wi.*
hōc *m.* hook.
~ede curved.
~iht hooked.
~īsern *n.* sickle.
hocc *m.* mallow.
~lēaf *n.* mallow.
hōcor *n.* derision.
~wyrde derisive.
hōd *m.* hood.
hof *n.* enclosure, dwelling, house; temple.
~rede confined to the house.
~weard *m.* ædile (!).
h f *m.* hoof.
~rec *n.* hoof-track.
gehōfod hoofed.
hofding *m.* chief, ringleader *vL.* [Scand.].
hōfe *f.* hove (a plant).
hofer *m.* hump; goitre, swelling.
~ede, ge~od, ~iend hump-backed.
hog-, hoh-, *LN.* hoga-, hogo-.
~fæst prudent, wise.
~full solicitous, anxious, sad; attended with anxiety.
~fulnes *f.* anxiety.
~līce *av.* prudently *LN.*
~scipe *m.* prudence.
hogian *w.* ymbe, be, *or* g. think about, consider, be intent on; intend, wish *wg.*
hoga thoughtful, careful *LN.*
hogu *f.* solicitude, care.

hōh, hō, *pl.* hō(a)s *m.* heel — on ~ behind; projecting ridge of land, promontory.

~fōt *m.* heel.

~hwierfing *f.* circle (?) Gl.

~scanca *m.* shank.

~seono *f.* heel-sinew.

~spor *n.* heel.

hol I. *n.* hole, cave, den. II. hollow — of his ~re hand hollow of hand.

hol-lēac *n.* a plant Gl.

hōl *n.* calumny, slander.

~inga, -unga *av.* in vain, without cause.

~tihte *f.* calumny, slander.

holian hollow out.

geholian obtain.

hōlian slander [hōl].

gehola† *m.* protector [helan].

hole *n.* hollow, cavity.

hold *m.* freeholder [*Scand.*].

hold *n.* carcase, dead body.

hold *wd.* gracious, friendly, kind; faithful, loyal; acceptable, pleasant.

~āþ *m.* oath of allegiance *vL.*

~e *av.* graciously, loyally.

~līce *av.* graciously, kindly; faithfully; attentively.

~rǣden(n) *f.* loyalty, discharge of duty.

~scipe *m.* loyalty *vL.*

holdian cut up, cut to pieces.

hole(g)n (*n.*) holly.

~lēaf *n* holly-leaf.

~rind *f.* holly-bark.

~stybb *m.* holly-stump.

holh *n.* hollow, hole. *Cp.* hol, holc.

holm *m.* ocean, sea, water†; land rising from water, island in river.

~ærn† *n.* ship.

~clif† *n.* cliff.

~ig† of the sea.

~mægen† *n.* ocean.

~þracu† *f.* tossing sea.

~weall† *m.* rampart of water.

~weard† *m.* coastguard.

~weg† *m.* way over the sea.

~wielm† *m.* surge of the sea.

holo-panne *f.* pan Gl.

holrian = heolorian.

holt *nm.* copse, wood; timber, wood.

~hana *m.* woodcock.

holt-wudu† *m.* copse, wood; timber, wood.

hōn *once pl.* tendrils of vine (?).

hona = heonu.

hōnede, ó having heels Gl. [hōh].

hop-pāda *m.* upper garment, cope Gl.

hop-scīete*, -ȳte *f.* sheet.

hōp-

~gehnāst† *n.* dashing of waves.

~ig†, ō† rough, running high (sea).

hopian hope; put trust in *w.* tō.

gehopp *once* (*n.*) small bag Gl.

hopp|ian leap; dance.

~estre *f.* dancer.

hoppe *f.* ornament; small bell (?).

hoppet(t)an leap; throb (*of* wound).

hopu (*f.*) privet Gl.

hōr *n.* adultery, fornication.

~cwene *f.* prostitute.

~ing *m.* adulterer, fornicator.

horian *once* cry out.

gehorian spit *lN.* [horh].

horas *pl. of* horh.

hōre *f.* prostitute.

hord *nm.* treasure, hoard, what is deposited.

~burg† *f.* treasure-city.

~cleofa, -y- *m.* treasury, storeroom, chamber.

~cofa† *m.* chamber; †mind, thoughts.

~ern, æ *n.* treasury, storehouse, storeroom.

~fæt *n.* coffer.

~geat *n.* treasury-door.

~loca *m.* coffer; †mind.

~mægen† *n.* riches.

~māþm† *n.* treasure.

~gestrēon† *n.* stored-up possessions, hoard.

~weard† *m.* guardian of treasure (dragon); king; heir, first-born.

~wela† *m.* hoarded wealth.

~weorþung† *f.* honouring with gifts.

~wynn† *f.* treasure.

hordian hoard up, store.

horder|e *m.* treasurer, steward.

~wice *f.* stewardship *vL.*

horeht = horwiht.

hor|h, ~u *mn., g.* ~(w)es, *pl.* ~as phlegm, mucus; filth.

~pytt *m.* mud-pit.

~usēaþ *m.* sink.

~wiell *m.* muddy stream.

horig = horwig.

horn *m.* horn, drinking-horn, cupping-horn; trumpet, horn; pinnacle, gable.

~bǣre horned.

~blāwere *m.* trumpeter.

~boga† *m.* bow.

~bora *m.* trumpeter.

~fisc *m.* garfish, kind of pike.

~fōtede horn-footed.

~gēap† with high *or* broad gables.

~pic *m.* pinnacle.

~reced† *n.* gabled house.

~sæl† *n.* gable hall.

~sceap- pinnacle *lN.*

~scip† *n.* beaked ship.

~sele† *m.* gabled hall.

~gestrēon† *n. for* hord~ (?).

gehornian insult (?) *lN.*

hōrnung-sunu *m.* bastard Gl.

hors *n.* horse.

~bǣr *f.* horse-bier.

~camb *m.* curry-comb.

~cniht *m.* groom, equerry.

~cræt *n.* chariot.

~(h)elene *f.* elecampane (a plant).

~ern *n.* stable.

~gærs-tūn *m.* horse-pasturing meadow.

~hierde *m.* groom.

~hwæl*, horsc- *m.* walrus.

~þegn, -þēn *m.* groom, a king's officer.

~wægn, -wǣn *m.* chariot.

~wealh *m.* king's officer.

~weard *f.* care of horses.

~weg *m.* bridle-path.

hors|ian provide with horses — ge~od folc cavalry.

horsc brisk, brave; intelligent, sagacious.

~līce, horx- *av.* intelligently.

hortan *pl.* whortleberries, bilberries (?) Gl.

horu = horh.

hor(w)ig muddy [horh].

hor(w)iht mucose; filthy.

hos *once f.* pod Gl.

hōs† *f.* troop of attendants.

hos|a *m.*, ~e, ~u *wk. f.* hose.

~ebend *m.* garter.

hosp *m.* contumely, insult; blasphemy, contempt, cause of shame, reproach.

~cwide† *m.*, ~sprǣc *f.* opprobrious language.

hosp-word *n.* word of contempt, opprobrious language.
hospettan ridicule.
hoss- = **hysse** vine-shoot.
hoþma† *m.* darkness.
hrā = **hrǣw**.
hracing *f.* detention (?) *LN.*
hrac|a *m.*; **-e, -u** *wk. f.* throat.
hrāca, ǣ *m.* expectoration; phlegm.
hrad|ian, *A.* **hr(e)aþian** *intr.* hasten.
-ung, hrǣding *f.* celerity, diligence.
hrade = **hraþe.**
hrǣ = **hrǣw.**
hrǣc|an clear throat, spit.
-ung *f.* clearing the throat, spitting.
hrǣc|a *m.* clearing the throat.
-gebrǣc *n.* expectoration, bronchitis Gl.
-tunge *f.* uvula.
hrǣc(e)t|an eructate.
-ung *f.* eructation.
hrǣd, rǣd *d.* **-um, hradum;** *A.* **hræþ** quick, swift; agile; clever, quick ; hasty.
-bita *m.* beetle.
-fērnes *f.* celerity.
-hygdig, -hȳdig hasty.
-hygdignes, -hȳd- *f.* precipitancy.
-lic short (period of time) ; premature ; sudden.
-lice *av.* quickly, soon, at once
-licnes *f.* quick lapse of time.
-mōd hasty.
-nes *f.* quickness; quick lapse of time.
-rīpe early (fruit).
-wǣgn, -wǣn *m.* swift chariot.
-wilnes *f.* precipitancy, haste.
-wyrde hasty of speech.
hrǣd-mōnaþ = **hrēp-.**
hrǣding = **hradung.**
hræfn, e, hremn, hremm, æ *m.* raven. **-es fōt** cinquefoil. **-es lēac** orchis.
-cynn *n.* raven-kind.
hræfn = **hæfern** crab.
hræg(e)l *n.* dress ; armour; ship's sail.
-ciest *f.* clothes-chest.
-gefrætwodnes *f.* dress-adornment.
-hūs *n.* vestry.
-sceara *fpl.* cloth-shears.
-talu *f.* vestment-fund.

hrægel|þegn, -þēn *m.* keeper of dresses.
-gewǣde *n.* dress Gl.
-weard *m.* keeper of dresses.
-ung *f.* clothing, clothes.
hræm(n) = **hræfn.**
hræn = **hærn** wave.
hrætel|e*, hra- *f.* a plant.
-wyrt *f.* rattlewort.
hræþ = **hræd.**
hræþe = **hraþe.**
hræþe-mūs = **hrēaþe-.**
hrǣw = **hrēaw** raw.
hrǣ̆(w), hrā(w), hrēaw *nm.* corpse, carrion; (living) body.
hrā|fiell† *m.* slaughter.
-gīfre deadly Gl.
-wērig† sore, wearied.
-wic*, hrēaw- *n.* place of corpses.
hrāgra *m.* heron.
hramma *m.* cramp.
hramsa *m.* broad-leaved garlic.
-cropp *m.* head of garlic Gl.
hran *m.* smaller kind of whale.
-fisc† *m.* whale.
**-mere† *m.*, -rād† *f.* sea.
hrān *m.* reindeer.
hrand.
-spearwa *m.* sparrow *LN.*
hratian*, r- rush, hasten. *Perhaps for* hradian.
hratele, *see* **hrætele.**
hraþian = **hradian.**
(h)raþe, hraþe *av.* quickly; soon —swā ~ swā as soon as ‖ *spl.* **(h)raþost, hrædest, radost** quickest, soonest — ~ is tō cweþenne (*or* secganne) in short.
hrāw = **hrǣw.**
hrēa *(f.)* indigestion (?) [hrēaw].
hrēac *m.* heap; (hay)rick.
-copp, -mete *m.* food given to labourers on completing a rick.
hrēam *m.* cry, shout, shouting, hue and cry, uproar.
-ig = **hrēmig.**
hrēaþe-mūs, æ, hrēaþa- *f.* bat. *Cp.* hrēre-mūs.
hrēaw, ēo, ǣ uncooked, raw.
-ian* *once, prt.* reawde be raw Gl.
hred-mōnaþ = **hrēp-.**
hredd|an rescue, recover, save ; take away *wda.*
-ing *f.* deliverance; redemption ; salvation.
hrēfan roof [hrōf].
hrefn = **hæfern** crab.

hrēmig† [ē = ǣ], ēa *w.g., i.* exulting ; lamenting (?).
hremm = **hræfn.**
hremm|an hinder *w.* æt; cumber (the ground).
-ing *f.* hindrance, obstacle.
hremn = **hræfn.**
hrēo = **hrēoh, hrēow** *aj.*
hrēoung, hrīung *f.* hard breathing, asthma.
hrēod *n.* reed.
-bedd *n.* reed-bed.
-brōc *m.* reedy brook.
-ig, -iht reedy.
-pōl *m.* reedy pond.
-wæter *n.* reedy piece of water.
-writ *n.* reed pen.
hrēodan* 7 — (ge)hroden† loaded, filled ; adorned *wi.*
hrēof rough ; scabby, leprous.
-nes *f.* leprosy.
hrēofl I. *f.* scab, leprosy. II. leprous.
-a *m.* leper ; leprosy.
-ig leprous.
hrēo(h) I. *pl.* hrēo stormy, rough ; troubled (in mind) ; fierce. *Cp.* hrēow. II. *(n.)* storm ; flood (?).
-lic stormy.
-mōd troubled (in mind), fierce.
-nes *f.* roughness (of weather) ; rough weather, storm.
hrēol reel.
hrēorig in ruins [hrēosan].
hrēos|an 7 fall, collapse, perish ; rush.
-endlic perishable.
hrēow I. *f.* penitence, repentance — ~e dōn *wg.* repent ; regret ; sorrow. II. hrēo(w) *aj.* sad, repentant. *Cp.* hrēoh.
-cearig† anxious, troubled.
-lic, ī, ȳ pitiable, deplorable, miserable.
-lice *av.* pitiably, miserably ; cruelly ; sadly.
-nes, *LN.* gehrēones *f.* penitence.
hrēow = **hrēaw** raw.
hrēow *occ. prt. of* **hrēowan.**
gehrēow *n.* lamentation.
hrēowan 7 *prt.* hrēaw, ēo *wd.* cause sorrow, repentance, *often impers.*
hrēowian repent *LN.*
hrēowig†, -ferhþ, -mōd sad.
hrēowsian, ȳ, ī repent, do penance ; be sorrowful, grieve.

hrēowsung _f._ repentance, penitence ; grief, lamentation.

hrep|ian, eo, (h)rẹppan touch ; treat (subject).

~ung _f._ sense of touch ; touching.

hrepsung = repsung.

hrēr half-cooked, underdone.

hrēr|an _tr._ move, stir, shake [hrōr].

~(ed)nes, ȳ _f._ movement, commotion ; haste.

hrēre-mūs _f._ bat. _Cp._ hrēaþe-mūs.

gehrespan† _once_ tear.

hrēþ† (_m._) victory ; glory.

~ēadig victorious ; glorious.

~lēas inglorious.

~sigor _m._ victory.

hrēþ-mōnaþ, hræd-, e _m._ March.

hrēþan triumph.

hrēþa _m._ cloak Gl.

hrēþe = rēþe.

hreþer† _m._ breast, womb, heart ; mind.

~bealo _n._ grief.

~cofa _m._ breast.

~glēaw prudent, wise.

~loca _m._ breast.

hrīung = hrēoung.

hrīcian cut, cut to pieces.

hricsc sprain (?).

hrĭddel (_n._), hrĭd(d)er coarse sieve.

hrĭdrian sift.

hrīefing _f._ scab [hrēof].

hrīefþo _f._ scurf [hrēof].

hrīeman make loud sound ; shout, call, cry out ; wail, lament ‖ exult [hrēam, hrēmig].

gehrīered destroyed Gl.

hrif _n._ womb ; interior of body ; stomach.

~tēung _f._ stomach-ache.

~wærc _m._ stomach-ache.

~wund wounded in the stomach.

gehrifian bring forth (young).

gehrifnian tear, seize.

hrīm _m._ rime, hoarfrost.

~cealdt icy cold.

~gicel† _m._ icicle.

hrīmig rimy.

~heard† hard-frozen.

hrīn|an 6 _w. g., i., a._ touch.

~ung _f._ touch _IN._

hrindan 3 thrust.

hrine _m._ touch.

hrinen(n)es, ge- _f._ touch, contact.

hring _m._ ring, gold ring, fetter, link ; circle ; circuit (of year).

hring|bān _m._ circular bone Gl.

~boga† _m._ serpent.

~fāg circle-spotted.

~finger _m._ third finger.

~īren† _n._ steel rings of corslet.

~loca† _m._ corslet.

~mǣl†, ~mǣled† adorned with rings.

~mẹre† _m._ bath.

~naca† _m._ ring-prowed ship.

~nẹtt† _n._ corslet.

~sẹle† _m._ hall in which gold rings are stored _or_ distributed.

~setl _n._ circus Gl.

~sittende sitting round Gl.

~þẹgu† _f._ receiving rings.

~weorþung† _f._ honour of receiving gold rings.

~gewindla _m._ globe, sphere Gl.

~wīse _f._ circular form.

hringan ring _tr. and intr.,_ resound.

hringe _f._ ring (to lift with).

hringed made of rings _or_ links.

~stẹfna† ring-prowed (ship).

hrīs _n._ twig.

~iht bushy.

hrisian shake _tr._

hrīscan = hrȳscan.

hrisel, ī† _m._ shuttle [hrisian].

hrist|ende creaking.

~ung _f._ noise (in throat) (?).

hristi|e _f._ rattle.

~ian rattle, creak.

hrip _m._, ~ādl _f._ fever.

hrīp† _f._ storm.

hrīp- = hrīþer-.

~fald _m._ cattle-pen.

hrip|ian have fever, be feverish.

~ing _f._ fever.

hrīþer, y _n._ ox, bull, cow, _pl._ cattle. _See_ hrīþ-.

~en of cattle, of ox.

~frēols _m._ cattle-festival Gl.

~hēawere _m._ butcher.

~heord _f._ herd of cattle.

~hierde, hrīþh- _m._ cowherd, herdsman.

hrōc _m._ rook.

(ge)hroden, _see_ hrēodan.

hroden† = *roden reddened.

hrōf _m._ roof, ceiling ; summit, top ; roof (of mouth) ; sky, heaven.

~fæst with a firm roof.

~lēas roofless.

~sẹle† _m._ roofed hall.

~stān _m._ roof-tile.

hrōf|tigel _f._ roof-tile.

~timber _n._ roof-timber.

~wyrhta _m._ roof-builder.

hrōp _m._ clamour, lamentation.

hrōpan† 1 shout, utter loud cries, howl, scream.

gehror _n._ ruin [hrēosan].

hrōr capable of motion, vigorous, strong.

hroren _ptc. of_ hrēosan.

gehroren(n)es _f._ ruin.

hrōst (_m._) perch.

~bēag† _m._ woodwork of roof.

hrot, r- _m._ thick fluid, scum.

hrōþor† _m., d._ ~, hrōþre solace, joy, benefit.

~lēas joyless.

hrūm (_m._) soot.

~ig sooty.

hrung† _f._ pole (?).

hrungeattorr† (?).

hrūse†, ū† _f._ earth, ground.

gehrusl = gehrūxl.

hrūtan 7 snore ; resound.

gehrūxl, -ūsl _n._ noise [hrȳscan].

hrycg _m._ back ; ridge, top, surface.

~bān _m._ backbone, spine.

~brǣdan _pl._ flesh on both sides of the spine.

~hǣr _n._ hair from animal's back.

~hrægl _n._ mantle.

~mearg _n._ spinal marrow.

~mearg-lip _n._ spine.

~ribb _n._ rib Gl.

~riple = ~brǣdan Gl.

~weg _m._ ridge-way.

hryding _f._ clearing, cleared land.

hryre I. _m._ fall ; destruction, ruin. II. _aj._ perishable [hrēosan].

hrȳscan*, i creak [gehrūxl].

hrypig† _once_ in ruins (building).

hryppa = ryppa.

hrȳwlic = hrēowlic.

hū _av. dir. interr._ how ; what ! _indir. interr._ how, _gen. w. indc., also w. sbj._ | _intens. w. ajs._ and _avs._ how, _w. cpv._ the : lufode hine leng hū geornor | _wg._ hū gēares hit sīe according to the time of year.

~hwega, -o, ~hugu _av._ about (quantity).

~lic of what kind _in dir. and indir. interr._

~meta _av._ how.

gehū _av._ somehow or other.

[94]

hūdenian shake.

hūf|e f. head-covering, hood.

~ian tr. put hood on (a person).

hui, huig interj.

huilpe = hwilpe.

hulc m. shed ; hut ‖ light ship.

hulfestre f. plover Gl.

hulu f. husk [helan].

hūn- (m.) cub*.

~spora m. spike (?) Gl.

~þȳrel n. hole in mast-head through which the halyard went.

hund m. dog, also as term of abuse. ~es pēo dog's parasite. ~es cwelcan berries of the wayfaring tree. ~es flēoge dog's parasite. ~es hēafod snapdragon. ~es lūs dog's parasite. ~es micge, ~es tunge cynoglossum (a plant). ~es wyrm dog's worm.

~lic doglike, canine.

~wealh m. dog-keeper.

hund n. hundred.

~feald hundredfold, hundred.

~wintre a hundred years old.

hund·eahtatig eighty.

~wintre eighty years old.

hund·endlufontig, -endleftig, -ænd- hundred and ten.

~oþa, -ælleftig- hundred and tenth.

hund·nigontig ninety.

~oþa, -nigontēoþa ninetieth.

~wintre ninety years old.

hundred, -od, -yd, lN. hundraþ n. hundred ; group of a hundred ; a territorial division, hundred. ~es ealdor president of hundred (district) ; centurion. ~es mann president of hundred (district).

~mann m. centurion.

~gemōt n. assembly of the hundred.

~pening m. tax for support of the chief of the hundred.

hund·seofontig, lN. unsefuntig seventy.

~feald seventy-fold.

~oþa seventieth.

~wintre seventy years old.

hund·tēontig hundred.

~feald(lic) hundredfold.

~gēare a hundred years old.

hund·twelftig hundred and twenty.

hund·twentig nundred and twenty.

---

hundtwentig-wintre hundred and twenty years old.

hūne f. horehound.

hungor m. hunger, also met. ; famine.

~biten suffering from hunger vL.

~gēar n. year of famine.

~lǣwe hungry, famishing.

~lic hungry.

hungrig hungry, starving.

hunig n. honey.

~æppel m. ball of honey (?) Gl.

~bǣre honeyed.

~binn f. vessel for honey.

~camb f. honeycomb.

~flōwende flowing with honey.

~gafol n. rent paid in honey.

~smæcc m. taste of honey.

~sūge, -sūce f. privet.

~swǣs honeyed Gl.

~swēte sweet as honey.

~tēar m. honey that flows from the comb, nectar (!).

~tēaren, ~tēarlic like nectar (!).

hunt|ian m. hunt.

~icge, ~igestre f. hunter.

~ung f. hunting ; game, prey.

~ing-spere†, -ig- n. hunting-spear.

hunta m. hunter.

huntoþ, -(n)aþ m. hunting, right of hunting ; game, prey.

~faru f. hunting-expedition.

hup- hip [hype].

~(p)bān n. hip-bone.

~seax n. short sword.

hūru av. at least, at all events, at any rate—not less than, at least (of quantity) ; especially ; certainly, indeed.

~þinga av. at least.

hūs n. house ; household, race.

~bōnda, ~bunda m., f. master or mistress of house [Scand.].

~bryce m. house-breaking, burglary.

~brycel house-breaking Gl.

~bryne m. fire.

~carl m. one of the king's bodyguard L. [Scand.].

~fæst having a house.

~heofon m. ceiling.

~hlāford m. master of a house.

~hlēow n. house-shelter.

~incel n. little house.

~rǣden(n) f. household.

ge~scipe m. household, race.

---

hūs|stęde m. site of building.

~ting n. (Danish) tribunal, meeting [Scand. hūsþing].

~wist f. household.

hūsian house, receive into one's house.

gehūsa, lN. hūsa m. fellow-inmate, fellow-monk.

hūsc, hūx (n.) mockery, insult.

~lic ignominious, shameful.

~līce av. ignominiously, shamefully.

~word n. insulting word(s).

hūsl n. Eucharist.

~bearn n. communicant.

~disc m. paten.

~fæt n. sacramental or sacrificial vessel.

~gang m. partaking of the Eucharist.

~genga m. communicant.

~hālgungf. attendance at Eucharist.

~lāf f. remains of Eucharist.

~portic m. sacristy.

~þegn, ~þēn m. acolyte.

~wer m. communicant.

hūsl|ian administer Eucharist or sacrament.

~ung f. administration of sacrament.

hūþ f. plunder, booty. Cp. hȳþ.

hūx = hūsc.

hwā no. who in dir. and indir. interr. — wg. : ~ is mancynnes þæt ne wundrie . . | indf. any one, some one, one wg. swā~ swā whoever, if any one. See neut. hwæt.

gehwā no., rare neut. gehwǣt, f. d., g. gehwǣm, gehwǣs, gehwǣre, ā any one ; each one, every one, wg. each, every. ānra ~ each one.

gehwǣd|e slight, small, young.

~nes f. smallness, insignificance ; subtlety, fineness.

hwǣder = hwider.

hwǣg (n.) whey.

hwǣl m. whale.

~en† once like a whale.

~hunta m. whaler.

~huntoþ m. whale-fishery.

~mere m. sea.

hwǣl = hwēall.

hwǣm, ā whom, what d.

ge~lic every (day) lN.

hwǣne whom a.

hwǣnne = hwonne.

hwǽr, hwǽr(a) *av.* where, whither *in dir. and indir. interr.* : ~ cwōm . . what has become of . .! ofseah ~ hē lǽdde saw him leading. *wg.* ~ eorþan where in the world | *indf.* anywhere, somewhere. ~ . . ~ at one place . . at another. swā ~ swā wherever, in whatever direction. wel ~ nearly everywhere.

gehwǽr, ā *av.* everywhere, in all directions; *time* on every occasion | *indf.* ~ . . ~ in some places . . in others.

hwǽs whose.

hwǽsan *or* hwēsan [ē = ǽ] I *prt.* hwēos wheeze.

hwǽss sharp, prickly.

hwǽst- blowing Gl.

hwǽstr|ian, ā whisper, murmur. ~ung *f.* whispering, murmuring.

hwæt brisk; brave, bold. ~līce *av.* quickly. ~mōd bold. ~nes, ge- *f.* quickness. ~rǽd† determined. ~scipe *m.* briskness; bravery.

hwæt *no. neut. of* hwā, *having similar meanings and constructions* I. what; who : nāt ic ~ gē sint — *wg. and indc. or sbj.* : ~ eom ic manna þæt ic mihte God forbēodan? what sort of a man am I to be able to . . ; ~ is þinga þe biterre sīe . . ?; hīe ne ācsodon ~ þāra gefarenra wǽre what was the number of the dead | *indf.* anything. something : lӯtles ~ a little, swelces ~ something of that sort. swā ~ swā whatever. II. *av.* why *dir. and indir. interr.* || *interj.* ah! lo! well! what!

~hwāra *av.* somewhat.

~hwegu, -a, -h(w)ugu I. *no.* something, a little. II. *av.* somewhat, slightly.

~hweguningas, -h(w)uguninges *av.* somewhat, a little.

hwǽte *m.* wheat [hwīt]. ~corn *n.* grain of wheat. ~cynn *n.* (kind of) wheat. ~gryttan *pl.* coarse wheatmeal. ~healm *n.* wheat-straw, -stalk. ~land *n.* wheat-land. ~melo *n.* wheat-flour. ~smedema *m.* fine wheat-flour.

hwǽte-wæstm *m.* corn.

hwǽten wheat(en).

hwǽþer I. *no.* which of two *dir. and indir. interr. w. g. or of, often w.* (þe) . . þe : ~ þāra twēgra . . ? ~ne of þisum twām . . ? ~ is māre þe þæt gold þe þæt tempel ? | *indf.* one or other of two, either *wg.* swā ~ swā whichever (of two or more) | both (?). II. *av., cj., often w.* þe . . (þe), *dir. and indir. interr.* whether *w. indc. or sbj.* : ~ gē willen on wuda sēcan gold ? ~ wæs his fulluht þe of heofonum þe of mannum? hē nyste self ~ hē mann wæs. befrān ~ þæs landes folc crīsten wǽre þe hǽþen. *See* hwǽþere *cj.*

gehwǽþer *no. wg.* each (of two), both : on ~e hand on both sides (in battle).

hwæþ(e)re I. *av.* however. þēah-þe . . ~ although . . yet. ~ (swā)þēah however. II. *cj.* = hwæþer.

gehwæþere *av.* nevertheless.

gehwæþeres *av.* on all sides.

hwām *d. of* hwā, hwæt.

hwamm *m.* corner, angle, prominence. ~stān *m.* corner-stone.

hwan = hwon *i. of* hwæt.

hwane *a. of* hwā.

hwanne = hwonne.

hwanon, ~e *av.* whence.

~hwegu *av.* from anywhere.

gehwanon *av.* from all quarters.

hwār(a) = hwǽr.

hwast- eunuch *lN.*

hwāstrian = hwǽstrian.

hwat|a *m.* diviner, augur. ~ian practise divination. ~ung *f.* divination.

hwat|a, ~an *fpl.* divination, omens.

hwatend iris illyrica (a plant).

hwaþerian, hwo- foam *or* surge (of sea).

hwealf I. *f.* vault, arch. II. vaulted; hollow, concave.

hweall*, hwal, hwall-, *vE.* hwæl impudent, bold. *Cp.* hwelan.

hwearf† *m.* crowd. *The allit. requires* *hwearf.

hwearf *m.* exchange; what is exchanged [hweorfan].

gehwearf exchange — tō ~e in exchange ; vicissitude.

gehwearfnes = gehwierfnes.

hwearf|ian, æ *intr.* turn, revolve, roll; wave (*of* banner); wander; change. ~ung *f.* change, vicissitude; exchange, barter.

hwearft *m.* circuit, expanse; lapse of time.

hwearftlian = hwierftlian.

hwel|an 4 resound. ~ung *f.* noise.

hwelian suppurate || make to suppurate.

hwelc, i, y *no. w. g., aj.* which (one), of what kind, what sort of *dir. and indir. interr.* | *indf.* any (one), some (one). elles ~ *wg.* any other. swā ~ swā whoever, whatever : swā ~e dæge swā whenever || as *correl. to* swelc : hit is scandlic ymb swelc tō sprecanne ~ hit þā wæs.

~hwegu, -a, -h(w)ugu *no., aj. the first element inflected* some (one), any (one).

~hwēne, oe *no., aj. lN.* some (one).

(ge)~nes *f.* quality (!).

gehwelc *no. wg., aj.* each (one), every (one) — ānra ~ *no. wg.* each one | *pl.* each one, all : ~e ǽnlīpige cendon . . each one singly made a declaration; ~e hālgan every saint; ~e ōþre lāc all || *indf. pl.* some : Loth and ~ē ōþre þe englas gesāwon.

hwelp *m.* whelp, cub.

hwemm *m.* corner [hwamm]. ~dragen sloping, leaning.

hwēne, oe *av.* somewhat, a little [hwōn].

hwēol, hweow(o)l, hweog(u)l *n.* wheel. ~fāg having a circular decoration. ~rād *f.* rut.

hwēop *prt. of* hwōpan.

hweorf|an, u 3 *intr.* turn, return; depart; wander, go; change, vary — feohtan mid ~endum sigum | onweg ~ depart, die || *tr.* turn, direct; change, convert (to religion).

hweor(f)-bān, u *n.* knee-cap.

hweorfa *m.* whorl (of spindle).

hwēos *prt. of* hwǽsan.

hwer *m.* kettle, cauldron ; pot, basin.

hwer-bān = hweorf-.

hwer-hwette *f.* cucumber

hwerfian = hwearfian.

hwerflic = *hwierflic.

hwergen *av.* — elles ~ elsewhere [hwër].

hwēsan, *see* hwǣsan.

hwęt-stān *m.* hone.

hwicce *f.* chest.

hwider, æ *av.* whither. swā ~ swā wherever (motion).

~ryne directed whither Gl.

gehwider *av.* in every direction ; in any direction.

hwięrf|an *tr.* turn ; change, transform ; convert (to religion) ; geoverturn, destroy ‖ *intr.* turn, revolve ; return ; wander, go, move ; change | *wg.* exchange, barter [hweorfan].

~lic*, hwerf-, hwirlic mutable, transitory.

~nes*, hwyrf- *f.* giddiness.

ge-(ed)nes, ea *f.* conversion (to Christianity).

~ung *f.* change, vicissitude.

hwięrfl|an.

~ung*, y, æ *f.* wandering ; period.

hwięrftlian*, y, ea revolve ; wander.

hwig = hwȳ.

hwīl *f.* space of time : ~ dæges ; ~e, tō ~e for a time ; tō scortre ~e ; gōde ~e for a long time | period of time : ǣr dæges ~e. nū ~e just now. þā ~e meanwhile, at the same time. ~e . . ~e at one time . . at another. *See* hwīlum. þā-hwīle-þe *cj. w. indc.* while, *correl.* þā-hwīle-þe . . þā hwīle while.

~hwega *av.* for some time.

~stycce *n.* period of leisure, odd time. sum ~ for some time.

~tīdum *av.* sometimes — ~ . . ~ at one time . . at another ; at certain times.

hwīl-(w)ęnd|e, ~lic temporary, transitory.

~līce *av.* temporarily.

hwīlen transitory.

hwīlende = hwīlwęnde.

hwīlpe† *f.* a sea-bird.

hwīl|um, ~on *av.* sometimes —

~ . . ~ sometimes . . sometimes, now . . now | some time, a little time : ~ ǣr | formerly (?).

hwīnan 6 make shrill sound, whizz.

hwiscet|tan.

~ung *f.* squeaking (of mice).

hwispr|ian murmur.

~ung *f.* murmuring.

hwistlian = wistlian.

hwīt I. white ; clear, bright ; fair, beautiful. II. *n.* white of egg.

~cwidu, ~cudu (*m.*) mastic Gl.

~fōt having white feet.

~lēac *n.* onion.

~locc†, ~loccede† fair-haired.

~nes *f.* whiteness.

hwīt|an *tr.* whiten ; polish.

~ian be white.

hwīte-hlāf *m.* wheat loaf.

hwītel *m.* cloak ; blanket.

hwīting-melo *n.* whiting.

hwīting-trēow *n.* whitten-tree.

hwiþa, eo *m.* breeze.

hwon *i.* of hwæt.

hwōn I. *av.* somewhat, a little. II. *no.* a little (of) *abs. or wg.* III. *aj.* some, a little, few.

~lic slight (quantity) ; unimportant.

~līce *av.* a little, moderately, slightly.

~lotum *av.* in small quantities Gl.

hwonne, a, æ *dir. interr.* when ; *indir. interr. w. sbj. and indc.* when, until : sege ūs ~ þās þing geweorpen | hit biþ lang ~ se hlāford cume | *indf.* : nū ~ eft at some future time.

hwōpan† 1 threaten, *wdi.* threaten one with.

hwōsta *m.* cough.

hwōstan cough.

hwoþerian = hwaþerian.

hwurf- = hweorf-.

hwurfol fickle [hweorfan].

~nes *f.* fickleness.

hwȳ, ī I. *i.* of hwæt. II. *av.* why *in dir. and indir. interr.*

hwylc = hwelc.

hwylca [y = e ?] *m.* tumour, boil Gl.

hwyrf-bān = hweorf-.

hwyrfe-pōl [= ię *or* eo] *m.* whirlpool, eddy Gl.

hwyrft *m.* turning, revolving ; orbit (of stars), circuit (of earth) ;

motion, course ; return ; period, course (of time) [hweorfan].

gehwyrft (*m.*) — ~ gēares anniversary.

hȳ-gedryht† *once f.* band of retainers (?). hȳ- = hīw-.

hycgan think of, be mindful of *w. a. or g. or* ymb ; meditate (evil), plot (against) ; be intent on, determine, endeavour — *w.* fram be averse to ; hope. *Cp.* hogian.

hȳd *f.* (human) skin, skin (of animal), hide — þǣre ~e þolian be flogged, þā ~ forwyrcan be liable to a flogging.

~gięld *n.* payment to escape flogging.

~ig of leather.

gehȳd having a skin.

gehȳd = gehygd.

hȳd|an hide, conceal ; sheath (sword) ; bury.

~els hiding-place, den (of thieves), place where a thing is hidden.

gehȳdnes *f.* comfort, security.

hydele, hn- *f.* — hǣwen ~ a plant.

hȳf *f.* hive.

gehygd, -hȳd *fn.* mind, thought — mid ~um carefully.

hygdig, hȳdig thoughtful ; modest, chaste.

~līce *av.* chastely.

~nes *f.* chastity.

hyge† *m.* mind, heart, mood, disposition ; courage ; pride.

~bend *m.* mind-bond, natural tie.

~blind infatuated.

~blīþe glad.

~clǣne pure-minded.

~cræft *m.* faculty, wisdom.

~cræftig wise.

~fæst, ~frōd wise.

~frōfor *f.* consolation.

~gǣlsa sluggish.

~gāl wanton.

~gār *m.* wile, device.

~gēomor sad.

~glēaw prudent, sagacious.

~grimm fierce, cruel.

~lēas thoughtless, foolish, reckless Pr.

~lēast *f.* levity, folly, recklessness Pr.

~mǣþ ~um reverently.

~mēþe mind-wearying.

~rōf brave.

hyge|rūn *f.* secret.
~sceaft *f.* mind, heart [*Old Saxon*].
~snottor wise.
~sorg *f.* sorrow, anxiety.
~tēona *m.* injury, wrong, insult.
~trēow *f.* faith.
~þanc *m.* thought.
~þancol thoughtful, wise.
~þrymm *m.* pride, courage.
~þrȳþ *f.* pride.
~þyhtig brave.
~wiẹlm *m.* agitation of mind, anger.
~wlanc proud.
hyht *mf.* hope ; joy, pleasure.
~full† joyful ; pleasant.
~giẹfa† *m.* giver of joy.
~giẹfu† *f.* pleasant gift.
~lēas† joyless ; incredulous.
~lic† joyful ; pleasant.
~lice *av.* joyfully.
~plega† *m.* sport, pastime.
~willa† *m.*, ~wynn† *f.* joy.
gehyht *n.* hope, comfort.
hyht|an hope, confide ; rejoice.
~ing *f.* exultation.
hylc *m.* bend, turn.
gehylced spread out, diverging Gl.
hyld|an flay, skin [hold].
~ere *m.* butcher.
hyld|o, hyld *f.* favour, grace ; allegiance, loyalty — his ~a swōron swo.e allegiance to him [hold].
~āþ *m.* oath of allegiance.
~emæg† *m.* kinsman.
~rǣden *f.* fidelity.
hyll *mf.* hill.
~wyrt *f.* pulegium.
hylle-hāma, hilh- *m.* cricket, grasshopper.
Hymbre *pl.* Northumbrians. *Cp.* Norþhymbre.

hymele *f.* hop-plant [*Lt.* humulus].
hymen = ymen hymn.
hym(b)lice *f.*, hymlic *m.* hemlock.
hynden(n) *f.* association of a hundred men [hund].
~mann *m.* head of a hynden.
hyngran, -ian be hungry ; *impers.* : hine (*or* him) hyngrede — *ptc.* gehyngred hungry [hungor].
hyngrig = hungrig.
hyp|e *m.* hip. *See* hup-.
~(e)bān = hup-.
~eseax = hup-.
~wærc *m.* pain in the hips.
hȳr *f.* hire, wages ; usury, interest.
hȳr|an, ~ian hire.
~geoht (*n.*) hired yoke of oxen.
~egiẹlda *m.* mercenary, hired servant.
~ling *m.* hireling *LN.*
~mann, hȳrig- *m.* hireling.
~oxa *m.* hired ox.
ge~ung *f.* hiring.
hyr|ian imitate.
~ing *f.* imitation.
hyra = hira.
hȳra *m.* hireling, servant.
hyrdel, *vE.* hyrþil *m.* hurdle.
hyre = hire.
hȳre-borg*, īe *m.* interest (on money).
hyrnan project [hyrne].
hyrn|e *f.* corner ; angle [horn].
~full angular.
~stān *m.* corner-stone.
hyrned|e horned ; having a projection.
~nebba horny-beaked.
hyrnen of horn [horn].
hyrnetu, *vE.* -ītu ; *L.* -et, -et(t)e, *pl.* -yttan *f.* hornet [horn].

hyrst(†), *vE. pl.* hryste *f.* ornament, jewel ; trappings, equipment, armour.
hyrst *m.* copse, wood.
~geard *m.* copse (?) Ct.
gehyrst *f.* ornament.
hyrstan adorn ; equip.
gehyrstan murmur *LN.*
hȳscan, hȳxan deride ; revile *w.* on *a.* [hūsc].
hyse†, *pl.* hyssas *m.* son ; youth ; man, warrior ‖ hisse, hoss- vineshoot Gl.
~beorþor *Pr. n.* bearing a son ; young man.
~berþling, ~byrding *f.* bearing a male child.
~cild *Pr. n.* male child.
~rinc *Pr. m.* man.
~wise *Pr. f.* the manner of youths.
hysp|an scorn, revile [hosp].
ge~endlic abominable.
~ing *f.* reviling.
~nes *f.* object of reproach.
hȳþ *f.* landing-place, harbour.
~giẹld *n.* port-due.
~lic of a harbour.
~weard† *m.* harbour-warden.
-hȳþ booty = hūþ.
~scip *n.* pirate-ship Gl.
gehȳþ convenient — naht ~es hæbbe no apparatus.
~lic convenient.
~lice *av.* comfortably (?).
~nes *f.* advantage.
hȳþan ravage, plunder.
hȳþelic convenient, suitable.
hȳþig.
~ian facilitate.
~ung *f.* advantage
hȳþþ *f.* benefit, advantage.
gehȳþþo *f.* subsistence, food.

I.

ia-, īa- = gea-, gēa-.

īacin(c)tus *m.* jacinth [*Lt.* hyacinthus].

ic, ig I.

icge-gold† *once.*

ī-dæges, ig- *av.* on the same day.

īdel I. empty; empty-handed; desolate, destitute *wg.*; useless, vain; unemployed, idle. II. *n.* frivolity; idleness; inattention, carelessness —on ~ in vain, to no purpose. ~georn lazy.

īdel-gield *n.*, ~offrung *f.* idolatry.

īdel|hende empty-handed; devoid *wg.* ~nes *f.* frivolity, folly; carelessness, inattention; uselessness; idleness — on ~se in vain. ~sprǣce talking idly.

ides *f.* virgin; †woman.

īdlian come to nothing, be useless.

īdol *nf.* idol [*Lt.*].

īe, see ēa.

īec|an increase; add [ēac]. ~end *m.*, ~estre *f.* increaser. ~nes *f.* increase.

īedisc*, ȳddisc (*n.*) furniture, household goods [ēad].

īeg *f.* island [ēa]. ~būend(e)† *m.* islander. ~clif, ecg-† *n.* sea-cliff. ~flota*, æg-† *m.* sailor. ~land *n.* island. ~strēam*, ēg-, ēh-† *m.* sea; river. ~weard*, æg-† *f.* watch by the sea (?).

īegoþ*, īg(e)oþ, īg(g)aþ *m.* island, *esp.* small island in river, eyot.

iėld|an *intr. and tr.* delay, dissimulate [eald]. ~end *m.* delayer *intr.* ~endlic dilatory. ~ing *f.* delay; dissimulation.

iėldcian = ėlcian delay.

iėlde† *pl.* men.

iėldest *spl.* of eald.

iėld(o) *f.* period, age (of the world); time of life, age; old age.

---

iėldr|a I. *cpv. of* eald. II. ~an *pl.* parents; ancestors.

iėlfe *pl.* of ælf elf.

iėlfen*, æ, e, y *f.* fairy [ælf].

iėlfetu, L. ylfet,t)e *f.* swan.

iėlfig* = ylfig chattering.

iėrfan inherit; demise, bequeath.

iėrf|e *n.* inheritance; property, possession; cattle. ~ebēc *fpl.* will. ~(e)cwealm *m.* cattle-plague. ~egedāl *n.* division of property. ~efirst *m.* legal delay before entering on inheritance. ~egeflit *n.* dispute about inheritance. ~hand *f.* administrator. ~elāf *f.* heirloom, inheritance; heir. ~eland *n.* heritable *or* inherited land. ~elēas without cattle. ~enuma *m.* heir. ~estōl† *m.* hereditary seat *or* dwelling.

iėrf(e)-weard *m.* heir, possessor. ~nes *f.* inheritance. ~ian inherit, possess. ~writend, ~writere *m.* testator. ~writend *m.* testator.

iėrfe|gewrit *n* will, testament.

iėrgan dishearten [earg].

iėrg(o) *f.* sluggishness, cowardice.

ier|lic angry [ierre]. ~scipe *m.* anger.

iėrman ill-treat, harass [earm].

iėrming, ea *m.* wretched one, poor wretch; pauper; little one.

iėrmþ(o) *f.* misery; poverty; bodily trouble, disease; crime.

iernan, *A.* eo; *prt.* arn, *A.* orn 3 run; flow (*of* river); turn *intr.*, grind (*of* mill) | ūp ge~ rise, grow (*of* plants) Bd.

geiernan 3 coagulate. *Cp.* gerinnan.

ierre I. *n.* anger. II. gone astray; perverse; angry. ~mōd angry, wild. ~þweorh*, yre- angry.

---

ierringa *av.* angrily.

iers|ian, eo be angry *w.* wiþ *a.*, on *a.*; make angry. ~igendlic passionate. ~ung *f.* anger.

iersinga *av.* angrily.

iėrþ, y, ea *f.* ploughing; crop, produce. ~land *n.* arable land. ~ling *m.* agriculturist, farmer, ploughman; a bird. ~tilia = eorþ-.

iesende = gesen entrails.

īeþ, ēaþ *cpv. of* ēaþe easily. ~bede exorable. ~begiéte easily obtained. ~bēne exorable. ~bylig, ~belig irritable, passionate. ~dǣde easy. ~fēre easy (road). ~fynde† easily found. ~georn amiable (?) Gl. ~giéte*, ~gete easily obtained, ready. ~hylde contented. ~lǣre docile. ~gesīene† easily seen. ~wielt easily turned.

īeþ|an lay waste, ravage; depopulate; kill. ~ung *f.* laying waste.

īepe† desolate, waste.

īeþ|e, ēaþe easy; indulgent, kind *wd.*; mild, not attended with hardship, easy (journey). *Cp.* ēaþe *av.* ~nes *f.* ease (of life), comfort; pleasure, satisfaction.

īeþelic, ēa easy || ēa- scanty, insignificant, weak. ~nes *f.* ease.

īeþelice *av.* easily; (treat subject) lightly.

īew|an, ēow(i)an *wda.* show, reveal [ēage].

īfegn = īflg.

ifig, ifegn *n.* ivy. ~bearo *n.* group of ivy-clad trees (?) Ct.

īfig|cropp(a) *m.* cluster of ivy-berries.

~lēaf *n.* ivy-leaf.

~tearo *n.*, -tara *m.* ivy-gum.

īfiht covered with ivy.

īl, ig(i)l *m.* hedgehog.

ilca same.

ilce *av.* — swā ~ in the same way; swā ~ swā in the same way as, as.

ile, y *m.*, *vE.* ill *n.* sole of foot; callosity.

ill = īle callosity.

illeroc|u*, -acu *f.* crapula.

ge~ad suffering from hot cockles, surfeited, crapulatus.

ilpen of an elephant [elpend, ylp].

imbe* = ymbe swarm of bees.

imberdling = inbyrdling.

imp|a, ~e *mf.* shoot, graft.

impian graft; *rfl.* be engaged in, *ptc.* associated with *w.* tō, on *d.*

in *rare in W. prp. w. a., d. (i.) of place and time* in, on, among, into, during, *also met.*

in- *A.* = on-.

in- *is sometimes written for* un- *through the confusion between* un- *and* on- = *A.* in-.

in-gebed† *once n.* heartfelt (?) prayer.

in-bend *mf.* internal fetter.

in-betȳnednes *f.* life of a recluse.

in-blāwan ɪ breathe on, ɪnspire (!).

in-boren native.

in-borg *m.* bail, security.

in-bryne *m.* fire (!).

in-bū|an inhabit (!).

~end *m.* inhabitant.

in-burg *f.* vestibule.

in-byrd|e born in master's house.

~(1)ing, im- *m.* slave born in master's house.

inc you two *a., d.*

inc|a ·*m.* cause of complaint, grudge; scruple, doubt; suspicion.

ge~fullian offend.

in-cempa *m.* soldier of the same company.

incer of you two.

in-cieg|an invoke (!).

~ung *f.* invocation (!).

incit you two *a.*

in-clēofa, -clyfa, i *m.* (inner) chamber; den, cave.

in-cniht *m.* house-servant.

in-cofa *m.* inner chamber; †breast, mind.

in-copu *f.* internal disease.

incund = innancund.

~līce *av.* inwardly.

~nes *f.* inward conviction; sincerity.

in-cūþ alien, strange.

~līce *av.* sadly.

in-dǣlan impart, infuse (!).

in-dīepan dip, immerse (!).

Indisc Indian.

in-dryhten† aristocratic, noble, magnificent.

in-dryhto† *f.* nobleness, glory.

in-eardian inhabit (!).

in-fær *n.* entering; place of entrance.

in-færeld *n.* entering; place of entrance, vestibule; interior.

in-fangen(e)-þēof *L.* jurisdiction over thieves within a certain space.

in-faru *f.* entering, invasion.

in-feoht, -fiht *n.* attack on person by inhabitant of the same house.

in-gefeoht *n.* civil war.

in-flēde full of water (*of* river).

in-gefolc† *n.* native race.

in-fōstor *n.* rearing *or* breeding at home.

in-frōd† very old *or* wise.

ing *the Runic letter* ng.

in(n)-gang *m.* entering; right of access; entrance-fee.

in-genga† *m.* invader.

in-gēoting *f.* pouring in.

in-gyte *m.* infusion.

in-heord *f.* herd of the lord and kept on his estate.

in-here *m.* home-army, native army.

in-hīernes *f.* possession.

in(n)-hīred *n.* household.

~mann, *lN.* innheard- *m.* member of retinue, soldier.

in-hīwa, -hīga *m.* member of household *or* convent, &c.

in-hold loyal.

in-gehrif *n.* womb.

in-gehygd, -hȳd *nf.* mind, thoughts; conscience; understanding, intelligence, knowledge; import (of what is said).

~nes *f.* intention.

in-īeddisc*, ē (*n.*) household furniture.

in(n)-ielfe, inifli *n.* intestines; womb.

in-ierfe *n.* household goods.

in·innan = on-.

in-lād *f.* right of inland passage; entrance-fee.

in-lagian 'inlaw,' restore (an outlaw) to legal rights.

in-land *n.* demesne land, land retained by the lord instead of being let out.

in-laþiend *m.* inviter (!).

in-lēgan *A.* inflame = *on·līē-gan (?).

in-lend|e native, of natives, of one's own country.

~a *m.* native.

~isc native.

in-lic internal; native.

in-līce *av.* internally; thoroughly; sincerely.

in-lichamung *f.* incarnation *lN.*

in-mǣþl(a)e *f.* recklessness *vE.* Gl. *Cp.* onmēdla.

in-mearg once *pl.* ~a marrow Gl.

in-mēde close to one's heart, important.

in-gemynd† *nf.* mind; remembrance.

in-gemynde† remembered.

inn *n.* house; chamber; quartering oneself (*of* soldiers).

inn *av.* in — on *wa.* in to. ~ tō in to: þā geatu ~ tō him. *Cp.* intō.

inn|ian enter; take up one's quarters, lodge.

~ung *f.* contents; revenue.

geinnian admit, receive (into house, church), entertain hospitably; include; fill; supply (loss).

inna womb *lN.*

inn-ādl*, ina- *f.* internal disease.

innan *prp. w. a., d., g.* in, into; from within (!); *of time* at.

innan, ~e, inne *av.* within, inside — ~ on *prp. wd.* inside.

innan-bordes *av.* at home (as opposed to abroad).

innan-burgware *pl.* townspeople.

innan-cund, inne-, in- internal, inward; inner (thoughts); earnest, thorough. *Cp.* incund.

innan-weard, in(ne)- I. internal, interior of, depths of; earnest; thorough — ~ *n.*, þæt ~e intes-

tines. II. *av.* within. *Cp.* in-weard.

inn-āwrīting *f.* inscription (!).

inne- = innan-.

innemest, *see* inn|era, ~or.

innera, inra *cpv.* inner; *spl.* innemest inmost.

in-nīwian renew (!).

innor *av. cpv.* more within; *spl.* innemest.

inn-orf *n.* household goods.

innoþ *m.* interior; interior of body, intestines; stomach; womb.

~tīedernes *f.* weakness of intestines.

~wund *f.* wound in the intestines.

in-gerec (*n.*) tumult Bd.

in-rēcels *m.* incense (!).

in-scēawere *m.* inspector (!).

in-scēawung *f.* inspection (!).

in-segel *n.* seal, signet. *Cp.* insigle [*Lt.* sigillum].

insegl|ian seal, seal up.

~ung *f.* sealing, seal.

in-geseted inserted.

in-set|tan institute (!).

~nes *f.* regulation (!).

in-sigle *n.* seal [insegel].

in-siht *f.* narrative, epitome.

in-sittende sitting within.

in-smoh (?) *m.* slough, what is cast off.

in-spinn (*n.*) spindle.

in-stæp|e, e I. *m.* entrance — ~es *av.* instantly. II. *av.* instantly.

in-stand|an 2 be at hand (!).

~endlic present, daily (bread).

in-gestealdt *n.* household goods.

in·stede, -styde *av.* at once.

in-stice *m.* internal stitch (pain).

in-stihtian arrange (!).

in-swān *m.* he who has charge of the lord's swine.

in-geswell *n.* internal swelling.

in-swōg|an 1 invade (!).

~ennes *f.* invasion.

in-tinga *m., lN.* inþing, *lM.* inting(a) affair, business ; cause of complaint ;' cause — for his

intingan because of him, for his sake [in, þing].

in-tō *prp. wd.* into.

in-trahtnung *f.* explanation (!).

in-gepanc *nm.* thought(s), mind; intention.

in-gepēod† *f.* nation.

in-picce very thick *or* coarse.

in-pīnen (*f.*) house-servant (?) Gl.

in-wærc, -wræc *m.* internal pain.

in-wæte *f.* internal humour (of body).

in-weard = innan-.

~lic internal.

~līce *av.* inwardly; earnestly, deeply, thoroughly.

in-geweaxen implanted.

in-weorc *n.* indoor work.

in-werod *n.* body of retainers, household.

in-widd, -witt, -wit deceitful, malicious, wicked.

in-widda *m.* adversary.

in-gewinn *n.* civil war.

in-wīse *once f.* condiment.

in-wit, -wid *n.* guile, deceit; malice ; evil.

~gecynd† *n.* evil nature.

~feng† *m.* hostile grasp.

~flān† *m.* treacherous shaft.

~full deceitful, malicious, evil.

~giest† *m.* evil guest.

~giren† *n.* treacherous snare.

~hlemm† *m.* gash of malice.

~hrōf† *m.* evil roof.

~nett† *n.* evil net.

~nīþ† *m.* enmity.

~rūn† *f.* evil counsel.

~scear† (?) *m.* slaughter.

~searo† *n.* treachery.

~sorg† *f.* sorrow.

~spell† *n.* tale of evil.

~stæf† *m.* wickedness.

~þanc† *m.* evil thought *or* purpose.

~wrāsen† *f.* evil chain.

in-gewitnes *f.* knowledge, conscience.

in-wræc = in-wærc.

in-wrītere *m.* private (?) secretary Gl.

in-wrīting *f.* inscription (!).

in-wund *f.* internal wound.

in-wunenes *f.* persistence.

io- = geo-.

ioc = geoc.

īor† a river animal; *the Runic letter* īo.

Īras *mpl.* Irish.

Īr(a)-land *n.* Ireland.

Īring — ~es weg Milky Way.

is is.

īs *n.* ice; *the Runic letter* i.

~gebind† *n.* bond of ice.

~geblæd *n.* chilblain (?).

~ceald† ice-cold.

~mere† *m.* frozen lake.

īsen, īsern, īren I. *n.* iron, steel; iron *or* steel implement ; †sword; ordeal. II. *aj.* of iron, steel.

~bend† *m.* chain.

~byrne† *f.* steel corslet.

~fetor *f.* iron fetter.

~græg iron-grey.

~heard iron-hard.

~hearde *f.* black centaury (a plant).

~here† *m.* armed host.

~hyrst fitted with iron.

~gelōma *m.* iron implement.

~ordāl *n.* ordeal with hot iron.

~ōre *f.* iron mine Gl.

~panne, -a *fm.* frying-pan.

~scofl *f.* iron shovel.

~scūr† *f.* shower of iron missiles.

~smiþ *m.* blacksmith.

~swāt *m.* iron dross (?).

~tang *f.* snuffers.

~þrēat† *m.* armed troop.

~wyrhta *m.* blacksmith.

isend = gesen entrails.

isig icy.

~fepera† icy-winged.

īsiht icy.

i-sīpes *av.* at once.

isn|ian — ~od iron-clad.

īu = gēo.

Iūdē|as *mpl.* Jews.

~isc Jewish.

īw, ēow, ēoh *m.* yew.

~berige *f.* yew-berry.

K = C.

L.

lā *interj.* oh! .ah! — **lā lēof!** O sir!; *intens.*: **hū lā ne wurpe wē þrȳ cnihtas intō þām fȳre?** þā cwæþ ic, hwæt is þæt lā? (then). **þæt lā wæs fæger** (indeed).

lāc *nf.* joyous activity, sport, game; †contest, battle | gift; offering, sacrifice; Epiphany: **fram ~um oþ sumormæssan** | booty† | message (?) | medicine.

~dǣd *f.* munificence.

~giéfa† *m.* liberal giver.

~lic sacrificial.

~sang *m.* offertory Gl.

gelāc† *n.* commotion (*of* sea, storms) — **sweorda~** battle; crowd.

lācan I *prt.* **lēolc, lēc** *intr.* move quickly *or* intermittently (*of* birds, flame, waves); play — †**daroþum ~** fight; †**wordum ~** sing, modulate.

gelācan I — **on hīe gelēc þæt hīe wunnon . .** persuaded them to . .

lācian present with a gift Gl.

lācn|ian, & treat medically, dress (wound); cure [**lǣce**].

~igendlic medical, surgical.

~ung *f.* medical treatment; cure; medicine.

lactuc|a *f.*, **-as** (?) lettuce [*Lt.*].

lacu *f.* stream Ct.; lake (?) [**lęccan**].

lād *f.* way, course; journey; carrying, conveying (goods); means of living, sustenance [**līþan**].

~mann *m.* guide, leader.

~rinc *m.* (king's) messenger (?).

~scipe *m.* leadership.

lād *f.* excuse; defence against a charge; clearing oneself from an accusation.

gelād† *n.* way, course — **dēop ~** ocean.

lādian find excuses for *w. a. of person or thing*; excuse, let off; *rfl. wag.* clear oneself of blame or

a legal charge: **~ hine þæs** (be **āþe, mid ordāle**), **~ hine þæt he nyste . .** prove that he did not know.

lād|igendlic excusable.

~ung *f.* excuse; clearing oneself, exculpation.

ladteow = **lāttēow.**

lǣ (*n.*) head of hair.

lǣccan *prt.* **lǣhte** seize, catch, arrest; **forþ ge~** carry off.

lǣce *m.* physician; leech.

~bōc *f.* medical book.

~cræft *m.* (art of) medicine; remedy, medicine; prescription.

~cræftig skilled in medicine.

~cynn† *n.* race of physicians.

~dōm *m.* remedy, medicine; salvation.

~dōmlic salutary.

~dōmnes *f.* plaster.

~feoh *n.* physician's fee.

~finger *m.* fourth finger.

~hūs *n.* hospital.

~sealf *f.* salve, plaster.

~seax *n.* surgical knife.

~wyrt *f.* drug; rib-wort.

lǣcnian = **lācnian.**

lǣd|an lead (*of* guide, general, road); carry, convey, bring; place, put — **on lyft ~** lift up | bring forth, produce | mark the bounds of land: **landgemǣre ~** | pass, lead (life); perform, do (praise) || *intr.* †**tānum ~** flourish with twigs.

~end *m.* bringer.

ge~endlic*, **~enlic** malleable.

~nes *f.* production, bringing forth Bd.

lǣd|an* excuse.

~end *m.* excuser, apologist.

Lǣden, *later* **ę, ȳ** [*through infl. of* **līeden**] I. *n.* Latin (language). II. *aj.* Latin. *Orig. perhaps the form* **lęden** *was used only as an adj.* [*Lt.* latinum].

~bōc *f.* Latin book.

Lǣden|isc Latin.

~nama *m.* Latin noun.

~gereord *n.* Latin.

~sprǣc *f.* Latin.

~stæf *m.* Latin letter.

~geþēode *n.* Latin.

~ware *mpl.* Romans.

~word *n.* Latin word.

lǣfan *wda.* leave, bequeath, not take away || *intr.* remain over, be left [**lāf**].

lǣfel, ę *m.* cup, bowl.

lǣfer *f.* rush, bulrush; thin plate of metal.

~bedd *n.* place where rushes grow, bed of rushes.

lǣg *prt. of* **licgan.**

lǣl *f.*, **~a** *m.* twig, whip || mark of whip, weal, bruise.

~(i)an become black and blue.

lǣmen of clay, earthen [**lām**].

lǣn *f.* lending, loan; thing lent; †gift; benefit; temporary grant, lease (of land) [**lēon**].

~dagas† *mpl.* transitory days of life, lifetime.

~land *n.* land granted on lease.

~(e)lic transitory.

lǣn|an *wda.* lend; grant; lease.

~end *m.* lender, creditor.

~endlic transitory.

~ere *m.* lender, creditor.

lǣne lent; leased; temporary, transitory; frail, infirm; frivolous, sinful.

lǣpe-wince, hlēape- *f.* lapwing (bird).

lǣpeldre *f.* dish.

lǣppa, a *m.* tag, end, skirt; lobe (of ear, liver); district.

lǣr-gedēfe (?) once† fit to be learned.

lǣr|an teach *w. a. of pers. or thing, wda., rarely waa.*: **~de him þæs þing**; **~de hīe on lifes weg, tō fulwihte** brought them by his teaching to . . | educate — **gelǣred** learned, clerical | exhort, advise,

persuade : ~de hine þæt hē for-lēte.

gelǣrednes *f.* learning, skill.

lǣrestre *f.* teacher.

lǣring* *f.* teaching.

~mǣden *n.* (female) pupil.

~mann *m.* disciple.

lǣr|e*, gelǣr empty, hungry.

~nes *f.* emptiness (of stomach).

lǣrest = lǣst.

lǣrig, *lǣrg† border (of shield).

lǣs *f.*, *g.* lǣs(w)e pasture.

lǣs *f.* letting (of blood), bleeding.

lǣs less, *see* lȳtel.

~boren of lower birth.

lǣsian = lǣswian.

lǣsest = lǣst.

lǣssa *cpv. of* lȳtel.

lǣst *once f.* boot Gl.

~wyrhta *m.* shoemaker.

~e *f.* (shoemaker's) last Gl.

lǣst *spl. of* lȳtel.

lǣst|an *wd.* follow; help ‖ *tr.* carry out, perform, do ; furnish ; pay ‖ *intr.* continue, last, suffice [lāst].

~end *m.* doer.

lǣswe, *see* lǣs.

lǣswian, lǣsian pasture, feed (sheep, &c.) *intr. and tr.*

lǣt, *spl.* A. ~est, ~(e)mest delaying, behindhand ; sluggish *wg.*, slow ; late.

~byrd *f.* delayed birth.

~hȳdig dull-minded.

~lice *av.* slowly.

~nes *f.* delay ; slowness (of lapse of time).

~rǣde deliberate, slow.

~sum (year) late (for crops) L.

lǣt|an 1 b *prt.* lēt, A. lēort leave : ~ hine þǣr ; hine dēadne ~ ; leave behind ; bequeath ; depart from, leave | ān ~ give up (the money, the attempt). aweg ~ let go, send away ; refrain from, ignore. tō gīemlēaste ~ neglect, be indifferent to ‖ make to go, place, put *gen. met.* : blōd ~ bleed ; ~ hit of gemynde dismiss it from the mind ; ~ hine ūp put him ashore | hand over, deliver up : lēt hī tō him, lēt hī him tō handa ‖ admit : ~ þā riht-wīsan intō heofenan rīce ; hine inn ~ | permit : hīe þǣr sittan lēt ; God lǣtt us costian be

tempted | cause (to happen), make : God lēt hī befeallan on þæt ēce fȳr ; God lēt hine frīgne left him free-will ; God lēt hine him (*rfl.*) swā lēofne þæt . . loved him so | grant (territory to a vassal), let (land on lease), *always w. tō of pers.* ‖ behave, be in a certain state of mind : ~ uncūþ-līce wiþ hine be unfriendly ; ēaþelīce ~ ymbe þæt take it easily | think : leohtlīce ~ ymbe þæt think lightly of ; lēton þæt hit micel unrǣd wǣre thought it bad policy ; hī hī selfe lēton for hēane thought themselves of no account ; hī ~aþ þæt tō wær-scipe þæt hī mægen . . think it clever | pretend : lǣtt swelce hē wǣre . . pretends to be (*or* thinks he is . .) | assert : hī ~aþ þæt menn mōten . . hī bēotlīce ~aþ þæt hī mægen . . boast ‖ *intr.* ~ of *d.* give up (property). hȳþe þe wē fram lēton set sail from. hē nō be þǣm ānum lēt, ac . . did not stop there (content himself). lēton tō rǣde þæt hī woldon . . determined after consultation.

gelǣt, ~e *n.* junction of roads.

lǣtt, *pl.* ~a, latta *f.* lath.

lǣttewestre *f.* guide [lǣttēow].

lǣþ (*n.*) division of land, district containing several hundreds.

lǣþan hate ; cause to shun ; revile [lāþ].

lǣþþo, lǣþo *f.* hatred, malice ; injury, wrong.

lǣw|an betray.

~end *m.* traitor.

~finger*, lēaw- *m.* forefinger.

lǣw|an, ~e, A. lēga *m.* betrayer, traitor.

lǣwede, ēa lay(man) [*Lt.* laicus].

lāf *f.* remnant, remains, remaining : wæs tō ~e remained — †hamera~ sword ; heirloom, legacy ; widow [-līfan].

lafian lave, wash, pour.

lagian ordain (laws) [lagu].

lagen *ptc. of* lēan.

lāgon *prt. of* licgan.

lagu *m.* sea, flood, water† ; *the Runic letter* l.

~cræftig nautical.

~fæsten(n) *n.* sea.

lagu|fæþm *m.* embrace of waters.

~flōd *m.* sea, stream, water(s).

~lād *f.* sea-way, sea.

~mearh *m.* ship.

~sīþ *m.* sea-journey.

~strǣt *f.* sea-road, sea.

~strēam *m.* sea, river, water.

~swimmend *m.* fish.

lagu L. *f.*, once *npl.* (?) law ; district (in which certain laws prevail), *esp. in* Dena ~ Danelag [*Scand.* log = *lagu *npl.*].

gelagu† *npl.* extent, surface (of sea) [licgan].

lah- = lag- law-.

~breca *m.* law-breaker.

~brecende lawless, impious.

~bryce *m.* breach of law.

~cēap *m.* payment for re-entry into lost legal rights.

~lic lawful.

~līce *av.* according to law.

~mann *m.* law-man, lawyer.

~riht *n.* legal right.

~slit, -tt, -t(t)e (*n.*) fine for breach of (Danish) law.

~wita *m.* lawyer.

lām *n.* clay, earth.

~fæt *n.* vessel of clay, the body.

~pytt, ~sēaþa *m.* clay-pit.

~wyrhta *m.* potter.

lam|a *aj. m.*, *f.* lame ; paralytic.

~byrd *f.* imperfect birth.

lamb, A. o, e, lombor ; *pl.* ~ru, L. ~, A. lombor, lomberu lamb.

~es cerse a plant.

lamprede *f.* lamprey [*Lt.* lampreda].

lān- = lǣn-.

land *n.* land, terra firma ; country, province, district ; country *as opposed to town* ; (cultivated) land, estate.

~ādl *f.* = hland- (?).

~ælf *f.* land-elf.

~āgend *m.* native.

~āgende owning land.

~ār *f.* landed property, estate.

~begang *m.* dwelling in a country.

~begenga *m.* cultivator of land, inhabitant.

~bōc *f.* charter in which land is granted.

~brǣce *f.* ploughing up fallow land.

~būend *m.* cultivator of land ; native.

~būend *f.* colony, settlement.

land|būende dwelling, native.
~būnes f. settlement, colony.
~cēap m. tax paid when land was bought.
~fæsten(n) n. naturally strong military position.
~feoh n. recognitory rent for land.
~fierd f. land-army.
~folc n. people of the country.
~fruma† m. king.
~gafol n. rent of land.
~hæbbende owning land; ruling a country.
~hæfen f. landed property.
~here m. land-army; native army.
~hlāford m. landowner, lord of the manor; ruler of a country.
~hredding f. redemption of land.
~gehwerf m. exchange of land.
~lagu f. law of the district.
~lēas without land.
~lēode pl., ~lēod f. people, natives; country.
~lyre m. loss of land.
~gemaca m. neighbour.
~gemǣre n. boundary.
~mann m. native.
~mearc f. boundary.
~gemierce n. boundary.
~openung f. breaking up fallow land.
~rǣden(n) f. local ordinance.
~rest† f. grave.
~rīca m. local magnate, lord of the manor.
~rīce n. estate; territory, region, continent.
~riht n. law of the land; legal rights of natives of the country; legal obligation connected with land or estate.
~sǣta m. colonist.
~scaru f. land, country; boundary.
~gesceaft† f. creation coll.
~sceap n. land.
~scipe† m. region, country [Old-Saxon].
~scoru f. piece of land Ct.
~seten f. estate; occupation of land.
~sepla m. tenant vL.
~sidu m. custom of the country, something habitual.
~sittende occupying land.
~sōcn f. search for land (dwelling-place).
~spēd f. landed property.

land|spēdig rich in land.
~splott m. plot of ground, small piece of land.
~stede m. land, country.
~stycce n. piece of land; tract, country.
~waru† f. people of a country, country.
~weard† m. king.
~wela† m. wealth of the earth, earthly possessions.
~geweorc† n. fortress.
~gewierpe n. mound (?) Ct.
gelanda m. fellow-countryman, kinsman.
landefen f. proportion of land vL. = *land-andefn.
gelandod having estates.
lan|e, ~u wk. f. lane; street.
lang cpv. lengra, spl. lengest long, tall. ~a frīgedæg Good Friday.
~fǣre lasting, durable; advanced (age).
~fērnes f. long duration.
~first m. long space of time.
~ieldo f. advanced age.
~līce av. for a long time.
~līf(e), cpv. lenglīfra (!) long-lived.
lang-mōd patient, long-suffering.
~līce av. patiently.
~nes f. long-suffering.
lang|nes f. length.
~sceaft having a long shaft.
~scip n. war-ship.
~strang patient (!).
~gestrēon† n. long-accumulated treasure.
langsum long, prolonged, lasting, tedious.
~līce av. for a long time.
~nes f. length.
lang|swēorede, ȳ long-necked.
~twidig† granted for a long time, lasting.
gelang at hand, attainable, dependent on, result of w. æt, on.
langian grow long (of days) | impers. w. a. desire, long for; feel tedium or discontent | summon | belong.
langung f. delay; desire, longing; tedium, weariness; grief.
~hwīl† f. time of longing or tedium.
lange av., cpv. leng, spl. lengest for a long time — (swā) leng

swā swīþor the longer the more | expressing extent, quantity: swā ~ swā . . swā ~ correl. to the extent which . . to that extent.
langoþ m. longing, desire; unsatisfied desire, discontent, tedium.
lann† (f.) fetter, bond.
lapian lick, lap up, sup (up liquid with bread).
lār f. what is taught, learning, doctrine, science; narrative; cunning (?) | act of teaching; exhortation, advice, instigation.
~bisn f. example.
~bōc f. book of instruction.
~cræft m. science.
~cwide m. precept, doctrine.
~hlystend m. catechumen.
~hūs n. school.
~lēast, ~līest f. want of knowledge; want of instruction.
~lic instructive, edifying; under instruction, learning.
~smiþ† m. teacher, sage.
~spell n. sermon, homily.
~swice m. deception.
~wita m. learned man.
lārēow, lN. lāruw, m. teacher, pedagogue, master; preacher [lār, þēow].
~dōm m. office of teacher; ecclesiastical authority or office.
~lic of a teacher.
~setl n. teacher's seat, pulpit.
laser (m.) tares, corn-cockle.
lāst, ǣ m. sole of foot (lǣst) | footprint, track : (him) on ~e behind (him). on ~ after, in pursuit; (look) back — on ~ faran return. ~ weardian remain behind; follow. ~as lecgan travel, wander | d. ~e, ~um wg. in the manner of : brȳde ~e as a bride, wreccan ~um as an exile, in exile.
~weard m. pursuer; successor.
~word† n. after-word, posthumous fame.
gelāst n. fulfilment; duty, due.
~full helpful.
lāt-tēah f. guiding-rein [lād].
latian be slow; be sluggish or torpid; delay wg. [læt].
lata aj. (m.), f. procrastinating, late wg.
late av. slowly; late: at last.
lāttēow, lād-, ǣ, -þēow, lātēow

m. guide; leader, general [lād, þēow].

lāttēowdōm *m.* guidance, leadership.

lāþ I. *aj. wd.* hostile : ne lēof ne~ neither friend nor foe; hated, unpopular; hateful to, noxious; grievous, unpleasant — him wæs ~ tō āmyrrenne he was unwilling to. II. *n.* injury, offence; what is unpleasant, pain.

~bite† *m.* wound.

~lēas harmless, innocent.

~lic hateful, unpleasant, horrible.

~līce *av.* hatefully, grievously, horribly.

~genīþla† *m.* enemy.

~scipe *m.* hardship, painful position.

~searo† *n.* hostile device.

~sīþ† *m.* hateful journey.

~spell *n.* bad news.

~getēona† *m.* enemy.

~trēow† *n.* hateful tree.

lāþ-wende hostile; pernicious.

~mōd hostile.

lāþ|weorc† *n.* evil *or* hostile work.

~gewinna† *m.* enemy.

gelāþ hostile.

lāþian invite, summon : hē hine him on fultum ~ode called upon him to help him.

(ge)~ung *f.* invitation, calling; congregation, church.

lāþian be hateful *wd.*

lāþe *av.* with enmity; in detestation.

lāþettan hate *wa.*; be hateful *wd.*

laur, lawer (*m.*) laurel [*Lt.*].

~bēam *m.* laurel.

~berige *f.* berry of laurel.

~trēow *n.* laurel.

lāwerce *f.* lark.

lēa, *see* **lēah** meadow.

lēan 2, *also wk., prt.* lōg, lēade *w. a. of pers. or thing, wda.* blame : hī him þone sīþfæt lōgon blamed him for the journey, hē him lōh þæt hē hæfde . . for having; find fault with, disapprove.

lēac *n.* leek; garlic.

~blæd *n.* leek-leaf.

~cerse *f.* nasturtium.

~tūn, lēhtūn *m.* kitchen-garden.

~tūn-weard *m.* gardener.

~weard *m.* gardener.

---

lēad *n.* lead; cauldron, kitchen-copper.

~gedelf *n.* lead-mine.

~gota *m.* plumber.

~stæf *m.* loaded stick, scourge Gl.

~gewihte *n.* 'lead-weight,' a scale of weight.

lēaden of lead.

lēaf, (ge)~e *f.* permission, leave; excuse.

lēaf *n.* leaf (of tree); leaf (of book).

~helmig having a leafy top.

~scead† *n.* place shaded by foliage.

~wyrm *m.* caterpillar.

lēaf-leoht easy.

gelēaf leafy.

gelēaf|a, lēafa *m. w.* tō, on *a.* belief, faith, trust.

~full believing, full of faith.

~fulnes *f.* belief.

~hlystend *m.* catechumen Gl.

~lēas unbelieving.

~lēasnes, ~lēast *f.* unbelief.

~lic credible.

~sum credible; faithful.

lēafnes *f.* permission.

~word† *n.* password.

lēag *f.* lye, ashes and water for washing.

lēagung *once f.* falsehood [lēogan].

lēah *f., d.* lēage, *m., d.* lēa meadow, field.

lēah-tūn = lēac-.

leahte *prt. of* leccan.

leahtor *m.* vice, sin; bodily defect, disease.

~cwide† *m.* opprobrious words.

~full vicious.

~lēas faultless.

~līce *av.* wickedly.

leahtr|ian blame, find fault with; accuse; revile; corrupt, vitiate.

~ung *f.* blaming, detraction.

leahtroc, -ic, leactrog, lectric *m.* lettuce [*Lt.* lactuca].

lēan *n.* reward, requital; gift; pay, wages.

~giefa *m.* recompenser.

lēanian reward, requite *wda.*

lēap *m.* basket; weel (for catching fish); a measure; trunk (of the body).

lēas I. devoid of, without *wg.*; sham, false, feigned; untruthful, false (witness); incorrect, faulty;

---

worthless, vain. II. *n.* false-hood.

lēas-bregd, ~brēd I. *m.* deceit, trick. II. deceitful, lying.

~nes *f.* deceit.

~ende deceitful.

lēas|cræft *m.* deception.

~ferht*, -y false, deceitful Gl.

~ferþnes *f.* levity, folly.

~giélp *n.* vainglory.

~lic sham.

~līce *av.* deceptively; incorrectly.

~licettan dissemble.

~licettung *f.* dissimulation.

~mōdnes *f.* inconstancy.

~nes *f.* falsehood; levity.

~ōleccung *f.* cajolery.

~sagol mendacious.

~spanung *f.* enticement.

~spell *n.* false story.

~spellung *f.* empty talk.

~tyhtan entice, seduce.

~tyhtung *f.* enticement.

~gewitnes *f.* false witness.

lēas|ian tell lies.

~ere *m.* liar; hypocrite; buffoon.

lēasung *f.* falsehood: deception; hypocrisy; artifice; frivolity.

~spell *n.* false statement, idle fable.

lēasettan pretend, feign; be a hypocrite.

lēaþor (*n.*) lather.

~wyrt *f.* soap-wort.

lēaw-finger = læw-.

leax *m.* salmon.

lēc *m.* looking at, sight [lōcian].

lecc|an, *prt.* le(a)hte wet; water, irrigate [lacu].

~ing *f.* irrigation.

lecgan *prt.* lēgde, lēde lay, put, *also met.* lāstas ~ go. ~ on *a.* put on; impose (taxes); commission with (an errand). on ~ *wd.* accuse of. (þider) inn ~ assign (lands) | lay (eggs) | bury | lower (ship's mast) | kill || *intr.* go : him on lāst ~ pursue.

lecþa *m.* leak *or* lowest part of ship (?) Gl.

lēde = lēgde *prt. of* lecgan.

leden = læden.

lēf, ē† I. infirm, diseased, ill; in bad condition (*of* ship). II. *once* (*n.*) damage, harm.

lēfan*, ie [*error*!] — *ptc.* gelēfed weak; old.

lēfung f. paralysis.
gelēfenscipe m. permission IN.
left weak = *lyft.
legde, prt. of lecgan.
legen, ptc. of licgan.
leger n. lying ; lying ill ; disease ; death-bed ; death | place of lying, lair, couch, bed ; burial-place, grave — clǣne ~ consecrated grave.
~bǣre ill.
~bedd n. couch ; sick-bed ; grave.
~fǣst ill.
~stōw f. burial-place, cemetery.
~tēam m. sexual intercourse.
~wīte n. fine for fornication.
geleger.
~gield n. lupercalia Gl.
~od confined to bed.
legie f. legion [Lt. legio].
lelopre f. a plant.
lemian lame ; cripple ; tame, break (horse) [lama].
lemp-healt limping.
lempedu f. lamprey [Lt. lampreda].
lempitu f. dish vE.
lencten, lengten I. m. spring ; Lent. II. aj. of Lent.
~ādl f. (tertian) fever.
~bryce m. breach of Lenten fast.
~dagas mpl. Lent.
~eorþe f. earth ploughed in the spring.
~fæsten n. Lenten fast.
~hǣto f. spring heat.
~lic of spring ; of Lent.
~sufl n. Lent food.
~tīd f. spring ; Lent.
~tīma m. spring.
~tīme of spring.
~wuce f. week in Lent.
lendan go ; arrive || tr. endow with land [land].
lenden|u npl. loins.
~bān n. loin-bone.
~brǣde f. loin.
~rēaf n. apron.
~wǣrc m. pain in the loins, kidney disease.
leng av. longer, see lang.
~līfra more long-lived.
~togra [=~togen-?] more prolix L., Gl.
lengan tr. prolong (action) ; delay ; disregard || intr. spread, extend ; belong.

lenge belonging to, having affinity with.
gelenge belonging to ; addicted to wd.
lengest, see lang, lange.
leng(o) f. of space length ; height, stature | of time length.
lengra, see lang.
lengten = lencten.
lengþ(o) f. length [lang].
lent (f.) lentil Gl. [Lt. lentem].
lēo mf., d. ~n, ~ne, ~nan lion. ~n fōt a plant [Lt. leo].
lēon, (hē) lihþ, n W. līþ, prt. lāh, ēa, ptc. ligen, A. imper. līh 7 lend ; grant.
lēod † m. king.
lēod m. fine for manslaughter LL.
lēod f. nation L. Formed from lēode by an. of þēod.
gelēod m. fellow-countryman.
lēodan 7 sprout, grow ; be descended (from).
lēoda m. fellow-countryman.
lēod|e, L. ~a pl. people ; soldiers ; country.
~bealo † n. harm to a nation.
~biscop m. bishop of a district.
~burg † f. city.
~gebyrga † m. chief, king.
~cyning † m. king.
~fruma † m. chief, patriarch, king.
~geard † m. territory, country.
~gield n. fine for manslaughter.
~gryre † m. general terror.
~hata m. tyrant, persecutor.
~hete † m. hostility.
~hryre † m. fall of a nation.
~mǣg † m. kinsman.
~mǣgen † n. flower of a nation ; body of warriors ; power, virtue.
~mearc † f. territory, country.
~riht n. law of the land.
~rūne f. sorceress.
~scaru † f. nation.
~scaþa † m. public enemy.
~scipe m. nation ; country.
~stefn † m. race, family, people.
~þēaw m. custom of a country.
~geþyncþ f. rank.
~weard † m. government.
~wer † m. man of a country.
~werod † n. assembled nation.
~gewinn † n. strife, war.
~wita m. sage.
~wynn † f. home joy.
lēof I. aj. wd. beloved, dear ;

friendly ; pleasant — him wæs ~re þæt hīe fuhten or him wæs ~re tō feohtanne þonne .. they preferred. II. interj. sir !
lēof|lic beloved ; pleasant ; precious ; beautiful.
~līce av. lovingly, kindly ; gladly, willingly.
~spell † n. pleasant news.
~tǣl(e) kind ; acceptable, pleasant, popular.
~wende kind, amiable ; acceptable ; pleasant, popular.
gelēof consanguineous, related.
leofian = libban.
lēofian be pleasant wd.
lēog|an 7 make incorrect statement (without necessarily implying an intention to deceive) : hē lēag mid þǣre race ; hē lēag be þām fȳre ; him man on liehþ he is credited with (good or bad) qualities which he does not possess ; deceive wd. (of hope).
~ere m. liar ; false witness.
leoht n. light ; (eye)sight ; candle, light.
~bǣre bright ; splendid, glorious.
~bēamede having bright rays.
~berend(e) m. Lucifer.
~berende luminous.
~brǣdnes f. manifestation, display.
~fæt n. lantern, lamp.
~fruma † m. creator of light.
~īsern n. candlestick.
~lēas without light.
~lic shining.
~sāwend m. author of light.
~scēawigend m. light-seeing.
~gescot n. contribution for church lights.
leoht bright ; clear ; beautiful ; easy to understand, clear ; cheerful.
leoht not heavy, light ; agile ; not oppressed, comfortable, tolerable ; slight, light (punishment)
~lic unimportant.
~līce av. slightly ; lightly, gently ; carelessly.
~mōd easy of temper.
~mōdnes f. levity.
leohtan = liehtan.
leoht|ian become light, dawn ; †shine, give light wd.
~ing f. lighting (candle) or giving light Gl.

leohte *av.* brightly; (understand) clearly.

leohte *av.* easily; without discomfort.

lēolc, *prt. of* lācan.

lēom|a *m.* ray of light, radiance. ge~od having rays of light.

lēona *m.* lion [lēo].

lēor|an, *A.*, *ptc.* ~ed, *once* loren depart, pass away *of place and time*; die.

~ende, ge~endlic transitory.

~(ed)nes, ge- *f.* departure; vision; death.

leorn|ian learn; think out, devise; study; read. [*From* *leonian *by infl. of* lǣran.]

~ere *m.* pupil, disciple; reader; learned man, scholar.

~igende docile (mind).

leornung *f.* act of learning, study, going to school; reading.

~cild *n.* pupil.

~cniht *m.* pupil, disciple.

~cræft *m.* learning, scholarship.

~hūs *n.* school.

~mann *m.* (male or female) pupil, student.

lēort, *prt. of* lǣtan.

geleoso, *pl. of* *gelise study.

lēoþ *n.* song; poem.

~cræft *m.* art of poetry, metre; poem.

~cræftig skilled in poetry.

~cwide *m.*, ~giédding *f.* poem.

~lic in verse.

~sang *m.* poem; metre, poetry.

~weorc *n.* poetry.

~wīse *f.* poetical form, poetry.

~word† *n.* word in a poem.

~wrence *m.* poem.

~wyrhta *m.* poet.

lēoþian† sing, recite poetry ‖ *intr.* sound.

leoþu-, leoþo-, liþe-, liþu-, leoþe-. *Cp.* liþ.

~bend *mf.* bond, fetter.

~bieg(e) flexible; meek, humble.

~cæge† *f.* key of limbs.

~cræft *m.* bodily agility, skill.

~cræftig† agile.

~fæst† firm, skilled (?).

~lic bodily.

~sār *n.* pain in joints.

~sierce† *f.* corslet.

~wāc flexible; agile.

~wācian mitigate.

leoþu|wǣcan *tr. and intr.* soften, assuage, grow calm.

leoþo-rūn†, eo† [*or* *lēoþr-] *f.* advice (?).

lēow *n.*, *pl.* ~er thigh, ham.

lēowe *f.* league [*lLt.* leuca, leuga].

lesan 5 collect, gather, pick, glean.

lett|an *wag.* hinder; procrastinate [læt].

~ing *f.* hindrance; delay.

leþer* *n.* leather.

~codd *m.* leather bag.

~helm *m.* leather helmet.

~hose *f.* leather gaiter.

~wyrhta *m.* leather-maker.

leþeren = liþeren of leather.

libban, leofian, lif- live, be alive, pass life, subsist.

līc *n.* living body (†); corpse. þæt micle ~ elephantiasis.

~beorg *f.* sarcophagus.

~burg *f.* cemetery.

~bysig† active.

~fæt† *n.* body.

līc-ham|a, līcuma *m.* living body; *rarely* corpse.

~lēas incorporeal.

~lic of the body, corporeal, carnal.

~līce *av.* in the body, corporeally. ge~od incarnate.

līc|hord† *n.* interior of body, body.

~hrægel *n.* winding-sheet.

~hryre† *m.* death.

~lēoþ *n.* dirge.

~lic funeral.

~mann *m.* undertaker, (corpse) bearer.

~pytt *m.* grave.

~rest *f.* burial-place, sepulchre.

~sang *m.* dirge.

~sār† *n.* wound.

~sierce† *f.* corslet.

~tūn *m.* burial-ground.

~þegnung *f.*, ~þēn- *f.* funeral.

~þēote *f.* pore.

~þrōwere *m.* leper, sufferer from ulcers.

~þrūh *f.* coffin.

~wiglung *f.* necromancy.

~wund† *f.* wound.

līc-wierþ|e, ge-, -weorþ *wd.* pleasing, acceptable; estimable, praiseworthy; sterling (money).

~nes *f.* being pleased with, good pleasure.

gelīc *wd.* similar; equal.

gelīc|a *mf.* equal; such a one as: þīnre ~an of the like of you.

~bisnung *f.* imitation.

~e, līce *av.* in the same way, equally, in a similar way. swā ~ similarly. ~and hē wǣre .., ~ost þǣm þe hē wǣre .. as if he were; ~ and spynge dēþ just as a sponge does.

~lic fit, proper.

~līce *av.* equally.

~nes, līcnes *f.* similarity; simile, parable.

līc|ian *wd.* please.

~(i)endlic pleasant.

~endlīce *av.* pleasingly.

~ung *f.* pleasing; pleasure.

licc|ian lick; lick up, lap.

~ung *f.* licking.

licett|an, liccet(t)an pretend *w. sbj.*, *w.* swelce *and sbj.*, *also rfl.* ‖ *wa.* simulate, feign.

~ere *m.* hypocrite.

~ung *f.* pretence, hypocrisy.

licg|an 5 *prt.* læg, *pl.* lāgon, ǣ lie, lie at anchor, be confined to bed, be ill ~ ~ mid *d.* lie (with woman); remain, be: þæt land læg wēste ~ tōgædre ~ join (*of* boundaries) | lie dead, die: þær libban oþþe þær ~ — ~ende feoh lifeless property (as opposed to cattle); ready money | be still (*of* wind); fail (*of* sword's edge); ge~ cease (*of* strife) | be situated; extend (*of* territory); *direction* lie, lead to (*of* road): se weg þe tō Stānlēage liþ; flow (*of* river) | belong (*of* land) *w.* tō, intō, þider inn | for hine ~ make his cause one's own | ~ ongēan *abs.* oppose a measure.

līcuma = līchama.

lid† (*n.*) ship, vessel.

~mann *m.* sailor.

~weard *m.* sailor.

~wērig weary of seafaring.

lida† *m.* sailor.

liden, *ptc. of* līþan.

lieden*, ȳ, ēo *n.*, *f.* (?) language. *Cp.* lǣden [lēode].

liefan allow *w. d. and a. or ger.*: ~ him hām disband them [lēaf].

gelief|an, *L.* bel-, *A.* (ge)lēfan believe, think true, take on trust, *w. d.*, *g.*, *rarely a.*, *w. sbj.*, *indc.*;

believe (in God) w. on a. (d.), be a true believer [gelēafa].

gelīefed believing, pious.

~**lic** permissible.

~**līce** av. believingly, credulously.

līeg mn. flame; lightning.

~**bǣre**, ~**berende** fiery.

~**bryne**† m. fire.

~**cwalu**† f. fiery death.

~**draca**†·m. fiery dragon.

~**egesa**† m. terror of fire.

~**fǣmende**, ~**fām-blāwende** vomiting flame.

~**fȳr** n. fire.

~**locc**, ~**loccede** with flaming locks.

~**rǣsc** m., ~**rǣscetung** f. lightning.

~**spīwol** vomiting flames.

~**þracu**† f. violence of fire, burning.

~**ȳþ**† f. wave of fire.

līegen fiery.

līeget|u f., L. also used as n. pl., g. līeget(t)e; **līget** m. (flash of) lightning.

~**rǣsc** m. flash of lightning.

~**slieht** m. flash of lightning; thunderbolt.

līegn(i)an deny [lēogan].

lieht|an shine; give light wd.; dawn [leoht].

~**ing**, ~**ung** f. giving light, shining; light; dawn.

~**nes** f. brightness.

lieht|an alleviate, ease (discomfort); release [leoht].

~**ing** f. alleviation, mitigation, release.

līes|an release, deliver; redeem [lēas].

~**ing** f. redemption, release.

~**nes**, ge-f. redemption.

līesing m. freedman.

līetan*, **līt-** once tr. bend, incline [lūtan].

līeþran lather, smear [lēaþor].

līex|an shine, glitter [līeg].

~**ende** av. splendidly IN.

~**ung** f. brightness.

līf n. life, period of life, way of life — ~es bēon be alive, survive; on ~e alive; tō ~e lǣfan let live | mynecena ~ nunnery.

~**brycgung** f. way of life (!) IN.

~**bysig**† struggling for life.

---

līf|caru† f. anxiety about life.

~**dæg** m. day of life.

~**gedāl**† n. death.

~**fadung** f. regulating life.

~**fæc** n. life(time).

~**fæst** living; life-giving; settled.

~**fæstan** endow with life.

~**frēa**† m. Lord of life.

~**fruma**† m. Author of life.

~**lād** f. way of life.

~**lēas** without life.

~**lēast** f. death.

~**lic** living; vital, life-giving; causing death.

~**līce** av. vitally.

~**lyre** m. loss of life.

~**neru**† f. sustenance, food.

~**gesceaft**† f. condition of life, life.

~**getwinnan**† mpl. twins.

~**weard**† m. Guardian of life.

~**weg** m. manner of life.

~**wela**† m. wealth.

~**wielle** living (water) IN.

~**wraþu**† f. support of life.

~**wynn**† f. joy of life.

lifer f. liver.

~**ādl** f. disease of liver.

~**bȳl** m. protuberance on liver.

~**hol** n. hollow in liver.

~**læppa** m. lobe of liver.

~**wærc** m. pain in liver.

~**wyrt** f. liverwort.

lifer once (f.) a weight (?) Gl. [Lt. libra.]

lifgan, **lifian** = **libban**.

lifrig of the liver [lifer].

geliger, ~e, **gelīre** n., ~**nes** f. fornication, adultery [licgan].

lihtan alight, halt.

lilie f. lily [Lt.].

lim n. limb, member (of body); branch (of tree).

~**hāl**† sound in limb.

~**lǣw** f. mutilation.

~**lǣwa***, ~**lǣweo** maimed, mutilated.

~**lama** crippled.

~**lēas** without limbs.

~**mǣlum** av. limb by limb.

~**nacod**† naked.

~**rǣden** (!) f. cloak Gl.

~**sēoc**† diseased in limbs.

~**wǣd**† f. garment.

~**wæstm**† m. stature.

~**wērig**† weary.

līm (m.) anything that causes adhesion, mortar, (bird)lime, paste.

---

līm|ian.

~**ing** f. plastering, cementing.

gelimp n. event; chance; vicissitude, fortune — on gōdum ~um in prosperity; calamity.

~**full** suitable.

~**lic** suitable.

~**līce** av. suitably.

~**licnes** f. opportunity.

(ge)**limpan** 3 happen often imps., wd., w. indc. | w. tō d. belong (of land); concern, be of importance to.

līn n. flax; linen; linen cloth.

~**æcer** m. flax-field.

~**hǣwen** flax-coloured.

~**land** n. flax-growing land.

~**lēah** m. flax-field.

~**sǣd** n. linseed.

~**wǣd** f. linen garment or cloth.

~**wyrt** f. flax.

lind, ~e only in first sense, f. lime, linden; †shield.

~**gecrod**† n. warlike troop, host.

~**croda**† m. shield-press, battle.

~**hæbbende**† m. warrior.

~(**h**)**rycg** m. ridge where limes grow.

~**hwæt***† shield-brave.

~**gelāc**† n., ~**plega**† m. battle.

~**gestealla**† m. companion in battle.

~**werod**† n. warlike troop.

~**wiga**†, ~**wīgend**† m. warrior.

linden of lime-wood.

līne, **ī**† f. rope; line, series; guidance, regulation [Lt. linea].

līnen of linen.

~**werd** clothed with linen.

līnetwige, -**igle**, **līnete** f. linnet.

linnan 3 desist, part from w. i. or g.

lippa m. lip.

līr|a m. fleshy parts of body, flesh.

~**eht** brawny.

gelīre = **geliger**.

gelīsian slip, glide.

gelise*, pl. -**leoso** n. study. Cp. **word-gecwide**.

liss, **lips** f. kindness, favour; forgiveness; saving (of life); joy [līþe].

lissan† once subdue.

list mf. skill; cunning; art, accomplishment — ~um skilfully.

~**hendig**† having skilful hands.

~**elīce** once av. carefully.

līste *f.* hem, border.
lits-mann = līps-.
lip *n.* joint ; limb.
~ādl *f.* gout.
~sēaw *n.* synovia.
~wærc *m.* pain in the joints.
lip *n.* fleet *vL.* [*Scand.*].
lip-wyrt, y *f.* dwarf elder.
lip *n.* strong drink.
~wǣge† *n.* drinking-cup.
lip, *see* licgan.
lip = lihþ, *see* lēon.
lipnes *f.* gentleness, lenity [līþe].
līp|an 6 *prt. pl.* lidon, lipon go by water, sail — *ptc.* geliden having travelled much.
~end *m.* wanderer, sailor.
līp|an soften, mitigate [līþe].
~ung *f.* alleviation.
līpian be kind, be gracious ; become alleviated.
Līþa *m.* — se ǣrra ~ June, se æfterra ~ July.
lipe- = leoþu-.
līþe soft ; mild (weather, ale), calm (sea), gentle (whistling, gestures), slight (illness) ; kind, gentle, gracious ; pleasant ; sweet.
~lic gentle (voice, words).
~līce *av.* kindly ; not severely, gently ; slightly.
līpercian soothe ; flatter.
liper|e *f.* sling [leþer].
~lic of a sling.
liperen, e of leather [leper].
līpig flexible ; yielding, pliant.
~ian, -eg- assuage ; be mild *or* gentle.
lipincel *n.* little joint.
līps = liss.
līps-mann, lits- *m.* (Danish) sailor [līp].
lipule (*m.*) 'joint-oil,' synovia [līp, ele].
līxan = līexan.
lobbe *f.* spider.
loc *n.* lock, bolt, bar ; anything shut in, prison, stronghold *esp.* (sheep)fold | settlement (of negotiations, dispute) ; conclusion (in logic) [lūcan].
~hyrdel *m.* sheep-fold.
~stān *m.* stone closing mouth of cave.
lōcian look, see *w.* on *a.*, tō | *w.* tō, intō belong.
loca *m.* enclosure, stronghold.
lōca, lōc *L.* -ever : ~ hū however,

~ hwonne whenever, ~ hwǣr wherever, ~ hwæþer whichever (of two), ~ hwæt whatever [lō-cian].
locc *m.* lock (of hair) ; hair.
~bore *f.* long haired (free woman) LL.
~feax *n.* head of hair.
~gewind *n.* head of hair.
loccian entice, soothe.
locer (carpenter's) plane.
gelod-wyrt *f.* silverweed.
geloda *m.* joint of the backbone ; brother.
loddere *m.* beggar, pauper.
gelodr once *f.* spine.
lodrung *f.* triviality.
lof *n.* praise ; glory ; song of praise, hymn.
~bǣre laudatory.
~dǣd *f.* praiseworthy deed.
~georn eager for glory.
~herung *f.* praise.
~lāc *n.* offering in honour of a god.
~lǣcan praise.
~lic praiseworthy.
~līce *av.* gloriously.
~mǣgen† *n.* glory.
~sang *m.* hymn, psalm.
~sealm *m.* psalm of praise.
~singende hymning.
~sum praiseworthy.
lof|ian praise ; appraise, set price on.
~ung *f.* praise ; appraising, valuation.
loft, *see* lyft.
lōg (*n.*) place — on his ~ instead of him.
lōg, lōh *prt. of* lēan.
lōg|ian place — ge~ ūp put away carefully, lay by | portion out, arrange (life), frame (speech) — ge~ð sprǣc good style | go into details, discuss *w.* be.
ge-~ung *f.* order.
logþor cunning, clever Gl.
gelōma, lōma *m.* tool, utensil, article of furniture.
gelōm|e, lōme *av.* often.
~lǣcan be frequent ; frequent Gl. ; -ende frequentative (verb).
~lǣcing *f.* frequency, frequenting Gl.
~(e)lic frequent.
~līce *av.* often, repeatedly.
~lician become frequent.
~licnes *f.* frequency, repetition.

loppe *f.* flea.
lop(p)estre *f.* lobster ; locust (!).
lor *n.* — tō ~e weorþan perish, be lost, be wasted [lēosan].
loren *ptc. of* lēoran depart.
-loren *ptc. of* -lēosan.
lorg *f.*, *pl.* *vE.* loerge pole ; weaver's beam.
los *n.* — tō ~e weorþan perish, be lost. *Cp.* lor, *of which* los *seems to be an Anglian form.*
~(e)wist *IN.f.* loss, waste, destruction, injury.
los|ian *w. d. of pers.* be lost : mē ~ode hit I lost it ; escape (from) ; perish.
~igendlic about to perish.
~ing *IN.f.* loss, destruction.
lot *n.* deceit, wile [lūtan].
lot-wrenc *m.* deceit, wile.
~cēast *f.* guile.
lopa *m.* cloak.
lox (*m.*) lynx.
lūcan 7 I. *tr.* close, shut up, confine ; interlace ; conclude (transaction) || *intr.* join together (so as to form one mass). II. pull up, weed.
lud-geat *n.* back- or side-gate, postern.
luf|ian love ; caress, fondle.
~estre *f.* lover.
~igend *m.* lover.
~igendlic loving, amiable ; worthy of love, pleasant.
lufestice *f.* lovage (a plant) [*Lt.* levisticum].
luf|u *f. st.*, *wk.*, *sometimes pl. in sg.* sense love, loving, passion, affection ; friendliness ; amicable arrangement (in law) ; sake : for Godes ~an (~e, ~um), for mīnre lufan.
~(e)lic loving, amiable ; pleasant.
~līce *av.* lovingly, amiably ; willingly.
~rǣden(n) *f.* love.
~sum amiable, kind ; worthy of love.
~sumlīce *av.* amiably, kindly.
~sumnes *f.* amiability, kindness ; pleasantness.
~tācen *n.* token of love.
~tīeme loving, philanthropic.
luf-wend|e, ~lic amiable, loving ; beloved, pleasant.
~līce *av.* amiably, gently.

luh lake *IN*. [*Celtic*].

gelumpenlic occasional [limpan].

lund.

~laga *m*. kidney.

lungen(n) *f*. lung(s).

~ādl *f*. lung-disease.

~sealf *f*. salve for lungs.

~wyrt *f*. lungwort.

lungre† *av*. quickly, shortly; at once, suddenly.

-luron *prt. pl. of* **-lēosan**.

lūs *f*., *pl*. **lȳs** louse.

~þorn *m*. spindle-tree.

lust I. *m*. pleasure; desire; lust. **on ~e** *wg*. glad, desirous. **on ~um** joyful. **~um** willingly. II. *aj*. willing (mind).

~bǣre, ~bǣrlic pleasant; desirous.

~bǣrlice *av*. with pleasure, pleasantly.

~bǣrnes *f*. desire; pleasure.

~full desirous.

(ge)~fullice *av*. joyfully, willingly.

(ge)~fulnes, -fyl- *f*. pleasure; desire.

~fullian enjoy, rejoice *w.g. or on d*.

(ge)~fullung *f*. pleasure.

~geornnes *f*. desire, lust.

~grin*† *f*. snare of pleasure.

~lice *av*. gladly, willingly.

~moce *f*. lady's smock (a plant).

~sumlic pleasant.

~sumlice *av*. willingly.

lūtan 7 *intr*. bow, bend, turn; prostrate oneself; fall; entreat *abs. w. sbj*. | *of time* — **geloten dæg** after part of the day.

lūtian lie hid, lurk, skulk.

lybb *n*. drug; poison.

~corn *n*. purgative grain *or* drug.

~cræft *m*., **-lāc** *n*. drugging, witchcraft.

-lǣca *m*. sorcerer.

lybbestre *f*. witch.

lycce mendacious [**lyge**].

lȳden = ****līeden** language, **lǣden** Latin.

lyfesn *f*. charm, amulet.

lyffet|tan, -et(i)an flatter.

~ere *m*. flatterer.

~ung *f*. flattery.

lyft, loft [*Scand*.] *fnm*. air; wind; sky; cloud. **on ~(e)** aloft.

~edor† *m*. clouds.

~fæt† *n*. aerial vessel (lamp?), moon.

~flēogend†, ~floga† *m*. air-flyer.

~helm† *m*. air, cloud.

~gelāc† *n*. motion through the air.

~lācende† sporting in the air.

~scapa† *m*. aerial robber (raven).

~geswenced† air-driven.

~wundor† *n*. aerial prodigy.

~wynn† *f*. air-joy, flying.

lyften aerial.

lyft*, e weak.

~ādl paralysis.

lyge I. *m*. falsehood. II. *aj*. mendacious, lying [**lēogan**].

~searo† *n*. lying, artifice, wile.

~spell *n*. falsehood.

~synnig† lying.

~torn*, lige-† *once m*. (!).

~word† *n*. falsehood.

~wyrhta *m*. liar.

lygnes (!) *f*. deceitfulness.

lygen *f*. falsehood.

~word† *n*. falsehood.

lyg(e)n|ian*, i *tr*. accuse of falsehood, give the lie to; convict of falsehood — **ge~od** perjured, lying.

lynd *f*. fat; fatness [**lund**].

gelynd *f*. fat.

gelyndu *npl*. joints of the spine.

lyne-bor *n*. borer, auger [**lynis**].

lynis *m*. axletree.

lypen.

~wyrhta *m*. tanner Gl.

lyre *m*. loss; being disabled, injury; destruction [**lēosan**].

lȳs *pl. of* **lūs**.

lyso, *inflected* **lysw-** I. bad, wrong. II. *n*. evil.

lystan, *impers. wag., w. d. of pers.*, *w. inf*. desire [**lust**].

lyswen purulent (urine) [**lyso**].

lyswen*, lyssen *once* (*n*.) purulence.

lȳt I. *av*. to a slight degree, little || *cpv*. **lǣs** *av*. less — **ān ~ fēowertig bēaga** 39. **noht(e) þon ~, nā þȳ ~** not less; nevertheless. **þȳ ~ (þe)** *cj. w. sbj*. lest. *n. indecl. wg*. fewer : **mid ~ worda** || *spl*. **lǣst, lǣsest** *av*. least. *n. indecl. wg*. fewest. II. *n. indecl. always wg*. few, little. III. *aj. indecl*. few : **mid ~ wordum**.

~hwōn I. *av*. very little (space, time, quantity). II. *n. indecl. wg*. very little, few.

lȳtel, *cpv*. **lǣssa, spl. lǣst, LA. lǣsest, ēa** ; *once spl*. **lǣrest** little, small. **lȳtlum** by degrees; in small pieces. **lȳtlum and lȳtlum** by degrees.

~fōta having small feet.

~hygdig†, -hȳd-, ~mōd pusillanimous.

~nes *f*. littleness, paucity.

lȳtes-nā, lȳtes(t)ne *av*. almost, nearly ['by a little not'].

lytig cunning, wily [**lot**].

~lic, lytelice deceitful.

~lice, lytelice *av*. cunningly.

~nes *f*. cunning.

lytigian act cunningly.

lȳtlian diminish *tr. and intr.*; shorten (fast); become ineffectual *or* weak (*of* laws); curtail, abrogate.

lȳtling *m*. little one, child.

gelyþen = **geliden**.

lȳþer|full, ~lic mean, sordid, vile.

~lice *av*. wickedly.

~nes *f*. wickedness.

lȳþre I. *aj*. contemptible, base; sordid; bad; wicked. II. *av*. badly, miserably.

M.

mā av. more, see micle.
~cræftig† mighty, for mægen- (?).
~fealdra L. cpv. of manigfeald.
~geïect augmented Gl.
maclian arrange, manage esp. in hīt~; cause; do, make gen. L.; put — ~ ūp, hang up (on walls) ‖ intr. act, behave : fare : befrān þæt cild hū hit ~ode how it had got on.
~ung f. doing.
gemaca = gemæcca.
maclic suitable LN.
mād.
~mōd† once m. folly.
gemād foolish, mad.
mādm = māþm.
mǣ, see micle.
gemæcc wd. well-matched, suitable (wife) ; equal, being a match for.
gemǣc lic conjugal Gl.
~nes f. intercourse, union.
~scipe m. cohabitation.
gemǣcc|a, -maca m. one of a pair, especially a male and a female animal, mate ; husband ; wife, g. þīnes, þīnre ~an.
mǣcg†, ę, once ~a† m. man, warrior; son.
mǣd f., pl. mǣd(w)a meadow.
~lacu f. meadow-stream.
~(we)land n. meadow or grassland.
~mǣweht mowing of a meadow.
~rǣden(n) f. grass mown on meadow.
~splott m. plot of meadow-land.
mǣdan — ptc. gemǣdd mad [mād].
mǣden = mægden.
mǣdere, mæddre f. madder.
~cīþ m. shoot of madder.
gemǣdla m. chatter.
mǣg vb., pl. magon, prt. mihte, ea, e have power, avail : ne ~ tō nahte is of no use. ~ wiþ a. (drug) cures (disease); hē ~ wiþ hine has influence with him | be

in good or bad health : āxode hū hē mihte ; ic mæg wel ∣ can, have the power, possibility, be allowed to w. inf. — ellipse of inf. þǣr him mon tō ne mehte could not get at him.
mǣg I. m., pl. mǣgas, ǣ m. kinsman, son. II.† f. kinswoman; woman.
~bana m. slayer of one's kinsmen.
~bōt f. compensation to the family of a man killed.
~burg f. family, kinsmen, tribe.
~cild n. young kinsman.
~cūþ related.
~cwealm m. murder of kinsman.
~cynren n. family, lineage.
~hǣmed n. incest.
~hand f. kinsman, natural heir.
~lagu f. law of responsibilities of kinsmen.
~lēas without kinsmen.
~lic of or belonging to kinsmen.
~lufe† f. love.
~morþor n. murder of kinsmen.
~gemōt n. meeting of kinsmen.
~myrþra m. murderer of a kinsman.
~racu f. genealogy.
~rǣden(n) f. relationship.
~rǣs m. attack on one's kinsmen.
~scir f. division of a people, containing the kinsmen of a particular family.
~sibb f. relationship ; natural affection.
~siblic of kin.
~slaga m. killer of a kinsman.
~slieht m. killing a kinsman.
~tūdor n. family, kindred.
~wine† m. kinsman.
mǣg-wlit|e m. appearance, form, species.
~ian fashion.
~lice av. figuratively (!).
mǣg-gewrit n. genealogy.
gemǣg, ā m. — wē sint ~as we are relatives.

mægden, mǣden n. girl, young woman ; virgin.
~ǣw f. marriage with a virgin.
~cild n. girl.
~hād m. virginity.
~hēap m. troop of girls.
~lic of girls, girlish ; virginal.
~mann m. girl; female servant ; virgin.
mǣge = māge.
mægen, mæg n. strength ; might, power; efficacy (of drug) ; miracle; troop, force.
~āgende† mighty.
~byrþen(n)† f. mighty burden.
~corþor† n. mighty troop.
~cræft† m. strength ; might, power.
~cyning † m. mighty king.
~dǣd† f. mighty deed.
~ēaca† m. help.
~ēacen† mighty, inspired with strength.
~earfeþe† n. great labour or hardship.
~ellen† n. mighty valour.
~fæst vigorous.
~folc† n. mighty people or crowd.
~fultum† m. mighty help.
~hēap† m. mighty troop.
~heard† strong.
mægen-lēas feeble.
~lice av. feebly.
~t f. weakness, impotence.
mægen|rǣs† m. vigorous attack.
~rōf† very strong or brave.
~scipe† m. might.
~spēd f. might, virtue.
~stān† m. big rock.
~strang† strong (in body) ; mighty.
~strengo † f. bodily strength ; might.
~strengþo f. strength ; might.
~þegen† m. mighty minister (angel).
~þrēat ⊦ m. mighty troop.
~þrymm m. power ; majesty, glory ; †Christ, †heaven, †angels.
~þrymnes f. majesty, glory.
~þyse† f. strength, force.
~weorc† n. mighty work.

E

mægen|wīsa† *m.* general.
~**wudu**† *m.* mighty spear.
~**wundor**† *n.* great prodigy.
mægenian gain strength.
gemægenod confirmed.
mæger lean.
~**ian** make lean.
mægester, ā, ā† *m.* master, teacher [*Lt.* magister].
~**dōm** *m.* office of teacher.
mæg(e)þ *f.* maiden, girl; virgin; †woman.
~**blæd** *n.* pudendum muliebre.
~**bōt** *f.* fine on unmarried woman.
~**hād** *m.* virginity, chastity; troop of young persons.
~**hādlic** virginal.
~**mann** *m.* girl, virgin.
mægþ *f.* family, kindred, group of kinsmen; generation; tribe, nation; province, country [**mǣg**].
~**hād** *m.* relationship.
~**lēas** plebeian.
~**rǣden(n)** *f.* = **mǣg-**.
~**sibb** *f.* kindred.
gemægþ *once f.* power, greatness.
mægþ|a *m.,* ~**e,** **mag(e)þe** *f.* Mayweed.
mæht- = miht-.
mǣl *n.* mark, token; ornament; †sword. Crīstes ~ cross, crucifix | measure | (appointed) time, occasion† — ~**a gehwelce** always; food-time, meal. *Cp.* māl.
~**caru**† *f.* trouble of the time.
~**dæg, māl-** *m.* fixed *or* appointed time, day.
~**mete**† *m.* food (!).
~**gesceaft**† *f.* fate.
~**sweord***, **māl-** *n.* ornamented sword.
~**tang** (*m.*), ~**tange** *f.* pair of compasses.
mǣl† *n.* talk, speech; contest, battle [**mæþel**].
mǣl-drop|a *m.* phlegm Gl.
~**iende** phlegmy Gl.
mǣl-scafa *m.* caterpillar, blight.
gemǣl marked, stained.
mǣlan mark, stain.
mǣlan† speak.
mǣle *m.* cup, bowl.
mǣn|an mean, allude to: gif hē .. þæt is þæt ic ~e, gif hē ..; hwæt hē mid þǣre sprǣce ~de | signify: nāt hwæt þā word ~aþ |

intend, mean | speak of, relate, complain (of) *abs., tr.*
mǣne false (oath); wicked [**mān**].
gemǣn|e I. *aj. wd.* common: uncer ~ bearn, wæs him cild ~; in common, public (road). II. *n.* fellowship, intercourse — habban ~ wiþ *a.* have to do with (an adversary) [**gemāna**].
~**(e)lic** common, general.
~**elīce** *av.* generally, collectively; in common, mutually.
~**elīcnes** *f.* generalness Gl.
~**nes** *f.* society, association, union.
~**scipe** *m.* fellowship, communion.
(ge)mǣnsum|ian partake of (Eucharist) *wg.*; communicate Bd., Gl.; marry *lN.*
~**nes** *f.* participation; the Communion.
~**ung** *f.* communion.
mǣran make known, proclaim, celebrate.
gemǣran fix limits, mark off, determine.
mǣrian become famous.
mǣre-torht = mere-.
mǣre pure (money).
~**hwīt***, e sterling (silver).
mǣr|e *n.* boundary.
~**āc** *f.* boundary oak.
~**apuldre** *f.* boundary apple-tree.
~**brōc** *m.* boundary brook.
~**cnoll** *m.* boundary hill.
~**dīc** *f.* boundary dyke.
~**hege** *m.* boundary hedge.
~**pōl, ~pul** *m.* boundary pool.
~**pytt** *m.* boundary pit.
~**stān** *m.* boundary stone.
~**þorn** *m.* boundary hawthorn.
~**weg** *m.* boundary road.
mǣr|e glorious, famous.
~**hlīsa** *m.* celebrity.
~**lic** famous, illustrious, splendid.
~**līce** *av.* gloriously, splendidly; excellently.
~**nes** *f.* celebrity.
~**weorc** *n.* splendid work.
gemǣr|e *n.* boundary.
~**haga** *m.* boundary hedge.
~**lacu** *f.* boundary stream.
~**weg** *m.* boundary road.
~**wiell** *m.* boundary stream.
mǣrels*, ā mooring-rope.
~**rāp** *m.* mooring-rope.
mǣring (*m.*) sweet basil (!).
mǣrs|ian declare, proclaim, make

known; celebrate (birthday), perform (ceremony); glorify, praise; enlarge (!) || *tr.* become known, be spread (*of* fame).
mǣrs|ere *m.* herald.
mǣrsung, ge- *f.* rumour; celebrity; celebration; glorification.
~**tīma** *m.* time of glorification.
mǣrþ(o) *f.* fame, glory — mǣrþum gloriously; glorious deed.
mǣscre *f.* mesh (of net).
mǣslen, mǣsling = mǣstling.
mǣssian say mass, perform (mass); come to mass.
mǣsse *f.* mass; mass-day, festival.
~**ǣfen** *m.* eve of a festival.
~**bōc** *f.* missal.
~**crēda** *m.* Nicene Creed.
~**dæg** *m.* festival.
~**gierela** *m.* surplice.
~**hacele** *f.* cope.
~**hrægel** *n.* surplice.
~**lāc** *n.* the host.
~**niht** *f.* eve of a festival.
mǣsse-prēost *m.* mass-priest; high priest.
~**hād** *m.* office of mass-priest.
~**scīr** *f.* district of a mass-priest.
mǣsse|rēaf *n.* mass-vestment.
~**sang** *m.* mass.
~**tīd** *f.* mass-time.
~**þegn** *m.* mass-priest.
~**þegnung** *f.* celebration of mass.
~**wīn** *n.* mass-wine.
mǣsser|e *m.* mass-priest.
~**bana** *m.* killer of a mass-priest.
mæst *m.* mast (of ship).
~**ciest** *f.* mast-hole.
~**lōn** *pl.* mast-pulleys.
~**rāp** *m.* mast-rope.
~**twist** *m.* stay.
mæst *m.* mast (of beech).
~**land** *n.* mast-land, swine-feeding land.
~**rǣden(n)** *f.* right of feeding swine in mast-land.
mǣst, *see* micel, micle.
~**licost** particularly Gl.
mǣstan fatten.
mǣstel-bearg*, -berg *m.* fattened hog *lN.*
mǣsten(n) (*m.*) swine-pasture.
~**rǣden(n)** *f.* right of swine-pasture.
~**trēow** *n.* tree yielding mast.
mǣs(t)ling, *A.* mǣslen *n.* a kind of brass; brass vessel.
~**smiþ** *m.* brass-smith.

mǣt|an dream *impers. w. a., d.*
~ing *f.* dream.
mǣte insignificant; small, few; bad [metan].
gemǣte of suitable dimensions, fitting well (*of* clothes).
gemǣtgan† = gemetgian.
mǣþ *f.* measure, degree, proportion: be þǣre ~e þe him tō gebyrige fair share of property | efficacy, (human) power, capacity *gen. w. negation stated or implied*: nis nā ēower ~ tō witanne; ofer ūre ~ þencan | rank | what is fitting, right | respect. ~e gecnāwan on *d.* reverence. ~e wāt (*or* cann) on *d.* feel respect for.
~full humane, courteous.
~lēas greedy.
~lic fitting.
~lice *av.* humanely, courteously.
mǣþ (*n.*) act of mowing; hayharvest [māwan].
mǣþian have consideration for, regard.
mǣþel† *n.* meeting; council; harangue, talking.
~ærn *n.* council-house.
~cwide *m.* discourse.
~hēgende attending a council; speaking.
~stede *m.* council-place; battlefield.
~word *n.* formal word.
mǣþ(e)re *m.* mower.
mǣþigian honour.
mǣþlan = maþelian.
mǣw, mēaw, mēg *m.* seagull.
~pōl*, māwpul *m.* seagull-pool Ct.
maffa *m.* caul.
māg- = mǣg-.
maga *m.* stomach.
maga strong, powerful [mæg].
māgat, āt, at *m.* son; man [mǣg].
māgas *pl. of* mǣg.
magdala-trēow *n.* almond tree [*Lt.* amygdala].
māge, ǣ *f.* kinswoman.
magepe = mægþa May-weed.
magister = mægester.
magu† *m.* child, son; man, warrior, attendant, servant.
~dryht *f.* band of warriors.
~geoguþ *f.* youth (period).
~rǣdend *m.* adviser of men.

magu|rǣswa *m.* chief.
~rinc *m.* boy, youth; man, warrior.
~timber *n.* child; progeny, population.
~tūdor *n.* progeny.
~þegn *m.* servant; retainer, man, warrior.
māh† *once* bad (?).
gemāh, -g importunate, shameless, wicked.
~nes *f.* importunity, shamelessness.
māl *n. L.* action at law; bargaining; agreement, pay — scylian scipu of ~e, settan litsmenn of ~e pay off, dismiss [*Scand.*].
māl *n.* mark, stain [mǣl].
māl-, *see* mǣl-.
gemā|lic, -mǣglic, -mǣhlic importunate; shameless; disgraceful, wicked [gemāh].
~līce *av.* importunately; peremptorily.
~licnes *f.* importunity; shamelessness, wantonness.
malscra *once pl.* spells = malscrunga.
malscrung *f.* witchcraft, spell.
mamme *f.* teat [*Lt.* mamma].
mamor sleep, stupor.
mamrian† *once* meditate, design (evil).
man *no. indf.* one, they [mann].
mān I. *n.* wickedness, crime — swerian ~ swear false oath. II. *aj.* false; wicked.
~āþ *m.* false oath, perjury.
~bealo† *n.* wicked injury.
~dǣd *f.* crime, sin.
~dǣde, -deorf wicked.
~drinc *m.* poison.
~fǣhþo *f.* guilt.
~feld *m.* field of crime.
~folm† *f.* hand that does evil.
~fordǣdla† *m.* wicked destroyer.
~forwyrht† *n.* sin.
~frēa† *m.* prince of evil, the Devil.
~fremmende† evil doing.
mān-full, ~ic wicked, sinful.
~īce *av.* wickedly.
~nes *f.* wickedness.
mān|genga *m.* evildoer.
~hūs *n.* dwelling of wickedness.
~īdel† vain (words).
~lic infamous, wicked.
~genīþla† *m.* wicked persecutor.
~scaþa† *m.* enemy; sinner.
~sceatt† *m.* usury.

mān-scyld† *f.* guilt, sin.
~ig† guilty.
mān|swara, -o- *m.* perjurer.
~swaru *f.* perjury.
~sweriende perjuring.
~swica *m.* traitor.
~wamm *m.* stain of sin.
~weorc I. *n.* crime. II. *aj.* wicked.
~word† *n.* wicked word.
~wræc- wicked Gl.
~(ge)wyrhta† *m.* sinner.
man *vb. prt.* munde *wg.* be mindful of; think, esteem: hine weorþne ~.
man-bryne [= mann- *or* mān-] *m.* conflagration.
geman having a mane [manu].
geman, man *vb., pl.* -munon, *prt.* -munde [*A.* often has y for u] *w. g., a.* remember.
man|ian remind *wag.*; admonish, exhort *w. sbj.*; advise; claim, exact *wag.*: sē þe (hine) þæs fēos ~ode the creditor.
~iend *m.* admonisher; claimer — gafoles ~ tax-gatherer.
~ung *f.* admonition, advice; claiming, exaction (of toll, &c.); tollplace; district liable to exacting or summoning; the people of such a district.
gemāna *m.* companionship, intercourse, sexual intercourse; community, association.
mancus, *pl.* -usas, -osas, -essas, *m.* a monetary unit, thirty pence.
mand *f.* basket.
mang* mixture — in ~ among *IN. Cp.* æg-mang.
gemang I. *n.* mixture, union, *pl.* sexual intercourse; business, affair; court of justice; troop, crowd — on (*or* in) . . ~ *wg.* into the midst of, among. II. *prp. w. d., a.* among; *time* — ~ þām meanwhile. *Cp.* ongemang.
mang|ian traffic, trade.
~ere *m.* merchant, trader.
mangung *f.* commerce, trade.
~hūs *n.* shop.
gemang(en)nes *f.* mingling Gl.
manig, æ, e, *pl.* ~e, ~a, *A.* monge; *A. spl.* mængist | *w. sg. no.* many a, *w. pl. no.* many: ~burg, ~e menn. *wg.* heora~ | *abs.* many people. *neut.* on ~dǣlan divide into many parts.

manig-brǣde*, **-bredæ** (law) relating to various matters Gl.

manig-feald manifold, various; complex; numerous, abundant; plural.

~**ian** multiply, increase.

~**lic** various, numerous.

~**līce** av. manifoldly, in many ways; in the plural.

~**nes** f. multiplicity; complexity; great number.

manig|fįeldan multiply; multiply (in arithm.): **gemænigfyld þā þrēo þurh fīf.**

~**siþes** av. often.

manig-tīew|e, -tēaw skilful.

~**nes** f. skill.

mann, pl. **męnn** human being; man; vassal, hero; the Runic letter m.

~**bǣre** producing or supporting human beings.

~**bōt** f. fine paid to lord of man killed.

~**bryne** m. conflagration. Or =mān-?

~**cwealm** m. pestilence, mortality, slaughter.

~**cwięld** f. pestilence, mortality.

~**cwięlmnes, -a-** f. homicide (!) lN.

~**cynn** n. mankind, human beings; race, nation, inhabitants.

~**drēam†** m. social joy.

~**dryhten†** m. (liege) lord, master.

~**ēaca** m. increase of population, birth of children.

~**faru†** f. expedition, troop.

~**fultum** m. troops, army.

~**lēas** uninhabited.

~**lica** m. human form, appearance; statue.

~**līce** av. manfully.

~**lufe†** f. love of human beings.

~**mægen** n. troop, cohort.

~**męnigo** f. multitude; number of men or soldiers.

~**mięrring** f. loss or destruction of men.

~**rǣden(n)** f. allegiance, homage; tenant's dues or service.

~**rīm** n. number of human beings.

~**scipe** m. humanity, kindness.

~**sįelen** f. selling people as slaves, abduction.

~**slaga** m. a homicide.

~**slęge, ~slięht** m. homicide.

mann|swica m. traitor.

~**þēaw†** m. custom. In some cases =mān- (?).

~**þēof** m. kidnapper.

~**þwǣre** gentle, kind.

~**þwǣrnes** f. gentleness, goodnature.

~**werod** n. troop (of soldiers); assembly.

~**weorþ** n. legal value of a man's life.

~**weorþung** f. worshipping human beings.

~**wīse** f. custom of men, custom.

mannian garrison.

manna m. man.

manna (n.) manna [Lt.].

man|u f., pl. ~**a(n)** mane.

mapuldor m., **mapuldre** f., **mapultrēo** m. maple tree.

mapulder(e)n of maple.

māra, see **micel**.

marc n. mark, half a pound L. [Scand.].

marcet, -ket n. market. lCt. [Fr.].

mare, vE. **maer(a)e** f. nightmare — **gif mon ~ rīde**; monster, satyr Gl.

mare f. silverweed.

margen, see **morgen**.

marma m. marble [Lt. marmor].

marm-stān, marman-, marmor- m. marble.

~**gedelf** n. marble quarrying.

martyr, -e m. martyr [Lt.].

~**dōm, ~hād** m. martyrdom.

~**racu** f. martyrology.

martyr|ian*, ge~ martyr.

~**ung** f. martyrdom, passion (of Christ).

mārūfie f. horehound [Lt. marrubium].

māse f. titmouse.

massere m. merchant.

matte, ea f. mat, mattress.

mattoc, ǣ, ea m. mattock, pick-axe.

maþ|a m., ~**u** f. worm, maggot.

gemaþel n. conversation [mǣl].

maþel|ian†, mǣþlan harangue, speak.

~**ere** m. orator.

~**ung** f. loquacity.

maþelig turbulent Gl.

maþu = maþa worm.

māþm, māþ(þ)um, L. **mādm** m. anything precious, treasure, gift.

~**ǣht** rf. precious thing, treasure.

~**ciest** f. treasury.

~**fæt** n. precious vessel.

~**gięfa†** m. prince, king.

~**gięfu†** f. giving treasures.

~**hierde** m. treasurer.

~**hord†** n. treasure.

~**hūs** n. treasury.

~**sęle†** m. treasure-hall.

~**sigle†** n. precious jewel.

~**gesteald†** n. treasure.

~**gestrēon†** n. treasure.

~**sweord†** n. precious sword.

~**wela†** m. treasure.

māwan I mow.

max = masc net.

max-wyrt f. mash-wort.

mē me.

mēagol firm (mind), earnest, vigorous [mæg].

~**līce** av. earnestly.

~**mōd** earnest.

~**mōdnes** f. earnestness.

~**nes** f. earnestness.

meaht- = miht-.

mealm (m.) soft stone, chalky earth.

~**iht** chalky (soil).

~**stān** m. = mealm.

mealt n. malt.

~**hūs** n. malt-house.

~**gescot** n. contribution paid in malt.

~**wyrt** f. malt-wort.

mealwe f. mallow [Lt. malva].

mēar-gealle, mergelle m. a kind of gentian (plant) [mearh, gealla].

mēaras, see **mearh**.

mearc f. mark; end, limit of given space, boundary; limit (of time), end of period; district.

~**bēce** f. boundary beech.

~**beorg** m. boundary mound.

~**brōc** m. boundary brook.

~**denu** f. boundary valley.

~**dīc** f. boundary ditch.

~**hof** n. dwelling.

~**īsen** n. branding-iron.

~**land** n. borderland, waste land; †country.

~**mōt** n. place where the assembly of a district was held.

~**pæþ†** m. path.

~**stapa†** m. waste-wanderer.

~**stęde†** m. borderland, waste land.

mearc|trēow *n.* boundary tree.

~þrēat† *m.* troop.

~wadu† *npl.* shallows, water by shore.

~weard† *m.* denizen of the waste, wolf.

~weg *m.* boundary road.

~wielle *m.* boundary stream.

gemearc *n.* — † tō þæs ~es þe in the direction that ..

mearc|ian make a mark, mark; take note of (the date); mark *or* plan out, design, appoint; create; determine *or* fix boundaries; describe.

~ere *m.* notary (!).

~ung, *lN.* ge- *f.* marking, mark, characteristic; marking out, description; constellation.

mearca *m.* space marked out.

mearg *nm.* marrow; pith.

~cofa† *m.* bone.

~gehæcc *n.* sausage.

~hæccel*, mearhæ- (*n.*) sausage.

~lic marrowy.

mearh†, -rg, *pl.* mēaras *m.* horse.

mearn *prt. of* murnan.

gemearr *n.* hindrance; heresy, wrong-doing.

mearrian go astray, err.

mearþ *m.* marten. *Cp.* merþern.

mearu, *pl.* mearwe tender, delicate.

~nes *f.* tenderness, frailty.

meatte = matte.

mēaw = mæw.

mec me *a.*

mēce† *m.* sword, blade [ē = æ̂; *the form is A.*].

~fisc, æ̂ *m.* mullet Gl.

mecg = mæcg.

mecgan mix, stir.

mechānisc mechanical [*Lt.*].

med-drosna *pl.* dregs of mead [medu].

mēd *f.* reward, requital — underfōn tō ~es *w. a., g.* as a requital.

~giélda *m.* hireling; mendicant (!).

~sceatt, mēt- *m.* wages, fee, payment; gift; bribe.

~wyrhta *m.* hireling.

gemēde I. *aj.* agreeable, acceptable [mōd]. II. *n.* what is agreeable, due observance (?); agreement.

medeme, -ume midway in size, amount, age, rank, excellence;

capable of *wg.*, suitable, excellent, worthy, perfect.

medem|lic moderate-sized, middling; excellent, worthy.

~līce *av.* moderately, slightly; suitably; kindly; ge- worthily *lN.*

~licnes *f.* mediocrity.

~micel of moderate size. *Cp.* medmicel.

~nes, *lN.* gemeodnis *f.* dignity, rank; benignity.

medem|ian, medm- *tr.* determine proportionate amount, fix measure; moderate Gl.; deem worthy, promote — ~ tō *d.* rank among, make equal to ‖ ge~ *intr., rfl.* condescend.

~ung *f.* fixing amount, proportioning.

mēder, *see* mōdor.

mederce = myderce.

mēdgian bribe [mēd].

medlic moderate, low (voice).

med-micel I. *aj.* small *of space, time, quantity*; unimportant, petty, mean, humble. II. *n.* a little.

~nes *f.* smallness.

med-micle *av.* meanly, humbly.

mēdren, mēd(d)ern I. maternal, of a mother. II. *n.* the mother's side (descent) [mōdor].

~gecynd *n.* nature inherited from mother.

~cynn *n.* descent on the mother's side.

~mǣg *m.* maternal kinsman.

~mǣgþ *f.* kinship on the mother's side.

gemēdren, *L.* -ed born of the same mother as *wd. Cp.* gefædren.

med-rīce plebeian.

med-sǣlþ *f.* bad fortune.

med-spēdig† poor, needy.

med-strang of middle rank.

med-trum, *see* mettrum.

medu *mn., g.* meda, medwes mead. *See* med-.

~ærn† *n.* mead-hall, hall where mead is drunk.

~benc† *f.* mead-bench.

~burg† *f.* mead-city, festive city.

~drēam† *m.* mead-joy, festivity.

~drenc *m.* mead-drink.

~drynce†, i *m.* mead-drinking.

~full† *n.* mead-cup.

medu|gāl† excited with mead.

~heall† *f.* mead-hall.

~rǣden(n)† *f.* strong drinks *coll.*

~scenc† *m.* mead-cup.

~seld† *n.* mead-house.

~setl† *n.* mead-seat.

~stīg† *f.* path to hall.

~wang† *m.* plain (round hall).

~wērig† overcome with mead.

medume = medeme.

med-wīs foolish, dull.

melc, eo giving milk, milch.

melcan 3 milk *tr., abs.*

melcing* *f.* milking.

~fæt *n.* milkpail.

meld *f.* proclamation.

~feoh *n.* informer's pay.

meld|ian declare, tell; display; inform against, accuse.

~ung *f.* information (against some one), betrayal.

melda *m.* narrator; informer (against), betrayer.

melde *f.* orach (a plant).

mele-dēaw, mildēaw *mn.* honeydew, nectar.

mēle = mǣle.

melsc, *see* milisc.

melt|an 3 *intr.* melt, be dissolved, be consumed; digest, be digested.

~ung *f.* digestion.

melu, eo, ea, -uw, *g.* mel(u)wes *n.* meal, flour.

~hēdern*, -hūd- *n.* meal-storehouse.

~hūs *n.* meal-house (!).

~gescot *n.* contribution paid in meal.

mene, y *m.* necklace.

~scilling *m.* coin worn as ornament.

menen, mennen [*infl. of* mann], i *n.* female servant *or* slave.

meng|an *tr.* mix: ic minne drenc ~de wiþ tēarum (*or* tēaras) *or* mid tēarum—mæþelcwidas ~ † converse; stir up; disturb; *rfl. w.* wiþ *d.* associate with, have sexual intercourse with ‖ *intr.* mingle, combine [gemang].

ge~edlic mixed.

ge~edlīce *av.* confusedly.

ge~(ed)nes *f.* mixture; connexion.

~ung *f.* mixture, composition; ge- confusion.

menga *m.* merchant [mangere].

menig = manig.

menigdo, -u *f.* multitude, troop.

menigo, *A.* mengu *f.* multitude, crowd; great number [manig].

menn, *see* mann.

mennen = menen.

mennisc I. *n.* people, men; crowd; nation. II. *aj.* human.

~lic human.

~līce *av.* humanly.

~nes *f.* human nature; incarnation; humaneness, good feeling.

~u *f.* state of man.

mentel *m.* cloak [*Lt.* mantellum].

~prēon *m.* brooch.

mēo (*f.*) sock.

gemeodnis = medemnes.

meodu = medu.

meoduma *once m.* part of loom, treadle (?) Gl.

meolc, meoluc, *A.* milc, *d. sg.* ~e, ~a, ~um *f.* milk.

~dēond *m.* suckling.

~fæt *n.* milkpail.

~hwīt milkwhite.

~līpe milky Gl.

~sūcend *m.* suckling.

meolcian, i, y milk; suckle.

meord *f.* reward; pay.

mēos (*m.*) moss.

~hlinc *m.* mossy ridge Ct.

~gelegeo *npl.* [= -lǣgo ?] mossy tracts Ct.

mēowle† *f.* virgin, maiden; woman.

meox, i *n.* dung, excrement, manure.

~bearwe *f.* dung-barrow.

~force *f.* dung-fork.

~scofl *f.* dung-shovel.

~wilige *f.* dung-basket.

meoxen = mixen.

merce = merece.

merian test; purify.

mere *m.* lake, pool; cistern; †sea.

~bāt† *m.* boat.

~candel(1)† *f.* sun.

~ciest† *f.* sea-chest (Noah's ark).

~dēaþ† *m.* sea-death.

~dēor† *n.* sea-beast.

~fara† *m.* seafarer.

~faroþ† *m.* surge.

~fisc† *m.* sea-fish.

~flōd† *m.* deluge; ocean, waters.

~grot *n.*, ~grota *m.* pearl.

~grund† *m.* bottom of the sea *or* lake.

~hengest† *m.* ship.

~hrægl† *n.* sail.

mere|hūs† *n.* sea-house (Noah's ark).

~hwearf† *m.* sea-shore.

~lād† *f.* sea-way.

~līpende† *m.* sailor.

~men(n)en, -menn *n.* siren.

~nǣdre *f.*, ~nǣddra *m.* lamprey.

~smylte† calm.

~strǣt† *f.* sea-road.

~strēam† *m.* sea, water.

~strengo† *f.* strength in swimming.

~swin *n.* dolphin.

~torht†, æ (rising) bright from the sea (*of* the sun).

~torr *m.* towering waters.

~þyssa *m.* ship.

~weard *m.* sea-guardian.

~wērig sea-weary.

~wīf *n.* water-witch.

mere mare, *see* miere.

mere (*f.*), mera *m.* nightmare, satyr Gl.

mere-hwīt = mǣre- sterling (silver).

mer(e)ce *m.* smallage (a plant).

mergelle = mēar-gealle.

mergen, *see* morgen.

mersc, merisc *m.* marsh [mere].

~land *n.* marsh *L.*

~mealwe *f.* marsh-mallow.

~mēargealle *f.* marsh-gentian.

~ware *pl.* marsh-dwellers.

merpern- (cloak) of martens' skins *vL.* [mearþ].

merze, mertze *f.* merchandise Gl. [*Fr.*].

mēsan eat, feed [mōs].

mesa *once fpl.* dung.

mēse, -y, ēo *f.* table [*Lt.* mensa].

met|cund(lic) metrical.

~(e)gierd, -geard *f.* measuring-rod.

~rāp *m.* sounding-line.

mēt-sceatt = mēd-.

gemet I. *n.* act of measuring; quantity (in the abstract); apparatus for measuring; a certain quantity, a measure (of wheat); metre | distance: six mīla ~; boundary; *met.* limits (to avarice) | self-restraint, moderation | regulation, law | capacity: ofer mīn ~ | manner, way : on manigum ~um. þȳ ~e þe, on þām ylcum ~um þe in the same way as, like. āne ~e to the same degree, uniformly. II. *aj.* fit, proper, right.

gemete *av.* fitly, properly.

gemet-fǣst moderate; modest; steadfast (?).

~an compare Gl.

~līce *av.* modestly.

~nes *f.* moderation; modesty.

gemet|fǣt *n.* vessel for measuring. Gl.

~lǣcan moderate.

~lic moderate; suitable *wd.*

~līce *av.* moderately; fitly.

gemēt = gemōt.

met|an 5 measure; mark off, fix bounds; compare *w.* wiþ *a.*; †traverse.

~end *m.* measurer; God.

mēt|an paint, draw.

~ere *m.* painter.

~ing *f.* picture.

gemēt|an, mētan, oe, *prt.* -mette, -mitte find, discover, come upon; hīe hīe ~ton met (in battle) *abs.*

~(ed)nes *f.* finding, discovery.

gemēting, -mitting, m- *f.* (!) finding; meeting; hostile meeting, meeting (of roads); assembly, convention.

mete *m.*, *pl.* mettas food.

~ærn, metern, *n.* refectory.

~ǣfliung *f.* atrophy Gl.

~belg*, metbælg *m.* wallet.

~corn *n.* corn for food.

~cū *f.* cow.

~cweorra *m.* (?) surfeit, indigestion.

~fæt, metf- *f.* dish.

~fǣtels *m.* wallet.

~gafol *n.* tax *or* rent paid in food.

~gearwa *fpl.* preparations of food, dishes.

~lāf *f.* leavings of food.

~lēas without food.

~līest, ēa *f.* want of food.

~scipe*, mets- *m.* refection.

~seax*, mets- *n.* knife.

~sōcn *f.* appetite.

~sticca *m.* spoon Gl.

~swamm *m.* mushroom.

~tīd *f.* meal-time.

~þearfende† in want of food.

~þegn *m.* steward.

~ūtsiht *f.* dysentery.

meter (*n.*) metre [*Lt.* metrum].

~cræft *m.* metre.

~cund metrical.

~fers *n.* hexameters.

~lic metrical.

meter|geweorc *n.* metre, verse.
~**wyrhta** *m.* versifier.
met(e)g|ian measure out, assign ;
moderate, regulate ; meditate.
(ge)~**ung** *f.* moderation, temperance ; regulation, rule ; meditation.
metod(†) *m.* fate ; God [metan].
~(ge)sceaft *f.* death.
~**wang** *m.* battle-field.
mets|ian feed, furnish with pro-
visions [mete].
~ung *f.* feeding, provisioning.
met(t)ian supply with food.
gemetta *m.* partaker (of food)
[mete].
mettas *pl. of* mete.
metten *once f.* Fate (goddess).
met-trum, med- weak in health,
ill ; weak.
~nes, -trym- *f.* ill-health, infirmity.
mēþ|e, oe weary ; sad ; trouble-
some (!).
~ian become weary.
~nes *f.* fatigue.
mēþg|ian — *ptc.* ge~od exhausted
(strength).
mēþig weary, exhausted.
gemeþrian honour *LL.* Cp. mǣþian.
micel, y, *L. pl.* miccle. I. *aj.,*
cpv. māra, *spl.* mǣst, *lN.* ā
I. *aj.* big, much ; *met.* great ;
many : mǣstra ǣlc heora
flāna nearly all their arrows.
micles tō (beald) much. miclum
greatly. II. *n. wg.* much, *cpv.*
māre, *spl.* mǣst. III. *av.*
greatly, much. Cp. micle.
~ǣte greedy.
~dōend doing great things.
~hēafdede big-headed.
~lic grand, magnificent, great.
~lice *av.* magnificently, greatly ; exceedingly.
~mōd magnanimous.
~nes *f.* bigness ; abundance ; magnificence.
~sprecende boasting.
micelo *f.* size.
micg|a *m.,* ~e *f.* urine [mīgan].
micgþa = migoþa.
micl|ian increase in size *or* quan-
tity *tr. and intr.* ; *tr.* extol, magnify.
(ge)~**ung** *f.* magnificence (!).

micle *av.* much : ~ swīþor to a
greater degree, much more, ~ swīþost especially ‖ *cpv.* mā, *A.*
mǣ *av.* to a greater degree,
more — mā and mā more and
more ; *time* longer, any more *gen.*
w. negation expressed or implied ;
preferably, rather. *n. gen. wg.*
more (number, bulk) ‖ *spl.* mǣst
to the highest degree, most,
chiefly ; *w.* eall nearly : mǣst
ealle his gefēran, þā ōþre ealle
mǣst, eall mǣst almost entirely.
n. wg. the greatest number.
mid, *A.* miþ I. *prp. w. d., i., A.*
a. together with, with, among
(heathens) — ~ strēame down
stream (of river) | *time* † at | *in-*
strument : ~ hlāfe āfēdan | *de-*
fining : hū him spēow ~ wīge |
manner : ~ unryhte unjustly ; ~
ealle entirely ; ~ horsum ~ ealle
with horses and all. II. mid-þām-
þe when ; through *cj.* : heora līf
gelengan midþāmþe hī gre-
miaþ God. mid-þām-þæt with,
through *cj.* : wǣron gebrocode
midþāmþæt . . forþfērdon.
mid-þȳ with that, by means of
that ; together, at the same time.
mid-þȳ-(þe), mittȳ, mitte,
mittes [s = þe] when ; while, because. III. *av.* : þā þe (him)
mid fērdon.
mid-dæg *m.* midday.
~lic midday, meridian.
~sang *m.* midday service.
~tīd *f.* noon.
middan-dæg* *m.* midday.
~lic midday, meridian.
middan-geard, middaneard *m.*
earth, world ; mankind.
~lic earthly, worldly.
middan-sumor, midde- *m.* midsummer.
middan-winter, midde- *m.* mid-
winter.
midde-, *see* middan-.
midde *f.* — on middan in the
middle.
midd|e, mide *aj.* middle (of) :
þurh ~e þā ceastre, on þām
fenne ~um ; *of time* : on midne
dæg, ær ~um wintra ‖ *spl.*
midmest, midemest middle ;
se ~a finger ; þā ~an menn of
intermediate merit.

middel I. *aj., spl.* midlest, middle ;
intermediate (in merit). II. *m.*
middle, centre ; midst : gesette
hine on hyra ~e (*or* midle) ;
waist.
~dæg *m.* midday.
~dǣl *m.* middle.
~engle *pl.* Middle Angles.
~finger *m.* middle finger.
~flēre *f.* partition (gristle of nose).
~fōt *m.* instep.
~gemǣru† *npl.* central district.
~niht† *f.* midnight.
~rīce *n.* middle kingdom.
~gescyldru, u *npl.* part between
shoulders.
~seaxe, -an *mpl.* Middle Saxons,
Middlesex.
middeweard middle (of), in the
middle *of place and time* : ~ lencten ; ~ hit (Norway) is þrītig
mīla brād. *Used as noun* : on
~an (= -um) innoþes mīnes.
midemest, *see* midd.
mid-fæsten(n) *n.* Mid-Lent.
mid-feorh *n.* middle age.
mid-ferhþ *mn.* middle age.
~nes, -ferht- *f.* middle age.
mid-help*, miþ- *f.* help *lN.*
mid-(h)rif (*n.*) diaphragm ; entrails.
mid-(h)riþ|er, ~re *n.* diaphragm,
membrane.
mid-ierfenuma *m.* co-heir.
mīdl, mīþl *n.* (horse's) bit ; oar-
thong.
~hring *m.* ring of bit.
midl|ian, ge- halve, divide.
~igend *m.* mediator.
~ung *f.* midst — of, on ~e *wg.*
~unga, -inga *av.* moderately.
midlian bridle ; muzzle (dog) ;
restrain.
gemid-leahtrod reproached (!).
midlen *n.* middle, centre ; midst :
þurh hyra ~ ; on fȳres ~e.
mid-lencten *nm.* Mid-Lent.
midlest, *see* middel.
midmest, *see* midd.
midne-dæg *m.* midday.
midnes *f.* — on ~se *wg.* in the
midst.
mid-niht *f.* midnight.
mid-rād *f.* riding with, accompanying.
midrif = midhrif.
mid-singend *m.* co-singer (!).

mid-sīþian accompany (!).
mid-spreca *m.* advocate.
gemid-sīþegad accompanied (!) Gl.
mid-sumor *m.* midsummer.
mid-weg *m.* midway.
mid-winter *m.* midwinter.
mid-wist *f.* presence, participation.
mid-wunung *f.* dwelling with, association.
mid-wyrhta *m.* co-operator.
mięltan *tr.* melt; refine (metals), *also met.*; digest || *intr.* melt [meltan].
Mięrc|e, ~an *pl.* Mercians, Mercia [mearc].
~isc Mercian.
mierce† dark; evil.
gemięrce *n.* boundary.
mięrcels *mf.* mark; seal; trophy; marked place; mark (to shoot at) [mearc].
mięre*, ~e, y *f.* mare [mearh].
mięrr|an hinder, be stumbling-block to; squander, waste; err [gemearr].
~a *m.* one who leads astray.
~else *f.* hindrance, stumbling-block.
~ing *f.* leading astray; waste, squandering.
mīg|an 6 make water.
~ung, ~ing *f.* making water.
migoþa, mi(o)gþa *m.* urine.
miht, ea, *A.* æ I. *f.* might, power; ability; miracle. II. *aj.* †mighty; possible *LN.* [mæg].
~(e)lēas powerless.
~(e)lic possible.
~mōd† *n.* anger, excitement.
mihte *prt. of* mæg.
mihtelic, *see* mihtiglic.
mihtig, ea, *A.* æ powerful, mighty; possible *LN.*
~lic*, miht(e)lic possible.
~lice *av.* powerfully, through power.
mil-dēaw = mele-.
mīl *f.* mile [*Lt.* milia].
~gemearc† *n.* mile-distance.
~gemet *n.* measure by miles.
~pæþ† *m.* milestone-road.
~getæl *n.* mile.
mil *n.* millet [*Lt.* milium].
milc- = meolc-.
milcen, y I. of milk. II. (*n.*) milk food [meolc].
mildian become mild.

mild|e I. *aj.* gentle, mild; merciful, kind. II. *av.* mercifully.
~beorht serene (light) Gl.
~elic propitious.
~elice *av.* kindly, humanely; propitiously.
~heort gentle; merciful.
~heortlice *av.* kindly, mercifully.
~heortnes *f.* mercy.
gemildgian mitigate Gl.
milds = milts.
milisc, mylsc, e honeyed, sweet [mele-].
~ian become sweet *or* mellow || *tr.* gemilscad sweetened.
mīlitisc military — ~mann soldier [*Lt.* miles].
milt|e *m.*, *f.* spleen.
~copu *f.* spleen-disease.
~esēoc spleen-sick.
~(e)wærc, -wræc *m.* pain in the spleen.
miltestre *f.* prostitute [*Lt.* meretrix].
~hūs *n.* brothel.
milts, milds *f.* kindness; mercy [milde].
milts|ian, mildsian pity, be merciful *w. d. or g.*; pardon (sins) *w. d.* || *tr.* make merciful.
(ge)miltsigend *m.* pitier.
~lic pardonable.
(ge)miltsung *f.* pity; mercy; pardon.
mimerian remember.
gemimor known, familiar (*of* language) *wd.*
~lice *av.* by heart.
mīn my; of me.
~lice *av.* in my manner (!).
min|n (!)† small; mean, vile.
~dōm (!)† *m.* abjectness.
~lic petty (favour).
mins|ian *intr. and tr.* diminish.
~ung *f.* parsimony.
minte *f.* mint [*Lt.* mentha].
mis-begān *vb.* disfigure (!) *LN.*
mis-bēodan do wrong to, ill-use *wd.*
mis-bisnian set bad example.
mis-boren misshapen (child at birth); degenerate.
mis-brogden, -brōden distorted Gl.
mis-byrd *f.* abortion.
mis-byrdo *f.* imperfection (of bodily organ).

miscian, mix- mix, apportion.
mis-cealfian mis-calve.
mis-cięrran pervert.
mis-cräcettan*, -crō- croak horribly.
mis-cweþan 5 speak incorrectly; curse *LN.*
mis-dǣd *f.* misdeed, offence.
mis-dōn *vb.* act wrongly, transgress.
mis-gedwield *n.* error.
mis-ęfesian tonsure wrongly.
mis-ęndebyrdan arrange wrongly.
misenlic = missenlic.
mis-fad|ian arrange *or* carry out wrongly.
~ung *f.* mismanagement; misconduct.
mis-faran 2 go astray, err, transgress; fare badly, turn out badly.
mis-fēdan misfeed (!).
mis-fēran go astray, transgress.
mis-fōn I fail to get hold of *or* find *wg.*; make mistake, err, go astray; *wi.* mistake (the day).
mis-gieman neglect.
mis-grētan insult.
mis-hæbbende ill, unwell.
mis-healdan I neglect.
mis-healdsum* negligent.
~nes *f.* negligence.
mis-hier|an *wd.* disregard, disobey.
~nes *f.* act of disobedience.
mis-hwierfed, mis-hworfen perverted; inverted.
mis-gehygd *n.* evil thought.
mis-lǣdan mislead *met.*
mis-lǣran misadvise.
mis-lār *f.* bad teaching *or* advice.
mis-libban lead bad life.
mislic = missenlic.
mis-lician be unpleasant to, displease *wd.*
mis-(ge)limp *n.* misfortune.
mis-limpan 3 *impers. wd.* turn out badly *or* unfortunately.
mis-gemynd *n.* evil record.
mis-rǣcan revile, abuse *wa.*
mis-rǣd *m.* misguidance; misconduct.
mis-rǣdan miscounsel; follow bad policy.
miss *n.* absence, loss.
missan miss (mark) *wg.*; escape notice of *wd.*
mis-scręnce distorted.

mis-scrȳdd misclothed, not in correct costume.

missenlic, misen-, mis(s)end-, misse-, mis(t)- dissimilar, various; wandering, erratic.

~nes f. variety; various colours or forms.

missenlíce, mis(t)- av. variously, differently; **~fēran** wander about.

misseret n. half a year.

mis-spōwan I succeed badly, fail impers. wd.

mis-sprecan 5 grumble, murmur LN.

mist m. mist.

~glōm† misty gloom.

~helm† m. veil of mist.

~hlip† n. misty slope.

~ian grow dim (of eyesight).

~ig misty.

mis-tǽcan misteach.

mistel m. basil; mistletoe.

~lām n. birdlime.

~tān m. mistletoe.

mis-tídan impers. turn out badly, fail.

mis-tímian impers. wd. happen amiss.

mistlic = missenlic.

mis-trīewan*, ī mistrust LN.

mis-tūcian ill-treat L.

mis-tyht|an misadvise; dissuade wrongly.

~endlic dehortative (adverb).

mis-þegnian, -þēnian misuse.

mis-þēon 6 degenerate.

mis-weaxende misgrown (branch).

mis-węndan pervert, lead astray; be perverted.

mis-węnde erring (morally).

mis-weorc n. evil deed.

mis-weorþan 3 impers. wd. turn out badly, be unfortunate.

mis-weorþian slight, neglect.

mis-(ge)wider n. bad weather, bad season.

mis-wissian misguide (of priest).

mis-wrītan 6 make mistake in writing.

mīte f. mite (insect).

gemitt-, see gemētan.

mitta m. a measure [metan].

mitte(s) when, see mid.

mittȳ when, see mid.

miþ = mid with.

mīþan 6 ptc. miþen conceal w.g.

or a., waa., wda.: ic his māþ I dissembled the fact, ic mīn māþ hid myself; †refrain from wi. ‖ intr. lie hid; wa. be hidden from Bd.

mix = meox.

mixian = miscian.

mixen(n), eo f. dunghill, dung.

~dynge, -i- f. dung.

~plante f. nightshade.

mōd n. mind, intellect, heart; pride; courage; violence (of waves).

~blind† blind met.

~blissiende† rejoicing.

~bysgung† f. anxiety.

~cearig† anxious, sad.

~caru† f. sorrow.

~cræft m. intelligence.

~cræftig intelligent.

~cwānig† sad at heart.

~earfoþ n. distress of mind.

~full arrogant.

~gēomor† sad.

~glæd† glad.

~glēaw† wise.

~hęte† m. hate.

~hord† m. mind.

~hwæt† brave.

~gehygd† n. thought.

~lēas spiritless.

~lēast f. want of courage.

~lēof† beloved.

~lufu† love, affection.

~gemynd† n. mind; intelligence.

~rōf† brave.

~sefa† m. mind, heart, soul; character, disposition.

~sēoc† sad.

~sēocnes f. weakness of the heart Gl.

~snot(t)or† prudent, wise.

~sorg† f. sorrow.

~stapol m. character, temperament.

~stapol(fæst)nes f. constancy, firmness of character.

~swīþ† resolute.

~geþanc m. thought(s), mind, heart, intelligence.

~geþoht n. mind, thought.

~þracu† f. courage.

~þrēa† f. trouble of mind.

~þwǽre gentle, mild.

~þwǽrnes f. gentleness.

~geþyldig† patient.

~welig† intellectual.

mōd|wēn† f. hope.

~gewinna† m. anxiety.

~wlanc proud.

gemōd I. n. mind, heart. II. unanimous; on good terms with wd.

mōdelic = mōdiglic.

mōdig high-minded, high-spirited; brave; headstrong, impetuous; proud.

~lic, mōdelic high-minded; brave; proud; magnificent (treasures).

~líce av. boldly; proudly.

~nes f. high-mindedness, magnanimity; pride.

mōd(i)gian become proud; be proud, exult w. on; bear oneself proudly; be impetuous, rage; be indignant, disdain.

gemōdod disposed — hetelíce ~ fierce.

mōdor, dd, -er, d., (g.) mēder f. mother.

~cynd f. nature inherited from mother.

~cynn n. descent on mother's side.

~healf f. mother's side.

~lēas motherless.

~lic maternal.

~slaga m. matricide.

mōdren, dd of a mother.

mōd(d)rige, mōderge f. maternal aunt; cousin.

gemōdsum.

~ian agree.

~nes f. concord.

mohþe = moþþe.

molcen n. curdled milk.

mold|e f. earth, dust; ground; world.

~ærn† n. grave.

~corn n. tuber of saxifraga granulata; the plant itself.

~græf† n. grave.

~hiepe f. heap of earth.

~hrērende† moving on earth.

~stōw f. grave.

~weg† m. the earth.

~wyrm m. earthworm.

molegn (n.) curds.

~stycce n. piece of curd.

mols (n.) decay.

molsnian become mouldy, decay.

mōn|a m. moon; month.

~anǣfen(n) m. Sunday evening.

~andæg, mōndæg m. Monday.

[119]

mōn|anniht *f.* Sunday evening.
~(e)lic lunar.
~sēoc lunatic ; epileptic.
mōnaþ, mōnþ, *pl.* **mōnþas, ~** *m.*
 month — **mōnþes ādl** menses
 [**mōna**].
~ādl *f.* menses.
~ādlig menstruant.
~blōd *n.* menses.
~bōt *f.* a month's penance.
~gecynd *f.* menses.
~fyllen*, ~fylen *f.* time of full
 moon Gl.
~lic lunar ; menstrual.
~sēoc menstruant ; lunatic, epileptic.
~sēocnes *f.* lunacy.
mōr *m.* moor ; mountain.
~bēam *m.* mulberry tree ; blackberry bush [*Lt.* morus].
~berige *f.* mulberry.
~denu *f.* swampy valley.
~fæsten(n) *n.* moor-fastness.
~hǣþ *n.* heath, moor.
~healdt (?).
~hop† *n.* marsh.
~ig marshy.
~land *n.* moorland.
~mǣd *f.* marshy meadow.
~pytt, ~sēaþ *m.* moor-pit.
~secg *m.* sedge.
~slǣd *n.* marshy valley.
~stapa† *m.* moor-traverser.
~wyrt *f.* a plant.
mōraþ, mōrod *n.* sweetened wine
 [*lLt.* moratum].
mor|e, ~u *wk. f.* (edible) root,
 carrot, parsnip.
morgen, e, a, *d.* **morgen(n)e,**
 mor(g)ne daybreak, morning —
 on ~(n)e, on ǣr(ne) mergen, o
 early | next day — tō ~, tō ~(n)e,
 on mor(g)ne, on mergen to-
 morrow ; þæs on ~(ne) the next
 morning.
~ceald† morning-cold.
~colla† *m.* morning terror.
~dæg *m.* daylight, morning ; to-
 morrow.
~drẹnc *m.* morning potion.
~giẹfu *f.* gift from husband to wife
 on morning after wedding.
~lang† tedious, long (day).
~leoht *n.* dawn, morning.
~lic, my-, morgendlic, morning,
 of to-morrow.
~mæsse *f.* first mass.

morgen|mẹte *m.* breakfast.
~regn *m.* morning rain.
~sēoc† sad in the morning.
~spell† *n.* morning tidings.
~sprǣc *f.* periodical assembly of a
 guild.
~steorra *m.* morning star.
~swēg† *m.* morning clamour.
~tīd† *f.* morning.
~torht† bright at morn.
~wacian rise early.
morn-, *see* **morgen.**
mōrod =mōraþ.
mortere *m.* mortar [*Lt.* mor-
 tarium].
morþ *n.* murder, homicide ; †death,
 destruction ; crime ; anything horrible.
~bealo† *n.* violence, murder.
~crundel *n.* corpse-pit (?) Ct.
~dǣd *f.* murder ; deadly sin ; crime.
~slaga *m.* murderer.
~sliẹht *m.* murder.
~weorc *n.* murder.
~wyrhta *m.* murderer.
morþor *not W.nm.* murder · crime,
 sin ; torment, misery.
~bealo† *n.* murder.
~bẹdd† *n.* (violent) death-bed.
~cofa† *m.* prison.
~crǣft† *m.* murder, crime.
~cwealm† *m.* murder, slaughter.
~hẹte† *m.* deadly hate.
~hof†, ~hūs† *n.* house of torment
 (hell).
~hycgende† plotting mischief.
~lēan† *n.* retribution.
~scyldig† guilty.
~slaga *m.* murderer.
~slagu *f.,* **~slẹge** *m.* murder.
~sliẹht† *m.* slaughter ; the slain.
~wyrhta *m.* murderer.
mōs, *often* ō *n.* marsh, moor.
mōs *n.* food.
mōste *prt. of* **mōt.**
mot *n.* atom, mote.
mōt toll, tax *lN.*
mōt-. *Cp.* **gemōt.**
~ærn, -e *n.* court-house.
~bell *f.* meeting-bell
~hūs *n.* court-house.
~lǣþ- *n.* court, assembly (?) *L.*
~gerēfa *m.* president of a court.
~stōw *f.* assembly-place, forum.
~weorþ entitled to attend an assembly.
mōt *vb., prt.* **mōste** be allowed,

have opportunity *w. inf.* —
 mōste ic would that I might . . .
 | must (?).
gemōt, once -ēt *n.* meeting,
 council, discussion — **witena ~**
 parliament | †battle.
~ærn, ~hūs *n.* senate-, council-
 house.
~mann *m.* orator Gl.
~stẹde *m.,* **~stōw** *f.* meeting-,
 council-place.
mōt|ian talk ; make speech ; dis-
 cuss, dispute.
~ere *m.* orator.
~ung *f.* conversation.
moþ|þe, *lN.* **mohþe** *f.* moth, in-
 sect.
~freten moth-eaten.
mu(c)g-wyrt *f.* mugwort.
mūl *m.* mule [*Lt.* mulus].
~hierde *m.* mule-keeper.
gemun remembering *wg.* [ge-
 man].
gemuning *f.* remembrance.
mund *f.* hand† ; hand (as measure) ;
 protection, guardianship ; protector, guardian.
~beorg† *m.* sheltering hill.
~bora *m.* protector, patron, guardian ; prefect.
~bryce *m.* breach of legal protection
 or guardianship ; fine for the offence.
~byrd *f.* protection, patronage ;
 help ; fine for breach of legal
 protection.
ge-byrdan protect.
~byrdnes *f.* protection ; protector,
 patron, advocate ; protection of
 rights granted by charter.
~crǣft *m.* power to protect.
~gripe† *m.* grasp.
~heals† *once* protection (?).
~leow, ~le(a)w (*m.*) hand-basin.
~rōf† strong-handed.
mund|ian protect, be guardian.
~iend *m.* protector.
gemunde *prt. of* **geman.**
munt *m.* mountain, hill [*Lt.*
 mons].
~ælfen *f.* mountain nymph.
~land *n.* hilly country.
munuc *m.* monk [*Lt.* monachus].
~behāt *n.* monastic vow.
~cild *n.* child intended for monastic
 life.
~gegiẹrela *m.* monk's dress.

munuc|hād *m.* monastic state.
~hēap *m.* body of monks.
~lic monastic.
~līce *av.* monastically.
~līf *n.* monastic life ; monastery.
~regol *m.* rule of a monastic order ; monastic order.
~stōw *f.* place for monks.
~þeaw *m.* monastic rule.
~wīse *f.* manner of monks.
munucian *rfl.* become a monk.
mūr *m.* wall [*Lt.* murus].
murc† *once* grievous (hunger).
murc|ian, murcn- complain, murmur ; grieve.
~nere *m.* complainer, murmurer.
~ung *f.* complaint, murmuring ; grief.
murnan 3 *intr.* be sad, anxious ; care, reck *w.* for *d.* || *tr.* lament ; care for, regard.
mūs *f.*, *pl.* mȳs mouse — ~e-pīse vetch.
~fealle, -ię *f.* mouse-trap.
~fealo mouse-coloured.
~hafoc *m.* mouse-hawk.
mūscelle, mūs(c)le, mūxle *f.* mussel.
must (*m.*) new wine, must.
~flēoge*, muscflēote *f.* must-fly Gl.
mūtung *f.* loan Gl. [*Lt.* mutuum].
mūþ *m.* mouth ; opening, orifice.
~ādl *f.* mouth-disease.
~bana† *m.* devourer.
~berstung *f.* breaking out of ulcers round mouth.
~copu *f.* mouth-disease.
~frēo free to speak.
~hæl† salutary words (?).
~hrōf *m.* palate.
~lēas without mouth.
mūþa *m.* mouth of river.
mūþettan let out (secret) *abs.*
mūwa = mūga.
mūxle = mūscelle.
mycel = micel.
mycg *m.* midge.
~nętt *n.* mosquito-net.
mydd *n.* bushel [*Lt.* modius].
myderce, mydrece, med-, *lN.* mudric- *f.* chest, coffer.
myl (*n.*) dust.
mylcen = milcen.
mylen *m.* mill [*Lt.* molina].

mylen|brōc *m.* mill-brook.
~dīc *f.* mill-pond (?) Ct.
~geard *m.* mill enclosure.
~hamm *m.* mill enclosure.
~hwēol *n.* mill-wheel.
~pōl, -pul *m.* mill-pool.
~scearp† sharp-ground.
~stān *m.* grindstone.
~steall *m.* mill.
~stede *m.* mill.
~stig *f.* mill-path.
~trog *m.* mill-trough (which brings water to mill-wheel).
~waru *f.* mill-dam.
~weard, mylew- *m.* miller.
~wer *m.* mill-dam.
gemynan, *see* geman.
gemynd *fn.* memory, remembrance ; memento ; caring for, solicitude.
~dæg *m.* commemoration-day.
~lēas, myndlēas insane, foolish.
~līest *f.* madness.
~stōw *f.* monument.
~ewierþe worthy of mention Bd.
gemynde† *once* mindful.
myndg|ian *intr.* *wg.* remember, bear in mind ; intend || *tr. wg.* remind ; demand payment. *Cp.* mynegian.
~iend *m.* reminder.
(ge)~ung *f.* remembrance ; admonition ; mynegung claim of payment.
gemyndig, m- *wg.* mindful.
~lic, gemyndelic to be borne in mind by *wd.* ; memorable.
~līce *av.* by heart.
~licnes *f.* remembrance.
myne† *m.* memory, memorial ; purpose ; desire ; love, affection.
~lic† desirable, pleasant.
myne *m.* minnow.
myne = męne.
gemyne remembering *lN.*
gemyne *sbj.* of geman.
mynecen(u) *f.* nun [munuc].
myneg|ian, myng- = myndgian.
~iendlic hortatory.
myn(e)le† *f.* longing, desire.
mynet *n.* coin ; coinage [*Lt.* moneta].
~cīepa *m.* money-changer.
~īsen *n.* coinage.

mynet|slege *m.* minting, coinage.
~smiþþe *f.* mint.
mynet|ian coin, mint.
~ere *m.* money-changer ; minter.
mynnan *or* mynian *intr.* direct one's course (to), intend.
mynster *n.* monastery, nunnery ; church, cathedral [*Lt.* monasterium].
~clǣnsung *f.* purification of a church.
~clūse *f.* cell.
~fǣmne *f.* nun.
~gang *m.* entering on monastic life.
~hām *m.* monastery.
~hata *m.* persecutor of monasteries.
~lic monastic.
~līce *av.* monastically.
~līf *n.* monastic life ; monastery.
~mann *m.* monk.
~munuc *m.* monk living in monastery.
~prāfost *m.* provost of monastery.
~prēost *m.* priest who conducts service in a church.
~scīr *f.* management of a monastery.
~stōw *f.* cathedral town.
~þeaw *m.* monastic custom.
~þegnung *f.* service in a monastery.
~wīse *f.* custom of a monastery.
myntan intend ; think.
myrgan rejoice.
myrgen = morgen.
myrig|e, myrge I. pleasant, delightful. II. *av.* pleasantly, delightfully ; (sing) sweetly.
~nes *f.* music.
myr(i)gþ *f.* delight ; pleasantness ; sweetness (of sound).
myrre, -a *f.* myrrh [*Lt.*].
myrten I. *aj.* (animal) having died of disease. II. *n.* flesh of such animals.
myrþr|an* murder [morþor].
~a *m.* murderer.
~ung *f.* murder.
mysci† *pl.* flies Ps.
mȳse = mēse table.
gemȳþe *n.*, *gen. pl.* waters'-meet, junction (of two streams *or* roads) [mūþ].
myx = meox.

N.

nā, *A.*, *W.* nō not, no — nā þȳ (*or* þe) lǣs *av.* nevertheless.

nabban = ne habban.

naca† *m.* boat, ship.

nacod, nǣced I. naked, bare; destitute; empty (words). II. *f.* nakedness.

~nes *f.* nakedness.

nǣcan, hn- kill Gl.; hn- check (disease).

nǣced = nacod.

nǣdl, *A.* nēþl *f.* needle.

nǣd(d)re *f.* snake.

nǣder|bīta *m.* ichneumon.

~fāh variegated like a snake.

~wyrt, ~winde, nǣdre- *f.* adderwort.

nǣfde *prt. of* nabban.

nǣfig poor *lN.* [ne, habban].

nǣfre *av.* never [ne, ǣfre].

nǣft poverty Gl.

~ig poor Gl.

nǣgan† address, speak to.

genǣgan†, ē assail; address (with words).

nǣgel *m.* nail (of finger, toe); peg, nail; plectrum.

~seax *n.* nail-knife.

~spere *n.* sharp nail (?) Gl.

nǣgen *once* = ne mǣgen *sb.* may not.

nǣgled|bord† with nailed planks (*of* ship).

~cnearr† *m.* ship with nailed planks.

~crǣt *n.* iron chariot.

nǣgl(i)an nail; nǣgled studded with silver.

nǣm|an.

~ing *f.* contract Gl.

nǣnig no(ne) *adj.*; *no. wg.* — ~e þinga not at all [ne, ǣnig].

~wiht *av.* not at all.

nǣniht = nān-wiht.

nǣnne, *see* nān.

nǣp, *pl.* ~as *m.* turnip, rape [*Lt.* napus].

~sǣd *n.* rapeseed.

---

nǣre = ne wǣre.

nǣs = ne wǣs.

nǣs *av.* not.

nǣs- nose. *Cp.* nosu.

~gristle *f.* nose-gristle.

~þȳrel *n.* nostril.

nǣsc skin Gl.

nǣss *m.* headland, promontory; †ground, earth, depths.

~hlip† *n.* slope of headland.

genǣstan† *once* contend.

nǣster *once* wild carrot (?) Gl.

nǣt|an annoy, oppress, subdue.

~ing *f.* blaming.

nafaþ, *see* nabban.

nafel|a *m.* navel.

~sceaft *f.* navel.

nafeþa *m.* nave (of wheel).

nafu *f.* nave (of wheel).

~gār *m.* auger.

genāg† R.

nāh = ne āh.

naht, o = nāwiht.

~fremmend† *m.* evil-doer.

~gītsung *f.* wicked avarice.

~lic worthless, of no avail.

~līce *av.* evilly.

~nes *f.*, ~scipe *m.* worthlessness, cowardice.

~wela *m.* false wealth.

nāhte = ne āhte.

nā-hwǣr, nāwer, nōwer *av.* nowhere; never; not at all.

nā-hwǣrn*, nāwern *av.* nowhere.

nā-hwæþer, nō-, nawþer, nāþor, nōþer I. *no. wg.* neither of two: of heora nāþrum; sē þe nāþor nele, ne leornian ne tǣcan. II. ~ ne .. ne (.. ne) *cj.* neither .. nor (.. nor): hē nolde āsendan nā(hwæþ)er ne engel ne hēahengel (ne wītegan).

nā-hwanon *av.* from nowhere.

nā-hwider *av.* to no place.

nālǣs not = nealles.

nalde = ne wolde.

nam = ne eom.

---

nām *f.* seizure [niman].

~rǣden(n) *f.* learning Gl.

namian mention (name of); appoint, nominate; give name to.

nam|a *m.* name; noun.

~bōc *f.*, ~bred *n.* register.

~cūþ celebrated, of note.

~cūþlīce *av.* by name.

~mǣlum *av.* name by name.

namnian call by name.

nān, *a. m.* nānne, ǣ no(ne), not one *aj.*; *no. wg.* — ~e þinga on no account (allow it).

~þing, nāþinc *n. wg.* nothing.

~wiht, nān(w)uht, *lN.* nǣniht I. *n. wg.* nothing. II. *av.* not at all.

nard (*m.*) spikenard [*Lt.* nardus].

nas = ne wǣs.

nāst = ne wāst.

nāt = ne wāt.

nāt|hwǣr *av.* somewhere [nāt I know not].

~hwæt *n.* something.

~hwelc *no.*, *aj.* some one or other, some.

nātes-hwōn, nāteþæshwōn, nātōhwōn *av.* not at all [nāwiht].

nātōhwōn = nāteshwōn.

nā-þe-lǣs nevertheless, *see* nā.

nāþer = nāhwæþer.

nāþinc = nān þing nothing.

nauht = nāwiht.

nauþer = nāhwæþer.

nāwa *once av.* never [ne, āwa].

nāwer = nāhwǣr.

nāwern = nāhwǣrn.

nā-wiht, nō-, -wuht, nauht, naht, noht I. *n. w. g.*, *w.* elles nothing; nothingness, naught: tō nauhte weorþan; anything worthless: for nauht tō habbenne consider worthless; wickedness; of no account: ēowre godas ne sind nahtes. II. *aj. indecl.* worthless, bad. *Cp.* āwiht. III. *av.* not.

nawþer = nāhwæþer.

ne, ni *av.*, *cj.* not; nor — ne . . ne neither . . nor.

nē-fugol, *see* nēo.

nēa-, *see* nēah.

nēa-lǣc|an, nēah-, nēo- *wd.* approach.

(ge)~ung *f.* approach.

nēa|lic, nēah- near.

~līce *av.* nearly, about.

~wist, -e *fm.* nearness, neighbourhood, presence | associating with, society; sexual intercourse.

nēad = nīed.

nēadian, ē compel *L. w.* tō, *w. ger. Cp.* nīedan, nēodian.

nēadig.

~nes *f.* obligation Gl.

nēadinga, nēadlunga = nīedinga.

nēah I. *av.*, *cpv.* nēar, ȳ, ē, *spl.* nīehst near *of place* — feorr oþþe ~, ge ~ ge feorr far and (or) near | *of time* near; lately — *spl.* last: þā ic hine nēhst geseah | *of quantity, degree* nearly — *spl.* dōn swā wē nȳhst magon act as nearly as we can accordingly; *so also* for·nēah, ful·nēah nearly. II. = *prp. wd.*, *also cpv. and spl.* near *of place*: nān ne sǣte hiere tīen mīlum ~ settle within ten miles of Carthage; nīehst þǣm tūne | *of time*, *impers.*: wēndon þæt hit nēar worulde geendunge wǣre þonne hit wǣre | *of manner* according to: ic dō ~ þām þe þū cwǣde. III. *aj.* very rare in positive nēah, nēag-, *which is gen. expressed by composition, as in* nēahfrēond *compared with* hiera nīehstan frīend | *cpv.* nēarra, ē, nēara nearer | *of time* later || *spl.* nīehsta, ēa, ē, nēxt, *A.* nēst nearest | *of time* latest, last — æt nīehstan at last, finally; next — þā æt nīehstan thereupon, then | next (of kin), nearest (friends): sēo nēste hond the nearest heir.

~būend† *m.* neighbour.

~gebūr *m.*, ~gebȳren, *IN.* ~gebȳrild *f.*, nē(a)h,h)eb- neighbour.

~cirice *f.*, neighbouring church.

~dūn *f.* neighbouring hill.

~ēa *f.* neighbouring river.

nēah|ēalond *n.* neighbouring island.

~frēond *m.* near relation *or* friend.

~gangol *wd.* (official) placed near (the king).

~hergung *f.* war close at hand.

~gehūsa *m.* neighbour.

~mǣg, nēam- *m.* near relation.

~mǣgþ *f.* neighbouring province.

~mann *m.* neighbour.

~munt *m.* neighbouring mountain.

~nes *f.* nearness, neighbourhood.

~sibb I. *f.* relationship. II. nearly related.

~stōw *f.* neighbouring place, neighbourhood.

~tīd *f.* time close at hand.

~tūn *m.* neighbouring farm, town.

~þēod *f.* neighbouring nation.

~wæter *n.* neighbouring piece of water.

~wudu *m.* neighbouring wood.

nēah-, *see also* nēa-.

geneah† *once n.* sufficiency, abundance.

geneah *vb.*, *pl.* -nugon suffice, not be wanting *impers.*; suffice, be competent *w. ger.*

geneahh|e, -neh(h)e, ~ige, neahhi(g)e *av.* sufficiently, abundantly; frequently; earnestly.

geneahlīce*, e *av.* frequently; usually (worn, *of* clothes).

neahhige = geneahhe.

genēahsen *once* near, close together.

neaht = niht.

nealles, nallas, nālæs, nālas, nals *av.* not. *Cp.* næs.

neam = ne eom am not.

nēan *av.* from near; near; about, nearly — for·nēan nearly.

nēar *cpv. of* nēah *av.*

nearo, nearw- I. *aj.* narrow, confined; limited, petty; causing *or* accompanied by difficulty, hardship, distress, difficult (breathing); strict, severe. II. *n.* (?) † narrow place; confinement, prison; position of difficulty, danger, hardship.

~bregd† *n.* cruel artifice.

~cræft† *m.* power of imprisoning.

~fāg† cruelly hostile.

~grāp† *f.* tight grasp.

~lic oppressive, grievous.

~līce *av.* briefly (narrated); grievously, oppressively; accurately, minutely.

nearo|nes *f.* strait; oppression (of asthma); anxiety, distress, misfortune.

~nīed *f.* urgent need.

~searo† *n.* imprisonment (?).

~sorg† *f.* sorrow, affliction.

~þancas *mpl.*, ~þancnes *f.* wickedness.

~þearf† *f.* severe straits.

~wrenc† *m.* cruel artifice.

nearwian *tr.* confine, compress; hard press, afflict || *intr.* become narrow, be diminished.

nearwe *av.* tightly (bound); oppressively, severely; anxiously; accurately, narrowly.

nēat *n.* ox, cow; animal.

genēat *m.* companion (with sense of dependency), hanger-on, vassal, tenant [nēotan].

~land *n.* land held by genēat.

~mann = genēat.

~riht *n.* regulations as to tenure of genēat-land.

~scolu *f.* troop.

nēawung *f.* nearness *IN.* [nēah].

nębb *n.* nose; face; beak; front.

~gebrǣc *n.* nose-mucus.

~corn *n.* pimple.

~wlatfull impudent Gl.

~wlite *m.* face.

nębbian snub, rebuke.

nefa *m.* nephew; grandson; stepson.

genefa *m.* nephew.

nefene *f.* niece; granddaughter [nefa].

nefne = nemne.

nefte, nepte *f.* cat's-mint [*Lt.* nepeta].

genēgan = genǣgan.

nēh = nēah.

genehhe, genehlīce, *see* geneahhe.

nēh(h)e-būr, *see* nēah-.

genēhwian approach *IN* [nēah].

nele = ne wile.

nellan = ne willan.

nęmn|an, ~ian, *prt.* nęm(n)de give name to *wanom.*; designate by name *w. a. and a. or* for *a.*, tō: þis līf hē nemde for weg, se dæg wæs eall ge~ed tō Sunnandæge included in; address, invoke; mention; nominate, appoint [nama].

~igendlic nominative.

nęmning *f.* name.
nemne, y, nefne *not W.* **I.** *cj.* unless, except. **II.** *prp. wd.* except. *Cp.* **nympe.**
nēo- corpse.
~będd† *n.* corpse-bed.
~fūgol†, nē- *m.* carrion-bird.
~sīþ† *n.* death.
nēod *occ.* = **nīed** need.
nēod *f.* desire, zeal, earnestness, pleasure — **~e** eagerly, diligently.
~fracu† *f.* greed.
~frēond, *see* **nīed-.**
~full earnest, zealous.
~laþu† *f.* friendly invitation (?).
~līce *av.* eagerly, zealously, diligently ; †greatly.
~lof *n.* diligent praise.
~spearwa† *m.* sparrow Ps.
~weorþung† *f.* honouring Ps.
nēodian *impers. wg.* be required, be advisab'e [= **nēadian**].
nēol = **neowol.**
neom = **ne eom.**
neoman = **niman.**
nēon = **nīwan.**
geneorþ contented Gl.
neorxna-wang *m.* paradise.
~lic of paradise.
nēos|an, ~ian *not W. w. a. or g.* investigate, inspect ; go to (bed), visit ; attack.
(ge)~ung *f. W.* visit, visitation.
nēotan 7 *wg.* use, enjoy.
neoþan, ~e, i *av.* beneath, below.
~weard, nioþo-, neoþe-, niþe-, nyþe- situated beneath, below ; lower part of, bottom of.
neoþor = **niþor.**
nēowe = **nīwe.**
neowol, niwel, nēol, *vE.* **nihol(d)** prostrate ; with face downwards ; headlong ; deep down, profound [= *ni-heald].
~lic depths of : **of niwellicum brēoste.**
~nes *f.* abyss, depth.
nēp.
~flōd *m.* neap-tide, very low tide.
nepte = **nefte.**
genęr, nęr *n.* refuge, safety — **on ~e healdan** harbour (Christians) [genesan].
~stęde *m.* place of refuge.
nęr|ian save, protect *w. a., d.*
ge~e(d)nes *f.* deliverance.
~(i)gend *m.* preserver, Saviour.

nęrung *f.* protection.
genesan, nesan 5 be saved ; *tr.* escape from, survive.
nese, nǣse *av.* no. *Cp.* **giese.**
nest *n.* nest ; young bird (!).
nest *n.* provisions, rations.
~pohha *m.* wallet.
nestan spin.
genęsta *m.* neighbour *IN.* [nēah].
nestlian build nest [nest].
nęt(e)le, nętel *f.* nettle.
nętt *n.* net (for hunting, fishing, flies) ; network (of clouds) ; spider's web.
~gearn *n.* net-yarn, string for making nets.
~rāp *m.* toil, snare.
nętte *f.* caul.
nēþ|an venture on, dare, *wi.* risk (life) [nōþ].
~ing *f.* daring, hardihood.
neurisn a kind of paralysis *or* aneurism (?).
nęwe-sēoþa, niwe-, nu-, ni- *m.* pit of stomach.
nēxt, *see* **nēah.**
nī- = **nīw-.**
nic *av.* not I !, no [ne, ic].
nicor *m.* water-monster ; hippopotamus Gl.
~hūs† *n.* water-monster's abode.
nīed, ēa, ēo *f.* inevitableness ; requirement, what is required ; duty ; compulsion ; hardship, distress ; *the Runic letter* n.
~bād *f.* enforced contribution, toll.
~bādere *m.* toll-exactor.
~bebod† *n.* command.
~behēfe, ~behēfedlic necessary.
~behēfednes *f.* necessity.
~behōf(lic) necessary.
~beþearf necessary.
~boda† *m.* violent messenger (?).
~bryce *m.* requirement, need.
~bysgo† *f.* distress.
~bysig† distressed.
~clamm *m.* distress, need.
~cleofa†, ~cofa† *m.* prison.
~costing† *f.* affliction.
~dǣda *m.* acting under compulsion (self-defence).
~gedāl† *n.* enforced separation (of body and soul), death.
~fara† *m.* one who journeys under compulsion.
~faru† *f.* enforced journey, death.
~gefēra† *m.* forced companion (?).

nīed|frēond *m.* close relation, intimate friend.
~gafol *n.* tribute.
~gęnga† *m.* miserable wanderer.
~giēld *n.* tribute, exaction.
~giēlda *m.* debtor.
~gripe*† *m.* violent grasp.
~hād *m.* force.
~hǣmed *n.* rape.
~hǣmestre *f.* concubine.
~hǣs *f.* compulsion.
~help *f.* help in need.
~hiernes *f.* servitude.
~mǣg, ge~ *m.* near relation.
~mǣgen *n.* force.
~māge *f.* near relation.
~micel† urgent (errand).
~nǣm *f.* taking by force, rapine.
~nǣman ravish, rape.
~nes *f.* necessity.
~nima *m.* one who takes by force.
~niman 4 take by force, abduct (woman).
~nimu *f.* rapine *IN.*
~nimung *f.* rapine, abduction (of woman).
~riht *n.* duty ; service ; office ; necessary payment, due.
~scyld *f.* duty, obligation.
~sibb *f.* relationship.
~gestealla† *m.* inseparable companion.
nīed-pearf I. *f.* inevitableness ; need (of), what is needed ; constraint ; distress, trouble. **II.** necessary ; useful.
~lic necessary ; useful.
~līce *av.* necessarily.
~nes *f.* necessity, compulsion ; need (of) ; trouble, distress.
nīed|þēow *m.* slave.
~þēowetling *m.* one enslaved for unfulfilled obligation.
~þēowian reduce to servitude, enforce service from.
~þing *n.* necessary thing.
~þrāfung *f.* reproof.
~wǣdla† *m.* wretch.
~geweald† *n.* tyranny.
nīed-wīs necessary ; due.
~līce *av.* of necessity.
~nes *f.* necessity.
nīed|wraca *m.* one who is forced to be an avenger.
~wracu† *f.* violence, distress.
~wrǣclīce *av.* violently.
~gewuna *m.* enforced custom Gl.

nīed-wyrhta *m.* one who acts under compulsion *or* involuntarily.
nīed|an compel *w.* tō, *w. sbj.* ~ ūt expel | press (debtor): ~ hīe æfter gafole. *Cp.* nēadian, nēodian.
ge~edlic compulsory.
~ing*, nēadung *f.* compulsion.
nīede *av.* necessarily.
nīedes *av.* of necessity.
nīedinga, -unga, -unge, nēad-(l)unga *av.* by force, against one's will.
nīedling *m.* slave ; sailor.
genīeh near — ~e māgas near relations.
nīehst *spl. of* nēah.
~a, nēxta *m.* neighbour.
nierw|an, -ian, *prt.* ~de, nier-(w)ede narrow, confine — ge~ed crowded (house) ; hem in ; afflict, persecute ; threaten (?) [nearo].
nierwett *n.* narrowness ; narrow place, pass ; shortness of breath.
nierwÞ *f.* prison.
nīeten *n.* animal [nēat].
~cynn *n.* species of animal.
~lic animal.
nifol† = neowol.
nift *f.* niece ; granddaughter ; stepdaughter [nefa].
nīg- = nīw-.
nigon nine.
~feald nine-fold.
~tēoþa nineteenth.
~tīene nineteen.
~tīenlic containing the number nineteen (!).
~tig = hundnigontig ninety.
~wintre nine years old.
nigoþa ninth.
nihstig, nistig, e, nixtnig fasting — on ~ fasting *av.*
niht, ea *f.* night ; darkness ; *w. numbers* = ' day.'
~bealo† *n.* nocturnal harm.
~butorflēoge *f.* moth.
~ēage able to see at night.
~eald a day old.
~egesa† *m.* nocturnal terror.
~feormung† *f.* night's shelter.
~egale *f.* nightingale ; night-jar.
~genga† *m.* (night) goblin.
~genge *f.* (goblin), hyena (!).
~gield *n.* night-service *or* sacrifice.
~glōm† darkness of night.
~helm† *m.* shades of night.
~hræfn, -(h)remn *m.* night-jar.

niht|hrōc *m.* raven.
~lang a night in length.
~langes *av.* for a night.
~lic, nihtelic nocturnal, of night.
~nihstig*, ~nestig fasting a night.
~rest† *f.* bed.
~rīm, ~gerīm *n.* number of days.
~sang *m.* seventh-hour service, compline ; copy of this service.
~scadu*, ~scada *m.* nightshade (plant).
~scu(w)a† *m.* shades of night.
~slǣp *m.* night's sleep.
~wacu, ~wæcce *f.* night-watch.
~waru *f.* night-wearing (of clothes).
~weard† *m.* night-guardian.
~weorc† *n.* nightwork.
nihtern|e, ea I. *aj.* nocturnal — ~um *av.* for a (whole) night. II. *av.* during the (whole) night.
~nes *f.* night-time.
nihtes, ea *av.* at night, by night — oÞ forÞ ~ till far on in the night.
nim|an 4 *prt.* nōm, nam, *pl.* nōmon, nāmon take hold of, hold ; contain, have room for ; take by force : on him heora ǣhta ~ ; catch ; receive, accept, take, *also met.* : sige ~ gain the victory, andan ~ tō him take dislike to him. ‖ *intr.* on ~ have effect (*of* remedy).
~ing *f.* plucking *IN.*
nimÞe = nymÞe.
genip *n.* mist, cloud, darkness [nīpan].
nīpan 6 grow dark.
nis = ne is.
nist|an, ~ian, ~lan build nest [nest].
niþ *n.* abyss [nīÞer].
nīþ *m.* enmity ; † contest, battle — ~e rōf warlike ; † affliction, trouble ; † wickedness.
~cwalu† *f.*, ~cwealm† *m.* violent death, destruction.
~draca† *m.* hostile dragon.
~full ill-disposed, malicious.
~fullice *av.* maliciously.
~giest† *m.* malicious stranger, fiend.
~grama *m.* anger, malice.
~grimm† fierce, hostile.
~heard† bold.
~hell *Pr. f.* hell.
~hete† *m.* hate ; affliction ; wickedness.

nīþ|hycgende† hostile.
~hygdig† brave.
~lice *av.* cowardly.
~loca† *m.* hell.
~plega† *m.* battle.
~scaþa† *m.* foe, persecutor.
~sele† *m.* hostile hall.
~synn*† *f.* sin.
~getēon† *n.* battle, attack (?).
~weorc† *n.* battle.
~geweorc† *n.* hostile deed.
~wracu *f.* severe punishment.
~wundor† *n.* portent.
niþan = neoþan.
niþas = niþþas.
niþemest, see niþerra.
niþer *av.* downwards ; down ; below.
~bogen bent down.
~dǣl *m.* lower part.
~gang *m.* descent.
~heald inclining downwards, bent down.
~hrēosende falling down.
~hryre *m.* downfall.
~lic low, lower ; inferior, humble.
~nes *f.* bottom.
~scyfe *m.* descent.
~sige *m.* setting (of sun).
~stige *m.* descent.
~weard downward.
~weard(es) *av.* downwards.
niþer|ian humiliate ; condemn.
(ge)~igendlic deserving condemnation.
(ge)~ung *f.* humiliation ; condemnation.
niþ(e)re *av.* below.
niþerra, -era, eo *cpv.* lower, *spl.* niþemest.
nīþing *m.* infamous man, villain.
genīþla† *m.* enemy.
niþor, eo *av.* lower.
niþþas†, niþas *mpl.* men.
nīw-, nī(g)-. *See* nīwe.
~bacen fresh-baked.
~cenned newborn.
~cielct, -cealt newly whitewashed.
~gecierred, ~cumen neophyte.
~fara *m.* new-comer, stranger.
~gehālgod newly consecrated.
~(ge)hwierfed, ~(ge)hworfen newly converted.
~lǣred newly initiated.
~lic fresh.
~lice *av.* recently.
~nes *f.* newness, novelty.

nīw|slīcod glossy.
~tiẹrwed† fresh-tarred.
nīw|ian renew ; renovate, re-store.
~ung f. rudiment (!).
nīwan, -e, nẹ̄o(wa)n av. recently
— nū ~ recently.
~ācẹnned newborn.
~cumen neophyte.
nīw|e, í, A. nẹ̄owe I. new, recent.
II. nīwe, nīge av. recently.
niwel = neowol.
nīwer(e)ne tender, young (child).
niwiht = nā-wiht.
niwunga, nẹ̄owinga av. anew.
noctern nocturn [Lt.].
genōg I. aj. enough ; abundant ;
much, many. II. av. sufficiently ;
very.
nōhwæper = nā-.
nolde = ne wolde.
nōm prt. of niman.
nōn n. ninth hour ; service at the
ninth hour, nones.
~mẹte m., ~gereord n. dinner.
~sang m. nones.
~tīd f., ~tīma m. ninth hour.
norþ av., cpv. ~or, spl. ~(e)mest
northwards ; in the north.
~dæl m. north part, the north.
~duru f. north door.
~ēast av. north-east.
~ēast-ẹnde m. north-east end.
~ēast-lang extending north-east.
~ẹnde m. north part.
~folc n. (people of the) north of
England, (people of) Norfolk.
~healf f. north side ; north.
~hẹre m. army in the north (of
England).
~hylde f. north slope (?) Ct.
~hymbre I. pl. Northumbrians.
II. aj. Northumbrian.
~hymbrisc Northumbrian.
~land n. northern land.
~lane f. the north lane.
~lẹ̄ode pl. Angles.
~lic northern.
~gemǣre n. north boundary.
~portic m. north porch.
~rihte av. due north.
~rodor m. northern sky.
~sǣ f. North Sea.

norþ|scēata m. northern promon-tory.
~þēod f. northern nation.
~wēalas, -walas mpl. the Welsh,
Wales.
~wēal-cynn n. the Welsh.
~(e)weard north.
~weard(es) av. northward.
~weg m. way north ; Norway.
~west av. north-west.
~west-ẹnde m. north-west end.
~west-gemǣre n. north-west boun-dary.
~wind m. north wind.
norþan av. from the north — be ..
~ prp. wd. north of.
~ēastan av. from the north-east.
~ēastan-wind m. north-east wind.
~hymbre pl. Northumbrians.
~weard north (part) of.
~westan av. from the north-west.
~westan-wind m. north-west
wind.
~wind m. north wind.
norþemest, see norþ, norþerra.
norþerne from the north, northern ;
Northumbrian, from the north of
England ; Scandinavian.
norþerra, -(e)ra cpv., spl. norþ(e)-
mest more northern.
norþmest, see norþ, norþerra.
nōse†, ō† f. promontory.
nos(t)le f. fillet, band.
nos|u, g. ~a, ~e, f. nose. Cp. næs-.
~gris(t)le, nosu- f. cartilage of the
nose.
~þȳr(e)l, ~terle n. nostril.
not m. mark ; sign [Lt. nota].
~wrītere m. scribe.
notian make use of, enjoy, dis-charge (office) [notu].
notere m. scribe Gl. [Lt. nota-rius].
not|u f. use, enjoyment ; discharge
(of office), employment [nēotan].
~georn industrious.
nōþ† f. boldness.
nōþer = nāhwæþer.
nōwend, -ent m. master of a ship ;
sailor.
nōwiht = nā-.
nōwþer = nāhwæþer.
nū I. av. now — nū-gēn, nū-gīet,

nū-þā, see gēn, gīet, þā. II.
cj. w. indic. now that, since
— correl. nū .. nū. III. interj.
nū, nū lā, nū ge lā behold !
nū|lā interj. now !
~na once av. now [nū, nū].
numol capacious Gl. [niman].
nunn|e f. nun, vestal [Lt. nonna].
~fǣmne f. nun.
~hīred m. nunnery.
~līf n. leading life of a nun.
~(an)mynster n. nunnery.
~scrūd n. nun's habit.
nybþe = nympe.
genycled, -cnycled bent, crooked
Gl.
genyht, once -hþ fn. sufficiency,
abundance [geneah].
~full abundant.
~līce av. abundantly.
genyhtsum satisfied wg. ; abun-dant.
~ian suffice wd. ; be abundant.
~nes f. abundance.
nyllan = ne willan.
nymne = nemne.
nympe, i, e, once nybþe not W.
cj. unless, except. Cp. nemne.
nypel (m.) trunk (of elephant).
nysse, nyste = ne wiste.
nytan = ne witan.
nyten ignorant [ne, witan].
~lic ignorant.
~nes f. ignorance, sloth ; igno-miny (!).
nytt I. f. use, advantage, profit ;
office, occupation ; duty. II. aj.
useful, advantageous, profitable,
beneficial [nēotan].
~lic useful, beneficial.
~licnes f. usefulness, useful pro-perty.
~nes f. use, advantage.
nyttwierþ|e, -weorþ, u useful,
profitable.
~lic useful.
~līce av. usefully.
~licnes f. utility.
nytt|ian wg. make use of, enjoy,
eat.
~ung f. use, advantage.
nyttol useful, beneficial.
nypan = neoþan.

O.

ō = **ā** ever.
ōcusta = **ōxta**.
oden *f.* threshing-floor; yard.
oemseten = *ymbseten shoot.
of I. *prp. wd. place, motion — starting-point* from, away from : Dryhten lōcaþ of heofenum; faran of stōwe tō stōwe. **ūt(e)** of out of, away from | *time* from — of þissum forþ henceforth | *origin* of : þā menn of Lundenbyrig ; *material* of : wyrcan mannan of eorþan ; = *genitive* of : ān mǣden of þām cynne | *causal* from : him stent ege of þē ; of yflum willan syngian ; ongietan micel of lȳtlum infer | *partitive* : genam of þǣs trēowes wǣstme some of | *change* from : āwendan (translate) of Lǣdene on Englisc | *deprivation* from : geniman ūs of Dēofles anwealde; of dēaþe ārīsan | *concerning* about : sǣdon him fela spella of hira lande. II. *av.* starting-point, motion away: stōd lēoma him of ; *origin* sēo þēod þe hē of cōm ; *privative* : him man slōg þā handa of.
of·ann *vb. wdg.* grudge, refuse to grant.
of·āscian, -āxian inquire, inquire for ; find out by asking, learn.
of·bēatan 1 beat to pieces, break ; beat to death.
of·blindian blind (!) *LN.*
of·call|an 2 — ic bēo ~en I am cold.
of·clipian summon by calling ; obtain by calling out *or* cries, call for (help).
of-cumende derivative (in grammar).
of·cyrf *m.* cutting off; what is cut off.
of-dǣl, æf- tending downwards.
of-dǣle *n.* downward slope, descent.

of·drǣdd (*ptc.*) afraid.
of·dūne *av.* down. *In comp. also* adūn(e)-, dūne- [of, dūn].
~heald directed downwards.
of·earm|ian have pity.
~ung *f.* pity.
ofen *m.* oven ; furnace.
~bacen baked in an oven.
~raca *m.*, **~racu** *f. st.* oven-rake.
ofer, -ær I. *prp. w. a., d. (d. not W.) place* over, above, on *rest, motion* : standende ~ hī ; his hūs ~ stān getimbrode ; *across* : ~ land ēodon ; *extension* throughout : ~ eall his rīce | *time* after : þæs ~ Ēastron ; *during* : ~ winter sǣton | *quantity* beyond, above : ~ þæt in addition ; †~ snāwe scīnende | *superiority, rule* : cyning ~ eall Angelcynn | contrary to, against : ~ willan ; ~ þā trēowa in violation of the truce | *object of verb* : wacian ~ ; †~ benne sprǣc. II. *av.* over; se cwellere him ~ stōd ; hiene ~ brohte ferried him over ; eall þæt ~ biþ tō lāfe.
ōfer *m.* edge, margin; bank (of river), shore (of sea).
ofer|ian exalt.
~ing *f.* superfluity.
ofer·ǣt *m.* gluttony ; feast.
~e gluttonous.
ofer·bæc *av.* back(wards`.
~getēung *f.* tetanus.
ofer·bebēodan 7 rule.
ofer·becuman 4 supervene (!).
ofer·bīdan 6 survive (a person) ; outlast, survive (hardships).
ofer·biternes *f.* (excessive) bitterness.
ofer·blica*, io *m.* superficies Gl.
ofer·blīþe (over) cheerful.
ofer·brǣd|an cover.
~els *m.* covering, veil, garment ; surface.
ofer·brǣw*, ā *m.* eyebrow.
ofer·brecan 4 break (agreement).

ofer·bregdan, -brēdan 3 cover ; be covered.
ofer·brū *f.* eyebrow.
ofer·brycgian make bridge over.
ofer·cǣfed covered with ornamental work.
ofer·ceald† very cold.
ofer·cīdan censure, reprove.
ofer·cierr *m.* passing over.
ofer·clif *n.* overhanging cliff Gl.
ofer·climman 3 climb (wall).
ofer·cræft *m.* cunning.
ofer·cuman 4 overcome ; get at, reach, obtain.
ofer·cyme *m.* arrival (!).
ofer·cȳþan disprove, confute.
ofer·dōn *vb.* overdo.
ofer·drenc *m.* drunkenness.
ofer·drencan intoxicate.
ofer·drīfan 6 cover (with drifting sand) ; disperse (darkness) ; refute ; outvote.
ofer·drinc|an 3 intoxicate.
~ere *m.* drunkard.
ofer·druncen I. *n.* drunkenness. II. *aj.* intoxicated.
~nes *f.* over-drinking, intoxication.
ofer-(ge)drync *m.* intoxication ; feast.
ofer-(ge)dyre *n.* lintel.
ofer-ēaca *m.* surplus, remainder.
ofer-eald very old.
ofer-ealdormann *m.* chief officer.
ofer-et(t)ol gluttonous.
~nes *f.* gluttony.
ofer-fær *n.* passing over.
ofer-færeld *n.* passage.
ofer-fǣtt very fat.
ofer·fæþman cover.
ofer·faran 2 *intr.* pass by, pass away || *tr.* pass, cross ; traverse ; go through (danger) ; come upon, meet with.
ofer·feallan 1 fall on, attack.
ofer·feng *m.* buckle, clasp.
ofer·feohtan 3 overcome.
ofer·fēran pass, traverse ; come upon, meet with.

ofer·fērnes *f.* possibility of being crossed, ford.

ofer-fierro *f.* great distance, remoteness.

ofer·flēdan overflow.

ofer·flēde overflowing, in flood.

ofer·flēon 7 flee from *tr.*; fly over.

ofer·flēogan 7 fly over (!).

ofer·flītan 6 beat (in competition); refute.

ofer·flōw|an 1 overflow *tr., intr.* ~ednes, ~en(n)es, ~nes, ~endnes *f.* superfluity ; abundance.

~ende superfluous.

~endlīce *av.* superfluously.

ofer·fōn 1 seize.

ofer·froren frozen over.

ofer-full over full.

ofer·fylgan *wd.* pursue; persecute; attack.

ofer·fyllan feed to excess, stuff.

ofer·fyllo *f.* repletion; excess in eating or drinking.

ofer·gān, -gangan *intr.* come to an end, pass away; *also impers. wg.*: †þæs oferēode that trouble is over ‖ *tr.* come upon (*of* sleep, disease); pervade; overrun, conquer (country); cross; pass beyond; transgress.

ofer·gǣg|an transgress.

~ednes *f.* transgression.

~end *m.* transgressor.

ofer·gapian disregard, neglect.

ofer·gēare old.

ofer-geat- oblivion.

ofer-gang, -geong *m.* going across.

ofer·genga *m.* traverser, traveller.

ofer·gēotan 7 cover by pouring, cover, wet.

ofer·gīem|an disregard, neglect.

~nes *f.* observation *IN.* (!).

ofer·giét|an 5 forget *wg.*

~ende forgetful.

~nes *f.* oblivion.

~ol, eo forgetful.

~olian, -geotel- forget.

~olnes *f.* forgetfulness.

ofer-gifre gluttonous.

ofer·glenged over-adorned.

ofer·grǣdig too covetous.

ofer·gūmian neglect, disregard.

ofer·gyldan gild, adorn with gold.

ofer·gylden gilded, adorned with gold.

ofer·gyrd *ptc.* girded.

ofer·hacele *f.* hood.

ofer-hēah† very high.

ofer·healdan 1 neglect to do.

ofer·healf-hēafod *n.* upper part of head.

ofer·hebban 2 fail to do, neglect; pass over, omit mention of.

ofer·helian cover, conceal.

ofer·helung *f.* covering, concealing.

ofer·helmian cover, overshadow.

ofer·heortnes *f.* vehemence of feeling.

ofer·hergian ravage.

ofer·hier|an not listen to, disregard; overhear, hear.

~e disobedient.

~nes *f.* disregard, *esp.* of legal enactment; fine for such disregard.

ofer·higian† (?).

ofer·hlæstan overload.

ofer·hlēap|an 1 leap over; pass over.

~end *m.* overleaper.

ofer·hlēopor not hearing, inattentive.

ofer·hlēoþrian outsound.

ofer-hliep *m.* leap of the moon in leap-year.

ofer·hlīf|ian tower above, excel; be threatening.

~ung *f.* sublimity, excellence.

ofer·hlūd clamorous.

ofer·hlȳde clamorous.

ofer·hlȳttrian clarify.

ofer·hog|a *m.* despiser; proud person.

~ian despise.

~iend *m.* despiser.

ofer·holt† *n.* phalanx of shields (?). *Cp.* oferhyrned.

ofer·hrǣgan† *once*, ǣ† tower above (?) *wd.*

ofer·hrēfan, ȳ roof, cover.

ofer·hrēran, ȳ overthrow.

ofer·hrops voracity.

ofer·hycgan despise.

ofer·hyge*, -hige (?) *m.* pride.

ofer·hygd, hȳd I. *fn.* pride. II. *aj.* proud. *mis-written or mispronounced for* oferhygdig, -hygdg- (?).

~ig proud.

~igian be proud.

ofer·hylmend† *m.* prevaricator.

ofer·hyrned† having horns above. *Cp.* oferholt.

ofer·ieldo *f.* great age.

ofer·iernan 3 come upon; overwhelm, run over, cross; go over (a subject).

ofer·lād *f.* carrying across *IN.*

ofer·lǣdan overwhelm, oppress.

ofer·lagu *f.* cloak Gl.

ofer·lecgan overload, surfeit.

ofer·lēof† very dear.

ofer·lēor|an *A. intr.* pass (by) of space and time; *tr. and intr.* transgress, prevaricate.

~nes *f.* transgression.

ofer·libban survive.

oferlīce *av.* excessively.

ofer·liehtan outshine.

ofer·līpan 6 cross (water).

ofer·lufu *f.* excessive love.

ofer-mǣcga† *m.* illustrious person.

ofer·mǣg *vb.* prevail (!).

ofer·mægen *n.* superior force, mighty power.

ofer·mǣstan over-fatten.

ofer·mǣt|e excessive, immense.

~lic immense.

~o *f.* presumption.

ofer-māþum† *m.* very valuable treasure.

ofer·mēd|e I. *n.* pride. II. *once aj.* proud [mōd].

~u (*f.*) pride.

ofer·mēdla *m.* pride, pomp.

ofer-gemet *n.* excess.

ofer·mete *m.* excess in food, feasting.

ofer·mētto *f. often pl.* pride [mōd].

ofer·micel excessive.

~nes *f.* excess.

ofer·mōd I. *n.* pride. II. *aj.* proud, self-confident.

~nes *f.* pride.

~ig proud.

~(i)gian be proud.

~ignes *f.* pride.

~(i)gung *f.* pride, presumption.

~lic proud.

~līce *av.* proudly.

~licnes *f.* pride.

ofer·nied *f.* extreme necessity.

ofer·niman 4 rape; carry off, get rid of (poison) (!).

ofer·nōn *n.* afternoon.

ofer·genyhtsumian superabound.

ofer·prūt arrogant.

ofer·rǣdan read through; consider (?).

[128]

ofer-ranc too sumptuous (clothes).
ofer-reccan confute.
ofer-renco *f.* extravagance, luxury.
ofer-ricsian rule over *wd.*
ofer-rīdan 6 ride across.
ofer-rōwan 1 row over.
ofer-sǣlic transmarine.
ofer-sǣlig very fortunate.
ofer-sǣlþ *f.* excessive enjoyment.
ofer-sǣwisc foreign.
ofer-sāwan 1 oversow.
ofer-scead(w)ian overshadow.
ofer-sceatt *m.* interest, usury.
ofer-scēaw|ian superintend.
~igend *m.* superintendent.
ofer-scīnan 6 illuminate.
ofer-scūan, -ȳan overshadow.
ofer-sēam *m.* bag *LN.*
ofer-sēcan† overcome (?).
ofer-segl *m.* top-sail.
ofer-seglian sail across.
ofer-sendan transmit (!).
ofer-sēon 5 survey, see; despise.
ofer-sēocnes *f.* serious illness.
ofer-gesett in authority.
ofer-sielfran, y, -seolfrian silver.
ofer-sīeman overload, oppress
(heart).
ofer-sittan 5 take possession of;
abstain from.
ofer-slǣp *m.* excessive sleep.
ofer-slēan 2 subdue (heat of body).
ofer-slege *n.* lintel.
ofer-slop *n.* surplice.
ofer-slype *m.* surplice.
ofer-smēaung *f.* excessive meditation.
ofer-sprǣc *f.* loquacity.
~e loquacious.
ofer-sprǣdan cover.
ofer-sprecan 5 speak too much;
be abusive.
ofer-sprecol loquacious.
~nes *f.* loquacity.
ofer-stǣlan confute; convict;
convince.
ofer-stǣppan 2 step over, cross;
go beyond, exceed.
ofer-steall *m.* opposition.
~a *m.* survivor.
ofer-stiellan leap over.
ofer-stig|an 6 mount above, sur-
mount, climb over; surpass, be
stronger than.
~endlic superlative (in grammar).
ofer-stige *m.* astonishment, exaltation (of mind).

ofer-stigennes *f.* passing over.
ofer-swimman 3 swim across.
ofer-swīþ|an *wk., also prt.* -swāþ
overcome, surpass.
~estre *f.* conqueror.
~nes *f.* oppression, distress.
~ung *f.* oppression, distress.
ofer-swīþe *av.* too much.
ofer-swīþrian prevail, conquer.
ofer-swōgan 1 cover, choke (with
weeds).
ofer-tǣl *n.* odd number.
ofer-teldan 3 cover.
ofer-tēon 7 cover; finish.
ofer-getilian overcome (!).
oferge-timbran build.
ofer-togennes *f.* being covered
(eyes with film).
ofer-trahtnian comment on, expound.
ofer-tredan 5 trample on, tread
under foot.
ofer-trūw|a *m.* over-confidence.
~ian be over-confident in *wi.* — ~od
over-confident.
ofer-þearf *f.* great necessity; extreme distress.
~a *m.* one in extreme need *or* distress.
ofer-þeccan cover.
ofer-þēon 6, 7 excel, surpass.
ofer-þrymm *m.* excessive power.
ofer-þungen *ptc.* of oferþēon *or*
*oferþingan surpass.
ofer-wadan 2 wade over.
ofer-weald|an 1 get the better of.
~end† *m.* ruler.
ofer-weaxan 1 overgrow.
ofer-weder (?) *n.* stormy weather.
ofer-wennan, -wenian become
insolent.
ofer-weorc *n.* tomb.
ofer-geweorc *n.* superstructure;
tomb.
ofer-weorpan 3 throw backwards,
throw down; sprinkle.
ofer-wiellan boil down.
ofer-wigan† overcome.
ofer-winnan 3 overcome, take
(fortress).
ofer-wintran get through the
winter.
ofer-wist *f.* gluttony.
~lic supersubstantial *LN.*
ofer-wlenced (*ptc.*) great (king).
ofer-wlenco *f.* great prosperity,
riches.
ofer-wrecan 5 overwhelm.

ofer-wrēon 6, 7 cover.
ofer-wrigels *m.* covering.
ofer-writ *n.* letter.
ofer-gewrit *n.* super-, in-scription.
ofer-wundennes *f.* trial, experi-
ment Gl.
ofer-wyrcan cover.
ofer-ȳþ *f.* great wave.
ōfesc = ōwisc.
ofet *n* fruit; pulse Gl.
of-faran 2 overtake, intercept
(army), *often w.* hindan.
of-feallan 1 kill by falling on.
of-fēran overtake (an army).
of-ferian carry off.
offerenda *m.* psalm sung during
the offertory [*Lt.*].
of-fiellan kill.
of-flēogan 7 fly away.
offrian sacrifice, bring offering [*Lt.*
offerre].
offrung, -ing *f.* offering a sacrifice;
offering, sacrifice.
~dagas *mpl.* offering-days.
~disc *m.* paten.
~hlāf *m.* shew-bread.
~sang *m.* hymn sung when offering
is made.
of-fylgan come up with, overtake.
of-gān, -gangan *vb. w.* æt exact,
extort, acquire; begin : ofgā his
sprǣce (suit) mid foreaþe.
of-gangend|e, ~lic derivative.
of-gēotan 7 moisten, soak; put
out (fire with water).
of-giefan 5 abandon, give up, leave;
wda. commit (corpse to the
earth).
of-habban detain.
of-hag|ian *impers.* — gif him ~ie
if it is inconvenient to him.
of-healdan 1 withhold.
of-hearm|ian *once, impers. wdg.*
cause grief : him ~ode þæs.
of-hende, æfhynde out of one's
possession.
of-hnītan 6 gore to death.
of-hrēosan 7 overwhelm; fall down.
of-hrēowan 7 pity *wg.* — *imper.*
wdg.; excite pity *wd. of pers.*
of-hyngred, -od hungry.
of-iernan 3 overtake (by running);
hē wæs ofurnen tired with
running.
of-lǣtan 1 b relinquish; let blood
wg.
oflǣte, -ete, -ate *f.* oblation,

offering ; sacramental wafer ; wafer [*lLt.* oblata].

of·lang|ian — ~od weorþan feel longing.

of·lecgan† lay down.

of·lēogan 7 lie, be false.

of·lician be displeasing *or* unpleasant *wd.*

of·licgan 5 overlay (child).

of·linnan 3 cease.

of·lysted, -lyst desirous *wg., w. sbj.*

of·man *vb , prt.* -munde recollect *wa.*

of·manian exact (fine).

of·myrþr(i)an murder.

of·nēadian extort *w.* æt.

ofnet receptacle, vessel.

of·niman 4 fail, be wanting *wd.*

ofost, of(e)st, oef-, o† *f.* speed, haste, hastening on — ~ is sēlest *w. ger.* the quicker the better. of·stum hastily [of, ēst].

~līce *av.* speedily, hastily.

of·rīdan 6 overtake by riding.

of·sacan 2 deny charge.

of·scacan 2 shudder Gl.

of·scam|ian *rfl. wg.* be ashamed : hē hine ~ode þæs | ~od weorþan be ashamed.

of·scēotan 7 shoot to death ; *ptc.* ofscoten elf-shot, (cattle) suffering from distension of the stomach.

of·scotian shoot to death.

of·sendan send after, summon, make one's summons reach.

of·sēon 5 see *wa.* or hwǣr *w. indc.*

of·seten(n)es *f.* siege.

of·sett|an press hard, afflict.

~ing *f.* pressing hard.

of·sittan 5 press down by sitting on ; oppress, afflict ; besiege ; repress, check ; occupy, take possession of.

of·slægennes, ę *f.* being killed.

of·slēan 2 kill.

of·slītan 6 bite to death.

of·smorian suffocate, strangle.

of·snīþan 6 slaughter (animal).

of·sprǣc *f.* utterance.

of·spring *m.* offspring.

of·spyrian find out.

ofst = ofost.

of·stæppan 2 trample on.

of·stand|an 2 *tr.* restore, make restitution Gl. || *intr.* stick fast, remain unmoved — *ptc.* ~en unmoved.

ofstende *once* hastening.

of·stician stab to death.

ofstig swift.

ofge·stignes *f.* descent.

of·stingan 3 stab to death.

of·swelgan 3 devour.

of·swingan 3 flog to death.

oft *av., cpv.* ~or, *spl.* ~ost often.

of·talu *f.* verdict against a claim.

of·tēon 7 *wda.* take away, withhold.

of·torfian stone *or* pelt to death.

oft-rǣd|e frequent ; ready at any time.

~lic frequent.

~līce *av.* frequently ; habitually.

of·tredan 5 tread down ; injure *or* kill by trampling.

oft-sīþ *m.* — on ~as often.

of·tyge, i *m.* withholding.

of·tyrfan stone to death.

of·þǣnan moisten.

of·þecgan† destroy.

of·þencan *once* remember.

of·þiestr(i)an darken, obscure.

of·þīnan 6 — ofþinen moist, damp.

of·þringan 3 *tr.* crowd, press on.

of·þrycc|an squeeze, choke ; oppress, afflict.

~ednes, ofþrycnes *f.* oppression, repression ; affliction, trouble.

of·þryscan beat down, repress.

of·þrysm(i)an choke.

of·þyncan *impers. wdg., w. indc.* be displeased, weary of.

of·þyrst(ed) thirsty, thirsting for *wg. or* æfter.

of·weorpan 3 kill with missile.

of·worpian stone (to death).

of·wundrian be astonished.

cga *m.* terror ; object of terror.

ō-gengel (*m.*) bar, bolt.

ō-hielde, -heald sloping.

ōhsta = ōxta.

oht† *f.* terror (?) ; persecution (?) [ōga ; ehtan].

oht = āwiht.

oht-rīp harvest *lN.*

ōhwǣr = ā-.

ōl-þwang *m.* strap Gl.

ōlǣcan = ōleccan.

ō-lecc|an, -lǣcan, -liccan, -lehtan *wd.* treat gently ; soothe ; please ; flatter ; propitiate.

~end*, -ehtend, ~ere *m.* flatterer.

~ung *f.* soothing ; flattery ; favour ; allurement.

olfend, -a *m.* camel [*Lt.* elephantem].

~miere *f.* she-camel.

ōliccan - ōleccan.

oll (*n.*) contumely, contempt.

ollung = andlang.

ōlyht-word *once n.* flattery. *Cp.* ōleccan.

ōm rust.

~an, hōman *pl.* erysipelas.

~cynn *n.* corrupt humour.

~ig rusty ; inflammatory, resulting from inflammation.

~iht full of inflammation, inflammatory.

ōmian become rusty Gl.

on *prp. w. a , d , i.* | *place, motion* in, on, into, on to, to, among. *Also met.* : on Englisc in English ; on his geweald onfēng | *time* in, at, during | *instrumental* : wurdon on flēame generede ; on Godes naman ! | *defining* : þæt gafol biþ on dēora fellum ; *attribute* : on nǣddran hīwe (form) | *hostility* : rǣdan on hīe plot against | *change to,* into : of Lǣdene on Englisc āwendan translate | *object of verb* : on Gode trūwian ; lōcode on hine | *to form adverbs* : on ōþre wīsan in another way ; tōdǣlan on fēower into four parts.

on·ǣht *f.* property.

on·ǣlan, *A.* in- ignite ; heat (oven) ; burn ; consume ; inflame (with desire).

on·æþele natural to, inherent in *wd.*

on·āl *n.* burning ; what is burnt.

onā·scunung *f.* detestation.

onā·sendednes *f.* immission (!).

on·bæc, ~ling *av.* back(wards).

on·bærn|an *tr.* kindle, *also fig.* ; heat, inflame, *also fig.* ; burn, consume ; incite *w.* tō.

~nes, in-*f.* incense.

on·bǣru *once*† *f.* [*or n. pl.*] — ~ habban *wg.* refrain from (?).

on·bāsnung *f.* expectation.

on·belgan* 3 — inbolgen exasperated.

on·bēn *f.* imprecation (!).

on·bēodan, in- 7 *wda.* announce, tell ; command.

on·beran 4 carry off, plunder ; weaken, injure.

on-bescēawung f. inspection.
on-bescūfan 7 thrust out (!) Gl.
on·bīdan 6 wait; *wg.* wait for, expect.
on·bīeg|an bend; subdue.
~nes f. curvature.
on·bierhtan illuminate; enlighten.
on·biernan, in-, eo 3 burn, kindle
  | *ptc.* onburnen inflamed (body), resulting from inflammation.
on·bindan, un- 3 unbind; disclose.
on·bītan 6 taste, partake of (food) *wg.*
on·blǣstan break in *intr.* (!) Gl.
on·blanden† *ptc.* mingled (with).
on·blāw|an, in- 1 breathe into; inspire.
~nes f. inspiration.
on·blāwan, in- 1 inflate.
on·blōtan 1 sacrifice, offer (sacrifice).
on-geboren inborn.
onbran = onbarn *prt. of* on-biernan.
on·bregdan, -brēdan, in- 3 *tr.* move quickly, jerk, pull open || *intr.* move quickly, start up (from sleep).
on·bring (n.) instigation.
~ellan *fpl.* instigations.
on-gebroht imposed.
on-bryce m. inroad Gl.
on·bryrd|an, in-, abr- inspire; incite, excite; excite to compunction.
~ing f. incitement.
~nes f. inspiration; excitement; contrition.
on·būgan 7 *intr.* bend; bow (to show respect) *w.* tō; submit, yield *wd.*; deviate.
on·būtan, ab- *av., prp. w. a., d.* around; *of time* about.
geon·byrdan attack, oppose *w.* on *a.*, ongēan.
on·byr(i)g|an, *lN.* ingeberigan taste *w. g.*, *rarely a.*
~ing f. taking food.
~nes f. tasting, taste.
on·cann *vb. w. a. and g. or for d.* accuse of, reproach with, be indignant with.
on·cennan bear (child).
on·(ge)cīegung (!) f. invocation.
on·cierran *tr.* change direction of, turn | change, pervert, influence (a person); revoke || *intr.* turn.
on·clifiende adhering.

on·cnǣwe known.
on·cnāw|an 1 know; understand; perceive; acknowledge.
~(en)nes f. knowledge; acknowledgement.
on·cnyssan strike down.
on·cunnes f. accusation [oncann].
on·cunning f. accusation.
on·cwepan 5 answer, respond, re-echo; cry out, protest.
on·cȳpan *once* make known.
on·cȳpig† *once wg.* devoid, without. *For* un- (?).
on·cȳp|þ| f. grief, distress.
~dǣd f. injury.
on·dǣl|an infuse *lN.*
~end m. infuser *lN.*
on·dōn *vb.* open.
on·dōung f. injection.
on·drǣd|an 1 b, *prt.* -ēd, A. -ēord; *also wk. prt.* -ǣdde fear *w. a. or g.*, *and often w. rfl. d.*, *also w.* fram.
~endlic terrible.
~ing f. fear.
on·drencan, in- inebriate.
on·drīfan*, in- 6 drive forth, utter (words).
on·drincan, in- 3 drink of *wg.*
on·druncnian get drunk.
on·dwǣscan extinguish *for* ā- (?).
one = ono.
on·ealdian grow old.
on·eardiend m. inhabitant.
onefn = onemn.
on·ēgan† fear [ōga].
on·ēgnan†, oe fear.
on·emn, -ef(e)n *prp. w. d., a., av.* close by, alongside; *of time* — ~ þǣm at the same time.
~þrōwian sympathize.
on·erian plough (field).
onerning = onierning.
ōnett|an hasten; be brisk, cheerful; *wd.* anticipate, be too quick for [*from* *onhātjan].
~ung f. precipitation.
on·ēpung, oe f. inspiration.
on·fægnian show gladness, fawn (*of* dog).
on·fǣreld n. entrance; attack; journey.
on·fæstnian pierce.
on·fæpmnes f. embrace.
on·fangen(n)es f. receiving.
on·fealdan 1 unfold.
on·feall, e (m.) swelling.
on·feallende invading, rushing on.

on·fēng m. taking hold of, seizing; appropriating; defence; †attack.
on·fēng|e I. m. receptacle. II. taken.
~nes f. reception, acceptance.
geon-fenge taken (!) *lN.*
on-gefeoht n. attack.
on·find|an, in- find out, discover; perceive; experience, suffer.
~end m. finder, inventor.
on·flǣscnes f. incarnation.
on-geflogen attacked with disease.
on·flyge m., onflīgn- infectious disease.
on·fōn 1 b *w. a., g., i.* take; receive; accept; take up (a person), take under protection, stand sponsor to; conceive (child).
on·fōnd m. taker up.
on·forhtian be afraid.
on·gefremming (!) f. imperfection.
on·fundelnes f. experience, proof.
on·fundennes f. experience, trial; solution (of riddle).
ongǣgn = ongēan.
ongēn = ongēan.
on·gal|an* 2 charm.
~end m. wizard.
on·gang m. entrance; irruption, attack.
on·geador *av.* together.
on·gēan, -geagn, -gēn, A. -gǣgn, ę, -gǣgum; *in comp. also* gēan-; *once* ongend I. *prp. w. a.; w. d.*, *rare in W. except when av.* | to wards, *also met.*; opposite, in front of; against; *contrast* : ~ þǣm on the contrary; *equivalence* : ~ þǣm in return, ~ þæt þæt hīe bohton .. in consideration of .. II. *av.* opposite; in the opposite direction; back — eft ~ back again; against: him ~ cōmon; in reply: †sohte gielpword ~ ; on the other hand; again.
ongēan-cierrendlic relative (in grammar).
ongēan-cyme m. return.
ongēan-fealdan 1 fold back.
ongēan-flōwende*, ongend-ongent- refluent Gl.
ongēan-hwyrf m. return.
ongēan-weard going towards *or* against.
~es *av.* towards.
~lic adversative.
~līce *av.* adversatively.

ongēan-wiþerian oppose.
ongegn = ongēan.
ongēn = ongēan.
ongend = ongēan.
on-gēotung f. pouring in.
on-giefan 5 give back; pardon.
on-gieldan 3 w. a., g. pay the
  penalty, be punished for; †forfeit,
  lose (life) wg.; wd. sacrifice (to
  idols).
on-giernan*, y inflict (!).
on-gierwan undress.
on-giet|an 5 †seize, assail | per-
  ceive, see, hear; feel; be told of,
  hear of; understand, know, re-
  cognize; know carnally.
~(en)nes f. knowledge; intellect;
  meaning.
on-ginn|an, ag-, once g- 3 w. inf.,
  ger. begin, often pleon.; undertake; try for, endeavour, carry
  on; attack || intr. begin; behave,
  act.
~endlic inchoative (verb).
~es f. undertaking.
on-gripe m. attack.
ongrislic = an-.
on-gunnennes f. undertaking.
on-gyrdan unbuckle.
on-hādian degrade from holy
  orders.
on-hæle† secret, hidden [helan].
on-hætan, in- heat; inflame
  (heart).
on-hag|ian impers. w. a. or d. of
  pers. and tō d., w. sbj., w. ger. be
  convenient, suitable; be within
  one's pecuniary means: gif him
  (or hine) tō þām ~ige if he can
  afford it; be contented; be inclined: þeah hine hwon ~ige
  has little inclination.
on-hātan 1 b promise wda.
on-hātian grow hot.
on-healdan*, a- 1 keep (peace).
on-hēaw m. chopping-block.
on-hebban, in- 2, also wk. raise,
  met. exalt; leaven; begin | take
  away.
on-hefednes f. exaltation.
on-hende on hand, demanding
  attention.
on-hield|an, in- tr. bend down;
  humble; incline (ear) met. || intr.
  decline, sink.
~ednes f. declining Gl.
on-hierdan encourage.

on-hindan av. behind.
on-hinderling av. back.
on-hlīdan 6 tr. open; intr. appear.
on-hlinian lean on (!).
on-hnīgan 6 bend down, bow tr.
  and intr.
on-hōn 1 b tr. hang, crucify.
on-hohsnian† once abominate,
  detest.
on-hrægl n. covering Gl.
on-hrēodan = onrēodan.
on-hrēran touch; stir up, agitate;
  agitate (mind); excite (anger).
on-hrīnan 6 w. g., i. touch.
on-hrine m. contact.
on-hrōp (m.) importunity; abusive
  language.
on-hūpian draw back, recoil.
on-hwelan 4 resound.
on-hweorfan 3 tr. change; re-
  verse, recall (curse) || intr. change;
  †wg. change from, be cured of.
on-hwierf|an tr. turn; change.
~ednes f. change, alteration.
on-hyr|ian w. d., a. imitate, emu-
  late.
~enes f. imitation.
~iend m. imitator, emulator.
~ing f. imitation, emulation.
on-hȳscan, ý ridicule; deceive;
  revile; detest.
on-iernan† 3 yield (of door burst
  open).
on-ierning*, e f. attack lN.
on-iewan show wda.
on-innan, in- prp. wd., av. in,
  within, into, among.
on-lǣnan wdg., da. lend; grant;
  lease, let.
on-lǣtan 1 b loosen, relax.
onlāh, -lēah prt. of -lēon.
on-lecgende (salve) to be laid on.
on-legen f. medicinal application.
on-lēon 6 wdg. lend; grant. W.gen.
  has only the prt. onlāh, ēa, using
  onlǣnan for the other parts of the
  verb.
on-lieht|an, in-, -eo-, -ian illu-
  minate, illumine; give sight to;
  enlighten (mind).
~end m. illuminator.
~ing f. illumination, enlightening.
~nes f. illumination.
on-līes|an untie, loosen; release,
  deliver.
~nes f. deliverance, redemption.
on-līexan*, in- become light, dawn.

on-līþian intr. yield || tr. untie
  (shoestring).
on-lōciend m. spectator.
on-lūcan 7 unlock; open; disclose,
  reveal.
on-lūtan 7 intr. bow (down).
on-mǣlan† speak wd.
on-man vb., prt. -munde wag.
  think worthy, esteem; consider
  (worthy) | rfl. care for, wish.
onge-mang, on-mang I. prp. wd.
  among; time — ~ þām meanwhile, ~ þǣm þe while. II. av.
  among (others), by way of inter-
  lude. Cp. gemang II.
on-mearcung (!) f. inscription.
on-middan, on . . middan wd. in
  the midst of.
on|o, ~e A. behold! | if, whether;
  interr. particle. Cp. heonu.
on-ōrettan† perform with effort,
  accomplish.
on-orþung (!) f. inspiration.
on-pennian unpen, open.
on-rād once (!) f. riding.
on-rǣs m. attack; violence.
onred (m.) a plant.
onrēod prt. = onrēad.
on-rēodan 7 redden.
on-rid (n.) riding-horse.
on-riht† once right, proper.
~līce av. rightly, properly.
on-ryne m. running, course; attack
  (of illness).
on-sac|an, L. occ. onsc- 2 w. a., g.
  deny, clear oneself (of accusation);
  excuse oneself; refuse, resist;
  †attack: hine fēores ~ aim at his
  life.
~nes*, onscea- f. excuse.
on-sǣc lN. excused; denying.
on-sǣgan prostrate.
on-sǣgdnes, -sęg(e)d-, -sǣgnes,
  once lN. sǣgednes f. sacrificing,
  offering; thing sacrificed.
on-sǣge assailing.
on-sǣlan untie, loosen.
on-sagu f. accusation.
on-sand (!) f. immission.
on-sang m. incantation.
on-sāwan 1 sow.
on-scacan 2 shake.
on-scōgan, an- unshoe wai.:
  ~ hine ōþre fēt —— ptc. unscōd.
on-scortian grow short (of days).
on-scrȳdan*, un- waa. undress,
  strip off.

on·scun|ian, -eon-, -yn- detest; reject; shun, fear; irritate (!).

~iend *m.* detester.

~iendlic detestable.

~ung *f.* detestation, abomination; exasperation (!).

on-scyte *m.* attack; calumny

on·sēcan require of, exact *wag.*

on·sēcg|an *wda.* sacrifice, offer || deny, abjure.

~ung *f.* sacrificing.

on·sendan send *wda.*; send out; give up (ghost); emit (odour).

on·setenes, -setnes *f.* laying on (of hands); founding.

on-gesetenes *f.* knowledge Bd.

on·setl *n.* riding.

on·setnis, on·settnung *f. LN.* [ē=ǣ?] snare.

on·settan oppress.

on·sīcan 6 sigh.

on·sīgan 6 sink, decline, *also met.* Cp. on-sīgan *wd.* attack.

on·sittan 4 *w. a., g.* fear, *often w. rfl. d.* Cp. on-sittan occupy; oppress.

onslǣge = onslege.

on·slǣpan, ā 1 b sleep, fall asleep.

on·slēan 2 once coin (money).

on-slege*, æ *m.* blow.

on·slūpan 7 become loose (*of shoe-string*).

on·spannan 1 unfasten; disclose (thoughts).

on·spornan, and- 3 stumble.

on·sprǣc *f.* claim, accusation.

on-spreca *m.* claimant, accuser.

on-sprecend *m.* plaintiff, accuser.

on·springan 3 *intr.* crack, burst; spring forth (*of streams*).

on·sprungennes *f.* defect, want.

on-stǣl† (*m.*) arrangement, creation. æ = ǣ, *or* -stǣl *A. form of* -steall (?).

on·stǣpe *m.* entrance.

on·stǣppan 2 walk, go.

on-stal *once m.* institution, supply (of teachers). -stal = stāl *or* -steall (?).

on·stāl (*m.*) charge, accusation.

on-standende urgent (!).

on·stellan institute; initiate, begin (flight); appoint.

on·stiepan raise.

on·stīgend *m.* mounter, rider.

on·sting *m.* authority; claim.

on·stīpian (!) make hard.

---

on·stregdan 3 sprinkle.

on·styr|ian *intr. and tr.* move; cause (fear); agitate (mind), disturb.

~enes *f.* movement.

onsundrian = āsundrian.

on·sundr|an, ~um *av.* apart, separately; especially [sundor].

on·swebban put to sleep; bury.

on·swifan 6 *tr.* turn, turn aside.

on-symbelnes *f.* festival Bd.

onsȳn = ansīen.

on-talu *f.* successful claim.

on·tend|an kindle; heat, *met.* inflame.

~nes *f.* burning; fire; inflammation (of body); *met.* fire of desire, passion, desire.

on·tēon 7 untie.

on·tīegan untie.

on-tige *m.* claim, usurpation.

on-timbernes (!) *f.* instruction.

on-timbran (!) instruct, edify.

on·tydran nourish, increase (fire).

ontydre = ortydre.

on-tyht*, i attentive, intent Gl.

~ing*, i *f.* attention Gl.

on·tyhtan incite, impel.

on·tȳn|an open; reveal.

~nes *f.* aperture.

on·pēon† 6 be of service.

on·pwǣgennes *f.* washing.

on·pwēan, in- 2 wash clean.

on·ufan *av., prp. wd.* upon.

on·uppan I. *prp. w.d., a.* upon, on. II. *av.* above; besides.

on·wacan 2 *intr.* awake; be born (from), originate.

on·waccan *f.* arousing *LN.*

on·wadan 2 enter, penetrate *met.*

on·wǣcan mollify.

on·wǣcn(i)an, -a- *intr.* awake; be derived, spring from.

on·wǣstem *m. LN.* increase = ōwǣstm.

on·wealcan, and- 1 roll.

onweard = andweard opposed.

on·weg, aweg, *in comp. also* weg- *av.* away.

onweg-ācierrednes *f.* apostasy.

onweg-ālǣdnes *f.* removal.

onweg-gewit *n.* departure.

onweg-gewitennes *f.* departure.

on·wendan, in- *tr.* change; exchange (for) *w.* mid; turn aside; invert; pervert; *wdg.* deprive || *intr.* return.

---

on·wend|edlic changeable.

~(ed)nes *f.* movement, change, alteration.

on·weorpan, in- 3 throw *or* turn aside; begin the web.

onweorpnes = onworpennes.

on·wīcan 6 retreat, yield.

on·wiellan cause to boil; cause passion.

on·windan 3 untie, loosen; retreat.

on-gewinn *n.* assault.

on·winnende aggressive.

on-wist *f.* dwelling in a place.

on-worpennes, -weorpnes *f.* throwing on; being inspired with a feeling.

on·wrēon, in- 6, 7 uncover; reveal; explain.

on·wreopian *once* reveal.

on·wrigen(n)es, -wrihnes *f.* uncovering, disclosing, displaying; exposure; revelation; explanation, exposition [onwrēon].

on·wrīting (!) *f.* inscription.

on·wrīpan 6 unwrap.

on·wrīpung*, -tung *f.* bandage.

on·wuldrian *once* extol, praise (!)

on·wun|ian (!) inhabit.

~ung *f.* dwelling; perseverance.

on·wyrtrumian*, un- root up *LN.*

on·ȳpan (!) pour in.

open open; evident.

~ears *m.* medlar.

~lic public.

~līce *av.* publicly, without concealment; clearly.

~nes *f.* publicity.

open|ian *intr.* open; become manifest || *tr.* open; disclose, manifest; discover.

~ere *m.* opener.

(ge)~ung *f.* opening; manifestation, revelation.

ōr beginning, origin; front, van.

ōra *m.* bank, shore.

ōra *m.* ore, unreduced metal.

ōra *m.* Danish monetary unit, eighth of a mark [*Scand. pl.* aurar].

or-blēde bloodless.

orc *m.* cup, pitcher [*Lt.* urceus].

orc *m.* demon.

or-cēap|e, -es, ~unga, ~ungum *av.* without payment gratis; without cause.

orceard = ortgeard.

or-cēas free from accusation, enjoying immunity.

~nes f. immunity.

or-cnǣwe, -āwe recognizable, evident.

orcnēast† *once* *mpl.* monsters.

ord *m.* point ; spear ; source, beginning ; front, van ; chief, prince, *coll.* flower (of nation).

~bana† *m.* slayer, murderer.

~fruma *m.* origin ; originator, creator ; †chief.

~stapu† *f.* prick, wound.

~wiga† *m.* warrior.

or-dǣle not participating in, exempt.

or-dāl *n.* ordeal.

~īsen *n.* iron used in the ordeal.

or-eald very old.

orel, orl *nm.* garment, veil, mantle [*Lt.* orarium].

ōret- battle [*from* *or-hāt].

~lof *n.* triumph Gl.

~mæcg(a)† *m.* warrior, champion, man.

~stōw *f.* arena.

ōretla *m.* contumely, insult.

ōretta †, -eta *m.* warrior, champion, man.

orf *n.* cattle. *Cp.* weorf.

~gebitt *n.* grazing.

~cynn *n.* cattle.

~cwealm *m.* cattle-plague.

or-fierm|e, -eo- untidy, squalid ; †destitute *wi.* ; †worthless [feorm].

~o, ~nes f. squalor.

organ *m.* song ; voice [*Lt.*].

org a)nian sing to accompaniment of musical instrument.

organe f. marjoram (a plant) [*Lt.* origanum].

organ|on ; ~a, ~an *pl.* a musical instrument [*Lt.*].

orgel, -ol, -al pride [*from* *orgāl].

~lic contemptible, beneath one.

~lice, orglice *av.* proudly, arrogantly.

~nes f. pride.

~scipe *m.* wantonness.

~word *n.* arrogant speech.

orgel.

~drēam *m.* music.

or-giète, ea to be perceived clearly, manifest.

or-gilde unpaid for, uncompensated.

orglice = orgellice.

or-hlyte devoid of, free from *wg.*

or-ieldo f. extreme old age.

orl = orel.

or-lǣg†, e (*n.*) fate.

or-leahtor (!) *m.* danger.

or-leahtre blameless.

or-leg|e† I. *n.* hostility, war. II. *aj.* hostile.

~cēap *m.* fighting (?).

~fram warlike, brave.

~gīfre, -lǣg- warlike.

~hwīl f. time of war.

~nīþ *m.* hostility.

~stund f. time of adversity.

~weorc *n.* battle.

or-mǣt|e immense, excessive.

~lic excessive.

~nes f. immensity, excess.

or-mōd discouraged, despairing.

~nes f. discouragement, despair.

orn *prt. of* iernan.

orne I. unhealthy, harmful. II. (*n.*) injury: ne wyrþ him nān ~.

ornest *n.* trial by battle L. [eornost].

or(o)þ *n.* breath.

orped grown up ; active, energetic ; intelligent.

~lice *av.* boldly ; clearly, definitely.

orrest battle *v L.* [*Scand.* orrusta].

orret|tan disgrace, put to shame [or-, riht ?].

~scipe *m.* infamy.

or-sāwle† lifeless.

or-sceattinga *av.* gratis.

or-sorg *wg.* without anxiety, unconcerned ; secure, safe ; prosperous.

~lic secure *wg.*

~līce *av.* without anxiety ; rashly ; securely, safely.

~nes f. freedom from anxiety ; security ; prosperity.

ort-geard, orce(a)rd, -ird *m.* orchard, garden.

~lēah*, orcerdleh f. orchard Gl.

~weard *m.* gardener.

or-trīew|e, -ēowe, -ū(w)e despairing ; perfidious.

~nes f. mistrust, doubt.

or-trūw|ian, -trīewan despair of *wg.* ; ge- *wa* disbelieve.

or-trūwung despair.

or-tȳdre barren ; on- effete (!).

orþ = oroþ.

orþ|ian breathe ; pant.

~ung f. breathing, breath ; pore.

or-þanc I. *mn.* mind, intelligence ; skill ; contrivance, invention — ~um skilfully. II. *aj.* skilful, cunning.

~bend† *m.* cunning band.

~pil† *m.* cunning point.

~scipe *m.* mechanical art.

or-pances† *av.* heedlessly.

or-wearde *once* † [ea = ie] without guardian *or* owner.

or-weg out of the way (road) Gl.

~nes f. inaccessibility.

georwēnan despair.

or-wēn|e, -wēna despairing *wg.* ; despaired of, desperate (circumstances).

~nes f. despair.

or-weorþ *n.* ignominy.

or-wīge without fighting *or* resisting ; not liable to charge of homicide.

or-wyrþ *M.,* -u ignominy ; vituperation.

~lic ignominious.

ōȝ *m.,* *gpl.* ēsa god; *the Runic letter* o.

ōsle f. blackbird.

ōȝt (*m.*) knot (in tree) ; knob.

~ig, ~iht knotty, rough.

oster|hlāf *m.* oyster patty.

~scill f. oyster-shell.

ostre f. oyster [*Lt.* ostrea].

ot = æt-, oþ-.

oter, ottor (*m.*) otter.

~hol *n.* otter's hole Ct.

oþ or I. *prp* *w. a., d.* (*rare*) up to, as far as *of extension and motion, and quantity* ; *time* until | oþ-þe, oþ-þæt, oþ-þæt-te *cj. w. indic.* (*sbj.*) until. II. *cj. w indic.* (*sbj.*) until.

ōþian *once* pant.

oþ·beran 4 carry (away), bring.

oþ·berstan 3 escape.

oþ·bregdan, -brēdan 3 take away, carry off.

oþ·cierran be perverted.

oþ·clifan 6 adhere *wd.*

oþ·cwelan 4 die.

oþ·dōn *vb.* put out (eye).

oþ·ehtian drive away (cattle).

ōþel = ēþel.

[134]

ōþer aj., no., always st. ; second —
on þām ōþrum dæge following ;
other (= Lt. alter, alius); the rest
of : þæs ōþres folces; different :
þā burh geseah on ōþre ge-
wend on ōþre hēo ǣr wæs
changed from what it was ; one of
two : wund þurh (þæt) ~ cnēow
— ~ . . ~ one . . the other ‖ either:
heora ōþrum fylstan. ~ (. .)
oþþe . . oþþe, ~ þāra oþþe . . oþþe,
~ twēga oþþe . . oþþe either . .
or. In this sense it may be a
shortening of ōhwæþer = āhwæþer.

~lice av. otherwise, cpv. ~licor.
oþ·fæstan entrust, commit.
oþ·faran 2 escape from wd.
oþ·feallan 1 wd. cease to concern
(a person) ; be wanting, fail (the
power of speech) ; lose power,
decay (of learning).
oþ·fēolan 3 adhere.
oþ·ferian carry off ; save (life).
oþ·flēogan 7 fly away.
oþ·flēon 7 flee ; escape wd.
oþ·flītan 6 get (land) from another
by litigation wda.
oþ·gān vb. escape.
oþ·glīdan 6 glide away.

oþ·grīpan 0 snatch away wda.
oþ·healdan 1 withhold.
oþ·hebban 2 exalt ; elate, make
proud.
oþ-hielde*, y, e wd. contented.
oþ·hlēapan 1 escape.
oþ·hrīnan 6 touch.
oþ·hȳdan intr. hide from wd.
oþ·iernan 3 run away ; escape wd.
oþ·īewan, ēo tr. show ; rfl. appear ; intr. appear.
oþ·lǣdan lead away, carry off ;
save (life).
oþ·rīdan† 6 ride.
oþ·rōwan 1 row away.
oþ·sacan 2 wg., w. sbj. deny (statement, charge): oþsōc þæt hē hit
nǣre denied that he was . .
oþ·scacan 2 escape.
oþ·scēotan 7 intr. turn away from
(faith) ; be lost to, escape wd.
oþ·scūfan 7 depart.
oþ·spornan 3 intr. strike against,
stumble.
oþ·standan 2 intr. cease from
motion, stop ; be lost (of hearing) ;
remain ; wd. be a hindrance or
offence to.
oþ·stillan tr. stop.
oþ·swerian 2 deny on oath w. sbj.

oþ·swīgan become silent.
oþ·swimman 3 swim away.
oþ·tēon 7 take away.
oþþe, oþþo(n), oþþa, eA. eþþa cj.
or. ~ . . ~ either . . or .
oþ-þe until, see oþ.
oþ·þēodan disjoin, dismember.
oþ·þicgan† 5 take away.
oþ·þingian usurp LL.
oþþo, oþþon = oþþe.
oþ·þringan† 3 force away from
one, deprive (esp. of life) wda.
oþ·wendan turn a thing away from
some one wda., deprive.
oþ·windan 3 escape.
oþ·wītan 6 reproach with, taunt
with, charge with wda.
oþ·wyrcan once injure (?).
ō-wæstm m. shoot, branch.
ōwana = āhwanon.
ō-webb, ōwef [infl. of wefan],
āweb(b), āb [not ōb] n. woof.
ōwer(n) = āhwǣr anywhere.
ōwiht = āwiht.
ōwisc, ōfesc Ct. border (?).
oxa m., pl. oxan, exen, oe ox.
oxan-slyppe f. oxlip. oxna-lybb
ox-heal (a plant).
ōxn f. armpit.
ōxta, ōcusta m. armpit.

P.

pād f. cloak.
pǣc|an deceive.
~a m. deceiver.
pǣgel m. gill, wine vessel.
pæll, e m costly cloak or robe ; purple, purple garment [Lt. pallium].
~en of purple, costly (clothes).
pætig = prættig.
pæþ, a m. path ; valley IN.
pæþþan†, e traverse.
pāl m. pole, stake ; hoe or spade
[Lt. palus].
palent(s)e f., pal(l)ent m. palace
[Lt. palantium].
palentlic palatial.

palester, palstr spike Gl.
palm, -a m., IN. pælme f. palm.
~æppel m. date.
~bearo m. palm-grove.
~dæg, ~sunnandæg m. Palm
Sunday.
~trēow n. palm-tree.
~twig n. palm-branch.
ge~twigod† decked with palm.
~wuce f. Palm Sunday week.
panic (m.) a kind of millet.
pann|e f. pan, frying-pan.
~mete m. cooked food.
pāp|a m. pope. ~anhād m. papacy
[Lt. papa].

pāp|dōm m. papacy.
~seld, ~setl n. papal see.
paper (?) papyrus Gl. [Lt.].
papig = popig.
papol-stān m. pebble.
part m. part [Lt. pars].
pāwa, pēa m. peacock [Lt. pavo].
pēa = pāwa.
pearroc m. enclosure.
pecg [= pygg ?] pig.
pell(en) = pæll(en).
pening, penig, pending m.
penny.
~hwierfere m. money-changer.
~mangere m. money-dealer.

pening|slieht*, æ *m.* coining money *lN.*

~wǣg *f.* pennyweight.

~weorþ *n.* pennyworth.

penn *m.* pen, fold.

penn kind of cataract (disease of the eye).

pēo, pīe (*f.*) insect, parasite.

peorþ† (*m.*) chess-man (?); *the Runic letter* p.

peose = pise.

per|e, ~u *f.* pear [*Lt.* pirus].

~ewōs *n.* perry.

pernex† (*m.*) a supposed bird [*misunderstanding of Lt.* pernix quick].

persoc *m.* peach [*Lt.* persicum].

~trēow *n.* peach-tree.

perwince, perv-*f.*periwinkle[*Fr.*].

petersili(g)e *f.* parsley [*Lt.* petroselinum].

pic *n.* pitch. hlūttor ~ resin.

~en of pitch.

~ian cover with pitch.

pīc (*m.*) point, pike.

~ian*, ~an pick, put out (eyes) *L.*

~ung *f.* pricking.

pīe = pēo insect.

pigment, pihm- drug [*Lt.*].

pihten part of loom [*Lt.* pecten].

pīl *m.* pointed stick *or* stake; spike; prickle [*Lt.* pilum].

pīl|ian pound in mortar.

~ere *m.* pounder.

pīl|e *f.* mortar [*Lt.* pila].

~stæf *m.*, ~stampe *f.*, ~stocc *m.* pestle.

pil(e)ce, py- *f.* robe of skin [*Lt.* pellicia].

pill-sāpe *f.* a plant (?).

pīn- [*Lt.* pinus].

~bēam *m.* pine-tree.

~hnutu *f.* fir-cone.

~trēow *n.* pine-tree.

~trēowen, ȳ of pine.

pīn|ian torture; afflict (mind) [*Lt.* poena].

~ere *m.* torturer.

~nes *f.* torment.

pīnung *f.* torture.

~tōl *n.* instrument of torture.

pine-wincle = wine-.

pinn peg, pin; *lN.* pen [*Lt.* penna].

pinne *f.* leather bottle.

pinsian weigh; estimate value of; examine, consider [*Lt.* pensare].

pintel (*m.*) membrum virile.

pīp|e *f.* tube; pipe (musical instrument).

~drēam *m.* sound of the pipe.

~ere *m.* piper.

pip(e)lian grow pimply.

pipeneale *f.* pimpernel (plant) [*Lt.* bipennula].

pipor *m.* pepper [*Lt.* piper].

~corn *n.* peppercorn.

~cweorn *f.* pepper-mill.

~horn *m.* horn for holding pepper.

~ian, piprian pepper.

pir|ige *f.* pear-tree [pere].

~grāf *m.* pear-orchard.

pīs.

~līce, pī- *av.* heavily *lN.*

pise, io, y *f.* pea.

~cynn *n.* kind of pea.

pisle *once f.* (warm) chamber Gl. [*lLt.* pisalis].

pistol *m.* letter, epistle; written agreement [*Lt.* epistola].

~bōc *f.* book of Epistles.

~rǣdere *m.* epistle-reader (in church).

~rǣding *f.* lesson in church-service.

~rocc *m.* vestment worn when reading the epistle.

pīþa *m.* pith.

plǣce, plæ(t)se *f.* open place, street *lN.* [*Lt.* platea].

plǣgan = plegian.

plǣ(t)se = plǣce.

plǣtt *m.* blow with flat hand, smack.

plǣttan smack, strike with open hand.

plagian = plegian.

plant|e *f.* plant, shoot [*Lt.*].

~ian plant.

~sticca *m.* a gardening-tool, dibble (?).

~ung *f.* planting; plant.

plaster (*n.*) plaster [*Lt.* emplastrum].

-plat|ian cover with plates of metal [*lLt.* platus].

~ung *f.* plate of metal.

pleah, *prt.* of plēon.

pleg|an, ~ian, æ, a play *in its various meanings*, frolic, amuse oneself; play (harp); applaud; strive for *w.* for.

~ere *m.* player, athlete.

plega *m.* quick movement; game, athletic sport; fighting†; applause.

pleg|hūs *n.* theatre.

~lic relating to games, theatrical.

~mann, plege- *m.* athlete, wrestler.

~sciéld *m.* small shield.

~scip *n.* small ship Gl.

~stōw, plege- *f.* (amphi)theatre.

plegol sportive.

plēo, *see* pleoh.

~lic dangerous; hurtful.

plēon, *prt.* pleah risk, expose to danger *wg.*

pleoh, *g.* plēos *n.* danger, peril (to the soul); injury; responsibility, risk.

plett (sheep)fold *lN.*

plicgan [i = y ?] scrape Gl.

pliht *m.* danger; damage [plēon].

~lic dangerous.

pliht|an bring danger upon, be liable to forfeit *wd.*

~ere *m.* look-out man (on ship).

plōg a measure of land.

plott plot of ground.

pluccian pluck, gather.

plūm- [*Lt.* pluma].

~feþer *f.* down.

plūm|e *f.* plum (fruit *or* tree) [*Lt.* prunus].

~blēd *f.* plum (fruit).

~sēaw *n.* plum-juice.

~slā *f.* sloe.

~trēow *n.* plum-tree.

plȳme *f.* plum (fruit *or* tree) [*Lt.* *prunea].

poc|c *m.* pustule.

~ādl *f.* pox.

pohh|a *m.* pouch, bag.

~ede baggy (clothes).

pōl, -pul, *d.* -pulle *m.* pool.

polente *f.* parched corn [*Lt.* polenta].

pollegie *f.* pennyroyal [*Lt.* pulegium].

pollup *once m.* an instrument of punishment.

popig, a (*m.*) poppy.

por|r, ~lēac (*m.*) leek [*Lt.* porrum].

port *mn.* gate, entrance; harbour; town [*Lt.* portus].

~cwene, -oe- *f.* prostitute *lN.*

~geat *n.* gate of a town.

~mann *m.* citizen.

~gerēfa *m.* mayor.

~geriht *n.* due paid by town.

~strǣt *f.* street.

~waran, -weor- *pl.* citizens.

port|weall *m.* town-wall.
~wer *m.* citizen *IN. From* ~waran.
portian pound (in mortar). *Cp.* pyrtan.
portic *m.* porch, portico; enclosed place; place roofed in; arched recess in church [*Lt.* porticus].
gepos *n.* cold in the head.
posa = pusa.
posel, posling *m.* pill.
post *m.* post [*Lt.* postis].
postol = apostol.
potian butt, gore; prog, prod.
pott *m.* pot.
prætt *m.* guile, trick; *pl.* prattas double dealing.
~ig, e, pætig, e cunning.
præfost, prō- *m.* officer, provost of a monastery [*Lt.* propositus, praepositus].
~folgoþ *m.*, ~scīr *f.* provostship.
prass (*m.*) array, pomp.
predic|ian preach [*Lt.* praedicare].
~ere, pry- *m.* preacher.
prēon *m.* pin, brooch.
prēost *m.* priest [*Lt.* presbyter].
~hād *m.* priestly office, priesthood.
~hēap *m.* body of priests.
~lagu *f.* law relating to priests.
~lic of priests.
~scīr *f.* parish.
prēowt-hwīl *f.* moment. *Cp.* be-priwan.
press *f.* press [*Fr.*].
pric|ian prick; stab; point out.
~ung *f.* pricking.
pric|a *m.*, ~e *f.* point, dot; particle of space; 'point,' fourth *or* fifth part of an hour.

pric-mælum *av.* by points (of time).
pricel *m.* sharp point, prickle.
pricels *m.* sharp point.
prīm (*n.*) six o'clock in the morning; six o'clock service [*Lt.* prima].
~sang *m.* prime-song, six o'clock service.
princ- winking Gl.
pritigian *once* chirp Gl.
prod-bor, prot- (*n.*) auger (?) *LM.*
prōfian assume to be (a thief) [*Lt.* probare].
prōfast = prāfost.
prūt proud.
~līce *av.* proudly, confidently; magnificently.
~scipe *m.* pride.
prūt|ian.
~ung *f.* pride.
prutene *f.* southernwood [*Lt.* abrotanum].
prȳd- = prȳt-.
prȳto, prȳte, prȳd- *f.* pride [prūt].
pūcian creep.
pūcel *m.* goblin.
pudd *m.* ditch.
pudoc *m.* wen, wart.
puerisc boyish [*Lt.* puer].
-pul = pōl pool.
~sper *n.* reed *IN.*
pullian pluck, twitch.
pumic pumice [*Lt.* pumicem].
~stān *m.* pumice-stone.
pun|ian pound (in mortar).
~ere *m.* pestle.
pund *n.* pound (weight *or* money) [*Lt.* pondo].

pund|mæte weighing a pound.
~wæg *f.* pound-weight.
pund* enclosure, pound. *Cp.* pyndan.
pundere *m.* weigher *IN.*
-pundern *n.* pair of scales.
~georn [*the* -georn *doubtful*] weighing, pondering Gl.
pundor plumb-line.
pung (*m.*) bag, purse.
pungetung *f.* pricking sensation. *Cp.* pyngan.
punt punt [*Lt.* ponto].
pūr (*m.*) bittern (?).
pūr — ~lamb lamb without blemish [*Lt.* purus].
purpur|e *f.* purple robe [*Lt.* purpura].
~en purple.
purs purse [*Lt.* bursa].
pusa, posa *m.* bag, wallet.
puslian pick out best pieces of food.
pyffan blow (with mouth).
pyle *m.* pillow [*Lt.* pulvinus].
pylece = pilece robe.
pynca*, i *m.* point Gl.
pynd|an shut up, confine [pund].
~ing *f.* dam.
pyngan prick [*Lt.* pungere].
pyretre *f.* pellitory [*Lt.* pyrethrum].
pyrtan beat. *Cp.* portian.
pytt *m.* pit; grave; pond; pustule [*Lt.* puteus].
~an dig, prog.
~ede pitted, marked with hollows (*of* sword).

Q = CW.

R.

rā, rāha *m.*, rāh-dēor *n.* roe-(buck).

rabbian rage (of the devil) [*Lt.* ?].

racian rule, direct *wd.* ; go, betake oneself to.

raca *m.*, racu *f.* rake.

racca *m.* cord forming part of rigging of ship.

racente, -ete *f.* chain, fetter.

racentēag, -e, racet- *f.* chain, fetter [*L. expansion of* racente *by infl. of* tēag].

~ian chain.

racu *f.* narrative, exposition ; explanation ; rhetoric ; reckoning, account ; comedy.

racu rake = raca.

racu *f.* bed of stream.

rad- = hrad-.

rād *f.* riding (on horse, in carriage, in ship) ; journey ; warlike expedition, raid ; *the Runic letter* r [ridan]. *Cp.* rǣd-, rǣde-.

~cniht *m.* = siexhynde-mann.

~ehere = rǣde-.

~hors *n.* horse for riding.

~pytt† *m.* draw-well (?).

~stefn *m.* term of cavalry service (?).

~wērig weary with riding or travelling.

rād† *once* furniture, harness (?).

gerād I. *n.* reckoning, account (of expenditure) ; accuracy ; wisdom, prudence ; condition — on þæt ~ þæt *sbj* , tō þǣm ~e þæt *sbj.* on condition that, on the understanding that. II. *aj.* straight (road) — ~sprǣc prose ; skilled (in) *wg.* ; wise, prudent ; circumstanced, conditioned — þus ~ of this kind, swā ~ of such a kind, hū~ what kind of (man) ‖ hū ~es how.

~ian, ~egian arrange ; call to an account *or* audit.

~līce *av.* accurately, learnedly.

~nes *f.* compact.

~scipe *m.* prudence.

radian = hradian.

rador = rodor.

rǣc|an, *prt.* rǣhte, a *tr.* stretch forth (hand) ; give, bring, offer ‖ *intr.* extend.

~ing, ā *f.* stretching out, presenting *lN.*

gerǣcan overtake ; get at, reach ; seize, take (fortress), obtain (victory) ; address (?) — hīe swā scandlīce gerǣht hæfde had put them to shame.

rǣcc *m.* dog that hunts by scent.

rǣced = reced.

rǣd = hrǣd.

rǣd *m.* advice ; discussion, council ; resolution, plan of action, policy ; decree ; scheme, conspiracy ; †rule, power ‖ sound policy, what is advisable, benefit : him tō ~e, swā him mǣst ~ sīe ; help ; good fortune ‖ sense, understanding ‖ way of life, state of things : on ēcum ~e to last for ever.

~bana *m.* deviser of homicide (as opposed to the perpetrator).

~bora *m.* counsellor ; consul (!).

~fæst wise, prudent.

~fæstnes *f.* reasonableness, readiness to take good advice.

~findende advising.

~giefa *m.* adviser, councillor ; consul (!).

~gift (!) *f.* consulship, senate.

~hycgende† wise, prudent.

~lēas foolish ; rash ; in confusion ; helpless, miserable.

~lic advisable.

~līce *av.* wisely, skilfully ; designedly.

~mægen† R. *n.*   *Or* rǣd- (?).

~snotor wise.

~geþeaht *n.* counsel.

~þeahtende† consulting, deliberating.

~þeahtere *m.* counsellor.

~þeahtung *f.* advice.

~wita *m.* counsellor.

rǣd-wǣn *m.* chariot. *Cp.* rād.

rǣd|an, *prt.* ~de, *also st.* 1 b, rēd *rare in W.*, *A.* rēord advise *wd* ; discuss, deliberate : ~de wiþ hīe hwæt hīe dōn sceolden ; decide : ~don þæt hīe wolden . . , ~don þæt . . wǣre . . ; decree ; plot, try to injure : ~ on hīe ‖ rule, possess *w.d.*, *i.* ‖ try to benefit, help, provide for *wd.* | guess : hēton hine ~ hwā hine hrepode ; solve (riddle), interpret (dreams), foresee (future fate) ; read (book) ; read aloud *wda.*

~end† *m.* ruler ; soothsayer.

~endlic decretal.

~ere *m.* reader ; lector (second order in the church) ; student ; soothsayer.

~estre *f.* reader.

rǣding *f.* act of reading ; what is read, homily.

~bōc *f.* lectionary.

~scamol *m.* reading-desk.

~gewrit = rǣden-.

gerǣd|an, *prt.* -de, -rēd bring about by advice : him þone tēonan ~ ; arrange (hair) ; *and the other meanings of* rǣdan.

~end *m.* disposer *lN.*

~nes, rēdnes *f.* decree ; condition — in þās ~se on this c.

~ung *f.* decree.

rǣde mounted ; ready (?).

rǣde *once f.* reading.

rǣde|cempa *m.* cavalry soldier.

~here *m.* cavalry.

~mann *m.* horseman.

~wiga *m.* cavalry soldier.

rǣde-gafol *n.* rent that can be paid all at once.

rǣde-scamol [æ = ǣ *or* ē] *m.* pulpit *or* couch (?).

gerǣd|e *n.*, *gen. pl.* ~u, ~a trappings (of horse) ; equipage ; armour ; ornament.

~od equipped, with trappings (horse).

gerǣde ready.

rædels *m.* riddle [rǣdan].

rǣdelse *f.* discussion, debate ; conjecture, imagination ; interpretation.

rǣden(n) *f.* rule, government ; reckoning, estimating ; stipulation, condition — on (*or* þuih) þā ~ne þæt *sbj.*

~gewrit *n.* written agreement.

rǣdes-mann *L. m.* adviser, councillor ; steward [*Scand.* rāþsmaþr].

rǣdic, hr- *m.* radish [*Lt.* radix].

rǣdnes, *see* rǣdan.

gerǣf, *see* gerǫsp [ārāfian].

ræfnan undergo ; perform, do.

ræfsan = rǫfsan.

ræfter *m.* rafter.

ræg-hār† grey with lichen [ragu].

rǣge, ā *f.* roe, wild she-goat [rā].

rǣge-rēose *f.* muscles along the spine.

rǣpan bind ; enslave [rāp].

rǣpling, rēping *m.* prisoner ; felon.

~weard *m.* jailer.

ræps, e *m.* response (in church service) [*Lt.* responsorium].

ræpsan = rǫfsan.

rǣran raise ; build ; establish ; excite, cause ; perform, do [-rīsan].

rǣs *m.* running ; rush, impetus ; onslaught, attack [-rīsan].

rǣs-bora† *m.* councillor, chief [rǣswa].

rǣsan rush ; attack ; enter on rashly.

rǣsian = rǣswian.

rǣsc *once m.* shower of rain Gl.

rǣscan coruscate (*of* lightning).

rǣscett|an coruscate ; crackle (*of* fire).

~ung *f.* coruscate.

rǣsele *f.* solution (of riddle).

rǣsn *n.* plank ; ceiling.

rǣsw|an, rǣs(w)ian conjecture ; suspect.

~ung *f.* conjecture ; reasoning.

rǣswa†, ge- *m.* counsellor ; chief, king.

ræt (*m.*) rat.

gerǣplan *pl.* trappings (of horse).

rǣw, ā, ēa *f.* row ; succession (in time) — on ~e in succession ; hedgerow.

geráw *n.* row — on ~e sǣton.

gerǣwod drawn up in line (regiment).

rāge = rǣge.

raggig shaggy.

ragu (*f*) lichen.

~finc *m.* a bird.

~hār*, *see* rǣg-.

rāha, rāh-dēor, *see* rā.

ram-hund *m.* a kind of dog.

ram|m, -a *m.* ram ; battering-ram.

~gealla *m.* (a plant).

rān rapine robbery *L.* [*Scand.*].

rān *occ. prt. of* rīnan rain.

ranc proud ; insolent ; brave ; showy (*of* dress).

~līce *av.* boldly ; showily (*of* dress).

rand *m.* margin (?) ; †boss of shield ; †shield.

~bēag *m.* boss of shield.

~gebeorg† *n.* protection as of a shield.

~burg† *f.* city ; wall (?).

~hæbbend† *m.* warrior.

~wiga†, wīgend† *m.* warrior.

rāp *m.* rope.

~lic of rope.

~gǫnga* *or* ~ganga*, ~gon *m.* rope-dancer Gl.

rāpincel *n.* cord.

rahte *prt. of* rǣcan.

gerār *n.* roaring.

rār|ian wail, lament ; bellow.

~ung *f.* bellowing.

rāre-dumle* *f.*, -dumla *m.*, rārabittern (a bird).

rāsian explore.

rāsettan rage (*of* fire) [rǣsan].

rape = hrape.

rāw = rǣw.

rāw|an — ge~ende *once* dividing, cutting Gl.

rēad red.

~basu reddish purple.

~e *av.* redly, with red.

~fāg† stained with red.

~gold-læfer *n.* gold plating Gl.

~nes *f.* redness.

~stalede having a red stalk.

rēadian be *or* become red.

rēadan *pl.* (?) tonsils.

rēaf *n.* spoil, booty ; robe, dress.

~lāc *mn.* robbery, plundering, spoil, booty.

rēaf|ian rob, plunder, seize ; ravage, destroy.

~ere *m.* robber, brigand.

rēaf|igend *m.* plunderer.

~igende rapacious.

~ung *f.* plundering.

rēafol rapacious.

~nes *f.* rapacity.

reahtigean *once* discuss.

rēam (*m.*) cream.

~wīn *n.* a drink Gl.

rēama = rēoma membrane.

rēaw = rǣw.

gerec *n.* government, rule ; decree ; explanation.

gerec (*n.*) tumult *lN.*

gereclice *av.* straight.

rēc *m.* smoke.

recan 5 go, rush (?) — in-rǣcan ingesserunt Gl.

rēcan steam *tr.*

recedōm *once m.* rule. *Cp.* reccenddōm.

gerecenian explain.

recc|an, *prt.* re(a)hte *tr.* stretch, extend, give — *met.* direct (mind) | govern, subdue ; decree ; guide ; reprove | explain, interpret ; prove ; correct (error) ; narrate ; tell, say | count, reckon || *intr.* go [racu].

~end *m.* ruler.

~enddōm *m.* ruling, government.

~ere *m.* ruler.

reccan, *prt.* rohte [*the orig. form* *rēcan *is perhaps preserved in* recelēas], *wg.* care for, reck.

reced†, æ *n.* house, hall, palace.

~lic palatial Gl.

gerecednes, ~recen(n)es, cc *f.* narrative, history — ānfeald ~ prose ; interpretation ; governing, correction.

recelēas [e = ē *or* ǫ ?], reccennegligent, indifferent.

~ian neglect *wg.*

~līce *av.* negligently.

~nes *f.* negligence.

rec(c)eliest *f.* negligence.

rēcels, ȳ (*n*) incense.

~būc *m.*, ~fæt *n.* censer.

~rēoce *once f.* burning of incense.

rēcelsian smoke with incense.

recen, recon prompt, ready, swift.

~e, ric- *av.* at once, quickly — swā ~ swā as soon as.

~līce, ricen- *av.* quickly.

recnian pay (?) Ct.

recon = recen.

recon remuneration Gl.

rede-stān *m. once* synophites (precious stone) Gl.

geref|a, oe, r- *m.* reeve, officer, prefect.

~ærn *n.* court-house.

~land *n.* (?).

~mæd *f.* reeve's meadow.

~mann *m.* official.

~scipe *m.*, ~scīr *f.* reeveship, prefecture.

refs|an, æ, ræpsan, e reprove Gl. *Cp.* geresp.

~ung *f.* reproving Gl. ‖ interval; evening.

reg(e)n, rēn *m.* rain.

~boga *m.* rainbow.

~dropa *m.* raindrop.

~ig, ~lic rainy.

~scūr *m.* shower of rain.

~wæter *n.* rain-water.

~wyrm *m.* earthworm.

reg(e)n-†, rēn-.

~heard very hard.

~meld *f.* solemn announcement.

~þēof *m.* arch-thief.

~weard *m.* mighty guardian.

regol, eo *m.* rule, regulation; pattern, standard; canon (ecclesiastical); rule (Benedictine) [*Lt.* regula].

~bryce *m.* breach of rule.

~fæst observing an (ecclesiastical) rule.

~lagu *f.* monastic law.

~lic according to rule, regular; canonical.

~lice *av.* in accordance with rules.

~lif *n.* life according to ecclesiastical rules.

~sticca *m.* ruler (instrument).

~þēaw *m.* monastic discipline.

~weard *m.* authority on rules; provost of monastery.

relic-; reliquias *mpl.* relics [*Lt.* reliquiae].

~gang *m.* visiting relics; procession of relics.

remp|an.

~ende precipitate, hasty.

rēn|ian, regnian arrange, prepare — ge~ tō bismere humiliate; set (jewel, trap); mend.

~iend *m.* arranger.

ge~ung *f.* arranging.

renco *f.* pride, ostentation [ranc].

rendan tear, cut *lN.*

gerēne *n.* ornament [rēnian].

---

renge, y *f.* spider [*Lt.* aranea].

rēo = rēowe blanket.

rēoc† *once* fierce.

rēocan *intr.* smoke, steam; stink.

rēod I. ruddy (complexion). II. *n.* red colouring, red [rēad].

rēodan 7 *tr.* redden; †kill (?)

rēofan 7 break, tear.

reohhe *f.* a fish.

rēoma, ēa *m.* membrane, ligament.

rēon lamentation.

rēon = rēowon *prt. pl.*

rēon|ian mutter.

~ung *f.* whispering.

gerēon|ian conspire.

~ung *f.* plot.

rēonig† sad, mournful, gloomy (place).

~mōd sad, weary.

reopian = ripian.

reord *f.* meal, food.

~hūs *n.* house where meals are taken.

reord† *f.* voice, speech; language.

~berend† *m.* man.

~ian speak; read.

gereord† *n.* voice; language.

gereord, ~e, r- *n.* meal, banquet; food.

~hūs *n.* refectory.

~ian, ~an feed, feast *tr., intr., rfl.*

~nes *f.* banquet; feasting.

gereordung *f.* meal.

~hūs *n.* refectory.

rēost rest (part of plough).

rēotan† 7 weep, lament.

rēotig† sad.

rēow = hrēoh fierce.

rēowe, rēo, rūwe, *vE.* rȳhæ, rȳe *f.* blanket, rug, carpet [rūh].

repan 5 reap. *Cp.* rīpan reap.

geresp, gerēf — on hine ~ weorþan be brought home to him, proved (*of* charge). *Cp.* refsan.

rest, æ, *lN.* ge- *f.* rest; sleep; resting-place, bed; grave, tomb.

~bedd† *n* bed.

~e(n)dæg *m.* day of rest, Sabbath.

~engēar *n.* year of rest.

~hūs *n.* bedroom.

~lēas restless, disturbed.

~gemāna *m.* sexual intercourse.

ge~scipe *m.* sexual intercourse.

restan *abs., rfl.* rest, ge~ *wg.* rest from; remain.

geresta *f.* consort, wife.

rēt|an cheer, gladden, comfort, soothe (wound) [rōt].

---

rētend *m.* comforter.

rēpian be fierce [rēpe].

repe† just = rēpe (?).

~hygdig right-minded (?).

rēpe, oe fierce; severe, stern; zealous.

~mōd† fierce; indignant.

rēpen *once L.* wild (beast).

rēp|lic fierce.

~lice *av.* fiercely.

~nes *f.* fierceness; severity, strictness.

~scipe *m.* rage.

rēpig fierce.

~ian rage.

~mōd† fierce.

rēpra, oe, ge- *m.* rower, sailor [rōpor].

rēpru, ge- *npl.* oars.

gerēpre *once* ready.

rēwet(t) *n.* rowing; ship, vessel [rōwan].

ribb *n.* rib.

~spācan *pl.* the brisket (?) Gl.

ribbe *f.* ribwort Gl.

rīca *m.* man in power, ruler.

rīce powerful, of high rank; strong (*of* things); rich.

rīce *n.* power, authority, reign; kingdom, diocese.

~dōm *m.* rule.

~lic magnificent, splendid.

~līce *av.* with power; splendidly.

rīceter(e), rīcc- *n.* power, dominion; domination; usurpation; violence.

rīcs|ian rule, reign; dominate, tyrannize; prevail (*of* things) [rīce].

~ere*, ~are *m.* ruler *lN.*

~igend*, ~and *m.* ruler *lN.*

~ung *f.* rule, dominion *lN.*

rīd|an 6 ride (*also of* fetters, ships, the pillar of fire); swing — on gealgan ~.

~end† *m.* horseman, knight.

~ere *m.* (Norman) knight *vL.*

~wiga *m.* mounted soldier.

gerīdan 6 *intr.* ride ‖ *tr.* ride up to; ride over, take forcible possession of (country, estate).

ridda *m.* rider; cavalry soldier [rīdan].

ridesoht fever *lN.* [*Scand.* riþusōtt. *Cp.* hriþ, suht].

ridusende swinging, swaying Gl.

rīepan spoil, plunder.

rīep|ere *m.* plunderer, robber.
~ung *f.* plundering, despoiling.
rīf fierce.
gerif *n.* catch (of fish), number caught (of fish).
rifelede wrinkled. *Cp.* gerifod.
rifeling *m.* kind of shoe or sandal.
gerifod wrinkled.
rift, *e W. and l A.* y, *l W.* e *n.* cloak : veil, curtain.
rifter *m.* sickle ; scythe.
riftere, ript-, riftre *m.* reaper.
riht, *e W.* y, *K.* eo, ia, *A.* e I. straight ; erect ; right *in most of its present meanings* — ~es *av.* straight (on). II. *n.* right *in most of its present meanings,* equity, justice, due (punishment), prerogative; law; duty — hē hæfþ ~ his statement is correct | correctness, truth — on ~ correctly, properly | account — ~ āgieldan render an account [*Lt.* rectu-].
~æpel-cwēn *f.* lawful wife.
~æpelo *f.* true nobility.
~ǣw *f.* matrimony ; lawful wife.
~andswaru *f.* reproof.
~cynecynn *n.* genuine *or* direct royal lineage.
~cynn *f.* genuine breed *or* lineage.
~dōnde right-doing.
~fæderen-cynn *n.* lineal descent *or* descendants on father's side.
~fæsten-dæg *m.* regular fast-day.
~fæsten-tīd *f.* regular time for fasting.
~gefremed orthodox.
~fremmende† acting rightly.
~full honourable, right *vL.*
~gegiělda *m.* regular member of a guild.
~hǣmed *n.* matrimony.
~hand *f.* right hand.
~hand-dǣda *m.* actual perpetrator.
~heort upright in heart.
~hīwa *m.* lawful spouse.
~hlāford *m.* lawful lord *or* husband.
~hlāforddōm *m.* lawful authority.
~hlāford-hyldo *f.* loyalty, fealty.
~lǣcan set right, amend, correct.
~lǣcung *f.* setting right, correction.
~lǣce *m.* qualified physician.
~lagu *f.* just law, equity.
~gelēaffull orthodox.

riht|gelēaflīce *av.* in an orthodox manner.
~gelīefed orthodox.
~gelīefende faithful.
~lic just, fair ; fitting ; having a right to, fitted ; righteous.
~līce *av.* justly ; correctly ; in accordance with rules ; virtuously.
~līcettere *m.* thorough hypocrite.
~līf *n.* right *or* moral life.
~līplic articulate.
~mēdren-cynn *n.* direct descent on mother's side.
~meter-fers *n.* correct hexameter verse.
~munuc *m.* true monk.
~nes *f.* perpendicularity ; justice, equity.
~norþan-wind *m.* direct north wind.
~raciend *m.* expounder of righteousness.
~racu *f.* correct account.
ge~recan guide, direct.
~regol *m.* rule of right conduct, canon.
~ryne *m.* right course ; proper channel (of river).
~scilling *m.* genuine *or* standard shilling.
~scrīfend *m.* lawyer.
~scytte† shooting straight.
~gesett rightly appointed, canonical.
~smēa(w)ung *f.* argument.
~tīd *f.,* ~tīma *m.* proper time.
~geþancod right-minded.
~þēow *m.* lawful slave.
~weg *m.* right way ; definite direction, course (of ship) : þæs ~es þe .. in the direction that.
~wer *m.* lawful husband.
~west-ende *m.* extreme western end.
~willende well-meaning, righteous.
rihtwīs righteous.
~end *m.* Sadducee.
~ian justify ; rule.
~lic righteous.
~līce *av.* reasonably.
~nes *f.* righteousness, justice ; reasonableness, reason.
ge~ung *f.* justification.
riht|gewitt *n.* reason : wæs of hire ~e insane.
~wrītere *m.* one who writes correctly.
~wuldriende orthodox.
~ymbren *n.,* ~ymbren-dagas

mpl. duly appointed Ember time.
riht|an direct ; put upright, restore ; make straight ; restore (people) to their rights ; correct, reform ; rule, govern.
~end† *m.* ruler.
~ere† *m.* director, ruler.
ge~nes *f.* correction.
rihtung *f.* direction, guidance ; correction ; reproof ; regularis (in computation).
~prǣd *m.* plumb-line.
rihte *av.* straight (on) ; *of time* at once ; rightly, honourably, fitly, well ; correctly ; exactly (square).
rihte-bred *n.* carpenter's square, rule Gl.
gerihte *n.* straight direction — on ~ straight onwards, straight, direct, ūp on ~ upright ; right, due ; religious rite.
rīm *n.* number.
~āþ *m.* oath taken by a person and the number of persons he brings with him as compurgators.
(ge)~cræft *m.* arithmetic, computation.
~cræftig skilled in arithmetic.
~getæl *n.* number.
~talu† *f.* number.
gerīm *n.* number.
~tæl *n.* number.
rīm|an count, calculate, enumerate ; take into account ; account, esteem.
~ere *m.* calculator.
rima *m.* border, bank, coast.
rimpan 3 — *ptc.* gerumpen contracted, wrinkled (?).
rīnan, *rare prt.* rān rain [regn].
rinc† *m.* man, warrior.
~getæl *n.* number of men, host.
rind *f.* bark ; rind, crust.
~en of bark.
~lēas without bark.
rinde-clifer *f.* 'bark-scratcher,' woodpecker (?) Gl.
rinnan 3 run ; flow [iernan].
gerinn|an 3 coagulate ; run together, be mixed.
~ing*, ~yrning *f.* accumulation (of phlegm).
rinnelle *f.* brook.
rip, *pl.* ~u *n.* reaping, harvest ; cut corn, sheaf of corn.
~īsern *n.* sickle.
~tīma *m.* harvest time.

gerip *n.* reaping; harvest.

rīp|an 6 reap; gain advantage. *Cp.* repan reap.

~ere *m.* reaper.

ripian*, eo reap.

ripa, eo *m.* sheaf [rīpan].

rīp|e ripe.

~ian ripen *intr.*

~nes *f.* ripeness, maturity; harvest.

~o (?) *f.* ripeness, maturity.

~ung *f.* ripening *intr.*, ripeness, maturity.

rīpe-mann*, hrip(p)emonn *m.* reaper *LN.*

riptere = riftere.

gerīs *n.* fury.

rīs|an seize.

~ende rapacious.

rīsan (?) 6 rise. *Cp.* ārīsan.

gerīsan, r- 6 *wd. gen. impers.* befit.

rise, y, e, ~e *f.*, rix- rush [*Lt.* ruscus].

~bedd *n.* bed of rushes.

~en of rushes.

~lēac *n.* rush-garlic.

~mere *m.* rushy pond.

~pytt *m.* rush-pool.

~steort *m.* rushy promontory.

~pȳfel *m.* bed of rushes.

riscende *once* sounding Gl. *Cp.* ræscettan.

gerisen *once* seizing [rīsan].

gerisen|lic, -rislic suitable, convenient.

~līce *av.* suitably.

gerisn|e, -en- proper, suitable, convenient [gerīsan]

~es *f.* fitness, congruity.

~ian suit, accord.

~u *npl.* what is fitting *or* seemly, honour, dignity.

risoda *once m.* rheum.

rīp *mf.*, ~e *f.* stream, rivulet.

rīpig *nf.* stream.

rix-, *see* risc rush.

roc (n.) cud.

rocc, rooc *m.* upper garment.

roc(c)ettan belch; utter (words).

rōd *f.* cross (for crucifixion).

~begenga *m.* worshipper of the cross.

~bora *m.* cross-bearer.

~fæstnian crucify.

~ehengen(n) *f.* crucifixion.

~weorpiend *m.* worshipper of the cross.

~ewierpe deserving crucifixion.

rodor, ra- *m.* firmament; (†) sky, heavens.

~beorht† heavenly bright.

~cyning† *m.* king of heaven, Christ.

~lic of the firmament, heavenly.

~lihting *f.* dawn.

~stōl† *m.* celestial throne.

~torht† heavenly bright.

~tungol† *n.* star of heaven.

rōf† strong, brave.

rōgian†, ō† *once* prevail (?).

rohte *prt.* of reccan care.

Rōm *f.*, ~eburg *f.* Rome [*Lt.* Roma].

~feoh *n.*, ~pening *m.*, ~gescot *n.* Peter's pence.

~ware, ~waran *pl.* Romans.

~wealh, Rūm- *m.* Roman.

rōmian† possess *wg.*

Rōmān *f.* Italy Gl. [*Lt.* Romania].

~e, ~an *pl.* Romans.

~isc Roman.

roop, *see* ropp.

rōp, oo liberal.

~nes *f.* liberality.

ropp, roop *m.* colon, intestine.

~wærc *m.* colic.

ros|e *f.* rose [*Lt.* rosa].

~en of roses.

~ig rosy.

rostian roast, dry Gl.

rot = hrot scum.

rōt cheerful, glad; excellent, good.

~hwīl *f.* time of cheerfulness *or* comfort.

~līce *av.* cheerfully.

~nes *f.* cheerfulness; comfort, protection.

rōtfæst firmly established *vL.* [*Scand.* rōt root].

rot|ian decay; suppurate, ulcerate.

~ung *f.* decay; ulceration.

rōts|ian* cheer.

~ung *f.* cheering, comfort.

rop, hrop [ryppa].

~hund *m.* mastiff.

rōper (?) *m.* sailor Gl. [rōwan].

rōpor (n.) oar.

rōw I. gentle, mild (disease). II. *f.* quiet, rest.

rōw|an 1 *prt. pl.* rēo(wo)n row.

~end *m.* rowing = rēwett.

~ett *n.* rowing = rēwett.

~nes *f.* rowing.

~ung *f.* rowing *LN.*

ruddoc (*m.*) robin.

rude *once m.* scab Gl.

rūde *f.* rue (a plant) [*Lt.* ruta].

rud|u *f.* red colour, rouge; redness, blush; countenance [rēodan].

~ig ruddy.

rūg-, *see* rūh.

Rugern (*m.*) a month.

rūh, *pl.* rū(g)e shaggy, hairy; knotty, rough; untrimmed (hedge), uncultivated, wild; unprepared, not ground (corn).

rūm I. spacious, wide (road); open (country); extended (period of time); unrestricted, lax; liberal, bountiful; noble, magnificent. II. space; space of time; sufficient space, room; sufficient *or* fitting time, opportunity — pā him ~ ā-geald when the opportunity was given him.

~e *av.* extensively, far and wide; liberally, bountifully; amply, abundantly, at length; cheerfully.

~gāl† rejoicing in ample space.

~giefa *m.* liberal giver.

~giefol liberal.

~giefolnes *f.* liberality.

~heort liberal; cheerful.

~heortnes *f.* liberality.

~lic liberal; gracious; abundant.

~līce *av.* largely, greatly; (speak) at length; liberally; graciously, kindly.

~mōd *wg.* liberal, profuse; gracious, kind.

~mōdlic liberal.

~mōdlīce *av.* liberally; graciously.

~mōdnes *f.* liberality; kindness.

~nes *f.* breadth; abundance.

~welle spacious *LN.*

gerūm *n* space.

gerūm† spacious, dilated.

~e† *once av.* (?) roomily.

rūmian become free from obstruction (*of* body).

rūma *m.* separation.

gerūma† *m.* place, station.

rūmed|lic ample, liberal [rūm, mōd].

~līce *av.* liberally; (speak of) at large, fully.

rūn *f.* mystery, secret; council, secret discussion, communing (with oneself) | Runic letter; writing.

~cofa† *m.* mind.

~cræftig† skilled in mysteries.

~lic mystical.

~stæf *m.* Runic letter, rune.

rūn-wita† *m.* confidant, councillor, sage.

rūn|ian whisper; mutter; conspire.

~ere *m.* whisperer.

~ung *f.* whispering, soft speech, hints.

gerūna *m.* councillor.

runol *once* [= hr- ?] foul *or* running (virus).

rūst (*m.*) rust.

~ig rusty.

rūw-, *see* **rūh**.

rūwe = **rēowe** blanket.

rūxlan make a noise *LN.*

ryn *vb.* roar.

geryd- prepared, ready.

ryden *n.* — þæt rēade ~ *once* a plant.

rȳe = **rēowe** blanket.

ryge (*m.*) rye.

rygen of rye.

ryht = **riht**.

rȳman clear (road), make clear space; enlarge; give way, retire: ~ him setl yield it to him [rūm].

rȳmet(t) *n.* space, extent; sufficient space, room; extension of landed property; benefit.

~lēas *f.* want of room.

rȳmþ *f.* amplitude.

rȳnan roar. *Cp.* **rȳn**.

ryne *m.* running; course (of ship); orbit (of sun and moon); flowing, flux (of blood); bed of river; period of time, cycle; course of life; course *in other met. meanings* [iernan].

~giest† *m.* swift guest (= lightning).

~strang† strong for the course.

ryne|swift† swift in its course.

~þrāg† *f.* space of time.

~wǣgn†, **~wǣn** *m.* chariot.

rȳne *n.* mystery, mysterious saying [rūn].

~lic mystical.

~līce *av.* mystically.

~mann† *m.* sage.

gerȳne *n.* mystery.

~lic mystical.

~līce *av.* mystically.

rynel *m.* runner, courier.

rynge = **renge**.

rȳnig†, **ȳ**† *once* good in debate (?) [rūn].

ryniga *m.* liquid that runs off (?).

rynning *f.* rennet.

rysc = **risc** rush.

rysel, rysl *m.*, **~e** *f.* fat.

ryþþa *m.* mastiff [roþ-].

S.

sā (*m.*) bucket.

saban *once* sheet Gl.

sac = **sæc** guilty.

sacan 2 disagree, quarrel; fight; lay legal claim to *w.* on *a.*; blame, accuse.

sacian wrangle, quarrel.

gesaca *m.* adversary.

sacc, æ *m.* sack, bag [*Lt.* saccus].

sācerd, ā† *m.* priest [*Lt.* sacerdos, *through Irish*].

~bana *m.* priest-killer.

~hād *m.* priesthood.

~land *n.* priests' land.

~lic priestly.

~gerisne befitting a priest.

gesacu † *once f.* hostility.

sac|u, sæcc- *f.* dispute, quarrel; fighting. war; lawsuit; jurisdiction in lawsuits; persecution, affliction.

~full quarrelsome, litigious, given to accusation.

~lēas innocent; secure *vL.*

sadian *intr.* become satiated *or* weary || *tr.* ge~ satiate [sæd].

sāda *m.* noose, snare

sadol *m.* saddle.

~beorht† having a splendid saddle.

~boga *m.* saddle-bow.

~felg *f.* pommel of saddle.

~ian saddle.

sǣ *fm.*, *g.* sǣ(s), *dpl.* sǣ(u)m sea ; lake.

~ǣl *m.* sea-eel.

~ælfen(n) *f.* sea-nymph.

~bāt† *m.* boat, ship.

~beorg† *m.* sea-hill.

~burg *f.* sea-town.

~ceaster *f.* sea-town.

~ceosol *m.* shingle.

~cierr† *m.* retreat of the sea.

~clif† *n.* sea-cliff.

~cocc *m.* cockle.

~col *n.* jet.

~cyning† *m.* sea-king.

~dene† *mpl.* Danes.

~dēor *n.* sea-monster.

~draca *m.* sea-dragon.

~earm *m.* arm of the sea.

~færeld *n.* passage of the (Red) sea.

sǣ fæsten(n)† *n.* sea-fastness, defence afforded by the sea.

~faroþ *m.* sea-shore.

~fisc *m.* sea-fish.

~flōd *mn.* flood(tide), sea-inundation ; †sea.

~flota† *m.* ship.

~fōr *f.* voyage.

~gēap† roomy (ship).

~gēatas† *mpl.* Goths.

~genga *m.* sailor ; †ship.

~grund *m.* bottom *or* depths of the sea.

~healf *f.* side next the sea.

~hengest *m.* hippopotamus ; †ship.

~hete *m.* violence of the sea.

~holm† *m.* sea.

~lāc † *n.* sea-booty.

~lād† *f.* sea-voyage, watery way.

~lāf† *f.* what is left by the sea, sea-spoils.

~land *n.* land by the sea.

~lēoþ *n.* sailors' song.

~lic of the sea.

~lida† *m.* sailor ; pirate.

F

sǣ|līþend(e)† *m.* sailor.

~līþende† seafaring.

~gemǣre *n.* coast.

~mann *m.* sailor; pirate, Scandinavian.

~mearh† *m.* ship.

~mēþe† sea-weary.

~minte *f.* a plant.

~naca† *m.* ship.

~nǣss *m.* sea-headland, cape.

~nett *n.* sea-net.

~rieric†*, ȳ island (?).

~rima *m.* coast.

~rinc† *m.* sailor; pirate.

~rōf† active *or* strong on the sea.

~scapa *m.* pirate.

~sciell *f.* sea-shell.

~geset *m.* maritime district.

~sīþ *m.* sea-journey.

~snægl, ~snēl *m.* sea-snail.

~steorra *m.* star of the sea.

~strand *m.* sea-shore.

~strēam† *m.* water of the sea *gen. pl.*

~swealwe*, hǣ- *f.* sea-swallow.

~ūpwyrp *n.* what is thrown up by the sea, jetsam.

~wǣg† *m.* sea-wave.

~wǣter *n.* sea-water.

~wang† *m.* shore.

~wǣr seaweed.

~waroþ *m.* shore.

~weall† *m.* cliff; wall of waters (in Red Sea).

~weard *f.* sea-guard, keeping watch on the coast.

~weg† *m.* sea.

~wērig† weary with the sea.

~wīcing† *m.* pirate, seaman.

~wielm† *m.* billow.

~wiht *f.* sea-animal.

~wudu *m.* ship.

~ȳþ *f.* wave.

sǣc, a guilty; hateful Gl

sǣc = sacc bag.

sǣcc (*m.*) sacking, sackcloth.

~ing *m.* bed.

sǣcce, *see* sacu.

sǣd *wg.* satiated (with), wearied.

~nes *f.* satiety, nausea.

sǣd *n.* seed (of plants and animals); fruit, crop; growth; sowing; source; progeny, posterity [sāwan].

~berende† seed-bearing.

~cynn *n.* kind of seed.

~ian sow.

sǣd|ere *m.* sower.

~lēap *m.* seed-basket.

~lic seminal.

~noþ *m.* sowing.

~tīma *m.* sowing season.

sǣde *prt. of* secgan.

Sǣfern *f.* Severn [*Lt.* Sabrina].

~(e)mūþa *m.* mouth of the Severn.

sǣgan cause to sink *or* set (sun); lay low, destroy [sīgan].

sǣgde *prt. of* secgan.

gesǣgdnes *f.* mystery (!) *lN.*

sǣgednes = onsǣgdnes sacrifice.

sǣgon *prt. of* sēon.

sǣl† *n.* hall.

sǣl *mf., dpl.* ~um, sǣlum occasion, time — æt sumum ~e one day, on nǣnne ~ never; proper time, opportunity — tō ~es in due time; happiness *often in pl.*; condition, state.

~wang†, ā *m.* plain.

sǣlan happen.

sǣlan† bind; restrain; repress [sāl].

sǣlen *once* of willow Gl. [sealh].

gesǣlig happy, prosperous [sǣl].

~lic, gesǣllic happy.

~līce *av.* happily.

-nes *f.* happiness.

sǣlmerige *f.* brine [*Lt.* salmuria].

(ge)sǣlþ *f., gen. pl.* prosperity; happiness.

sǣm-* *aj.* only in *cpv. and spl.* ~ra, ~ost bad; unimportant, worthless.

sǣmtinges = samtinges.

sǣne sluggish, slow (in) *wg.*; cowardly [āsānian].

sǣp *n.* sap.

-ig sappy, succulent.

~spōn *f.* sappy shaving *or* chip.

sǣppe *f.* spruce-fir [*Lt.**sappium].

sǣran *once* be exalted.

sǣre = sāre.

sǣt *f.* ambush [sittan].

sǣt|ian, ~an, ~nian *wg.* lie in wait for, plot against.

~ere *m.* robber, waylayer; spy; seducer (the devil).

~ung, -ing *f.* lying in wait; snare; treachery; sedition (!).

Sǣtern(es)-dæg, Sǣter-, Sǣtresm. Saturday [*Lt.* Saturni dies].

Sǣter-niht *f.* Friday night.

sǣperige *f.* savory (a plant) [*Lt.* satureia].

sǣprene-wudu = sūperne-.

sǣwett *n.* sowing [sāwan].

safine *f.* savine (a plant) [*Lt.* sabina].

saftriende *once* rheumatic Gl.

saga *imper. of* secgan.

sāgol, *pl.* sāglas, sāhlas *m.* staff, club.

sag|u *f.*, ~a *m.* saw (tool).

sagu *f.* statement, report; testimony; foretelling [secgan].

sāh *prt. of* sēon 6.

sāh = sāg *prt. of* sīgan.

sāl *mf.* rope; bond; rein.

salfige *f.* sage (plant) [*Lt.* salvia].

sallettan play on *or* sing to the harp, sing psalms [*Lt.* psallere].

sālnes *once f.* silence.

salo, ea dark-coloured.

~brūn dark-brown.

~nebb† dark-faced.

~pād† dark-coated.

salnes *f.* darkness. *Cp.* sālnes.

salor† hall, palace [sæl].

saltere *m.* psaltery; the Book of Psalms, psalter [*Lt.* psalterium].

sal|u*, ~a *once f.* sale.

sālum, *see* sǣl.

salwian *tr.* darken, blacken.

sal(o)wig- [salo].

~feþera† dark-winged.

~pād(a)† dark-coated.

sam *cj.* — ~ . . ~ whether . . or *w. sbj.*

sām-bærned half-burnt.

sām-boren abortive.

sām-bryce *m.* partial breach *or* violation.

sām-cwic, -cucu half-dead.

same *av.* — swā ~ similarly; also. swā ~ swā as.

samen *av.* together *lN.*

sām-geong young (grown up).

sām-grēne backward (*of* plant).

sām-hāl in bad health.

sam-heort of one heart, unanimous.

sam-hīwan *pl.* members of a family; ge~ married couple.

sām-hwelc some *no., aj.*

sām-lǣred half *or* badly taught.

samlīce *av.* together, at the same time.

sam-mǣle agreed, having come to an agreement.

sām-mielt half-digested.

samnian *tr.* collect; cause to

unite (wound) ; glean ‖ *intr.* assemble ; unite.

samnung *f.* assembly, council.

~**cwide** *m.* collect.

gesamnung *f.* assembly ; congregation ; synagogue ; union.

samnunga = semninga.

samod I. *av.* together — **weras wīf** ~ men and women ; ~ **ætgædere** together ; ~ mid *d.* together with. II. *prp. wd.* at (dawn).

~**cumende** flocking together.

~**eard**† *m.* dwelling together, common home.

~**fæst**† joined together.

~**geflit** *n.* strife.

~**hering** *f.* praising (!).

~**līce** *av.* together *vL.*

~**rynelas** *mpl.* runners together Gl.

~**gesīþ** *m.* companion.

~**spræc** *f.* colloquy.

~**swēgende** consonantal.

~**þyrlic** concordant.

~**wiellung***, e *f.* welding Gl.

~**wunung** *f.* living together.

~**wyrcende** co-operating.

sam-rād united, unanimous.

sām-soden half-cooked.

sām-swǣled half-burnt.

sam-swēge*, sum- harmonious, in unison (song) Gl.

sam-tinges, æ, e *av.* without interval (of space or time), immediately.

sam-þe *av. correl.* both . . and, whether . . or.

sam-winnende struggling together.

sām-wīs dull-witted, foolish.

~**līce** *av.* foolishly.

sam-wist *f.* living together ; matrimony.

sām-worht half made *or* built.

sam-wrǣdnes *f.* union.

sām-wyrcan do incompletely.

sanct *m.* saint [*Lt.* sanctus].

sand *f.* sending, message ; messenger ; course *or* dish of food [sendan].

sand *n.* sand ; sea-shore.

~**beorg** *m.* sand-hill, sand-bank.

~**brōc** *m.* sandy brook.

~**ceosol** *m.* sand, gravel.

~**corn**, ~**grot**, *n.* grain of sand.

~**hliþ**† *n.* sand-slope.

~**hof**† *n.* grave.

~**hrycg** *m.* sand-bank.

sand|hyll *m.* sand-hill.

~**ig** sandy.

~**iht** sandy, dusty.

~**land**† *n.* sea-shore.

~**rid** (*n.*) quicksand.

~**sēaþ** *m.* sandpit.

~**geweorp** *n.* sand-bank, quicksand.

~**gewierpe** *n.* sand-heap.

sander-mann *m.* ambassador *vL.*

sang song ; singing ; poem.

~**bōc** *f.* music-book, hymn-book.

~**cræft** *m.* music ; poetical composition.

~**drēam** *m.* song, music.

~**ere** *m.* singer, poet.

~**estre** *f.* singer.

~**pīpe** *f.* pipe.

sang* bed, *see* **song**.

sāp *f.* ? amber, resin, pomade.

~**box** *m.* resin-box.

sāpe *f.* soap [*Lt.* sapo].

sār I. *n.* pain (of body and mind), sore, wound ; grief. II. *aj.* painful (wound) ; severe (hardship) ; causing sorrow, grievous : **þæt wæs him** ~.

~**benn**† *f.* wound.

~**bōt**† *f.* compensation for wound.

~**clāþ** *m.* bandage.

~**cwide** *m.* † bitter *or* reproachful speech ; lament.

~**e**, **ǣ** *av.* sorely, with suffering ; (speak) bitterly ; excessively.

~**ferhþ**† sore at heart.

~**lic** causing pain ; causing sorrow ; expressing sorrow (*of* voice, song).

~**līce** *av.* with pain ; lamentably ; in a way expressing sorrow.

~**nes** *f.* pain ; grief.

~**sēofung** *f.* complaint.

~**slege** *m.* painful blow.

~**spell**† *n.* lament.

~**stæf**† *m.* insult, reproach.

~**wielm**† *m.* pain.

~**wracu**† *f.* tribulation.

sār|ian be painful (*of* wound) ; be sad ; pity (!).

~**ung** *f.* lamentation.

sārcren once disposed to soreness (stomach).

sārettan complain of, lament.

sārg|ian *tr.* wound ; grieve ‖ *intr.* suffer.

~**ung** *f.* grief, lamentation.

sarga *m.* trumpet.

sārig feeling grief, sad ; expressing grief (*of* voice, song).

sārig|ferhþ† sad.

~**mōd** sad.

~**nes** *f.* sadness.

saturege *f.* savory (plant) [*Lt.* satureia].

sāul = sāwol.

sāw|an I sow.

~**end**, ~**ere** *m.* sower.

sāwol, **sāwl** *f.* soul; life.

~**berend**† *m.* human being.

~**cund** spiritual.

~**gedāl**† *n.* death.

~**drēor**† *n.* life-blood.

~**hord**† *n.* life ; body.

~**hūs**† *n.* body.

~**lēas** lifeless ; without soul.

~**sceatt** *m.*, ~**gescot** *n.* soul-scot, payment to church on death of person.

~**þearf** *f.* soul-need, what is necessary for salvation.

sāwl|ian expire.

~**ung** *f.* expiring, point of death.

gesāwlod having a soul.

sāwon *prt. of* sēon see.

scacan 2 *intr.* shake ; move quickly, flee, depart, proceed ‖ *tr.* shake.

scacol *m.* shackle ; ! plectrum.

scād *n.* account.

~**līce***, ~**elīce** *av.* reasonably, rationally.

~**wīslīce** *av.* with discretion, rationally.

~**wīsnes** *f.* sagacity, reason.

gescād I. *n.* separation ; distinction ; discrimination ; reasoning, understanding — ~ **witan** *wg.* understand ; statement ; argument ; (render) account ; truth (of statement). II. *aj.* accurate ; wise.

~**lic** reasonable.

~**līce** *av.* rationally ; accurately.

gescādwīs rational, intelligent, sagacious.

~**lic** rational.

~**līce** *av.* rationally ; sagaciously, prudently ; accurately.

~**nes** *f.* intelligence, reason.

gescād-wyrt *f.* oxeye (a plant).

scādan, ēa 1 b *tr.* divide, separate ; distinguish; scatter, sprinkle (small particles), shed (blood) ‖ *intr.* separate ; differ ; be scattered, fall (*of* small particles).

scāda *m.* crown of the head.

scāde-sealf*, ea *f.* medicinal powder (for sprinkling).

scāden-mǽl*, sceaþen-† with divided (branching) ornaments or patterns (sword).
scǽcdōm*, sǽc- m. flight [scacan].
scǣn|an break.
ge~ingnes(!) f. collision Gl.
scǣr = scear prt. of sciéran.
scǽþþa = sceaþa nail.
scāf.
~fōt splay-footed.
scafan 2 shave, polish; scrape, shred.
scafa m. plane (a tool).
scafoþa m., sceafþ, ǣ what is shaved or scraped off.
scaga m. copse.
scalu f. shell, husk; dish; scale (of balance), pair of scales.
scam|ian be ashamed, also impers. w. a. or L. d. of pers., w. g. or for d., w. sbj.: hē ~aþ þǣs, wē ~iaþ ūre, menn (a.) ~aþ for gōddǣdum, him ~aþ þæt hē cume.
~ung f. being put to shame, disgrace.
scamol m. bench; stool.
scam|u f. feeling of shame, modesty; disgrace; private parts.
~fǣst ashamed; modest.
~full modest, chaste.
~isc to be ashamed of, private (parts).
~lēas shameless, bold, wanton.
~lēaslic shameless, wanton.
~lēaslīce av. shamelessly.
~lic bashful; disgraceful.
~līce av disgracefully.
~liest, ēa f. impudence, wantonness.
~lim n. private member.
scanc|a m. shank of leg; leg.
~bend m. garter.
~gebeorg n. greave.
~forod with broken leg.
~gegierela m. garter.
~līra m. calf of leg.
scand m. buffoon; infamous man or woman. Cp. scand f.
scand f. disgrace; what is disgraceful; infamous woman. Cp. scand m.
~full infamous.
~hūs n. brothel.
~lic infamous; unchaste; disgraceful; obscene; causing shame.
~līce av. disgracefully; unchastely; ignominiously; insultingly.
~licnes f. what is accompanied with disgrace; disgraceful action.

scand|lufiende loving disgracefully Gl.
~word n. abusive word; obscene language.
gescapen ptc. of sciẹppan.
~nes f. creation.
scaru f. groin, private parts.
scaru f. (hair)-cutting; (sheep)-shearing; tonsure [sciéran].
scaþ|ian do mischief; steal.
ennes, ~ung f. injury.
scaþa m. one who does harm, (public) enemy, criminal; thief; fiend; †warrior.
scaþa† once m. injury, misfortune.
scaþel (m.) weaving-implement.
scea- often = sca-.
sceabb, ǣ m. scab.
~ede scabby.
scēac(e)re m. robber LN.
scead n. shade; protection.
~iht shady.
sceadd (m.) shad (a fish).
~genge – þonne ~ biþ when shad are in season.
sceadu, pl. scead(w)a, f. shadow; shade, darkness; shady place, arbour, &c.; protection; something unreal or unsubstantial, shadow.
~geard m. shady enclosure, ! Tempe.
~genga† m. one who walks in darkness.
~helm† m. darkness.
sceadw|ian, -dew- overshadow.
~ung f. overshadowing.
scēaf m. bundle, sheaf [scūfan].
~mǽlum av. sheafwise.
sceaft m. shaft (of spear, arrow); spear; pole; measure of length six inches.
~lō, pl. ~lōn shaft-strap (to help in throwing spear).
~riht(e) av. in a straight line.
sceaft f m. creation; what is created [sciẹppan].
gesceaft f n. creation; condition, nature; created thing, creature. coll. creation — þā ~a elements; decree (of fate, God).
sceagg a, cg m. hair of the head.
~ede hairy-headed.
sceal, L. sceall vb., pl. sculon, sbj. scyle, u, prt. scolde wdg. owe (money); obligation of duty, reasonableness, command, compulsion shall; to show that a statement is made at second-hand: hī

sǣdon þæt þæs hearperes wīf sceolde ācwelan died | often w. ellipse of infin.: hīe tō helle sculon go; ne ~ cyrcan timber tō ǣnigum ōþrum weorce be used for.
scealc m. servant; †man, warrior.
sceald.
~þȳfel; pl. vE. scald(t)hȳflas, scaldhūlas m. bush, shrub.
scealga m. a fish.
sceallan pl. testicles.
scēam†, ēa† once m. white horse(?).
scēan-feld = scíen-.
sceap (n.) private part.
gesceap n. creation; created thing, creature; form, shape; nature; destiny, decree (of fate); private part.
~hwīl† f. fated hour (of death).
~līce av. fitly.
scēap, ǣ, ē, LN. scíp n. sheep.
~en sheep's.
~heord f. flock of sheep.
~heorden hovel, shed.
~hierde m. shepherd.
~scaru f. sheep-shearing.
~wǣsce f. place for washing sheep.
~wīc n. sheepfold.
scear n. ploughshare [sciéran].
~bēam m. wood to which plough-share is fixed.
scear-seax, sciér- n. razor.
scear prt. of sciéran.
sceard I. notched, with pieces broken off or out; gashed, mutilated; deprived wg. [sciéran].
scearf|ian scrape, shred [sceorfan].
~ung f. scraping, scarifying.
scearflian scrape.
scearn (n.) dung.
~wibba, ~wifel m. beetle.
scēaron prt. pl. of sciéran.
scearp sharp; rough; pungent, acid, acrid; sharp of speech; severe (pain, hunger); energetic, strong, sharp (medicine, sight, intellect) [sciéran].
~e av. sharply, keenly (of seeing).
~ecged sharp-edged.
~līc keen (inquiry), severe (temptation).
~līce av. (heal) effectually, (see) keenly; painfully.
~nes f. pungency, acidity; keenness (of sight, intellect).

scearp|numol efficacious (medicine).

~sīene sharp-sighted.

~smēaung f. argument.

~þanclīce, ~þancfullīce av. efficaciously.

~þancol acute (of mind).

scearp|e f. scarification.

~ian scarify.

~ung f. scarifying.

scēarra, scēara, vE. scērero, -uru pl. shears, scissors [sciēran].

scēat m. piece of cloth, cloak, garment; lap, bosom, surface; region, quarter (of the earth); inlet (of the sea) Bd.; corner; projection [scēotan].

~codd m. wallet.

~līne f. sheet of sail, rope fastened to lower end of sail.

gescēat-wyrpan [y = iẹ ?] betroth Gl.

scēata m. cloth, napkin; bosom, lap; corner, lower corner of sail.

sceatt m. property; money, sum; payment, tribute, rent — tēoþa ~ tithe; bribe; coin; penny.

scēaþ, ǣ f. sheath.

sceaþa, eo, scæþþ- m. nail IN.

scēaw|ian see; scrutinize, reconnoitre; regard (with favour); seek out, select, provide; grant L.

~end-sprǣc, ~wīse f. buffoonery.

~ere m. spectator; spy; watchtower; mirror.

~ung f. seeing, contemplation; examination; regard for; ! pretence; spectacle, show.

gescēawian wda. make manifest, show (honour); see.

scegþ, sceiþ mf. swift ship [Scan. skeiþ].

~mann m. pirate. Scandinavian.

scẹnc m. cup; draught.

~an give to drink wda.

~ing-cuppe f. cup from which drink is poured.

scend|an, i, y put to shame, injure [scand].

(ge)~nes, ea f. shame, confusion.

~ung, ~ing f. abuse; injury.

scẹndle f. reproach, abuse IN.

scẹnn† once plate of metal on handle of sword (?).

gescẹnto, -scẹndþo f. shame, confusion [scand].

sceo- often = sco-, occ. = scu-

sceō- often = scō-, occ. = scū-.

scēo † once cloud (?).

scēon† wk. vb. happen — vL. sceet happens wd.

scēofan = scūfan.

sceoh† timid (?).

~mōd timid (?).

sceolh wry, oblique.

scēol|ēagede, ~iege, scy- squinting.

sceolon = sculon.

scēone = sciene.

sceorf = scurf.

gesceorf n. scurf.

sceorfan 3 gnaw; scarify; gescrape, shred.

sceorp n. dress.

sceorpan 3 scrape, cause irritation [screpan].

scēot quick, ready.

gescēot once quick, ready.

scēotan 7 tr. shoot or throw missile; hit with missile; move quickly, push, throw; contribute, pay (money); refer case to person or court w. tō ‖ intr. move quickly, rush, flow, run (of road), also met.; shoot (of pain).

~end† m. warrior.

scēota m. trout.

sceoþa = sceaþa nail.

scep = scyp patch.

sceran = sciēran.

scerero = scēarra.

scericge, scern- f. female buffoon, actress.

scernicge, see scericge.

scẹþ-. Cp. scẹþþan.

~dǣd f. crime Gl.

~nes f. injury.

~wrǣc once noxious, wicked.

scẹþþ|an 2, prt. †scōd, also wk. scẹþþede wd. injure [scaþa].

~end† m. enemy.

ge~endlic hurtful IN.

scẹþþu, ǣ f. injury.

scia (m.) shin, leg Gl., IN.

sciccels, scyccel m. cloak.

sciccing, scic(g)ing, scinccing (m.) cloak Gl.

scid n. piece of wood split thin, stick (for lighting fire).

~hrēac m. heap of sticks.

~weall m. fence.

scielian*, y, e divide, remove — ~ of māle put (ships) out of commission.

sciẹlcen f. female servant or slave; prostitute [scealc].

sciẹld m. shield; protection.

~burg† f. phalanx, testudo.

~freca† m. warrior.

~hrēoþa, ~rēþa, ~hrēada m. shield; testudo, phalanx.

~truma m. phalanx.

~weall† m. phalanx, testudo.

~wiga† m. warrior.

~wyrhta m. shield-maker.

gesciẹld n. refuge, protection.

sciẹld|an protect w. a. and wiþ a. — abs. ~ ongēan make defence (against accusation).

~en(n)*, i f. protection.

(ge)~end m. protector.

~ere m. protector.

(ge)~nes f. protection.

~ung f. protection.

sciẹlfan 3 intr. shake.

scielfor yellow Gl.

sciẹll f. shell; scale (of fish, snake) [scalu].

~fisc m. shell-fish.

~iht having a shell.

sciẹll*, scylt resonant (?) R.

sciẹllan 3 intr. sound.

sciẹlle*, e destruction, slaughter Gl.

scīen|e, ēo beautiful.

~feld*, ī, ēa m. Elysian field, Tempe.

scīenes = scȳnes suggestion.

sciẹpp|an 2, prt. scōþ, ptc. sc(e)apen, ǣ, ẹ create; form; destine (a person to anything), adjudge, wda. assign, give (name).

~end, ge- m. Creator.

scier-seax = scear-.

sciẹr|an, A. e(o), prt. scear, pl. scēaron, A. scǣr, scēron cut, shear — ptc. scoren cut short off, precipitous.

~ing f. shaving.

sciẹr|ian wda. allot, assign, grant [sciẹran].

~iendlic derivative (in grammar).

~ung f. expulsion.

sciẹrdan injure, destroy [sceard].

sciẹrden of shards [sceard].

sciẹrfe-mūs*, i f. shrew-mouse [sceorfan].

sciẹrpan tr. sharpen; incite, stimulate [scearp].

sciẹrpan clothe, equip (soldiers) [sceorp].

gescierpla *m.* clothing, clothes.
sciete *f.* sheet, a cloth [scéat].
sciftan divide (land); arrange, appoint.
scilling *m.* shilling, a monetary unit of varying value.
~rim *m.* reckoning by shillings.
scim|a *m.* shadow, gloom.
~ian be dark; be dazzled (*of eyes*); be bleared (*of eyes*).
scim|a, ï† *m.* light, brightness.
~ian shine, glitter.
scimrian shine, gleam.
scin|an 6 shine; *also fig.* be conspicuous, &c.
~endlic bright.
gescinan 6 *tr.* shine upon, illuminate.
gescincio *npl.* the fat about the kidneys.
scin|n, scin, ï† [*or* *scinn], ï phantom, demon, devil.
~cræft, scinn-, scin- *m.* magic, magic art *or* trick.
~cræftiga *m.* magician.
~gedwola *m.* phantom.
~hīw *n.* phantom; magic trick.
~lāc *n.* phantom; magic, magic art *or* trick; superstition; frenzy, rage.
~gelāc *n.* magic art *or* trick.
~lǣca, ~lāca *m.* magician.
~lǣce *f.* sorceress.
~lǣce, ~lāc-, *LN.* scinelāc- magic; spectral.
~lic*, *LN.* scinelic spectral.
~seoc spectre-haunted.
scinn*, y *n.* skin, fur *vL.* [*Scand.*].
scinna *m.* spectre, demon.
scinnere *m.* magician.
scinnes*, scinis *f.* light *LN.*
scin|u *f.* shin.
~bān *n.* shin-bone.
~hosu *f.* greave.
scip *n.* ship.
~bīeme *f.* ship-trumpet.
~broc *n.* hardship on board ship.
~gebroc *n.* shipwreck.
~brucol causing shipwreck.
~bryce *m.* what drifts ashore from wrecked ships.
~cræft *m.* naval power, force of ships.
~drincende drowning *LN.*
~fǣreld *n.* voyage.
~fæt *n.* vessel *or* dish in the form of a ship.

scip|farend *m.* sailor.
~gefeoht *n.* naval battle.
~gefēre *n.* going by ship.
~fērend *m.* sailor.
~fierd *f.* naval expedition, fleet.
~fierdung, -ing *f.* naval expedition; fitting out fleet; fleet.
~flota *m.* sailor, pirate.
~fultum *m.* naval reinforcements.
~fyllep private jurisdiction exercised over a group of three hundreds.
~fyrprung, ~fyrpung, ~forpung *f.* fitting out ships.
~gield *n.* tax for maintaining fleet.
~hamor *m.* hammer whose sound directed rowers.
~here *m.* fleet; crew of a warship.
~herelic naval *Gl.*
~hlǣd(d)er *f.* ship's ladder.
~hlæst *m.* transport (ship); crew.
~hlāford *m.* master of ship.
~incel *n.* small ship.
~lād *f.* sailing.
~lic naval.
~lip *n.* naval force *L.* [*Scand.*].
~lipende going in ship.
~mǣr(e)ls *m.* ship-rope.
~mann *m.* sailor, rower; one who goes on trading voyages.
~rāp *m.* cable.
~rēpra *m.* sailor.
~rōpor *n.* oar; rudder.
~rōwend *m.* rower, sailor *Gl.*
~ryne *m.* passage *or* channel for ships.
~setl *n.* rowers' bench.
~sōcn *f.* = ~fyllep.
~steall *m.* place for ship(s), docks.
~steorra *m.* Pole-star.
~stiera, eo *m.* steersman, pilot.
~getāwu *pl.* fittings of a ship.
~teoro *n.*, ~teara *m.* pitch.
~toll *m.* fare, passage-money.
~wealh *m.* one liable to serve in the fleet (?).
~weard† *m.* ship-master.
~werod *n.* crew.
~wise *f.* form of a ship.
~wyrhta *m.* ship-builder.
scip-ǣtere, -et- *m.* sheep's carcase *LL. Cp.* scēap.
scip|ian equip *or* man (ship) ‖ *intr.* embark.
~ere *m.* sailor.

scipe *m.* dignity, office; wages, stipend.
scipen, y *f.* stall, fold (for cattle or sheep).
scīr *f.* office, administration; district, shire, diocese, parish.
~biscop *m.* bishop of a diocese.
~lett (*n.*) piece *or* measure of land *Ct. Cp.* geoc-led.
~(e)mann, scīrig- *m.* official, steward; procurator; native of a district.
~gemōt *n.* shire-mote.
~gerēfa *m.* judicial president of a shire, sheriff.
~gesceatt *n.* property of a see.
~pegen *m.* thane of a shire.
~(e)wita *m.* chief man of shire.
scīr transparent, clear (weather); bright, glittering, white, brilliant; pure (wine); clear (voice); splendid.
~baso bright purple.
~e *av.* brightly; clearly (*of voice*).
~ecg bright-edged.
~ham† in bright armour.
~mǣled† with bright ornaments (sword).
~wered bright (light).
scīr|an declare, tell, speak; make a distinction, distinguish, decide; *wg.* get clear *or* rid of.
~nes *f.* explanation.
scītan 6 cacare.
scitol purgative.
scitte *f.* diarrhœa.
sco, *see* scōh.
scōd *prt. of* sceppan.
scofettan drive (hither and thither) [scūfan].
scofl *f.* shovel [scūfan].
scōg(e)an, scōian, scōan, *ptc.* gescōd shoe, put on shoes, furnish with shoes.
scōung *f.* supplying with shoes.
scōh, scō *m.*, *pl.* scōs shoe.
~cnyll *m.* signal for putting on shoes.
~ere *m.* shoemaker.
~nægl *m.* shoe-nail.
~pegn *m.* servant who attends to shoes.
~pwang *m.* boot-lace.
~wyrhta *m.* shoemaker, worker in leather.
scolde *prt. of* sceal.
scōl [*Fr.*], scolu [*Lt.*] *f.* school. *See* scolu.

scōl-mann *m.* learner.
gescola *m.* debtor [sceal].
gescola *m.* schoolfellow.
scol(i)ere *m.* pupil, learner.
scol|u *f.* troop, host [*Lt.* schola school *in L. sense of* corporation, body-guard].
~mann *m.* client, follower.
scōm.
~hylte (*n.*) thicket Gl.
scop *m.* poet.
~cræft *m.* poetry.
~lēop *n.* poem.
~lic poetical.
~gereord *n.* poetical language.
scōp *prt. of* scięppan.
scoppa *m.* shed, booth.
scorian *intr.* refuse.
scorian project (*of* stones from cliff).
scoren *ptc. of* sciēran.
scort, *cpv.* scyrtra, *spl.* scyrtest, short, not tall ; *of time* short, brief.
~ian *intr.* shorten (*of* days) ; run short, fail.
~lic short (time).
~lice *av. of time* quickly, soon ; (narrate) briefly.
~nes *f.* shortness (of time); short space of time ; epitome, summary.
~wierplic*, y (dream) of early fulfilment.
scot *n.* shot, shooting ; †*once* eo rush, darting (of salmon) [scēotan].
~frēo free from impost *L.*
~spere *n.* javelin.
scot-lira *m.* calf of leg.
gescot *n.*, *often coll.* missile weapons, bow and arrow ; arrow ; shooting, darting (missiles) ; flight of missiles | contribution, payment | part of building shut off from the rest, chancel.
~feoht *n.* fight with missiles.
scot|ian shoot (a person); shoot *or* hurl (weapon) || *intr.* move rapidly.
~ung *f.* shooting ; missile.
Scot|tas *mpl.* Irish ; Scotch.
~land *n.* Ireland ; Scotland.
scrād† R.
scræf *n.* cave ; den ; hovel.
scræf*, *vE.* scræb, e (*m.*) cormorant (?).
gescræpe = gescrēpe.
scrætte *f.* adulteress, prostitute.
scrallettan† sound loudly *intr.*

scrēad, ~e *f.* shred, paring.
~ian pare.
scrēadung *f.* pruning, trimming ; what is pared off, shred.
~īsen *n.* pruning-knife.
scrēawa *m.* shrew-mouse.
scremman make to stumble [scrimman].
scręnc|an put stumbling-block in the way of, trip up ; injure morally [scrincan ; *cp.* scręmman].
ge~ednes *f.* tripping up.
gescrence withered *LN.*
screpan 5 scrape.
gescrēp|e, scrēpe, oe, ǣ suitable, fit.
~elice *av.* fitly.
~nes *f.* convenience.
screpu*, eo *f.* curry-comb, strigil Gl.
scrīc shrike (a bird).
scrid *n.* carriage, chariot, litter [scrīþan].
~wægn *m.* chariot.
~wīsa *m.* charioteer.
scride*, -peþ† *once* course, orbit (of stars) [scrīþan].
scriden *ptc. of* scrīþan.
gescrif *n.* edict [scrīfan].
scrīfan 6 decree; *wda.* allot, assign, impose (penance), *wd.* shrive || care for, reck *w. g.*, *d. or for d.*
scrifen† R.
scrift *m.* legal penalty ; penance ; judge ; confessor, priest who hears confession [scrīfan].
~bōc *f.* book stating penances to be imposed after confession, confessional ; discourse on penance.
~scīr *f.* confessor's district.
~sprǣc *f.* confession.
scrimman 3 be drawn up *or* permanently bent (*of* limbs).
scrīn *n.* receptacle for valuables, coffer ; shrine ; ark (of the covenant) ; cage in which a criminal is confined [*Lt.* scrinium].
scrincan 3 *intr.* wither, fade ; shrink, contract ; be dispirited.
scripp (*m.*) bag, wallet.
scritta *m.* hermaphrodite Gl.
scrīþan 6 move smoothly, glide, go, wander ; come on, go on (*of* light, darkness, time).
scripe = scride.
scrofell (*n.*) scrofula [*Lt.*].
scrūd *n.* dress, garment.
~fultum *m.* supplying clothing.

scrūd|land *n.* land to provide clothing.
~waru *f.* dress.
scrūdn|ian, scrūtn- investigate.
~ung *f.* investigation.
scruf = scurf.
scrybb *f.* underwood.
scrȳdan dress ; provide with clothes, clothe ; put on (clothes), dress oneself in *waa.*, *w. a. and* mid *d.* [scrūd].
scrȳdels-hūs*, scru- *n.* vestry.
scrynce *once* withered *LN.* [scrincan].
scua = scuwa.
scucc|a, sceo- *m.* demon, devil.
~gield *n.* idol.
scūfan, sceo-, *ptc.* scofen, *LN.* y, 7 *tr.* push — ~ūt launch (ship) ; ~ him tō handa deliver up ; push (a person's cause) ; prompt (thought) ; † cause to appear (night, dawn) || *intr.* move, fall.
scūdan†, ūt *once* hasten (?) *intr.*
sculdor *m.*, *pl.* -dru, -a shoulder.
~hrægl *n.* cape.
~wærc *m.* pain in the shoulders.
gesculdru = gescyldru.
sculon, *see* sceal.
scult-heta = scyld-.
scun|ian, *LN.* giscynia avoid ; fear ; abhor.
~ung *f.* abomination.
scūr *m.* shower (of rain, hail) ; gust (of wind) ; shower (of missiles).
~beorg† *m.* roof.
~boga† *m.* rainbow.
~fāg showery (winter).
~heard† hardened by striking (sword).
~mǣlum*, scyr- *av.* stormily.
~sceadu† *f.* protection against storms *or* weather.
scurf, eo, scruf (*m.*) scurf.
~ede, ~ende scurfy.
scutel (*m.*) dish [*Lt.* scutula].
scu(w)a, uþ *m.* shadow ; darkness ; protection ; unreality.
gescȳ, *A.* oe *n.* pair of shoes [scōh].
scȳ|an, scyh- suggest, persuade, tempt.
~nes*, scīenes *f.* suggestion.
scyfe *m.* falling headlong ; precipitation, hastiness ; furtherance ; instigation [scūfan].
scyfel, scyfle *f.* woman's headdress Gl.

gescȳgean provide with shoes Ct. [gescȳ].

scyhtan† instigate. *Cp.* scȳan.

scyl = sciell.

scyld *f.* guilt ; debt, due [sceal].

~frecu†*f.* wicked greed.

~full guilty.

~hǣta, scultheta *m.* bailiff.

~hata† *m.* wicked persecutor, enemy.

~lēas guiltless.

~wrecende punishing guilt.

~wyrcende evil-doing.

gescyldan, -ian charge, accuse.

scyldian = scyldan, scyldgian.

scyldg|ian, scyld|ig|ian sin.

~ung *f.* criminal charge.

scyldig *w. g.* (*i.*) guilty; responsible for ; bound by obligation ; liable to (punishment) ; having forfeited, liable to lose (life, property).

~nes *f.* guilt *LN.*

gescyldru, -sculdru, -sculdre *pl.* shoulders [sculdor].

scyle, *see* sceal.

scylf *m.* peak, crag ; pinnacle, turret.

scylfe *f.* shelf, ledge ; floor, story.

scylfig*, scylp̄ig rocky Gl.

scylfrung [y = ie ?] *f. once* swinging (of lamps) *intr.* (?), brightness (?).

scynian = scunian.

scynd|an hasten *intr. and tr.* ; incite, exhort.

~endlīce *av.* hastily.

scyndel *m.* disreputable one, cad (*of* Jupiter !).

scyp, e *m.* patch piece of cloth.

scypian *once* take shape, be formed.

scypen = scipen stall.

scyr-mælum = scūr-.

scyrft *once* cutting (?) Gl. [sceorfan].

scyrt|an *tr.* shorten || *intr.* run short, fail *LN.* [scort].

~ing *f.* abridgement, epitome.

scyrte *f.* skirt, tunic Gl.

scyrtest, scyrtra, *see* scort.

scyte *m.* shooting ; stroke, blow ; missile, dart [scēotan].

~fingor, scytel- *m.* forefinger.

~heald, ~healden sloping, oblique ; steep.

~rǣs *m.* headlong rush.

---

scytel (*m.*) missile, dart, arrow [scēotan].

scytel (*m.*) dung [scēotan].

scytels, tt, scytel, tt *m.* bar, bolt [scēotan].

scyttan discharge (debt).

scytta *m.* archer.

scyttel(s) = scytels.

Scyttisc I. Irish ; Scotch. II. *n.* the Irish *or* Scotch language [Scottas].

se, *neut.* þæt, *i.* þȳ, þon that one, he — þæt wǣron Finnas they were Finns ; *rel.* who ; the.

se- = swā-.

sēada *m.* hiccup (?), heartburn (?). *Cp.* sēaþa [sēoþan].

seah *prt. of* sēon see.

seald *ptc. of* sellan.

~nes *f.* giving.

ge~nes *f.* grant (of land).

sēalas *pl. of* sealh.

sealf, ~e *f.* ointment.

~box *m.* box of ointment.

~cynn *n.* kind of ointment.

~ian salve, anoint.

~lǣcnung, ~lǣcung *f.* treatment with ointments, pharmacy.

sealh, *pl.* sēalas *m.* willow.

~beorg *m.* willow-hill.

~(h)angra *m.* willow-slope.

~.h)yrst *f.* willow-copse.

~rind *f.* willow-bark.

sealm, (p)salm, psealm *m.* psalm [*Lt.* psalmus].

~cwide *m.* psalm.

~fæt *n.* psalm-vessel (!).

~glīw, ~glīg *n.* psalmody.

~ian play on the harp.

~lēoþ *n.* psalm.

~lof *n.* psalm.

~lofian sing psalms.

~sang *m.* psalm ; psalmody ; composing psalms.

~scop *m.* psalmist.

~getæl *n.* number of psalms.

~traht *m.* commentary on psalms.

~wyrhta *m.* psalmist.

sealma = selma.

sealt I. *n.* salt. II. *aj.* salt, salted.

~ærn, ~ern *n.* salt-works.

~brōc *m.* brook running from saltworks.

~en salted.

~ere *m.* salt-worker.

fæt *n.* salt-cellar.

~hālgung *f.* benediction of salt.

~herpaþ *m.* road to salt-works.

---

sealt|hūs *n.* salt-house.

~lēaf *n.* a plant (?).

~lēag *f.* salt meadow Ct.

~mere *m.* brackish pool.

~nes *f.* saltness.

~sǣlepa *m.* saltness.

~sēaþ *m.* salt-spring.

~stān *m.* rock salt ; pillar of salt.

~strǣt *f.* road to salt-works.

~wīc *n.* place where salt is sold.

~wielle *f.* salt-spring.

~ȳþ† *f.* salt-wave.

sealt|ian, a dance [*Lt.* saltare].

~icge *f.* female dancer.

sēam *m.* seam [sīwian].

~ere *m.* tailor.

~estre *f.* sempstress, dressmaker ; tailor (man).

~sticca *m.* a weaving implement.

sēam *m.* burden, load ; furniture of a beast of burden ; bag ; supplying the lord with beasts of burden [*Lt.* sagma].

~hors *m.* pack-horse.

~pen(d)ing *m.* toll of a penny on a load (of salt).

~sadol *m.* pack-saddle.

sēamere *m.* beast of burden, mule Gl. [*lLt.* sagmarius].

sēar, ēa† dry, withered ; barren.

~ian wither ; pine away.

searo *n., g.* searwes (good or bad) device, contrivance ; skill | work of skill, machine ; armour, arms | cunning ; treachery.

~bend† *mfn.* cunning clasp.

~bunden† cunningly bound.

~cǣg† *f.* insidious key.

~cēap† *n.* curious object.

~cēne† brave.

~cræft *m.* skill ; artifice ; treachery ; plot ; machine.

~cræftig skilful ; wily.

~fāᵹ† cunningly variegated.

~gimm *m.* precious stone.

~grimm† fierce, brave.

~hæbbend(e)† *m.* warrior.

~hwīt *m.* (clear) whiteness.

~lic clever, ingenious.

~līce *av.* cunningly, ingeniously, with art.

~nett† *n.* corslet ; net of guile, snare.

~nīþ† *m., gen. pl.* treachery ; hostility ; warlike enterprise.

~pīl† *m.* pointed instrument.

~rūn† *f.* cunning mystery.

searo|sæled† cunningly bound.
~þanc *m., gen. pl.* skill; sagacity; artifice, wile.
~pancol clever, wise.
~geþræc† *n.* treasure.
~wrenc *m.* artifice, wile.
~wundor† *n.* wonderful object.
searw|ian act treacherously *or* unfairly.
~ung *f.* treachery, artifice.
sēaþ *m.* pit, cistern; pond, lake.
sēaþa *m.* heartburn (?). *Cp.* **sēada** [**sēoþan**].
sēaw, sēa *n.* juice, liquid part of anything.
gesēaw succulent.
seax *n.* knife; short sword, dagger.
~benn† *f.* wound.
Seax|e, ~an *mpl.* Saxons.
~land *n.* England.
sēc|an, oe, *prt.* **sohte** seek, try to find; try to get; try to find out, investigate, inquire; visit, go to; attack.
~nes*, oe *f.* visitation *IN.*
secg† *m.* man, warrior.
secg *m.* sedge, flag (a plant).
~ihtig sedgy.
~lēac *n.* rush garlic.
~scara, ~escere *m.* corncrake (bird).
secg† *f.* sword.
~plega† *m.* battle.
secg*, segg, seeg the sea Gl. *Cp.* **gār-secg.**
secg-rof† (?).
secg|an, *prt.* **sægde, sǣde,** *imper.* **saga** *wda.* (*wg.*) say, tell (story), recite — ~ on *a.* accuse: ~ on hine **selfne**; attribute to on ~ *wda.* accuse: **him gylt on ~**; signify, mean.
~a *m.* informant.
~et *f.* speaking, speech.
~end *m.* speaker; narrator.
gesēdan† satisfy [**sǣd**].
sedl = setl.
seding-līne = steding-.
sefa† *m.* mind, heart.
sēft *cpv. of* **sōfte.**
sēft|e, ge- not accompanied with discomfort, easy, mild, comfortable; mild, gentle (person).
~nes *f.* quiet; easy life.
segen, sæ- *f.* assertion, statement; report, story; narrative [**secgan**].

gesegen, æ *f.* conversation, statement.
gesegen *ptc of* **sēon.**
segl *nm.* sail.
~bōsm *m.* swelling out of sail, sail swelled out by the wind.
~gierd *fm.* sail-yard.
~rād† *f.* sea.
~gerǣdu *npl.* tackle.
~rōd *f.* sail-yard.
segl|an, ~ian = siglan sail.
ge~ed provided with a sail (*of* ship).
~ing *f.* sailing.
segn *mn.* sign, mark; banner [*Lt.* signum].
~berend† *m.* warrior.
~bora *m.* standard-bearer.
~cyning† *m.* king.
segn|ian, sēn- make sign of cross on, bless.
~ung *f.* blessing, consecration.
segne *f.* drag-net [*Lt.* sagena].
seht **I.** *mf.* agreement, settlement: peace, friendship. **II.** *aj.* agreed, at peace.
~an, ~ian bring to an agreement with one another; settle (dispute).
(ge)~nes *f.* reconciliation, agreement.
*sehtlian, æ, a bring to agreement *L.*; come to agreement *vL.*
sēl, oe, sēlor *av. cpv.* (*no positive*), *spl.* **~est, ~ost** well *in its various meanings, especially as regards health and liking:* **sōna him biþ ~** he will soon be better (well); **þā menn þe ic mīnes erfes soelest onn. sēl** *appears sometimes to have the meaning of a positive.*
seld† *n.* seat, throne; residence, hall.
~guma† *m.* (?).
geselda† *m.* companion, retainer.
seld|an, ~on, ~um *av., cpv.* **~(n)or,** *spl.* **~ost** seldom.
~cūþ, selcūþ unfamiliar; wonderful.
~cyme *m.* rare visit.
~hwonne, a, æ *av.* rarely.
~sīene unfamiliar, rare.
selde *once* *f.* porch Gl.
seldlic = sellic.
seldor, seldost, *see* **seldan.**
sele† *m.* hall, dwelling, house [**sæl**].
~drēam *m.* festivity.
~full *n.* festive cup.

sele|giest *m.* stranger in hall.
~rǣdend *m.* hall-ruler, house-owner.
~rest *f.* bed in hall.
~(ge)scot *n.* tabernacle, dwelling Gl.
~secg *m.* retainer.
~þegn *m.* chamberlain.
~weard *m.* hall-guardian.
gesele *m.* tabernacle Gl.
selen, y, sellen *f.* gift; grant; liberality [**sellan**].
sel(e)nes *f.* ! tradition.
geselenes *f. IN.* giving; tradition.
sēlest, *see* **sēl, sēlra.**
self, i, y, eo, ~a self; same.
~ǣta *m.* cannibal.
~ǣte *f.* a plant.
~bana, ~cwala *m.* suicide (person).
~cwalu *f.* suicide (action).
~(e)dēma *m.* independent (a kind of monk).
~dōm *m.* doing as one likes, independence.
~lice **I.** *n.* conceit, egotism. **II.** *aj.* conceited.
~līces *av.* voluntarily.
~myrþra *m.* suicide (person) Gl.
~myrþrung *f.* suicide (action).
~sceafte| not born of woman (*of* Adam).
~swēgend *m.* vowel.
~wealdlice *av.* arbitrarily.
~will *n.* one's own will.
~wille spontaneous.
~willende voluntary.
~willes *av.* voluntarily.
selfe *av.* — **swā ~** in the same way, also.
sell|an, *IW.* **y,** *prt.* **sealde** *wda.* give *in its various meanings* — **~ wiþ weorþe** sell; give up, surrender, betray — **feorh ~** die; sell [salu].
~a *m.* giver.
~end *m.* giver; betrayer.
sellic, syllic, seldlic strange, wonderful; excellent, admirable.
sellice, y *av.* wonderfully; excellently.
sēlla = sēlra.
selma, *once* **ea** *m.* couch, bed.
sēlra, sēlla, sȳlla *cpv.* (*no positive*), *spl.* **sēlest, oe, sēlost** good *in its various meanings, also as regards rank, value, prosperity, health. Cp.* **sēl.**

seltra, *vE.* **sæltna** *m.* a bird (robin ?).

selþ*, æt† *once f.* dwelling [sele].

gesēm *n.* reconciliation.

sēm|an *tr.* bring to an agreement (two persons) ; settle (dispute) ; satisfy (person *in matter of doubt*) ‖ *intr.* arbitrate [sōm].

~a *m.* arbitrator.

~end *m.* arbitrator, umpire.

semnendlīce *av.* by chance Gl.

semninga, samn-, -unga *av.* suddenly, forthwith.

semtinges = **samtinges**.

sēnian = **segnian**.

sencan *tr.* sink [sincan].

send|an send ; throw ; put ; emit (sound).

~lic to be sent.

~nes *f.* dismissal.

senep, sin-, -op *m.* mustard [*Lt.* sinapi].

~sǣd *n.* mustard-seed.

sengan *m.* singe, scorch [singan].

senoþ = **sinoþ**.

sēo *f.* pupil of eye [sēon].

sēo *fem. of* se.

sēo, *see* **sēon**.

sēo = **sīe** *sbj.*

sēon, *gen* ge- *in W., prt.* seah, *pl.* sāwon, *A.* sēgon, *ptc.* sewen, ē, *A.* segen see : geseah hine standan *or* standendne ; see fit, decree ; him wæs gesewen þæt . . it appeared to him.

sēon, (hē) sihþ*, *A.* sīþ, *prt.* sāh, *ptc.* siwen, eo, sigen 7 strain. filter ‖ *intr.* exude, flow.

sēoc ill, †wounded ; morally diseased ; sad.

~nes *f.* illness, disease.

sēod *m.* purse, pouch.

~ciest *f.* coffer Gl.

seodo = **sidu**.

seof|ian, e, y, eo† sigh ; lament.

~ung *f.* lamenting.

seofon, syfon, sibun seven.

~feald sevenfold.

~fealdlīce *av.* sevenfold.

~lēafe *f.* setfoil (a plant).

~nihte seven days old (moon).

~stierre (*n.*) the Pleiades.

~teogoþa, ~tēoþa seventeenth.

seofon-tiene seventeen.

~nihte seventeen days old (moon).

~wintre seventeen years old.

seofontig = **hund-** seventy.

seofon-wintre seven years old.

seofoþa seventh.

seoh *imper. of* **sēon**.

seoh-þe*, *A.* sehþe *interj.* behold ! [seoh, þu].

seohhe *f.* strainer [sēon].

seohtre, i *f.* drain, ditch Ct. [sēon].

sēolas *pl. of* seolh.

seolc = **seoloc**.

seolfor, i, y *n.* silver.

~fæt *n.* silver vessel.

~hammen plated with silver (horn).

~hilte, ~hilted silver-hilted (sword).

~smiþ *m.* silversmith.

~stycce *n.* piece of silver, coin.

~gewiht *n.* scale of weight by which silver is weighed.

seolfren, y, i of silver.

seolh, *pl.* sēolas *m.* seal (animal).

~bæþ† *n.* sea.

seoloc, seolc (*m.*) silk.

~en, silcen of silk.

~wyrm *m.* silkworm.

seoloþ†, eo†~siolepa bigong sea.

seomian†, e, eo† lie, lie heavy ; hang, heavy (*of* clouds) ; stand, remain.

seono, sen-, sinu, sin(e)we, *pl.* seon(o)wa, sina *f.* sinew.

~bend *mf.* bond made of sinews.

~benn† *f.* sinew-wound.

~dolg *n.* sinew-wound.

~wind, sine~ artery.

seono-wealt = **sine-**.

seonoþ, sen-, sin- *m.* synod, meeting, council [*Lt.*].

~bōc *f.* book containing decrees of synod.

~dōm *m.* decree of a synod.

~lic synodal.

~stōw *f.* place for synod, meeting-place.

~gewrit *n.* records of synod.

sēoslig *once* † afflicted [susl].

sēoþan 7 *tr.* boil ; cook ; *met.* purify ; afflict.

sēow(i)an = **sīwian**.

serede *prt. of* **sierwan**.

sescle *f.* sixth part [*Lt.* sextula].

sess (*n.*) seat, bench.

~ian† subside.

sester, seoxter *m.* jar, pitcher ; a measure (wet or dry) [*Lt.* sextarius].

set *n.* camp *gen. pl.* ; stall (for animals), fold ; sunset, place of sunset [sittan].

~gang *m.* sunset.

~hrægl *n.* cloth for covering seat.

set-þorn *m.* a tree Ct.

geset-, *pl.* ~u† *n.* seat, dwelling.

gesēt- ambush *LN.*

seten *ptc. of* **sittan**.

seten *f.* shoot, slip ; plantation.

setl, *A.* sedel, sepel *n.* sitting; residence ; siege ‖ seat, throne ; abode ; see ‖ setting (of sun, &c.) : sīgan tō ~e, gān on ~ ‖ hind quarters, podex.

~gang *m.* setting (of the sun, &c.).

~gangende setting (sun).

~hrægl *n.* covering for a seat.

~rād† *f.* setting (of the sun).

setl|an settle *tr.*

~ung *f.* sitting down, setting of the sun.

gesetla *m.* fellow-judge.

gesetnes,tt,-setednes,-seten(n)es *f.* foundation, creation ; position ; institution, arrangement; law; will, testament ; narrative ; literary composition, figure of speech ; sentence, paragraph.

sett|an put, set *in their various meanings* ; make to sit.: sette hine tō him by his side ; set down (what one is carrying) ; plant ; lay foundations of, build, found (city) ‖ set *met.* : ~ hine on borg make him security ; ~him naman ; ~ ongēan *a.* compare with ; ~ tō gafole let land ; ~ hine of his rīce depose ‖ fix (day), establish (law) ; appoint (officer) ; create ; compose (book) ‖ make a statement ‖ make, do : sīpas ~ go ‖ allay, settle (quarrel) ‖ *intr.* settle, alight *w.* on, ofer *a.* ; diminish (*of* swelling), subside (*of* flood), abate (*of* pain) ‖ æfter ~ go in pursuit. him on ~ put on (crown) ; issue (summonses) ; expel ; dismiss (from service).

~end† *m.* ordainer, appointer.

gesett|an people, garrison *w.* mid *d.* ; *and the meanings of* settan.

~endlic appointed.

sēþ|an assert, protest ; prove [sōþ].

(ge)~end *m.* asserter.

(ge)sēþung f. assertion; proof.
sepēana = swā·þēana however.
seppe = sehþe.
gesewen *ptc. of* sēon.
~lic, -sāw-, -seg- visible.
~līce av. visibly.
sex = siex.
sī is *sbj.*
sibb I. f. relationship; spiritual relationship; friendliness; peace, public security; peace of mind, happiness. II. *aj.* related, akin.
~æpeling† m. related prince.
~gebyrda† pl. relationship.
~cwide m. fair words.
~gedryht f. band of kinsmen; peaceful band.
~fæc n. degree of relationship.
~georn(n)es f. pacific disposition, friendliness; love.
~lāc n. peace-offering.
~leger n. incest.
~lic of peace.
ge~līce av. peacefully.
(ge)~ling m. kinsman.
~lufu f. friendship, love.
~gemāgas† mpl. kinsmen.
ge~nes f. relationship.
~rǣden(n) f. relationship.
~gesihþ f. vision of peace.
sibbsum, ge- peaceable, pacific; friendly.
ge~ian reconcile.
(ge)~līce av. peaceably.
(ge)~nes f. peace.
ge~ung f. peace-making.
gesibb related, akin.
sibbian reconcile.
sīc n. watercourse.
sīcan sigh; long (for) w. æfter d.
sice m. sigh.
sicerian ooze (*of* water into leaky ship) [sīc].
sicett|an, cc sigh; lament.
~ung f. sighing, sigh; lamentation.
siçol m. sickle.
sicor secure, certain of wg. [*Lt.* securus].
sīd spacious, capacious, broad (shield), long (clothes).
~e av. widely, extensively — ~ and wīde, wīde and ~ far and wide.
~fæþme†, ~fæþmed† broad-bosomed (ship).
~feaxe, ~feaxode long-haired.
~folc† n. multitude, great nation.
~land† n. spacious land.

sīd|rand† m. broad shield.
~weg† m. long way, pl. distance.
sīd|ian† once extend int/ . (?).
~ung f. augmentation, extension.
sīdan av. — wīdan and ~ far and wide.
sīd|e f. side (of body, of house, &c.); to mark direction (on the other) side; of descent (on the father's) side.
~ādl f. pleurisy.
~ece m. side-ache.
~wærc, ~wræc m. pain in the side.
sīd|e f. silk [*Lt.* seta].
~en of silk.
~wyrm m. silkworm.
sideware f. zedoary [*Lt.* zedoarium].
sīdling-weg m. oblique or side road (?) Ct.
sid|u, eo m. custom, habit; observance; good morals, chastity.
~efull chaste; decorous (dress); respectable, good.
-efullīce av. virtuously.
~efulnes f. morality, chastity.
~elic sedate, modest.
~elīce av. suitably, properly.
sīe is *sbj.*
siecl|ian sicken, be ill — wearþ or wæs ge~od was taken ill [sēoc].
sieltan salt, season [sealt].
sīeman load [sēam].
sīen f. power of seeing, sight [sēon].
gesīene visible; evident.
~lic visible.
~līce av. visibly.
sierce f., serc, syr(i)c m. shirt; tunic.
sierpan*, e have intercourse (with woman) *lN.*
sierw|an, syrewian, syrian, *prt.* ~de, sierede, syrode tr. devise; lie in wait for, plot, conspire: ~ ymb hine, ~ ymb his feorh; *ptc.* ge~ed armed [searu].
~ung f. lying in wait for, plotting, artifice.
siéx, i six.
~ecge hexagonal.
~feald sixfold.
~fēte (verse) of six feet.
~gilde requiring sixfold payment or fine.
~hynde of a class whose wergield is 600 shillings.

siéx|hyrnede six-cornered.
~nihte six days old.
~ta, *lN.* se(i)sta sixth.
~tēoþa sixteenth.
siéxtig sixty.
~ǣre sixty-oared (ship) [ār].
~feald sixty-fold.
~oþa, sixteogoþa sixtieth.
~wintre sixty years old.
siéx-tīene sixteen.
~nihte sixteen days old.
~wintre sixteen years old.
sife n. sieve.
sifeþa, sifþa, seof- *fpl., msg.* siftings, bran; tares, weeds (!).
siftan sift.
sīg = sī = sīe.
gesig n. victory *lN.*
sīgan 6 intr. fall, descend *also fig.*; move, go; of time come: Agustus (the month) sīhþ tō mannum.
sīgan 6 = sēon 6 intr. drain out, ooze; tr. strain, filter.
sige (m.) setting (of the sun) [sīgan].
sige m. victory, success.
~bēacn n. trophy; banner.
~bēag, *lN.* sigbēh m. crown.
~bēam† m. tree of victory, the cross.
~bearn† n. Christ.
~beorht triumphant.
~beorn† m. victorious warrior.
~bīeme† f. trumpet proclaiming victory.
~brōþor† m. victorious brother.
~cempa† m. victorious warrior.
~cwēn† f. victorious queen.
~dēma† m. triumphant judge, God, Christ.
~dryhten m. victorious lord, king; God.
~ēadig victorious.
sigefæst, ge- victorious, triumphant; glorious.
~an, *lN.* gesigfæstnian triumph; crown.
~nes f. triumph.
sige|gefeoht n. victory Bd.
~folc† n. victorious people.
~gealdor† n. victory-bringing charm.
~gierd f. rod that brings success.
~hrēmig triumphant.
~hrēþ† (?).
~hrēþig† triumphant.
~hwīl† f. time of victory.
~lēan† n. reward of victory, prize, palm.

sige|lēas defeated; unsuccessful (expedition); (song) telling of defeat.

~**lēoþ** *n.* song of triumph.

~**lic** victorious Gl.

~**mēce**† *m.* victorious sword.

~**rēaf** *n.* triumphal robe Gl.

~**rīce**† triumphant.

~**rōf**† triumphant, glorious.

~**sceorp**† *n.* triumphal apparel.

~**sīþ**† *m.* successful expedition.

~**spēd**† *f.* success, ability.

~**tācn** *n.* sign of victory; sign.

~**tiber**† *n.* sacrifice.

~**torht**† triumphant.

~**tūdor**† *n.* victorious progeny.

~**þēod** *f.* victorious people.

~**þrēat**† *m.* triumphant band.

~**þūf***† *n.* victory-banner.

~**wǽpen** *n.* victorious weapon.

~**wang**† *n.* plain of victory.

~**wīf**† *n.* victorious woman.

sigel†, segl, i† (*n.*) sun; *the Runic letter* s.

~**beorht**† sunny, bright as the sun.

~**hearwa**, sīl- *m.* Ethiopian.

~**hearwen** Ethiopian.

~**hweorfa** *m.*, ~**hweorfe** *f.* heliotrope (a plant).

~**torht**† radiant.

~**waru** *f.*, ~**ware** *pl.* Ethiopians.

sig(e)l (*n.*) brooch, jewel.

sīgend *m.* wave Gl.

siger|e, *pl.* **sīras** *m.* glutton Gl.

~**ian** be gluttonous Gl.

siglan sail [segl].

sig(e)le *n.* necklace.

sigle *f.* rye [*Lt.* secale].

sigor(†) *m.* triumph, victory.

~**bēacn**†*n.* sign of victory, the cross.

~**beorht**† triumphant.

~**cynn**† *n.* victorious race.

~**ēadig**† victorious.

~**fæst** victorious.

~**fæstnes** *f.* victoriousness.

~**lēan**† *n.* reward of victory, prize.

~**lic** triumphal Gl.

~**spēd**† *f.* success.

~**tācn**† *n.* convincing sign.

~**tiber**† *n.* sacrifice.

~**weorc**† *n.* victory.

~**wuldor**† *n.* glory.

sigor|ian, sig(e)rian triumph.

~**iend** *m.* victor.

sigsonte *f.* a plant.

siht|e marshy (?): on ~re mǽde Ct. [sēon 6].

---

sihtre = seohtre ditch.

gesihþ, -**siht** *f.* power of sight; act of seeing *or* looking at; what is seen; vision, apparition [sēon].

gesihþ (he) sees.

Sil = **Sigel-**.

silf = **self**.

silfren = seolfren.

silfring*, y *m.* silver coin.

sīma† *m.* bond, chain.

simbel, y, sibl — on ~ always.

~**farende** nomadic.

~**gefēra** *m.* constant companion.

simering-wyrt = sy-.

siml|e, **simble**, y *av.* continuously, always.

~**es** *av.* always.

~**ian** frequent *IN.*

~**unga**, ~**inga** *av.* always.

gesinlīce *av.* often.

sīn† *and IN.* his, its, her, their.

sin-biernende ever-burning.

sinc† *n.* treasure, anything precious, gold, jewels.

~**brytta** *m.* king *Pr.*

~**fæt** *n.* precious vessel.

~**fāg** variegated *or* adorned with gold.

~**giefa** *m.* giver of treasure, lord.

~**giefu** *f.* costly gift.

~**gimm** *m.* jewel.

~**hroden** adorned with gold.

~**māþm** *m.* treasure.

~**stān** *m.* jewel.

~**gestrēon** *n.* treasure.

~**þegu** *f.* receiving treasure.

~**gewǽge** *n.* R.

~**weorþung** *f.* costly gift, jewel.

sin-caldu = *sin-cieldo.

sincan 3 sink; be easily digestible, act as aperient (*of* food).

sin-cieldo*, -**caldu**† *f.* perpetual cold.

sind are.

sinder cinder; impurity of metal, dross.

~**ōm** *m.* rust.

sin-dolg*, syn-† *n.* great wound.

sin-drēam† *m.* everlasting joy.

sindon are.

sineht, *see* seono.

sine-wealt, sin-, seono-, sione-, -weald round, circular; spherical, globular; (building) with a dome.

~**ian** reel, totter.

~**nes** *f.* roundness.

sin-frēa† *m.* husband.

sin-fulle *f.* houseleek.

---

singal continuous, lasting; everlasting; daily.

~**e**, ~**a**, ~**es** *av.* continually, always.

~**flōwende** ever-flowing.

ge~ian continue.

~**lic** continual.

(**ge**)~**līce** *av.* continually, always.

~**nes** *f.* perseverance Gl.

~**ryne** *m.* continuous flow Gl.

sing|an 3 sing *in its various meanings*; resound; crow; recite; narrate.

~**endlic** that may be sung Gl.

gesinge *once* † *f.* wife. *Cp.* gesinhīwan.

sin-grēne I. green, uncooked (vegetables). II. *f.* houseleek.

sin-grimm† very fierce.

sin-here† *m.* great army.

sin-hīw|an, ge-, -hīgan, -hīna *npl.* (tū ~), *gpl.* -hī(g)na married pair.

~**scipe** *m.* matrimony.

sin-hweorfende*, -**hwurfende** round Gl.

sin-hwurful, -**yrfel** round.

(**ge**)**sinig** marriage *IN. Cp.* gesinhīwan.

~**an** marry *IN.*

~**scipe** *m.* marriage *IN.*

sinnan† care for, heed *wg.*

sin-niht, -**neaht**, ~**e**† *n.* eternal night — ~**es** *av.* in eternal night.

sinrǽden(n) *f.* state of marriage.

sinscip|e, ge- *m.* sexual intercourse; marriage; ge-*pl.* married people.

ge~lic conjugal.

sin-snǽd† *f.* — ~**um** *av.* in continuous (*or* huge) bites.

sin-sorg† *f.* continual sorrow.

sint are.

sin-tredende *once* round Gl.

sin-tryndel, -**trændel** round.

sin-þyrstende ever-desiring *wg.*

sin|u = seonu sinew.

~**eht** sinewy.

sin-wrǽnnes*, syn- *f.* continual lechery Gl.

sioleþ = seoloþ.

sīpian macerate *abs.*, be soaked.

sīras, *see* sigere.

sise-mūs *f.* dormouse.

sittan 5, *ptc.* seten sit, sit down, perch — on cnēowum ~ kneel; wiþ earm gesæt leant; dwell, stay; encamp; remain (in a certain

[154]

condition), be. ~ on *d.*, on ~ *wd.* afflict, attack ‖ *tr.* = gesittan occupy (bishopric).

gesittan 5 sit down; post oneself (*of general*); occupy (country); inhabit; take possession of, possess; preside over (synod); finish (term of military service); *and other meanings of* sittan.

sīþ *m.* going, movement; journey; expedition; *rarely* road, path; departure (from life), death; course of life, experience, fate, conduct; time (once, twice) — on ǣnne ~ once, all at once, fēower ~um seofon bēoþ. . .

~**bōc** *f.* itinerary.

~**boda**† *m.* guide (the pillar of cloud).

~**fæt** *mn.* journey, expedition; road, path; course (of ship); course of life, experience, conduct; period of time.

~**fram**† about to depart.

~**gēomor** sad from travelling.

~**stapel** *once f.* footstep Gl.

~**werod**† *n.* band on expedition.

sīþ = sihþ, *see* sēon see, filter.

sīþ I. *av.* late, with delay — ~ **and late** at last | afterwards. ǣr and~ always. ǣr oþþe ~, ~ oþþe ǣr ever, at any time. ne ~ ne ǣr never ‖ *cpv.* ~**or** afterwards ‖ *spl.* ~**ost.** II. *prp. wd.* — ~ þǣm aiter that, afterwards = sīþþan.

~**boren** late-born Gl.

~**dagas**† *mpl.* later times.

~**līce** *av.* lately, after a time.

gesīþ *m.* †companion, retainer, warrior; king's officer, count.

~**cund** having the rank of a gesīþ.

~**cundlic, ~līc** intimate Bd.

~**mægen**† *n.* troop of warriors.

~**mann** *m.* = gesīþ.

~**rǣden(n)** *f.* troop Gl.

~**scipe** *m.* association, companion-ship.

~**wīf, sīþ-** *n.* countess, lady of rank.

sīþian travel, depart, go.

sīþ|e, sigþe *m.* scythe.

~**berend** *m.* mower Gl.

sīþest, *see* **sīþra.**

sīþmest, *see* **sīþra.**

sīþra *aj. cpv.* (*no positive*) later, latter (time) | *spl.* sīþ(e)mest, sīþest, -ost — æt sīþ(m)estan in the end, at last.

sīþþ *f.* journey.

---

gesīþþ (*n.*) companionship, company.

siþþan, eo, siþþa I. *av.* afterwards, since; *of number* beyond that. II. *cj.* after, since [sīþ, þon = þǣm].

sīwian, sēow(i)an sew.

siwen, sēon 6.

~**īege** blear-eyed.

six = siex.

slā = slāh.

slā-wyrm *m.* blindworm.

slacian, ea *intr.* relax efforts, slacken [slæc].

slacor.

~**nes*, ea** *f.* remissness, laziness.

slæc, sleac slothful, languid; negligent; lax (conduct); gentle, stealthy (movement); easy (servitude); enervating (sleep).

~**full*, a** slothful.

~**lic** slow.

~**līce** *av.* slothfully.

~**nes** *f.* sloth; slowness (of movement, action); mental sloth; remissness (in doing duty).

slǣd *n.* valley.

slǣgen *ptc. of* slēan.

slǣhtan = slīehtan.

slǣp, ā *m.* sleep.

~**ærn, ~ern** *n.* dormitory.

~**bǣre** soporific.

~**full.**

~**fulnes** *f.* sleepiness.

~**lēas** sleepless.

~**lēast** sleeplessness.

~**nes** *f.* sleepiness.

~**wērig**† drowsy.

slǣp|an, ā ı b, *also prt.* ~**te** sleep — mid~ *wd.* lie with.

~**ere** *m.* sleeper.

slǣt = slīehþ *from* slēan.

slǣt|an set dogs on, hunt.

~**ing** *f.* hunting.

slǣw = slāw.

slǣwþ *f.* sloth [slāw].

slaga *m.* homicide [slēan].

slagen *ptc. of* slēan.

slagu (*f.*) slag, dross.

slāh, slā, *pl.* slān *f.* sloe.

~**hyll** *m.* sloe-hill.

slāhþorn *m.* blackthorn.

~**ragu** (*f.*) lichen from blackthorn.

~**rind** *f.* blackthorn-bark.

~**weg** *m.* blackthorn-road.

slāpan = slǣpan.

slāpian *impers.* be sleepy.

---

slāþol sleepy.

~**nes** *f.* sleepiness.

slāpor*, ǣ sleepy.

~**nes** *f.* sleepiness.

slarige *f.* clary (a plant).

slāw, ǣ, ēa sluggish, lazy.

~**ian** be *or* become sluggish.

~**līce** *av.* sluggishly, with delay.

slēa, ǣ, *vE.* slahǣ *f.* weaver's reed Gl. [slēan].

slēan 2 *prt.* slōg, *ptc.* slagen, æ, e strike, sting (*of* snake); play (harp); forge (metal), coin (money); drive in (stake), pitch (tent) | make by striking (fire, signal) | kill | *met.* strike (bargain); afflict (with punishment); | make move, drive — of~ *wd.* cut off (head) ‖ *intr.* strike: on īren ~ (*of* smith), tōgædre ~ collide; move: þǣr slōg micel mist came on. ~ ofdūne precipitate himself. ~ ūt on sǣ set sail; ūt ~ break out (of eruption).

geslēan 2 strike down, slaughter — wæl ~ make a slaughter; gain by fighting, conquer (country); *and the other meanings of* slēan.

sleac = slæc.

sleaht = slīeht.

slēaw = slāw.

sleccan, *prt.* **sleahte** weaken [slæc].

slecg (*f.*) sledge-hammer [slēan].

~**ettan** palpitate.

sleg-, *see* **slege.**

~**nēat** *n.* beast to be killed.

slege *m.* stroke, blow, beating; stinging (*of* snake); collision; clap (of thunder); killing, slaughter, murder [slēan].

~**bīetel** *m.* mallet.

~**fǣge**† doomed to slaughter.

slegel (*m.*) plectrum.

slegen *ptc. of* slēan.

slēow = slīw.

slic [ī?] smoother, sleek-stone.

slīc *once* cunning.

slicc *once* hammer *lK* Gl. = slecg (?).

slīd|an 6 glide, slide; *met.* make false step, err; *in prs. ptc.* be transitory.

slide *m.* slip; fall (into misfortune *or* error) [slīdan].

slidor, dd I. slippery. II. *n.* slippery place.

~**nes** *f.* slipperiness; slippery place (!).

slidrian, -der- slip.
slief|an slip *or* put dress (on a person).
~escōh *m.* slipper.
slief|e, slief *f.* sleeve.
ge~ed sleeved.
~lēas sleeveless.
slieht, i, ea *m.* killing, slaughter, mortality (from pestilence) ; *coll.* animals to be killed for food [slēan].
~swīn *n.* pig to be killed.
geslieht† *n.* conflict.
sliehtan*, æ kill *LN.*
sliep|an slip *or* put off *or* on (*of* yoke, ring) [slūpan].
~escōh *m.* slipper.
sliepa, y, i *m.* paste. *Cp.* slyppe.
slīm (*n.*) slime.
slinc|an 3 creep.
~end *m.* reptile.
slingan *once* creep *for* slincan (?).
slipig slimy.
slipor slippery ; unstable (in character) ; ! morally impure, foul Gl.
~nes *f.* (!) moral impurity Gl.
geslit *n.* rending ; biting, bite ; calumny.
~glīw *n.* scoffing Gl.
slīt|an 6 tear, rend, *also met.* (*esp. of* hunger) ; irritate (wound) ; destroy *met.* ; slander ‖ *intr.* tear.
~endlic consuming.
~ere *m.* destroyer ; glutton.
~ung *f.* biting.
slit|e *m.* tear, rent (in cloth), bite.
~cwealm *m.* death from being bitten.
slite [ī?] *f.* cyclamen (a plant).
sliten- *once* heretic *LN.*
slitennes*, slitnes *f.* laceration ; destroying, waste [slītan].
slitol pungent.
slīpan injure.
slip|e† I. severe, dangerous, painful, cruel (*of* things). II. *av.* cruelly (slain).
~heard fierce ; cruel (bonds).
slīpen† severe, evil, cruel (*of* things).
slīw, ēo, slī (*m.*) tench (a fish).
slōg, slōh *prt. of* slēan.
slōh, *d.* slō *nm.* slough, mire.
slota *once m.* morsel Gl.
sluma *m.* slumber.
slūpan 7 glide, move smoothly.
slyppe *f.* paste, slime. *Cp.* *sliepa.

smacian pat.
smæcc *m.* taste, savour.
~an *tr.* taste.
smæl narrow, slender ; small ; fine (powder).
~e *av.* = smale.
~pearmas *mpl.* intestines.
~pearme *n.* lower abdomen.
smǣte refined *or* pure (gold).
~gylden of pure gold.
smale, æ *av.* finely (ground) ; not loudly, softly [smæl].
smal|ian become slender.
-ung *f.* making slender, reducing (flesh).
smēa|gelegen *f.* syllogism Gl.
~lic searching (inquiry), profound (reasoning) ; exquisite Gl. [smūgan].
~līce *av.* searchingly, (reasoning) profoundly ; (see) clearly.
~mettas *mpl.* delicacies.
~panclīce *av.* in detail.
smēapancol, ~lic subtle.
~līce *av.* thoroughly, sagaciously.
~nes *f.* exactness.
smēa|wrenc, smēh- *m.* artifice, crafty device.
~wyrhta *m.* artisan.
~wyrm, smēga- *m.* penetrating worm.
smēan = smēagan.
gesmēag *n.* intrigue *vL.*
smēag sagacious ; ēo penetrating (worm) [smūgan].
smēag|an, smēan (penetrate) ; scrutinize, investigate ; meditate, reflect *w.* ymb ; seek (opportunity) ; suppose, assume.
~endlic meditative Gl.
~ung, smēawung, smēa(u)ng *f.* search ; investigation, meditation ; intention, intrigue.
smearcian, e smile.
smeart causing pain [smeortan].
smēap (*f.*) *once* meditation.
smed(e)m|a, smeo-, i *m.* fine flour.
~en of fine flour.
smelt, y *m.* smelt (a fish).
smēocan 7 *intr.* smoke ‖ *tr.* fumigate.
smēog = *smēag penetrating.
smeolt = smolt.
smeortan* smart. *Cp.* fȳr-smeortende.
smeoro, *g.* sme(o)r(u)wes, *n.* fat, grease, suet, tallow.

smeoro|mangestre, smere- *f.* butter-woman, dealer in butter and cheese.
~sealf *f.* unguent.
~wig*, smearuwig fatty.
~pearm *m.* entrail.
~wyrt *f.* a plant.
smer- = smier-.
smercian = smearcian.
smēp|e, oe smooth, polished ; not irritating (food, medicine) ; soothing, flattering, suave (manners) ; harmonious (sound) ; without discomfort, pleasant [smōp].
~an smooth, polish ; alleviate.
~ian become smooth ; make smooth.
~nes *f.* smoothness ; level surface Gl.
smicer elegant, beautiful.
~e *av.* elegantly, beautifully ; delicately.
~nes *f.* elegance.
ge~od elegantly wrought Gl.
smidema = smedema.
smiec*, ī *m.* smoke [smēocan].
~an *intr.* smoke ; *tr.* fumigate.
smiell*, æ *m.* slap *LN.*
smiellan *intr.* crack (*of* whip).
smielting *f.* amber.
smier|wan, ~an, ~ian, smer(u) w(i)an anoint [smeoru].
~els *m.*, ~enes *f.* ointment.
smiering, e *f.* anointing ; ointment.
~ele *m.* oil for anointing.
smītan 6 daub, smear ; pollute.
smite *once m.* pollution (?) Gl.
smitt|a *m.* smear, spot [smītan].
~ian smear ; pollute.
smip *m.* smith, carpenter.
~cræft *m.* smith's or carpenter's art.
~cræftiga *m.* smith, carpenter.
~ian forge, fashion (out of metal or wood).
~līce *av.* like a smith, skilfully Gl.
smippe *f.* smithy.
smoc|a *m.* smoke [smēocan].
~ian *intr.* smoke ; *tr.* fumigate.
smocc *m.* smock-frock, shift.
smolt, eo serene, peaceful, gentle (rain).
~e *av.* gently (blowing wind).
~līce *av.* gently (flowing).
smolt *once no.* fat.
smorian *tr.* choke, suffocate.

smōþ *once* serene (countenance) [smēþe].
smūg|an 7 creep *or* penetrate gradually.
~endlic creeping.
smygel, -els *m.* burrow [smūgan].
smylt|e I. serene, calm, mild, gentle (rain, wind); placid, cheerful; prosperous. II. *av.* gently (blowing wind) [smolt].
ge~an appease.
~lic serene, mild (weather).
~nes *f.* calm, quiet (*of* sea, weather); peace, tranquillity; placidity, composure; gentleness (in action).
snaca *m.* snake.
snacc (*m.*) war-ship.
snādas, *see* snǣd.
snǣd *m.* handle (of scythe).
snǣd [ē?], *pl.* snādas *m.* piece of land (?) Ct. [snīþan?].
~feld*, snæþ- *m.* enclosed field (?).
snǣd *f.* morsel *or* slice of food [snīþan].
~mǣlum *av.* (eat) bit by bit.
snǣdan cut into slices; hew, trim (stone); prune ‖ lunch.
snǣding *f.* lunch.
~hūs *n.* eating-house.
~scēap *n.* sheep to be killed.
snǣdel, ~þearm *m.* the great gut.
snǣgl = snegl.
snǣs = snās.
snǣsan run through (with spear), spit.
snǣþ-feld = snǣd-.
snās, ǣ (*f.*) spit, skewer.
snāþ (*n.*) killing [snīþan].
snāw, snā *m.* snow.
~gebland *n.* snowstorm.
~ceald cold as snow.
~hwīt white as snow.
~ig, ~lic snowy.
sneare *f.* noose, snare.
snegl, ǣ, snǣl *m.* snail.
snel|l quick, swift; active, strong; bold, brave.
~lic swift, bold.
~lice *av.* rapidly.
~nes *f.* quickness, activity.
~scipe *m.* boldness.
snēome† *av.* quickly; immediately.
gesneorcan 3 shrivel *intr.*
snēowan†,ēo†*intr.*hasten,proceed.
snēr [ē = ǣ] *f.* string (of harp).
snīcan (6) creep, crawl; ! spread imperceptibly (*of* wounds).

snid, ~e saw [snīþan].
snid *n.* slice, cut.
snid-īsen [*or* ī?] *n.* lancet.
gesnid *n.* slaughter.
snide (*m.*) incision; killing.
snierian†, snyrgan *intr.* hasten.
snīte *f.* snipe.
snīþ-strēo carline thistle (?).
snīþ|an, *ptc.* sniden 6 cut into, lance (boil, &c.), hew (stone); cut off, amputate; cut (hair, corn); cut into pieces; slaughter (animal).
~ung *f.* incision; wound; slaughtering.
snīwan snow.
snōd *f.* fillet, head-dress.
snoffa *once m.* nausea.
snofl mucus of the nose.
~ig full of mucus; having a cold in the head.
snoru *f.* daughter-in-law.
gesnot *n.* mucus of the nose.
snotor, tt prudent, wise.
~lic wise, philosophical Gl.
~lice *av.* prudently, wisely; philosophically Gl.
~nes *f.* wisdom.
~wyrde plausible.
snūd I. coming quick, sudden. II. *n.* speed.
~e *av.* quickly; at once.
snyring [y = ȳ, īe?] *once* sharp rock Gl.
snȳt|an* clear the nose.
~ing *f.* sneezing Gl.
snytrian, tt be wise; be a philosopher.
snytre† *once* wise [snotor].
snytro, tt, ge-*f.* prudence, sagacity, wisdom.
snyþian† *once* go with nose to the ground (*of* plough).
soc, ge- *n.* sucking [sūcan].
socian soak *tr.*, *intr.* [sūcan].
socc *m.* sock [*Lt.* soccus].
sōcn *f.* (seeking); investigation; asking; frequenting, going (to church); asylum, refuge; †persecution, attack; exercise of judicial power, jurisdiction [sēcan].
gesod *n.* boiling, liquefaction [sēoþan].
soden *ptc.* of sēoþan.
sōft|e I. quiet (sleep); luxurious, comfortable (bed); not stern, gentle *vL.* II. *av.* gently; peaceably, without discord; easily; at

ease, comfortably; not harshly, kindly [sēfte].
sōftnes *f.* ease, comfort; luxury, effeminacy.
sogoþa *m.* hiccup; eructation [sūgan].
sohte, *prt.* of sēcan.
sol *n.* mud, wet sand; wallowing-place.
sōl† sun Ps. [*Lt.*].
Sol-mōnaþ *m.* February.
sōlāte *f.* heliotrope. *Cp.* solsece.
sole *once f.* shoe, sandal [*Lt.* solea].
solor (*m.*) upper room [*Lt.* solarium].
solsece *f.* heliotrope [*Lt.* solsequia].
sōm *f.* concord, reconciliation, agreement.
~rǣden(n) *f.* wedlock.
gesōm unanimous, reconciled, friendly.
sōn *m.* musical sound, music [*Lt.* sonus].
~cræft *m.* music.
sōna *av.* immediately — ~ swā as soon as.
song [o = a *or* ō?] bed *lN.*
sopa *m.* draught, sup [sūpan].
sopp|e *f.* sop.
~cuppe *f.* sop-cup.
~ian sop.
sore mote (in eye) *lN.*
sorg *f. wg.* grief; anxiety; affliction.
~byrþen(n) *f.* grievous sorrow.
~cearig† anxious, sad.
~cearu† *f.* anxiety, sadness.
~full anxious, sad; causing anxiety *or* sadness.
~lēas free from anxiety *or* sorrow.
~lēast *f.* security.
~lēoþ *n.* dirge.
~lic grievous.
~lice *av.* grievously.
~lufu† *f.* sad love.
~stafas† *mpl.* sorrow, affliction.
~wielm† *m.* sorrow.
~wite *n.* torment.
~word† *n.* word of sorrow.
sorg|ian, *vE. prs. ptc.* soergendi, grieve; be anxious, solicitous *w.* ymb.
~ung *f.* sorrowing, grief.
sorig *once* sorry.
sōt, oo (*n.*) soot.
ge~ig grimy, dirty Gl.
sotel = setl.

sot|t I. stupid, foolish. II. *m.* fool [*Fr.*].

~scipe *m.* stupidity, folly.

sōþ I. true, real; righteous Ps. II. *n.* truth, reality, certainty; asseveration; justice, righteousness. **for ~,** tō ~ə with certainty, truly; as a fact, really. **tō ~um þingum witan, for ~ witan** know for a certainty.

~cwed, ~cweden veracious *LN.*

~cwide *m.* true saying, righteous saying; proverb, parable.

~cyning† *m.* king of justice, God.

~e *av.* truly, really; faithfully.

~es *av.* truly; verily.

~fæder† *m.* father of justice, God.

sōþfæst truthful; just, righteous.

~ian justify.

~lic true; sincere.

~līce *av.* truly; faithfully.

~nes *f.* truth; good faith, justice.

sōþ|giedd† *n.* true tale.

~hwæþre (!) *av.* however *LN.*

~lic true.

~līce *av., cj.* truly; verily, indeed; for.

~sagol veracious.

~sagu *f.* truth; history.

~secgan tell truth, declare *LN.*

~segen *f.* statement of the truth.

~spell *n.* history.

~spræc *f.* true saying *LN.*

~tācn *n.* prodigy *LN.*

~word† *n.* true word.

sōþ- = *Lt.* pro- (!) *LN.*

sōþian prove.

spāca *m.* spoke of wheel.

spad|e, ~u *wk. f.* spade [*Lt.* spatha].

spǣc, spǣc = spr-.

spær, ~lic sparing, frugal.

~hende, ~hynde frugal.

~līce *av.* frugally; (speak) briefly.

~nes *f.* parsimony, frugality.

spær-lir|a, speoru- *m.* calf of leg.

~ede having large calves.

spær* plaster, mortar.

~en of plaster, mortar.

~stān *m.* gypsum, chalk.

spǣt|an spit; syringe (wound).

~ung *f.* expectoration.

spǣtl = spātl.

spǣtlan, -ian spit foam.

spala = gespelia substitute.

spāld = spātl.

spaldor, *L.* **spelter** asphalt [*Lt.* asphaltum].

gespan *n.* persuasion, allurement.

span|an 2, *prt.* spōn, spēon instigate, persuade, allure.

~ere *m.* enticer.

span|e, ~u, *pl.* **~an, ~a** *f.* teat.

spang *f.* clasp, buckle.

gespang *n.* fastening, clasp.

spann *f.* span (measure).

gespann *n.* fastening, bond, web *met.*

spann|an 1 *prt.* spēon, spēnn clasp, fasten, attach.

~ing *f.* span (measure).

sparian *wa., also wd.* spare, show mercy to; *wa.* not use, abstain from, preserve.

spātl, ǣ, *A.* **spāpl, spādl, spåld** *n.* saliva.

~ian spit out, expectorate.

~ung *f.* saliva, what is expectorated.

spear-hafoc *m.* sparrow-hawk [spearwa].

spearc|a, ǣ *m.* spark; small portion, (not a) trace.

~ian emit sparks, scintillate.

spearnlian *intr.* kick, sprawl [spornan].

gespearrian shut, bar.

spearwa *m.* sparrow.

spearwa *m.* calf of leg Gl.

specan = sprecan.

spēd, œ *f.* success — **on ~** successfully, with good results; prosperity; wealth, plenty; progeny *once* Ps.; power, faculty; opportunity, means; speed *in av.* **~um** quickly [spōwan].

~līce *av.* effectually.

~sumian prosper.

spēdan, ge- succeed, *w.* tō in; make to succeed Gl.

sped phlegm, gum (in eye) Gl.

~iende? Gl.

sped-dropa [e *or* ē?] *once* †drop (of ink).

spēdig prosperous; wealthy, powerful, abounding in.

ge-līce *av.* prosperously.

~nes *f.* opulence.

spel|ian act as representative of, stand for.

~igend *m* representative.

~ing *f.* deputyship.

spelc, i [*infl. of* spilcan] (*m.*) splint (for broken limb).

spelcan = spilcan.

speld *n., pl.* **~ru, ~** splinter, piece of wood, torch.

gespelia, *L.* **spala** *m.* representative, deputy [spelian].

spell *n.* narrative, history; (idle) tale; prose; discourse, homily; philosophical argument; saying; message.

~bōc *f.* homily-book.

~boda *m.* messenger, angel, ambassador, prophet; public speaker Gl.

~cwide *m.* historical narrative.

spell|ian *intr.* discourse; *tr.* announce, tell.

~ung *f.* conversation; narrative, tale; discourse, homily.

spelt (*m.*) spelt, corn [*Lt.* spelta].

spelter = spaldor asphalt.

spend|an spend [*Lt.* expendere].

~ung *f.* spending.

spennels *once* (*m.*) clasp Gl. [spannan].

speoftian, -an spit, spit on *LN.*

spēon *prt. of* spanan, spannan.

spēow- = spīw-.

spere *n.* spear.

~brōga† *m.* spear-terror.

~healf *f.* (inheritance on) the male side.

~lēas (shaft) without a spear-head.

~nīþ† *m.* battle.

~wyrt *f.* a plant.

gesperod armed with spear Gl.

spic, e *n.* bacon, lard.

~hūs *n.* larder.

spic-māse *f.* titmouse (bird).

spice, spīca *f.* (?) aromatic herb, spikenard (?) [*Lt.* spica].

spicing *m.* spike, nail.

spierc|an *intr.* sparkle; sputter [spearca].

~ing *f.* sprinkling.

spierr|an strike.

~ing *f.* striking.

spigettan = spīwettan.

spilian play.

spilæg (*m.*) kind of snake *LN.* [*Lt.* spilagius].

spilc = spelc.

spilcan, e [*infl. of* spelc] bind with splints.

spild, *vE.* **spilþ** *m.* destruction, ruin.

~sīþ† *m.* destructive expedition.

spildan = spillan destroy.

spill|an, spildan destroy.
~ing *f.* waste (of money).
spind fat.
spinel, -nl *f.* spindle.
~healf *f.* (inheritance on) the female side.
spinnan 3 spin; *intr.* kick, struggle.
spir tapering shoot (of reed).
spitel *m.* spud, spade.
spittan dig.
gespittan spit, spit upon *lN.*
spittian spit *lA.*
spitu *f.* spit.
spiunge = sponge sponge.
spiw|an 6, **~ian** vomit *abs., wa, wi.*; spit.
~ettan*, spīgettan spit.
~ere *m.* vomiter.
~ing *f.* vomiting.
spīw|e (*m.*) vomiting.
~(e)drenc, -inc *m.* emetic.
spīweþa, spīwþa, spīwda, spēow- *m.* vomiting; what is vomited.
spiwol emetic.
splott *m.* spot; plot of land.
ge~od spotted.
spōn *mf.* shaving, chip.
sponge, spiunge *f.* sponge; spongy excrescence. *Cp.* **spynge** [*Lt.* spongia].
spor *n.* track, footprint; tracking; trace, vestige.
~wrecel *m.*? Ct.
spor|a, u *m.* spur.
~leþer *n.* spur-strap.
sporett|an *once* kick.
~ung, *sporteng *f.* kicking (?).
sporn|an, spu- 3 strike foot against; reject, contemn.
~ere *m.* fuller.
~ing *f.* stumbling, stumbling-block.
spornettan kick.
spōw|an 1 succeed; *impers. wd.* fare, succeed.
~endlīce *av.* prosperously.
spracen *n.* alder.
spræc (*n.*) shoot, twig.
spræc, spæc *f.* talking, conversation, conference; power of speech, eloquence; what is said, statement, report; language; subject of discussion, (difficult) question; suit, claim; decision; place of public speaking *lN.* [sprecan].
~cynn *n.* mode of speaking Bd.
~ern *n.* court-house *lN.*

spræc full loquacious.
~hūs *n.* auditory, parliament-house Gl.
~lēas speechless.
gespræc *n., not W.* [*miswriting of* gesprec, *taken for A.* *gesprēc?] speaking, way of speaking; what is said.
gespræce eloquent; affable.
~līc 'loquelar' (in grammar).
spræd|an spread.
~ung *f.* propagation *lN.*
spranca *m.* shoot, twig.
sprangettan palpitate.
sprēawlian *intr.* move convulsively.
gesprec *n.* speaking; power of speech.
sprec|an, specan 5 speak. ~ on *a.*, on ~ *wd.* make a claim against, sue, *so also w.* æfter, ymb.
~a† *m.* councillor.
~ol talkative.
~olnes *f.* loquacity.
gesprec|an 5 speak — him betwēonum gespræcon agreed; speak to, converse with *wa.*
~a *m.* interlocutor, one who consults with another.
~endlic to be spoken.
sprengan *tr.* scatter; sprinkle. apply clyster || *intr.* burst, crack [springan].
sprēot *m.* pole.
sprincel (*m.*) wicker basket.
sprind, spryngd active, vigorous.
~līce, sprinlīce *av.* actively, vigorously.
sprindel tenter-hook.
spring = spryng.
springan 3 leap; spring back (through elasticity); burst forth, fly, spirt; rise — ūp ~ rise (*of* sun); grow; . be diffused (*of* report, fame).
sprot *n.* shoot, twig [sprūtan].
sprota *m.* sprout, shoot; peg.
sprott *n.* sprat (a fish).
spryng *m.* source of water, spring; flux; sprinkling; ulcer [springan].
~wyrt*, spring- *f.* wild caper.
sprytle [y = īe?] *f.* twig.
sprytt|an *intr.* sprout, germinate || *tr.* put forth (shoot), bear (fruit); incite: ~ hine tō þǣm [sprūtan].
~ing *f., once* m. shoot, plant.

spurul given to kicking *or* trampling (?) Gl.
spynge *f.* sponge [*Lt.* spongia].
spyr|ian *w.* æfter follow track; go; investigate, inquire into [spor].
~emann, spe- *m.* tracker.
~igend *m.* investigator.
~igung *f.* investigation.
spyrd *m.* stadium, (foot) racecourse; furlong *lN.*
spyrte *f.* basket [*Lt.* sporta].
stac|a *m.* stake. drīfan ~an on mann a kind of witchcraft, injuring a person by piercing an effigy of him.
~ung *f.* a kind of witchcraft, *see* staca.
stæf *m.* staff, stick; letter (of alphabet) — *pl.* stafas piece of writing, literature.
~cræft *m.* grammar; learning, literature.
~cræftig versed in grammar *or* literature.
~cyst *f.* literature, learning — ~e leornian learn to read.
~gefēg *n.* combination of letters, syllable.
~leornere *m.* student.
~līc literal (meaning); literary.
~lipere *f.* catapult.
~plega *m.* literary game Gl.
~rǣw *f.* line (of writing); alphabet.
~sweord *n.* sword-cane Gl.
~wīs versed in literature.
~writere *m.* grammarian.
stæg *once* (*n.*) pool, pond Gl. [*Lt.* stagnum].
stæg (*n.*) stay, mast-rope Gl.
stǣgel steep [stīgan].
stǣger *f.* stairs [stīgan].
stǣl, ǣt† *n.* place; stead, relation — on fæder ~e in the position of a father; assistance; condition, state.
stæl- [stelan].
~giest† *m.* thievish stranger.
~here *m.* predatory army.
~hran *m.* decoy reindeer.
~tihtle *f.* charge of theft.
stæl-wierþe serviceable.
stæl-wyrt *f.* water starwort (a plant).
stǣlan institute. do, inflict: †fǣhþe on weras ~; impute (crime) to *w.* on *of pers*, *wda.*

gestællan *once* stall, stable.

gestæn = *gesten.

stǣn|an throw stones at, stone (to death) ; adorn with gems *or* mosaic [stān].

~ing *f.* stoning (to death).

stǣna *m.* earthenware jug [stān].

stǣnen of stone.

stǣner stony ground *IN.*

stǣnig, ~lic stony.

stǣniht = stāniht.

stæp|e, ę *m., pl.* ~as, stapas, stepping, step ; pace (measure) ; going | step (of stairs, ladder) ; pedestal, step (of mast) ; degree || in ~ instantly.

~egang* stę-† R.

~mǣlum *av.* step by step, by steps ; gradually.

stæpp|an, stę- 2, *prt.* stōp, step, go, proceed.

~escōh *m.* slipper.

stær *m.* starling.

stǣr, ē, eo [= oe ?] *n.* history [*Lt.* historia].

~leornere (?) *m.* student of history.

~trahtere *m.* historian.

~writere *m.* historian.

stær-blind, stære-, sta- quite blind.

stærced- = stęrced-.

stærling *m.* starling [stær].

stæþ *nm.* bank, shore.

~fæst† firm on the shore.

~hliepe steep.

~hlieplice *av.* precipitously.

~swealwe *f.* sand-martin.

~weall† *m.* barrier of the shore.

~wyrt *f.* a plant.

stæþþan† *once* stay, support.

stæþþig, ge- sedate, serious.

~nes *f.* sedateness, seriousness.

stafian dictate (oath) [stæf].

stagan impale, fix (on spit).

stagga *m.* stag *L.*

-stāl place [stapol].

~ern *n.* court of justice Gl.

~ian strengthen (supports).

gestāl *n.* impeachment, accusation.

stal|ian steal ; go stealthily, steal [stalu].

~ung *f.* robbery.

gestala *m.* accomplice in theft [stelan].

stalaþ (*m.*) stability Gl.

stal|u *f.* stealing, theft [stelan].

~gang† *m.* stealthy step.

gestalu *f.* theft.

stal|u *f.* — hearpan ~a pieces of wood into which the harp-strings are fixed (?).

stam-, *see* stamm.

~wlisp, scom- stammering.   *Or two words* (?).

stamm, scomm stammering.

~ettan stammer.

stamor stammer.

~ian, stam(e)rian stammer.

stān *m.* stone, rock.

~æx *f.* stoneworker's axe (?) Gl.

~bæþ *n.* vapour bath.

~beorg *m.* rocky hill.

~berende stony Gl.

~bill *n.* stone-working implement Gl.

~boga† *m.* natural stone arch.

~brycg *f.* stone bridge.

~bucca *m.* mountain goat.

~burg† *f.* stone-built town.

~carr (*n.*) *IN.* rock.

~ceastel, i *m.* chestnut (?) Ct.

~ceosol *m.* gravel.

~ciėst*, y *m.* chestnut (?) lCt.

~clif† *n.* cliff ; crag, rock.

~clūd *m.* rock.

~cræftiga *m.* stonemason.

~cropp *m.* stonecrop (a plant).

~crundel *m.* stone-hollow (?) Ct.

~gedelf *n.* stone-quarry.

~fæt *n.* stone vessel.

~fāg† paved (road).

~gefeall *n.* heap of stones.

~gefōg *n.* masonry.

~gaderung *f.* masonry.

~geat *n.* opening between rocks.

~giėlla *m.* pelican.

~gripe† *m.* stones seized.

~hęge *m.* wall.

~hiepe *f.* stone-heap.

~hiewet(t), ~hīfet *n.* quarry.

~hliþ† *n.* rocky slope.

~hof *n.* stone house.

~hol *n.* cave.

~hrycg *m.* ridge *or* reef of rocks Gl.

~ig, ǣ stony, rocky.

~iht, ǣ I. stony, rocky. II. *n.* stony ground.

~incel *n.* little stone.

~lesung *f.* masonry (without mortar) Gl.

~līm *m.* mortar.

~merce *f.* parsley.

~rocc (*m.*) Gl. high rock, obelisk.

~scalu *f.* shale, shaly ground (?) Ct.

~sciėlig*, y stony (ground).

stān|scræf *n.* cave.

~scylf *m.* peak, rock Gl.

~strǣt *f.* paved road.

~stycce *n.* piece of stone.

~getimbre *n.* masonry.

~torr *m.* stone tower ; high rock, crag.

~wang *m.* stony plain.

~weall *m.* stone wall.

~weg *m.* paved road.

~weorc *n.* masonry.

~geweorc *n.* art of building ; masonry.

~weorþung *f.* worship of stones.

~wurma *m.* colour got from a stone *or* mineral Gl.

~wyrht (*f.*) stone building (?) Gl.

~wyrhta *m.* mason.

stand *m. IN.* delay.

standan 2 *prt.* stōd stand ; stand still, stop, stay, remain (undisturbed), last | be valid, in force (of laws) ; *w.* on *d.* consist of ; be : gif nīed on handa stande in case of necessity, sē sceatt þe on þām lande stent the sum with which the land is charged | start from (of direction), *also fig.* : him stōd stincende stēam of þām mūþe, micel ege stōd deōflum fram ēow.

gestandan 2 stand up (as opposed to sitting), keep one's feet ; oppose (attacker) ; attack, assail, *also met.* (of illness) ; perform ; *and the other meanings of* standan.

stapol *m.* pillar, prop, *met.* foundation ; flight of steps.

~weg *m.* ? Ct.

starian gaze.

stare-blind = stær-.

stapol *m.* foundation, base (of pillar), *also met.* ; stability, *met.* security ; firmament, sky ; position, place ; state (of things).

~ǣht† *f.* estate (?) R.

stapolfæst firm, stationary ; firm (in mind).

~lic stable.

~līce *av.* firmly ; with firm mind.

~nes *f.* firmness, stability.

ge~nian, -fæstian establish.

~nung *f.* Gl. foundation.

stapol|ian fix, establish ; make steadfast (in mind).

(ge)~iend *m.* founder.

(ge)staþolung *f.* founding, foundation, settling.

staþol-wang† *m.* plain to dwell in.

stealc steep.

stealc|ian.

~ung *f.* walking cautiously.

steald *ptc. of* stellan.

gesteald† *n.* dwelling, abode.

stealdan† I possess *wi.*

steall *m.* act of standing; place; stead — on his ~; stall (for cattle), stable; fishing-ground; state (of affairs).

gesteall† *n.* structure, frame (of the earth).

steallere, a *m.* marshal *L.*

stēam *m.* exhalation, hot vapour, steam; †moisture (blood).

stēap *m.* drinking-vessel, flagon.

stēap lofty, tall, mounting high (*of* fire); prominent (gem, eyes).

stēapol (*m.*) tumulus (of stones) (?) Ct.

stearc rigid; rough (wind, weather); attended with hardship; obstinate; stern, severe; violent, strong.

~ferhþ† stern, fierce.

~heard violent (weeping).

~heort† stout-hearted.

~ian stiffen *intr.*

~līce *av.* vigorously.

stearn *m.* a sea-bird, tern (?).

steartlian stumble.

gestēd.

~hors *n.* stallion.

stēda *m.* stallion; entire camel [stōd].

stede, styde *m.* act of standing; standing still; place, *also met.*; stability; fixity (of condition); strangury; condition Gl. | of ~ immediately.

~fæst steadfast; firm (mind).

~fæstnes *f.* constancy.

~heard† firm.

~lēas having nothing to stand on, unstable.

~wang† *m.* plain.

~wist *f.* constancy.

stedig sterile, barren.

~nes *f.* sterility.

steding.

~līne *f.* stay, mast-rope Gl.

stefn-, *see* stemn-, stemn-.

stefnian *L.* summon *w. d. and* tō [? *Scand.* stefna].

stelan 4 steal.

stel|a, æ *m.* stalk; support.

~mēle *m.* vessel with handle.

~scofl *f.* shovel with (long) handle (?) Gl.

stellan, *prt.* stealde, place, set [steall].

stemn ¹, stefn *f.* voice — mid miclum ~um *of a single voice.*

stemn ², stefn *m.* period, time — ymb ~ by turns; nīwan stefne a second time, afresh; turn of military service.

~mǣlum*, stemmǣlum *av.* alternately.

stemn ³, stefn *m.* stem (of tree); foundation; (race, family); prow or stern of ship [stæf].

stemna*, stefna† *m.* prow of ship.

stemn|an, stefnan institute, regulate ‖ alternate Gl.

~byrd*, stefn- *f.* regulation.

~ing *f.* turn of military service.

stemn|an, stefnan provide with fringe.

~ing *f.* fringe, border.

stemnettan stand firm.

stemp|an pound (in mortar) [-stampe].

~ing-īsern *n.* stamping-iron.

gesten*, æ *n.* groaning.

stenan (5) groan.

stenc *m.* sense of smell; odour (good or bad) [stincan].

~bǣre stinking.

~brengende (!) odoriferous *LN.*

stenc|an scatter [stincan].

(ge)~nes *f.* odour *LN.*

gestenc fragrant.

stenecian pant [stenan].

steng *m.* pole, stake, bar, cudgel [stingan].

stēop- step-.

~bearn *n.* orphan.

~cild *n.* orphan; unprotected one.

~dohtor *f.* step-daughter.

~fæder *m.* step-father.

~mōdor *f.* step-mother.

~sunu *m.* step-son.

stēor *m.* steer, young bull; young cow.

~oxa *m.* steer.

stēor- *occ.* = stīer-.

stēor, ȳ [*infl. of* stīeran] *f.* (steering; rudder); guidance; regulation, rule; restraint; discipline; reproof; punishment; fine.

~bord *n.* starboard, right side of ship.

stēor|es-mann *L. m.* steersman, captain [*Scand.*].

~lēas not under control, ungovernable; profligate; uninstructed, foolish.

~mann *m.* steersman, captain.

~nægl *m.* handle of a helm.

~rēþra *m.* steersman, captain.

~rōþor *n.* rudder.

~scofl *f.* rudder.

~setl *n.* stern.

~stefn *m.* stern.

~wierþe, -weorþ deserving reprobation.

stēoran = stīeran.

stēora, īe *m.* steersman.

steorf|an 3 die.

~a *m.* pestilence.

steorn.

~ede having a forehead Gl.

steor|ra *m.* star.

~glēaw skilled in astronomy.

~scēawere *m.* astronomer, astrologer.

~wigl, ~wiglung *f.* astrology.

steort *m.* tail; tongue of land.

stēpan, oe initiate, consecrate Gl.

ster|an, ȳ burn incense; fumigate [stōr].

~ing *f.* incense.

sterced-ferhþ†, stæ-[= ie] brave, resolute.

sti- = stig-.

stic-, *see* stycce.

stic-fōdder *n.* ? case for spoons [sticca].

stic-tǣnel basket Gl.

stic|ian *tr.* prick, goad (ox), stab, gouge out (eyes); kill ‖ *intr.* remain fixed, stick; be inside; lie (*of* direction, boundary).

~ung *f.* piercing; killing (pigs).

sticc- *once* viscous (?).

sticca *m.* stick, peg; pointer (of dial); spoon.

stic|e *m.* stab, puncture; pricking sensation, stitch.

~ādl *f.*, ~wærc *m.* stitch (in side).

~wyrt *f.* agrimony.

sticel *m.* goad.

sticels *m.* goad; instigation.

sticol lofty, high up; steep; rough (road), scaly; difficult Gl.

stīel|e *n.* steel.

~ecg† steel-edged (sword).

~ed hardened, tempered.

~en of steel.

stiell *m.* leap.
stiellan *prt.* stielde, ? ea leap.
stiem|an *intr.* give out odour, smell sweet [stēam].
~ing *f.* fragrance.
stiep|an† raise ; build ; exalt, make illustrious, honour *wai.* ; ge- help [stēap].
~ere *m.* prop, pillar.
stiep-†, īe† *once* deprivation (?) ; downfall (?).
stiepel *m.* tower [stēap].
stier|an, *A.* ēo *w. d.* (or *a.*) steer (ship) ; guide, govern, restrain ; reprove ; punish ; *wdg.* restrain from, check : ~de him unrihtəs [stēor].
~end *m.* governor ; corrector ; reprover.
~ere*, ēo *m.* steer-man.
~nes *f.* discipline.
stierc*, i, y, io, styric *m.* calf.
stiern|e stern.
~inga† *av.* inexorably.
~lic harsh (word) ; severe (weather).
~līce *av* sternly, rigorously.
~mōd† stern.
stīf rigid.
~ian be or become rigid.
stig *n.* (pig)-sty ; ? hall.
~fearh, stī- *m.* young pig kept in sty.
~ian put (swine) in sty.
stīg *f.* path.
stig-rāp, stīrāp *m.* stirrup Gl.
stig-wita, stīwita† *m.* householder (?).
stīgan 6 rise ; descend, *gen. w.* niþer, ofdūne ; move on, go || *tr., gen.* ge-, ascend.
stige *m.* going up *or* down.
stīgend *m.* sty (in eye) Gl.
stignes *f.* descent *IN.*
stigol *f.* place of climbing over (fence) ; stile.
~hamm *m.* enclosure reached by stile.
stiht|an, -ian arrange ; regulate, govern ; incite.
~end *m.* ruler.
~ere *m.* director.
(ge)~ung *f.* arrangement ; dispensation, providence.
stille at rest ; silent ; not loud ; secret — hit eall ~ lǣtan keep it dark ; unchanging, stable ; gentle, quiet ; *wg* abstaining from, being exempt.

stillan *intr.* become calm (*of* storm) || *tr. w.d. or a.* make calm, assuage (pain).
stil|līce *av.* silently.
~nes *f.* quiet ; silence ; tranquillity, peace ; *wg.* exemption.
stincan 3 rise (*of* dust) ; emit vapour ; emit odour (good *or* bad) ; ? sniff, follow scent.
gestincan 3 have power of smell || *tr.* smell.
sting, y *m.* pricking, stab, stinging ; place stung.
stingan 3 thrust, insert ; stab, pierce | ~on *a.* lay claim to, usurp ; *rfl.* hine ~on *a.* meddle with.
stīþ stiff ; thick (paste) ; strong ; resolute, obstinate ; austere, severe ; accompanied with effort or hardship, severe (battle, winter), rigid (discipline), ascetic (life) ; harsh (to taste).
~e *av.* strongly, excessively ; severely, cruelly ; austerely, strictly.
~ecg† strong-edged.
~ferhþ† resolute ; stern.
~hycgende† resolute.
~hygdig, -hȳdig† resolute, stern.
~lic firm, strong ; severe (storm, battle) ; harsh (words) ; fierce.
~līce *av.* firmly (fixed) ; vigorously ; fiercely ; harshly ; with hardship, (live) austerely ; strictly, severely ; excessively, very.
~mægen† *n* strong troop.
~mōd† resolute ; obstinate ; stern ; fierce.
~nes *f.* stiffness, hardness ; constancy ; strictness.
~weg† *m.* rough road.
gestīþian become hard ; become strong ; grow up.
stōc.
~līf *n.* habitation ; town.
~weard *m.* townsman.
~wīc *n.* habitation.
stocc *m.* stock, trunk, log, pillory ; trumpet *IN.*
~en of logs, wooden (church).
stod (*n.*) post.
stōd *n.* stud, herd of horses.
~fald *m.* stud-enclosure.
~hors *n.* stud-horse, stallion.
~miere *f.* brood-mare.
~þēof *m.* horse-thief.
stōd *prt. of* standan.

stodla *m.* slay, part of loom.
stof|a, ~u *mf.* bath-room.
~bæþ *n.* vapour bath.
stofn *fm.* stem, trunk ; shoot, twig ; progeny ; foundation.
stōl *m.* stool, chair ; throne ; bishop's see.
stole *f.*, stol *n.* stole [*Lt.*].
stōp *prt. of* stæppan.
stōpel *m.* footprint.
stoppa *m.* bucket, pail.
stōr *m.* frankincense [*Lt.* storax].
~cylle *f.* censer.
~sæp *n.* resin.
~sticca *m.* incense-rod (for stirring ?).
stōr *once* strong, violent (thunder) *vL.* [*Scand.* stórr great].
store (*m.*) stork.
storfe *f.* flesh of animals that have died by disease [steorfan].
storm *m.* storm ; †uproar, tumult ; †attack.
stōw *f.* place.
~lic local, confined to one place.
~līce *av.* locally, as regards place.
stōwian restrain.
strāc|ian stroke [strīcan].
~ung *f.* stroking.
strǣc = strec.
strǣde *once f.* pace, step *IN.*
strǣl *fm.* not *W.* arrow, missile.
~bora *m.* archer.
~ian shoot.
~wyrt *f.* a plant.
strǣl, stregl (?) *f.* rug, bed, curtain [*Lt.* stragula ?].
strǣt *f.* (Roman) road, street [*Lt.* strata].
strand *n.* shore.
strang, *cpv.* strengra, *spl.* strengest strong, mighty, vigorous, potent ; severe, fierce ; accompanied with hardship, severe (winter).
~e *av.* violently ; severely.
~hende, y strong of hand.
~lic strong ; firm ; attended with effort *or* hardship.
~līce *av.* strongly ; firmly ; vigorously ; fiercely, bravely ; sternly.
~mōd resolute.
~nes *f.* strength, violence.
strang|ian be *or* become strong ; prevail || *tr.* strengthen, confirm, comfort.
~ung *f.* vigour ; strengthening *act.*, *pass.*

strapolas *mpl.* a kind of trousers.
straw = **strēaw**.
streaht *ptc. of* **streccan**.
strēam *m.* flowing, current ; running water, river ; †*pl.* waters, sea.
~faru† *f.* current, flow.
~lic of water.
~racu *f.* water-course, bed of river.
~rād *f.* bed of river ; †way over sea.
~ryne *m.* — strēamrynes in a stream.
~stæþ† *n.* shore.
~weall† *m.* shore.
~wielm† *m* surge.
~gewinn† *n.* strife of waters.
strēaw, ēo, *A.* strē(u) *n.* straw.
~ian = **strewian**.
strēawberige, ~wīse, straw- *f.* strawberry.
strec, ̂e I. *aj., dpl.* **~um,** stræcum vehement, violent, mighty ; obstinate ; stern, rigorous. II. *n.* violence, force ; strictness, rigour.
~lic strict.
~līce *av.* violently ; strictly.
~nes *f.* perseverance.
streccan, *prt.* stre(a)hte hold out (hand), extend ; spread out ; *rfl.* prostrate oneself.
streced-nes *f.* couch Gl.
strēdd *ptc. of* **strēgdan**.
strēgan *not W., prt.* **strēde,** *vE.* strēide strew, spread [**strēawian**].
stregdan, strēdan 3, *prt.* strægd, strēd (*lN.* strǣgde, strugde), *ptc.* strogden strew, spread, sprinkle. **stregdan** *is more frequent in W.*
stregd|an, strēdan, *prt.* strēdde (*lN.* strǣgde, strugde) strew, spread, sprinkle (water, a place) ‖ *intr.* disperse.
~nes *f.* sprinkling.
strēn = **strēowen**.
streng *m.* string (of harp, bow), rope, cable ; sinew, ligament ; lineage.
gestrengan strengthen *lN.* [**strang**].
streng|e severe.
~lic† strong.
strengel† *m.* chief.
strengest *spl. of* **strang**.

strĘngo *f.* strength, vigour ; firmness ; virtue.
strengþ(o) *f.* strength ; violence ; severity ; efficacy ; prime of life.
strengra *cpv. of* **strang**.
strēon = **strēowen**.
gestrēon, *lN.* strēon *n.* gain, profit ; usury ; procreation ; property, wealth.
~full precious, sumptuous.
strēowen, strēon, *A.* strēn *f.* bed, resting-place.
strēow = **strēaw**.
strēowian = **strewian**.
strew|ian, ēo, ēa strew, scatter.
~nes *f.* bedding, bed.
~ung *f.* bed.
stric [ĭ ?] (*n.*) plague (?) ; sedition (?).
gestric *n.* strife.
strīcan 6 rub, wipe ‖ *intr.* move, go.
gestrician mend (nets) *lN.*
strica *m.* stroke of pen, mark ; line of motion, orbit.
stricel (*m.*) strickle, implement for smoothing corn in a measure [**strican**].
stricel (*m.*) breast, teat.
strīdan 6 stride — ~ uppan hors mount.
stride *m.* stride, pace (measure).
strīen|an, *A.* ēo *w. g.* (*a.*) acquire ; ! augment ; beget [**gestrēon**].
ge~endlic genitive.
strīmende resisting, striving Gl.
strīþ *m.* struggle, contest [*Old Saxon*].
stroccian stroke.
gestrod *n.* plunder [**strūdan**].
(ge)strogdnes *f.* sprinkling *lN.* [**stregdan**].
stropp (oar) thong [*Lt.* struppus].
strūd|an 7 plunder, carry off ; ravage, destroy.
~end *m.* robber ; usurer Gl.
~ere *m.* robber.
~ung *f.* robbery, plundering.
strūtian stand out stiffly, be rigid.
strūta = **strȳta**.
strȳdan rob, deprive *wda* [**strūdan**].
strydere waster = **stryndere**.
strynd *f. not W.* lineage, race ; *lN.* tribe.
strynd|ende*, ~ed- prodigal Gl.
~ere, strydere *m.* waster, prodigal Gl.

strȳta, ū *m.* ostrich [*Lt.* struthio].
studu, stuþu *f., pl.* styde, styþe pillar, post, buttress.
stuf- = **stof-**.
stulor furtive, insidious [**stelan**].
~līce *av.* furtively.
gestun *n.* noise, whirlwind [stenan].
stunian *intr.* resound ; dash (against).
gestund *n.* noise.
stund *f.* point *or* short period of time ; fixed time, hour ; signal of time (bell) | ~et at once. ymb ~e from time to time. ~um from time to time — ~um . . ~um sometimes . . sometimes ; with effort, eagerly, fiercely, earnestly.
~mǣlum *av.* gradually ; alternately.
stunt stupid, foolish.
~lic foolish.
~līce *av.* foolishly.
~nes *f.* stupidity, folly.
~scipe *m.* foolishness.
~sprǣc *f.* foolish talk.
~sprǣce, ~wyrde talking foolishly.
stūpian *intr.* stoop, curve downwards.
sturtende *once* leaping *lN.*
stūt (*m.*) gnat.
stuþan-sceaft *m.* prop.
stuþu = **studu**.
stybb *m.* stump of tree.
stycce *n.* piece ; piece of money Gl. ; short space of time — ymbe ~ after a time.
~mǣlum, sticm- *av.* piecemeal ; here and there ; gradually.
styde = **stede**.
styde, *see* **studu**.
stȳfic|ian, -ecian root up.
~ung *f.* cleared ground (?) Ct.
styltan, ge- be stupefied, astonished *lN.*
styntan stupefy [**stunt**].
gestyr*, i *n.* movement *lN.*
stȳran = **stēran** fumigate.
styr|ian move *tr., intr., rfl.* ; set in action (voice, harp) : stir up ; agitate, excite (mind) ; cause.
~enes *f.* motion, commotion.
ge~enes *f.* tribulation *lN.*
~igendlic moving.
~ung *f.* motion ; setting in action, practice ; commotion, tumult ; trouble, agitation, emotion.

styrfig — ~flǣsc flesh of an animal that has died by disease [storfe].
styria, styr(g)a *m.* sturgeon.
styric = *stierc calf.
styrman be stormy; make noise, shout [storm].
styþe, *see* **studu.**
sū = **sugu.**
sub-diacon *m.* sub-deacon [*Lt.*].
sūcan, sūgan 7 suck.
sufl, -el *n.* what is eaten with bread, relish.
gesufl — ~ hlāf ? loaf of fine flour.
suftlere = **swiftlere.**
sūgan = **sūcan.**
sugian = **swīgian.**
sugga, sucga *m.* a bird.
sugu, sū *f.* sow.
suht† *once* (*f.*) illness [*Old Saxon*].
suhter|ga, suhtriga *m.* brother's son; uncle's son, cousin.
~(ge)fæderan *mpl.* uncle and nephew.
sūl = **sulh.**
sulh, sūl, *pl.* **sylh, syll** *f.* plough; furrow, gully (?) Ct.; ? = **sūlung** a measure of land.
~æcer *m.* strip of land for ploughing.
~ælmesse *f.* ecclesiastical tax on ploughed land.
~bēam *m.* plough-tail.
~gang *m.* as much land as can be tilled by one plough.
~hæbbere *m.* ploughman Gl.
~(h)andla *m.* ploughman Gl.
~(h)andle *f.* plough-handle *or* -tail.
~scear *n.* ploughshare.
~gesidu *npl.* ploughing apparatus.
~geteoh *n.* ploughing apparatus.
~geweorc *n.* plough-making.
sūlincel *n.* small furrow Gl.
sūlung, swu- *n.* 'plough-length,' *in Kent* a hide of land. *See* **hīd** [sulh, lang].
sum *no. wg.* a certain one, some one — **sixa** ~ one of six, with five others. *correl.* ~e . . ~e some . . others. *aj.* some — ~ hund scipa about 600 ships; ~ə þā tēþ some of the teeth || ~es in some degree. ~e dǣle somewhat. ~era þinga in some respects.
sūmnes *f.* delay *lN.*
sumor *m., d.* **sumera, -e** summer.
~hǣte *f.* summer heat.
~lǣcan *impers.* draw near to summer.

sumor|lang (day) long as in summer.
~lic summer.
~lida *m.* summer army of Danes (which does not winter in the country).
~mæsse *f.* midsummer.
~rǣding-bōc *f.* lectionary for summer.
~selde *f.* summer-house Gl.
sund *n.* power *or* act of swimming; †sea, water.
~gebland† *n.* commotion of waters, surge.
~būend(e)† *mpl.* men, people.
~corn *n.* saxifrage.
~gierd *f.* sounding-pole.
~helm† *m.* covering of water, the sea.
~hengest† *m.* ship.
~hwæt active in swimming.
~līne *f.* sounding-line.
~mere *m.* swimming-bath.
~nytt† *f.* act of swimming.
~plega† playing in water.
~rāp *m.* sounding-line.
~reced *n.* sea-house, the Ark.
~wudu *m.* ship.
gesund uninjured; in good condition; sound in health.
~full sound; prosperous.
~fullian make prosperous.
~fullic sound, good.
~fullīce *av.* safely; prosperously.
~fulnes *f.* health; prosperity.
~ig favourable (wind).
~elic prosperous.
~līce *av.* safely; prosperously.
sundēaw *m.* sundew (?), rosemary [= sund-dēaw ?].
sundor I. *av.* apart; severally; asunder; differently. II. *See* **onsundran.**
~anweald *m.* monarchy.
~cræft *m.* special art or power.
~cræftiglīce *av.* with special skill.
~gecynd *n.* peculiar nature.
~cȳþþo *f.* intimacy.
~feoh *n.* private property.
~folgoþ *m.* appointment, office.
~frēodōm, ~frēols *m.* special immunity, privilege.
~genga *m.* one who goes alone.
~giefu *f.* special gift *or* grace, privilege.
~hālga *m.* Pharisee.
~ierfe *n.* special inheritance *or* property.

sundor|land *n.* land set apart, private land.
~lic special.
~līce *av.* apart.
~liepe.
~liepes *av.* separately, specially Gl.
~līf *n.* private life.
~mǣd *f.* private meadow.
~mǣlum *av.* singly.
~notu *f.* special office.
~nytt *f.* special office *or* use.
~gerēf-land *n.* land reserved for the jurisdiction of a gerēfa (?) Gl.
~riht *n.* special right.
~seld *n.* throne.
~setl *n.* hermitage.
~sprǣc *f.* private conversation, conference.
~stōw *f.* special place.
~weorþung *f.* special honour, privilege.
~wīc *n.* separate dwelling.
~wine† *m.* intimate friend.
~wīs† specially wise.
~wundor† *n.* special wonder.
sunn|e *f.,* ~a *m.* sun.
~an-ǣfen(n) *m.* Saturday evening.
~an-corn *n.* gromel (a plant).
~an-dæg *m.* Sunday.
~an-niht *f.* Saturday night.
~an-uhta *m.* time before daybreak on Sunday; Sunday matins.
sun|bēam *m.* sunbeam.
~bearo† *n.* sunny grove.
~beorht† sunny.
~bryne *m.* sunburn.
~feld *m.* Elysium.
~folgend *m.* heliotrope.
~ganges *av.* in the direction of the sun's movement.
~gihte solstice.
~lic solar.
~sceado *f.* sunshade, veil.
~scīene† beautiful as the sun.
~scīn *n.* mirror (!) Gl.
~set West *lN.*
~stede *m.* solstice.
~wlītig† beautiful with sunshine (*of* summer).
sunor *fn.* herd (of swine) *lN.*
sun|u, *pl.* ~a *m.* son; young of animals.
~sunu *m.* grandson.
sūpan 7 sup, drink; **ge~** absorb.
sūpe *once f.* sup, draught.
sūr *f.* sour, acid.
~ēagede, ~īege blear-eyed.

sūr|mil(i)sc, ~melsc sour-sweet (apple).

~nes f. acidity.

sūre f. sorrel.

sūsl nf. torment.

~bana† m. demon.

~cwalu† f. torment.

~hof† n. abode of torment.

suster = sweostor.

sūtere m. shoemaker [Lt. sutor].

sutol = sweotol.

sūþ I. av. southward ; in the south. II. aj., see sȳþerra.

~dæl m. south (part).

~duru f. south door.

sūþēast south-east.

~ende m. south-east end.

~erne south-eastern.

Sūþ|engle pl. South Anglians ; people of the south of England.

~eweard = ~weard.

~folc n. southern people ; Suffolk.

~gārsecg m. southern ocean.

~heald southward.

~healf f. south side.

~hymbre mpl Mercians.

~land n. southern land.

~mægþ f. southern tribe or province.

~gemǣre n. south boundary.

~mann m. southern man.

~mierce pl. southern Mercians.

~portic m. south porch.

~rihte av. due south.

~rima m. south coast.

~rodor, ~rador m. the south.

~sǣ mf. English Channel.

Sūþseax|e, ~an pl. South Saxons ; Sussex.

~isc of Sussex.

sūþ|stæp n. south shore or coast.

~wāg m. south wall.

sūþ(e)weard southward.

~es av. southwards.

sūþ|weg m. south road or quarter.

~west av. south-west.

~westerne south-western.

~wind m. south wind.

sūþan av. from the south, on the south side — be ~ wd., wiþ ~ wa. south of ; southwards.

sūþanēastan av. (from) the south-east.

~wind m. south-east wind.

sūþan|ēasterne south-eastern.

~hymbre pl. Mercians.

~weard = sūþweard.

---

sūþanwestan av. (from) the south-west.

~wind m. south-west wind.

sūþan-wind m. south wind.

sūþerige = sæþerige (?) a plant.

sūþerne southern — ~ wudu, sæprene- southern - wood, abrotanum.

sūþ(er)ra = sȳþerra.

sūþmest, see sȳþerra.

suwian = swīgian.

swā, swǣ, weak se(þeah) av., cj. w. indc., sbj. also doubled swāswa without change of meaning || dem. so, often nearly = that no. : hē þā swā dyde did as he was asked ; hē ārās āblendum ēagum, and his gefēran hine swā blindne (blind in the manner mentioned) tō þære byrig gelǣddon; æt menn fīftīene peningas, and æt horse healf swā half of that sum | succession, then : fōr tō Sandwīc, and swā þanon tō Gipeswīc | therefore : hē him þæt land forbēad, and hē hit swā ālēt. ic mæg rǣdan on þȳs rīce ; swā mē þæt riht ne þynceþ þæt . . — swā and swā indf. in such and such a manner : þēah þū nyte for hwȳ hē swā and swā dō | degree : ne gemētte ic swā micelne gelēafan ; mid þrim scipum . . mid swā fela scipa | emphatic : wīne swā druncen so drunk, very drunk | pleon., referring to rel. clause : swā hraþe swā hī bēoþ dēade, swā bēoþ hī mid ealle geendode. swāswā hē hīe genamode, swā hī sindon gȳt gehātene | in such a manner that, so that : gif hwā stalie swā his wīf nyte ; ic hīe geleornode swāswā ic hīe forstōd ; dō rysle tō, swāswā sīen twā pund about two pounds | swā þæt in such a manner that, so that gen. w. indc. : hē wæs swīþe fæger swā þæt hē wæs gehāten Leohtberend || rel. as, like : swā(swā) ic ær sǣde ; bēoþ glēawe swā nǣddran ! ; heora hlāford weorþodon swā-swā wuldres cyning as being. nǣfre næs swilc sibb swilc swā wæs on his gebyrdtīde. swā hit = which rel. : fēng tō þǣm westrīce swā hit his fæder

---

hæfde | which : þon gelīc swā-(swā) lǣcas cunnon such as doctors know | where | when : swā þā ōþre hām cōmon | since | because | although | as if w. sbj. : flēah swā hē āfyrht wǣre | if : hē him þæt land forbēad swā hē ǣniges brūcan wolde || swā w. spl. = as : fōr æfter swā hē raþost mehte his fird gegadrian as soon as || swā . . swā dem., rel. as . . as : swā oft swā þā ōþre hergas ūt fōron, þonne fōron hīe ; swā gelǣrede biscepas swāswā nū sindon ; swā ealde swā hīe wǣron hīe gefuhton in spite of their age. Sometimes the place of the second swā is taken by an equivalent word : þā habbaþ beardas swā sīde oþ heora brēost | swā hwelc swā whoever, swā hwelc mann swā whatever man, if any man . . . See hwelc, hwæt &c. | either . . or, whether . . or : sīe þæt on cyninges dōme swā dēaþ swā līf, swā hē him forgifan wille ; God sealde him āgenne cyre, swā hē wǣre gehȳrsum, swā hē wǣre ungehȳrsum. Sometimes the second swā stands alone = or : dēm þū hī tō dēaþe, swā tō līfe lǣt ! || w. cpv. the . . the : Norþmanna land is simle swā norþor swā smælre ; swāswā hē lengra biþ swā hī bēoþ unge-sēligran. Omission of first element : hit mē gelīcaþ leng swā swīþor the longer the more.

swācendlic (?) convenient Gl.

swǣ = swā.

swæcc, e m. sense of taste ; taste, flavour (of food) || sense of smell ; odour.

ge~an smell.

swǣlan burn tr. [swōl ; ǣ = ōe].

swǣm m. trifler, contemptible creature.

geswǣpa, -āpa, -ēpo, pl. rubbish [swāpan].

swǣpels (m.), ~e f. cloak, garment.

swǣr, ~e, swǣr(e) heavy ; excessive, heavy (sleep) ; grievous (hardship, sin) ; sad (voice) ; sluggish ; weak.

geswǣred made uncomfortable (*of the body*).

swǣr|e, swāre *av.* grievously, oppressively.

~lic excessive (lamentation).

~līce *av.* excessively, (sleep) heavily.

~mōd sluggish.

~mōdnes *f.* sluggishness.

~nes *f.* weight; sluggishness.

geswǣre I. afflicted. II. gisuoere *n.* affliction *LN.*

swǣs(†) own; familiar, dear (kinsman); *Pr.* ~ mann native; gentle (speech); kind; pleasant; sweet (honey).

~lǣcan flatter.

~lic kind (words); pleasing (gift).

~līce *av.* kindly, graciously; pleasantly; (deceive) plausibly; ! properly.

~nes *f.* blandishment; pleasure.

~wyrde pleasant of speech Gl.

geswǣs dear, familiar; kind, gentle; pleasant, alluring.

~e *av.* blandly.

~lǣcan flatter.

~līce *av.* kindly.

~nes *f.* flattery.

swǣs|an.

~ung *f.* alleviation.

swǣsend|e *n., gen. pl.* ~u, food, refection, dinner; blandishment Gl.

~dagas, swǣsing- *mpl.* ! ides (of March, &c.).

swǣsing- = swǣsend-.

swǣtan perspire; toil; exude *wi.*; †bleed [swāt].

swǣþ *n.* footprint, track; trace, vestige. *Cp.* swaþu.

swǣþer, swaþor *wg.* whichever | *w.* swā . . swā either . . or: gewylde man hine ~ man mæge, swā cucenne swā dēadne; hī mōston dōn swā gōd swā yfel ~ swā hī woldon [swā, hwæ-þer].

swǣþriaṇ = sweþrian cease.

swāmian† *once* become dark.

swamm *m.* fungus, mushroom.

swan *m.* swan.

~rād† *f.* sea.

swān *m.* swineherd, herdsman; †man, warrior.

~gerēfa *m.* swineherd-superintendent.

~riht *n.* law concerning swineherds.

swān-steorra *m.* evening star.

swancor pliant, supple; agile, graceful; weak.

swangor sluggish (physically and mentally).

~nes *f.* sluggishness.

swāpan I *tr.* sweep (with broom); brandish (sword) || *intr.* rush, dash (*of* wind, &c.).

geswāpa = geswǣpa.

swār(e) = swǣr.

swarnian = swornian coagulate.

swāt *n.* perspiration; exudation; (†)blood; toil.

~clāþ *m.* handkerchief, napkin.

~fāg† blood-stained.

~lin *n.* handkerchief, napkin.

~swaþu† *f.* gory track.

~þȳrel *n.* pore.

swātan [*or* a ?] *pl.* beer.

swātig perspiring; †blood-stained, bleeding.

~hlēor† with sweating face.

geswapian*, æ investigate Gl.

swā·pēah *av.* however.

~hwæpere *av.* however.

swā·pēana, sepēana *av.* however.

swapor = swæper.

swaporian = sweprian cease.

swaþ|u *f.* track — on ~e behind; scar; vestige. *Cp.* swǣþ.

swē = swā.

swealwe *f.* swallow.

swearcian become dark (*of* sun) [sweorcan].

sweard, swearþ (*f.*) skin, rind (of bacon).

swearm *m.* swarm.

sweart black, dark; gloomy; evil.

~e† *av.* evilly; grievously, miserably.

~hǣwen violet-coloured.

~ian become black.

~lāst† leaving a black track.

~nes *f.* blackness; ink.

swearþ = sweard.

swebban, *prt.* swefede, put *or* lull to sleep; †kill [swefan].

swefan 5 sleep; †cease; †be dead.

swefed *ptc. of* swebban.

swefl, æ *m.* sulphur.

~en of sulphur.

~rēc *m.* sulphurous vapour.

~sweart sulphurous (?) Gl.

~þrosm *m.* sulphurous vapour.

swefn *n. often pl. w. sg. meaning* sleep; dream.

~racu *f.* interpretation of dream.

swefn-rĘccere *m.* interpreter of dreams.

swefn|ian *w. a. of pers.* appear in a dream: swā hwæt swā hine swefnaþ; *w. nom. of pers.* dream.

~igend *m.* dreamer.

swēg, oe *m.* noise, sound; melody; ! person.

~cræft *m.* music, musical performance.

~dynn† noise, din.

~hlēopor† *m.* melodious sound, melody.

~lic sonorous.

swēg|an *intr.* sound, resound || *tr.* signify, mean [swōgan].

~endlic vocal, vowel.

~ing *f.* noise.

geswēg|e sonorous; harmonious.

~sumlīce *av.* unanimously.

swegl† *n.* sky, heaven; sun.

~befealden encompassed by heaven.

~beorht heaven-bright.

~bōsmas *mpl.* interior of heaven.

~candel(l) *f.* sun.

~cyning *m.* king of heaven.

~drēam *m.* joy of heaven.

~horn *m.* a musical instrument Gl.

~rād *f.* music (?).

~torht heavenly bright.

~wered (?).

~wuldor *n.* glory of heaven.

~wundor *n.* heavenly wonder.

sweger, -gr *f.* mother-in-law [swēor].

swegle† I. bright. II. *av.* brightly.

swelan 4 *intr.* burn, be burnt up; inflame (*of* wound).

swelc, i, y *aj., no.* such, such a one, he: þā þā se cāsere eall swylc geseah the magician's tricks — ~ and ~ this and that, different things | hine ~es and ~es wundraþ | as much, as many: medmicel pipores and ōper swilc cymenes an equal quantity of cummin || *correl.*: ~ scolde eorl wesan ~ Æschere wæs. *correl. with other words*: ymb ~ tō sprecanne hwelc hit þā wæs. So also ~ . . swā || *w. the correl. word omitted* such as, which: eall gedǣlan ~him God sealde [swā, līc].

~nes (!) *f.* quality.

swelca *m.* pustule.

swelce *av. cj.*; as *w. indc.*, like;

as if *w. sbj.*; so also, also — ~ ēac, ēac ~ also.

swelg|an 3 *w. a., i.* swallow; absorb, *also fig.*; devour, consume, destroy.

~end *m.* devourer, glutton.

~end, ge~*fnm.* gulf, abyss, whirlpool.

~ end)nes *f.* whirlpool.

~ere *m* glutton.

geswell *n.* swelling, tumour.

swell|an 3 swell.

~ing *f.* swelling (of sail).

swelt|an, y, *prt.* swealt, eo 3 die; *wg.* become dead to *met.*: ~ synna.

~endlic about to die.

swenc (*m.*) tribulation *lN.* [swinc-an].

geswenc *n.* toil, affliction.

swenc|an afflict, torment; bring (jailer) into trouble (by escaping); mortify (flesh).

ge~ednes *f.* affliction.

sweng *m.* stroke, blow [swingan].

swengan *tr.* dash (aside) || *intr. w.* on *a.* spring on (*of* lion).

sweofot (†) *n.* sleep [swefan].

sweoloþ = swoloþ heat.

Swēo|n *pl.* Swedes.

~land, †~rīce *n.* Sweden.

~þēod† *f.* the Swedes, Sweden.

swēor, swehor *m.* father-in-law; cousin Gl. [sweger].

geswēor *m.* cousin Gl.

swēor, swēr, ȳ *mf.* column, pillar.

swēor|a, ī, ȳ, ū *m.* neck.

~bān *n.* neck-bone; neck.

~bēag *m.* necklace.

~clāþ *m.* collar.

~cosp, ~cops *m.* pillory.

~coþu *f.* quinsy.

~hnitu *f.* neck-nit.

~racenttēag *f.* chain for the neck.

~rōd *f.* cross hung from neck.

~scacol *m.* pillory.

~tēag, ~tēh *f.* collar.

~wærc *m.* pain in the neck.

gesweorc *n.* cloud, mist.

~nes *f.* gloom.

sweorc|an 3 become dark, be obscured — *ptc.* gesworcen dark; become sad; become grievous *or* troublesome.

~end-ferhþ† gloomy-minded.

sweord, u, y, *lN.* o *n.* sword.

~bealo† *n.* sword-hurt.

~berende† sword-bearing.

~bite† *m.* sword-cut.

sweord|bora *m.* sword-bearer, attendant; swordsman, gladiator.

~fætels *m.* sword-belt.

~freca† *m.* warrior.

~giéfu† *f.* gift of a sword.

~gripe† *m.* sword-stroke.

~hwīta *m.* sword-polisher.

~lēoma† *m.* glitter of swords.

~genīþla† *m.* warrior.

~plega† *m.* battle.

~rǣs† *m.* onslaught.

~slege† *m.* sword-stroke.

~geswing† *n.* sword-brandishing.

~wegende sword-bearing.

~wīgend† *m.* warrior.

~wund† wounded by the sword.

~wyrhta *m.* sword-smith.

gesweorf *n.* filings.

sweorfan 3 scrub, file.

geswēoru, ī, y† *npl.* hills (!).

sweostor, y, u, o, suster, *not W.* swester, *pl.* ~, sweostra, -u *f.* sister; nun.

gesweostren — ~u bearn *pl.* children of sisters, cousins.

gesweostru, -a, gesweostor *pl.* sisters, *esp. in* twā ~.

swēot†, ēo† *n.* troop, crowd.

sweotol, u, y, sutol distinct (to senses); evident; manifest; clear.

~e *av.* see (clearly); evidently; openly; (understand) clearly.

~lic clear, distinct.

~līce *av.* distinctly, clearly, openly.

sweotol|ian manifest; explain, state.

sweotolung, ge- *f.* manifestation (Epiphany); explanation, exposition; evidence, proof.

~dæg *m.* Epiphany.

swer|ian 2, *prt.* swōr, ~ede, *ptc.* sworen swear, swear (by) *w.* on *d.*, þurh *a.*

~igendlic jurative (adverbs).

swertling (*m.*) titlark Gl.

swēt|e, oe I. sweet, pleasant to taste; fragrant; untainted; agreeable, pleasant. II. *n.* sweetness, sweet [swōt].

~an *tr.* sweeten; make pleasant.

~ian be sweet.

~lǣcan sweeten Gl.

~līce *av.* pleasantly.

~mettas *mpl.* dainty, delicacy.

~nes *f.* sweetness, pleasantness to taste; fragrance; pleasantness.

~swēge melodious.

swēt-wyrde bland of speech; ! stuttering.

swepel, æ, eo *m.* bandage.

swepolian relent *vL.*

sweþr|ian, sweoþerian, swa-, swæ-, swī-, ge- cease, subside, abate (*of* fire, sound, storm, prosperity).

ge~ung*, æ *f.* ceasing — mōdes ~a loss of mental power.

sweþung *f.* poultice.

swī-tīma = swīg-.

swic (*n.*) deception [swīcan].

~cræft *m.* treachery.

~dōm *m.* deceit, treachery, treason; offence, scandalum.

~full deceitful.

geswic *n.* offence, scandalum.

swīc|an 6 †wander; †depart — †fram — *wd.* desert, withdraw favour *or* allegiance | *w.g. or* fram desist, cease; ge- withdraw (from expedition) | *wd.* desert; not be of service, fail (*of* sword); be traitor to || *? tr.* deceive *not W.*

~end *m.* betrayer, deceiver.

ge~ing *f.* intermission.

~ung *f.* deceit; offence, scandalum.

swician wander; ~ fram *d.* depart | *wd.* deceive, be treacherous — ~ on æhtum, ~ ymb þā sāwle as regards; offend, scandalizare | blaspheme.

swica *m.* deceiver; traitor.

swice *f.* trap.

swice deceitful, treacherous.

swicc (*m.*) odour. *Cp.* swæcc.

geswicennes *f.* cessation, abstention; repentance.

swicn, ge- *f.* clearance from criminal charge.

ge~an clear from criminal charge. *gen. rfl. w.* be *d.*

geswicnefull (?) treacherous.

swicol, eo deceitful, treacherous, crafty.

~lic deceitful; causing offence (scandalum).

~līce *av.* deceitfully, treacherously.

~nes *f.* deceit.

swierman swarm (*of* bees) [swearm].

swifan 6 *intr.* move, sweep — on ~ intervene, interfere *abs.*

geswifornes = geswipornes.

swift swift.

~līce *av.* swiftly.

swift|nes *f.* swiftness.
~o *f.* swiftness.
swift *once* reciprocal Gl.
swiftlere, suftlere *m.* slipper [*Lt.* subtalaris].
swīgan = swīgian.
swīg|ian, ī†, eo, u, sweowian, u, sugian, suwian; swīgan *rare in W.* be silent, not speak; not make sound (*of* things), *w. g. or a.* not speak of ‖ ge~ed bēon be silent.
~iendlice *av.* silently.
~ung *f.* silence; quiet; delay *LN.*
swīg|e, ī† *f.* silence; quiet.
~dagas *mpl.* silence-days (last three days of Holy Week).
~tīma *m.* time of silence.
~uht *m.* dawn of silence-days.
swīg|e silent; quiet.
~nes *f.* time of silence.
swigen *f.* silence.
swīglunga, swīlunge *av.* silently.
swill|an, swilian (hē swileþ) wash.
~ing, swiling *f.* washing.
swīma, ī† *m.* giddiness; dizziness; swoon.
swimm|an 3 swim, float.
~endlic able to swim Gl.
swīn *n.* swine, pig; †image of boar on helmet.
~en of swine.
~haga *m.* swine-pen.
~hierde *m.* swineherd.
~līc† *n.* image of boar on helmet.
swinc *n.* affliction.
~full disastrous *vL.*
~lēas without exertion.
~lic of labour.
geswinc *n.* labour; result of labour, work; effort; hardship, affliction.
~dagas† *pl.* time of hardship.
~full laborious; troublesome.
~fulnes *f.* tribulation.
~lic toilsome.
swincan 3 labour; be in pain *or* distress; not thrive (*of* crops).
swind = spind fat.
swindan 3 waste away; be torpid.
geswing† *n.* fluctuation, swell (of sea).
swing|an 3 beat, strike, chastise; whip (top, cream); ? beat *or* flap (wings); afflict.

swingere *m.* scourger.
swinge, y *f.* stroke (of rod), stripe, beating, *also met.* chastisement, affliction.
swingell, swingel(l)e, swingle *f.* stroke (of rod), beating, *also met.* chastisement, affliction; stick to beat with, whip.
swingl|ian.
~ung *f.* giddiness.
geswins*, -swin† *once n.* melody.
swinsian make melody; sound harmoniously.
swinsung *f.* melody, harmony.
~cræft *m.* music.
swip|e, ~u *wk. f.* whip, scourge, *met.* chastisement, affliction; some weapon (sword?, spear?).
swipor, swifor (?), ge- cunning.
ge~lice *av.* cunningly.
ge~nes *f.* cunning.
swippan*, (hē) swipeþ† scourge, beat.
swira = swēora.
geswiria, -swirga, *vE.* -swigra *m.* sister's son, nephew; cousin [swēor].
swīþ strong; efficacious (drug) | *cpv.* ~ra right (hand, side). ~re *f.* right side.
~fæst.
~fæstnes *f.* excessiveness, violence.
~feorm wealthy, fruitful; violent.
~feormende growing violent.
~ferhþ† brave, impetuous.
swīþfram, ge- strenuous.
~līce *av.* strenuously.
sw:þ|hwæt† very active.
~hycgende of strong purpose.
~lic excessive, great; violent, vehement; effective (drug); severe, strict.
~līce *av.* exceedingly; energetically; severely, strictly.
~licnes *f.* excess.
~mihtig powerful.
~mōd great of soul; brave; stern; proud.
~mōdnes *f.* greatness of soul.
~nes *f.* excessiveness; violence.
~snell† very quick.
~sprecol loquacious.
~stincende of strong scent.
~strang of great force (stream).
~strīeme (river) with strong current.
~swēge strong-sounding, heroic (verse) Gl.

swīþ|swīge taciturn.
swīþan make strong *met.*, support.
swīþian be *or* become strong; fix.
swīþe *av.* exceedingly, very | *cpv.* swīþor more | *spl.* swīþost most; especially, chiefly; almost, nearly.
swīþrian = sweþrian cease.
swīþrian be *or* become stronger, prevail; avail [swīþ].
swodrian *once* be drowsy, sleep heavily.
swōg|an *intr.* (re)sound — on ~ enter by force, invade Bd. | *ptc.* geswōgen in a swoon; dead; silenced.
ge~ung, -swōw- *f.* swooning.
swol, o† (*n.*) burning; heat (of sun, of fever) [swelan].
swolgettan use as a gargle [swelgan].
swoloþ, sweo-, *once* swa- *m.* heat, burning.
sword = sweord.
sworen *ptc. of* swerian.
sworett|an draw deep breath, sigh, pant.
~endlic panting.
~ung *f.* sighing; panting.
swornian *once* a coagulate Gl.
swostor = sweostor.
swōt sweet [swēte].
~e *av.* (smell) sweetly.
~lic savoury (food).
~mettas *mpl.* dainties.
~nes *f.* sweetness (of smell).
~stence odoriferous.
*-stincende, ~ste- odoriferous.
swūgian = swīgian.
swulung = sulung.
swūra = swēora.
swurd = sweord.
swuster = sweostor.
swutol = sweotol.
swūwian = swīgian.
swylc = swelc.
swyle *m.* swelling (on body), tumour, abscess.
swylt† *m.* death; perdition (of the soul).
~cwalu† *f.* death; perdition (of the soul), torment.
~dæg† *m.* day of death.
~dēaþ† *m.* death.
~hwīl† *f.* hour of death.
swyra = swēora.
swyrd = sweord.

geswyrf *n.* filings [sweorfan].

swyster = sweostor.

swytol = sweotol.

sȳcan, ī suckle [sūcan].

gesyd *n.* wallowing-place [sēoþan].

sȳdung = sīdung.

syde (*m.*) decoction (of herbs) [sēoþan].

syfian = seofian.

syfan = seofon.

sȳfer-, *see* sȳfre.

~ǣte abstemious.

~lic cleanly, pure.

~lice *av.* with cleanliness; abstemiously; chastely; carefully, prudently.

~nes *f.* moderation; abstemiousness; sobriety; chastity.

syfl|an — gesyfled provided with seasoning (*of* bread) [sufl].

~ige *f.* seasoning, food eaten with bread.

~ing *f.* seasoning, food eaten with bread.

sȳfre temperate, abstemious; sober; (morally) pure.

syl, *once* ~en, *pl.* ~a (*n.*) wallowing-place, miry place [sol].

sȳl *f.* pillar, column.

sylian make muddy *or* dirty; pollute [sol].

sȳla *once m.* ploughman Gl. [sulh].

sylen = syl.

sylen = selen gift.

sylf = self.

sylfor = seolfor.

syl.h), syll, *see* sulh.

(ge)sylhþe *n.* team (of oxen) [sulh].

syll, *once* ~e *f.* foundation beam *or* plank; support, foundation.

sȳlla = sēlra.

syllan = sellan.

symbel I. *n.*, *d.* symb(l)e; *occ.* sym(m)el- *in compos.* feast; (religious) festival. II. *aj.* of a feast *or* festival Gl.

symbel|calic *m.* chalice.

~cennes *f.* birthday festival *LN.*

~dæg *m.* † feast-day, feasting; (religious) festival day.

~gāl† excited with feasting.

~giéfa† *m.* entertainer.

~hūs *n.* banquet-hall.

~lic of a festival, solemn.

~lice *av.* solemnly.

~mōnaþlic comitial Gl.

~nes *f.* feasting; festival, solemnity.

~gereord† *n.* feast.

~tīd *f.* (religious) festival, solemnity.

~wērig† weary with feasting.

~wlanc† elate with feasting.

~wynn† *f.* exhilaration of feasting.

symbel, syml = simbel.

symbl(i)an feast.

symering-wyrt, si- *f.* a plant.

syml|ian frequent *LN.* *Cp.* simbel.

~inga *av.* continually *LN.*

gesyndgian make to prosper.

gesyndlic prosperous [gesund].

synder-, *LN.* syndur- [sundor].

~ǣ *f.* special law *LN.*

~lic separate; remote Gl.; private; ordinary (day, as opposed to festival); special; exceptionally good.

~lice *av.* apart, in private; separately, severally, in several ways; exclusively; specially.

~licnes *f.* speciality; excessiveness.

~liepe special.

~liepes *av.* singly.

~weorþmynt *f.* prerogative.

syndig skilled in swimming [sund].

syndr|ian separate [sundor].

~igendlic discretive (adverb).

~ung *f.* separation.

syndrig apart, separate, several; *distributive* one each: þā on-

fēngon hī ~e penegas; ~ stān pure rock (as opposed to earth); set apart, special, private; remarkable, exceptional, special.

syndrig|e *av.* *LN.* apart, singly.

~lic special.

~lice *av.* specially; singly.

syng|ian sin.

~ung *f.* sinning.

syn|n *f.* sin; †wrongdoing. injury, hostility.

~bōt *f.* penance.

~byrþen(n) *f.* burden of sin.

~bysig† wicked.

~dǣd *f.* sinful deed.

~dolg† *n.* hostile wound (?), *or* = sin-?

~fāh† hostile, wicked.

~full sinful.

~grīn *f.* snare of sin.

~leahtor *m.* sin, vice.

~lēas sinless.

~lēaw *f.* sinful injury.

~lic sinful.

~lice *av.* sinfully.

~lust *m.* sinful desire, lust.

~rǣs *m.* sinful impulse.

~rūst† *m.* rust of sin.

~scapa† *m.* malefactor.

~scyldig† wicked.

~wracu† *f.* punishment.

~wrǣnnes *f.* = sin-.

~wund *f.* sin-wound.

~wyrcende† sinning.

synn|ecge *f.* sinner.

~ig sinful; guilty.

gesynto *f.* *often pl.* *w.* *sg.* *meaning* health; welfare, safety, salvation [gesund].

syp|e, y† *m.* absorbing [sūpan].

~ian absorb (moisture).

syrf|e *f.*, ~trēow *n.* service-tree [*Lt.* sorbus].

sȳring *f.* sour whey [sūr].

sȳþerra, sūþ(e)ra *aj.* *cpv.* more southern, *spl.* sūþmest [sūþ].

T.

tā, tāhǣ f., pl. tān toe. See tāh-.

tā = tān.

tabule f., once m. table ; tablet (for writing on) ; board used as gong ; diagram, table [Lt. tabula].

tacan 2 take vL.

taccian once tame Gl.

tācn, -en, tānc n. sign in its various meanings, token, signal, sign of the Zodiac ; emblem, symbol ; prognostic ; miracle ; event ; symptom (of disease) ; proof ; banner [tēon 6].

~berend m. standard-bearer.

~bora m. standard-bearer ; ! guide.

~circul m. indiction, lunar cycle.

tācn|ian put mark on, mark ; point out, indicate ; ge- signify, mean ; be symbol of, express ; portend.

ge~iendlic emblematic.

~ung, ge- f. signification ; decree, dispensation ; emblem ; prognostic ; symptom ; proof.

tācor m. husband's brother.

tadde = tādige.

tādige, once tadde f. toad.

tæbere once an implement of weaving.

tǣc|an, prt. tǣhte, a wda. show ; direct, enjoin, teach.

tācn|an, ~ian show ; prove ; appoint [tācn].

~end m. indicator Gl.

~ing f. showing, proof.

tæfl f. chess-board ; chess, draughts, game of chance ; die (for gambling), piece [Lt. tabula].

~stān m. die or piece used in game.

tæfl|an, ~ian gamble.

~ere m. gambler.

~ung f. gambling.

tæflet given to gambling.

tægl m. tail.

~hǣr n. tail-hair.

tæhher = tēar.

getǣlt once, pl. -tale, swift, prompt.

tǣl, tāl f. fault-finding, censure ; calumny ; blasphemy — tō tāle

habban blaspheme against ; derision.

tǣl|hleahtor m. derision.

~lēas blameless.

~lēaslīce av. blamelessly.

~lic, ā calumnious ; blasphemous ; reprehensible.

~līce, ā av. blasphemously ; reprehensibly.

tǣlwierþ|e, ~lic reprehensible.

~līce av. reprehensibly.

~licnes, eo f. reprehensibility.

tæl, ę [infl. of tęllan] n. number [talu].

~cræft*, tęl- m. arithmetic, chronology.

~mearct f. date, period.

~mett n. amount (of time).

~sum rhythmic Gl.

getæl, ę n. number ; series ; catalogue ; tribe ; estimation, opinion.

~circul m. cycle, series.

~cræft*, e m. arithmetic.

~fæst measurable.

~rīmt n. series, succession.

~scipe*, getal- m. number lN.

~wīs skilled in arithmetic ; sagacious Gl.

tǣl|an blame ; calumniate, speak evil of ; deride, insult.

~end m. reprover ; detractor, slanderer ; derider.

~ende censorious ; slanderous.

~ere m. derider.

~ing f. reproof ; calumny.

~nes f. rebuke ; vituperation, detraction.

tǣnel m. basket [tān].

tǣnen of twigs [tān].

tæpp|a m. tap.

~ere m., ~estre f. tavern-keeper.

~ian tap (cask).

tæppe f. tape, ribbon.

tæpped, tæppet, teped n. carpet, curtain [Lt. tapete].

tæppel-bred n. footstool lN.

tǣsan pull to pieces, tease (wool) ; †wound ; once soothe (?).

getǣs|e I. convenient ; advantageous ; pleasant. II. n. convenience, advantage ; pleasure ; implement (?) Ct.

~lic convenient.

~līce av. conveniently ; pleasantly, gently.

~nes f. convenience.

tǣsel — wulfes ~ teasel (a plant).

tǣso = teoso injury.

tǣtan caress [tāt].

tættec- rag.

tagantes-helde f. a plant Gl.

tāh-. See tā toe.

~spura m. point of the toe (?) Gl.

tāh prt. of tēon 6.

tahte occ. prt. of tǣcan.

tāl = tǣl.

tal|ian [orig. part of tęllan ; cp. folgian, fylgan] enumerate ; consider (a thing to be so-and-so), account : hē ~aþ hine selfne wīsne ; ~ungōd tō gōde ; think ; impute wda., w. a. and tō d.

tal|u f., g. ~e, also indecl. series ; statement ; discussion ; claim ; excuse, defence ; legal case, action at law.

tam tame.

tama m. tameness.

tān m. ; tā f., pl. tān twig, branch, twig used in casting lots.

~hlyta, ~hlytere m. diviner.

tānc = tācn.

getang wd. in contact with.

~līce av. together.

tange, tang f. tongs, forceps.

tann|ian — getanned tanned.

~ere m. — tannera hol Ct.

taper-æx f. small axe [Russian, through Scand.].

tapor m. taper.

~berend m. acolyte.

tar- = teoru tar.

targ|e f., ~a m. small shield.

ge~ed furnished with a shield.

taru f. tear, rent [teran].

tasol = teosol die.

tāt- cheerful. Only in proper names.

tāwian prepare (land for sowing); treat (ill) : ~ tō bismere ; afflict : sē wæs yfele getāwod suffering (from cancer).

getāw|e, ~a *fpl.* apparatus, trappings, armour, arms — mannes ~ genitals [tāwian].

taxe *once f.* toad Gl.

tēn (?) *vb., prt.* tēde grow tough Gl. [tōh].

getēad *occ. ptc. of* tēon *wk.*

tēafor *n.* red pigment, vermilion.

tēag *f.* bond, chain, tape; case, casket; enclosure, paddock.

teagor = tēar.

tēah *prt. of* tēon 6.

tēah = tēag *prt. of* tēon 7.

teala = tela.

teald *ptc. of* tellan.

tealgor = telgor.

tealt unsteady, heaving (ship); precarious, fleeting.

~ian be unsteady, not stand firm.

tealtrian stagger, not stand firm; be uncertain (*of* calculation).

tealtrig unsettled.

tēam *m.* child-bearing; progeny, race; *coll.* parents and children, family; team (of oxen) ‖ vouching to warranty, right of jurisdiction in matters of warranty. *See* tīeman. [tēon 7.]

~byrst *m.* failure to produce an avoucher. *See* getīema.

~full prolific.

~pōl *m.* breeding-pool.

getēama = getīema.

tēar, teagor, *lN.* tæhher *m.* tear; drop, exudation.

~gēotende tear-shedding.

~ian, *lN.* tæherian shed tears.

tēarig tearful, watery (eyes).

~hlēor† weeping.

tēarlic tearful.

tearflian roll *intr.*

tearo = teoro.

teart severe (pain, discipline).

~lic severe.

~līce *av.* severely.

~nes *f.* severity.

~numol efficacious (drug).

tēde *prt. of* tēn.

tege *lW. m.* being fastened; series. *Cp.* tēag.

tel-trēow*, -trēo, -trē *n.* implement of weaving.

tela, ea, teolo I. *av.* well, thorough-

ly; prosperously, beneficially; very. II. *interj.* good !, well !.

teld (*n.*) tent.

teld|sele*, tyldsyle *once m.* tent Gl.

~sticca *m.* tent-peg.

~wyrhta *m.* tent-maker.

geteld *n.* tent.

~gehliwung *f.* tabernacle.

~weorþung *f.* feast of tabernacles.

teldian spread (tent).

teled *occ. ptc. of* tellan.

telg, æ *m.* dye, colour.

~berend what produces a dye.

~(e)dēag *f.* dye, purple Gl.

telg|an, ~ian dye.

~ung *f.* dyeing, dye.

telg|a *m.* branch, bough.

~ian† put forth shoots, flourish *once.*

telgor, ea *mf.* shoot, twig, plant.

telgra *m.* shoot, twig; branch; sucker.

tellan *ptc.* -teald, -teled count, reckon, calculate; consider (a thing to be so-and-so), account : ~ hine gōdne, ~ hit for nāht, tō wīsdōme; think; impute *wda.*; enumerate, state (case); *L.* narrate, say [tæl, talu].

temian tame, subdue [tam].

Temes *f.* Thames [*Lt.* Tamisia].

temes* sieve.

~ian, temsian sift.

tempel, templ *n.* temple [*Lt.* templum].

~geat *n.* temple-gate.

~hālgung *f.* dedication of the Temple.

~lic of a temple Gl.

~geweorc *n.* temple.

templic of a temple Gl.

tempr|ian moderate, regulate; mingle [*Lt.* temperare].

~ung *f.* moderation.

tengan *intr.* hasten, press forwards — ~ on *a.* attack [getang].

getenge *wd.* lying on, close to; occupying (mind); hard-pressing (object of pursuit), afflicting; oppressive (thirst).

tēon, *ptc.* togen 6 draw, drag, pull, tug, *also met.*; *abs.* swīpor ~ be heavier (when weighed in balance); ge- draw (sword); row (boat); make vibrate (strings of harp), play; string (harp), tighten — getogen wamb; bring, put,

take *also met.*; bring up, educate, instruct ‖ *intr.* go, travel *w. cognate a.*

tēon 7, 6 *prt.* tēah, *ptc.* -togen, i accuse *w. a. and g. or sbj.*

tēo|n, *lA.* tēagan, *eN prt.* tīadæ make, create; arrange, institute, ordain; furnish; adorn.

ge~ung*, getīung *f.* preparation.

teofonian† *tr.* join together.

teogopa = tēopa.

getēoh† *n.* R.

teohh *f., m. or n.* race, generation; troop, body of men.

teohh|ian think *w. sbj.*; consider, account : ælc mann ~aþ him (*rfl.*) þæt tō sēlestum gōde þæt þæt hē swīþost lufaþ; determine (on), intend *w. a., sbj., ger.*

ge~ung *f.* arrangement.

teola = tela.

teolian = tilian.

tēon|a *m.,* ~e *f.* injury, suffering; injustice, wrong; insult, contumely; quarrel.

~cwide *m.* abusive language; blasphemy.

~cwidian calumniate.

~full grievous, painful; malicious, hostile; calumnious, abusive, reviling.

~hete† *m.* dire hostility.

~lic hurtful.

~līce *av.* grievously; shamefully.

~lieg† *m.* dire flame (of hell).

~rǣden(n) *f.* injury, wrong.

~smiþ† *m.* evil-doer.

~word *n.* calumny; arrogant word.

tēond *m.* accuser.

tēon|ian irritate; calumniate. *Cp.* tīenan.

~ere *m.* slanderer.

tēontig = hundtēontig hundred.

tēor|ian, ēo† *intr. wd.* fail, not be up to the mark; be tired ‖ *tr.* tire.

ge~igendlic failing, defective.

ge~odnes *f.* exhaustion, fatigue.

(ge)~ung *f.* exhaustion, fatigue.

teoro, teoru *n.,* tier(e)we *f., wk. forms* -tearo, -tare, -tara (*m.*) tar, resin; ear-wax.

teors *m.* membrum virile.

teoso†, e, æ injury; fraud; wickedness, wrong.

~sprǣc *f.* deceitful speech.

teosol, e, *vE.* a *m.* die [*Lt.* tessera].

teoswian*, tesw- injure, annoy.

tēoþian, teogoþ- take tenth part, tithe; give tenth part, pay tithe.

tēoþung f. tenth part; tithe; association of ten men, tithing.

~cēap m. tithes.

~dagas mpl. the thirty-six tithing-days (amounting to a tithe of the year) in Lent.

~ealdor m. chief of ten monks, dean.

~georn sedulous in paying tithes.

~land n. land subject to tithe (?).

~mann m. captain of ten; head of a tithing.

~sceatt m. tithes.

tēoþa, teogoþa tenth [tīen].

geter n. tearing, laceration; tumult, discord Gl.

teran 4 tear, lacerate, bite — mid wordum ~ backbite; be pungent.

tẹrgan = tiẹrgan.

termen m. term, end, fixed date [Lt. terminus].

teter m. ringworm (skin disease).

~wyrt f. celandine.

tēþ pl. of tōþ.

tīadæ prt. of tēon create.

getīung = getēoung.

tīber, ī† fn. sacrifice, offering.

~nes f. slaughter, destruction.

ticcen, y, IN. cg n. kid.

ticia [for *ticca, or i = ī?] m. tick (insect).

tīd f. time, date, period, (bad) times; proper time — on ~e; hour; season (of year); church service at one of the canonical hours; festival, anniversary; tense.

~dæg† m. lifetime.

~fara† m. (?).

~gẹnge periodical.

~lic temporary; opportune; of time.

~lice, tīde- av. temporarily, in this world; conveniently, seasonably; in good time, quickly — þæs ful ~ soon after.

~licnes f. opportunity IN.

~rēn m. seasonable rain.

~sang m. service at one of the canonical hours.

~scēawere m. astrologer Gl.

~scriptor m. chronographer Gl. [Lt. scriptor].

~þegnung f. service at one of the canonical hours.

~weorþung f. service at one of the canonical hours.

~wrītere m. annalist.

---

tīd-ymbwlātend m. astrologer.

tīd|an happen wd.

~ung f. tidings.

tīeder-, tydder-.

~lic frail, weak.

~nes f. frailty, weakness (physical, mental, moral), ill-health, sinfulness.

tīedre, tȳddre, tīdder fragile; weak, frail (bodily, mentally, morally), having bad health; not lasting, fleeting.

tīedrian become weak or infirm; be perishable, decay.

tīefr|an, ~ian paint [tēafor].

~ung f. picture.

tīeg|an tie; connect; ge~ draw — hine onsundran getīgde drew aside [tēag].

~ing f. connexion.

tīeman be pregnant; ~ wiþ a. have sexual intercourse (of male); have (young), breed || w. a. and tō vouch to warranty, prove right to property by referring it to the person from whom it was obtained: tīeme hē (hit) tō þām menn þe him sealde; refer for confirmation (to authority, precedent) abs. w. tō [tēam].

getīema, ēa m. avoucher, surety. See tēam.

getīeme suitable.

getīeme n. team or yoke (of oxen).

tīen ten.

~amber containing ten ambers.

~feald tenfold.

~nihte ten days old.

~strẹnge, ~strẹnged with ten strings.

~wintre ten years old.

tīen|an annoy, irritate; revile, calumniate [tēona].

~end m. annoyer.

tiẹrg|an, ẹ, tyri(g)an, tyrw(i)an irritate, annoy, afflict.

~ing f. zeal (!).

tierw|e = teoro.

~en tarry; resinous.

tife f. bitch.

Tīg = Tīw.

tigel|e f. tile, brick, potsherd [Lt. tegula].

~ærn n. house of brick, brick-kiln (?) Ct.

~en of earthenware.

~fāg† adorned with mosaic.

---

tigel|lēag f. brick-field.

~stān m. tile.

~getæl n. number of bricks.

~geweorc n. brick-making.

~wyrhta m. potter.

tigen ptc. of tēon 6.

tiger tiger [Lt.].

tigrisc of a tiger.

tigþian = tiþian.

tiht m. charge, crime [tēon 6].

~bysig accused, of bad repute.

tihtan, y [confusion w. tyhtan] charge with offence.

tihtl|e f. accusation, charge.

~ian accuse wag.

til I. good in its various meanings, competent, serviceable, morally good — ~e hwīle av. long enough or a long while (?); gentle; liberal. II. n. goodness, kindness.

~frẹmmende doing good.

~lic capable, good.

~līce av. well.

~mōdig noble-minded.

til prp. wd. to of place and met. N.

til|ian, eo wdg., ger., sbj. strive after, intend, attempt; obtain, provide: hī him (rfl.) metes ~odon; w. g. or a. provide for, support: hē wæs fiscere and mid þām cræfte his (rfl.) ~ode; w. g. or d. or a. treat (medically), cure; wa. till land vL.

~ung f. striving after; labour, employment; gain, produce; (medical) treatment, cure, help.

tila = tela.

tilia, -iga m. cultivator of land, labourer.

till† (n.) point, station.

getillan attain, reach; touch.

tilþ, ge~, ~e f. employment, agriculture; gain, produce, crop [tilian].

getīmian wd. impers. happen.

tīm|a m. time, date; proper time wg., opportunity — on ~an, tō ~an in time, soon enough, tō ~an at once; period of time, time (of woman for bearing child), age (of world) — on mīnum ~an in my lifetime; season (of the year); quantity (of syllable).

~lic temporal, earthly.

~līce av. soon.

timber n. timber; edifice; act of building; material.

timber|hrycg *m.* wooded ridge (?) Ct.

~land *n.* timber-land.

~geweorc *n.* cutting timber.

ȝetimbernes *f.* edification *met.* Bd.

timbr|an, ~ian build, construct; edify, instruct; cut timber.

~end *m.* builder.

(ge)~ung *f.* act of building; what is built; edification *met.*

ȝetimbre *n.* edifice.

timpane *f.* timbrel [*Lt.*].

timpestre *f.* female timbrel-player.

timple *once, a.* timplean *f.* an implement of weaving.

tin *n.* tin.

~en of tin.

tinclian tickle.

tind *m.* prong, spike.

~ig, ~iht pronged, spiked.

ȝeting|an† *once* 3 press against *intr. wd.*

~cræft *m.* mechanics.

tinn beam Gl.

tinnan stretch, bend (bow); † R.

tintreg, tinterg *n.,* ~a *m.* torment, torture.

~end *m.* torturer.

~ian, tintrian torment, torture, afflict.

~lic tormenting, of torment.

~stōw *f.* place of torment.

~þegn *m.* torturer, executioner.

~ung *f.* torment, torture.

tīr *m.* glory†; *the Runic letter* t.

~ēadig, ~fæst glorious.

~fruma *m.* source of glory, God.

~lēas inglorious.

~meahtig glorious.

~wine *m.* follower.

titel|ian *wda.* ascribe.

~ung *f.* giving titles *or* headings Gl.

titol superscription [*Lt.* titulus].

titt *m.* teat.

~stricel*, y (*m.*) nipple of breast.

tīþ, ȳ *f.* grant(ing) — ~e fremian grant.

~e, tygþ- *also indecl.* ~a — ~ bēon, weorþan *wg.* have one's request granted, obtain.

~ian, tygþian *wdg. w.d. of thing* grant.

Tīw, tīg *m.* Mars; *the Runic letter* t.

Tīwes|dæg *m.* Tuesday.

~niht *f.* Monday night.

tō I. *prp. w. d.* (*g.*) | *of motion* to, *of rest* at, by, *also met.* | *time:* tō

middre niht, tō dæg(e) to-day, tō seofon nihtum mete for; þæt hit wǣre þrītig þūsend wintra tō þīnum dēaþdæge to | *order*, next to: þū bist se þridda mann tō mē on mīnum rīce; *degree:* fæstan tō ānum mǣle to the extent of taking only one meal a day; in addition to: . . and fela ōþre tō him | *source:* sohton fultum tō him | *result:* ceorfan tō styccum, God gescōp hine tō engle; *aim:* Gode tō lofe | *equivalence, price:* sellan tō miclum weorþe | *definition:* hīe hæfdon him tō gewunan þæt ..; *object of verb:* cweþan tō . ., fōn tō rīce | *to form avs.:* ic secge ēow tō sōþum þæt .. | *to form ger.:* tō cumenne, cumanne, cuman || tō-hwȳ, -hwām, -hwon why. tō þæs, tō þǣm (*or* þon) to that degree, so. tō-þæs-þe until. tō þām .. swā þū oftost mæge as often as you can. tō-þǣm-þæt *result* that *w. indc.:* *purpose* that *w. sbj.* II. *av.* to *of motion:* gang tō, and ārǣr hine !; *addition:* hī habbaþ ēac māre tō || too *w. ajs. and avs.*

tō-ætīec|an increase *tr.* Bd.

~nes *f.* increase Bd.

tō-āmearcian assign (!).

tō·bēadan exalt Gl.

tō·bēatan 1 beat to pieces, break.

tō·beran 4 *tr.* disperse; carry off (*of birds*) || *intr.* separate.

tō·berst|an 3 *intr.* burst asunder, break; break out in sores *in ptc.* tōborsten.

~ung *f.* bursting (*of boil*).

tō·blǣd|an — ~d bēon be inflated (with pride).

tō·blāw|an 1 blow away *or* about (dust); distend, inflate *lit. and fig.*

~ennes *f.* distension.

tō·borstennes *f.* abscess.

tō·brǣd|an *tr.* broaden, enlarge, expand; extend, diffuse; increase || *intr.* spread.

~(ed)nes *f.* extent, breadth Gl.

tō·brecan 4 break (to pieces); destroy, take (city); annul (laws), infringe, break (promise); cut short (sleep). *See* tōbrocen.

tō·bregdan, -brēdan 4 separate with violence, tear to pieces;

destroy, injure | *wi.* shake off (sleep); bacum ~ turn their backs on one another.

tō·brīesan, -ian crush.

tō·brīet|an break to pieces; destroy — ~t contrite.

~ednes *f.* Gl. bruise; trouble.

~endlic Gl. breakable.

~ing *f.* Gl. destruction; contrition.

tō·brocen broken; suffering from eruptions [tōbrecan].

~lic perishable.

tō·ceorfan 3 cut in pieces, cut; cut off.

tō·cēowan 7 chew to pieces, masticate.

tō·cierr|an *intr.* part, go different ways.

tōcir-hūs (!) *n.* inn.

tō·cīnan 6 *intr.* split, crack.

tō·clēofan 7 *tr.* cleave, split, break.

tō clifrian scratch all over.

tō·clip|ian call to, address.

~igendlic (adverb) of address.

ung *f.* address, appeal.

tō·cnāw|an 1 discern, distinguish; understand, know.

~ennes *f.* knowledge.

tō·cnyssan shatter, break.

tō-gecoren(n)es *f. lN.* adoption.

tō·cumende foreign.

tō·cweþan 5 forbid, prohibit.

tō·cwielman torment.

tō·cwies|an crush, break to pieces || *intr.* be crushed.

~ednes *f.* crushed condition.

tō·cyme *m.* approach, arrival.

tō·dæg, ~e *av.* to-day.

tō·dǣl|an divide; divide (in arithmetic) *w.* þurh; distribute, share; disperse; destroy; make difference between, separate; discern, distinguish || *intr.* be different *w.* fram; be separated from one another.

~edlīce *av.* separately.

~(ed)nes *f.* separation; part, division; point of separation, break.

~endlic divisible.

~endlīce *av.* separately, distinctly.

tō·dāl, ǣ *n.* dividing; part, section; dividing-point, division, comma; distribution; dispersion; distinction; discretion; dissension.

tō·dēman judge between, distinguish.

tō·dihtnian dispose.
tō·dōn *tr.* separate; open.
tō·drǣf|an dispel, disperse; expel.
~(ed)nes *f.* dispersion; expulsion.
tō·drēosan 7 fall to pieces, fall away.
tō·drīfan 6 separate, disperse, drive away; dispel, put an end to; destroy.
tō·dwǣscan extinguish (fire).
tō·dwīnan 6 disappear.
tō·ēacan *av., prp. wd.* besides.
tō·emnes *prp. wd.* alongside, on a level with.
tō·endebyrdnes (!) *f.* order Bd.
tō·fær *n.* departure, death *LN.*
tō·faran 2 *intr.* separate, disperse; cease to exist, disappear.
tō·feallan 1 fall to pieces; fall off.
tō·fēran *intr.* separate, disperse.
tō·ferian *tr.* disperse, put off; get rid of (rain); digest.
tō·fesian disperse, rout.
tō·fiellan cause to fall asunder, destroy.
tō·flēon 7 be dispersed.
tō·flēogan 7 *intr.* fly in pieces, be broken, crack.
tō·flēotan 7 *L.* be carried away (by flood).
tō·flōw|an 1 *intr.* flow away or apart; be melted; spread; be separated; be destroyed, come to nothing.
~e(n)dnes *f.* flowing, flux.
tō·foran *prp. w.d.* (*g.*) in front of, before; *of time* before; *of degree, quantity, superiority* above, beyond.
tō·forlǣt|an 1 dismiss.
~ennes *f.* intermission.
toft (*n.*) piece of ground [*Scand.* topt].
tog|ian drag [tēon].
~ung *f.* spasm.
tō·gān, -gangan *intr.* separate; be split or divided; disperse; cease to exist, pass away.
tō·gǣd(e)re *av.* together — ~ cuman, fōn join battle; continuously.
~weard *av.* (go) to meet one another; together.
tōgægnes = tōgēanes.
tō·gǣlan profane.
tō·gǣnan utter.
tō·gang *m.* approach, access.

tō·gēan*, -geægn *prp. wd.* towards *LN.*
tō·gēanes, ē, -gægnes, ę, ea I. *prp. w. d.* (*a.*) towards, to meet; to wait for, against (his coming); to resist, against. II. *av.* in direction of, again — grīpan ~ *abs.*; in return, requital; in reply.
tōgegnes = tōgēanes.
togen *ptc. of* tēon 7, *occ. of* tēon 6.
tōgēnes = tōgēanes.
tō·gengan *intr.* separate.
tō·gēotan 7 diffuse *tr., rfl.*; tō-goten used up, dried up (*of* ointment).
togett|an *intr.* : ~eþ betweox sculdrum there are spasms [togian].
tō·gīnan 6 *intr.* yawn, split, open.
tō·glīdan 6 glide or slip or flow away; collapse; disappear, cease to exist.
tō·gotennes *f.* diffusion [tōgēotan].
toh-, *see* togian.
~line *f.* tow-line.
tōh, ~lic, tōlic tough; glutinous.
~lice *av.* tenaciously Gl.
~nes *f.* toughness.
tō·haccian hack to pieces.
tō·heald leaning, inclined.
tō·hēawan 1 cut to pieces.
tō·hīgung *f. LN.* affectus, effectus.
tō·hladan† 2 *intr.* disperse.
tō·hlēotan 7 divide by lot.
tō·hlīdan 6 *intr.* open, split, crack
tō·hlystend *m.* listener.
tō·gehlytto *f* fellowship *LN.*
tō·hnęscian *intr.* soften away.
tō·hop|a *m.*, ~ung *f.* hope, expectation.
tō·hrēosan 7 fall to pieces, collapse, decay.
tō·hrēran shake to pieces, destroy.
tō·hrīcian cut, separate Gl.
getoht† *n.* battle.
tohte† *f.* battle, war.
tō·hwega *av., n. wg.* a little — ~ eles some oil.
tō·hweorfan 3 *intr.* separate, disperse.
tō·hyht† *m.* hope, what cheers.
tō·geīecendlic adjectival.
tō·iecnes *f.* increase Bd.
tō·geīehtnes *f.* addition [īecan].
tō·iernan 3 run about.

tō·iernende approaching.
tōl *n.* tool, instrument, *coll.* apparatus.
tō·lǣt|an 1 b *tr.* relax; *intr.* relax self-control.
~ennes *f.* abandonment, despair.
tolc|ian.
~endlice *av.* wantonly, luxuriously
tolcett|an be luxuriant, wanton.
~ung*, tolgetung *f.* incitement.
tolgetung, *see* tolcettan.
tōlic = tōhlic.
tō·licgan 5 *intr.* divide, diverge; extend (*of* boundaries) ‖ *tr.* divide, separate.
tō·lies|an loosen, undo; separate relax, relieve (pain); weaken destroy, put an end to.
~(ed)nes *f.* dispersion; destruction death.
~end *m.* destroyer.
~endlic destructive.
~ing *f.* destruction; redemption *LN*
tō·lipian dismember, disjoint.
toll *n.* tax, toll; toll-rights; freedom from toll; money due for rent, passage-money, fare, &c. tax-gathering, toll-house.
~ere *m.* tax-gatherer.
~frēo exempt from toll.
~scamol *m.* toll-seat, custom house.
~scīr *f.* business or district of tax gatherer.
~setl = ~scamol.
toln *f.*, (*n.*) toll.
~ere *m.* tax-gatherer.
tō·lūcan 7 pull asunder, dislocate destroy.
tōm† free from *wg.*
tō·mearc|ian distinguish; enumerate, describe.
~odnes *f.* enumeration.
tō·meldian*, (hē) tōmǣldeþ *once* destroy (peace) by tale-bearing.
tō·middes *prp. wd.* in the midst of.
tonian thunder Gl.
tō·nam|a *m.* cognomen, nickname
~ian give cognomen to.
tō·nemnan distinguish (by name)
tō·niman 4 divide; take away.
topp *m.* summit; whipping-top (plaything) (?).
tor-begīete*, -gete difficult to get.

tor-cierre hard to convert.
torcul wine-press *lM.* [*Lt.* tor-
cular].
tord *n.* piece of dung.
~wifel *m.* dung-beetle.
toren-īege blear-eyed.
tō·rendan tear asunder.
torf|ian throw ; pelt, stone.
~ung *f.* throwing ; stoning.
torht(†) bright ; beautiful ; illustrious.
~e *av.* (sound) clearly ; beautifully.
~ian make clear, show.
~lic glorious.
~līce *av.* splendidly.
~mōd glorious, illustrious.
~nes *f.* glory.
tō·rīepan scratch all over.
tō·rinnan 3 *intr.* disperse (*of*
water).
torn(†) I. *m.* anger, indignation ;
grief. II. *aj.* grievous.
~cwide† *m.* bitter speech.
~e† *av.* with indignation *or* grief :
mē is ~ I am grieved.
~lic† grievous, bitter.
~mōd† angry.
~gemōt† *n.* hostile meeting.
~geniþla† *m.* fierce enemy.
~sorg† *f.* anxious care.
~word† *n.* bitter word.
~wracu† *f.* grievous persecution.
~wyrdan address angrily, vitu-
perate.
torr *m.* tower ; rock, tor [*Lt.* tur-
ris].
tō·sǣlan *impers. wdg.* lack, fail in :
him tōsǣleþ þæs.
tō·samn|e *av.* together — ~ cuman
join battle.
~ian assemble, bring together Bd.
tō·sāwan 1 *tr.* disperse ; dissemi-
nate (doctrine).
tosc|a, ~e (?) *m., f.* (?) frog.
tō·scacan 2 *tr.* shake, disturb ; disperse ; get rid of (disease).
tō·scād, ēa *n.* discrimination ; distinction ; difference, diversity.
tō·scād|an, ēa 1b, *also prt.* ~de
divide, separate, *also met.* ; disperse, *also met.* ; make a distinction, make distinct ; discriminate,
discern ; decide, judge ; dispose,
appoint *lN.* ; expound *lN.* ‖ *intr.*
differ.
~end *m.* separator Gl.
~ennes *f.* separation ; distinction.

tōge·scādan*, ēa 1 *lN.* expound.
tō·scænan *tr.* break to pieces.
tō·scēacerian devastate, scatter.
tō·scēotan 7 *intr.* disperse.
tō·scierian *tr.* separate, divide Gl.
tō·sciftan *L. tr.* divide (troops).
tō·scrīpan 6 *intr.* disperse (*of*
water).
tō·scūfan 7 *tr.* disperse ; do away
with (sins).
tō·sendan *tr.* disperse ; destroy
once.
tō·sēoþan 7 boil to pieces.
tō·settan (!) dispose.
to·sēpan discriminate truth of,
prove.
tō·sīgan 6 fall to pieces, be worn
out (*of* clothes).
tō·sittan 5 be separated.
tō·slacian be remiss.
tō·slēan 2 break ; demolish ; drive
away (thoughts).
tō·slīfan 6 *tr.* split.
tō·slītan 6 tear to pieces, break,
lacerate, bite (*of* snake) — *ptc.*
tōsliten serrated (leaf) ; sever,
separate ; destroy, dissipate ‖ *intr.*
be different *lN.*
tō·slitnes *f.* laceration ; dissension.
tō·slūp|an 7 be loosened, relaxed,
untied (*of* bonds), *also met.* ; be
paralysed, be destroyed *or* dissi-
pated.
~ing *f.* dissolution (of life) Gl.
tō·smēagan investigate.
tō·snīþan 6 cut, cut up, cut off.
tō·sōc|nes, ~nung *f.* seeking, ac-
quisition *lN.*
tō·sprǣc *f.* address, conversation.
tō·sprǣdan *tr.* spread out, expand.
tō·springan 3 *intr.* break to pieces :
burst open ; crack, be chapped (*of*
hands).
tō·sprytting instigation *vL.*
tō·standan 2 be distant ; differ ;
be delayed, not be forthcoming.
tō·stencan *tr.* disperse ; dissipate,
destroy ‖ *intr.* perish *once.*
~(ed)nes *f.* dispersion, destruction.
~end *m.* prodigal.
tō·stician stab severely.
tō stincan 3 distinguish by smell.
tō·stingan 3 pierce, perforate.
tō·stregdan, -strēdan 3 ; -streg-
dan, -strēdan *wk. tr.* scatter ;
destroy ‖ *intr.* be scattered.
tō·sundrian *tr.* separate.

tō·swāpan 1 *tr.* disperse (flame).
tō·swellan 3 *intr.* swell.
tō·swengan disperse (flame).
tō·sweorcan 3 become dark.
tō·swīfan 6 *intr.* separate.
tō·syndr(i)an *tr.* separate ; distinguish.
tot-rida *m.* swing (?), see-saw (?)
Gl.
getot *n.* pride, pomp.
tōtian peep out, protrude.
tō-talu *f.* reputation *lN.*
tō·tellan distinguish.
tō·tēon 7 pull to pieces ; pull
away ; destroy.
tō·teran 4 tear to pieces ; destroy ;
harass (mind).
tō·torfian throw about.
tō·trǣglian pull to pieces *or* off
Gl.
tō·tredan 4 tread to pieces (?) Gl.
tō·twǣm|an *tr.* divide, separate ;
set at variance ; scatter ; do away
with ; discern.
~ednes *f.* disassociation, separation.
tō·tyhting *f.* instigation *vL.*
tōþ, *pl.* tēþ, toeþ *and* tōþas *m*
tooth, tusk.
~ece *m.* toothache.
~gār *m.* toothpick.
~lēas toothless.
~mægen† *n.* strength of tusks.
~rima *m.* gum.
~sealf *f.* tooth-paste.
~sticca *m.* toothpick.
~wærc, ~wræc *m.* toothache.
~wyrm *m.* worm in tooth.
tō·pegnung (!) *f.* administration.
tō·þen|ian.
~ednes *f* distension.
tō·geþēod(e)d adjacent Bd. ; adhering Gl.
tō·þerscan 3 beat to pieces.
tō·þindan 3 *intr.* swell ; be arrogant.
tō·þringan 3 *tr.* press asunder, disperse.
tōþunden|nes *f.* swollenness ;
arrogance [tōþindan].
~līce *av.* arrogantly.
tō·þuniende (!) astonishing.
tow.
~cræft *m.* skill in weaving *or*
spinning, spinning.
~hūs *n.* spinning-house Gl.
~lic of weaving Gl.

tow|myderce f. chest (?) Ct.

~tōl n. spinning implement.

tō-weard, a, o, e I. aj. facing; approaching | future, is to come or happen, coming; imminent. II. av., sometimes used where we should expect the aj. approaching; future, imminent. III. prp. w. g., d. towards. Often tmesis: tō þǣre sunnan weard.

~es av., prp. wd. towards. Gen. follows its word.

~lic future.

~līce av. in the future.

~nes f. future; future coming.

tō·weccan† stir up (strife).

tō·wegan 5 tr. disperse.

tō-gewegen applied Bd.

tō·wendan overthrow; demolish, destroy; abrogate (law).

tō·weorp|an 3 scatter, disperse, also met.; throw; break; pull down, demolish; destroy, abrogate, put an end to.

~endlic*, y destructible.

tō·wesnes, -wesennes, -wisnes f. separation; discord, dissension.

tō·wiþere†, -wiþre prp. w. a., d. against; in answer to.

tō·worpennes,-worpnes,-ednes, lN. -wyrp- f. dispersion; destruction; lN. expulsion [tōweorpan].

tō·wrecan 5 tr. disperse.

tō·writennes f. description, enumeration.

tō·wrīþan (!) 6 distort.

tō-wyrd f. occasion Bd.

trǣf n. tent; †building.

trǣglian pluck.

trǣppe*, e f. trap.

trāg† I. f. affliction, evil. II. aj. bad.

~e† av. evilly, cruelly.

traht mf. text, passage (in Scripture); commentary, exposition [Lt. tractus].

~bōc f. commentary.

traht|ian, trahtnian expound, explain; w. be discuss, treat of.

~ere m. commentator, expounder, interpreter.

~ung f. exposition.

trahtaþ m. commentary.

traisc tragic Bd. [Lt.].

tramet m. page (of book).

trandende precipitous, steep Gl.

getrēagian sew together.

tred|an 4 intr. tread || tr. tread down, trample, also fig.; walk over, traverse.

~end m. treader Gl.

treddan trample; investigate [tredan].

treddian intr. tread, walk.

trede [e = ǣ?]† once firm to tread on (of sea).

tredel m. step (to mount by).

treg|a (†) m. grief; affliction.

~ian tr. grieve; afflict, oppress.

trehing (?) m. third part of a shire, Riding. Cp. þrihing.

trem = trym footstep.

tremes = trimes.

trendel m. ring, circle.

trendl|ian — ~ed made round.

trēow, A. trē(o) n. tree; forest, wood; wood (material); gallows, the cross.

~cynn n. kind of tree.

~fēging f. boarding.

~fugol m. tree-bird.

~steall, ~stede m. plantation.

~teoro n. resin.

~wæstm m. vL. fruit of trees.

~geweorc n. wooden structure.

~weorþung f. tree-worship.

~gewrid n. thicket.

~wyrhta m. carpenter.

~wyrm m. caterpillar.

trēow, ȳ sometimes in pl. w. sg. meaning f. truth (to promise), faith: ~e healdan, habban keep faith; fidelity, loyalty; grace, favour; engagement, agreement; trust, belief.

~fæst faithful.

ge~fæstnian be faithful lN.

ge-full faithful.

ge-fullīce av. faithfully.

(ge)~lēas faithless; infidel.

(ge)~lēasnes f. faithlessness; unbelief, heresy.

ge~lic faithful.

(ge)~līce av. faithfully.

~loga m. traitor.

~lufu† f. faithful love.

~rǣden(n) f. fidelity.

~geþofta† m. trusty companion.

~þrāg† f. R.

trēowan = trīewan.

trēowian = trūwian.

trēowa = trūwa.

getrēowe = getrīewe.

trēowen, i, ȳ wooden; of a tree.

trēowsian, ȳ pledge oneself w. wiþ a. | rfl. pledge oneself w. wiþ a.; clear oneself = trīewan.

(ge)trēowþ, ie f., often in pl. w. sg. meaning good faith; fidelity; agreement, covenant, terms (of capitulation).

treppan*, (hē) trepeþ once tread lK Gl.

treppe = *trǣppe trap.

getricce once wd. contented with, adhering to (regulations) [i = y? Cp. getryccan].

trīew|an, ēo trust in w. d., on d.; make credible; ge- persuade, suggest lN. | rfl. clear oneself (of accusation) wg. [trēow].

~nes f. what is trusted in, protection.

(ge)trīewe, ēo faithful, trusty, honest.

trifol|ian pound, grind [Lt. tribulare].

~ung f. pounding.

trifot, -et tribute [Lt. tributum].

trimes, try-, tre-, pl. vE. trimsas, y mf.; trymesse f.; þrims, y a weight (drachm?); coin; a coin of the value of threepence [lLt. tremissis, tremisia].

trind|e f. round lump.

~hyrst m. circular copse (?) Ct.

triwen = trēowen.

trod n., ~u f. track [tredan].

trog m. trough; wooden vessel, canoe, cradle.

~hrycg m. Ct.

~scip n. canoe.

tropere m. trope-book (a Church-service book) [Lt. troparium].

trūcian fail (in doing something); be wanting, run short; wd. not be true, faithful.

trūgian = trūwian.

truht trout Gl. [Lt. tructa].

trum firm; substantial, strong; healthy; able to resist w. wiþ; steadfast.

~lic firm; substantial, stable, hortatory Bd.

~līce av. firmly; steadfastly.

~nes f. firmness; firmament; health; confirmation, support.

getrum n. troop; multitude.

trum|ian recover (from illness); ge- make strong Gl.

~ing f. recovery (from illness).

truma *m.* troop, legion; array, regular order (of troops).
getruma *m.* troop, regiment.
trumaþ *m.* strengthening.
trūþ *m.* trumpeter; buffoon.
~horn *m.* trumpet.
trūwa, ge-, ēo, ȳ, trūa *m.* (good) faith; confidence, faith; word (of honour), covenant; protection.
trūw|ian, ēo, ȳ, *A.* trūgian trust in (person) *w. d.*, on *a.*; *wda.* entrust *IN.*; trust in (thing) *w. g.*, be *d.*, tō *d.*; believe (confidently) *w. sbj.*; be true to *wd.* | gemake treaty; plot | *rfl.* clear oneself = trīewan.
ge-ung *f.* confidence, trust.
getryccan trust *IN.* *Cp.* getricce.
trymt, e — fōtes ~ *av.* a foot's length.
getrymt *once* (*n.*) firmament.
trymendlic = trymmendlic.
trymenes = trymnes.
trymes = trimes.
trymman, trym(m)ian make strong, build strongly; arrange, array (troops), *also met.*; encourage, exhort; confirm (agreement), corroborate; give (hostages) | ge- *rfl. wg.* recover from (illness) Bd. [trum].
trymmend *m.* encourager; party to an agreement.
~lic, trymendlic hortatory.
trymming *f.* strengthening; foundation (of house); confirmation, edification, edifying matter.
trymnes, trymenes, ge- *f.* firmness; firmament; prop, *also met.*; ge- arraying (army); confirmation; exhortation.
trymþ *f.* firmness, support.
tryndel = trendel wheel.
tryndled (dress) ornamented with wheel-shaped pattern (?) [trendel].
trȳw = trēow.
trȳwa = trūwa.
trȳwen = trēowen.
tū, *see* twēgen.
tūcian adorn ‖ ill-treat, *gen. w.* defining tō : ~ tō scame, ~ tō iermþe.
tūddor, tūdor *n.* progeny; fruit.
~fæst prolific.
~fōstor *m.* nourishment of offspring.

tūddor|full prolific.
~spēdt *f.* abundance of progeny.
~tēondet producing progeny.
tulg — under tungan ~e root of tongue.
tumb|ian dance, tumble.
~ere *m.* dancer, tumbler.
tūn *m.* enclosure round house, yard, garden; manor, estate, farm — ~es mann man living on a manor; village; town; dwelling, *coll.* the world: lenctentīma gæþ tō ~e on vii. id. febr. comes, falls.
~gebūr *m.* inhabitant Gl.
~cerse, æ *f.*, ~cressa *m.* nasturtium.
~cirice *f.* church in a tūn.
~incel *n.* small farm *or* estate.
~land *n.* land of estate.
~lic rustic Gl.
~mann *m.* man belonging to a tūn.
~melde *f.* orach (plant).
~minte *f.* garden mint.
~prēost *m.* village priest.
~ræd *m.* municipality.
~gerēfa *m.* bailiff.
~scipe *m.* inhabitants of a tūn.
~scir *f.* stewardship.
~steall *m.* farmstead (?) Ct.
~stede *m.* village.
~weg *m.* private road.
tunec|e *f.* tunic, coat [*Lt.* tunica].
ge-od in a tunic Gl.
tung|e *f.* tongue; anything tongue-shaped; speaking, speech; language.
~full loquacious.
~eþrum ligament of the tongue.
~wōd abusive Gl.
tungl|en of the stars.
~ere *m.* astronomer, astrologer.
tungol *n.* heavenly body, star; constellation.
~æ *f.* astronomy.
~bǣre starry.
tungolcrǣft *m.* astronomy, astrology.
~iga, -crǣfta astronomer, astrologer.
~wise *f.* astronomy Gl.
tungol|gimmt *m.* star.
~gescēad *n.* astronomy, astrology.
~witega *m.* astrologer.
tuning-wyrt = tunsing-.
tunne *f.* cask.
~botm *m.* bottom of cask Gl.
tunsing-wyrt, tuning- *f.* white hellebore.

tūr *m. vL., IN.* tower [*Fr.*].
turf *f., g.* tyrf turf.
~haga† *m.* grassy enclosure.
~hlēow *n.* turf-shelter (?) Ct.
turl (*f.*) ladle [*Lt.* trulla].
turn|ian *intr.* turn, revolve; be giddy. *Cp.* tyrnan [*Fr.*].
~igendlic revolving.
~ung *f.* rotation.
turtl|e *f.*, ~a *m.*, turtur *m.*, ~e *f.* turtle-dove [*Lt.* turtur].
tūsc, tūx, twū- *m.* canine *or* molar tooth; tusk.
~el, tūxl *m.* canine *or* molar tooth.
tuwa = twiwa.
tūx = tūsc.
twā, tū I. *nf.* two, *see* twēgen.
II. *av.* twice.
~dæglic = twi- lasting two days Bd. *See* twi-.
~lic double.
~nihte two days' old (moon).
twǣde *aj., av. = n.* two-thirds: dō (put in) þæs meluwes ~ and þæs sealtes þriddan dæl, se cyning āh twǣdne dæl weres.
getwǣfan *wag.* separate from; deprive; prevent | *wa.* put an end to (fighting).
twǣm *d. of* twēgen.
twǣm|an separate, part; put an end to (strife) ‖ *intr.* part *w.* fram *d.*
~endlice *av.* separately.
~ing *f.* separation; distinction.
twǣm *d. of* twēgen.
twēgen, ēt, *fem. and neut.* twā, *neut.* tū; *g.* twēga, twēgra; *d.* twǣm, ā two. on twā (cut) in two, apart. twām and twām *av.* by twos, two and two. ōþer twēga either, *see* ōþer. *See* twā.
twelf twelve.
~feald twelvefold.
~gilde to be restored twelvefold.
~hynd|e (person) whose wergield was 1,200 shillings; (wergield) of a person of that rank | *used as a noun in* ~es mann = ~ mann.
~nihte twelve days old (moon).
~wintre twelve years old.
twelfta twelfth.
twelftig = hund·twelftig.
twengan pinch, squeeze.
twentig twenty [twēgen, -tig].
~feald twenty-fold.
~oþa twentieth.

twentig-wintre twenty years old.
tweo- = **twi-**.
twēo, ȳ *m.* doubt ; hesitation, delay.
~**lic** doubtful, uncertain ; ambiguous.
~**līce** *av.* dubiously ; ambiguously.
twēon = **twēogan.**
twēog|an, twēon doubt *wg., impers. wag.* : hē twēoþ þæs, hine twēoþ þæs.
~**endlic** doubting ; doubtful.
~**endlīce, twīend-** *av.* doubtingly.
~**ung, twēoung** *f.* doubt.
twēon, ȳ (*m.*) doubt.
twēon|ian, ȳ doubt *wg., impers. w. a. or d. and g.*
~**igend** *m.* doubter.
~**igendlic** dubitative (adverb).
~**eleoht,** *see* **twēonol.**
~**ol** doubtful — ~**leoht, twēone-leoht** twilight Gl.
~**ung** *f.* doubt.
twēonum — be . . ~ *wd.* between : be sǣm ~. *See* **betwēonan.**
twi-, y, eo two-.
twi-bēte requiring double compensation.
twi-bill *n.* two-edged axe.
twi-bleoh, *pl.* -**blēo,** twice-dyed.
twi-browen twice-brewed.
twicc|ian pluck, gather (fruit) ; twitch.
~**ere** *m.* carver.
twicen, ~e *f.* place where two roads meet.
twi-dæglic, twā- lasting two days.
twi-dǣl *m.* two-thirds.
~**an** *tr.* divide in two ; *intr.* differ Gl.
twi-ęcge (de), two-edged.
twiendlīce = **twēogendlīce.**
twi-feald twofold, double ; ambiguous.
~**an** double.
ge~ian *tr.* double ; multiply, increase.
~**lic** double.
~**līce** *av.* doubly.
~**nes** *f.* duplicity.
twi-fēr|e accessible by two ways Gl.
~**lǣcan** dissociate Gl.
twi-fēte two-footed.
twi-fięldan double.
twi-fingre two fingers thick.
twi-fiþerede, -fe- forked (?) Gl.
twi-fȳrede two-furrowed Gl.

twig, *pl.* ~**u,** *n., once gpl.* ~**ena** twig, branch, stalk (of nettle).
twiga = **twiwa.**
twi-gǣrede cloven.
twi-gilde *n.* double payment, *or av.* with double payment.
twih —†**mid** unc ~ between us two. *Cp.* **twēonum.**
twi-hēafdode two-headed.
twi-heolor *f.* a balance.
twi-hīw|e of two forms ; of two colours.
~**ian** dissimulate.
twi-hlidede having two lids.
twi-hwēole two-wheeled.
twi-hwyrft *m.* double period Gl.
twi-hynde (person) whose wergield was 200 shillings ; (wergield) paid for a person of such rank [hund].
twi-icce *lKt.* = -**ęcge.**
twi-lǣpped having two skirts.
twi-lafte two-edged (axe) Gl.
twili double, woven with double thread.
~**brocen** (*of* woman's cyrtel) Ct.
twin-wyrm *m.* an insect Gl.
twin *n.* linen.
~**en** of linen.
twinclian twinkle.
twi-nębbe having two faces.
twi-nihte two days old.
twinihte*, *see* **twynihte.**
twinn, ge- double.
getwinn *m.* twin — ~**as** twins, triplets.
getwinnes *f.* junction.
twi-rǣd|e irresolute, un-unanimous.
~**nes** *f.* discord ; sedition.
getwis (brothers) having the same parents.
~**a** *m.* twin.
twi-sceatte *av.* to the extent of a double payment.
twi-scyldig liable to a double penalty.
twi-seht discordant.
~**nes** *f.* dissension.
twisel-tōþe having forked *or* double teeth.
twisl|a *m.* fork of a river.
~**ed** forked.
~**ian** *intr.* fork, branch off (*of* roads).
~**iht** forked.
~**ung** *f.* partition.
twi-snæcce cloven.
twi-snǣse cloven.

twi-sprǣc *f.* insincerity ; detraction.
~**e** insincere ; detracting.
~**nes** *f.* insincerity ; detraction.
twi-sprecan 5 murmur *IN.*
twi-spunnen double-spun.
twi-stręnge two-stringed.
twi-tęlged double-dyed.
twi-þrāwen double-twisted.
twiwa, eo, u, tu(w)a, twi(g)a *av.* twice.
twi-wǣg *f.* pair of scales Gl.
twi-weg *m.* meeting of two roads.
twi-winter period of two years Gl.
twi-wintre of two years.
twi-wyrdig contradictory, discordant [word].
twūsc, twūx = **tūsc.**
twuwa = **twiwa.**
twȳ = **twēo.**
twȳn = **twēon.**
twȳnian = **twēonian.**
twynihte *f.* — **māre** ~ a plant.
tȳn, *prt.* **tȳd(d)e** educate, train.
getȳd *ptc. of* **tȳn.**
~**nes** *f.* learning, skill.
tȳdr|an, tȳddr(i)an *tr.* bring forth (young, fruit), breed ; rear ; cultivate [tūdor].
~**ed** provided with offspring.
~**iend** *m.* propagator, producer.
~**ung** *f.* propagation ; ! branch.
tyge *m.* pull, dragging ; conducting, diverting (course of water) ; draught (of drink), deduction ; matter (of statement) [tēon].
~**hōc** *m.* hook to pull with.
~**horn** *m.* cupping-glass.
tygel (*m.*) trace (of harness).
tygþian = **tīþian.**
tyht *m.* training ; habit, way (of life) ; movement, march [tēon].
tyht|an incite, persuade *w.* on *a.,* tō *d.* ; suggest, bring to the mind ; educate, teach.
~**end** *m.* instigator.
~**endlic** hortative.
~**ere** *m.* instigator.
~**ing** *f.* incitement, persuasion, allurement.
~**nes** *f.* instigation.
tyhten(n) *f.* incitement.
tyld-syle = **teld-sęle** tent.
tylg *av. cpv.* used also as *aj.* more willingly ; hē wæs tilg better (in health) ; on the contrary, rather

[178]

| *spv.* ~est, ~ost best; chiefly, most.
tȳnan fence, enclose; shut, close [tūn].
tyncen *once* (*n.*) barrel (?); bladder (?) [tunne?].
tynder, tyndre *f.* tinder.
~cynn *n.* combustibles.
tyndre = tynder.

getȳne *n.* court.
getyng|e, t- eloquent, fluent [tunge].
~līc eloquent.
~līce *av.* eloquently.
~nes *f.* eloquence.
tyrdel *n.* piece of dung [tord].
tyrn|an *tr., intr.* turn, revolve. *Cp.* turnian [*Lt.* tornare].

tyrn|geat *n.* turnstile.
~ing *f.* revolving; roundness.
tyrw(i)an = tiergan.
tysca *m.* buzzard.
tysl|ian *rfl.* dress: gē ~iaþ ēow on Denisc adopt Danish fashions.
~ung *f.* style of dress.
tȳtan† *once* appear, shine (*of* stars).

Þ.

ÞĀ   ÞÆRRIHTE   ÞAFUNG

þā *av., cj.* then, thereupon; when — *correl.* þā . . þā when . . (then); *non-temporal* then, and; *causal* since | þāþā when – *correl.* þāþā . . þā when . . (then); *causal* since | þā-þe when *rel.*
þā, *see* se.
pac|a *m.* roof.
~ian thatch.
paccian *tr.* pat, flap.
þæc *n.* roof, thatch.
~tigele *f.* roof-tile.
þæcele *f.* torch. *Cp.* fæcele.
þæder = þider.
geþæf *wg.* consenting to [þafian].
þæge, þāge *nW. no.* these, they.
þǣm *d. of* se.
þǣnan moisten. *Cp.* þwǣnan. [þān.]
þǣnian = þānian.
þæne = þone *a. of* se.
þænne – þonne.
þǣr, ā, þāra I. *av., cj.* there, thither; *rel.* where, whither — *correl.* þǣr . . þǣr where (whither) . . there (thither) | *indf.* there: þǣr cōmon six scipu. *often w. rel. pronoun:* se dǣl þe þǣr onweg cōm | in that case, then | *of time* then | because, since || þǣr-þǣr *rel.* where, in whatever direction; when. II. = *no. when combined with prps. and the av.* bī = be: ~æfter after that; ~bī g) thereby; ~nīehst next to that. *Also w. the place avs.* inne, ūte: ~inne, ~ūte inside, outside.

þǣr·riht|e, ~es *av.* immediately.
þǣra = þāra.
þǣre, *see* se.
þærscwald = þerscold.
þǣs I. *g. of* se. II. *av.* after: raþe ~, ~ ymb þrēo niht; †so: þū wurde ~ gewitlēas þæt . . || þæs-þe *av.* the *w. cpv.:* hī clipodon ~ mā | *cj.* after: sōna ~ hīe cōmon; in proportion as, as far as, according as, as: ~ wē mihton, ~ bēo secgaþ; because, that: wā mē ~ ic swīgode (þæs *governed by* wā).
þæs-lǣcan suit, agree.
þæslic, ge- suitable, fit; not conflicting, harmonious (testimony); elegant, beautiful.
~nes *f.* fitness.
þæslīce *av.* so; suitably.
þæsma *m.* leaven.
þæt, a I. *neut. of* se. II. *av. sequence* then, *esp. in enumerating boundaries in charters:* andlang Temese, þæt (*or* þonne) ūp on Lygean. III. þæt, þætte = þæt þe [*see* þe] *cj.* that — *correl.* þæt (*no.*) . . þæt (*cj.*): ic þæt wāt þæt hē ūs gescildeþ, þæs wēnan þæt . .; so that *of result w. indc., sbj.*; in order that *w. sbj.*; *rarely* because.
þætte [*from* þæt þe] I. *no.* which; that which: dō ā ~ duge! II. *cj* = þæt that; so that; in order that.
þafian, a†, *w. a., d.* consent to,

permit, tolerate; *wa.* endure, suffer.
(ge)þafung *f.* consent.
geþafa *m* supporter, helper | ~ bēon *wg.* assent to; be convinced.
geþafsum consenting *LN.* [geþæf].
~nes *f.* consent *LN.*
þafet|an.
~ere *m.* one who is too indulgent to wrong-doers, condoner.
þāge = þǣge.
þā·gīet, *see* gīet.
þāh *prt. of* þicgan, þēon.
þām *d. of* se.
þan = þon; *occ.* = þām.
þan I. moist, irrigated (land). II. *n.* irrigated land. *Cp.* þawenian. [þīnan.]
~ian, ǣ be *or* become moist.
þanc *m.* thought; favour, grace — †~e graciously; pleasure, satisfaction, *esp. in* on ~(e), tō ~es pleasant, to (his) delight; thanks; will *esp. in g.:* ~es voluntarily, mīnes ~es through me, of my own accord, Godes ~es by God's will (*or* grace).
~full thoughtful; spirited; pleasing· grateful; contented.
~fullīce *av.* gratefully.
~hycgende† thoughtful.
~metian† *once* think, deliberate.
~metung, -meo- *f.* deliberation.
~snotor† wise.
~wierþe, ~weorþ(līc) acceptable, pleasing; memorable.
~weorþlīce *av.* gratefully.

þanc-word† *n.* thanks.
geþanc *mn.* mind; thought.
þanc|ian *wdg.* thank; requite | *wi.* rejoice in Gl.
~ung *f.* thanksgiving, thanks; gratitude.
þancol thoughtful; sagacious.
~mōd thoughtful; sagacious.
geþancol thoughtful; sagacious; desirous; *lN.* suppliant.
þane = þone, *a. of* se.
þanne = þonne.
þanon, ~e, þonan *av.* thence *motion, extension*; *time* after that; *origin* thence; because of that | *rel.* whence; *origin* whence | ~ þe *rel.* whence—*correl.* ~ þe (*rel.*) . . ~ (*dem.*).
~forþ *av.* thenceforth.
~weard departing.
þār(a) = þǣr.
þāre = þǣre.
þās, *see* þes.
þat = þæt.
þāwian *tr.* thaw.
þawen|ian *once,* *ptc.* ge~ed moisten.
þe, þi, þy *av.* *weak form of* þȳ ‖ *w. cpv.* the, any ‖ *gives rel. meaning to other words*: þe ic I who; wē, þe ūs befæst is . . to whom; sē þe he who, who: þanon þe whence | = *indecl. rel. pro., gen. nom. but also = other cases*: þǣm īglonde þe mon þæt folc Mandras hǣtt of which. *w. separated prp.* : þǣre rōde dǣl þe Crīst on þrowode | *rel. cj.* that, &c.: ēac wæs þæt (*no.*) þe stōd . . there stood . . [*hence* þætte, *which see*]; hit is þǣm gelīcost þe ic sitte on ānre dūne as if; þȳ gēare þe . . when; betera þe than [= þonne]; þēah þe although (*without modifying the meaning of* þēah) ‖ or : is hit ālȳfed, þe nā? — þe . . þe *whether* . . or *referring back to some other word*: hwider hē gelǣded sȳ, þe tō wīte, þe tō wuldre.
þēah, þēh *av.* however, yet ‖ þēah, þēah-þe *cj. w. sbj.* although ; if; that: nis ēac nān wundor, þēah ūs mislimpe | *correl.* þēah (þe) . . þēah although . . yet.
þēah·hwæþere *av.* however, yet.
þēah = þāh, *prt. of* þicgan, þēon.

þeaht *f.* advice; plan, policy.
þeaht *ptc. of* þeccan.
geþeaht *nf.* thought, device, counsel, resolution, plan; advice; assembly, council.
þeaht|ian consider, form plan; take counsel, deliberate.
(ge)~end, (ge)~ere *m.* counsellor.
ge~endlic deliberative.
~ung *f.* consultation.
geþeahta *m.* counsellor.
þēana, *see* swā·þēana.
þeara = þāra.
þearf *f.* need, want, necessity; what is needed; duty, employment; advantage, benefit — tō ~e usefully, profitably; trouble, hardship.
~lēas without having cause; without achieving result.
~lēase *av.* needlessly.
~lic useful, profitable *wd.* ; necessary Gl.
~līce *av.* profitably, to good purpose.
~licnes *f.* poverty.
þearf *vb.*, *pl.* þurfon, *prt.* þorfte, *prs.ptc.* ~ende, þy-, *lN.* þo- be in want, be poor; *w.g., a.* require, need; *w. inf.* require, be under obligation *or* constraint | *wda.* owe.
þearf|ian be indigent | †him swā ge~od wæs the necessity was imposed on them.
~ednes *f.* poverty.
þearfa I. *aj. wg.* destitute. II. *m.* poor man, pauper.
þearfend|e in want.
~lic poor, (life) of poverty; scanty, insufficient.
þearl strict (judge); severe (illness), excessive.
~e *av.* severely; excessively, very.
~lic severe, painful.
~līce *av.* sternly, severely; violently.
~mōd† severe, stern, fierce.
~wis severe, stern, fierce.
~wislic severe, painful.
~wislīce *av.* severely, strictly.
~wisnes *f.* severity, strictness.
þearm *m.* entrail.
~gyrd, ~gyrdel *m.* girth.
~gewind, ~wind *n.* intestines (?).
þēaw *m.* custom, habit, usage | *pl.* ~as conduct; virtue.

þēaw|fæst moral, virtuous; gentle, kind.
~fæstlīce *av.* speak (correctly).
~fæstnes *f.* morality, discipline.
~full moral, virtuous.
~lēas without morality, ill-conditioned.
~lic customary; moral; figurative Gl.
~līce *av.* properly.
geþēawod mannered — wel ~ virtuous, wīslīce ~ prudent, wise.
þec *a. of* þū.
þecc|an, *prt.* þe(a)hte cover [þæc].
~end *m.* protector.
þecen *f.* roof, cover.
þecgan *twice* — hine þegeþ þurst troubles.
þefian pant.
þegen, þegn, þēn, þeng *m.* servant, attendant, retainer; official; soldier; disciple; aristocrat, nobleman, thane; †warrior, hero, man.
~boren of gentle birth.
~gilde *n.* wergield of a thane.
~hyse *m.* attendant.
~lagu *f.* law relating to thanes.
~lic manly, brave.
~līce *av.* bravely, nobly.
~rǣden(n) *f.* thaneship, service.
~riht *n.* privilege of a thane.
~scipe *m.* thaneship: body of retainers; allegiance [*Old Saxon*]; bravery.
~scolu *f.* body of retainers Gl.
ge~sum*, -þēn- helpful, obedient.
~werod† *n.* body of retainers.
~wer *m.* wergield of a thane.
þegeþ, *see* þecgan.
þegnest = *þēnest.
þegn|ian, þēnian *wd.* serve, attend upon; *wda.* supply, provide; *wa.* administer (an office).
~estre *f.* attendant, servant.
þegnung, þēn-, þēnig (*in comp.*) *f.* service, use; official service; church service; retinue; meal.
~bōc *f.* (religious) service-book.
~fæt *n.* kitchen utensil.
~gāst *m.* ministering spirit.
~hūs *n.* workshop.
~mann *m.* attendant; retainer.
~werod *n.* body of attendants *or* retainers.
þēh = þēah.
þel, þell, *pl.* þelu *n* plank (of ship), plate (of metal).

þel|brycg *f.* plank bridge *or* foot-path.
~fæsten(n)† *n.* (Noah's) ark.
~trēow*, wel-† *n.* tree.
þelma (?) *once m.* inflammation.
þēn = þegen.
þenian = þennan.
þenian = þegnian.
þencan, *prt.* þohte, ō (?) think, think of, consider; be intent on, determine, wish *w.* tō *d., g., inf., ger.* [þanc].
geþencan remember.
þenden, *LN.* þende *av., cj.* meanwhile, while.
þēnest*, þegnest [*anglicized form*] *f.* service *L.* [*Scand.* þjōnusta *f.*].
~mann, þēo- *m.* thane *vL.*
þeng = þegen.
þengel† *m.* prince. *Cp.* fengel.
þenn|an, þenian *tr.* stretch; prostrate Gl. || *intr.* exert oneself (!).
~ing *f.* stretching out.
þēo = þēow.
þēo, *see* þēoh.
þēon 6, 7, (hē) þihþ, *A.* þīp, *prt.* þāh, ēa, *pl.* þigon*, u, *ptc.* þigen*, o, *prs. ptc.* þēonde, þīendi, *intr.* grow up; lengthen (*of* days); become vigorous, flourish; prosper *w. i. or* on *d.*; be profitable *or* successful. *Cp.* þingan.
geþēon 6, 7 *intr.* grow, flourish, prosper *w.* on *d. or i.*: on lāre ~ increase in *or* acquire knowledge : gōde ~ [*or* Gode *d.* !] increase in virtue | *ptc.* geþogen grown up; virtuous, excellent; yfele ~ degenerate; prosperous.
þēon = þīen press.
geþēon*, -þīan *once* receive *eKt.*
þēod *f.* nation, race — *pl.* ~a Gentiles; people, men; country; language.
~bealo† *n.* great evil.
~būend† *pl.* men.
~cwēn† *f.* empress.
~cyning *m.* (†)monarch; †God.
~egesa† *m.* great terror.
~eorþe† *f.* world.
~fēond *m.* arch-enemy.
~fruma *m.* prince, lord.
~guma† *m.* warrior, man.
~here *m.* army.
~her-paþ, -poþ *m.* highway.
~isc I. Gentile. II. *n.* language.

þēod|land *n.* country; the Continent.
~lic of a people.
~līcettere *m.* arch-hypocrite.
~loga *m.* arch-impostor.
~mægen† *n.* tribal force.
~scaþa *m.* arch-malefactor.
~scipe *m.* nation, people. *See also* þēodan.
~stefn† *m.* people.
~gestrēon† *n.* great treasure.
~þrēa† *fm.* great calamity.
~weg *m.* highway.
~wiga† *m.* mighty warrior.
~wita *m.* councillor; sage, learned man.
~wundor† *n.* great wonder, miracle.
þēod|an = þīedan.
ge~endlic copulative.
ge~lic social, intimate.
ge~nes, þēodnes *f.* juncture; conjunction; conjugation; translation.
ge~rǣden(n) *f.* fellowship.
~scipe *m.* connexion, association; injunction; instruction, discipline; authority, rank; conduct; erudition; testimony *lN.* *See also* þēod.
ge~sumnes *f.* agreement.
geþēode *n.* language; translation.
þēoden(†) *m.* chief, lord, prince, king; God, Christ.
~gedāl *n.* separation from one's lord (by death).
~hold loyal.
~lēas without a lord.
~māþm *m.* princely treasure.
~stōl *m.* throne.
þēof *m.* thief.
~denn *n.* thieves' cave (?) Ct.
~feng *m.* obligation of land-holder to arrest those who committed theft on his land.
~gield *n.* compensation made by one convicted of theft.
~mann *m.* brigand.
~scip *n.* piratical ship.
~scolu *f.* band of thieves.
~scyldig guilty of theft.
~slege, ~sliht *m.* thief-killing.
~stolen stolen.
~wracu *f.* punishment of thief.
þēofian thieve.
þēofend, -ent, *lN.* -unt *f. only in pl.* theft.

þēoging *f.* thriving, progress, Gl. [þēon].
þēoh *n., d.* þēo, *gpl.* þēona thigh.
~ece *m.* thigh-ache.
~hweorfa *m.* knee-joint.
~gelǣte *n.* thigh-joint.
~scanca *m.* thigh.
~seax *n.* short sword.
~wærc, -wræc *m.* pain in thigh.
~geweald *npl.* genitals.
þēonest = þēnest.
þēor (*m.*) inflammation (?).
~ādl *f.* = þēor.
~drenc *m.* drink for þēor.
~gerid *n.* = þēor.
~wærc *m.* = þēor.
~wenn *m.* carbuncle (!).
~wyrm *m.* worm accompanying þēor.
~wyrt *f.* ploughman's spikenard.
þeorf I. unleavened; fresh (milk) (!). II. *n.* unleavened bread.
~dæg *m.* day on which unleavened bread was eaten.
~hlāf, ~ling *m.* loaf of unleavened bread.
~nes *f.* (unleavenedness), purity.
~symbel *n.* feast of unleavened bread.
þēos *fem. of* þes.
þeoss-, *see* þes.
þēoster-, īe, þ(r)īestre-, *see* þīestre.
~cofa† *m.* dark chamber, darkness.
~full dark, hidden.
~fullnes *f.* darkness.
~lic dark.
~loca† *m.* tomb.
~nes *f.* darkness.
þēostre, -o = þīestre, -o.
þēostr|ian, īe *tr., intr.* darken, dim.
~ung *f.* darkness.
þēostrig, þr-, īe *not W.* dark.
geþēot *n.* howling.
þēotan, þūtan 7 howl; resound.
þēote *f.* water-pipe, channel; torrent, cataract.
þēow I. *m.* servant, slave. II. *aj.* not free.
~boren slave-born.
~byrde, e slave-born.
~cnapa *m.* slave-boy.
~dōm *m.* servitude, slavery; divine service.
~dōm-hād *m.* service Bd.
~hād *m.* service.

þéow|incel n. young slave.
~lic of a slave.
~ling m. slave.
~níed, þéon- f. enslavement, oppression.
~weorc n. slave's work.
þéow-racu = *þíew-.
þéowan = þíen.
þéowan = þéowian.
þéow|ian, ~an intr. wd. serve, be servant or slave, serve (God); be engaged in, perform || tr. enslave.
þéowian = þíen.
þéowa m. servant, slave.
þéow|e, ~u wk. f. servant, slave.
þéowen(n), þíwen, þéowene f. servant, slave.
þéowot, þéow(e)t, -et(t) n. servitude, slavery.
~dóm m. service.
~lic of a slave, servile.
~ling m. servant, slave.
~scipe m. service.
þerh = þurh.
geþersc n. continued beating (horse).
þerscan 3, prt. þærsc beat, batter, thresh (corn).
þerscel, y, þriscel (m.) flail.
~flór f. threshing-floor.
þerscold, þrexwold, þyrsc-, -wald, ea m. threshold.
þes, neut. þis, aj. this, the | no. this one, this thing. ǽr þissum formerly.
þéwan = þíen press.
geþían = geþéon receive.
þic-, see þicce.
~feald dense.
ge~fieldan make dense Gl.
~lice av. densely, thickly; in quick succession.
~nes f. denseness, viscosity; thickness, depth (of earth); thicket (!); a solid body; darkness.
þicc|e I. thick-set, dense, viscous, solid; thick. II. av. densely, thickly; frequently.
~et(t) n. thicket.
~ian intr. thicken; crowd || tr. thicken.
~ol corpulent.
þicgan 5, imper. þige, prt. þáh, éa, pl. þǽgon, ptc. þegen; in W. wk. prt. þigede, þigde, ptc. þiged take, receive, accept; take (food, medicine), eat.
þider, æ av. thither; rel. whither,

to there where | ~ þe rel. whither, correl. ~ þe . . þider.
þider|geond av. thither.
~léodisc of that people, native.
~weard, -es av. in that direction, on the way thither: hé wæs ~.
þidres av. thither.
þíen*, ȳ, éo, prt. þȳde, þȳdde; þȳwan, é, éo, -ian press, lie heavy on, impress (mark); drive on; stab, pierce | rebuke, threaten; oppress, subjugate.
(ge)þíed|an, éo tr. join, associate, also rfl. — ~ fram separate; rfl. w. tó betake oneself (to prayer); gə- translate. See þéodan.
geþíede*, ȳ† once virtuous.
þíefe-feoh n. stolen property [þéof].
þíefþ, éo, þéoft f. act of thieving; what is stolen [þéof].
þíestre, éo, lN. þíostor dark, gloomy, also met. [þéoster-].
þíestro, þr-, éo f. often pl., A. þíostre n. darkness.
þíewan = þíen.
þíewrac|u, ~e, í, ȳ, éo, ww f. threatening, threat.
~ian threaten.
geþíewe customary [þéaw].
þigde prt. of þicgan.
þigen f. partaking of food or drink; food or drink [þicgan].
þigen ptc. of þicgan.
þignen(n), þínen f. attendant, servant; midwife [þegen].
þil|ian, þill(i)an lay down planks, make (bridge) [þel].
~ing f. structure of planks, flooring.
þilc = þyllic.
þille (f.) structure of planks, flooring [þel].
þín of thee.
þínan 6 become moist.
geþind [i = y?] n. swelling.
þindan 3 swell; be angry Gl.
þínen = þignen.
þing n. thing in its various meanings; object of value, gen. pl. goods; event; action; condition, state, pl. affairs, concerns; terms (of peace); meeting, court of justice | in adverbial phrases cause: for þisum ~um therefore; for his ~um for his sake | purpose: ~um purposely; tó þám ~um þæt w. sbj. in order that | respect: ǽlces ~es in every respect; sumera ~a

in some respects; ǽnige ~a at all; náne ~a, nǽnig(e) ~a not at all; ~a gehwelce in every respect, under all circumstances, anyhow | tó écum ~um to eternity; tó sóþum ~um truly; be fullum ~um completely; mid nánum ~um not at all. ǽrest ~a in the first place; raþost ~a at the earliest.
þing|léas innocent, exempt.
~gemearc† n. computed or allotted time.
~rǽden(n) f. intercession, pleading.
~stede† m. place of meeting, public place.
~stów f. place of meeting, public place.
þingan (?) address Gl.
(ge)þingan 3 flourish, prosper, be exalted [þéon, geþungen].
þing|ian intercede, plead, arrange w. d. (or for, fore a., d.) = for, and tó d., wiþ a = with, and a.: earmum ~ tó þám rícum; se cyning him ge~ode wiþ Éadgife his bóca edgift | make terms (for . . with . .), reconcile same construction | come to terms (with) w. wiþ a. | determine | pray abs., w. d. of thing: hé his (rfl.) life ge~ode æt Gode || tr. settle (dispute) || †make a speech, speak intr. w. wiþ, ongéan.
~ere m. intercessor, advocate, priest.
~estre f. intercessor.
~ung f. intercession, mediation.
geþing|e n. meeting, council; agreement, compact; result, destiny.
~sceatt m. ransom.
þirda = þridda.
þis this neut.
þis(s)-, see þes.
þisl = þixl.
þistel m. thistle.
~gebléd n. blister caused by prick of thistle.
~twige f. goldfinch.
þíwen = þéowen.
þixl, þísl, ~e f. wagon-pole, shaft.
þó, vE. þóhæ f. clay.
-iht clayey.
þocerian run about.
þoddettan prod, push.
þoden m. whirlwind;! whirlpool Gl.
þoft rower's bench.
(ge)~rǽden(n) f., (ge)~scipe m. fellowship.

geþoft|a *m.* companion.
~ian *intr.* associate *w.* wiþ *a.* : confederate.
þogen, *ptc. of* þeon.
geþoht, *LN.* þoht *m.* thought [þencan].
pohte *prt. of* þencan.
þol, *L.* þoll (*m.*) oar-peg, rowlock.
þole-, þolo-, þol-, *see* þolian.
~byrd patient.
~byrdnes *f.* patience.
~mōd I. patient. II. *m.* patience.
~mōdnes *f.* patience.
þolian *tr.* suffer, undergo ; *wg.* lose, be deprived of || *intr.* hold out, endure.
þolle *f.* frying-pan Gl.
þon *i. of* se.
þon = þonne.
þone, *see* se.
þon·ēcan *av.* whenever.
þonne, a, æ *av. cj.* then *of time* ; *of* succession *in place* ; *succession in narrative* then, again, *often pleon.* | *rel.* when | *correl.* ~ . . ~ when . . then | *cause* since ; although || þonne, þon *w. cpv.* than.
þōr = þūr.
þor|fæst useful *LN.* [þearf, fæst].
~lēas useless *LN.* [þearf, lēas].
þorfend, ~e *m.* pauper, one in want *LN.* [þearf].
~nes *f.* poverty *LN.*
þorfte *prt. of* þearf.
þorh = þurh.
þorn *m.* thorn ; thornbush ; *the* Runic letter þ.
~geblǣd *n.* blister caused by prick of thorn.
~grǣfe *f.* thorn-copse.
~ig, ~iht thorny.
~rǣw *f.* thorn-hedge.
~rind *f.* thorn-bark.
~stybb *m.* thorn-stump.
þorp = þrop.
þost *m.* dung.
þoter|ian howl, wail [þeotan].
~ung *f.* howling, wailing.
þōþer *m.* ball, sphere.
geþræcen adorned, prepared.
þracu† *f., g.* þræce pressure, force, violence.
þræc-†, *see* þracu.
~heard brave.
~hwil *f.* hard times.
~rōf brave.
wīg *n.* fighting, battle.

þræc-wudu *m.* spear.
geþræc(†) *n.* pressure, force, violence || *once* equipment Gl.
þrǣd *m.* thread [þrāwan].
geþrǣf — on ~ unanimously.
þrǣft† *once* (*n.*) quarrel.
þrǣgan†, ǣ† run [þrāg].
þrǣl *m., g.* þrǣl(l)es slave, servant, serf [*Scand.* þrǣll].
~riht *n.* serf's right.
þrǣs fringe Gl.
þrǣsce *f. once* thrush Gl. *Cp.* þrysce.
þrǣst|an twist ; press ; torture, afflict.
ge~ednes, þrǣstnes *f.* affliction ; contrition.
~ing *f.* torment, affliction.
þrǣwen *occ. ptc. of* þrāwan.
þraf|ian urge ; reprove, correct.
~ung *f.* rebuke, censure.
þrāg *f.* time ; evil times ; paroxysm | ~e for a time. ~um sometimes ; ? at regular intervals.
~bysig† periodically busy (?).
~mǣlum *av.* at intervals.
þrang *once* (*m.*) crowd Gl.
geþrang *n.* crowd, tumult [þring-an].
þrāw|an *ptc.* ~en, ǣ, ō *tr.* twist ; rack || *intr.* turn round ; revolve ; ~ende curling (hair).
~ing-spinel *f.* curling-iron.
þrēa, þrawu *st. f., wk. m., n.* ; threat, rebuke ; punishment, oppression, severity ; affliction, calamity | ~m cruelly, miserably.
~lic† miserable, calamitous.
~nied† *nf.*, ~nīedla† *m.* misery, affliction.
~nīedlic† calamitous.
~weorc† *n.* misery.
þrēa|n, þrēagan, *A.* þrēgan rebuke ; threaten, try to compel *w. sbj.* ; punish, chasten ; oppress, afflict.
~gend *m.* reprover.
~ung, ~ng, ~gung, ~wung *f.* reproof, correction ; threat ; punishment.
þrēagan = þrēan.
þrēal *f.* correction, rebuke ; threat ; punishment, discipline.
þrēap|ian rebuke.
~ung *f.* rebuke.
þrēat *m.* crowd, troop ; violence, ill-treatment, punishment ; threat [þrūtian].

þrēat-mǣlum *av.* in troops.
þrēat|ian urge on, press ; afflict | rebuke ; threaten ; compel by threats, urge : ~ode hine fram Crīstes gelēafan ; *w. æfter d.* demand with threats.
~end *m.* violent person *LN.*
~ung *f.* compulsion ; ill-treatment ; rebuke, correction ; threatening.
þrēatnian force.
þrēaw|ian reprove, correct [þrēa].
~ung *f.* rebuke, correction.
þrec *once* grievous.
þrece *m.* violence ; weariness [þracu].
þrehtig*, oe (?), *see* þreohtig.
þreo- = þri-.
þrēo *fn.*, þrīe *m., d.* þrim, *g.* ~ra three.
~hund-wintre three hundred years old.
~tēoþa, þrēott- thirteenth.
þrēot(t)iene thirteen.
~gēare thirteen years old.
þreodian = þridian.
þreohtig, oe (?) steadfast, enduring.
þrēora *g. of* þrēo.
þrēotan 7 *impers. wa.* (?) weary.
þrēowian = þrowian.
þrescold = þerscold.
þri-, y, eo three-.
þri-beddod three-bedded (room).
þrid|ian, eo, y deliberate ; hesitate.
~ung, ~ing *f.* deliberation ; hesitation.
þri-dæglic lasting three days.
þri-dǣled tripartite.
þridda, *LN.* þirda third.
þrīe, *see* þrēo.
þrīepel (*m.*) instrument of punishment, kind of cross [þrēapian].
þrīetan *tr.* weary ; urge, force [þrēotan].
þri-feald threefold.
~lice *av.* triply.
þri-fe(o)þor triangular.
þri-fēte three-footed.
þri-fieldan triple.
þri-fingre three fingers thick, *av.* three fingers' breadth.
þri-flēre three-storied.
þri-fōtede, -fōtod three-footed.
þri-fyrede three-furrowed.
þriga = þriwa.
þri-gǣrede three-pronged.

þri-gēare I. three years old. II. *n.* space of three years.

þri-gięld *n.* — ~e (compensation) with a triple payment.

þri-hēafdede three-headed.

þrihing (?) *m.* third part of a shire, Riding. *Cp.* **trehing**.

þri-hīwede having three forms.

þri-hlidede three-lidded.

þri-hyrne, -hyrnede triangular.

þri-lēafe*, ē *once f.* trefoil Gl.

þrilen woven with three threads.

þrili *vE.* threefold Gl.

þrilic threefold.

þri-līþe (year) having three months named **līþa**, having an intercalated month.

þrim *d. of* **þrīe**.

þri-milce May.

þrims = **trimes**.

þrinen threefold.

þrines, þrynnes *f.* trinity.

geþring *n.* crowd, troop; tumult (of waters).

þringan 3 *tr.* press on, crowd; pinch (with cold), oppress, afflict | *intr.* crowd, throng; press on, make one's way | *impers.* †þǣre tīde is nēah geþrungen it is near the time.

þri-nihte three days old.

þrinnes = **þrines**.

þrintan swell.

þri-rēþre having three banks of oars, trireme.

þriscel = **þerscel**.

þri-scīete triangular.

þrisel.

~lic tripartite.

þri-slite three-forked (tongue).

þrīst, ~e bold, brave; shameless.

~e *av.* boldly, bravely; shamelessly; vigorously, exceedingly.

~full presumptuous.

~hycgende† bold, brave.

~hygdig†, **~hȳdig** bold, brave.

~lǣcan presume.

~lǣcnes *f.* presumption.

~(e)līce *av.* boldly, presumptuously.

~ling (*m.*) ? Ct.

~nes *f.* boldness, temerity.

þrīstian dare, presume.

þri-strenge three-stringed.

þrītig, tt, ī† [*or* -itt-] thirty.

~feald thirtyfold.

~oþa thirtieth.

~wintre thirty years old.

þrittēoþa = **þrēotēoþa**.

þriwa, eo, þriga, þria *av.* thrice.

þri-winter period of three years Gl.

þri-wintre three years old.

þroc *n.* piece of timber on which the ploughshare is fixed; table.

þrōh (?) hatred, envy Gl.

þrōh, d. þrō(gu)m rancid Gl.

þroht† I. *m.* affliction, hardship. II. *aj.* grievous.

~heard having fortitude; grievous.

þrohtig (?), *see* **þreohtig**.

þrop, þorp, -þrep *m.* farm, estate; village.

þrosm *m.* vapour, smoke.

~ig smoky.

þros(t)le *f.* throstle, thrush.

þrot|e, ~u *f. wk.* throat.

~bolla *m.* gullet, windpipe.

þrow|ian, ō†, ēo be passive; suffer (pain) — *abs.* suffer martyrdom; pay for, expiate.

þrower|e *m.* martyr.

~hād *m.* martyrdom.

þrowiendlic capable of suffering, passive (verb).

þrowung *f.* passivity; suffering (pain); martyrdom, anniversary of martyrdom; painful symptom (in illness).

~rǣding *f.* martyrology.

~tīd *f.* date of martyrdom; time of suffering.

~tīma *m.* time of suffering.

þrōwen, occ. ptc. of þrāwan.

þrowend *m.*, *gpl.* **~ra** scorpion.

geþrūen, ptc. of þweran.

þrūh, g. þrȳh, fnm. water-pipe, trough; coffin.

þrūst-fell *n.* leprosy [þrūst- *from* þrūts-].

þrūt|ian swell with pride or anger; threaten.

~ung *f.* anger, arrogance; threatening.

þry- = **þri-**.

þryc|can *tr.* press, trample; impress (mark) || *intr.* press, force one's way.

~nes *f.* affliction *LN.*

þrydian = **þridian**.

þrydlice = **þrȳþlice**.

geþrȳde, ȳ *prt.* bound (book) (?) *LN.*

þrȳh, *see* þrūh.

geþryl- *n.* crowding, crowd.

þrymm *m.* strength, might; glory,

[184]

---

magnificence; anything glorious; host, army, body (of water).

þrym|cyme† *m.* glorious coming.

~cyning† *m.* Deity.

~dōm *m.* glory.

~fæst† glorious, illustrious.

~full† powerful, severe (storm); glorious.

~lic glorious, magnificent.

~līce *av.* gloriously, magnificently.

~rīce *n.* kingdom of glory, heaven.

~seld, ~setl *n.* throne.

~sittende† dwelling in glory.

~wealdende ruling in glory.

þrymma† *m.* warrior.

þryms = **trimes**.

geþryscan afflict, depress (mind) [þerscan].

þrysce *f.* thrush.

þrysman (suffocate); oppress [þrosm].

þrȳþ† *f.*, *gen. pl.* strength, might — **~um** vehemently, very; troop, host, body (of water).

~ærn *n.* palace.

~bearn *n.* mighty youth.

~bord *n.* shield.

~cyning *m.* mighty king, God.

~full strong, brave.

~lic brave.

~līce*, þrȳd- *av.* mightily.

~gesteald *n.* splendid abode.

~swīþ mighty.

~weorc *n.* splendid work.

~word *n.* brave word, noble speech.

þū thou.

þū-þistel, þūfe-þistel *m.* sow-thistle.

þūf *m.* tuft; banner.

~bǣre leafy.

~ian become leafy.

~ig leafy.

geþūf leafy, luxuriant.

þūfe (?) tufty, bushy. *See* **þū-þistel.**

þūft *m.* thicket.

geþuhtsum *once* abundant (rain).

þuhte *prt. of* **þyncan**.

þullic = **þyllic** such.

þūma *m.* thumb.

þumle entrails Gl.

þun-wang, -wange, ę *f.* temple (of head).

geþun *n.* loud noise.

þun|ian be prominent *or* erect; be proud | resound, creak.

~ung *f.* creaking; a rattle.

þung *m.* aconite, poisonous plant, (vegetable) poison.

geþungen full-grown; capable; excellent, good [þingan, þeon].

~líce *av.* virtuously.

~nes *f.* growth; goodness, perfection.

þunor *m.* thunder, thunderbolt; the god of thunder, Jupiter.

~bodu *f.* gilthead (a fish).

~cláfre, ǽ *f.* bugle (a plant).

~lic of thunder Gl.

þunorrád *f.* thunder.

~lic of thunder Gl.

~stefn *f.* voice of thunder.

þunor-wyrt *f.* houseleek.

þunres|dæg, þures- *m.* Thursday. *See* þur.

~niht *f.* Wednesday night.

þunr|ian thunder.

~ing *f.* thunder *L.*

þúr, ó *m.* Thor, god of thunder, Jupiter [*Scand.* þórr].

~es-dæg = þunres-.

geþuren *ptc. of* þweran.

þurh, -uh, *A.* o, e, þerih *av.*, *prp. w. d.* (*d.*, *g.*) place, extent through | *time* throughout, during |*cause, means, instrument*through, because of; *motive* through, out of (humility); *aim* with a view to; *agent w. pass.*=fram | *to form avs.*: ~ líegett in the form of lightning; ~ wíte as a punishment.

þurh-beorht very bright, splendid.

þurh-bitter very bitter.

þurh·bláwen inspired.

þurh·borian perforate.

þurh·brecan 4 break through.

þurh·bringan bring through.

þurh·brogden transported Gl.

þurh·brúcan 7 enjoy thoroughly.

þurh·burnen thoroughly burnt.

þurh·clǽnsian clean out.

þurh·créopan 7 penetrate.

þurh·delfan 3 pierce.

þurh·dréogan 7 pass (time).

þurh·drífan 6 drive out; pierce; permeate.

þurh·dúfan 7 dive through.

þurh·etan 5 eat through, consume (*of* rust).

þurh-fǽr (!) *n.* secret place.

þurh·fæstnian (!) transfix.

þurh·far|an 2 pass, traverse *tr.*, *intr.*; pass beyond, transcend; pierce; penetrate.

þurh·farennes (!) *f.* secret place.

þurh-gefeoht (!) *n.* war.

þurh·féran *tr.* pass · through . penetrate.

þurh-fére I. pervious. II. (!) *n.* secret place.

þurh·fléogan, -fléon, 7 fly through.

þurh·lón 1 penetrate.

þurh·gán, -gangan traverse; permeate; pierce.

þurh·géotan 7 cover (by pouring); saturate; imbue, inspire.

þurh·gléded† filled with live coals.

þurh·hǽlan heal thoroughly.

þurh-hálig very holy.

þurh-hefig very heavy.

þurh-hwít very white.

þurh·iernan 3 run through, traverse; pierce.

þurh·lǽran persuade Gl.

þurh·lǽred very learned.

þurh-láþ very hateful Gl.

þurh·léoran pass through.

þurh·lócung *f.* preface, summary (of book) Gl.

þurh·rǽsan† rush through.

þurh·scéotan 7 shoot through, transfix.

þurh·sciene*, ý [*or* y=i ?] transparent Gl.

þurh·scínendlic splendid Gl.

þurh·scrípan 6 traverse.

þurh·scyldig very guilty.

þurh·sécan seek out.

þurh·séon 5 *tr.* see through, penetrate with the sight, *also fig.*

þurh·sléan 2 cut through; kill Gl.

þurh·sméa(ga)n inquire into thoroughly, investigate.

þurh·smierian anoint thoroughly.

þurh·smúgan 7 creep through, penetrate; traverse; study *or* consider thoroughly.

þurh·spédig very wealthy.

þurh·stician transfix, pierce.

þurh·stingan 3 pierce.

þurh·swimman 3 swim through.

þurh·swíþan be very strong Gl.

þurh·swógan penetrate.

þurh·téon 7 carry out, perform, accomplish; obtain (request); continue; afford (expense); undergo; drag Gl.

þurh·togennes *f.* collatio, a religious reading in monasteries.

þurh·trymman confirm Gl.

þurh·þíen*, ý pierce.

þurh·þráwan 1 *tr.* penetrate.

þurh·þýrel perforated.

þurh·þýrelian pierce.

þurh-út *L. av.*, *prp. w. a.* (?) quite through.

þurh-wacol vigilant; sleepless (night).

þurh·wadan 2 *tr.* pass through; pierce.

þurh·wæccendlic very vigilant.

þurh·wlítan 6 look through, penetrate with the sight.

þurh·wrecan 5 *tr.* thrust through, pierce.

þurh·wund wounded right through.

þurh·wun|ian continue, persist, last.

~igendlíce *av.* perseveringly.

~ung *f.* residence; perseverance.

þurruc (*m.*) small ship; bottom part of ship.

þurst *m.* thirst.

~ig, y, *lN.* þrystig thirsty.

þus *av.* thus, so.

~lic = þyllic such.

þúsend *nf.* thousand.

~ealdormann *m.* chiliarch Gl.

~feald thousand (fold).

~híwe milleform Gl.

~lic numbered by thousands.

~mǽle thousand.

~mǽlum *av.* in thousands.

~mann, ~ríca *m.* ruler of a thousand men.

~gerím† *n.* counting by thousands.

~getæl *n.* a thousand.

þútan=þéotan.

geþuxod dark (?).

þwægen *ptc. of* þwéan.

þwǽle *f.* band, fillet Gl. = towel (?) [þwéan].

þwénan *tr.* moisten, soften. *Cp.* þénan, þawenian.

geþwǽr|e not at variance, united; harmonious (sound); yielding to, obedient *wd.*; pleasing *wd.*; peaceful, gentle; prosperous.

~ian, þ- *tr.* reconcile || *intr.* agree; *wd.* consent to; suit, fit.

~lǽcan, þ- *wd.* agree, comply; suit.

~(e)líce *av.* in accord.

~nes, þ- *f.* concord; tranquillity; gentleness.

þwǽre *f.* churn (?), olive-press Gl. [þweran].

þwagen *ptc. of* þwēan.
þwang *mf.* thong.
þwastrian *once* whisper.   *Cp.* hwastrian.
þwēan 2, (hē) þwihþ, *prt.* þwōg, *ptc.* þwǣgen, a, o wash; ! anoint *LN.*
þwēal, þwæhl, a *nm.* washing; ! ointment *LN.* [þwēan].
þwearm (*m.*) a cutting instrument Gl.
þwęng *f.* (?) band *LN.* [*Scand.* þwęngr thong; *cp.* þwang].
geþwēor *n.* curds.
þwēor-, þwȳr- *see* þweorh.
~a *m.* peevishness.
~es *av.* across, crosswise; from the side, obliquely; perversely.
~ian be adverse, be at variance, oppose.
~lic reversed; adverse; perverse, bad.
~līce *av.* reversedly, in wrong order; obstinately; perversely, wrongly.
~nes *f.* crookedness; obstinacy; depravity, wickedness.
~scipe *m.* perversity.
~tīeme contentious; perverse.
þweorh, þwēor, ȳ, *g.* þwēores, ȳ (across, crosswise); adverse; angry; perverse, bad — on ~ perversely, wrongly.
~fȳre, ~fu- *n., also pl.* ~fȳro crossfurrow, rough place.
þweran 4, *ptc.* þworen, þuren, þrüen, þroren, þrofen stir, churn; †beat (metal), forge.
þwere = þwǣre.
þwihþ, *see* þwēan.
þwīnan 6 dwindle. *Cp.* dwīnan.
geþwinglod — ~e loccas.

þwirel (*m.*) whisk (for whipping milk) [þweran].
geþwit *n.* what is shaved off, chip [þwītan].
þwītan 6 cut, shave off.
þwōg *prt. of* þwēan.
þwogen *ptc. of* þwēan.
þwȳr- = þwēor-.
þȳ, þī(g) I. *i.* of sē. II. *av., cj.* therefore; because — *correl.* þȳ .. þȳ because.   þȳ-þe so that | *w. cpv.* the — *correl.* þȳ .. þȳ the .. the.
~dæges *av.* on that day.
~lǣs, *see* lȳt.
þȳn = *þīen press, stab.
þȳd(d)e *prt. of* þīen.
þȳfel *m.* bush, leafy plant; thicket, rank growth [þūf].
þyften *f.* female servant [geþofta].
geþyht† *aj.* R.
þyhtig strong.
þylc = þyllic.
geþyld, *LN.* þ- *fn.* patience — ~um patiently [þolian].
~elic = ~iglic.
~ig patient.
~(i)gian, ~ian bear (patiently), endure.
~iglic, ~elic patient.
~iglice, ~elice *av.* patiently.
~mēdan*, *ptc.* geþylmēd humbled.
~mōd patient.
þyl|e *m.* orator; buffoon, jester Gl.
~cræft *m.* rhetoric Gl.
geþyll *once* (*n.*) breeze *LN.*
þyllic, þylc, i; þyslic, u; þullic, -uc *no., aj.* such [þus, -lic].
þȳmel *m.* thumbstall [þūma].
þȳmele thumb thick (fat of swine) [þūma].

þyn|hlǣne *Gl.* shrunk [þynne].
~nes *f.* thinness, weakness.
~wefen thin-woven.
þyncan, *prt.* þuhte *impers. wd.* seem; seem good *or* fit [þęncan].
geþyncþ|o *f.* honour, rank, dignity — ~um honourably | court, legal assembly [geþungen].
geþyng|o *f.* honour, advancement *LN.*
þynn|e thin.
~ian make *or* become thin.
~ol lean.
~ung *f.* making thin.
þȳr(e)l I. *n.* aperture, hole. II. *aj.* perforated [þurh].
~ian perforate.
~ung *f.* perforation.
~wamb† having a pierced stomach.
þyrfe, *see* þearf.
þyrfende, *see* þearf.
þyrncin thistle [þorn].
þyrn|e *f.* thorn-bush, bramble.
~en of thorns.
~et(t) *n.* thorn-thicket.
~iht(e) thorny.
þyrr|e dry; withered.
~an† *once* dry, wipe.
þyrs *m.* giant, demon.
þyrscel = þerscel.
þyrscwald = þerscold.
þyrst|an *wg.* be thirsty, thirst (for) *pers. and impers. wa., ptc.* geþyrst thirsty [þurst].
~ig = þurstig thirsty.
þȳs *i. of* þes.
þyslic = þyllic such.
þys(s)-, *see* þes.
þyss*, þys storm.
þȳw-racu = þīew-.
þīȳwan = þīen press.

U.

ū *m. the letter* u.
ūder (*n.*) udder.
ūf *m.* owl ; vulture Gl.
ūf *once* uvula (?) Gl.
ufan *av.* from above, downwards; above.
~cumende coming from above.
~cund from aloft, celestial.
~weard upper part of.
ufemest, *see* ufor.
ufenan, -on I. *av.* from above. II. *prp. wa.* above, on ; besides.
ufer|ian elevate, exalt ; delay *tr.* [ufor].
~ung *f.* delay.
uferra, -era, y- *cpv., spl.* yfemest, u, ymest, higher, upper ; later, after.
ufeweard, ufw- upper part of ; further up ; later part of.
ufor *av. cpv., spl.* yfemest, u-, to a greater height, higher, *also met.* ; further, further away ; later.
ufweard = ufe-.
uht, ~a *m.* time just before day-break — foran tō ~es before dawn ; nocturns (the earliest canonical service).
~gebed *n.* matins.
~caru† *f.* care that comes at dawn.
~floga† *m.* dawn-flyer.
~hlemm† *m.* noise at dawn.
~lic of early morning ; of matins.
~sang *m.* nocturns, matins.
~sanglic of nocturns.
~scapa† *m.* depredator at dawn.
~tīd *f.* time before daybreak.
~þegnung *f.* matins.
~wæcce *f.* vigil before daybreak.
uht = wiht.
ūle *f.* owl.
ulm-trēow *n.* elm-tree [*Lt.* ulmus].
uma, ām† reed (of loom).
umbor† *n.* child.
ume *once f.* a plant.
un-, on- un-. *The stress is sometimes on the second element.*

un- = on-.
un-ābeden unasked.
un-āberend|e*, -beriende intolerable.
~lic intolerable.
~lice *av.* intolerably.
un-ābīegendlic inflexible.
un-ābindendlic indissoluble.
un-āblinn (?) *n.* non-cessation.
un-āblinnend|e unceasing.
~lic incessant.
~lice *av.* incessantly.
un-ābrecendlic inextricable Gl.
un-ācennend unbegotten.
un-ācnycendlic indissoluble *IN.* [cnyccan].
un-ācumendlic, -cumenlic intolerable.
~nes *f.* unbearableness.
un-ācwencedlic inextinguishable.
un-ādrēogendlic unendurable.
un-ādrūgod not dried.
un-ādrysnend|e inextinguishable *IN.*
~lic, -drysenlic inextinguishable *IN.*
un-ādwǣsc|ed not extinguished.
~en(d)lic inextinguishable.
un-ǣmt|a, -ǣmetta *m.* want of leisure ; occupation.
~igian deprive of leisure, take up another's time.
un-geǣsc unheard of.
un-ǣt *m.* gluttony.
un-ǣtspornen not hindered.
un-ǣpel|e plebeian.
~boren not of noble birth.
~ian degrade, debase.
~lice *av.* ignobly.
~nes *f.* infamy.
un-geǣwed unmarried.
un-ǣwfæstlice *av.* irreligiously.
un-ǣwisc modest (*or* immodest ?).
un-āfandod untried.
un-āfeohtendlic not to be contended against.

un-āfunden undiscovered ; untried.
un-āfȳled undefiled.
un-āfyllend|lic, -edlic insatiable.
~lice *av.* insatiably.
un-āga *m.* pauper.
un-āgān not lapsed (*of* lease).
un-āgǣledlice *av.* unremittingly.
un-āgen not one's own.
un-āgiefen not repaid.
un-āgunnen without a beginning.
un-āliefed unlawful.
~lic, -endlic unlawful.
~lice *av.* unlawfully.
~nes *f.* what is unlawful ; licentiousness.
un-āliesed not remitted.
un-āmānsumod not excommunicated.
un-āmeten immeasurable.
~lic immense.
un-āmetgod immense.
un-āmielt unmelted.
un-andcȳpignes *f.* ignorance.
un-andergilde *once* (riches) that may be kept (?).
un-andett unconfessed.
un-andgiet|full unintelligent.
~ol*, -angyttol unintelligent.
un-andhēfe*, -oife insupportable *A.*
un-andweard not present.
un-andwīs inexperienced.
un-ānrǣdnes *f.* inconstancy.
un-āpinedlic unpunished.
un-ār *f.* dishonour.
ge~ian dishonour.
~lic dishonourable, disgraceful ; unkind, unnatural (will, testament).
~lice *av.* dishonourably ; unmercifully.
un-āræfn|ed intolerable.
~e(n)dlic intolerable.
un-āreccendlic indescribable.
un-āreht unexplained.
un-ārimed innumerable.
~lic innumerable.
~lice *av.* innumerably.

un-ārodscipe *m.* remissness, cowardice.
un-ārweorþ|ian dishonour.
~nes *f.* irreverence, indignity.
un-geārwierd*, y not honoured.
un-āscended unhurt.
un-āscier|ed*, -scyrod not separated.
~igendlic inseparable.
un-geāscod unasked.
un-āscruncen not withered.
un-āsecgend|e ineffable Bd.
~lic ineffable.
~līce *av.* ineffably.
un-āsedd unsatiated.
un-āseolcendlic energetic.
un-āsēpen(d)lic insatiable.
un-āsiwod without a seam.
un-āsmēagendlic inscrutable.
un-āsolcenlīce *av.* energetically.
un-āspringende unfailing.
un-āsporiendlic, -spyriendlic unsearchable.
un-āstīpod not made firm.
un-āstyr|od unmoved.
~iende, ~iendlic motionless.
un-āsundrodlic inseparable.
un-āswundenlīce *av.* not languidly.
un-ātalodlic innumerable *IN.*
un-āteald uncounted.
un-ātellendlic innumerable.
un-ātemed untamed.
~lic untameable.
un-ātēoriend|e indefatigable.
~lic lasting ; indefatigable.
~līce *av.* permanently ; indefatigably.
un-ātēorod unwearied.
un-āþrēotende unwearied, unfailing.
un-āþroten unwearied, indefatigable.
~līce *av.* unceasingly, indefatigably.
un-āwæscen, -waxen unwashed.
un-āwegendlic immovable.
un-āwemmed immaculate.
~lic immaculate.
~nes *f.* incorruptibility.
un-āwend, ~ed unchanged, inviolate.
~lic, ~edlic unchangeable.
~ende, ~endlic unchangeable.
un-āwīdlod undefiled.
un-āwierded unhurt.
un-āwriten unwritten.
un-beald timid, irresolute.

un-bealo† *n.* innocence.
~full innocent.
un-gebēaten unwrought.
un-beboht unsold.
un-bebyriged unburied.
un-becēas indisputable.
un-becrafod not subject to claims.
un-becweden unbequeathed.
un-beden unasked.
un-befangenlic incomprehensible.
un-befliten undisputed.
un-befohten not attacked, unopposed.
un-begān uncultivated ; unadorned.
un-begrīpendlic incomprehensible.
un-begunnen without beginning.
un-behēafdod not beheaded.
un-behēfe inconvenient.
un-behel|ed uncovered, naked.
~endlīce *av.* openly.
un-behrēowsigende impenitent.
un-belimp *n.* mischance.
un-gebeorglīce *av.* rashly (?) ; unbecomingly (?).
un-beorhte *av.* not brightly.
un-berēafigendlic not to be taken away.
un-berend|e intolerable *IN.* ; barren.
~lic intolerable.
~nes *f.* barrenness.
un-besacen undisputed.
un-bescēawod inconsiderate.
~līce *av.* inconsiderately.
un-bescoren unshorn, untonsured.
un-besenged unsinged, not burnt.
un-besēondlic incomprehensible.
un-besmiten undefiled.
~nes *f.* spotlessness.
un-besorg unconcerned.
un-bēted unatoned.
un-gebętt unamended, unatoned for.
un-bepierfe*, y† useless, vain.
un-bepohte *av.* unthinkingly.
un-beweddod unbetrothed ; unmarried.
un-bewielled not boiled away.
un-biddende not praying.
un-gebīeg|ed unbent.
~endlic indeclinable.
un-bieldo *f.* want of boldness; irresolution.
un-gebierde, -ard- beardless [beard].

un-biermed*, e unleavened, unfermented.
un-biernende not burning *intr.*
un-biscopod not confirmed (by a bishop).
un-blanden unmixed.
un-bleoh† not coloured, white, bright.
un-geblētsod unblessed.
un-blētsung *f.* curse.
un-blinnendlīce *av.* incessantly.
un-bliss *f.* unhappiness ; affliction
un-blīþe sad.
un-blōdig bloodless.
un-boht, unge- unbought.
un-boht *av.* gratuitously *IN.*
un-boren, unge- unborn.
un-brād narrow.
un-bræce† unbreakable.
un-brocen, unge- unbroken.
un-brocheard delicate, tender.
un-gebrocod not afflicted *or* injured.
un-brosn|igendlic, ungebrosnendlic indestructible.
~ung, unge- *f.* soundness.
un-gebrosnod undecayed.
un-bryce† unbreakable, indestructible.
un-brȳce useless.
un-brygde*, -brȳde *av.* honestly
un-gebunden not bound.
un-gebyde uncongenial (to) *wd.*
un-bȳed desert *IN.*
un-gebyrde uncongenial.
un-gebyredlic incongruous.
un-bȳrego *npl.* desert *IN.*
un-byrged unburied.
unc us two.
un-cāfscipe *m.* sloth.
un-capitulod not divided into chapters.
un-camprōf unwarlike.
un-cēap|od*, -ed gratis.
~unga *av.* gratis.
un-cēas, -cēast *n.* peace.
un-cenned not begotten.
uncer of us two.
un-cīepe gratuitous.
un-gecierred unconverted.
un-clǣmod not smooth.
un-clǣn|e not clean, impure.
~līce *av.* in an unclean manner.
~nes *f.* impurity.
~o *f.* impurity *IN.*
un-clǣns|ian soil, pollute.
~od, unge- unpurified.

[188]

un-clǣnsung *f.* pollution.
un-gecnāwen unknown.
un-gecnyrdnes *f.* negligence.
un-gecōp|lic unsuitable, trouble-some.
~līce *av.* unsuitably.
un-gecoren not chosen — ~ āþ, *opposite of* cyre-āþ; reprobate, evil.
un-gecost reprobate, bad.
un-cop|a *m.*, ~u *f.* disease.
un-cræft *m.* evil practice.
~ig powerless.
un-crafod free from claim.
un-cristen infidel.
un-cumlīþe inhospitable.
un-cūþ unknown, uncertain; un-friendly, unkind.
~lic unknown.
~līce *av.* unkindly.
un-cwaciende firm.
un-cweden revoked, = on- (?).
un-gecwēme unpleasing.
un-cweþende speechless; inani-mate.
un-cwidd in undisputed possession (of property).
un-cwisse speechless.
un-gecydd undeclared.
un-cyme unseemly, paltry.
un-gecynde, uncynde alien; un-natural.
~lic unnatural.
~līce *av.* unnaturally.
un-cyn|n unsuitable, improper.
~lic unsuitable, improper.
un-cyst *f.* defect; disease; vice; parsimony.
~ig niggardly.
un-cȳþig ignorant; †devoid of *wg.*
un-cȳþþ(o) *f.* ignorance ‖ foreign country.
un-dǣd *f.* crime.
un-gedǣft|līce, und-, -elīce *av.* unsuitably.
~nes *f.* unseasonableness.
un-dǣled undivided.
un-gedafen|lic improper; trouble-some.
~līce *av.* improperly, unseasonably.
~licnes *f.* inconvenience.
un-gedafniendlic unseemly.
un-dēaded not deadened.
un-dēad|lic, -dēap- immortal.
~līce *av.* (rise) to immortality.
~licnes *f.* immortality.

un-dearnunga, eo, -inga *av.* openly.
un-dēaw without dew.
un-declinigendlic indeclinable.
un-gedēfe troublesome.
~līce *av.* unbecomingly.
un-dēogollīce = undīe-.
un-dēop shallow.
~þancol shallow-minded.
un-dēore I. cheap, common. II. *av.* cheaply.
under I. *prp. w. d. and a.* (*gen. expressing motion*) under; among ‖ while — under-þǣm-þe *cj.* while ‖ *met. protection*; *subjection*; *exposure, suffering*: ~ fǣr-gripum; *rank, degree*; *manner*; *pretext.* II. *av.* under, beneath. on ~ beneath.
under-ǣgenlic subnixus *LN.*
under-andfōnd *m.* receiver *LN.*
under·bǣc, ~ling *av.* backwards, back.
under·beginnan 3 begin, under-take.
under·beran 4 support Gl.
under·bīegan subject.
under·brǣdan (!) spread under *LN.*
under·būgan 7 *wd.* submit.
under-burg *f.* suburb (!).
~ware *mpl.* inhabitants of a suburb.
under·cierran (!) subvert *LN.*
under·crēopan 7 enter surrepti-tiously *also fig.*
under·cuman (!) 4 assist.
under-cyning *m.* under-king, viceroy.
under-delf cavity beneath Gl.
under·delfan 3 undermine, dig out.
under-diacon *m.* sub-deacon.
under·drencan (!) suffocate Gl.
under·drifennes (!) *f.* subjection.
un-gedȳred uninjured.
under·etan 5 sap, undermine *fig.*
under-fang = -feng.
under·fangennes, -fangelnes *f.* assumption.
under-feng, -fang *m.* undertaking, acceptance; one who undertakes Gl.
under·flōwan 1 flow under *tr.*
under·fōn 1 b receive; receive sur-reptitiously (stolen property) (?); undertake.
under·fōnd *m.* one who receives Gl.
~lic*, -fōnlic to be received Gl.

under·fylgan (!) follow *LN.*
under·gān, -gangan 1 undermine *fig.*, deceive ‖ undergo.
under-geoc tamed *LN.*
under·ginnan 3 begin, undertake.
under·gietan 5 understand, per-ceive.
under·hebban (!) 2 lift *LN.*
under·hlyst|an (!) supply (omitted word).
~ung (!) *f.* supplying (omitted word).
under·hnigan 6 go beneath *tr.*; submit to, undergo *w. a. or d.*
under-holung *f.* cavity beneath Gl.
under-hwītel *m.* under-cloak Gl.
under·īecan (!) add.
under·iernan 3 run beneath *tr.* ‖ ! help *LN.*
un-derigend|e, ~lic harmless, innocent.
under-lāttēow *m.* consul.
under·lecgan support.
under·licgan 5 submit *wd.*
underling *m.* subordinate *L.*
under·lūtan 7 stoop under, lift *tr.*
undern *m.* third hour, nine in the morning; morning.
~giefl *n.* breakfast.
~mǣl *n.* morning.
~mete *m.*, ~gereord *n.* breakfast.
~rest *f.* rest in the morning.
~sang *m.* tierce (a church service).
~swǣsendu *npl.* breakfast.
~tīd *f.* third hour; tierce.
~tīma *m.* third hour.
~geweorc *n.* breakfast.
under·neopan, -nyþan *av.*, *prp. wa.* underneath, below.
under·niman 4 take upon oneself; take in (with mind); steal.
under·niþemest *av.* lowest.
under·plantian (!) supplant.
under-gerēfa *m.* under-officer, pro-consul.
under·scēotan 7 intercept, cut off; support.
under-scyte *m.* intercepting.
under·sēcan investigate.
under-sierc *m.* under-shirt.
undersmēagan = -smūgan.
under·smūgan 7 come upon unawares, surprise.
under·stand|an 2 understand, perceive, take for granted.
~ennes (!) *f.* substance.
~ing *f.* intelligence *L.*

under·stapplian supplant Gl.
under·stingan 3 support.
under·strégdan strew under *tr.*
under-tódál (!) *n.* sub-distinction.
under-tunge *f.* sublingua Gl.
under·pencan consider.
under·þéow *m.* slave, subject.
under·pied|an, *A., W.* ēo subject
— *ptc.* ~d, undergeþéoded subject, subordinate ; add Bd. ; support Gl.
~endlic subjunctive.
~nes *f.* subjection, submission.
under-wedd *n.* pledge, security.
under-wrǽdel waist-band.
under·wreþ|ian, eo, i support.
~ung *f.* support.
under·writan 6 sign.
under·wyrtwalian supplant Gl.
un-díegellīce, ēo *av.* openly.
un-dierne I. manifest. II. *av.*
openly, clearly.
un-dīlegod not effaced.
un-dōm *m.* unjust judgement.
~līce *av.* indiscreetly Gl.
un-dréfed not made turbid.
un-gedrehtlīce *av.* indefatigably.
un-gedríeme inharmonious.
un-drifen not driven.
un-druncen sober.
un-drysnende inextinguishable
IN.
un-(ge)dyrstlic timorous.
un-éacniendlic sterile.
un-geeahtendlic, e inestimable ;
indescribable.
un-earfoþlīce *av.* without difficulty.
un-earg, ~lic intrepid.
un-éaþe, *cpv.* -ieþ, with difficulty ;
grievously ; unwillingly ; scarcely.
un-éaplǽcne, -ácn- not easily
cured.
un-emn, -fn unequal, irregular.
~e *av.* unequally.
~lic diverse.
un-endebyrdlīce *av.* irregularly,
in a disorderly manner.
un-geend|igendlic infinite ; infini-
tive.
~od endless ; infinite.
~odlic infinite.
un-ered unploughed.
un-estful unkind.
un-fǽcne, ǽ without deceit *or*
fraud.

un-fǽderlīce *av.* in an unfatherly
manner.
un-fǽg|e not fated to die.
~lic, unge- not serious (symptom).
un-fǽger ugly, horrible.
~e *av.* unpleasantly, cruelly.
~nes *f.* abomination *IN.*
un-fǽhþ *f.* abstention from prose-
cuting a feud.
un-fǽle uncanny, evil.
un-fæst not firm.
~līce *av.* not firmly, vaguely.
un-fæstende not fasting.
unfæstrǽd inconstant.
~nes *f.* inconstancy.
un-fáh not regarded as an enemy,
exempt from hostility.
un-gefandod untried.
un-gefaren impassable.
un-geféalīce *av.* unhappily.
un-feax bald.
un-feferig free from fever.
un-gefége unsuitable.
un-gefél|e, ~ed without feeling.
un-félende without feeling.
un-feormigende inexpiable.
un-feorr not far *wd.*
un-fér|e incapacitated, infirm.
~nes *f.* infirmity.
un-gefér|e impassable, impervious.
~ed inaccessible.
~endlic*, ~enlic impassable.
un-gefér|lic unsocial, civil (war,.
~līce *av.* in civil war.
un-gefērne impassable.
un-gefepered not feathered.
un-firn, y *av.* not long ago ; soon.
un-gefirn *av.* soon — ~ þæs soon
after that.
un-flitme*† ? *av.* without dispute.
un-gefōg, ~līc immense, excessive ;
impetuous, unrestrained.
~e, ~līce *av.* excessively, immoderately.
un-forbærned not burnt.
un-forboden not forbidden.
un-forbūgend|līc inevitable.
~līce *av.* (gazing) fixedly.
un-forburnen not burnt.
un-forcūþ noble, good [*Cp.* fra-
coþ].
~līce *av.* nobly, well.
un-fordytt unobstructed.
un-forebyrdig impatient.
un-foresceáwod unconsidered,
hasty.
~lic hasty, rash.

un-forgiéfen not forgiven ; not
given in marriage.
un-forgiétende mindful *wg.*
un-forgolden unremunerated.
un-forhǽf(e)dnes *f.* incontinence.
un-forhladen inexhausted Gl.
un-forht fearless.
~e *av.* fearlessly.
~igende fearless.
~līce *av.* fearlessly.
~mōd fearless.
un-forlǽten not left.
un-formolsnod not decayed.
un-formolten unconsumed, undigested.
un-forod unbroken, inviolate.
~lic indissoluble.
unforrot|igendlic, ~odlic incor-
ruptible.
un-forsceáwodlīce *av.* unexpectedly, suddenly ; without forethought *or* consideration.
un-forswǽled not burnt.
un-forswigod not passed over in
silence.
un-forswīþed unconquered.
un-fortredde *f.* knot-grass.
un-fortreden (grass) not killed by
treading.
un-forwand|igendlīce *av.* with-
out bashfulness.
~odlic unhesitating, fearless.
~odlīce *av.* without swerving,
directly ; unexpectedly, suddenly ;
unhesitatingly, fearlessly ; inconsiderately, rashly.
un-forwealwod *once* unwithered
(fruits) (?).
un-forwordenlic undecayed.
un-forworht innocent ‖ unrestricted, free.
un-fracoþlīce *av.* honourably, virtuously.
un-gefrǽg|e, ~elic unheard of,
extraordinary.
~līce *av.* extraordinarily.
un-(ge)frætewod unadorned.
un-fram† feeble.
un-gefrēdelīce *av.* without sensation.
un-gefremed unfinished.
un-frem|u *f.* damage, loss.
~full not advantageous.
un-gefrēod not freed.
un-frēondlīce *av.* unfriendlily.
un-fricgende not questioning.

un-friþ *m.* hostilities, war; being out of the king's peace.

~flota *m.* hostile fleet.

~here *m.* hostile army.

~land *n.* hostile country.

~scip *n.* war-ship; ship of a hostile country.

un-frōd† young.

un-fulfremed imperfect; imperfect (tense).

~nes *f.* imperfection.

un-fulfremming *f.* imperfection Gl.

un-fūliend|e, ~lic incorruptible.

un-(ge)fullod, -fulwad not baptized.

un-gefullod unfulfilled.

un-fulworht unfinished.

un-gefyll|ed, ~e(n)dlic insatiable.

un-gefynde worthless (corn).

un-gēara *av.* lately; soon, *gen. w.* nū.

un-gearo not ready (to act); unprepared (against attack) — on ungearwe by surprise, suddenly; uncultivated (land).

un-gegearwod not clothed.

ungel *m.* fat.

un-genge useless *LN.*

un-georn|e *av.* reluctantly; negligently.

~full negligent.

un-giefende (?) unforgiving. *For* unfor- (?).

un-giéfu *f.* evil gift.

un-giéld, ~e *n.* excessive tax.

~a *m.* one who is not a member of a guild.

~e not entitled to compensation.

un-gíem en(n) *f.* carelessness.

~ende careless.

un-giered not clothed.

un-gifeþe† not granted.

un-gifre† pernicious.

un-ginn† not ample.

un-glæd sad, cheerless (*of* stormy sea).

~lic stern, gloomy Gl.

un-glēaw† dull, not keen (*of* edge of sword) (?) || not sagacious; ignorant *wg.*

~līce *av.* unwisely, imprudently.

~nes *f.*, ~scipe *m.* folly, imprudence, ignorance.

un-g'enged unadorned.

un-gnieþe† not scanty, liberal.

un-gōd I. evil, bad. II. *n.* evil.

un-grāpigende not handling (*of* hands).

un-grēnet not green.

un-gegrēt not greeted.

un-griþ (?) *n.* hostility.

un-gryndet bottomless, deep R.

un-gyltig innocent.

un-(ge)hādod not in holy orders.

un-gehǣl|edlic, ~endlic incurable.

un-hǣl(o) *f.* bad health, unsoundness (in an animal); †misfortune.

un-hǣlþ *f.* bad health.

un-(ge)hǣmed unmarried.

un-gehǣplic unsuitable.

un-hāl in bad health, unsound (animal).

~wendlic incurable.

un-(ge)hālgod unconsecrated.

un-hālig not holy.

un-handworht not made with hands.

un-hār† bald (?) *or* very grey-haired (?).

un-gehāten not promised.

un-gehēafdod (swelling) not come to a head.

un-hēah not lofty, low.

un-gehealdsum, -healt- incontinent.

~līce *av.* incontinently.

~nes *f.* incontinence.

un-hēanlīce *av.* nobly, bravely.

un-hearmgeorn inoffensive.

unheld = -hyld.

un-gehend|e distant.

~nes *f.* distance.

un-hēore = -hīere.

un-geheort disheartened.

un-hered not praised.

un-herigendlic not praiseworthy.

un-hier|e, ēo I. fierce, cruel, grievous. II. fiercely.

~lic fierce; strong (wind); doleful (poem).

un-gehiered unheard of.

un-gehiernes *f.* deafness.

un-(ge)hiersum disobedient.

~līce *av.* disobediently.

~nes *f.* disobedience.

~od disobedient.

un-gehiert cowardly.

un-hīredwist *f.* unfamiliarity !.

un-hīwe formless.

un-hīwed colourless.

un-gehīwod unformed; unfeigned.

un-gehlēopor inharmonious.

un-hlēowe† chill (wave).

un-hlīse disreputable.

un-hlīs|a *m.* infamy.

~bǣre, ~ēadig, ~full, ~ig disreputable.

un-hlitme† = *unflitme (?).

un-hnēaw† liberal; abundant (gifts).

un-hoga foolish *LN.*

un-hold hostile; not loyal.

~a† *m.* fiend.

un-hrædsprǣce slow of speech.

un-hrēoflig not leprous.

un-gehrepod untouched.

un-gehrinen untouched.

un-hrōr not moving *intr.*

un-hūfed bare-headed Gl.

un-gehwǣde much.

un-hwearfiende unchanging.

un-hwīlen† eternal.

un-hygdig, -hȳd- foolish.

un-hyldo *f.* disfavour, hostility.

un-hȳpig unhappy.

un-īeþe, ēa difficult; grievous.

~lic difficult, impossible; grievous.

~līce *av.* with difficulty; with hardship.

~licnes *f.* difficulty.

unīep-, ēa.

~ian molest Gl.

~lǣce, ~lǣcne, ǣ not easily cured.

~mielte not easily digested.

~nes *f.* hardship, affliction; severity; anxiety, grief.

un-lācnigendlic incurable.

un-(ge)lācnod uncured.

un-gelādod not cleared (of charge).

un-gelæccendlic irreprehensible.

un-lǣce *m.* bad physician.

un-lǣd(†), ~e poor; unhappy, wretched; wicked; causing trouble *or* dispute, unlucky (*of* stolen cattle).

~līce *av.* miserably.

un-lǣgne = -liegne.

un-lǣne permanent.

un-(ge)lǣred not learned, ignorant.

~līce *av.* unskilfully.

~nes *f.* want of learning.

un-lǣt not slow, energetic *wg.*

un-lǣtto *f.* sin [unlǣd].

un-lāf *f.* posthumous child.

un-lagu *f.* bad law; injustice.

un-land *n.* what is not land†; barren land.

~āgende not possessing land.

un-lār *f.* bad teaching *or* advice.

H

un-gelaþod uninvited.
un-gelēaf unbelieving.
un-gelēaf|a *m.* unbelief.
~**full** unbelieving.
~**fullic** unbelieving; incredible.
~**fullice** *av.* incredibly.
~**fulnes** *f.* unbelief.
~**lic** incredible.
~**sum** infidel.
~**sumnes** *f.* infidelity.
un-leahtorwierþe irreprehensible.
un-lēanod not repaid.
un-lēas true, honest.
~**līce** *av.* truly.
~**nes** *f.* truth.
un-lēof odious.
un-libbende dead.
un-lichamlic incorporeal.
un-licwierþe unpleasing.
un-gelīc different.
~**a** *m.* one not like another.
~**e** *av.* differently.
~**lic** improper.
~**lice** *av.* improperly.
~**nes** *f.* difference.
un-gelief|ed infidel.
~**end** infidel *LN.*
~**e(n)dlic** incredible.
~**nes** *f.* unbelief.
un-(ge)liefed not allowed.
un-liefe(n)dlic unlawful.
un-liegne not to be denied, incontrovertible LL.
un-līf *n.* — -es dead.
un-lifigende dead.
un-gelimp *n.* misfortune.
~**lic** unseasonable; unfortunate.
~**lice** *av.* unseasonably; unhappily.
un-līþe severe, cruel.
un-līþuwāc, -leo- inflexible, severe.
~**nes** *f.* inflexibility, severity.
un-lofod not praised.
un-lust *m.* disinclination, tedium; want of appetite | evil desire, lust.
ge-ian loathe.
un-lyb|ba, ge- *m.* poison, drug; sorcery.
~**wyrhta** *m.* sorcerer.
un-lyft *f.* bad air, malaria.
un-(ge)lygen truthful.
un-lȳt *n.* much.
un-lȳtel I. big; great; much.
II. *n.* much.
un-gemaca *m.* not a match *or* equal.

un-gemæcc dissimilar.
un-mǣg *m.* bad kinsman (?) *or* alien (?).
~**e** not of kin, alien.
un-mǣgnes = *-mēagolnes.
un-mǣle spotless, immaculate.
un-mǣne without evil, sincere (oath); devoid *w.* fram.
un-mǣr|e without fame, obscure.
~**lic** ignoble.
un-mǣt|e immense, excessive.
~**lic** immense.
~**nes** *f.* immenseness, excess.
un-gemǣt|e I. excessive. **II.** *av.* excessively.
~**lic** immense.
un-mǣþ *f.* wrong.
~**lic** excessive.
~**lice** *av.* immoderately, excessively; violently, cruelly.
un-mag|a *mf.,* ~**u** (?) *f.* helpless *or* needy person; one who is dependent on others, ward.
un-manig few.
un-mann *m.* bad man.
un-mēagol insipid.
~**nes*, -mægnes** *f.* weariness.
un-gemēd|e incompatible; unpleasant.
~**nes** *f.* adversity *LN.*
un-medom|e unfit, unworthy.
~**lice** *av.* improperly.
un-meltung [= ię (?)] *f.* indigestion.
un-gemenged, unm- unmixed.
~**nes** *f.* purity.
un-mennisclic anti-human, unnatural.
un-gemet I. *n.* immensity, large quantity; want of moderation —
~**e, ~es, ~um** excessively. **II.** *av.* excessively, very.
~**ceald**† very cold.
~**fæst** excessive; intemperate ‖ very firm†.
~**fæstlic** irretentive.
~**fæstnes** *f.* intemperance.
~**gīemen(n)**† *f.* excessive care.
~**hleahtor** *m.* immoderate laughter.
~**lic, unm-** immense; excessive.
~**lice, unm-** *av.* immoderately; excessively.
~**nes** *f.* extravagance.
~**þurst** *m.* excessive thirst.
~**wæcce** *f.* excessive wakefulness.
~**wæl** *n.* great carnage.
~**wilnung** *f.* excessive desire.

un-gemetg|od excessive; intemperate.
~**ung** *f.* excess, intemperance.
un-mett- excess.
un-micel small.
un-(ge)mīdlod unrestrained.
un-gemielt*, y, e undigested.
~**nes*, e** *f.* indigestion.
un-miht I. *f.* weakness. **II.** impossible *LN.*
~**elic, ~lic** impossible.
geun-miht, un-gemiht without strength, weak.
un-mihtig, ~lic weak; impossible *LN.*
~**nes** *f.* weakness, impotence.
un-mild|e ungentle, harsh.
~**heort** merciless.
un-milts *f.* anger (of God).
~**igendlic** unpardonable.
~**ung** *f.* impiety, cruelty.
un-mōd *n.* despondency.
un-gemōd at variance.
~**nes** *f.* contentiousness.
un-mōdig pusillanimous; diffident.
un-gemōdignes *f.* contentiousness.
un-gemolsnod undecayed.
un-gemunucod not made a monk.
un-murn† without anxiety, unconcerned.
~**lice**† *av.* without anxiety.
un-gemynd *f.* madness.
~**ig** unmindful *wg.*
un-myndlinga *av.* undesignedly; unexpectedly.
un-mynegod not demanded.
un-myrg|e sad (?) Gl.
~**þ** *f.* sadness, misery.
unn|a *m.,* ~**e** *f.* permission; liberality; what is granted, grant [ann].
un-nēah I. *av., prp. wd.* far (from). **II.** *aj.* distant *LN.*
unnend *m.* one who grants *LN.* [ann].
un-geniedd uncompelled.
un-nied|ig uncompelled.
~**unga** *av.* without compulsion.
un-nīþing *m.* honest *or* respectable man *vL.*
un-nyt|t, -net I. useless, frivolous. **II.** *n.* what is useless, folly, frivolity; detriment.
~**lic** useless, unprofitable.

un-nyt|līce *av.* to no purpose ; to ill purpose.
~licnes *f.* unserviceableness.
~nes *f.* uselessness, triviality.
~wierpe useless.
~wierplīce *av.* uselessly, to no purpose.
un-ofercumen unconquered.
un-oferfēre impassable.
un-oferhrēfed not roofed over.
un-oferswiþ|ed unconquered.
~edlic, ~ende, ~endlic invincible.
un-oferwinnendlic invincible.
un-oferwrigen not covered over.
un-oferwunnen*, -innen unconquered.
un-ofslægen not killed.
un-onbindendlic, -bundenlic indissoluble.
un-onstyrigendlic motionless.
un-onwęndedlic, -węndlic unchangeable.
un-onwęndend|lic unchangeable.
~līce *av.* unchangeably.
un-orn|e mean, humble ; old (clothes).
~lic mean, of small value.
un-plēo|lic safe.
~līce *av.* safely.
un-gerād I. discordant, at variance *wd.* ; unskilful *wg.* ; boorish, foolish. **II.** *n.* discord, folly.
~nes *f.* discord.
un-ræd *m.* bad policy, wickedness, folly ; injury, detriment.
~fæstlīce *f.* ill-advisedly, foolishly.
~lic ill-advised, foolish.
~līce *av.* ill-advisedly, foolishly.
~siþ *m.* unprofitable course.
un-geræd stupid. *Cp.* ungerād.
~elīce *av.* rudely.
~nes *f.* discord.
un-ræden(n) ?†   *f.* ill-advised action.
un-ræfniendlic*, on- intolerable.
un-geręc|e *n.* tumult.
~lic tumultuous.
~līce *av.* tumultuously.
un-geręgnod, -rēnod not ornamented.
un-gereord barbarous Gl.
un-gereordod unfed.
~lic, -reordlic insatiable.
un-rēt|an make sad.
~o *f.* sadness, anxiety.
un-rēþe gentle.
un-rīce humble, poor.

un-riht, y I. wrong, wicked, unjust. **II.** *n.* wrong, wickedness, injustice.
~cyst *f.* vice.
~dǣd *f.* evil-doing.
~dǣde evil-doing.
~dēma *m.* unjust judge.
~dōm *m.* iniquity.
~dōnde evil-doing.
~e *av.* wrongly.
~fēoung *f.* evil hatred.
~gięld *n.* unjust tax *vL.*
~gięlp *n.* vainglory.
~gītsung *f.* covetousness.
unrihthǣm|an commit fornication *or* adultery.
~ed I. *n.* fornication, adultery. **II.** adulterous.
~dere *m.* adulterer.
~end *m.* adulterer.
~ere *m.* adulterer, fornicator.
unriht|lic wrong, wicked, unjust.
~līce *av.* wrongly, unjustly.
~lust *m.* improper desire.
~lyblāc *n.* sorcery.
~nes *f.* iniquity, injustice.
~gestrēon *n.* unrighteous gain.
~weorc *n.* improper work.
~wīf *n.* loose woman.
~wīfung *n.* unlawful matrimony.
~willende ill-disposed.
~(ge)wilnung *f.* evil desire.
unrihtwīs evil, wicked, unjust.
~līce *av.* unrighteously.
~nes *f.* iniquity, injustice.
unriht|wrigels *m.* veil of error.
~wyrcend(e) evil-doing, -doer.
~wyrhta *m.* evil-doer.
un-rīm I. *n.* countless quantity. **II.** *aj.* innumerable.
~e innumerable.
~folc *n.* innumerable people.
un-gerīm I. *n.* countless quantity. **II.** *aj.* innumerable.
~ed, ~(ed)lic innumerable.
un-rīpe immature.
un-gerīpod immature ; premature.
un-gerisende unbecoming.
un-gerisen|e, -risne I. unsuitable; improper. **II.** *n., often pl.* inconvenience ; unseemliness, disgrace.
~lic unseemly.
~līce *av.* disgracefully.
~nes, -risnes *f.* disgrace.
un-rōt sad.
~ian be sad ‖ *tr.* make sad.

un-rōt|lic gloomy (sky).
~mōd sad.
~nes *f.* sadness.
~sian be sad ‖ *tr.* make sad.
un-rōtlic — ~e dōn *pl.* exterminate *lN.* (?).
un-rūh smooth.
un-geryd|e I. boisterous, rough. **II.** *n.* rough place.
~elīce *av.* violently, very.
~nes *f.* tumult.
un-ryne *m.* diarrhoea. *For* ūt- (?).
un-sac free from accusation.
un-gesadelod not saddled.
un-sǣd unsatiated.
unsǣd *n.* evil seed.
un-sǣgd, -sǣd unsaid.
un-sǣl *m., gen. pl.* unhappiness.
~e evil, wicked.
~ig unhappy ; wicked ; calamitous.
~þ, unge- *f.* unhappiness, misfortune.
un-gesǣlig unhappy ; calamitous.
~līce *av.* unhappily ; wickedly.
~nes *f.* misery.
un-gesǣllīce *av.* unhappily.
un-sǣpig sapless.
un-samwrǣde opposed, contrary.
un-sār free from pain.
un-sāwen not sown (field).
un-gescād, ēa I. *n.* want of intelligence, indiscretion. **II.** *aj.* unreasonable. **III.** *av.* unreasonably, excessively.
~lic unreasonable.
~līce, unscēadelīce *av.* unreasonably ; excessively.
ungescādwīs irrational, foolish.
~lic, unsc- irrational, indiscreet.
~līce *av.* indiscreetly.
~nes *f.* want of intelligence, indiscretion.
un-scam|fæst shameless.
~fulnes *f.* shamelessness.
~iende not ashamed.
~ig unabashed.
~lic shameless.
~līce *av.* shamelessly.
un-gescapen unformed ; uncreated.
un-scearp not sharp (wine).
~nes *f.* dullness (of mind).
~sīene not sharp-sighted.
un-scęnde†, y not bringing disgrace, honourable (gift).
un-(ge)scęnded uninjured.
un-scęnnan *once* unharness.
un-scęþed uninjured.

un-scępful|l, æ, ea innocent.
~līce *av.* innocently.
~nes *f.* innocence.
un-gescępped uninjured.
un-scęppende, æ, -sceaþþiende harmless, innocent.
un-scęppig, æ, ea harmless, innocent.
~nes *f.* innocence.
un-scielliht without shells (fish).
un-scierped not clothed.
un-scōgan = on-.
un-scoren unshorn, unshaved.
un-scortende not running short *lN.*
un-gescrēp|e, ǣ inconvenient.
~nes *f.* inconvenience.
~o *f.* inconvenience.
un-scyld *f.* innocence ‖ grievous fault.
~ig guiltless, innocent ; not accountable (for ill result).
~iglic innocent.
~ignes *f.* innocence.
un-scynde = -scęnde.
un-seald not given.
un-sealt without salt.
un-gesegnod, -sēnod not marked with the sign of the cross.
un-sęht I. *mfn.* discord. II. *aj.* at variance, mutually hostile.
un-seldan *av.* often.
un-gesēonde blind.
un-gesewen unseen.
~lic, uns- invisible.
~līce *av.* invisibly.
un-sibb *f.* enmity ; strife, war ; disagreement, dissension.
~ian disagree.
un-gesibb not related *or* akin ; at variance.
un-gesibsum quarrelsome.
~nes, uns- *f.* quarrelsomeness ; discord.
un-sideful|1 unchaste.
~nes *f.* unchastity.
un-sidu *m.* vice.
un-gesięlt not salted.
un-gesīen|e, ~lic invisible.
un-sigefæst unvictorious.
un-sīþ *m.* evil *or* rash expedition ; misfortune.
un-slæc, ea energetic.
~līce *av.* energetically.
~nes *f.* diligence.
un-slǣpig sleepless.
un-slāw, ǣ, ēa active, energetic.

un-slāwlīce *av.* actively.
un-slit (*n.*) fat, tallow Gl.
un-sliten not torn.
un-smeoruwig not greasy.
un-smēþ|e rough.
~nes *f.* roughness.
un-smōþ (?) rough.
un-snotor, tt foolish.
~līce *av.* unwisely.
~nes *f.* folly.
un-snytr|o, tt *f.* folly — ~um foolishly.
un-(ge)soden not boiled *or* cooked.
un-sōft|e *av.* in discomfort : him ~ wearþ he felt discomfort ; severely ; with difficulty.
~līce *av.* not gently.
un-sōm *f.* disagreement.
un-gesōm at variance.
un-sorg without anxiety.
un-sōþ I. not true. II. *n.* untruth.
~fæst unveracious ; unjust.
~fæstnes *f.* injustice, iniquity.
~ian falsify, disprove.
~sagol mendacious.
un-spēd *f.* poverty, want.
~ig poor ; barren (soil).
un-spiwol not emetic.
un-sprecende speechless.
un-stæfwīs illiterate.
un-gestæþþig, unst- unstable, inconstant.
~lic*, -stæþþelic unstable.
~līce *av.* unsteadily.
~nes, unst- *f.* unsteadiness.
un-staþolfæst not stationary ; desiring change, unsettled ; not steadfast, wavering (in mind)
~nes *f.* inconstancy.
un-stędeful|1*, unstydful apostate *lN.*
~nes*, onstydf- *f.* instability *lN.*
un-stęnc *m.* stench.
un-still|e not still ; restless, turbulent ; not at peace, troubled.
ge~ian disturb.
~nes *f.* motion ; disturbance, bustle ; breach of peace ; restlessness, unruliness ; agitation (of mind).
un-strang weak.
~ian be weak.
~nes *f.* weakness.
un-strenge weak.
un-gestrēon *n.* ill-gotten treasure.
un-gestroden not liable to confiscation.
un-styrigende stationary.

un-styrigendlic insupportable (burden).
un-swǣs unpleasant.
~lic grievous, unpleasant.
un-swefn *n.* bad dream.
un-geswēge discordant.
un-geswęncedlic indefatigable.
un-sweotol not discernible.
un-swēte sour, bitter ; fetid.
un-swicen not betrayed, safe.
un-swīcende loyal.
un-geswicendlīce *av.* incessantly.
un-swicigende unfailing, loyal.
un-swicol honest.
un-swīp weak.
~e *av.* not vigorously.
un-geswuncen unlaboured Gl.
un-sȳfer|lic impure.
~nes *f.* impurity.
un-sȳfre dirty ; (morally) impure.
un-synn *f.* — †~um guiltlessly, without having deserved it.
un-synnig guiltless, innocent ; undeserved (punishment).
un-getæl, e innumerable.
un-tǣl|e blameless.
~ed unblamed.
~lic*, -tǣllic irreprehensible.
~līce, ā *av.* blamelessly.
~wierpe irreprehensible.
~wierþlīce *av.* laudably.
un-getǣs|e I. inconvenient, unpleasant. II. *n.* inconvenience, trouble.
~līce *av.* inconveniently.
~nes *f.* inconvenience.
un-tǣllic = -tǣllic.
un-tamlic*, -tamcul untameable.
un-teald uncounted.
un-tealt steady (ship).
un-tela, eo, ea, a *av.* badly.
un-tęllendlic indescribable *vL.*
un-tęmed untamed.
un-getęmprung *f.* rough weather (!).
un-teogoþod = -tēopod.
un-getēon- = ungetien-.
un-tēorig untiring, unceasing.
un-getēor|igendlīce *av* indefatigably.
~od unwearied.
un-tēoþod*, -tiogoþad untithed.
un-tīd* *f.* wrong time.
~fyllo *f.* feasting at wrong times.
~lic unseasonable.
~līce *av.* unseasonably.
~sprǣc *f.* unseasonable talking.

un-tīd|weorc *n.* work at wrong times.

~gewidere *n.* unseasonable weather.

un-tīedre*, -tyddre firm (mind).

un-tīemende barren.

un-getīen-, ēo, *pl.* ~a misfortune, trouble.

un-tilod without provision made, unprepared.

un-tīm|a *m.* wrong time; bad season, calamity.

~e ill-timed, bringing misfortune.

~nes *f.* bad season, calamity.

un-tīþa*, -tygþa unsuccessful in obtaining a request.

un-tōbrocen not broken in pieces.

un-tōclofen not cloven (foot).

un-tōdǣled not divided *or* separated.

~lic, -dǣllic, -dǣlendlic indivisible, inseparable.

~lice *av.* indivisibly, inseparably.

~nes *f.* undividedness.

un-tōdǣllic, -dǣllic indivisible, inseparable.

un-getogen uneducated.

un-tōlǣtendlice *av.* unremittingly.

un-tōliesende inextricable.

un-tōscacen not destroyed.

un-tōslægen not beaten to pieces.

un-tōsliten not torn.

un-tōsprecendlic (!) ineffable.

un-tōtwǣmed undivided, unseparated.

un-trāglice† *av.* well, honestly.

un-trēow *f.*, *gen. pl. w. sg. meaning* perfidy, fraud.

~e = -trīewe.

~fæst untrustworthy.

~sian, unge- act unfairly, defraud *abs.*; offend: untrēowsod bēon scandalizari.

~þ, ie, unge- *f.* perfidy, treachery.

un-trīew|e, ēo, unge- not faithful *wd.*

~lice *av.* perfidiously.

~þ = -trēowþ.

un-getrīewnes *f.* infidelity.

un-trum, unge- weak; in bad health.

~ian be weak || *tr.* enfeeble.

~lic weak.

~nes, -trym- *f.* weakness; illness.

un-trymed unconfirmed (by bishop).

un-trymig weak, in bad health *LN.*

~o *f.* illness *LN.*

un-trymi(g)an become weak *or* ill *LN.*

un-trymnes = -trumnes.

un-trymp *f.* weakness; illness.

un-twēo *m.* certainty.

~lic undoubted.

~lice, -twȳlice *av.* undoubtedly; without feeling doubt.

un-twēod unwavering (courage).

un-twēogend|e I. not doubting, unhesitating, unwavering. II. *av.* without doubting.

~lic certain.

~lice *av.* unhesitatingly; unequivocally.

un-twēonigend*, ȳ indubitable.

un-twifeald united; simple-minded, sincere.

un-twȳlice = -twēo-.

un-(ge)tȳd, -dd untrained, unskilled.

un-tȳdre† *once*, *m.* monster.

un-tȳdrende barren.

un-tygþa = -tīþa.

un-tȳned unfenced.

un-getyng|e, -full not eloquent.

un-þærfe = -þierfe.

un-þæs|lic, unge- unsuitable, unseemly.

~lice *av.* improperly.

~licnes *f.* unseemliness.

~licu *f.* incongruity *once L.*

un-þanc *m.* displeasure, ill-will; *opposite of* thanks : him ~ sǣde þæs; act of ill-will, offence | ~es against one's will *wg.*: his ~es.

~full, unge- ungrateful *wg.*

~wierþe, -weorþ, u unacceptable; ungrateful.

un-geþanc *m.* evil thought.

~full ungrateful.

un-geþeaht *n.* bad counsel.

~endlice *av.* hastily.

un-þearf *f.* disadvantage, detriment.

~es *av.* needlessly.

un-þēaw *m.* bad habit, vice.

~fæst vicious, unmannerly.

~fæstlice *av.* viciously.

~full undisciplined.

un-geþēaw|e opposed to one's habits.

~fæst ill-regulated.

un-geþenlice *av.* basely.

un-geþēod separate.

un-þierfe*, æ useless *LN.*

un-þinged, unge- unexpected, sudden.

un-þingod unatoned.

un-þol|emōdnes *f.* impatience.

~igendlic intolerable.

un-þrīste timid, diffident.

un-þrow|endlicnes *f.* impassibility.

~igendlic incapable of suffering.

un-geþungen vile.

un-þurhscēotendlic impenetrable.

un-þurhtogen not performed.

un-þwægen, o unwashed.

un-geþwǣr|e, unþ- I. at variance, quarrelsome; troublesome, unpleasant. II. *n.* disturbance *LN.*

~ian, geunþwǣrian be at variance.

~lic discordant.

~lice *av.* ungently.

~nes, unþ- *f.* discord, quarrel; vexation, trouble.

un-þyhtig weak.

un-geþyld *fn.* impatience.

~ig, unþ- impatient.

~iglice, ~elice *av.* impatiently.

un-þyldlicnes *f.* difficulty (!) Bd.

un-wāc|lic† splendid.

~lice† *av.* resolutely; splendidly.

un-wǣded not clothed.

un-gewǣpnod unarmed.

un-wǣr not on one's guard; heedless | unwær, on ~, ~es, on unwaran (= -um) *av.* unexpectedly.

~lic heedless.

~lice *av.* heedlessly, carelessly.

~nes *f.*, ~scipe *m.* heedlessness.

un-wǣscen not washed.

un-wǣstm *m.* failure of crops; weed *LN.*

~bǣre unproductive, barren.

~bǣrnes *f.* barrenness.

~berendlic barren.

~berendnes *f.* barrenness.

~fæst barren.

~fæstnes *f.* barrenness.

un-wæterig without water.

un-wandiende unhesitating.

un-warnod unwarned.

un-geweald — ~es *av.* involuntarily, by chance.

un-gewealden disordered (stomach) (!).

un-wealt steady (ship).

[195]

un-wearnum† *av.* without hindrance, irresistibly.
un-weaxen not grown up.
un-weder, unge- *n.* bad weather, storm.
~līce *av.* so as to threaten bad weather.
un-wegen not weighed.
un-węm|me without blemish, uninjured, inviolate.
~lic immaculate.
~nes *f.* immaculateness.
un-węmm|ed immaculate.
~ing *f.* incorruption Gl.
un-gewęmmed, ~lic uninjured; immaculate.
~līce *av.* inviolably.
~nes, -węmnes *f.* purity.
un-gewęnd|nes *f.* unchangeableness.
~endlic unchanging, chronic (illness).
un-wēn|e hopeless; unexpected.
~ed unexpected.
~lic unpromising.
~unga *av.* unexpectedly.
un-wēod *n.* weed.
un-weorcheard infirm, delicate.
un-weorclic*, unwo- (time) not suitable for work.
un-weorþ = -wierþe.
~ian dishonour, disgrace ‖ become contemptible Gl.
~lic unimportant, petty; not creditable, infamous.
~līce *av.* improperly; ignominiously; with indignation.
~scipe *m.* disgrace; indignation.
~ung *f.* disgrace; indignation.
un-weotod = -witod.
un-węred uncovered.
un-wērig not weary.
un-gewērigod unwearied.
un-werod not sweet.
un-widere *n.* bad weather, storm.
un-gewider|e *n.* bad weather.
~ung *f.* bad weather *vL.*
un-widlod not polluted.
un-gewięld, ~e unsubdued.
~elic unyielding.
un-gewięrded uninjured.
un-wierþ|e, -weorþ, u of no value; not esteemed, contemptible; ignominious; wanting in merit, unworthy *wg.*
~nes *f.* contempt; disgrace.
un-wierþe *av.* unworthily.

un-will — ~es against one's will *w. g., poss. pro.*
un-gewill unpleasing *vL.*
un-will|a *m.* what displeases | ~an, ~um against one's will *w. g., poss. pro.* : his ~an, ūrum ~um.
~ende unwilling.
un-wilsumlīce *av.* against one's will.
un-wine *m.* enemy.
un-gewintred not grown up.
un-wīs foolish, stupid; ignorant *wg.*
~dōm *m.* folly, stupidity; ignorance.
~lic foolish.
~līce *av.* foolishly.
~nes *f.* ignorance; wickedness *LN.*
un-gewiss I. uncertain | ignominious. II. *n.* uncertainty, doubt | unconsciousness. on ~e without knowing it. ~es *av.* involuntarily | ignominy.
~lic uncertain.
~nes *f.* uncertainty.
un-wita *m.* ignorant person, fool.
un-witende not knowing, unconscious, frenzied.
un-gewītendlīce *av.* permanently.
un-wītn|igendlīce, unge- *av.* with impunity.
~od, unge- unpunished.
~ung *f.* impunity.
un-witod, eo uncertain.
unwit|t.
~weorc *n.* foolish work.
un-gewit|t *n.* insanity; folly.
~fæstnes *f.* madness.
~full insane; foolish.
~fulnes *f.* insanity.
~lic foolish.
un-wittig unintelligent, stupid.
un-gewittig mad; irrational; foolish.
~līce, -wittelīce *av.* foolishly.
~nes *f.* foolishness.
un-wittol ignorant.
un-wiþerweard not adverse.
un-wiþmeten|lic, -endlic incomparable.
~līce *av.* incomparably.
un-wlite *m.* disfigurement.
un-wlitig, unge- ugly, disfiguring.
~ian deprive of beauty ‖ become ugly.
~nes *f.* disfigurement.
~ung *f.* disfiguring.
un-(ge)worht not made.

un-wrǣne not lustful.
un-wrǣst, ~e weak, untrustworthy, contemptible.
~līce *av.* feebly.
un-wrecen unavenged; unpunished (crime).
un-wręnc *m.* spiteful trick, artifice; vice.
un-(ge)writen unwritten.
un-writere *m.* careless scribe.
un-wriþen not bound.
un-gewun|a I. *m.* bad habit. II. unaccustomed.
~elic unusual, exceptional; unfrequented.
~elīce *av.* unusually.
un-wunden I. not wound. II. unwound = onwunden.
un-wundod not wounded.
un-wunigendlic, unge- uninhabitable.
un-wynsum unpleasant.
~nes *f.* unpleasantness.
un-wyrd *f.* misfortune.
un-gewyrht *nf.* — be ~um without cause.
un-ymbwęndedlic unalterable *LN.*
ūp, ūpp [*by infl. of* uppan] *rest* above, up; erect | *motion* upwards; up (a river), up (the country) — cuman ~ land, lǣtan put ashore, *also fig.* | *separation* ~ forlǣtan divide (course of river).
ūp-āhafen|līce, æ *av.* arrogantly.
~nes *f.* lifting up; exaltation; exultation; pride.
ūp-āhęfed|līce *av.* proudly.
~nes *f.* lifting up; exaltation; pride.
ūp-āsprungennes, -springnes *f.* rising; origin.
ūp-āstigennes, -stignes *f.* ascent; means of ascent.
ūp-āwęnd upturned.
ūpcund celestial.
ūp-cyme *m.* rise.
ūp-eard† *m.* dwelling on high (heaven).
ūp-ęnde *m.* upper end.
ūp-ęngel† *m.* angel of heaven.
ūp-fǣreld *n.* ascension.
ūp-feax having hair above, bald in front Gl.
ūp-flēring *f.* upper story *or* chamber.
ūp-flōr *f.* upper story *or* chamber.
ūp-gang *m.* rising (of sun); land-

ing, going up the country; access, approach.

úp-godu *npl.* celestial deities.

úp-hafennes, -hæfenes *f.* raising.

úp-héafod *n.* top end (of field).

úp-héah upright; tall; distinguished, noble.

úp-heald *n.* supporter, maintenance.

úp-hebbe† *f.* 'tail-lifter,' waterfowl, coot.

úp-hebbing *f.* rising *lN.*

úp-hefnes *f.* exaltation.

úp-heofon *m.* lofty heaven, sky.

úp-hús *n.* upper chamber.

úp-land*, uppel- *n.* up-country, rural districts *vL.*

úp-lang upright; tall.

úp-legen *f.* hair-pin.

úp-lendisc up the country, rustic.

úplic on high, lofty, celestial, sublime.

úp-lyft *fnm.* upper air.

úp-gemynd† *n.* thoughts of heaven.

úpnes *f.* height.

uppian rise.

uppan, -on *prp. w. a., d.* upon, on; above | *of time* on; after | *opposition, attack* against *wa.* | in addition to *wa.*

uppe *av.* on high, up; up (*of the* sun) | on land; present (*of* arrival) | ~ weorþan be revealed *or* known; ~ bringan bring to pass.

uppe- = úp-.

úp-riht upright, erect; with the face upwards Gl.

~e *av.* erect; overhead, in the zenith.

úp-rodor†, a *m.* sky, heaven.

úp-ryne *m.* rising (of the sun); beginning (of day).

úp-spring *m.* rising (of the sun); beginning (of day); bursting forth (of water); birth; what springs up Gl.

úp-stige *m.* ascent, (Christ's) ascension; means of ascent Gl.

úp-stígend *m.* ascender Gl.

úp-wæstm *m.* stature, height (of man).

úp-ware *mpl.* denizens of heaven Gl.

úp-weard I. *aj.* up-turned, up; moving upwards. II. *av. motion* upwards; up (the country)

| (counting days) backward (from end of month).

úp-weardes, uppew- *av.* upwards.

úp-weg *m.* way to heaven.

úp-gewend upturned.

úp-wiellende*, y flowing up Gl.

úr *m.* bison; *the Runic letter* u.

úre of us.

~lendisc (!) of our country.

úrig.

~feþera† dewy-winged.

~lást† with dewy track.

urnen *ptc. of* iernan.

ús us.

úsic us *a.*

ússer = úre.

út *av.* out *motion* | outside; out (at sea); abroad.

útian expel; alienate (property).

úta- = útan-.

úta-cumen = útan-.

utan = uton let us.

útan *av.* outside, from outside.

útan-bordes *av.* abroad.

útan-cumen, útac-, -ymen, útcymen foreign, strange; belonging to some one else.

útane,-one, -ene *av.* from outside; outside; *met.* outwardly.

útan-landes *av.* abroad.

útan-weard outside.

út-cwealm *m.* complete destruction Gl.

út-cymen = útan-cumen.

út-dráf *f.* expulsion.

~ere *m.* expeller Gl.

úte *av., cpv.* útor, út(t)er outside, in the open air; away from home, abroad | *motion* out.

úter *cpv. of* úte.

~mere *m.* open sea.

úterra, -era, út(t)ra *cpv.* outer, exterior; *met.* external | *spl.* **ýtemest, út(e)mest** outermost, extreme; last.

úte-weard outside, at the extremity — on ~um outside.

út-fær *n.* exit.

út-færeld *n.* going out.

út-faru *f.* going out.

út-gefeoht *n.* war abroad.

út-fór *f.* evacuation (of body).

út-fús† ready to sail (*of* ship).

út-gang *m.* going out, exit, protrusion; evacuation (of body);

end (of period) | place of going out, passage; what is evacuated (from body) | anus; privy.

út-gársecg† *m.* furthest ocean.

út-geng- exit *lN.*

út-healf *f.* outside.

út-here *m.* foreign army.

út-iern|ende purgative (drug); diarrhoeic (disease); suffering from diarrhoea.

~ing*, ~iorning *f.* flux *lN.*

út-lád *f.* right to carry things out of a place.

út-lǽs *f.,g.* ~we pasture away from the house.

ut-lag*, -h *L.* outlawed; connected with *or* necessitating outlawry [*Scand.* útlagr].

~a *m.* outlaw.

~ian outlaw.

~u (!) *f.* outlawry.

út-land *n.* foreign country; outlying land.

út-lend|a *m.* foreigner.

~e, ~isc foreign.

útlic external, foreign.

út-gemǽre *n.* extreme boundary.

útmest, *see* úterra.

uton, wu-, *lN.* wutum, *lM.* wutu let us! *w. inf.* : ~ (wē) gán !.

út-ryne *m.* running out, exit; what flows out.

út-scyte *m.* place where a stream or road runs into another.

út-scytling *m.* stranger Gl.

út-siht, ~e, ~ádl *f.* diarrhoea.

út-síþ *m.* going out, egress.

ut-spíwung*, usspiung *f.* expectoration.

út-wǽpnedmann *m.* stranger Bd.

út-wærc *m.* dysentery.

út-waru *f.* defence (military service) away from home.

út-weald *m.* outlying wood.

út-weard outside of; †striving to escape.

úp-genge departing — ~ weorþan *wd.* pass out of one's possession†; transitory (wealth).

úp-mǽte immense.

úp-wit|a, *lN.* up(u)uta *m.* sage, philosopher, scholar.

~ian study philosophy.

~igung *f.* study of philosophy, philosophy.

~lic philosophical.

W.

wā, A. also wǣ I. indecl. no. used as av. wdg. evil, suffering : him wæs ~ þæs it caused him pain or grief. II. interj. wdg. : ~ him þæs sīþes ! [wāwa].

~lic lamentable.

wāc I. weak; timid, slothful ; pliant; slender ; insignificant, mean ; bad (state of things). II.(n.) weakness.

~e av. weakly, slothfully.

~ian become weak ; become torpid or cowardly.

~lic insignificant, mean.

~lice av. weakly ; meanly.

~mōd weak-minded, timid, irresolute.

~mōdnes f. weakness of mind, cowardice.

~nes f. weakness ; insignificance.

~scipe m. weakness ; insignificance.

wacan 2 intr. (awake) ; be born ; originate.

wac|ian, A. æ; prs. ptc. ~iende, wæccende be awake ; keep watch w. ofer.

wacnian = wæcnian.

wacol awake ; watchful ; vigilant ; attentive.

~lice av. vigilantly.

wacon = wæcen.

wacor, wæc(c)er watchful, vigilant.

~lice, wocor- av. vigilantly.

wacsan = wascan wash.

wād n. woad.

~sǣd n. woad-seed.

~spitel m. woad-spade.

wad|an 2 go, advance ; lead life. behave ; wade ‖ tr. ge- penetrate.

~ung f. going.

wǣ = wā.

~nes f. iniquity.

wǣ-werþlice, -wærþ-, -werd-, y av. vigorously, boldly.

wǣc|an weaken ; afflict [wāc].

ge-ednes f. weakness.

wæccan = wacian, esp. in lN.

wæcce f. keeping awake, vigil ; watch (part of night) [wacan].

wæccer = wacor.

wæcen, wacon f. keeping awake, watching (over), guarding.

wæcn|an, ~ian be born ; have origin (from) [wacan].

wǣd† n. water, sea gen. in pl.

gewǣd n. ford, shallow [wadan].

wǣd f. dress, clothes ; sail-yard, rope.

~brēc fpl. trousers.

~lēas without clothes.

~erāp m. stay, pl. rigging.

gewǣd|e n. dress, clothes, equipment.

~ian dress, equip, furnish.

wǣdelnes f. poverty.

wǣdl, A. wēþl, ǣ† f. poverty.

~a m. pauper.

~ian be poor.

~ig poor.

~ung f. poverty.

gewǣf = gewef.

wǣfan supply with clothes, clothe [wefan].

wǣfung = wāfung.

wǣfels m. covering ; dress, cloak.

wæfer-gang m. cobweb [wefan].

wǣfer|hūs n. theatre, amphitheatre.

~lic of a theatre.

~nes f. pomp, pageant.

~sīen f. spectacle, display.

~stōw f. theatre.

wǣflian talk foolishly Gl.

wǣfre wandering, restless, flickering (flame).

wæfs = wæsp wasp.

wǣfþ f. show, spectacle Gl.

wǣg m. wave [wegan].

~bora† m. wave-traverser.

~bord ⊢ n. ship.

~dēor† n. sea-monster.

~dropa† m. tear.

~fǣt† n. cloud.

~faru ⊢ f. sea-way.

~flota† m. ship.

~hengest† m. ship.

~holm† m. sea.

wǣg|līþende† seafaring.

~rāp† m. wave-bond.

~stæp† n. sea-shore.

~strēam† m. sea-current.

~sweord† n. sword with wavy pattern.

~þel† n. ship.

~þrēa† m. violence of waves.

~þrēat† m. violence of waves, flood.

wǣgan afflict ; frustrate ; deceive.

wǣge† n. cup.

wǣg|e f. scales, balance ; a certain weight, wey (of cheese) [wegan].

~pundern n. pair of scales.

~(e)scalu f. scales, balance.

~etunge f. tongue of a balance.

gewǣge n. weight, measure.

wægn, wǣn m. carriage, cart, chariot.

~ere n. charioteer.

~faru f. chariot-journey.

~scilling m. tax on vehicles.

~eþixl, wǣnes þīsl f. carriage-shaft; Great Bear (constellation).

~þoll cart-pin (?) Gl.

~gewǣdu npl. lining of a carriage.

~weg m. cart-road.

~wyrhta m. wheelwright.

gewǣgnian once frustrate Gl.

wǣl n. slaughter, carnage ; field of battle ; bodies of those who have fallen in battle coll.

~bedd† n. bed of death.

~bend† f. deadly bond.

~benn† f. wound.

~blēat† pale.

~ceald† deadly cold.

~cēasiga ⊢ carrion-picking (raven).

~clamm† m. deadly bond.

~cræft† m. deadly art.

~cwealm† m. violent death.

~cyrige, walcrigge f. sorceress.

~dēaþ m. violent death.

~drēor n. blood.

~fǣhþ f. deadly feud.

~fæþm† m. deadly embrace.

~fāg† blood-stained.

wæl|feld † *m.* field of battle.
~fiell†, ea *m.* slaughter.
~fūs† hastening to death.
~fyllo† *f.* fill of slaughter.
~fȳr† *n.* deadly fire ; funeral pyre.
~gār† *m.* spear.
~giest*, æ† *m.* murderous stranger.
~gīfre† sanguinary, murderous.
~gimm† *m.* deadly jewel.
~grǣdig† cannibal.
wælgrim|m fierce, cruel.
~līce *av.* fiercely.
~nes *f.* cruelty.
wæl|gryre† *m.* deadly terror.
~here† *m.* bloodthirsty army.
~hlemm† *m.* fatal stroke.
~hlence† *f.* corslet.
wælhrēow fierce, cruel.
~līce *av.* cruelly.
~nes *f.* ferocity, cruelty.
wæl|hwelp† *m.* deadly whelp.
~mist† *m.* deadly mist.
~nett† *n.* deadly net.
~nīþ† *m.* violence, war.
~notu*, wæll-† *f.* deadly mark *or* letter, rune.
~pīl† *m.* arrow of death.
~rǣs† *m.* deadly onslaught.
~rēaf† *n.* spoils, booty.
~rēc† *m.* deadly vapour.
~regn*, wæll-† *m.* fatal rain, the Deluge.
~rēow = ~hrēow.
~rest†, æ *f.* bed of slaughter, grave.
~rūn † *f.* war-song.
~sceaft† *m.* spear.
~sciell*, -scel slaughter.
~seax† *n.* dagger.
~sliht, ea *m.* slaughter ; †battle.
~slītende biting to death.
~spere † *n.* spear.
~steng† *m.* shaft (of spear), spear.
~stōw *f.* battle-field.
~strǣl† *mf.* deadly arrow.
~strēam† *m.* deadly flood.
~sweng† *m.* deadly stroke.
~wang† *m.* field of slaughter.
~wulf† *m.* warrior, cannibal.
wǣl *mn.* whirlpool, pool ; ocean.
wǣl-wyrt = wēal-.
wǣlan torment, afflict.
wǣlisc = wielisc.
wǣlm = wielm.
wǣlt part of the body, sinew (?) LL.
wǣmn = wǣpen.
wǣn = wǣgn.
wǣp-mann = wǣpned-.

wǣpen, wǣmn *n.* weapon ; membrum virile.
~ ora *m.* soldier, knight.
~hete† *m.* violence, war.
~hūs *n.* armoury.
~lēas without weapons.
~lic male.
~strǣl† *m.* arrow.
~getæc-, ~tac *n. L.* vote of consent expressed by touching weapons ; district governed by such authority [*Scand.*?].
~pracu† *f.* battle.
~geþræc *n.* battle.
~wīfestre = wǣpned-.
~wiga† *m.* warrior.
~gewrixl *n.* hostile encounter.
wǣpn|ian arm.
~ung *f.* armour.
ge-ung *f.* army.
wǣpned male.
~bearn, ~cild *n.* male child.
~cynn *n.* male race.
~hād *m.* male sex.
~hand, ~healf *f.* male line of descent.
~mann, wǣpm- *m.* man.
~wīfestre *f.* hermaphrodite.
wǣps = wǣsp.
wǣr cautious | *wg.* aware ; attending (to), heeding.
~gēapnes *f.* argument Gl.
~lǣcan warn.
~lēas (?) careless.
~lic cautious.
~līce *av.* cautiously ; intently.
~licnes *f.* caution.
~lot *n.* cunning Gl.
~nes *f.* caution.
~scipe *m.* caution.
~word *n.* word of warning.
~wyrde cautious in speech.
wǣr† *n.* sea.
wǣr† true [*Old-Saxon*].
wǣr *f.* agreement, treaty ; promise ; faith, fidelity, friendship.
~fæst† faithful, honourable, true.
~genga† *m.* one seeking protection, client ; stranger.
~lēas† faithless.
~loga *m.* traitor.
~sagol truthful.
gewǣr *wg.* aware.
wǣrc, wræc *m.* pain [weorc].
~an *intr. wa.* be in pain.
wǣrlan go, pass *LN.*
wǣrna = wrǣnna wren.

wǣron were.
gewǣrpan = gewierpan.
wǣrriht = wearriht.
wǣrtere = weartere.
wǣs was.
wǣsc *f.* washing [wascan].
~ere *m.* washer.
~estre *f.* washer, *also of man.*
~ern, ~hūs *n.* laundry.
~ing *f.* washing.
gewǣsc *n.* flood, overflow.
wǣsend = wāsend.
wǣsma *m.* growth.
wǣsp, wæfs, wæps *m.* wasp.
wǣstling *m.* sheet, blanket.
wǣstm, -em *mn.* growth ; stature, form | crop, produce ; fruit, plant ; usury ; progeny | plenty, prosperity *also pl.*
wǣstmbǣr|e fertile, fruitful.
~ian be fruitful ; make fruitful Gl.
~o, ~nes *f.* fertility.
wǣstmberend|e fertile.
~nes *f.* fertility.
wǣstm|lēas unfruitful.
~sceatt *m.* usury.
wǣstmian grow, thrive, bear fruit.
wǣt I. wet, moist. II. *n.* liquid ; drink.
~a *m.* moisture.
~an wet, moisten.
~ian be wet Gl.
~ung *f.* moistening, moisture.
wǣter *n.* water ; sea.
~ādl *f.* dropsy.
~ǣdre *f.* spring, torrent.
~ælfen, e *f.* nymph.
~berere *m.* water-carrier Gl.
~geblǣd *n.* a kind of blister.
~bōg *m.* succulent shoot.
~bolla *m.* dropsy.
~bora *m.* water-carrier.
~brōga† *m.* water-terror.
~būc *m.* pitcher.
~bucca*, ~buca *m.* water-spider (?) Gl.
~burne *f.* stream.
~byden *f.* water-cask.
~clāþ *m.* towel.
~crōg *m.* water-jug.
- crūce *f.* water-jug.
~egesa† *m.* water-terror.
~elfen = ~ælfen.
~fæsten(n) *n.* protection by water (fortress).
~fæt *n.* water-vessel.
~gefeall *n.* waterfall.

wæter|flasce, -axe *f.* flagon.
~flōd *m.* flood, deluge.
~full dropsical.
~fyrhtnes *f.* hydrophobia.
~grund† *m.* depths of the sea.
~gyte, **~scyte** *m.* Aquarius (sign of the Zodiac).
~hæfern *m.* crab.
~hālgung *f.* consecration of water.
~helm† *m.* ice.
~ig, **~isc** watery.
~gelād *n.* conduit.
~gelǣt *n.* aqueduct Gl.
~lēas without water.
~līest, **ēa** *f.* want of water.
~mēle *m.* bowl, basin.
~nǣdre *f.* water-snake.
~ordāl *n.* water-ordeal.
~pund *n.* spirit-level.
~pytt *m.* water-pit.
~rāp *m.* cable.
~rīþe *f.* water-channel, brook.
~scēat *m.* towel.
~scīete *f.* towel, napkin.
~scipe *m.* piece of water; conduit.
~scyte = **~gyte**.
~sēaþ *m.* water-pit.
wætersēoc dropsical.
~nes *f.* dropsy.
wæter|sol *n.* swamp.
~spryng *m.* spring.
~steall *m.* watery place, piece of water.
~stefn† *f.* voice of waters.
~stoppa *m* bucket.
~strēam† *m.* river.
~trog *m.* water-trough.
~þēote *f.* torrent.
~þis(s)a†, **y** *m.* water-traverser (whale, ship).
~þrūh *f.* water-pipe.
~þrȳþ† *f.* violence of water.
~wǣdlnes *f.* dearth of water.
~gewǣsc *n.* flood.
~weg *m.* water-course.
~wiell *m.* spring.
~write *f.* water-clock Gl.
~wyrt *f.* water-starwort.
~ȳþ† *f.* wave.
wæt(e)r|ian water, irrigate; make to drink (cattle), water.
~ung *f.* watering.
wætla *m.* cloth, bandage.
wæþ *n.* ford *vL.* [*Scand.* vaþ].
wǣþan wander; hunt [wāþ].
wǣþl = **wǣdl**.
wafian wave, brandish.

wāfian, **ā†** gaze in wonder, be astonished, wonder at *wg.*; hesitate.
wāfung, **ǣ** *f.* amazement; pageantry.
~stede *m.*, **~stōw** *f.* theatre.
wāg *m.* wall.
~fleohta *m.* hurdle Gl.
~hrægl *n.* tapestry.
~rift *n.* tapestry, curtain.
~þiling *f.* wainscoting.
wag|ian *intr.* move, wag [wegan].
~ung *f. intr.* moving, shaking.
wāgon, **ǣ** *prt. pl. of* wegan.
wāh once fine (meal).
wā-lā, **weglā**, **wellā** *interj.* wₒ. alas!; oh!.
wā-lā-wā, **weilāwei**, **wellāwell** *interj.* alas!.
walcrigge = **wæl-cyrige**.
walde = **wolde** would.
walu *f.* weal, mark of blow.
wamb *f.* stomach.
~āblāwung *f.* distension of the stomach.
~ādl *f.* stomach-ache.
~coþu *f.* stomach complaint.
~frǣcnes *f.* gluttony.
~heardnes *f.* costiveness.
~hord† *n.* contents of the stomach.
~sēoc ill in the stomach.
~wærc *m.* stomach-ache.
wam|m I. *m.* stain; defilement; crime; injury. **II.** *aj.* wicked.
~cwide† *m.* evil speech, curse.
~dæd† *f.* sin.
~full† defiled, impure.
~scaþa† *m.* foe, fiend.
~scyldig† sinful.
~wyrcende† evil-doing.
wan wanting, deficient *wg.*, *gen. uninfl.* — **ānes ~ þrītig, ānes ~ þe þrītig** twenty-nine.
wana *m.* want, deficiency — **~ bēon** be wanting, fail.
gewan wanting, diminished.
wan|ian *tr.* diminish; curtail; give away, part with (property); take as plunder; deprive *wag.*; injure; infringe, annul ‖ *intr.* diminish; decline; fade; wane (*of* moon).
~iendlic diminutive.
ge~od waning (moon).
~ung *f.* decrease; waning (of moon); injury.
wānian *intr.* complain ‖ *tr.* bewail.

wānung *f.* lamentation.
wan-ǣht *f.* poverty.
wanan-bēam *m.* spindle-tree.
wancol unstable.
wand mole (animal).
~eweorpe *f.* mole (animal).
gewand *n.* being ashamed *wg.*; hesitation, scruple [windan].
wand|ian hesitate; be neglectful; care for, regard; stand in awe of.
~odlīce *av.* slowly.
wandlung *f.* changeableness.
wandrian wander.
wan-fōta once *m.* pelican Gl.
wang *m.* plain, field.
~stede *m.* place.
~turf *f.* meadow.
wang|e *n.* jaw; cheek.
~beard *m.* beard.
~tōþ *m.* molar tooth.
wangere *m.* pillow, bolster.
wan-hæfenes, **-hafnes** *f.* poverty.
wan-hǣlan weaken.
wan-hǣlp *f.* weakness, illness.
wan-hafa poor.
wan-hafol poor.
~nes, **-hæfel-** *f.* poverty.
wan-hāl unsound, weak, ill.
~ian make weak *or* ill.
~nes *f.* infirmity.
wan-hlīete*, **ȳ** devoid of Gl.
wan-hoga *m.* thoughtless one.
wan-hygd, **-hȳd** *f.* carelessness, heedlessness.
~ig careless, rash.
wan|n dark.
~fāg† dark.
~feax† dark-haired.
~fȳr† *n.* lurid fire.
~hǣw- bluish.
wann-hāl = **wan-**.
wanniht pale.
wansian diminish [wan].
wan-sǣlig unhappy.
wan-sceaft† *f.* misfortune.
wan-sceafta(n) *pl.* a disease.
wan-scrȳdd scantily clothed.
wan-sīþ *m.* unhappy journey.
wan-spēd *f.* poverty.
~ig poor.
wapol bubble, froth.
~ian bubble.
wār seaweed.
~ig† seaweedy, sea-stained (clothes).
~iht full of seaweed Gl.
warian *tr.* guard, watch over; †inhabit, possess; guard against,

ward off: ~ him (*rfl.*) **wīte,**
~ hine wiþ *a.* || warn [*for*
warnian?] [wær].
warenian = warnian.
warht = worht.
wari-trēo = wearg-trēow.
warn|ian, waren-, wearn- warn |
rfl. take warning; beware of *w.*
wiþ *a.* || *intr.* refrain *w. sbj.* [wær].
~**ung** *f.* warning; caution.
waroþ, ea, *lN.* **wearþ** *n.* shore.
~**faroþ†** *m.* surf.
~**gewinn†** *n.* surf.
wāroþ† *once n.* seaweed.
waru *f.* ware, article of merchandise.
waru *f.* defence, guard; precaution,
care.
wascan, æ, waxan 1, 2, *prt.*
wōsc (?), **wēox** wash. *See*
wæsc.
wāse *f.* mud.
~**scite** [i = y *or* ī?] *f.* cuttle-fish.
wāsend *fm.* throat, gullet; ruminating stomach Gl.
wāst, *see* **wāt.**
wāt *vb.,* (þu) **wāst,** *pl.* **witon,** *prt.*
wiste, wisse know; observe;
feel — **ege** ~ fears.
watol *m.* wattle, hurdle; *pl.* thatch-
ing, roof.
wāþ† *f.* wandering, travelling |
hunting.
~**an** *once, prt.* ~**de** wander.
waþol [ā?]† *once* wandering (?) (*of*
the moon).
waþum† *m.* wave.
~**a, -ema†** *m.* wave.
wāwan† 1 blow (*of* wind).
wāwa *m.* woe, misery [wā, wēa].
wax-georn = *weax-.
wē we.
wēn bend — *ptc.* **gewēd** crooked
Gl. [wōh].
wēa *m.* grief, pain; misfortune; sin
[wāwa, wā].
~**dǣd†** *f.* crime.
~**lāf** *f.* survivors of calamity.
~**lic** sad, painful.
~**mētto** *f.* grief, anger.
wēamōd peevish.
~**nes** *f.* peevishness.
wēa|gesīþ†, *Pr. m.* companion in
misery.
~**spell†** *n.* bad news.
~**tācen†** *n.* sign of grief.
~**þearf†** *f.* sore need.

weahte, *prt. of* **weccan.**
weal-, *see* **weallan.**
~**hāt** boiling hot, red hot (iron).
wēalian speak indistinctly *or*
strangely [wealh].
wēal- = wealh-.
wēalas, *pl. of* **wealh.**
gewealc *n.* rolling — †ȳþa ~ sea;
struggle, battle *vL.*
wealc|an 1 *intr.* roll, fluctuate ||
tr. roll, whirl; twist, wring;
revolve in one's mind, scheme,
reflect on; discuss; ge- traverse
Gl. | hī ne mihton nānþing
ongēan ~ could not prevent it,
could not do anything.
~**ere** *m.* fuller.
~**ol** rolling, unsteady.
wealcian *intr.* roll.
wealca *m.* †wave; light robe.
weald, *d.* ~**a** *m.* forest; †foliage.
~**swaþu†** *f.* forest-track.
weald *cj. w. sbj.* lest.
weald-geng|a *m.* robber.
~**e** *f.* robbery.
weald-hwænne *once cj.* whenever.
weald-leþer = geweald-.
geweald *n.* power — ~**es** *av.* inten-
tionally, of one's own accord;
control, dominion; subjection;
protection | groin; *pl.* muscles of
the neck.
~**leþer, weald-** *n.* rein, bridle.
weald|an 1 *w.g., i., a.* have con-
trol over, wield (weapon); govern;
possess; cause; *wdg.* provide with,
bestow on.
~**nes** *f.* domination Gl.
gewealden I. under control, sub-
jected | inconsiderable, small.
II. *av.* moderately.
~**mōd** self-controlled.
wealdend, -en *m.* ruler, king,
controller.
ge~līce *av.* powerfully.
wealg lukewarm.
wealh, *pl.* **wēalas** *m.* foreigner;
Briton, Welshman; slave, serf.
In comp. also wēal-.
~**baso** vermilion.
~**cynn** *n.* the Welsh.
~**gefēra** *m.* = ~**gerēfa** (?).
~**hafoc** *m.* falcon.
~**hnutu** *f.* walnut.
~**land*, wēa(l)land** *n.* foreign
country.

wealh|more, -u *wk. f.* carrot.
~**gerēfa** *m.* commander of a force
which patrolled the Welsh border (?).
~**sāda*, wēal-†** *m.* rope. *For*
wǣl- (?).
~**stod** *m.* interpreter; mediator.
~**þēod** *f.* Welsh nation.
~**wyrt** *f.* dwarf elder.
weall *m.* wall, rampart; †rocky
shore [*Lt.* vallum].
~**gebrec** *n.* making breach in wall.
~**clif†** *n.* cliff.
~**dor†** *n.* door in a wall.
~**fæsten(n)†** *n.* fortification, city.
~**geat†** *n.* rampart-gate.
~**lim*, weallīm** *m.* cement, mortar.
~**rēaf** *n.* tapestry.
~**stān†** *m.* wall-stone, corner-stone.
~**steall†** *m.* foundation.
~**stēap†** with steep walls; steep as
a wall.
~**stielling** *f.* scaling a wall.
~**prǣd** *m.* plumb-line.
~**wala†** *m.* foundation (?).
~**weg** *m.* wall-road Ct.
~**weorc** *n.* masonry.
~**geweorc** *n.* building a wall.
~**wyrhta** *m.* mason.
weall|an 1 *intr.* boil; be hot;
flow — **ūp** ~ rise (*of* river); go in
waves, be agitated (*of* fire, stormy
sea), *also met.* be fervid, &c.:
swarm.
~**ende** boiling; fiery (arrow);
fervid.
~**ung*, wall-** *f.* zeal *lN.*
weall|ian, *prs. ptc.* ~**ende** wander;
boil (?).
wealle *f.* starwort.
(ge)weallod walled.
wealt shaky, unsteady.
wealwian roll *tr. and intr.*;
wallow || fade, wither.
wēar *once m.* cup. *Or* = wearr (?).
wearnes, *see* **wearr.**
weard *m.* watchman, sentry;
guardian, protector; †lord, king;
†possessor.
weard *f.* keeping watch; guarding,
protection; keeping, holding, *also
met.*
~**mann** *m.* watchman, guard.
~**seld, -setl** *n.,* ~**steall** *m.* guard-
place, watch-tower.
~**wīte** *n.* penalty for not keeping
guard Ct.

weard av.—**wiþ** him ~ towards him.
weardian watch over, guard; keep, possess | **lāst** ~ follow *wd.*; remain behind. **swaþe** ~ remain behind.
wearf*† *m.* crowd *written* hw-.
wearg-brǣde *f.* eruption, ringworm [**wearr**].
wearg *m.* outlaw, felon.
~**rōd** *f.* gallows.
~**trafu**† *npl.* abode of felons (hell).
~**trēow***, **waritrēo** *n.* gallows.
weargincel *n.* butcher-bird.
wearh = **wearr**.
wearm warm.
~**ian** become warm.
~**lic** warm.
~**nes** *f.* warmth.
wearmille = **wurmille**.
wearn *f.* reluctance, refusal; resistance, reproach, abuse [**waru**].
~**wīslice** *av.* obstinately.
wearn = **worn**.
wearnian = **warnian**.
wearoþ = **waroþ**.
wearp (*m.*) warp [**weorpan**].
~**fæt** *n.* basket.
~**sticca** *m.* shuttle-stick (?).
wearr, **wearh**, **waar** (!) *m.* callosity, wart. *Cp.* **wearg-brǣde.**
~**ig** warty.
~**iht**, **wēariht** warty.
~**nes***, **wearnes** *f.* knottiness.
wearte *f.* wart.
weartere, æ *m.* warder, dweller.
wearþ *prt. of* **weorpan.**
wēas *av.* by chance.
~**gelimp** *n.* accident, chance.
weax *n.* wax.
~**æppel** *m.* ball of wax.
~**berende** *m.* candle-bearer.
~**bred** *n.* writing-tablet; diagram, table.
~**candel**(l) *f.* taper.
~**en** of wax.
~**hláf** *m.* cake of wax.
~**hláf-sealf** *f.* wax-salve.
~**(ge)scot** *n.* contribution in wax.
~**sealf** *f.* wax-ointment.
weax-georn*, a *once* gluttonous.
weax|**an** 1, 2 *prt.* **wēox**, *lN.* **wōx** *intr.* grow, flourish, propagate; happen, arise; increase, wax (*of* moon); **ge~** grow up.
(ge)~**nes** *f.* increase, growth.
~**ung** *f.* increase; increase of prosperity.

weaxan = **wascan.**
węb|**b** *n.* web; tapestry [**wefan**].
~**bēam** *m.* weaver's beam.
~**hōc** *m.* weaver's comb.
~**hūs** *n.* weaver's shop.
~**lic** of weaving.
~**gerēþru** *npl.* implements of weaving.
~**gerod** *n.* a weaving-implement.
~**sceaft** *m.* warp-beam.
~**tāwa** *m.* (?), ~**tēag** *f.* an implement of weaving.
~**geweorc** *n.* weaving.
~**wyrhta** *m.* cloth-maker.
wębb|**ian** weave; contrive.
~**ung** *f.* plotting, conspiracy.
wębb|**a**, ~**ere** *m.* weaver.
~**e**, ~**estre** *f.* female weaver.
węcc|**an**, **wr-**, *prt.* **we(a)hte** *tr.* awake, arouse; refresh, encourage; stir up, move; cause [**wacan**].
~**end** *m.* instigator.
węcg *m.* wedge; lump (of metal).
węcgan, *prs.* (hē) **węgeþ**, *prt.* **węg(e)de** *tr.* move, stir ‖ *intr.* move, be stirred [**wagian**].
gewōd, *see* **wēn.**
wēd|**an** be mad, rage [**wōd**].
~**ung** *f.* frenzy.
węd|**d** *n.* pledge; agreement, covenant.
~**brōþor** *m.* associate.
~**bryce** *m.* breach of agreement.
~**fæstan***, **wet-** betroth Gl.
~**lác** *n.* wedlock.
~**loga** *m.* violator of agreement, traitor.
wędd|**ian** make contract; promise, agree to *wg.* — **weres** ~ agree to marry a man; *wa.* betroth, give in marriage.
~**ung** *f.* pledging; betrothal.
wēd(e)-beorge, **woe-** *f.* hellebore.
wēde-hund *m.* mad dog.
gewēde *n.* madness; boisterousness [**wōd**].
wēden-heort frenzied.
~**nes** *f.* frenzy.
wēden-sēoc mad.
weder *n.* sky; air; breeze; weather; season, time of day.
~**blác** (?).
~**burg**† *f.* city.
~**candel**(l)† *f.* sky-candle, sun.
~**dæg**† *m.* fine day.
~**fæst** weatherbound.
~**ráp** *m.* cable.

weder|**tácen**† *n.* sun.
~**wolcen**† *n.* cloud.
wederung *f.* (bad) weather.
gewef, **-wæf** = **gewif(e)** fate.
wefan 5 weave; arrange, contrive, do.
wefl *f.* warp.
wefta *m.*, **weft**, **wift** *f.* weft.
weg *m.* path, road; way, direction | **on weg** away. **wearþ** him on **wege** (**awege**) went away. **ealneweg**, **ealneg** *av.* always. on **ealne weg** continually, incessantly.
~**brǣde**, ǣ *f.* plantain, dock.
~**gedál** *n.* cross-way.
~**fǣreld** *n.* journey.
~**farende**, ~**fērende** wayfaring.
~**fōr** *f.* journey.
~**gelǣtu** *npl.* place where two or more roads meet Gl.
~**lēas** out of the way.
~**līest** *f.* wilderness.
~**nest** *n.* provisions for a journey; viaticum.
~**rēaf** *n.* highway robbery.
~**gesīþ** *m.* travelling companion.
~**twislung** *f.* branching of roads.
weg- = **onweg-.**
weg-lā, *see* **wā-.**
wegan 5 *tr.* carry; weight | kill ‖ *intr.* move | **ge~** fight.
węhte *prt. of* **węccan.**
weiláwei = **wā-lā-wā.**
wel *av.*, *cpv.* **bęt**, *spl.* **bętst** well — **wel þām þe** . . ! he is fortunate who . . **swā wel swā wē bętst magon** as well as we can; in good health: **him wæs sōna bet** he recovered; nearly; in a great degree, very; fully; *pleonastic in* **wel·nēah** nearly, &c.
wela *m.*, *often pl.*, prosperity, happiness; riches.
wēlan bind.
wel-(ge)boren of good family.
welcn = **wolcen.**
wel-gecwēm|**e**, ~**edlic** acceptable.
~**nes** *f.* favour.
wel-dǣd *f.* good deed, benefit.
wel-gedōn well done.
wel-dō(e)nd *m.* doer of good, benefactor.
wel-dōnnes *f.* kindness *lN.*
weler *m.* lip.
wel-fręmming *f.* doing good.

welgá *interj.* hail!.
wel-hǣwen beautifully coloured.
wel-gehealden contented.
wel-hwā each, every.
wel-hwǣr, wel-gehwǣr, ge-wel-hwǣr *av.* (nearly) everywhere.
wel-hwelc, ge- (nearly) every.
welig prosperous; wealthy.
~ian enrich.
welig, y *m.* willow.
wellā = wā-lā.
wellere = wellyrge.
wel-libbende leading a respectable life.
wel-gelīc|ian please well; be well pleased.
~wierþe acceptable.
~wierþnes *f.* good pleasure.
wel-līcung *f.* agreeableness.
wellyrge, wellere bosom, fold, hollow.
wel-gestemned having a good voice.
wel-stincende fragrant.
wel-þungen prosperous.
wel-willend|e benevolent.
~līce *av.* benevolently.
~nes *f.* benevolence.
wel-gewlite beautiful.
wel-gewlitegod well adorned.
wel-wyrcend *m.* well-doer.
~e well-doing.
wēm|an *intr.* sound ‖ *tr.* announce, persuade, entice, seduce [wōma].
~ere *m.* enticer.
wemm|an defile, pollute; profane; injure, destroy [wamm].
(ge)~ednes *f.* defilement.
~end *m.* defiler.
~ing *f.* defilement.
ge~ing *f.* profanation.
ge~odlice *av.* corruptly.
wēn, oe *f.* hope, expectation; belief, opinion; probability : hit is ~, ~ is, is ~ *w. sbj.* it is probable that; *the Runic letter w.*
~a *m.* hope, expectation; opinion.
wēn|an hope, expect *w. g., a., sbj., rarely inf.*; think, have an opinion *wa., w. indc., sbj., also without þæt* : ic ~e wit sind oferswīþde — him tō ~ wa attribute (fault).
wēnung *f.* expectation, hope.
~a, -unge, -inga *av.* perhaps; by chance.

wenian, wennan accustom, train *also rfl.*; wean (child) | †treat — ~ mid wynnum treat kindly.
~ tō wiste feast *tr.*, entertain. hringum ~ give gold to.
wencel I. *n.* child; maidservant.
II. *aj.* †weak.
wend|an *tr.* turn, *met.* direct (thoughts, &c.); convert (to Christianity); change, bring (to life again); translate; bring about, compass ‖ *rfl.* turn; go ‖ *intr.* turn; go; change [windan].
~ere *m.* translator.
~ung *f.* turning; change.
Wendel-sǣ *m.* Mediterranean [Wendle].
Wendle *pl.* Vandals.
gewenge *n.* cheek [wang].
wenlic [e = ē *or* y ?] beautiful.
wen|n *mf.* tumour.
~bȳl *m.* carbuncle.
~sealf *f.* ointment for tumour.
~spryng *m.* carbuncle.
~wyrt *f.* a plant.
wen-sēoc having the falling sickness (?).
~nes *f.* falling sickness (?).
Went|e, ~as, ~sǣte *mpl.* people of Monmouthshire.
wēobed = wēofod.
weoce = wuce week.
weoce = wice wick.
wēod *n.* weed.
~hōc *m.* hoe.
~ian weed.
~mōnaþ *m.* August.
~ung *f.* weeding.
weodu = wudu.
weoduwe = wuduwe widow.
weofan = wefan.
wēofod, wī(g)bed, wigbid, ēo†*n.* altar [= wīg-bēod idol-table].
~bōt *f.* fine for injuring priest, which was applied to the support of the altar.
~heorþ *m.* altar-hearth.
~hrægl *n.* altar-cloth.
~scēat *m.* altar-cloth.
~steall *m.* altar-place.
~þegn, ~þēn *m.* priest.
~þegnung, -þēn- *f.* altar-service.
~wīglere *m.* soothsayer Gl.
wēoh, wīg, ī†, *pl.* wēos *m.* idol.
See wīg.
~steall *m.* sanctuary.
weola = wela.

weolc = weoloc.
weoloc, weolc *m.* whelk.
~baso purple.
~baso-hǣwen purple.
~rēad crimson.
~sciell *f.* whelk-shell.
~telg *m.* purple dye.
~wyrm *m.* murex.
wēop *prt. of* wēpan.
weorad = werod.
weoras, *see* wer man.
weorc, o, A. e *n.* work (act and thing), action; building (act and thing), fortification | †hardship, pain, grief, annoyance, *often used like adj.* : þæt wæs him ~ tō þolianne. ~um with effort *or* difficulty.
~dǣd *f.* action.
~dæg *m.* work-day.
~ern *n.* workshop.
~full laborious.
~hūs *n.* workshop.
~mann *m.* working man, labourer.
~nieten *n.* working cattle.
~rǣden(n) *f.* corvée-work Ct.
~gerēfa *m.* foreman.
~stān *m.* stone for building.
~sum laborious; grievous.
~þēow *m.* servant, slave.
geweorc *n.* act of working; act of building | what is done, work; what is built; fortification.
weorce†, *Pr. av.* [*i. of* weorc] painfully, grievously *used like adj.* [*cp.* ange] : him wæs ~ on mōde.
weorf, o, -uf *n.* beast, cattle — wilde ~ unbroken colt. *Cp.* orf.
~tord *m.* dung.
weornian fade [wesan, wisnian]
weorold = woruld.
geweorp *n.* throwing, tossing *tr. and intr.* — †waroþa ~ surf; heap (of earth, thrown up by beetle).
weorp|an, u, *lN.* o 3 *w. a.*, i throw, lay (hands on) — ~ hlot, ~ tān cast lots | throw off (cloak); throw down; expel | † ~ hine wæteres sprinkle with water ‖ ~ him on accuse.
~ere† *m.* thrower down.
weorpan *wk.* = wierpan.
weorþ, u, y, *lN.* o *n.* worth; price, price-money; ransom, redemption | honour, dignity.

[203]

weorþ|full worthy, honourable (dress), glorious, good (man).
~**fullic** honourable, distinguished.
~**fullice** *av.* honourably.
~**fulnes** *f.* glory.
~**georn** ambitious.
~**lēas** worthless.
~**lic** conferring distinction, glorious (victory).
~**lice** *av.* with distinction, gloriously; befittingly.
~**licnes** *f.* distinction, glory.
~**mynd**, ~**mynt** *fmn., often pl.* honour, dignity, glory; insignia of office Gl.
~**myntan** honour.
~**scipe** *m.* showing honour to; dignity (of office); glory.
weorþ *aj.* = **wierþe**.
weorþ *occ.* = **worþ**.
weorþ|an, u, y 3, *ptc.* **worden** happen, be made (*of* peace), be fulfilled (*of* God's will); come into being, arise | become: **ge~aþ tō nāhte, wearþ on fielle fell**; be | *auxiliary, pass.*: **wierþ gesewen**; *pret.*: **wearþ āfeallen fell.**
geweorþan 3 *in all the meanings of* **weorþan**, *esp. the first group, very rare as aux.* | *impers. w. a.* (*L. d.*) *of person, ag.*: **hū hine hæfde geworden wiþ hīe** how he had fared with her; **þā gewearþ hīe þæt man tōwurpe . .** the senators agreed to . .; **swāswā him bām gewearþ** as they had agreed; **hū gewearþ þē þæs þæt þū woldest . .?** what made you think of . . (determine to . .)?; **þæs manige gewearþ þæt . . w.** *indc.* many thought that . .
weorþ|ian, u, y *occ. wd.* honour, distinguish; worship; praise; adorn; endow.
~**ere**, ~**iend** *m.* worshipper, adorer.
weorþung *f.* honouring; worship; praising; dignity, glory; ornament.
~**dagas***, **weord-** *m.* festival Gl.
~**stōw** *f.* place of worship.
weorþe = **wierþe**.
weorþig = **worþig**.
weoruld = **woruld**.
wēos *pl. of* **wēoh** idol.
weosnian = **wisnian**.
weota = **wita**.

weotoma = **wituma**.
weoxian keep clean (house).
wēp|an, oe 1, *ptc.* **wōpen** weep || *tr.* bewail, weep for [**wōp**].
~**endlic** deplorable.
wer *m.* man; †hero; husband.
~**bēam**† *m.* warrior.
~**cynn** *n.* human race.
~**hād** *m.* virility; male sex.
~**lēas** unmarried (woman).
~**lic** male; manly.
~**lice** *av.* manfully, bravely.
~**mægþ** *f.* nation.
~**met** *n.* stature.
~**(e)mōd** *m.* wormwood.
~**scipe** *m.* married state.
~**þēod**† *f.* nation, *pl.* people.
~**(e)wulf** *m.* werewolf, monster, fiend.
wer, were, æ *m.* legal money-equivalent of a person's life, wer, wergield.
~**borg** *m.* pledge for payment of wer.
~**fǣhþ** *f.* feud involving wer.
wergield *n.* wer.
~**þēof** *m.* thief redeemed by payment of his wer.
wer|lād *f.* exculpation of a man by oaths in proportion to the amount of his wer.
~**tihtle** *f.* charge involving liability to pay wer, homicide.
wer *m.* weir, dam; fish-trap [**werian**].
~**hierde** *m.* keeper of a fishing-weir.
~**stede** *m.* weir-place.
wer-nægl *m.* wart [**wearh-**, *infl. of* **wer** man (?)].
wer|ian I. defend; †*once* inhabit [*cp.* **warian**]; ward off. II. dam up (pool) [**wer, waru**].
~**iend** *m.* defender.
~**ing** *f.* weir, dam.
werian wear (clothes, ring); clothe (body) [**waru**].
were|mod = **wer-** wormwood.
~**wulf** = **wer-**.
wergulu *f.* crab-apple.
werig-, *see* **wiergan**.
wērig, oe weary [**wōrian**].
~**fer(h)þ**† weary; disheartened.
~**mōd**† weary; disheartened.
~**nes** *f.* weariness.
wēr(i)gian weary, exhaust.
wērig = ***wīerig** accursed.

werod *n.* multitude, troop; regiment, army [**wer, rād**].
~**līest** *f.* lack of soldiers.
werod, -ed I. sweet. II.† *n.* sweet drink, mead.
~**an** become sweet.
~**lǣcan** make sweet *or* pleasant.
~**lice** *av.* sweetly.
~**nes** *f.* sweetness.
wesan, bēon; (ic) **eom**, *A.* **eam**, *LN.* **am, bēo**, *A.* **bēom**; (þŭ) **eart, bis(t)**, *A.* **earþ**, *LN.* **arþ**; (hē) **is, biþ**; (hīe) **sind, bēoþ, wesaþ**, *occ.* **biþon**, *A.* **earun**, *LN.* **aron**; *sbj. prs.* **sīe** (*also A.*), **sī(g), bēo**, *Kt. also* **sē(o)**; *prt.* **wæs, a**, *pl.* **wǣron**; *ptc. prs.* **wesende, bēonde|** exist; happen; be; *auxiliary* | **nǣre þæt w.** *sbj.* if it had not been that, unless.
gewesan*, giwos(s)a (*n.*) intercourse, conversation *LN.*
gewes|an† *once* strive, contend.
~**nes** *f.* dissension.
wēsan soak, macerate [**wōs**].
wēse *once* moist, macerated [**wōs**].
wesend, eo *m.* bison.
~**horn** *m.* bison's horn.
wesole, eo, wesle *f.* weasel.
west *av.* west(wards), in the west.
~**centingas** *mpl.* people of the west of Kent.
~**dǣl** *m.* west part, the west.
~**dene**† *mpl.* West Danes.
~**ende** *m.* west end.
~**eweard** = **weard**.
~**healf** *f.* west side.
~**heowag** (*m.*) a part of a church.
~**lang** extending west.
~**mearc** *f.* west boundary.
~**norþ-lang** extending north-west.
~**norþ-wind** *m.* north-west wind.
~**rīce** *n.* western kingdom.
~**rihte** *av.* due west.
~**rodor** *m.* western sky.
~**sǣ** *m.* Baltic.
~**seaxe, -an** *mpl.* West Saxons; Wessex.
~**sūþ-ende** *m.* south-west end.
~**sūþ-wind** *m.* south-west wind.
~**wēalas** *mpl.* Cornishmen.
~**(e)weard** *av.* westward.
~**weg** *m.* west way.
~**wind** *m.* west wind.
wēst|an ravage.
~**nes** *f.* desolation.

westan, -ane *av.* from the west — be ~, wiþ ~ *prp. wd.* west of.

~healf *f.* west side.

~sūþan-wind *m.* south-west wind.

~wind *m.* west wind.

wēst|e, oe waste, uninhabited.

~ig, oe waste, desert *lA.*

westema, *see* **westerra.**

wēsten(n), *lN.* **woestern** *n.* desert, wilderness.

~gryre *m.* terror of the wilderness.

~setla *m.* hermit.

~stapol *m.* desert place.

wēstern = wēsten.

westerne western.

westerra, -era, westra *cpv.* more westerly, *spl.* **westema, westmest.**

westmest, *see* **westerra.**

westra = westerra.

wēþ|e pleasant, mild.

(ge)~nes *f.* suavity, mildness.

weþel bandage.

weþer *m.* wether, sheep.

~cynn *n.* wether kind.

wēþla = wǣdla.

wibba *m.* beetle [wefan].

wībed = wēofod.

wīc, ii, í *nf.* dwelling, village, villa ; *pl.* camp ; street, market-place ‖ bay, creek.

~eard† *m.* dwelling.

~gefēra *m.* = **~gerēfa.**

~friþu† *m.* protection of dwelling.

~gerēfa *m.* bailiff ; tax-gatherer.

~sceawere *m.* harbinger (of Christ).

~steall† *m.* camp.

~stede† *m.* dwelling.

~stōw *f.* dwelling ; camp.

~tūn *m.* court, vestibule.

wīcan 6 give way, collapse.

wīcian dwell ; encamp ; anchor.

wicca *m.* wizard.

~rǣd *m.* divination.

wicce *f.* witch.

~crǣft, ~dōm *m.* witchcraft.

wiccian use witchcraft.

wiccung *f.* witchcraft.

~crǣft, ~dōm *m.* witchcraft.

wicclian stagger Gl.

wice *m.* wych-elm.

wice, eo *f.* lamp-wick.

wīce *f.* office, commission ; *vL.* officer.

wice = wuce week.

wicel *aj.* ? (*of* drinking-cup).

wicg† *n.* horse.

wicga *m.* beetle.

wīcing *m.* pirate.

wīcn|ere *m.* steward, bailiff.

~ian attend upon.

wīd wide — ~ and **sīd** far and wide. tō ~an ealdre for ever.

~brād† ample.

~cūþ widely known, famous.

~fæþme† capacious, extensive.

~farend *m.* wanderer.

~fērende† coming from afar.

~floga† far-flier (= dragon).

~folc† *n.* great nation.

~gal = ~giell.

~gangol wandering.

wīdgiel|l, ~gal extensive ; wandering.

~nes *f.* amplitude.

wīd|land† *n.* extensive country.

~lāst† I. *m.* long journey. II. *aj.* wandering far.

~mǣre far-famed.

wīdmǣrs|ian divulge, celebrate.

~ung *f.* disgrace Gl.

wīd|rynig† far-flowing.

~sǣ *mf.* open sea.

~sceop† *once* extensive.

~scripol erratic.

~sīþ† *m.* long journey ; great traveller.

~wegas† *mpl.* great distance.

wīdian become wider.

wīdan *av.* from afar. *Cp.* sīdan.

wīde *av.* widely — **sīde** and ~, ~ **landes** far and wide.

~feorh† ; ~ferhþ†, y *mn.* long life, eternity *used adverbially.*

gewider, *pl.* **~u** *n.* weather ; good weather ; bad weather ; storm [weder].

~ian *impers.* be fine weather.

wīdl (*n.*) defilement, impurity.

~ian defile.

wido-bān = wiþo-.

widu = wudu wood.

widwe = wuduwe widow.

wiĕl|ian*, y, *lN.* **æ,** *prt.* **~ede** roll. *Cp.* **wiĕlwan.**

gewiĕlcþ*, i *f.* rolling [wealcan].

gewiĕld|an overpower, subdue, dominate ; compel ; temper (with oil) [wealdan].

~end *m.* subduer.

wiĕlde strong, victorious.

gewiĕlde under one's control, con-

quered : hē dyde hīe him (*rfl.*) tō gewildon subdued them.

wiĕlede *prt. of* **wiĕlwan.**

wīel|en *f.* female slave [wealh].

~incel *n.* little slave.

~isc, -e, y, *vE.* **welhisc** foreign ; Welsh.

wiĕll, ~a *m.,* **~e** *f.* fountain, spring [weallan].

~eburne† *f.* spring.

~cerse *f.* watercress.

~flōd† *m.* flood.

~(e)spryng *m.* spring.

~egespryng *n.* spring.

~(e)strēam† *m.* stream.

~weorþung *f.* worship of springs.

wiĕllic of a fountain.

wiĕlm *m.* boiling ; surging, raging (of fire) ; flowing, bursting forth [weallan].

~hāt† blazing (fire).

wiĕlwan, wiĕlian, *prt.* **wiĕlede** roll [wealwian].

wiĕrd|an injure.

~ing*, oe *f.* injury *lN.*

~nes *f.* injury.

gewiĕrdlan injure.

wiĕrg-cwedol, wyrig- cursing, given to cursing.

~ian curse.

~nes *f.* malediction.

wiĕrg|an, *L.* **wyrian** curse, revile [wearg].

~end, *pl.* **~endras** *m.* reviler ; †weĕrgend maligner.

~ing, *L.* **wyriung** *f.* cursing, curse.

~nes, wyrig-, i *f.* cursing, curse.

~þo *f.* cursing.

wiĕrgen(n)† *f.* she-wolf [wearg].

wiĕrig*, ē†, y accursed, wicked.

~nes*, ē *f.* malice *lN.*

wiĕrm|an warm, keep warm [wearm].

~ing *f.* warming.

wiĕrnan *wdg.* prevent from ; withhold, refuse [wearn].

wiĕrp, *see* **wyrp** throwing.

gewiĕrpan, æ recover (from illness) [weorpan].

wiĕrpe*, y *m.* change for the better, relief, recovery (from illness).

wiĕrrest, *spl. of* **yfel.**

wiĕrs, ~a, ~t, *see* **yfel, yfle.**

~ian become worse.

~lic bad.

[205]

gewierþan*, y estimate value of, appraise.

wierþ|e, y (also eW., and A.), eo, weorþ, u deserving (good or evil) wg. ; honoured, esteemed, dear (to) wd. ; of high rank [weorþ].

~nes f. worth ; worthiness ; dignity, splendour.

gewierþe*, y, -wyrde n. amount, contents wg.

wierþig*, y deserved (punishment).

wīf n. woman, lady ; wife.

~cild n. female child.

~cynn n. female sex.

~cȳþþ f. company of a woman.

~fæst married.

~feax n. woman's hair.

~frēond m. female friend.

~gāl lecherous.

~geornnes*, ~geornes f. lechery.

~gift f. dowry.

~hād m. womanhood ; female sex.

~hand, ~healf f. female side in inheritance or descent.

~hīred n. nunnery.

~gehrin, ~lāc n. intercourse with women.

~lēas without a wife.

~lic feminine, female.

~līce av. in the manner of a woman.

~lufu f. love for a woman.

~gemǣdla m. woman's talk.

~gemāna m. intercourse with a woman.

~mann, L. wimman m. woman.

~myne m. love for a woman.

~scrūd n. woman's clothes.

~þegn m. woman's attendant Gl.

~þing n. intercourse with a woman.

gewif n. a disease of the eye.

gewif, -e, pl. ~u w. sg. meaning, n. fate, fortune [wefan].

~sǣlig fortunate.

gewif|ian marry (of man) ; hē ~ode on hire.

~ung f. marrying (of man).

wifel m. beetle.

wifel, wifer, wiber arrow, dart Gl.

wifre f. weaver [wefan].

wift = weft weft.

wīg n. war.

~bǣre warlike.

~bealo† n. war.

~bill† n. sword.

~blāc† in bright armour.

wīg|bora m. soldier.

~bord† n. shield.

~cierm m. noise of battle.

~cræft m. prowess ; military skill.

~cræftig valorous.

~freca† m. warrior.

~fruma† m. warrior.

~gār*, wīgār m. spear.

~gryre† m. war-terror.

~hafola† m. helmet.

~haga† m. phalanx.

~hēap† m. band of warriors.

~heard† warlike.

~hęte m. hostility. war.

~hryre† m. fall in battle.

~hūs n. battlement, turret.

~hyrsta† fpl. war-trappings.

~lēoþ† n. war-song, signal.

~lic martial.

~līce av. valiantly.

~mann m. soldier.

~plega† m. battle.

~rād*, o† f. war-path.

~rǣden(n)† f. battle.

~sigor† m. victory.

~sīþ† m. warlike expedition.

~smiþ† m. warrior.

~spēd† f. success in war.

~spere n. spear.

~steall† m. entrenchment, fortress.

~strang brave.

~getāwe† pl. war-trappings.

~trod*, wītrod† (?).

~þracu† f. battle.

~þrīst† bold in war.

~wǣgn m. war-chariot.

~wǣpen n. weapon.

wīg = wēoh idol.

~gięld† n. idol.

~smiþ† once m. maker of idols. Cp. under wīg war.

~weorþung f. idolatry.

wīg|an, -ian fight — ~ende mann soldier.

~end†, wiggend m. warrior.

wīgian = wigan.

wiga†, i† m. warrior, man.

wiggend = wīgend.

wigl|ian practise divination.

~ere m. diviner, soothsayer.

(ge)~ung f. divination.

wīgol once belonging to divination (birds) Gl.

wiht, u I. fn., lpl. ~u thing ; creature, being ; sprite, demon | ~e av. at all. II. pron. wg. anything. III. av. at all.

Wiht f., ~land n. Isle of Wight [Lt. Vectis].

~sǣte, ~ware pl. Isle of Wight people.

wiht n. weight.

wiht-mǣres-wyrt f. scurvy-grass (?).

gewihte n. weight.

wihtel*, y quail.

wil- = will-.

Wil-sǣt|e, ~an pl. people of Wilts.

wīl n. wile, trick vL.

wilde wild, untamed — ~ fȳr wildfire (heaths, &c., on fire) ; uncultivated, desert.

wildēor, dd = wilder.

~en, ~lic animal, fierce.

~līce av. like an animal.

~nes f. desert.

wilder, wild(d)ēor n. wild beast ; deer, reindeer [wilde, dēor].

wile, see willan.

gewile = gewill.

wile-wīse = wilig-.

wilig|e f. basket [welig].

~wīse* f. — on wiliwīsan basketwise.

wiliht*, y full of willows [welig].

will (n.) — his ~es of his own accord.

wil(1)-, see willa.

~boda† m. messenger of joy, angel.

~gebrōþor† mpl. brothers.

wilcum|a m. welcome guest — used also like aj. or interj. : ~an lā mīne hlāfordas !.

~ian welcome.

wil(1)|dæg m. day of joy.

~gedryht† f. devoted retinue, faithful band.

~fægen† glad.

~fǣmne f. beloved woman.

~fullīce av. willingly Gl.

~giefa† m. king.

~giest* m. welcome guest.

~gehlēpa† m. familiar associate.

~hrēþig† exulting.

~sęle† m. pleasant dwelling.

~sīþ†, Pr. m. pleasant or desired journey.

~gesīþ† m familiar companion.

~spell† n. glad tidings.

~gesteald*, -eall† n. riches.

~gesweostor† pl. sisters.

wilsum desirable, pleasant.

~lic desirable.

~līce av. willingly.

wil(l)|sumnes *f.* willingness.
~þegu† *f.* acceptable food.
~geþofta† *m.* familiar associate.
~wang† *m.* delightful plain.
~weg† *m.* pleasant path.
gewil|l, -wile *n.* wish, will — on hiora gewill in order to please them.
~bod *n.* command.
~sum desirable.
will|an *vb.*, (he)wile, *prt.* wolde, *A.* a | wish, be willing; desire; attempt. wile ~ desire righteousness. gif heo wolde hine would marry him | *habit, repetition* be used to | *auxil. w. inf.* wile will =*future*; wolde would = *prt. sbj.*
~endlice *av.* willingly.
will|ian wish, desire || *intr. wd.* following the will of: Gode ~igende.
ge~ung *f.* desire.
will|a, *gpl.* ~ena, wilna *m.* will — his selfes ~um of his own accord; be his ~an permission | desire; pleasure — ~um joyfully; object of desire *or* pleasure.
wilna *occ. gpl. of* willa.
wiln|ian *w. g., a., sbj., ger., inf.* desire; ask for: hie ~odon him (*rfl. pl.*) friþes tō him (*sg.*).
(ge)~iendlic desirable.
(ge)~ung *f.* desire.
wīm-mann = wīf-.
wimpel *m.* neck-covering, cloak.
wīn *n.* wine [*Lt.* vinum].
~ærn, ~ern *n.* wine-cellar; tavern; †hall.
~bēam *m.* vine.
~bel(i)g, æ *m.* wine-skin.
~ber(i)ge *f.* grape.
~bōg *m.* vine-shoot.
~brytta *m.* innkeeper Gl.
~burg† *f.* festive city.
~byrele *m.* innkeeper.
~clyster *n.* bunch of grapes.
~gedrinc† *n.* wine-drinking.
wīndruncen wine-drunk.
~nes *f.* wine-intoxication.
wīn|drync *m.* draught of wine, wine.
~fæt *n.* wine-vat.
~gāl† elated with wine.
wingeard *m.* vineyard.
~bōg *m.* vine-shoot.
~hōc *m.* vine-tendril.
~hring *m.* bunch of grapes (?) Gl.

wīngeard-seax *n.* pruning-knife.
wīn|hāte† ? *f.* invitation to wine.
~hūs *n.* tavern.
~lēaf *n.* vine-leaf.
~lic vinous.
~mere *m.* wine-vat.
~reced† *n.* festive hall.
~repan*, eo gather vintage Gl.
~sæd† satiated with wine.
~sæl† *n.*, ~sele† *m.* festive hall.
~sester *m.* wine-vessel.
~tæppere *m.* tavern-keeper.
~tīber *n.* libation.
~(ge)tredde *f.* wine-press.
~trēow *n.* vine.
~trēowig of a vine Gl.
~trog *m.* wine-vessel.
~twig *n.* vine-shoot.
~þegu† *f.* receiving wine, banquet.
~wringa *m.* wine-press.
winc|ian, *prs. ptc.* ~(i)ende shut eyes, blink, wink.
wince *f.* pulley.
wincel (*m.*) corner.
wincel *n.* child.
wincettan nod, beckon.
wind *m.* wind.
~ǣd(d)re *f.* artery Gl.
~bland† *n.* violence of the wind.
~fana *m.* Gl.
~fann, gefon *f.* fan.
~ig windy.
~rǣs *m.* rush of wind.
~scofl *f.* fan.
~sele† windy dwelling (=hell).
~swingell *f.* fan.
gewind *n.* anything spiral, winding path, vine-tendril Gl.
windan 3 *tr.* wind, twist, weave — †wunden (gold) made into rings; brandish || *intr.* turn, move; *met.* gewand ymbe his þearfe looked after his interests | rush, fly (*of* birds, spears); roll; slip | delay, hesitate.
winde-cræft = wynde-.
winde-locc *m.* curl Gl.
gewinde — hit wæs ~ on þā burg the wind was towards the town.
windel *m.* basket.
~stān *m.* spiral shell.
~strēaw *n.* windle-straw (a plant).
~trēow *n.* willow.
windwian *tr.* blow; winnow.
windwig.
~ceaf *n.* chaff.

windwig|sife *n.* winnowing-sieve.
wine†, *occ. gpl.* winigea, *m.* friend; protector, lord.
~dryhten *m.* lord.
~gēomor mourning for friends.
~lēas friendless.
~mǣg *m.* kinsman.
~scipe *m.* friendship.
~trēow *f.* (conjugal) fidelity.
~þearfende in need of friends.
wine-wincle, p- *f.* winkle, shell-fish.
winigea *occ. gpl. of* wine.
wining*, wynyng *m.* garter, legging.
gewinn, w- *n.* labour, effort; hardship; war, hostility; gain, profit.
~dæg *m.* day of trouble; day of battle.
~full troublesome.
~fullic laborious, full of hardship.
~fullice *av.* laboriously, with an effort.
~stōw *f.* wrestling-place Gl.
~tīd *f.* time of trouble *or* affliction.
~woruld† *f.* world of hardship.
winnan 3 *intr.* toil; endure hardship, suffer: ~ of feferādle; strive *w.* æfter for, *w.* ongēan *a.*; protest, contradict; make war, fight *w.* wiþ *a.*, on *a.* | on ~ *wd.* make war on, attack. mid ~ *wd.* fight with (as ally). wiþ ~ *wd.* resist || *tr.* endure (hardship).
gewinn|an 3 *tr.* gain, acquire; conquer, take (fortress) || *intr.* (*rare*) make war, fight.
~a, w- *m.* adversary.
winnung *f.* winnowing, chaff. *Cp.* windwian.
winpel = wimpel.
winstre, wine- I. *wk. fem. aj.* left: sēo ~ hand. II. *f.* left hand.
winter *m., d.* wintra, *pl.* winter, wintru, winter; *in reckoning* year.
~biter† bitterly cold.
~burna *m.* winter torrent, stream which flows only in winter.
~ceald† wintry cold.
~cearig† winter-sad.
~dæg *m.* winter day.
~dūn *f.* down on which sheep are kept in winter (?).
~feorm *f.* winter provisions.
~fylleþ October.

winter|gegang *n.* fate Gl.
~lǣcan grow wintry (*of* season).
~lic winter, wintry.
~rǣding-bōc *f.* lectionary for the winter.
~(ge)rīm† *n.* number of years.
~scūr *m.* winter shower.
~seld, ~setl *n.* winter quarters.
~steall ? an animal LL.
~stund† *f.* short period.
~sufl *n.* food for winter.
~getæl*, e† number of years.
~tīd *f.* winter time.
~gewǣde† *n.* winter garment (=snow).
~geweorp† *n.* snow-fall.
gewintred grown-up ; aged.
wintrig of winter, wintry.
wiota = wita.
wīpian wipe.
wīr *m.* wire.
~boga† *m.* twisted wire.
wīr, ȳ myrtle Gl.
~grǣfa *m.* myrtle-grove.
~trēow *n.* myrtle.
gewīred made of *or* ornamented with wire (brooch).
wircan = wyrcan.
wīs = wīse manner.
wīs wise, sensible, learned.
~dōm *m.* wisdom ; learning.
~e *av.* wisely.
~fæst† wise.
~fæstlic† wise.
~hycgende† wise.
~hygdig, hȳdig† wise.
~lic advisable.
~līce *av.* wisely.
~wyrde prudent in speech.
wīs-bōc† *f.* book Ps.
wis|ian *wd.* guide ; point out, show.
ge~ung *f.* direction. *For* gewissung (?).
wīsa† *m.* leader.
wis|e *f.* growth, (strawberry) plant — fugeles wyse a plant.
~lēag *m.* meadow (?) Ct.
wīse, wīs *f.* manner, way ; testamentary disposition, arrangement | occurrence, affair ; state, condition, (material) thing | direction | melody.
wis|lic certain. *Cp.* gewiss.
~līce *av.* with certainty, certainly.
wisnian, eo dry up, wither [we-ornian].

gewiss, wiss I. certain (fact) — tō ~an [= ~um] þinge for a certainty, certainly ; feeling certain (about), acquainted with *wg.* II. *n.* certainty, definite information — mid ~e, tō ~e, tō ~um, tō wissum with certainty.
~līce *av.* with certainty ; accurately | moreover Gl.
wiss|ian *w. a., d.* guide, direct ; indicate, show *wda.*
~iend *m.* driver (of chariot) ; governor, mistress.
(ge)~ung *f.* guidance, direction, government.
wisse *prt. of* wāt.
Wissi-gotan *mpl.* Visigoths.
wist *f.* sustenance, food ; feast *gen. pl.* ; luxury.
~full productive.
~fullian feast.
~fullīce *av.* sumptuously.
(ge)~fullung *f.* abundance, feasting.
~fulnes *f.* dainties.
~fyllo† *f.* full meal.
~giefende plentiful.
~lǣcan feast.
~męttas *mpl.* dainties.
gewistian feast.
wiste *prt. of* wāt.
wistl|e, hw- *f.* whistle, flute, pipe.
~ian whistle.
~ere *m.* piper.
~ung *f.* whistling, piping.
wit we two.
wītan 6 *wda.* reproach with, blame for.
gewit|an 6 depart ; cease to exist, die out (*of* family), die | ūt ~ go out (*of* fire).
~endlic transitory.
~endnes = gewitennes.
witian, eo decree ; destine.
wit|a, io, ge- *m.* sage, wise man ; councillor, senator — ~ena-gemōt *n.* parliament ; = gewita [wāt].
gewita, io, w- *m.* witness ; accomplice ; = wita.
wīte *n.* punishment ; fine ; torture ; misery.
~ærn*, wītern *n.* prison.
~bęnd† *mf.* cruel bond.
~brōga† *m.* terror of torment.
~fæst under arrest ; legally enslaved.
~hrægl *n.* penitential dress.

wīte|hūs *n.* house of torture, amphitheatre Gl.
~lāc† *n.* punishment.
~lēas without punishment *or* fine.
~līest *f.* freedom from punishment *or* fine.
~lic, wītiglic of punishment.
~rǣden(n) *f.* punishment.
~rn = ~ærn.
~scræf† *n.* hell.
~stęng *m.* rack.
~stōw *f.* place of torment *or* execution.
~swing *m.* flogging.
~tōl *n.* instrument of torture.
~þeow, ~þeowmann *m.* freeman legally enslaved, convict.
wīte-dōm, wītig- *m.* prophecy.
~lic prophetic.
wīteg|a, ĭ, í, wītga *m.* wise man, prophet.
~estre *f.* prophetess.
~ian prophesy.
~endlic*, wītendlic prophetic.
wītegung *f.* prophecy.
~bōc *f.* book of prophecy.
gewītennes *f.* departure, death.
wītga = wītega.
wītig, ī† [*or* -itt-], wittig wise ; in one's right mind.
wītig-dōm = wīte-.
wīting- = wītnung-.
gewit(t)nes *f.* witnessing, seeing, knowing ; testimony, concurrence, cognizance | one who witnesses *or* gives evidence.
witn|ian punish ; torture.
~ere *m.* executioner, torturer.
wītnung, ge- *f.* punishment ; torture.
~stōw, wīting- *f.* purgatory.
witod = witodlīce.
witodlīce, witod *av., cj.* truly, certainly, indeed ; for, and.
witol, tt wise.
witon *prt. pl. of* wāt.
witrod = wīg-trod.
(ge)witscipe *m.* testimony, evidence.
wit|t *n.* understanding, sense ; right mind, senses.
~līest *f.* folly.
~sēoc insane.
gewit|t *n.* intellect, understanding ; right mind, senses : of his gewitte wearþ ; consciousness.
~fæst of sound mind.

gewit|lēas foolish, mad.

~lēast *f.* folly ; madness.

~loca† *m.* mind.

~sēoc insane.

witter wise *L.* [*Scand.* vitr].

wittig = wītig.

gewittig, -wītig wise, clever; sane.

wittol = witol.

witum|a, weotoma, wetma *m.* dowry.

~bora *m.* bridesman.

wiþ *av., prp. w. a., d., g., in W. gen. a., except where specially marked d. or g.* | *rest* opposite ; near, (lean) against : **hēt delfan his byrgene ~ þæt weofod ; ~ earm gesæt** | *extension* along : **on þǣm lande ~ þā West-sǣ** ; as far as, to | *motion* towards *wg.* : **ēode ~ þæs Hǣlendes** | *opposition, hostility, protection* against : **fuhton ~ Brettas ; fuhton ~ þām cyninge ; healdan ~ besmitennysse** *also wg.* | *separation* from | *exchange, price* for *wd.* : **him feoh gehēton ~ þām friþe** | *association* with (*of* mixture, share, &c.) : **dǣlan rīce ~ God** ; *obj. of verb, &c.* (angry, make peace) with, (speak, be reconciled) to : **gebealg ~ hine ; cīdan ~ God** || **wiþ-þǣm-þe, wiþ-þǣm-þæt** in exchange for, in consideration of, provided that || **wiþ . . weard** *wd.* towards : **wiþ hire weard.**

wiþ·æftan I. *prp. wd.* behind. II. *av.* behind.

wiþ·blāwan 1 *w. g.* [*or d.* ?] blow away.

wiþ·bregdan, -brēdan 3 *wa.* withhold, keep back | *wd.* oppose, resist ; admonish.

wiþ·cēosan, wiþer- 7 reject *ptc.* **-coren (Gode)** rejected (by God).

wiþ·coren rejected.

~nes *f.* reprobation.

wiþ·cwedennes, wiþercwednes *f.* contradiction.

wiþcwedolnes = wiþer-.

wiþ·cwepan 5 deny *w.a., sbj.* | reject, refuse *w.d., sbj. w. neg.* : **wiþcwǣþ þæt hē nǣre . . refused to be . .** ; *wdg.* refuse a person a request *or* command : **hīe him þæs wiþcwǣdon** | oppose, refuse

---

to follow teaching of *wd.* ; dispute (sentence), object to *wd.* ; remonstrate with *wd.*

wiþ·drīfan 6 repel, renounce.

wiþer† *once prp. wd.* (?) against.

wiþer- *occ.* = wiþ-.

wiþerian resist *w.* ongēan.

wiþer-breca = -broca.

wiþer-broc|a, -bre-, eo *m.* adversary.

~ian oppose.

wiþer-cierr *m.* rearing (of a horse).

~an rear.

wiþer-cora *m.* adversary.

wiþer-coren = wiþ-.

wiþer-cwednes = wiþcwedennes.

wiþer-cwedol, -cwidel contradicting.

~nes *f.* contradiction.

wiþer-cwide *m.* contradiction ; resistance.

wiþer-cwidel = -cwedol.

wiþer-feohtan 3 resist.

wiþer-flitan 6 resist.

wiþer-flita *m.* adversary, opponent.

wiþer-gield *n.* recompense.

wiþer-hlinian lean against ; resist.

wiþer-hycgende ; -hygdig, -hȳdig hostile, refractory.

wiþer-lēan *n.* requital.

wiþerling *m.* opponent.

wiþer-māl *n.* counter-plea, defence *L.*

wiþer-mēd|e antagonistic.

~nes *f.* antagonism.

~o *f.* antagonism.

wiþer-mōd.

~nes *f.* adversity.

wiþer-rǣd|e the opposite of, antagonistic to *wd.* ; adverse ; rebellious ; disagreeing (*of* food).

~lic adverse.

~nes *f.* opposition ; adversity.

wiþer-riht *n.* recompense Gl.

wiþer-rihtes*, -rǣhtes† *av.* opposite.

wiþer-sac|a *m.* adversary ; betrayer ; apostate.

~an = wiþsacan.

~end*, -sacerd *m.* blasphemer.

~ian become an apostate.

~u *f.* = ~sǣc.

~ung *f.* apostasy.

---

wiþer-sǣc *n.* hostility, opposition ; apostasy.

wiþer-sienes *av.* in full view, visibly (?).

wiþer-sprǣc *f.* contradiction.

wiþer-stǣger steep.

wiþer-steall *m.* defence, resistance.

wiþer-talu *f.* contradiction.

wiþer-tīeme opposed, the opposite of *wd.*

wiþer-tihtle *f.* counter-charge.

wiþer-trod† *n.* retreat.

wiþerweard, -word adverse ; rebellious.

~ian oppose.

~lic perverse.

~lice *f.* perversely.

~nes *f.* opposition, adversity.

wiþer-winn|an 3 oppose Gl.

~ung*, we- *f.* controversy Gl.

wiþer-winna *m.* adversary.

wiþe-winde = wiþo-.

wiþ·faran 2 escape *wd.*

wiþ·feohtend *m.* adversary.

wiþ·ferian† rescue *w.a. and d. or of.*

wiþ·fōn *vb.* grab at *wd.*

wiþ·foran I. *prp. wd., place* before ; *time* before. II. *av.* previously.

wiþ·gān, -gangan *vb.* go away, disappear.

wiþ·geondan *prp. w. a.* (*or d.* ?) beyond (?).

wiþ·grīpan 6 *wd.* oppose.

wiþ·habban *wd.* resist, hold out against.

wiþ·hæftan seize.

wiþ·hindan *av.* behind.

wiþ·hogian despise, reject.

wiþ·hycgan reject, despise.

wīþig willow ; band, bond.

~bedd *n.* plot of willows.

~pȳfel *m.* thicket of willows.

~wielle *m.* willow-spring.

wiþ·innan I. *prp. w.* within. II. *av.* within.

wiþ·lǣd|an take away ; rescue *w.a. and d. or of.*

~nes *f.* abduction.

wiþ·lecgan refuse.

wiþ·licgan 5 *wd.* oppose.

wiþ·met|an 5 compare to, liken to *wd.*

~enlic comparative (degree).

~en(n)es, wiþgemetnes *f.* comparison.

wiþ·metung f. comparison.
wiþ·neoþan, i, y av. beneath.
wiþo.
~bān, wido- n. shoulder-blade.
~winde, wiþe- f. bindweed, convolvulus. Cp. **wuduwinde.**
wiþre † n. resistance.
wiþ·sac|an 2 deny w. a , g., sbj. | reject, refuse w. d., sbj. w. neg. : **wiþsōcon þæt hīe nolden** . . refused to . . | wd. oppose, revolt from, renounce (idols) ; w. **wiþ** a. conspire against.
~endlic negative (in grammar).
~ung f. renunciation.
wiþ·scorian wd. refuse, reject.
wiþ·scūfan 7 repel, refute.
wiþ·sēon 5 wd. rebel against.
wiþ·set|tan wd. resist.
~nes*, wit- f. opposition.
wiþ·slēan 2 wd. frustrate (conspiracy).
wiþ·spornan 3 offend against.
wiþ·sprecan 5 contradict.
wiþ·stæppan 2 depart.
wiþ·stand|an 2 wd. resist, oppose.
~end m. opponent.
wiþsteall = **wiþer-.**
wiþ·stunian dash against.
wiþ·styllan retreat.
wiþ·styltan hesitate.
wiþ·tēon 7 take away, withdraw.
wiþ·tremman step back.
wiþþe f. withy, bond ; chaplet, crown.
wiþ·ufan I. prp. wd. above. II. av. previously.
wiþ·uppan av. above.
wiþ·ūtan I. prp. wd. outside of ; except ; without. II. av. outside.
wiþ·weorpan 3 reject, repudiate.
wīwar- (n.) park, fishpond (?) [Lt. vivarium].
~awīc n. Ct.
wixlan = **wrixlan.**
wlac|ian, ge~od bēon become lukewarm.
wlacu = **wlæc.**
wlæc, wlacu lukewarm.
~lic lukewarm.
~līce av. lukewarmly met.
~nes, wlacu- f. lukewarmness.
wlæffetere m. one who speaks indistinctly Gl.
wlætan defile, debase.
wlætta, ea [Middle E. spelling] m. nausea [**wlātian**].

wlanc proud, elated ; aristocratic ; showy, fine (horse), grand, solemn (day).
~ian be proud.
~lic proud.
~līce av. arrogantly.
wlātian gaze [**wlītan**].
wlāt|ian impers. : **mē ~aþ** I feel nausea.
~ung f. nausea.
wlęccan make tepid [**wlæc**].
wlęncan make proud ; adorn, exalt, endow [**wlanc**].
wlęnco f. pride | pl. prosperity, riches ; high birth.
wlisp, wlips lisping.
~ian lisp.
wlītan 7 look.
wlite m. †brightness ; beauty, splendour ; appearance, form ; legal value, wer: **gieldan be his ~ or be his ~s weorþe.**
~beorht† beautiful.
~full beautiful.
~lēas† ugly.
~līce [= **wlitiglīce** ?] av. beautifully.
~sciene* beautiful.
~sīen*, ēo † f. spectacle, sight.
~torht, wlitig-† beautiful.
~wamm m. disfigurement of the face.
~weorþ n. legal value of person's life, ransom.
wlitig beautiful.
~e av. beautifully.
~fæst† beautiful.
~ian beautify, adorn ; form, fashion || intr. become beautiful.
~līce, wlitelīce av beautifully.
~nes f. beauty.
wlitu f. form, species.
wlō, d. of wlōh.
wlōh f.) fringe, tuft.
gewlōh*, -wlō † adorned.
wō, see wōh.
~lic perverse, wicked.
~līce av. wickedly.
~nes, wōgnes f. crookedness ; error ; wickedness.
wōcor f progeny, coll. living creatures ; usury [**wacan**].
wōd mad, frenzied.
~frec, æ furious, ravenous (of the devil).
~lic, ~elic mad, unrestrained.
~līce av. madly, fiercely.
~nes f. madness.

wōd|scinn, ~scīn n. frenzy.
~scipe m. madness.
~sēoc mad.
~sēocnes f. madness.
~þrāg f. paroxysm of madness.
Wōden m. the god Woden, identified with Mercury—**Wōdnes-dæg** Wednesday, **Wōdnes-niht** Tuesday night.
woff|ian talk wildly or foolishly ; blaspheme.
~ung f. wild talk ; blasphemy.
wōg-, see **wōh.**
~nes = **wōnes.**
wōg|ian woo.
~ere m. wooer.
wōh, g. wōs, L. wōges I. aj., pl. **wō(ge), dpl. wō(gu)m, wōn** crooked ; perverse, wrong, unjust. II. n. error, wrong ; wickedness | **on wōh** wrongly, wickedly ; **on wōn gebringan** lead into evil.
~bogen crooked.
~cēapung f. illegal traffic.
~dǣd f. sin.
~dōm m. unjust judgement.
~fōtede crooked-footed Gl.
~fręmmende evil-doing.
~full wicked.
~fulnes f. wickedness.
~georn inclined to evil.
~god n. false god.
wōhhǣm|ed n. fornication, adultery.
~end, ~ere m. fornicator, adulterer.
wōh|handede having deformed hands.
~lic = **wōlic.**
~nębb n. grimace.
~gestrēon n. ill-gotten gain.
~sum evil.
wōhs, prt. of wascan.
wōl mf. pestilence.
~bærnes f. pestilence.
~berende pestilential.
~berendlic pestilential.
~bryne m. pestilence (!).
~dagas† mpl. time of pestilence.
~gewinn n calamitous war.
wolc = **wolcen.**
wolcen, wolc n. cloud.
~faru † f. drifting of clouds.
~gehnāst † n. collision of clouds.
~wyrcende cloud-making (!) Gl.
wolc(en)-rēad = **weoloc-.**
wolde prt. of **willan.**
wollen ptc.

wollen-tēar-† weeping.

wōm, *see* **wōh.**

wōma, *once* **wōm**† *m.* tumult; terror.

wōn, *see* **wōh.**

wōp *m.* weeping, *also pl. in sg. meaning.*

~dropa† *m.* tear.

~ig flowing (tears).

~lēoþ *n.* dirge Gl.

~lic tearful.

~lice *av.* tearfully.

~stōw *f.* place of mourning.

wōpen *ptc. of* **wēpan.**

wōperian weep.

wōr.

~hana *m.* moorcock.

~henn . moorhen.

wōr|ian wander; crumble.

~ung *f.* wandering.

worc = weorc.

word, *L.* ō, u *n.* word; what is said, speech; sentence; verb. **wǣron þǣs wordes** *w. indc.,* **hæfdon him tō ~ e** *w. indc.* said | command, *pl.* directions | news, report; fame, glory.

~(ge)bēot† *m.* promise.

~bēotung† *f.* promise.

~cræft† *m.* art of poetry, eloquence.

~gecwide, -æde, *pl.* -eodu *in sg. meaning, n.* agreement.

~fæst true.

~full fluent.

~giédd† *n.* song.

~glēaw† eloquent.

~hlēopor† *n.* speaking, speech.

~hord† *n.* store of words — ~ on-lūcan speak.

~ig verbose.

~lāc *n.* speech.

~laþu† *f.* conversation.

~lēan† *n.* reward of eloquence.

~loc *npl.* dispute, logic Gl.

~loca† = **~hord.**

~loga† *m.* liar.

~gemearc† *n.* statement.

~mētung*, ~mittung *f.* debate Gl.

~gerȳne† *n.* word, information.

~samnere *m.* catalogue (!) Gl.

~samnung *f.* debate Gl.

~sāwere *m.* word-sower *met.*

~snoterung *f.* sophism Gl.

~snotor eloquent.

~wīs — se ~a the sophist Gl.

~wrītere = wyrd-.

~wynsum affable.

worden *ptc. of* **weorpan.**

wordl|ian talk, discuss, argue.

~ung *f.* talk, discussion.

worf' = weorf cattle.

worht *ptc. of* **wyrcan.**

world = woruld.

worms, y, *E.* **worsm** *nm.* pus, matter.

worn *m.* troop, multitude.

~mǣlum *av.* in troops.

worpian throw, hurl [weorpan].

worsm = worms.

worþ, eo *nm., d.* ~ a (?) enclosure adjoining house, courtyard, farm, street (!).

worþig, eo, *dpl.* ~(n)um court-yard, enclosure by house, street (!).

~netele *f.* nettle.

woruf = weorf cattle.

woruld, world, weorold *f.* world; age, aeon — on ~a, on ealra ~a ~, tō ~ə for ever; mankind; life, period of life, way of life.

~ǣht *f.* worldly possession.

~afel- worldly possessions.

~ār *f.* worldly prosperity.

~bearn† *n.* human being.

~bisgo *f.* worldly occupation.

~bisgung *f.* troubles of the world.

~bliss *f.* worldly joy.

~bōt *f.* compensation in this world.

~būend *m.* human being.

~gebyrd *f.* origin.

~camp *m.* secular warfare.

~candel(l)† *f.* sun.

~caru *f.* worldly care.

~cræft *m.* worldly wisdom *or* occupation.

~cund worldly, secular.

~cundlice *av.* in a worldly spirit *or* manner.

~cyning† *m.* earthly king.

~dǣd† *f.* action in this life.

~gedāl† *n.* death.

~dēad† dead.

~dēma *m.* secular judge.

~dōm *m.* earthly judgement.

~drēam† *m.* earthly joy.

~dryhten† *m.* God.

~dugoþ *f.* worldly possessions.

~earfoþ† *n.* earthly trouble.

~ege *m.* earthly fear.

~ende† *m.* end of the world.

~feoh† *n.* earthly goods.

~folgoþ *m.* earthly occupation.

~frætwung *f.* earthly adornment.

~frēond†, *Pr., m.* earthly friend.

woruld|friþ *m.* worldly peace.

~fruma *m.* patriarch.

~gālnes *f.* sensuality.

~giéfu *f.* worldly gift.

~giélp *n.* worldly boasting, pride.

~gītsere *m.* covetous person.

~gītsung *f.* covetousness.

~gleng *m.* worldly pomp.

~gōd *n.* earthly good.

~hād *m.* secular state.

~hlāford *m.* secular lord.

~hogu *f.* earthly care.

~hyht *f.* earthly joy.

~iermpo† *f.* earthly misery.

~lǣce *m.* earthly physician.

~lagu *f.* civil law.

~lēan *n.* earthly reward.

~lic of the world, terrestrial; secular, worldly.

~lice *av.* in the world, in this life.

~līf *n.* this life.

~lufu *f.* love of the world.

~lust *m.* worldly desire *or* pleasure.

~mǣg *m.* earthly kinsman.

~mann *m.* man; layman.

~mēd *f.* earthly reward.

~nīed *f.* temporal need.

~nytt *f.* worldly use *or* advantage.

~rǣden(n)† *f.* course of things, destiny.

~rīce† I. having worldly power or riches, mighty. II. *n.* earthly kingdom; the world.

~riht *n.* secular law.

~geriht *n.* worldly justice.

~gerisnu *npl.* worldly usage.

~sacu *f.* worldly strife.

~gesǣlig prosperous in this world.

~(ge)sǣlþ *f.* worldly prosperity.

~scamu *f.* public disgrace.

~sceaft† *f.* earthly creature *or* thing.

~gesceaft† *f.* earthly creature *or* thing; the world.

~scēat *m.* quarter of the globe, district.

~scipe *m.* worldly affair.

~snotor prudent in worldly matters.

~sorg *f.* earthly care.

~spēd† *f.* earthly riches *or* prosperity.

~spēdig prosperous.

~sprǣc *f.* worldly talk.

~stēor *f.* earthly rule.

~strengo† *f.* strength.

~gestrēon *n.* worldly possessions.

~strūdere *m.* arch-robber.

~stunda† *fpl.* period of life.

~geswinc† *n.* earthly hardship.

woruld þearfa†*m.*,~þearfende†
poor.
~þēaw *m.* worldly usage.
~þegen, ~þēn *m.* secular servant.
~þēowdōm *m.* secular service.
~þīestro *f.* earthly darkness.
~þing *n.* worldly affair; worldly
possession.
~geþoht *m.* worldly thought.
~geþyncþ *f.* worldly honour or
dignity.
~wǣpen *n.* worldly weapon.
~wela† *m.* earthly prosperity or
wealth.
~weorþscipe *m.* worldly honour.
~wīdl† (*n.*) earthly defilement.
~wīg *n.* worldly contest.
~wilnung *f.* earthly desire.
~wīs learned, scientific.
~wīsdōm *m.* science, philosophy.
~wita *m.* scientist, philosopher.
~wīte† *n.* martyrdom.
~wlenco *f.* worldly ostentation.
~wrenc *m.* worldly artifice.
~gewrit *n.* secular treatise, philosophy.
~wrītere *m.* philosopher.
~wuldor *n.* worldly glory.
~gewuna *m.* worldly custom.
~wuniende†dwelling in the world.
~wynn *f.* earthly joy.
~ȳþ *f.* worldly wave.
wōs *n.* moisture, juice.
~ig moist, juicy.
giwosa = gewesan.
wōþ† *f.* sound, clamour, melody,
song.
~bora *m.* poet, prophet.
~cræft *m.* art of poetry.
~gīefu *f.* gift of melody.
~sang *m.* song, poem.
wōx *prt. of* weaxan, wascan.
wracian be exiled or in exile
[wracu].
wracnian = wræcnian.
wrac|u, *g.* ~e, wrǣce *f.* revenge,
vengeance, punishment, persecution; cruelty; distress, misery
[wrecan].
wræc *n.* exile; misery [wrecan].
~fæc† *n.* time of misery.
~full miserable.
~hwīl† *f.* time of misery.
~lāstas† *mpl.* exile, wandering.
~lāstian banish.
~lic wretched; †wonderful [*for*
wrǣttlic?].

wræc|līce *av.* in exile.
~līf *n.* life of exile or misery.
~mǣcg† *m.* outcast, wretch.
~mann† *m.* exile.
~scipe*, e *m.* exile.
~setl† *n.* place of exile.
~sīþ *m.* exile; misery.
~sīþian be in exile.
~stōw† *f.* place of exile or punishment (=hell).
~wīte *n.* punishment.
~woruld *f.* miserable world.
wrǣcca *m.* stranger; exile; wretch,
despicable one.
wrǣcnes = wrecennes.
wrǣcnian, a be in exile.
wrǣd, -þ *m.* band, bandage, wreath
| troop, herd [wrīþan].
~mǣlum *av.* in troops.
wrǣn|e lecherous.
~nes *f.*, ~scipe *m.* lechery.
wrǣnna, wǣrna *m.* wren.
wrǣnsa *once m.* lasciviousness Gl.
[wrǣne].
wrǣsn = wrāsen.
wrǣsnan† change, modulate
(voice).
wrǣst vigorous, strong, efficient.
~e *av.* vigorously.
wrǣstan twist.
wrǣstl|ian, ā,wrāxlian, ǣ wrestle.
~ere *m.* wrestler.
~ung *f.* wrestling; struggle, contest.
wrǣt|t† *f.* ornament, work of art.
~lic† artistic, ornamental; rare,
wondrous.
~lice† *av.* splendidly.
wrǣtte *f.* a plant.
wrǣþ-studu = wraþ-.
wrǣþ = wrǣd.
gewrǣþan *rfl. w.* ongēan, *intr. w.*
tō be fierce, savage [wrāþ].
wrǣþþo, ā, wrǣþu *f.* anger.
wrǣxlian = wrǣstlian.
wrāh *prt. of* wrēon.
wrang *L. n.* injustice, wrong
[*Scand.*].
wranga*, pranga, wrong *m.* hold
(of ship) Gl.
wrāse *f.* knot, lump.
wrāsen†, ǣ chain.
wrāst, ~lic delicate Gl.
wrāstlian = wrǣstlian.
wrāþ angry, fierce; hostile — ~um
fiercely; harsh (to taste); grievous,
terrible.
~e *av.* angrily, fiercely; grievously.

wrāþ|lic severe (punishment).
~līce *av.* fiercely, severely.
~mōd† wrathful.
~scrafu† *npl.* caves of misery
(=hell).
gewrāþian *rfl.* be angry *vL.*
wrǣþþo = wrǣþþo.
wrāþ|u *f.* support, prop; help,
benefit.
~studu, wre-, -þu *f.* support.
wrāxlian = wrǣstlian.
wrēah *occ. prt. of* wrēon.
wrec|an 5 drive, push; expel;
avenge: ~ hine on his fēondum,
~ his tēonan on *d*; punish:
on him (*pl.*) gewræc þæt hīe
slōgon . . || *intr.* advance, go.
~end *m.* avenger.
~ennes, wrecnes, æ *f.* vengeance.
wrecca = wrǣcca.
wreccan = weccan.
wrecnes = wrecennes.
wrecnian = wrǣcnian.
wrecscipe = wrǣcscipe.
wrēg|an stir up†; accuse [wrōht].
~end *m.* accuser.
~endlic accusative (case).
~ere *m.*, ~istre *f.* accuser.
~ung *f.* accusation.
wrenc *m.*; modulation (of the
voice); artifice, trick.
~an twist, turn; play tricks, be
deceitful.
wrenna = wrǣnna.
wrēon 6, 7 *prt.* wrāh, ēa, *pl.*
wrigon, u, *ptc.* wrigen, o cover
rare in W.
wreoþen-hilt = wriþen-.
wreþ-studu = wraþ-.
wreþian prop, support [wraþu].
gewrid, w- *n.* thicket [wrīdan].
wrīd|an 6, ~ian, ī†, wrīp(i)an
grow, flourish.
wrigian, ī†strive, tend, go forward.
wrigels *mn.*covering,veil[wrēon].
wrigen *ptc. of* wrēon.
wrincl|e *f.* wrinkle.
~ian wrinkle.
wring-hwǣg (*n.*) strained whey.
gewring *n.* liquor, drink.
wringan 3 wring, press out; ge~
squeeze (out of shape).
gewrisc = gewrixl.
wrislan = wrixlan.
wrist, wyrst *f.* wrist.
writ- [wrītan].
~bōc *f.*, ~bred *n.* writing-tablet.

writ|īren, ~seax *n.* style.

gewrit, writ *n.* what is written, writing; letter; legal document, deed; book, Scripture.

writ|an 6 engrave; draw, depict; write.

~ere *m.* writer.

wrīting *f.*

~feþer *f.* pen.

wrīþan 6 twist; bind.

wrīþ(i)an = wrīdan.

wrīþa *m.* bridle; ring; torture [wrīþan].

wrīþels *m.* band.

wrīþen-hilt*, wreo-† with twisted hilt (sword).

wrixend|līc mutual.

~līce *av.* mutually; in turn.

wrixl *f.*, ~a *m.* exchange.

gewrixl, ~e, gewrisc *n.* change; exchange, requital; purchase; turn (in rotation).

gewrixl *aj.* changing.

wrixl|an, ~ian, *IN.* wixl- |†change *intr.*, change colour, be variegated *w. or without* blēom | exchange — †wordum ~ converse; requite.

~ung *f.* exchange.

gewrixlan obtain.

wrogen *ptc. of* wrēon.

wroht = worht.

wrōht *f.* accusation; recrimination, quarrelling; crime | *once* talebearer *m.* ?; calamity, misery [wrēgan].

~bera *m.* accuser.

~berend *m.* accuser.

~bora *m.* accuser.

~dropan† *mpl.* wicked drops (of blood of murdered man).

~georn contentious

~lāc *n.* accusation, calumny.

~līc accusing.

~gemǣne involved in quarrel.

~sāwere *m.* causer of strife.

~scipe† *m.* crime.

~smiþ† *m.* criminal.

~spitel slanderous Gl. [spittan].

~stafas† *mpl.* crime.

~getīeme† *n.* crime.

wrōt *m.* snout, trunk (of elephant).

~an root up (*of* pig).

wrugon, *prt. pl. of* wrēon.

wryhta = wyrhta.

wrynd|an — ge~ed founded (*of* house) *IN.*

wucu, wice *wk. f.* week.

wuc|ubōt *f.* week's penance.

~(e)dæg *m.* week-day.

~þegn, ~þēn *m.* servant (monk) appointed for a week's duty.

~þegnung, -þēn- *f.* week's service.

wud|ian cut wood.

~i(g)ere *m.* woodcutter, servant Gl.

~ig wooded.

~iht wooded.

wudu, wi(o)du *m., pl.* wuda(s) wood, forest; timber, wood; †ship.

~ælfen, e *f.* dryad.

~æppel *m.* crab-apple.

~bǣre wood-bearing.

~bærnett *n.* burning wood.

~bāt† *m.* boat, ship.

~bēam† *m.* tree.

~bearo *m.* grove, forest.

~bill *n.* hatchet.

~binde, ~bindle *f.* woodbine.

~blēd† *f.* wood-blossom.

~brūn *n.* bugloss (plant).

~bucca *m.* wild goat.

~cerfille *f.* cow-parsley.

~cocc *m.* woodcock.

~culfre *f.* wood-pigeon.

~cūnelle *f.* wild thyme.

~docce *f.* dock.

~elfen = ~ælfen.

~fæsten(n) *n.* forest-cover, place protected by forest; †ship.

~feld *m.* wooded plain.

~fīn pile of wood.

~fugol *m.* forest bird.

~gāt *f.* wild goat.

~hana *m.* woodcock.

~hēawere *m.* woodcutter.

~henn *f.* quail.

~holt *n.* forest, wood.

~hunig *m.* wild honey.

~hwistle = ~wistle.

~lǣs *f.* wood-pasture.

~land *n.* woodland.

~leahtric *m.* wild sleepwort.

~līc woody.

~mǣr *m.* wood-nymph, echo.

~merce *f.* wild parsley.

~rǣden(n) *f.* forest regulation.

~rēc† *m.* wood-smoke.

~rima *m.* border of a forest.

~rofe *f.* woodruff.

~rose *f.* wild rose.

~snīte *f.* snipe.

~telga *m.* branch of a tree.

~trēow *n.* forest tree.

wudu|pistel *m.* hellebore.

~wāsa *m.* faun, satyr.

~weald *m.* forest.

~weard *m.* forester.

~weaxe *f.* wood-wax (a plant).

~wēsten(n) *n.* wooded waste.

~winde *f.* woodbine.

~wistle, ~hw- *f.* hemlock.

~wyrt *f.* wood plant.

wuduw|e, wid(e)we *f.* widow.

~anhād, widuwhād *m.* widowhood.

wuh(h)ung *f.* fury, frenzy.

wuht = wiht.

wuldor *n.* glory; praise.

~bēag *m.* crown of glory.

~bēagian crown.

~blǣd† *m.* glorious success.

~cyning† *m.* king of glory, God.

~drēam† *m.* joy of heaven.

~fæder† *m.* glorious father, God.

wuldorfæst glorious.

~e†, ~līce *av.* gloriously.

wuldor|full glorious.

~fullian glorify.

~fullīce *av.* gloriously.

~gāst† *m.* holy spirit.

~giefa† *m.* giver of glory.

~giefu† *f.* glorious gift *met.*

~gimm† *m.* sun.

~hama† *m.* robe of glory.

~helm *m.* crown of glory.

~lēan† *n.* heavenly reward.

~līc glorious.

~līce *av.* gloriously.

~māga† *m.* saint.

~magu† *m.* saint.

~micel† wonderfully great.

~nytting† *f.* great usefulness.

~spēd† *f.* glory.

~spēdig† glorious.

~gesteald† *n.* heavenly possessions *or* dwelling.

~torht† gloriously bright; illustrious, noble.

~þrymm† *m.* glory.

~werod† *n.* heavenly host.

~word† *n.* glorious word.

wuldr|ian glorify, praise; boast |¦ *intr.*|live in glory.

~ig glorious.

~ung *f.* glorying.

wulf *m.* wolf. ~es camb *m.* wild teasel. ~es fīst toadstool.

~hēafod-trēow† *n.* gallows.

~heort† savage, cruel.

~hlīþ† *n.* wolf-slope.

[213]

wulf|hol *n.* wolf's hole.
~sēap *m.* wolf's hole.
~slæd *n.* wolf-valley Ct.
wull, ~e *f.* wool.
~camb *m.* wool-comb.
~cnoppa *m.* tuft of wool.
~flīes *n.* fleece.
~ic woolly.
~mod distaff.
~tewestre *f.* wool-carder.
wullian wipe with wool.
wullen = **wyllen.**
gewun I. *(n.)* custom. **II.** *aj.* usual.
wun|ian dwell; remain, continue (in time and space) ‖ *tr.†* inhabit, remain in.
~enes, wunes *f.* dwelling.
~ung *f.* dwelling (act and place).
gewunian dwell; continue | be in the habit of *w. ger.*, habituate oneself to *w.* tō.
gewun|a, wuna I. *m.* habit, custom. **II.** *aj. indecl.* accustomed.
~elic customary.
~elice *av.* usually.
wund I. *f.* wound. **II.** *aj.* wounded.
~iht ulcerous.
~lāc *n.* wounding, wound.
~swaþu *f.* scar.
wundian wound.
wundel (*f.*) wound.
wunden|feax† with braided hair.
~heals† with twisted prow (ship).
~locc† with braided locks.
~mǣl† with twisted ornaments.
~stefna† with twisted prow (ship).
wundor *n.* wonder; wonderful thing; miracle. **wundrum** *av.* wonderfully. terribly.
~āgræfen† wonderfully carved.
~bēacen *n.* strange sign.
~bebod† *n.* strange command.
~bleoh† *n.* wonderful colour.
~clamm† *m.* wonderful bond.
~clofe, u *f.* camphire (plant).
~cræftiglice *av.* marvellously.
~dǣd *f.* wonderful deed.
~dēaþ† *m.* terrible death.
~fæt† *n.* wonderful vessel.
~full wonderful.
~fullīce *av.* wonderfully.
~giefu† *f.* wonderful gift *met.*
~lǣcan magnify.
~lic wonderful.

wundor|līce *av.* wonderfully.
~māþm† *m.* wonderful treasure.
~sīen*, ēo† *f.* wonderful sight.
~smiþ† *m.* wonderful smith.
~tācen† *n.* prodigy.
~(ge)weorc *n.* wonderful work, miracle.
~woruld† *f.* wonderful world.
~wyrd† *f.* strange occurrence.
wundr|ian *wg.* wonder (at), admire.
~ung *f.* wonder, admiration.
wurd = **word.**
wurdon, *prt. pl. of* **weorþan.**
wurm = **wyrm.**
wurma *vE. m.* murex, purplefish; purple.
wurm|ille, ~ele *f.* wild marjoram.
wurpan = **weorpan.**
wursm = **worms.**
wurþ- = **weorþ-.**
wūsc* wish [**wȳscan**].
~bearn *n.* little child *lN.* *Cp.* **gewȳscan.**
wutodlice = **witodlīce.**
wuton = **uton.**
wylf *f.* she-wolf [**wulf**].
wylfen I. *f.* she-wolf. **II. †**savage, cruel.
wylig willow = **welig.**
wyliht full of willows = **wiliht.**
wyllen, u of wool [**wull**].
wynde-cræft, i *m.* art of embroidery [**windan**].
gewynde *n.* weaving (?) Gl.
wyndle *f.* wound. *Cp.* **wundel.**
wyn|n *f.* joy. **wynnum** joyfully.
~bēam† *m.* tree of joy, the Cross.
~burg† *f.* pleasant city.
~candel(1)† *f.* sun.
~dæg† *m.* day of joy.
~drēam† *m.* joy.
~ele† *m.* pleasant oil.
~fæst† pleasant.
~full joyful.
~grāf† *mn.* pleasant grove.
~land† *n.* pleasant country.
~lēas joyless.
~lic pleasant, beautiful.
~lice *av.* joyfully.
~lust *m.* pleasure.
~mǣg† *f.* saint.
~rōd† *f.* the Cross.
~gesīþ† *m.* acceptable companion.
wynsum pleasant.
~ian rejoice.

wynsum|lic, ge- pleasant.
~lice *av.* pleasantly.
~nes *f.* loveliness, pleasantness.
wyn|psalterium *n.* psalm of joy.
~werod *n.* chorus Gl.
~wyrt† *f.* pleasant plant.
wynnung, i *f.* tares *lN.* *Cp.* windwian.
wȳr = **wīr** myrtle.
wyrc|an, A. i, y; *prt.* **worhte,** *A.* **wyrcte,** *ptc.* **worht,** *lN.* **wroht** | *w. a., g.* work *tr. and intr.*, build, perform, keep (festival); cause; amount to (in reckoning) | *wg.* strive after | deserve, acquire.
~end *m.* worker, doer.
~nes *f.* work.
~ung *f.* working.
gewyrce, i *n.* inwards (of pig).
wyrd *f.* fate; event, phenomenon [**weorþan**].
~gesǣlig fortunate.
~gesceapum *av.* by chance Gl.
~stafas† *mpl.* destiny.
~wrītere *m.* historian; scientist.
gewyrd *f.* fate; event, circumstance, state of things.
~elic historical.
gewyrd, ~e *n.* talking, eloquence; ordinance [word].
gewyrde = **gewierþe** amount.
gewyrde|lic* eloquent.
~lice *av.* eloquently, accurately.
~licnes *f.* eloquence.
wyrgan, ie [*error ?*], *lN. prt.* **-wrigde** strangle.
gewyrht *nf., gen. pl.* deed, transgression, desert, merit: **be his ~um, būton ~um** undeservedly, **mid ~um** deservedly; **†**fate (?) [**wyrcan**].
wyrhta, wryhta *m.* worker, maker.
gewyrhta *m.* doer; co-operator, accomplice.
wyrm *m.* reptile; serpent, dragon; worm [**wurma**].
~ǣte worm-eaten.
~baso red.
~geblǣd *n.* a kind of blister *or* swelling.
~cynn *n.* species of serpent.
~fāg† with serpentine ornaments.
~galere, galdere *m.* snakecharmer.
~geard† *m.* abode of serpents.
~hǣlsere *m.* diviner by serpents.
~hīw *n.* form of a snake.

wyrm|hord† *n.* dragon's treasure.
~lic† *n.* serpentine ornament.
~melo *n.* worm-meal (?).
~rēad scarlet.
~sele† *m.* hall of serpents (= hell).
~slite *m.* being eaten by worms.
~wyrt *f.* a plant.
wyrmella = wurmille.
wyrms = worms pus.
~ig purulent, festering.
~tĕung*, wyrshrtĕung, ~spī-wung*, wyrsnsspīung *f.* phthisis Gl.
wyrms|an,   wyrsman   fester — ge~ed purulent [worms].
wyrp, ie *once, lN.* y, oe *m.* throwing; blow, stroke, shot [weorpan].
wyrpe = wiĘrpe recovery.

gewyrpe *n.* heap (?) Ct.
wyrpel† *m.* foot-ring (of hawk).
wyrrest = wierrest.
wyrsa = wiersa.
wyrsman = wyrmsan.
wyrst = wrist.
wyrt *f.* vegetable, plant, herb, spice; crop; root.
~bĘdd *n.* bed planted with herbs.
~box *m.* perfume-box.
~brĘþ *m.* fragrance of flowers.
~cynn *n.* species of herb.
~cynren *n.* species of herb.
~drĘnc *m.* herbal drink.
~fæt *n.* perfume-box.
~geard *m.* kitchen garden.
~ig — ~ hamm garden.
~gemang *n.*, ~gemĘngnes, a *f.* spice, perfume.

wyrt|mĘte *m.* dish of vegetables.
~tūn *m.* garden.
wyrt-wal|a *m.* root.
~ian root *or* pull up *or* out.
wyrt-weard *m.* gardener.
wyrt-(t)rum|a *m.* root, root-stump.
~ian root up.
wyrtian spice, perfume.
wȳscan wish *wdg., w. sbj* [wūsc].
gewȳsc|an wish | adopt : ~hīe him (*rfl.*) tō bearnum.
~ednes, ~ing *f.* adoption.
~endlic desirable; optative (mood) | adoptive (child).
~endlīce *av.* (child) by adoption.

Y.

ȳce *f.* toad, frog.
ȳdæges = īdæges on the same day.
ȳddisc = *īedisc furniture.
yfel I. *aj., cpv.* wiersa, y, *spl.* wierrest,   wyr(re)sta   bad; wicked; painful, miserable. II. *n.* evil; wickedness; mischief, damage; misery.
~cund evil.
~cwepende evil-speaking.
~dĘd *f.* evil deed.
~dĘda *m.* evil-doer.
~full evil, wicked.
~georn(n)es *f.* wickedness.
~lic, yfelic evil, bad; mean, untidy (in dress).
~nes *f.* badness, wickedness.
yfelsac|ian blaspheme.
~end *m.* blasphemer.
~ung *f.* blaspheming, blasphemy.
yfel|sōþ unhappily true, too true.
~sprĘce evil-speaking.
~willende vicious.

yfel|willendnes *f.* malice.
~wyrcende evil-doing.
yfele, yfle *av., cpv.* wiers, y badly, wrongly; miserably.
yfelian, yfl- *intr.* become bad || *tr.* injure.
yfemest *spl. of* uferra.
yferra, -era = uferra.
yfes *f.* eaves of house. *Cp.* efes.
~drype*, yfer- *m.* drip from eaves Gl.
ylcian = Ęlcian delay.
ylca = ilca same.
ylfig chattering, raving Gl.
ylp *m.* = elpend elephant — ~es-bān ivory.
yltsta *spl. of* eald old.
ym- = ymb-.
ymb, *L.* ~e, embe *prp. wa.* [*the av.* ymbe *takes d.*] | *place* around | *time* about, at: ~e gangdagas oþþe Ęr after: hē fōr ~ āne niht tō Īglēa, þæs ~e lȳtel soon

after.   ~ twelf mōnaþ every twelve months | concerning, about: georn ~ lāre, smēan ~ God. ~ (bēon) be busy about, aim at: se dēofol is Ęfre ~e yfel; hū hē ~e hī sceolde how he should deal with them; *also abs.*: hū hē ~e wolde how he would act.
ymb·bĘtan*, ymbe- † curb, enclose.
ymb·beorgan 3 protect.
ymb·beran 4 surround.
ymb·biegnes, ymbe- *f.* bend (of river).
ymb·bindan 3 bind round.
ymb·būgan 7 bend round.
ymb·cĘfian embroider round.
ymb·ceorfan 3 circumcise.
ymb·cięrr *m.* migration *lN.*
~an go round, make the circuit of.
~ing *f.* embrace.
ymb·clypp|an embrace.
ymb·cyme *m.* assembly.

[215]

ymbe *av.* [*the prp. is* ymb, *L.* ymbe] around. *In compos.* ymb- *is older and more frequent than* ymbe-.

ymb|e [y = i] (*n.*) swarm of bees.

~stocc *m.* stump with swarm of bees in it Ct.

ymbe- *occ.* = ymb-.

ymb·eardiende neighbouring Gl.

ymb-fær, ymbe- *n.* circuit.

ymb-færeld *n.* circuit.

ymb·fæstnes *f.* enclosure.

ymb·fæþmian encompass.

ymb·faran 2 surround; traverse.

ymb-fęng *m.* envelope, covering.

ymb·fēran go round, traverse.

ymb·flēogan 7 fly round.

ymb·fōn 1 b grasp, clasp; encompass, surround.

ymb·frætwian surround with ornaments, adorn.

ymb·gān, -gangan *vb.* go round; surround.

ymb-gang *m.* circuit, circumference.

ymb·gyrdan encircle, surround.

ymb·habban surround, include.

ymb-haga *m.* hedge, enclosure.

ymb·hammen surrounded Gl.

ymb·healdan 1 encompass.

ymb·hēapian heap round.

ymb·hęgian hedge round.

ymb·hōn 1 b *tr.* hang round — *ptc.* -hangen surrounded, hung (with), covered (with).

ymb-hog|a *m.* consideration, reflection, purpose; care, anxiety.

~ian be anxious about.

ymb·hring|an surround.

~end *m.* attendant Gl.

ymb·hūung *f.* circumcision *LN.* [hēawan].

ymb·hweorfan 3 *intr.* revolve || *tr.* go round, encompass; tend, cultivate.

ymb·hwięrf|an revolve round; encompass; traverse.

~nes *f.* change, revolution.

ymb-hwyrft, -e, -i, -eo, -ea *m.* rotation; orbit (of stars); circuit, extent; world.

ymb·hycgan reflect on, consider.

ymb·hygd, -hȳd *f.* solicitude, anxiety.

~ig solicitous, anxious.

~iglīce*, ~elīce *av.* carefully.

ymb-hygdignes *f.* solicitude.

ymb·iernan 3 run round.

ymb·lǣdan lead round.

ymb·lǣrigian provide with a rim.

ymb·licgan 5 surround, encompass, confine.

ymb·līþan 6 sail round.

ymbren *n.* Ember-tide, the Ember days [ymbryne].

~dæg, ymbrig- *m.* Ember-day.

~fæsten(n) *n.* fast at Ember-tide.

~wuce *f.* Ember week.

ymb·ryne, emrene *m.* motion round, revolving; orbit (of stars) | *time* lapse, course.

ymb·sceadwian overshadow.

ymb·scēaw|ian look round.

~iendlīce *f.* circumspectly.

~ung *f.* looking round.

ymb·scīnan 6 shine round *tr.*

ymb·scrīpan 6 make the circuit of.

ymb·scrȳdan clothe, dress.

ymb·sellan surround.

ymb·sēon 5 look round.

ymb·sēon *f.* beholding.

ymb-set *n.* siege.

ymb-seten*, *vE.* oemseten *f.* shoot, slip.

ymb-setl *n.* siege.

ymb·sētnung *f.* sedition.

ymb·sęttan encompass; besiege.

ymb·sittan 5 encompass, besiege *also w.* ūtan.

ymb-sittend, ymbe-† *m.* neighbour (nation).

~e *intr.* sitting round; neighbouring (people).

ymb·smēagung*, ymbe- *f.* consideration.

ymb·snidennes *f.* circumcision [ymbsnīpan].

ymb·snīpan 6 circumcise.

ymb·spannan 1 clasp round, embrace.

ymb·sprǣc, ymbe- *f.* conversation, discussion.

~e spoken about, well known.

ymb·stand|an 2 surround.

~en*, ymbe-† surrounded.

ymb·standende† standing round, enclosing.

ymb·stand(en)nes *f.* encompassing; guardianship.

ymb·styrian stir about, overturn.

ymb·swǣpe, -ā- *f.* digression Gl.

ymb·swāpan 1 environ; clothe, dress.

ymb·trymian, -trymman surround; fortify.

ymb·trymming *f.* surrounding; fortifying.

ymb·tȳnan surround.

ymb·tyrnan surround Gl.

ymb·þanc*, ymbe- *m.* reflection.

ymb·þridung *f.* deliberation, reflection Gl.

ymb·þringan 3 throng round, surround.

ymb·ūtan, abūtan *av., prp. wa.* around, about — ymb hīe ūtan = ~ hīe.

ymb·wǣfan envelop, clothe.

ymb·wǣrlan turn towards *LN.*

ymb·weaxan 1 grow round, surround.

ymb·węnd|an turn round.

~nes *f.* change.

~ung *f.* reviving; behaviour.

ymb·weorpan 3 surround.

ymb·wician besiege.

ymb·windan 3 enfold, encompass.

ymb·wlāt|ian contemplate.

~ung *f.* contemplation.

ymb·wyrcan enclose, surround.

ymel, e caterpillar.

ymele, ymle *f.* document, piece of writing.

ymen *m.* hymn [*Lt.* hymnus].

~bōc *f.* hymn-book.

~sang *m.* hymn.

ymesene blind.

ymest *spl. of* uferra.

ymnere *m.* hymn-book [*Lt.* hymnarium].

ynce inch [*Lt.* uncia].

yndse, entse *f.* ounce [*Lt.* uncia].

ynne-lēac *n.* onion [*Lt.* unio].

ȳplen, ypplen *n.* top, summit Gl. [ūp].

yppan bring out *or* up; ge- produce (flowers); make manifest, disclose, betray; ge- utter (words) [uppan].

yppe I. evident, known. II. *n.* upper room Gl.; dais, throne; show, spectacle Gl.

ypping† *f.* (?).

~iren*, i- *n.* crowbar.

ȳr, ē back of axe.

ȳr† bow (?); *the Runic letter* y.

yrse-binn *f.* a kind of box (?).

ysl|e *f.* ash.
~ende glowing Gl.
ysope *f.* hyssop [*Lt.*].
ȳst *f.* whirlwind, storm.
~ian storm, rage.
~ig stormy.
ȳt|an expel [ūt].
~end *m.* expeller.
~ing *f.* journey.
ȳtemest *spl. of* ūterra.
yteren of an otter [otor].

ȳterra = ūterra.
ȳtmest = ȳtemest.
ȳþ *f.* wave.
~gebland† *n.* surge.
~bord† *n.* ship.   *Cp.* wǣgbord.
~faru† *f.* flood.
~hengest *Pr. m.* horse.
~hof† *n.* ship.
~ig rough (sea).
~lāde† *fpl.* sea-passage.
~lāf† *f.* shore.

ȳþ|lid† *n.*, ~lida† *m.* ship.
~mearh† *m.* ship.
~mere† *m.* sea.
~naca*† *m.* ship.
~gewinn† *n.* life in the water.
~wōrigende wandering on the waves Gl.
ȳþg|ian, ȳþian fluctuate, surge; rage.
~ung *f.* fluctuation.
ȳþung *f.* inundation; agitation.